Archaeology, Economy, and Society

GW00750219

This book examines the contribution of archaeology to the study of the social, economic, religious, and other developments in England from the end of the Roman period at the start of the fifth century to the beginnings of the Renaissance at the end of the fifteenth century.

The first edition of the book was published in 1990, and it remains the only synthesis of the whole spectrum of medieval archaeology. This new edition is completely rewritten and extended but uses the same chronological approach to investigate how society and economy evolved. It draws on a wide range of new data, derived from excavation, investigation of buildings, metal-detection, and scientific techniques. It examines the social customs, economic pressures, and environmental constraints within which people functioned; the technology available to them; and how they expressed themselves, for example in their houses, their burial customs, their costume, and their material possessions such as pottery. Their adaptation to new circumstances, whether caused by human factors such as the re-emergence of towns or changing taxation requirements, or by external ones such as volcanic activity or the Black Death, is explored throughout each chapter.

The new edition of *Archaeology, Economy, and Society* will be essential reading for students and researchers of the archaeology of medieval England.

David A. Hinton is an Emeritus Professor of Archaeology, University of Southampton. He is a former editor of the journal *Medieval Archaeology*, published by the Society for Medieval Archaeology, of which he is an Honorary Vice-President. He served as President of the Royal Archaeological Institute from 2013 to 2016. His published work includes *Gold and Gilt, Pots and Pins* (Oxford University Press, 2005), which reflected his specialist interest in medieval artefacts. He has also written numerous articles on topics such as cemeteries, churches, houses, and sculptures.

Archaeology, Economy, and Society

England from the Fifth to the Fifteenth Century

New edition

David A. Hinton

Routledge
Taylor & Francis Group
LONDON AND NEW YORK

Cover image: Stokesay Castle, Shropshire. The stone tower and part of the great hall owned by a thirteenth-century merchant. Photo: Paul Stamper.

Second edition published 2022
by Routledge
4 Park Square, Milton Park, Abingdon, Oxon, OX14 4RN

and by Routledge
605 Third Avenue, New York, NY 10158

Routledge is an imprint of the Taylor & Francis Group, an informa business

© 2022 David A. Hinton

The right of David A. Hinton to be identified as author of this work has been asserted in accordance with sections 77 and 78 of the Copyright, Designs and Patents Act 1988.

All rights reserved. No part of this book may be reprinted or reproduced or utilised in any form or by any electronic, mechanical, or other means, now known or hereafter invented, including photocopying and recording, or in any information storage or retrieval system, without permission in writing from the publishers.

Trademark notice: Product or corporate names may be trademarks or registered trademarks, and are used only for identification and explanation without intent to infringe.

First edition published by Routledge 1990

British Library Cataloguing-in-Publication Data
A catalogue record for this book is available from the British Library

Library of Congress Cataloging-in-Publication Data
Names: Hinton, David Alban, author.
Title: Archaeology, economy, and society : England from the fifth to the fifteenth century / David A. Hinton.
Other titles: England from the fifth to the fifteenth century
Description: New edition. | Abingdon, Oxon ; New York, NY : Routledge, 2022. | "First edition published by Routledge, 1990." | Includes bibliographical references and index.
Identifiers: LCCN 2021058864 (print) | LCCN 2021058865 (ebook) | ISBN 9780367440800 (hbk) | ISBN 9780367440824 (pbk) | ISBN 9781003007432 (ebk)
Subjects: LCSH: Excavations (Archaeology)—England. | England—Economic conditions—1066-1485. | England—Social conditions—1066-1485. | England—Social conditions—To 1066. | Archaeology, Medieval—England. | England—Antiquities.
Classification: LCC DA130 .H56 2022 (print) | LCC DA130 (ebook) | DDC 942—dc23/eng/20211221
LC record available at https://lccn.loc.gov/2021058864
LC ebook record available at https://lccn.loc.gov/2021058865

ISBN: 978-0-367-44080-0 (hbk)
ISBN: 978-0-367-44082-4 (pbk)
ISBN: 978-1-003-00743-2 (ebk)

DOI: 10.4324/9781003007432

Typeset in Times New Roman
by Apex CoVantage, LLC

Contents

Illustrations

Acknowledgements for Illustrations

Most of the illustrations in this book are from the previous edition and are acknowledged there (Hinton 1990, vi). I am grateful to Penny Copeland for her help in processing most of the following, which are additional, and to those who have given permission for their reproduction:

> 1.1: Nick Bradford, for author; 1.3; 2.1–3: Nick Griffiths, for author; 2.4: Penny Copeland and James Miles, for author; 2.7: Faith Vardy for Museum of London Archaeological Service; 3.3a and 3.3b: Society of Antiquaries of London; drawing by Chris Fern; 3.5a and 3.5b: Dave Watt, for author; 4.1: the late Bill Putnam; 7.1: Thames Valley Archaeological Services.

Introduction

The intention of this book is to present a chronological consideration of the role of archaeology in the study of the Middle Ages in England, as was that of the original edition (Hinton 1990). It has been completely rewritten, and its extra length is a mark of the amount of new information that has been published. Two major factors account for this: more excavation and fieldwork and more discoveries of artefacts. Planning regulations, notably the introduction of the principle that developers should ensure that a record is made of any archaeological remains that their work destroys, has led to an upsurge in discoveries wherever ground is disturbed – in towns and the countryside, in gravel-pits and quarries, and along the routes of new roads, railways, and pipelines. Another major introduction has been the Portable Antiquities Scheme, which began with pilot studies in 1995 and quickly built up into a nationwide network of recorders, with results entered on to an invaluable website. Most metal-detector hobbyists adhere to its guidelines, report their finds, and add to existing knowledge; this is particularly seen in the discussions of coin numbers and uses in this book for which the Early Medieval Coin Corpus maintained at the Fitzwilliam Museum, Cambridge, has been a great help.[1]

The last 30 years has also seen the continuation of an upsurge of interest in specific areas of study, reflected in the expansion of journals such as *Vernacular Architecture* and *Castle Studies Group Bulletin*. New outlets for publications on the Middle Ages include *Early Medieval Europe* and *Journal of Medieval History*. These take papers from across Europe, as increasingly has *Medieval Archaeology*, a widening of outlook that this book does not reflect. I still believe that a chronological outline is a useful prelude both to both in-depth and to broadening studies, however. Inevitably, some people will think that I have not paid enough attention to a topic of particular interest to them, such as church archaeology and the development of building styles and sculptures, not only tomb monuments on the inside but also the 'exhibitionist' creatures and humanoids on the outside. Some people will be disappointed that I have not dealt with a town, castle, or early medieval cemetery of particular interest to them. Others will take an opposite view and regard the book as too processualist, not paying enough attention to new approaches.[2]

DOI: 10.4324/9781003007432-1

Contributions to two books in particular are referenced frequently: the Oxford University Press *Handbook* series covering the archaeology of the early and later Middle Ages. With a cruel irony, the spectacular discovery of a hoard was made in a field in Staffordshire only a few days after the first of those had gone to press; not long afterwards, the 'Prittlewell Prince' was excavated. The Staffordshire hoard was an assemblage that no-one had even conceived of as having once existed; the chamber-burial excavated in Essex was something that could have been imagined, but was something that no-one expected ever to have survived to be recovered. They overshadow many other discoveries, some of which have led to the recognition of a new type of site. Nor would the two early eleventh-century massacre sites have been anticipated. Important as those all are, in the long term it is the everyday sites and finds that are most informative about the lives of medieval people and their struggles with work, health, dearth, social relations, and death. These subjects can also be studied at different times and in different ways, using documentary evidence; some of the footnotes in this book may seem excessively long, but they are intended to show some of the light that can be thrown by historians on issues addressed by archaeologists studying the Middle Ages.[3]

Some unexpected controversies have arisen during the last 40 years, which are not about the true purpose of archaeology and its relationship with history alone. In the early Middle Ages, there were peoples and tribes such as Angles and Saxons but not 'anglo-saxons', a word that has become controversial, particularly in the United States where it has overtones of white supremacy – although I always assumed that the term 'White anglo-saxon Protestant' was used ironically as 'WASP'. The word was coined by a seventeenth-century translator of William Camden's sixteenth-century *Anglo-Saxones*, and therefore has the Lewis Carroll advantage of meaning what I want it to mean, but out of deference to sensibilities I have either avoided using it or given it lower case initials. How far to take such practice is problematic, and I have gone to the extreme of giving religions lower case initials, so as not to imply that one belief is superior to another, but I have used capitals for languages. 'Viking' is also deliberately spelt with a lower case 'v' because the people for whom it is convenient to use the term were also from a variety of tribes, peoples, and modern countries. For a specific tribe and so on, a capital latter is appropriate, as in 'English', 'Saxon', or 'Norman', although all may have been less uniform than the names might imply.[4]

The book has been written in 2020 and 2021, during the various restrictions imposed by the COVID-19 pandemic, which has not only given a little poignancy to Chapter 10 on the Black Death, but has also greatly reduced the possibilities of visiting libraries and archives and of procuring suitable new illustrations. The latter is not an enormous problem, as a reader can find multiple images of almost anything with the press of a couple of buttons – images that are nearly all in colour and lack the density required for reproduction. Other buttons give access to many books and journals, though far from all – and I am very grateful to colleagues in the Hartley Library at the University of Southampton who instituted a 'click and collect' system without which I would have been unable to proceed.

The previous edition of this book was written with a fountain pen on the back of scrap paper. The manuscript was typed up for me, and I carried it by hand to the publisher, with the illustrations. The typescript had to be recast manually by the printer, the illustrations were turned into plates, and the first proofs were then sent to me on paper to be checked line by line, approved, and posted back. This edition so far has been, and presumably all will be, done electronically. Despite the change of working practice that all this has entailed, however, I hope that I have nevertheless taken to heart my own long-ago instruction to students, which I found when preparing this book on a sheet of paper that I had reused for notes: 'Anything written needs to have clarity; it is for a writer to make a point clear, not for a reader to have to work out what is intended.'

Notes

1 Lewis *et al.* 2011 for an introduction particularly relevant to early medieval studies.
2 For 'exhibitionist' sculpture, see Woodcock 2005. For new approaches to the later Middle Ages: see Gilchrist and Reynolds 2009 and Gilchrist 2008; 2009; 2012.
3 Handbooks: Hamerow *et al.* (eds) 2011; Gerrard, C. M. and Gutiérrez (eds) 2018. See Chapters 2, 3, and 5 for the Prince, the hoard, and the massacres.
4 J. Hines, 'Who did the Anglo-Saxons think they were?', *Current Archaeology* 366 (Sept. 2020), 52–5 explains the origin and reasons for *Angli* and *Saxones* verbally coalescing.

1 The Fifth Century

Living Without the Legions

Anyone living in Britain in A.D. 400 who had any information about what was happening beyond their immediate neighbourhood, or who knew how much the province had changed during the previous century, would probably have been very worried about the future. With barbarians within the Empire and repeated struggles for the imperial title, occasional episodes of stability must have seemed something to be hoped for rather than expected. An observer could have seen how towns were losing their temples and grand houses, how defensive walls had become necessary as raiders from outside the Empire – from modern Ireland, Germany, and Scotland – took slaves and property because garrisons were insufficient for protection, and how opulent villas were becoming grain-processing and industrial centres. The new religion, christianity, may have promised salvation in the next world but could not offer it in the living one.[1]

Social and economic changes in the fifth century are signalled as much by what ceases to be present in the archaeological record as by what is actually found. In particular, the large towns reveal very little sign of urban use: streets and buildings were not maintained; butchered bones and broken pots were not being discarded; build-up of 'dark earth' layers may have resulted from silt overflowing from uncleared drains and from rotting straw roofs, or might contain soil spread over streets and building rubble so that some sort of market-gardening could take place, but anyone living within the old towns was not leading an urban life, and they were not building houses that could be identified. A few people were being buried within the walls, however, a sign of the breakdown of control, for such burial had been strictly forbidden by the Empire; in Canterbury, a pit containing a male, a female, two children, and two dogs may have represented a family group. In Lincoln, a building identified as a christian church inside the forum-basilica had a burial within it that contained a repaired sixth- or seventh-century hanging-bowl, but whether that proves uninterrupted use of the site is highly contentious, and there is only a very little other evidence of activity. Open space would have remained in a forum-basilica for a while, so assemblies might have taken place in some of them but not for everyday marketing, or there would be butchered animal bones.[2]

Marketing was inhibited by another of the fifth-century absences. Roman Britain had made extensive use of base-metal and silver coins for buying, selling, and

DOI: 10.4324/9781003007432-2

paying taxes and presumably wages but had ceased to mint any of its own. New supplies of the copper-alloy coins had virtually ceased to arrive by the end of the fifth century's first decade, and existing stocks could not have lasted long enough to be used in everyday small-scale transactions. A few gold and base-metal coins continued to come into Britain, but, more significantly, silver *siliquae* show both that new coins were very hard to come by and that they were still in demand: many that are found in hoards had been clipped, reducing their silver content. This was not done furtively, as the trimming of the edges is so visible. Furthermore, the image of the emperor's head was always left undamaged. These coins must have been acceptable, at least for some purposes. Perhaps it was generally believed that order would be restored by Rome, as it had been in the past, and that the *siliquae* would again be currency used at face value.[3]

Disruption is also indicated by one particular presence – that of hoards. Several have been found, usually with silver plate from dinner services, either complete or cut up into pieces that could be weighed, valued, and used as rewards, allowing wealthy Britons to offer incentives to those whom they wanted to serve them, even perhaps as mercenaries to defend them. The huge hoard found on the hillfort Traprain Law near Edinburgh may not have resulted from a successful raid by Picts into Britain but may represent an attempt to pay one frontier group to stave off attacks by others. Without new supplies, any coins in the hoards may already have been quite old when buried, so dating is difficult, and deposition could have continued long into the fifth century, but a single hoard that has in it coins of the 460s points towards an earlier date for the rest.[4]

The third great fifth-century absence is an abundance of wheel-made pottery. Some production continued, such as coarse shell-tempered wares in the south and calcite-gritted in the north, but the big industries could not be maintained, partly because supplies to garrisons were not required and partly because the big urban markets disappeared. Romano-British weaving techniques survived, although the quantities of cloth produced cannot be estimated. Without large groups of pottery and frequent finds of base-metal coins, the dating of sites becomes more difficult; recent work has revealed far more Romano-British rural settlements than previously known, and possibly therefore more may have survived into the post-Roman period than previously realized, all but untraceable without the pottery and coin evidence. Similarly, some of the large Romano-British cemeteries may have continued in use without new burial modes by which to identify the latest interments.[5]

Whether there was a fourth great absence of an abundance of people or not has therefore become contentious. The evidence that suggests a population peak of 3.6 million people in Roman Britain does not exist for the fifth century, but the loss of large towns and the reduced scale of use indicated at many other sites, even where it continued in some form, point to a substantial diminution. How that came about is another question: populations can be reduced suddenly by disease, but the 'Justinian plague' was to come in the next century. Mass famine is unlikely: low-lying fenlands and marshes flooded over, but whether that was because there was not enough labour to keep drainage cuts and sea-banks operational, or because the sea-level rose, is debatable; dendrochronology indicates warm conditions in the second half of the fourth and in the fifth centuries which might have been enough to melt some icebergs.[6]

A few people may have emigrated; strong links with Britanny are suggested by place-name similarities but not by a sudden growth in settlement numbers there. Slavery is another form of emigration, and successful raiding parties would have taken captives to sell. Warfare would have killed some of the combatants but not the bulk of the population. More difficult to understand are self-limiting strategies; in times of perceived crisis, people have smaller families and, at present, that seems the most feasible explanation for post-Roman population decline.[7]

Without the demand for grain to be supplied to towns and to the garrisons on the Rhine, much less arable land would have been needed and, therefore, fewer people for the labour-intensive work of ploughing, sowing, harvesting, and processing (Illus. 1.1). Pollen sequences show increases in grasses, but few fields were abandoned altogether; trees and woodland did not grow over them, so they were used for raising animals. Unfortunately, cereals are harvested for their grains before they can pollenate, so intermittent ploughing of fields predominantly used for grazing may be disguised. The different types of cereal grown depended both upon soil and climatic suitability and upon personal preference; a trend towards growing bread-wheats may be because their taste was preferred, not because they required less threshing and were therefore labour-saving. Medieval field boundaries more often than not overlie Roman ones, though some of those may reflect the lie of the land rather than continued maintenance.[8]

The bones of the animals reared, mainly sheep and cattle, may show slight changes in size from the Roman period, but they were certainly not seriously malnourished and left to fend for themselves; many lived for several years to provide wool, milk, and traction before being slaughtered for meat, hides, and bones for tools. Pigs were mostly killed in their second year, when at their most productive for meat, as they have no use but as pork; they were therefore being closely controlled, even when feeding in woodland in the autumn. Chickens, ducks, and geese were kept. Wild boar, deer, and wild birds figured little in people's diet; horses may sometimes have been eaten, but most died when too old to be much use for meat. Agriculture was not practised for basic subsistence alone, as some things like iron had to be acquired, and rents in kind, termed renders, almost certainly had to be given to chiefs and overlords, but farmers were able to practise 'risk-aversion' strategies, avoiding over-reliance on any one product.[9]

Without the imperial troops to maintain order for the civilian magistrates, 'post-colonial' conditions came into play. In some areas, opulent Roman villas seem to have been the country retreats of people who made large profits from supplying goods and services to the Empire and receiving bribes for helping to administer it, but were also in use as estate centres. The suspicion that too many excavations of Roman villas used to be focused on walls and mosaic floors, shovelling off the overlying layers in order to reach them and dismissing evidence of craft and agricultural processing activity as squatter occupation, has been justified by some recent work. Perhaps the most surprising, albeit preliminary, results have been reported from Chedworth, Gloucestershire, where a very large villa has produced

Illustration 1.1 An excavated Romano-British barn at Worth Matravers, Dorset. In the foreground is a grain-dryer; hot air from the stoke-pit on the right was drawn under the partly surviving stone-flagged floor, on to which grain would have been piled to 'parch' it for easier milling or to stop it from germinating if it was wanted for ale. Production of cereals in an area of thin soils, so close to the sea that salt-laden winds would have affected their growth, reflects imperial demand for British grain. The dryer was filled in and floored over; either the barn was still roofed, or it was a hard-standing for animals. After its demolition, a grave was cut through the wall at the top right, undated but probably of the same sixth- to seventh-century date as a small cemetery excavated nearby; the stone slab structure annexed to the middle of the barn's wall may have been a cist grave from which all trace of a skeleton had gone. The photograph therefore demonstrates the pressures placed on farmers by Rome, reduction in demand at the end of the Roman period, and new early medieval uses: the Decline and Fall of the Roman Empire in a Dorset field (Graham *et al.* 2002, 19–25; Ladle 2018, 78–93).

fifth- and sixth-century radiocarbon dates, including one for a wall which bounded a mosaic, so that the mosaic itself must have been laid no earlier than the year 424. It was not of top quality, but even for a second-rate work to have been possible well in the fifth century would suggest more survival of skills and patronage than previously realized. Late Roman shelly pottery was found as were imported fifth- and sixth-century wares from the Mediterranean. At least part of the villa remained as a high-status place, therefore, but other parts were, more typically, downgraded, with a grain-dryer inserted where wealthy occupants used to stroll. Also in the Cotswolds, a villa at Frocester, Gloucestershire, remained in use, with relatively large amounts of pottery, albeit not of high quality, and some other items that are likely to run on well into the fifth century.[10]

Wealth, or at least serious attempts to signal it, has also been found in the west of *Londinium* in the modern Trafalgar Square area. A large kiln was still producing bricks and tiles in the first half of the fifth century; no demand was coming from within the city as it was being abandoned, so the supplies must have been for a villa or a shrine. Nearby, burials included one in a reused stone sarcophagus. Other cemeteries were in use around London; one to the east contained a grave of someone buried with a belt-buckle of a type usually associated with military costume. It raises the possibility that a soldier had been hired to defend the city in the early fifth century, but he also had a 'cross-bow' brooch, an imperial symbol of authority. Despite being unoccupied, London could have been seen as still usable in an emergency, as might Silchester, Hampshire, where the very recent discovery of a buckle of late fourth-/early fifth-century type joins a scatter of post-Roman objects from inside and outside its walls. Shore forts like Portchester (Illus. 1.2) and Pevensey also have fifth-century objects and could have been retained in use, as might have been the signal station or small fort at Filey, Yorkshire. Some of the forts along Hadrian's Wall were also still used, like Birdoswald and Vindolanda; those might have become power bases for former garrison leaders, who had to live by extortion because they were no longer receiving wages. At the west end of the Wall, Carlisle remained in some sort of use, with a timber building and a belt fitting found in one excavated site. Belt fittings with military connotations are widespread, usually as stray finds, and may show that people were claiming that they would fight for their position in life; some have christian imagery.[11]

Silchester is particularly interesting because it has good evidence about its final years and because it is one of the sites with evidence of people from outside the Empire being in Britain. Found in a well was a stone column with a personal name incised into it, in Irish ogam, a script of the fourth/fifth century; its deposition looks like a deliberate 'closing' act no earlier than the mid fifth century. Studies of isotopes in teeth that may reveal where someone was brought up are indicating that many people who were buried in the large Romano-British cemeteries had come from overseas and some from far east beyond the Alps. Whether anyone in them arrived in the fifth century remains in doubt. In a fort just outside Gloucester, the burial of a man with some late fourth- or fifth-century silver dress fittings and other objects inside an existing stone building may be that of a recruit from eastern Europe; the fort was later to be the site of a royal residence, Kingsholm, though

Illustration 1.2 Portchester Castle, Hampshire, was a Roman shore-fort where the stone walls required little subsequent maintenance to remain usable, like the circuit defences of many towns. Excavation has shown that the interior was used from the third century onwards, but whether it had a defensive role in the fifth century is not known; the only objects excavated are not 'military'. Occupation of the sixth to eighth centuries was not substantially different from that of other sites, but it was a *burh* and probably a thegn's residence in the ninth to eleventh centuries, becoming the site of a castle. The lower part of the Water Gate, on the left, is early Norman; the keep was built in three stages (the buttress tops show where its roof was originally). Behind the keep, the ruined hall complex provided the context for the entertainment and display expected of a fourteenth-century king. In the left corner, Assheton's Tower was a late fourteenth-century innovation for gunnery. The church is what remains of a twelfth-century Augustinian Priory, a frequent but usually unhappy combination with a castle – in this case, leading to relocation. Eighteenth- and nineteenth-century barrack blocks show up as parchmarks to the west of the church (Cunliffe 1976; Cunliffe and Munby 1985).

there is no other evidence of continuity within it; inside the city itself are a few possible traces of activity.[12]

What is not in doubt is that during the course of the fifth century, people living in most of the eastern side and the central zone of England were increasingly likely to be buried with objects that had either come from, or were made in close imitation of, things made on the continent, mostly outside the boundaries of the Roman Empire, from southern Scandinavia down to the Low Countries, but also in northern France, in an area that seems to have been overrun by tribes who moved south across the Rhine and established the kingdom of the Franks. Whether grave-goods signal immigrants, or natives adopting new customs, remains in debate, as does whether the people buried without goods were natives, forced to come to terms with incomers; there are even a few instances of people buried with objects that suggest a Romano-British mode. Isotopes are opening up new ways of considering these questions but can only reveal whether someone had grown up in an environment significantly different from the one in which they were buried and then only if the enamel in their teeth is used; children of migrants, or anyone from an area with a chemical geology not unlike that of their resting-place, will not be signalled. DNA extracted from bones has the problem that immigrants may have the same ancient shared ancestry as the native population. Differences in height, with newcomers slightly taller than indigenes, may not be significant, as different diet, with more meat available, could account for slight changes. How many people crossed the North Sea or the Channel to settle in England remains incalculable; the language spoken in most of the country changed from various forms of Celtic or Brittonic into Germanic Old English, but that may have been achieved as much by political as by numerical dominance.[13]

During the fifth century, new types of brooches and other objects appeared in the south and east of England, introduced from the northern continent but not clustered in particular zones. The early fifth-century 'wide equal-arm' brooch is found on the continent mostly in north Germany, and in small numbers in East Anglia near the coast, but also in the Upper Thames Valley, Surrey, and Wiltshire (Illus. 1.3). A little later in date are the first 'bracteates', round pendants of thin sheet gold with designs that at first were clearly modelled on imperial coins; one found at Scalford, Leicestershire, has a crowned head drinking from what is recognizable as a glass cone beaker, an early allusion to the importance of feasting for those who could afford the conspicuous consumption involved. On the continent, bracteates were mostly made in modern Denmark, but in England they are not found solely in the zones closest to the shortest sea-crossing. The earliest 'great square-headed brooches', which appear probably at the end of the fifth or early in the sixth century, are few but have been found from the Isle of Wight to the Warwickshire Avon and Lincolnshire, unlike their successors which are less showy but have become more localized. The glass cone beaker shown on the Scalford bracteate is a type well known on the continent as well as in England and is one of several different vessel shapes, some of which may have been made in Kent but are not confined to it. All these objects may have signalled elites rather than regional or tribal allegiances.[14]

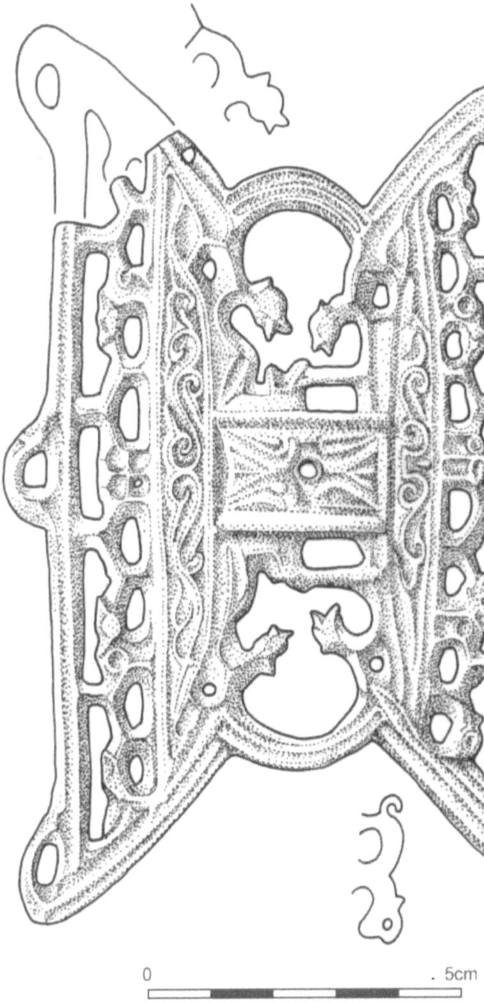

Illustration 1.3 A fifth-century 'wide equal-arm brooch' made of gilded copper alloy, from an adult female's grave at Collingbourne Ducis, Wiltshire. The brooch had had long use so some of the detail is not clear, but the drawings show how animals can be recognized in its pattern. It had been damaged and repaired: the small hole in the side upper left is present where a rivet had been used to hold a repair patch in place, unsuccessfully as it was not still with the brooch when it was buried. Brooches of this type were usually worn in the middle of a woman's chest to hold a shawl or cloak in place, with the arms horizontal; this brooch was found upright by the shoulder, so unless it had been displaced after burial by burrowing animals, it might have been placed in the grave by people who did not know how it was supposed to be worn; either it was of a type that had passed out of normal modes of costume, or it had come from an area where people had different customs. It has been identified as a Nesse Type, emphasizing its close connections with, if not manufacture in, an area of north Germany. The cemetery is only some 250 metres away from where a settlement has been excavated but was on higher ground (Gingell 1975/6, 68 and 76; Walton Rogers 2007, 121; Egging Dinwiddy and Stoodley 2016, 2 and 116–17).

As well as inhumation, cremation was used for many burials. A few cremation cemeteries in eastern England were very large, numbering in thousands and probably drawing on populations that did not all live in the immediate area. The funeral pyre had to be carefully prepared if the whole of a corpse was to be consumed, and the heat had to be high enough for the bones to be reduced to powdery ash so that they could be gathered after the pyre had cooled down, and buried in a pottery urn or a bag. The whole process therefore took time and effort, rather more than an inhumation, although what ceremonies, including funeral meals at the graveside, took place is unknowable for either method. Two large cremation cemeteries studied recently are Spong Hill in Norfolk and Cleatham in Lincolnshire; differences between them include several cases in the latter where one burial cut into and overlay another, while in Spong each seems to have been kept carefully separate even in the same pit. Indeed, the urns at Spong are more like those in a cremation cemetery in Germany at Issendorf than those at any cemetery in England, suggesting regular cross-North Sea contact maintained by two communities rather than a wholesale migration. Urns were often stamped or otherwise decorated, but many show signs of wear, so they were not new and specially made for burial; they were built up by hand, not thrown, usually in fairly coarse fabrics, though the exteriors were often burnished to give a sheen, and stamps with various designs appear on many. Occasionally, wheel-turned Romano-British pots were used as urns, possibly taken from second- or third-century cremation cemeteries, or from old kilns, but there is a possibility that they were made in the fifth or even sixth century, if the skill required to throw them on a wheel had survived.[15]

Broadly at the same time and in the same areas as cremation and grave-goods began to appear, so did new settlements with distinctive types of building. The most easily located is the 'sunken-featured', having a rectangular pit of varying size from about 2 metres by 1 metre up to 4 or 5 metres by up to 3 metres, usually with two or more post-holes inside them at their ends. When first identified, it was thought that the 'sfbs' were houses, with the occupants living a squalid semi-troglodytic existence that was difficult to reconcile with the quality of the objects found in graves. Subsequent excavation has found evidence for much larger rectangular structures with floors at ground level, indicating a higher standard of living. The ground-level buildings vary a little in size but do not at first show differences in either their location within a settlement or in their method of construction, which involved setting timber posts into individual holes, which would clearly denote a dominant family. At first glance, therefore, they seem unlike the cemeteries, with their swords and brooches suggesting elites; but with exceptions, the graves may reflect internal family structures, not that one group of people had greater resources than another. No fifth-century 'chieftain' sites have been found in eastern England or the Midlands.[16]

The use of the 'sfbs' probably varied; some may have been for grain storage, although cereals would have had to be dried first to prevent mildew. Rows of clay loomweights, as though from a collapsed loom or shelf, found on the floors of a few suggest that some were weaving huts, with roofs high enough for an upright loom. That arrangement would have kept the cloth away from the smoke and dirt of cooking fires, and the loom would not have needed to be disassembled to create space when people came home from work out in the fields. The textiles produced can be identified from very rare surviving fragments or from mineralized remains on objects; the warp-weighted loom could produce good woollens, which seem more like Romano-British types than Germanic or Scandinavian, so indigenes survived, perhaps as slaves, at least long enough to imbue succeeding generations with their techniques. The rows of weights present another question, however; it would have been so easy to stoop down and pick them up that it seems that they must have been deliberately left, as though their owner had passed on, and it was not appropriate to use them again. Some 'sfbs' seem to have been more carefully backfilled than others, with objects in them that look likely to have been deliberately deposited; such 'closure' may have taken place because the owner had died.[17]

Dating of buildings is problematic, as even the 'sfbs' can usually reveal only when they were backfilled, not when they were constructed, and the sizes of their post-holes imply big enough timbers to have survived for some years, if their thatched roofs were maintained. How long a timber dug into damp ground will last is an important aspect of discussion, particularly about the Vale of Pickering in Yorkshire, where 130 'sfbs' and 90 ground-level buildings were reported, which would indicate a large population if each had been used by several generations. The alternative is that buildings did not have long lives because of an association with the dead, and people moved a few metres to a new site, unhindered by fixed property boundaries, living in small groups, as is usually advocated for sites like Mucking, Essex, and West Stow, Suffolk.[18]

The settlement sites must have relied mainly on their own resources for food, fuel, and building materials. They were not isolated, however, as iron, glass vessels, and lava quernstones were reaching them, and although gold bracteates may have been beyond the reach of most, the objects in burials show that many people had access to copper alloy for their brooches, many of which were gilded, so both a little gold and a little mercury were available. The bracteates were made by stamping very thin metal sheets over iron dies, but most of the jewellery was cast, requiring crucibles and charcoal to melt the available alloys and pour it into the moulds. More time and knowledge were needed for this process than an everyday farmer could have had, but who the smiths were and how they were supported have to be assessed as much from their finished products as from direct evidence, of which there is little for the immediate post-Roman period: broken moulds and crucibles are rare finds in the 'sfb' sites, and metalworking hearths have not been definitely recognized. If the smiths travelled from one place to another, their brooches would in theory show the zones in which particular types and designs were acceptable, but some brooches may subsequently have been taken out of the areas in which they normally circulated, if marriage took a girl away from her roots. A recent study of cruciform brooches, introduced early in the fifth century, demonstrated not only how widespread they were initially, but also that many had been repaired or damaged before burial, so may have passed through different owners, ending up some way from where they were made. A smith working in copper alloys may also have had to be a skilled ironsmith, capable of producing the elaborate pattern-welded blades of many swords.[19]

Brooches were clearly valued for their symbolism and meaning rather than for what their metal was worth. At a different level, hand-made pottery that could be fired in a simple bonfire, although not to a high temperature, might have been made in every household or might already have been acquired from local specialists. It was used in quantity; West Stow produced over 50,000 sherds. Some pottery was made using organic materials as a binder, such as chopped grass or straw; it has now been found so widely that it can no longer be used as a sign of immigrants. The cremation urns hint at specialists able to spend time on the decoration of different stamps and patterns; the Cleatham possibility of wheel-turned products would certainly indicate people with special knowledge. Exchange mechanisms that brought glass and querns to settlement sites would also have brought salt, essential for every household. Gift exchange may explain many of the elite objects but not the everyday items; renders to lords could have been reciprocated with commodities such as salt and iron, but more likely is the possibility that at least some coinless trading was taking place, possibly when people assembled for meetings or at funerals; neighbours may have trusted one another enough for reciprocal arrangements, and itinerant traders may have brought goods that they would barter for textiles.[20]

Nearly all the settlements with many 'sfbs' do not overlie earlier Romano-British buildings, although they may not be very far away (Illus. 1.4), and a few are within the walls of the old towns, though not in the large ones except for Canterbury. Similarly, the burials with grave-goods show no direct continuity with Romano-British sites, with a single exception, which is a cemetery in Warwickshire at Wasperton, well inland and where perhaps new customs arrived later than to the east and therefore the likelihood of continuity might seem less. Despite that, burials of traditional type were joined by some with occasional grave-goods. The two groups were contiguous but do not seem to have overlapped, so people with the new and the old customs may not have integrated; the remarkable thing is that only at that one site can they be seen coming together at all, although Stretton in the same area has only 60 metres between two similar groups. Immigrants replacing natives is the obvious interpretation, but natives accepting new customs is another. Stretton had an abnormally high proportion of male burials with weapons, and skeletal differences raise the possibility that they were incomers, but that the women were native.[21]

Questions of differences between migrants and natives are also raised by the only hoard with coins datable to the second half of the fifth century, found in West Sussex at Patching; it contained gold coins, including two minted in the 460s, and so were recent imports. It also had *siliquae*, a few clipped, suggesting that they had been acquired in Britain. Two gold rings, one of very pure metal and not therefore made from melted-down coins, and a piece of Germanic silver derived from no obvious source in Britain, together with the absence of any large pieces of plate, show that Patching is not in the same category as the earlier British hoards.

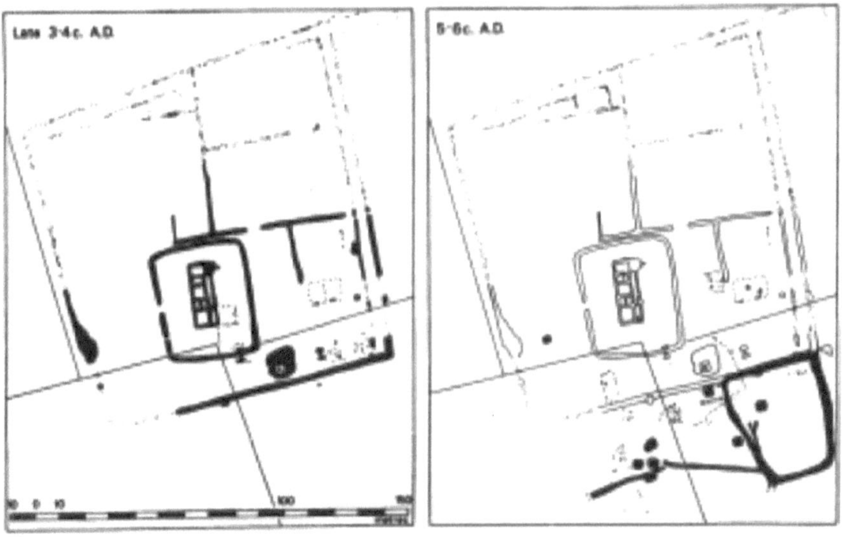

Illustration 1.4 Romano-British and later phases at Barton Court Farm, Oxfordshire. An eight-roomed stone house was demolished after *c.* 370, other buildings surviving a little longer. 'Sunken-featured buildings', fence-lines, and burials followed, but not in arrangements which suggest that they had any direct connection with the previous use of the site, though burials close to Roman ruins occur quite frequently, cf. Illus. 1.1 and Shapwick, Somerset: Gerrard and Aston 2007, 964–5. The new enclosure emphasizes the changes in ownership and use (Miles (ed.) 1986).

It may have been owned by someone with continental support and who had built up a treasure-hoard which he could disburse to followers in a power-grab or by someone who was hoping to use it to enable him to cling on to inherited authority and land. He was not a heroic figure like the supposed King Arthur, with an overarching mission to defend the native people and christianity against the incomers, but someone operating out of self-interest. Such leaders were able to arrange occasional alliances, and some had more followers than others, but their power was fleeting.[22]

*

Even by the end of the fifth century, some areas in eastern England have not produced furnished inhumations, cremations, or 'sfbs'. Some proposed gaps have been filled by subsequent discoveries, but one that still remains significant is north of London, modern Hertfordshire. The walled area of Verulamium was slower to lose occupation than London, finally being used for agricultural processing with a barn and a water pipe; extra-mural cemeteries seem to have remained in use, without grave-goods and aligned on the later abbey, which suggests that they were christian. A fragment of a penannular brooch of late fourth- or fifth-century date is not a type associated with immigrants, but with the west. A christian cult-centre may have survived to become today's St Albans. Another Hertfordshire town, Baldock, has substantial evidence of burials and occupation likely to run throughout the fifth century.[23]

Christianity may account for vestiges of continued use elsewhere. In Devon, the Roman *Isca*, now Exeter, had a fourth-century forum and basilica, used for burials, aligned on the Roman street grid, not west-east, and radiocarbon-dated from the fifth to the early seventh centuries; only six graves were found, but others might have been beyond the excavation site's limits. Their presence may show continued use at least of the central part of the town, unless the dead were brought for burial where Roman lustre might be bestowed on them by people who had forgotten the Roman ban on intra-mural cemeteries. Some sherds of Palestinian and north African amphoras might be either of fourth- or fifth-century date, and perhaps three fifth-/sixth-century imported sherds have been found. There were also 'dark earth' layers.[24]

In north Somerset, the Roman *Aquae Sulis* had become *Bathum* by the end of the eighth century; the walled circuit contained temples, baths, and fine stone houses in the Roman period, with most of the evidence for normal urban activity being extra-mural, beside the River Avon along Walcot Street. The intra-mural area was already changing in the fourth century, with reduction in the scale of the religious complexes, leading to collapse or deliberate demolition. The central baths were still visited in the fifth century, however, with enough visitors to wear down a path through the rubble; one of them dropped a penannular brooch of fifth-/sixth-century type, proving post-Roman use. Other hot springs there seem to have been given no attention, and 'dark earth' formed in at least one area. No imported pottery has been found, so whether the place had any residential, religious, defensive, or trading use is unknown.[25]

In south Somerset, Ilchester had been a fort on the Fosse Way in Roman times. A late Roman military-style buckle may indicate that a garrison was there in the late fourth century or that someone was wearing it in the fifth century to claim military rights. Coarse shell-tempered pottery may also indicate fifth-century occupation, although the quantities are small. One of several cemeteries had late Roman types of burial, with hobnails, and a coin in one skeleton's mouth; another cemetery reportedly had west–east burials, some in coffins, and possibly were christian. Two Byzantine coins may show sixth-century use, if they were contemporary imports. Ilchester as a place where authority was exercised was superseded by the reuse of the Iron Age hillfort at South Cadbury, where the upper rampart was restored with a drystone, timber-laced wall, and a timber gateway; traces of a possible building, 19 metres long, with curved ends and a hearth, placed on the most conspicuous part of the hill, would have been suitable for a chief's hall.[26]

South Cadbury was not the only old hillfort to come back into use. Badbury Rings in Dorset has been shown in a recent excavation to have a late or post-Roman mortared wall built over the inner Iron Age rampart, and surfaces nearby gave fifth-/sixth-century radiocarbon dates. Cadbury Congresbury, Somerset, is another, with buildings, craftworking, and some signs of restructuring of the defences. Budbury hillfort overlooking Bradford-on-Avon has an undated drystone wall, and a post-Roman buckle was found in it. Nearby, excavation of a Roman villa discovered what may well have been a christian baptistery, so continued use is possible. Another possibility is Poundbury outside Dorchester in Dorset; the hillfort had a drystone wall, unfortunately undated, but suggestive because it overlooks a late Roman extra-mural cemetery which continued in use for burials before being replaced by timber buildings that might include a shrine.[27]

Elsewhere, direct evidence of hillforts is slight or lacking. Irthlingborough, Northamptonshire, had some late Roman use, and its ditches may have been widened soon afterwards. In Northumberland, Yeavering Bell looms over a site that developed into a major complex and may have had some use in the Roman period but has no trace of subsequent refortification. The Patching hoard was found near Highdown Hill, but its interior has not been shown to have been in use; another Sussex hillfort, the Caburn outside Lewes, has also been mooted but similarly has no positive evidence. In Shropshire, Wrekin Hill has been proposed on the basis that a group of people, the *Wreaconsaete*, took their name from it, but that may simply have been because it was a landmark, not that it was a successor to Wroxeter, a Roman town where the claim for large post-Roman buildings has been scrutinized and found unlikely, although a few post-Roman objects and burials have been found, and outside it was an inscribed stone with an Irish name, probably dating from the fifth century. Lichfield, Staffordshire, however, has some evidence suggesting use, and it may be that some smaller towns, serving local market needs, lasted longer than the major centres.[28]

Christianity may not have achieved total dominance in fourth-century Roman Britain, but it seems likely to have become unchallenged in the fifth century among those who did not adopt the new inhumation and cremation practices. A few older customs such as burial with a coin in the mouth or with hobnails at the feet may have survived for a while, but only in the south-west have enough cemeteries been excavated for distinctions to be clearly apparent. At Cannington, Somerset, several graves had small objects in them but were probably mostly residual from earlier occupation on or near the site, possibly at the nearby hillfort, apart from some iron knives and beads with children. Burnt grain in one grave and charcoal in another suggest pre-christian beliefs, as might a few non-standard cases of flexed legs and a crouched female – use of the cemetery probably began in the fourth, even possibly the late third, century, as identified by radiocarbon dating; traces of a structure that could have been a shrine that lasted into the late seventh century, the longest timespan of any yet investigated, were also found. As elsewhere, christianity was not overtly displayed but was probably practised after the fourth century, with most people laid supine, with their heads to the west. Low mounds provided foci, one of which contained the grave of a 13-year-old, suggesting someone special; some graves were lined with stones, something seen at other cemeteries, and might denote people of higher status. A small number of imported sherds might show that feasting had taken place at the grave-sides.[29]

The mounds at Cannington could have been for small buildings, as has been suggested at other cemeteries. At Henley Wood, Somerset, a pagan temple might have remained in use for a while as burials there continued – though with no clear-cut transition to christianity and with no direct evidence of association with the nearby Cadbury Congresbury hillfort established. A few buildings elsewhere may be fifth-century christian churches, such as at Uley, Gloucestershire, where the pagan temple had been demolished and its dedications to Mercury smashed to be replaced by at least a baptistery. Christian use of villas like Budbury could account for an occasional instance of a much later church overlying a Roman building, but the conversion of temples as suggested for Uley and even Bath seems occasional at best; Lydney, Gloucestershire, has been reappraised and shown to have no features later than the fourth century, and the temple outside Badbury Rings was demolished, but not so that it could be rebuilt or replaced – its stones were quite possibly used for the refortification of the hillfort. Although the inscribed stones in Silchester and outside Wroxeter are not necessarily christian, a growing number in Cornwall and Devon, some with Irish ogam inscriptions as well as Latin, show connections with christianity overseas.[30]

The south-west of England's connections overseas are also shown by imports of pottery made in the Mediterranean, notably found at Tintagel, Cornwall, and it is likely that Cornish tin was a return cargo. The next largest amounts are from two coastal sites in south Devon, Bantham and Mothecombe, from which Dartmoor tin may have been shipped, as perhaps were hides from cattle that grazed the lush pastures of the South Hams in winter and spent the summer on the moor, if transhumance was practised. The coastal sites were probably also only used seasonally, operated from places inland better sheltered in winter. Smaller amounts of imports found elsewhere could indicate that the Mendips were still producing lead; Exmoor, and possibly the Forest of Dean iron ore; and even wool or woollen cloth from sheep fed on the Cotswolds and the Wiltshire Downs are possibilities. On the coast in east Dorset, industrial activity involving charcoal-burning for iron-smelting furnaces continued, but the amounts produced may not have been enough to interest exporters. Roman Britain had had well-developed inland salt production in Cheshire and at Droitwich, Worcestershire, where the natural brine springs may have been temporarily abandoned but were coming back into use perhaps late in the fifth century, presumably not for export, but as a sign of returning demand.[31]

The imported pottery was a mix of tableware using red clay and much thinner than anything made in England, and amphoras which contained wine and olive oil. Even if those luxuries had been much available in Roman Britain, a couple of generations had passed, and so it is questionable whether anyone would still have eaten food cooked in oil, not the animal fat that they must have been used to, and the wine was probably fairly sour after its long journey; both could have been for church use. The wine could have been made more palatable by sweetening it with honey, however, which would account for traces of wax found in two amphora sherds from Tintagel analysed by gas chromatography. Other sherds had fatty acids indicating a different use, or rather reuse – large numbers of stoppers show that the amphoras were not discarded after their original contents had been consumed. The glass vessels, the pottery tableware, and the sweetened wine all point to high-status consumption by such people as those who had the resources to commission the memorial stones.[32]

A large fragment of slate inscribed with names and Latin words excavated at Tintagel is another example of the literacy seen on the stones. One of the names is 'Artognou[s]', possibly a rendering of Augustus, implying Roman officialdom; the tin trade may have been an imperial monopoly, like Mendip lead. There is little evidence of use of Tintagel, or of the Devonshire coastal sites, in the Roman period, but a takeover of the metal distribution by power-grabbers can easily be envisaged. On a wider scale, the villas' late Roman roles as processing centres suggest that people were accustomed to bringing produce to them as part of their rent, so it would have seemed no great change to continue to bring grain and animals to wherever they were instructed in return for holding a farmstead and enjoying the protection of a lord from the incursions of outsiders and for the maintenance of laws and customs. The lord, or chief, needed men with him to enforce obedience and to deter raiders, so needed to maintain a household by receiving food and other supplies from the producers. Meetings were probably held, with assent given to the lord's proposals, and the lord then probably gave a feast to cement the people's loyalty and togetherness, but with the hierarchy probably maintained by the exotic tableware and sweetened wine being reserved for the favoured few. The headland at Tintagel where the pottery and glass have been found has not produced any buildings that seem of sufficient size to have been a feasting-hall, but at Mothecombe traces of what are interpreted as being oval buildings would certainly have been large enough to hold a feast in, and the large number of bones from young animals suggests that prime meat was being served.[33]

Another issue for the fifth century is whether it is possible to reconstruct the areas controlled by the people who exercised power. The Roman system of provinces with – presumably – known boundaries was probably not deeply embedded and would not have survived. A revival of Iron Age tribal territories has been mooted but is controversial; the far south-west may have perpetuated the Dumnonian zone but only because it is a peninsula. Its characteristic settlement form, the 'round', was widespread in the Roman period but reduced in number either in the fifth century as part of the post-Roman retraction seen elsewhere or because of political reorganization subsequently. Crouched and flexed burials, as in a cemetery outside Sherborne in Dorset as well as at Cannington, are reminiscent of Durotrigian practices, but they are too few when set against the very many full-length burials to make revival seem likely. Similar ones have been found in Yorkshire, where a territory around Leeds called Elmet was still thought 'British' in the seventh century and seems likely to have retained a cultural difference until then. The boundary between Dorset and Wiltshire is marked by Bokerley Dyke, a late Roman bank and ditch that suggests a frontier that might have been maintained by the Durotiges in the fifth century against the Atrebates but was perhaps more likely perceived to be needed against newcomers in the Salisbury area. Large-scale dykes and hillforts required communal effort, willingly given or otherwise. Maintenance of roads and tracks may have been another obligation carried forward from Roman Britain. Organization of people, and of the supplies needed to sustain those who lived too far away to get home each evening, could have been achieved by an egalitarian social structure where everyone gathered at a meeting-place and assented to the work, but direction by a chieftain centred on a Tintagel or a South Cadbury seems more likely.[34]

A degree of prosperity in Wiltshire is suggested by the likelihood that distinctive metalwork was produced in the northern part of the modern county. Penannular brooches like the one found in Bath and many 'hanging-bowls' have enamelled decoration, a characteristic of Romano-British work which continued into the post-Roman period. Some of those things found their way eastwards and ended up in inhumation graves, but the melted glass technique involved in enamelling seems not to have been adopted in eastern England until the sixth century, and rarely then. Perhaps surprisingly, the decoration does not have overt christian symbolism. In eastern England, many of the 'military' and other fittings had been cut down and adapted by the time that they were buried or lost, and smiths depended heavily upon recycling until late in the fifth century, when new supplies of copper became available to them.[35]

Christianity was also being practised in Northumberland in the fifth century, at least at the Roman forts that remained in use: part of a lead vessel incised with a variety of motifs including chi-rhos and crosses, as well as letters in Latin, Greek, and possibly ogam, is a recent discovery justifying suggestions that buildings there and elsewhere were churches. Settlement was also taking place in the lower valley of the River Glen, with post-built rectangular structures up to 10 metres long near Milfield, dated by radiocarbon to the fifth/early sixth century. Barley may have been the main crop, as other grains were not found in the post-holes; unfortunately, the absence of 'sfbs' or pits in which rubbish might accumulate hinders further comparison with other settlements, but the overall impression is of a substantial farmstead.[36]

*

A descendant of the observer of the condition of Britannia at the start of the fifth century would probably by its end have had no more than a vague concept of a province once ruled by Rome. Instead, the breakdown from a semblance of unity to a chaos of competing chiefdoms is the image presented by Britain's only recorder and might have been the observer's also. The chiefs had warbands that protected their territories and undertook raids into others' territories for loot and to coerce their rivals into paying tribute. In some areas there was christianity and literature, and contact with the Mediterranean; elsewhere, there were people with little concept of such a civilization but with their own ideas of what to believe and how to behave. Materially, those people may have been better off, however, less dominated by the demands of their leaders for luxuries and better able to enjoy the fruits of their agricultural labours for themselves. Even for them, however, worse was to come.[37]

Notes

1 Some time ago, a German historian counted 210 reasons that had been offered to explain the Fall of Rome: cited by Ward-Perkins 2005, 33, whose account of it is the liveliest that I know. Esmonde Cleary 1993 remains a useful overview of Britain. The future St Patrick was captured by Irish raiders from somewhere in Britain, who spent time as a slave; unfortunately, slaves are almost impossible to identify in the material record in this period.

2 'Dark earth' in London was first analysed by MacPhail 1981; other examples include McCarthy 2014, 240–1, on Carlisle, and Ottaway 2015, 54, on York. Bartholomew's argument (1982) that the instruction from the Emperor in A.D. 410 that the *civitates* should look to their own defences applied only to Italy is not unequivocally accepted, but the troop withdrawal of 409–13 is the last reasonably reliable date. Honorius's letter would have implied that a formal administration based on the cities remained viable. A Greek writer also thought that Britain still had cities to defend: Charles-Edwards 2013, 40–4. Canterbury: Bennett 1980 (the group is unprecedented). Lincoln: Vince 2003, 145–9. Silchester's forum-basilica has been mooted as another possibility, on the basis of some window-glass: Fulford *et al.* 2006, 280; the Gloucester forum may also have been kept clear but without any evidence of church use: Heighway 2010, 39–40. Crabtree 2018, ch. 2 for an interesting comparison between Romano-British towns and modern Detroit for the speed and nature of decay. Speed 2014 was also a useful overall discussion.

3 Base-metal coinage: Abdy 2006, 91–4; Moorhead 2006; Moorhead and Walton 2014, 112–14. Naismith 2017, 32–4 for clipping. He pointed out that clipped *siliquae* seem to be exclusively British and that finds made on the continent were probably owned by soldiers who had served in the province.

4 Hoards: Guest 2014, 119–20 for numbers and dating (the exception is Patching) and 124–7 for reasons, which might not simply have been a fear of loss to barbarian raiders; also Naismith 2017, 28–31 and 34–5. Traprain Law: Hunter, F. 2014.

5 Pottery: Gerrard, J. 2010 for a very revealing type made well into the fifth century in south-east Dorset, but nothing like the quantities and distribution of the earlier Black-Burnished wares were made there, which were regularly taken as far away as the forts on Hadrian's Wall; their successors filtered along the south coast as far west as Exeter but made no inroads east into Hampshire or the Isle of Wight or more than a few miles north except for Bath. See also Gerrard, J. 2013 (general overview) and 2014 (pottery) (and see Cleatham). Weaving: Walton Rogers 2007, 230–2. Romano-British settlement density: Allen, M. [a] *et al.* 2017, 12. Even where direct 'continuity' has been identified, it seems to have been on a reduced scale, as at Combe Down, Wiltshire: McOmish *et al.* 2002, 100–10. The reduction in evidence from field walking is exemplified by an intensive study in Essex: Williamson, T. 1988. Cemeteries: see also Ch. 2.

6 R-B population estimate: Allen, M. [a] *et al.* 2017, 179. A number as low as a million is arguable for the fifth/sixth centuries in eastern and southern England (Hedges 2011, 81) but would be higher for the whole country. Sea-level, fens, and marshes (some already being lost in the fourth century): Rippon 2006, 80–1; Murphy 2009, 33–8; Rippon 2017; but Oosthuizen 2017, 10 put the sea rise as late as *c.* 600 for the Wash and preferred an eleventh-century, not Roman, date for the Sea Bank: pp. 44–6.

7 Slavery: Pelteret 1995.

8 Pollen, fields, and boundaries: Rippon 2018, 271–5, summarizing the work of the 'Fields of Britannia' project; for northern England: Higham, N. J. 1986, 243–4. Woodland: Hooke 1998, 144–5, noting that tree growth is also actively managed; Jones, R. and Page 2006, 3–5. Wheat: Moffett, L. 2011, 348–50.

9 West Stow, Suffolk, with some 180,000 bones studied, has the most complete excavation report: Crabtree 1985; 1989; goats are difficult to distinguish from sheep, but at

West Stow the distinction was negligible at around 1%, which is probably typical for most zones. The West Stow sheep were slaughtered a little earlier than most, indicating that they were wanted there for meat as much as for wool. Summaries: Sykes 2006; O'Connor 2011; Banham and Faith 2014, 76–137; Holmes, M. 2018; early anglo-saxon agriculture was 'unfocused and designed to produce a range . . . of meat, milk, wool and traction for local consumption': Crabtree 2018, 66.

10 Villas as estate centres: Allen, M. [a] *et al.* 2017, 362. Chedworth: Papworth 2021a, 21–5; the mosaic dating might yet be challenged, as the charcoal and bone used for it came from a foundation trench, so is it possible that that was originally left open, perhaps for a drain, only later being infilled? Frocester: Price, E. 2000. 'Post-colonial' theory has to some extent displaced 'systems collapse' as a model to explore, but Halsall (2013, 176) noted that the model 'fails' because fourth-century administrators would have been British, not outsiders, so the trajectory to new control systems would have evolved differently. An aspect of urban collapse would have been the disappearance of the emperors' tax-gatherers: Charles-Edwards 2013, 40–4; Wickham 2005 for southern European developments generally, p. 44 for Britain's nearest neighbour. Deliberate rejection of the outside ruler's coinage is another aspect of 'post-colonial' theory, but the clipped *siliquae* and later copying of Roman coin designs do not support its application to post-Roman Britain.

11 St Martin site: Telfer 2010, 52–4; see Ch. 3 for its development. London buckle: Barber, B. *et al.* 1990, 11; Cowie and Blackmore 2008, 128–9. Soldiers might have been former *foederati*, officially brought in from outside the Empire to defend it, and who had subsequently avoided service on the continent. The brooch seems to signal higher status, so may have been worn by a man of authority; a similar belt-set has now been found in a Leicester cemetery: *Current Archaeology* 319 (Oct. 2016), 23. A buckle found in Cemetery I, grave 117 at Mucking, Essex, could also signal a 'soldier' but was not new when buried: Hirst and Clark 2009, 663. London abandonment: Perring 2015, who suggested that a scatter of intra-mural burials could be 'closing' events. Frontier forts: Willmott, T. 2010; Birley 2014. Carlisle: McCarthy 1990, 10–11 and 181; work reported at the cathedral produced a penannular brooch that could date to the fifth century but had had long usage, and pottery that could have been made in the fifth century: McCarthy 2014, 231, brooch report by C. Batey, 210–1; McCarthy 2018, 310–11. Belt fittings that were specifically for soldiers became symbols of rank more generally: Swift 2000, 8–9 and 230; Blaylock 2008; Gerrard, J. 2013, 106; Harland 2019; Swift 2019; during the fifth century, their styles transitioned from males to females. Imagery includes peacocks, symbolic of eternal life through baptism. Ager 1985; Inker 2003: for belts and brooches of the distinctive 'quoit-brooch' style. Silchester belt-buckle: Michael Fulford and Barry Ager, personal communication. An old suggestion that extra-mural amphitheatres might have been defensible has not been supported by subsequent work. Filey: Ottaway 2000; calcite-gritted pottery and a substantial earthwork there may be of post-Roman rather than late Roman period.

12 Silchester: Fulford *et al.* 2006, 274–80. Gloucester: Hurst, H. 1975; Hills and Hurst 1989; Heighway 2010, 44 – none of the contents appears to have been 'military', however; other activity traces: Heighway 2010, 39–40.

13 Isotopes and ancient DNA: Hedges 2011. Isotopes: Ottaway 2017, 178 for Winchester; teeth are used because enamel does not change over time, unlike signatures in bones. Some early results from isotopes seem doubtful to me, such as that a large number of people moved from the Pennines east into Yorkshire. See Carver (2019, 54–6) for a clear discussion of DNA issues; a skeleton from Oakington, Cambridgeshire, gave a 'British' signature but had an above-average number of grave-goods in the new style, so rapid acceptance of new modes by indigenes should not be ruled out, nor that they were not the least prosperous. I have disbelieved the relevance of modern DNA results to ancient populations since reading that a study of people in present-day Welsh towns

found them different from people living in England; as most Welsh towns were settled in the twelfth and thirteenth centuries by English immigrants, the DNA should have given the opposite result. Heights: Hines and Bayliss (eds) 2013, 102–4 and 130. How many people crossed the sea in the post-Roman period is one question, and how they did it is another – the best evidence of boats is still the large open rowing-boat found in a Danish bog at Nydam. The pace of language change is measurable only by the written record, which favoured what the elites could understand, unless it was Latin for the educated; see Coates (2007) for an admirably clear review. See Ch. 2 for further discussion of grave-goods.

14 'Wide Equal-Arm' brooches: Bruns 2003; the Portable Antiquities Scheme website has a few further examples as well as an extremely clear introduction by H. Geake to the different types of brooches. Bracteates: Behr 2011; another has now been found near the Scalford one: Scott and Sharp 2019, 120. 'Great square-headed brooches': Hines 1997, 202 and 226–30 for his Group 1. The magisterial survey using radiocarbon dating, Hines and Bayliss (eds) 2013, does not include the fifth/first half of the sixth centuries, because of the plateau in the curve: pp. 35–7; a sequence for East Anglia starts *c.* 450, when grave-goods become sufficiently common for meaningful study between cemeteries: Penn and Brugmann 2007, 99. Glass: Evison 2008, 11–13 and 49–52 for cone beakers; in upper society, drink was proffered by ladies, for example in *Beowulf*, and see Crawford 2009, 48. Discussions are often made in terms of Angles, Saxons, and Jutes, because of the early eighth-century writer Bede, but archaeology does not correlate with an image of large numbers of migrants crossing the sea from specific continental regions and establishing themselves in specific regions in England: Richardson, A. 2011 set out some of the issues very clearly.

15 Food remains: Lee 2007. Spong Hill: McKinley 1994, 82–105 for the practices involved; Hills and Lucy 2013, 318–19 for Issendorf, 335–43 for summary of other sites. Cleatham: Leahy 2007, 126–7 for the problem of wheel-thrown urns; Squires 2012, 313 for numbers – and 2013. Both sites also had inhumation burials. On cremation, see also Ch. 2.

16 Hamerow 2012, 17–66; nothing directly comparable to the enormous continental long-houses with the provision for cattle at one end has been found, unless a recent excavation in Suffolk has located one. A few Roman 'sfbs' are known but do not have internal post-holes so are not in the same tradition. 'Sfbs', or *Grubenhaüser*, are widespread in northern Europe outside the Empire. Some ground-level buildings might have had sunken features below them, floored over, but various objections to that include the access, requiring a heavy trap-door: Hamerow 2011, 146–51 for the 'suspended floor' issue. Continuous trenches may have joined or replaced individual post-holes at a later date, but they still had posts set into them, not stone wall footings.

17 Hamerow 2012, 61–2 for grain storage, 70–2 and 62–4 for weaving; also Walton Rogers 2007, 30–2. Weaving methods: Owen-Crocker 2007. Housing for most animals can be excluded, as the beasts could not get down into them, but pig coprolites in some areas at West Stow suggest another use – the pigs could be fed on scraps and could not climb out; housing for slaves cannot be totally excluded; slave labour: Faith 1999, 61–70. 'Sfb' fills and their meanings, including human body parts: Morris, J. and Jervis 2011; Sofield 2015, 354–5; Carver 2019, 197–9. See Ch. 2 for further discussion.

18 Vale of Pickering: Powlesland 1999; 2014, 117–19; Blair 2018, 140–1; Hamerow 2011, 135–6 for post longevity.

19 Mercury is needed for fire-gilding and has to be imported from Spain, Italy, or Slovenia: Coatsworth and Pinder 2002, 129–30. Metalworking fragments have been excavated in early 'sfbs' at Witton, Cambridgeshire, and Mucking, Essex, and a few have been found elsewhere: Hinton 2003, 261–2, to which Carlton Colville, Cambridgeshire, can now be added: Lucy *et al.* 2009, 173–4 and 249–62, with contribution by J. Cowgill on smithing, 372–81. Cruciform brooches: Martin, T. F. 2015, 126–33 for 'crafting'

and repairs, 171–6 for early distribution. Swords: Brunning, S. 2019; pattern-welding (Illus. 5.1) involves great skill in welding together separate bars of iron, some often twisted for extra effect; the blades could have been imported, but the wide spread of the objects, not all swords, argues against that: Gilmour, B. 2010; Leahy 2003, 123–8; Birch 2013.

20 West Stow: West, S. 1985, pottery contribution by A. Russel. Chaff-tempered pottery: J. Timby, contribution to Price, E. 2000. Trading would have involved land and water routes, and although maintenance obligations are only documented much later, they could have been applied: Langlands 2019, 165–80 – bridges may have been mostly beyond anglo-saxon capabilities, but clearance, rerouteing to fords, and laying down causeways can all be envisaged: Harrison 2007.

21 Small towns may have been more of a focus than large ones: Heybridge, Essex, and Dorchester-on-Thames, Oxfordshire, are examples: Fitzpatrick-Matthews 2014. Wasperton: Carver 2019, 324–30, and discussion on 389 of other claims. Stretton: Ford 1996, 66–9; Härke 2011, 14 (I have not seen discussion of this cemetery in subsequent publications but suspect that the height difference in males may be a factor of diet rather than of birth: cf. Gowland 2007, 58–9; Hines and Bayliss (eds) 2013, 102–6.).

22 See White, S. *et al.* 1999 for the details and Guest 2014, 120 for its 'singularity'. For 'King Arthur', see Higham 2002 and Halsall 2013; the British victory at Mons Badonicus reported by Gildas could have resulted from one such co-operative venture, and 'Catraeth' from another; see notes 34 and 37 for Gildas, Ch. 2 for 'Catraeth'.

23 Verulamium/St Albans: Niblett 2010, 129–32. A continental account of a victory there may have been of orthodoxy over a British heresy, not a military one. Baldock: Fitzpatrick-Matthews 2014, with discussion of the area generally. Rippon (2018, 268–79) noted various such 'gaps'.

24 Exeter basilica: Bidwell 1979, 112–13; pottery: Campbell, E. 2007, 125–6; Rippon and Holbrook (eds) 2021, 221–2, contribution by J. Allan; Byzantine coins of the period found in Exeter are probably recent souvenirs, as they do not have the corrosion to be expected of British conditions; see further Ch. 2; the burials were originally attributed to the fifth century, but recent dating spans the fifth-to-seventh centuries, pp. 222–4. See Holbrook (2015) for a review of towns in the south-west, including on p. 103 consideration of new data from Dorchester, Dorset, where extra-mural settlement in addition to Poundbury has also been found: Davies, S. M. *et al.* 2002, 171–9.

25 A useful summary by Davenport 2002, 13–21 is augmented by Davenport *et al.* 2007, 97–8; Costen 2011, 8; and the important revision of the baths' dating is augmented by Gerrard, J. 2007. 'Religion' is included as a possibility because a christian church, even one with a bishop, has been postulated, helping to account for the later establishment in Bath of a minster. Bath, Cirencester, and Gloucester were named as three *ceastra* purportedly in 577, but that may mean no more than the fact that old Roman centres were still remembered, not that they were used; the usual translation 'cities' is misleading. *The Ruin* could have been composed with Bath in mind, but Babylon and Aachen might also have informed the poem. Bath was also *Acemannes ceastra* in the tenth century, where *Ace* is from *Aquae*, and the second element is perhaps a British word: Mills 2011, 7; Akeman Street, the Roman road from the east, was not therefore renamed because aching people went along it to seek a cure. Walcot might come from *wealas*, the Old English term for Welsh or British, possibly because a native settlement remained in use, though no archaeological evidence has been found, and the 'cottage [outside the] wall' is a more prosaic alternative.

26 Ilchester: Leach 1982; 1994, 11–12. South Cadbury: Alcock, L. 1995; the element Cad- that appears in several hillforts and other names is thought to be Celtic, meaning 'battle' and/or Cata, a myth-figure hero: Nottingham University on-line ('mist' or 'brook' have also been mooted). Imported pottery: Campbell, E. 2007.

27 Badbury: Papworth 2019, 145–69. The Bad- element which like Cad- was widely used, is Old English for the word 'battle' and/or an Old English personal name, possibly

reconstructed from a Celtic one: Nottingham University on-line. Cadbury Congresbury: Rahtz *et al.* 1992. Budbury hillfort: Brown, R. *et al.* 2019, 100–1; the buckle is not one of the military type; Budbury villa baptistery: Corney 2003, 16–20. Bradford-on-Avon was later recorded as a battle site, though it is not clear whether that was an attack on the hillfort or a skirmish by the river, cf. Old Sarum, Wiltshire (Illus. 2.6) was also named as a battle site, but that might just be that two 'armies' met at the junction of roads there. Poundbury and other south-western sites: Webster, C. J. 2008, 172–86.

28 Irthlingborough: Parry 2006, 97 and 139–42. Yeavering Bell: Frodsham 2005. Wroxeter: Lane, A. 2014; he noted a defensive use of the lower slopes of the Breiddin hillfort across the modern boundary with Wales, pp. 509–11. *-saeta* names are usually associated with rivers, but *-ingas*, *-wara*, *-ge*, and *scir* do not conform to set, widespread patterns of kins, tribes, chiefdoms, peoples, or areas: Yorke 2000; Eagles 2015; Baker, J. 2017. Lichfield: Sargent 2013.

29 Cannington: Rahtz *et al.* 2000. See also Chs 2 and 3.

30 Henley Wood: Watts and Leach 1996; they noted that a later parish boundary separated the cemetery from the hillfort and speculated about its antiquity. Uley and baptisteries: Woodward 1992, 103–9. Budbury: Brown, R. *et al.* 2019. Lydney: Casey and Hoffman 1999. Badbury: Papworth 2019, 168. Inscribed stones: Okasha 1993; Handley 2001; Petts 2014.

31 See Campbell (2007) for the different types of pottery and glass (only some from the Mediterranean, pp. 56–9); imports from France seem to be of later times: see Ch. 2. Many of the ships may have come from southern France and Spain, not directly from the Mediterranean. Bantham: Reed *et al.* 2011; Mothecombe: Agate *et al.* 2012. Imported sherds have been reported at Pevensey, Sussex, but seem to be absent from anywhere in Dorset, Hampshire, or the Isle of Wight, and at Pevensey they may have arrived from northern rather than south-western France. Exmoor has at least one iron-smelting site with fifth-century radiocarbon dates, which increase in the sixth century and are joined by Somerset's Blackdown Forest: Webster, C. J. 2008, 175; Dorset: Ladle 2012; over 1000 charcoal pits and four furnace bottoms were excavated, but spread over the fifth to the ninth centuries, production seems small-scale – but see Ch. 3. Romano-British mineral exploitation: Allen, M. [a] *et al.* 2017, 179–98; silver usually occurs in the same strata as lead but probably only in very small amounts in the south-west. Droitwich: Hurst, J. D. (ed.) 1997, 17–27; the radiocarbon dates are broad but centre on the sixth century: see Ch. 2. Transhumance, the grazing of animals on unfenced summer pastures at a distance from the farmstead, would have required agreements between different communities and might be very ancient, but whether such arrangements could have survived the widespread reorganization of agriculture and estates assumed to have taken place in Roman Britain, or were substantially renegotiated subsequently, remains in doubt; the former view has been strongly promoted by Oosthuizen 2019, 104–5 and 109–19.

32 Amphoras and mead: Moffett, C. 2017 (cooking in oil becomes less likely with the revelation of secondary use of amphoras for animal fats – the diners were not enduring funny tastes). Gerrard, J. 2013, 176 suggested that oil was used cosmetically, noting the incidence of combs and tweezers at Cadbury Congresbury as evidence of human body awareness.

33 See Moffett, C. 2017, 119–21 for recent summary of Tintagel. Cist-graves in the churchyard on the mainland (Thomas, C. 1988, 427–31; Nowakowski and Thomas 1990) could indicate that further investigation on the mainland opposite the peninsula might be revealing. Mothecombe: Agate *et al.* 2012, 387–92 for the buildings; they also cite a number of places where grain-dryers indicate 'some control of production', 386–7. South Cadbury did not produce enough animal bones for comparison.

34 Provinces and tribal zones: Rippon 2018, 8–9. South-western 'rounds': Rose, P. and Preston-Jones 1995; Turner, S. 2006, 78–9; Rippon 2008, 119–22. Linear earthworks: Higham, N. J. and Ryan 2013, 52–4, with map. Sherborne: McKinley 1999. Elmet:

Roberts, I. 2014. Bokerley Dyke: Eagles 2001, 212–15; Mees 2019, 43. Writing in the late fifth or sixth century, Gildas mentioned Dumnonia but no other such tribal groups in modern England: Morgan Evans 2014, 177–9; Gildas called their leaders *reges*, 'kings', and *rix*, from *rex*, led to many personal names with *ri* in them, probably coming to indicate high status rather than kingly power: Birley 2014, 200; 'chiefs' gives a better idea of such leaders' authority. Roman law on road maintenance: Langlands 2019, 177–9.

35 Enamelled work was also characteristic of Wales and Ireland: Youngs 1989; 1995. Metal analyses: Swift 2019, 23–31.

36 Vindolanda vessel: *Current Archaeology* 368 (Oct. 2020); forts' christian and other use: Willmott, T. 2010. Milfield Basin site: Johnson, B. and Waddington 2008, 155–61.

37 Calling Gildas a 'recorder' suggests that he was dispassionate, but he was a writer of diatribes which by chance contain snippets of useful information about the society that he knew. Of many discussions of monetary and non-monetary systems, Bolton 2004 is particularly useful; Screen 2007, 159 showed that cattle numbers were particularly considered as representing wealth, *feoh*, appropriate for tribute payments; see also Crawford 2009, 140. No medieval equivalent to the iron 'currency bars' of the pre-Roman period is suggested, but salt might have been used as it is easily weighed.

2 The Sixth Century

Adjusting to Change

For archaeologists, the sixth century is dominated by discussion of cemeteries because of their quantity and the information that they contain about the human condition – both cultural and physical. Few have been excavated in their entirety, because of modern constraints of developments like road lines, and because their limits are hard to establish anyway, as they were not generally enclosed by banks and ditches and, to judge from graves dug slightly away from main groups, not by permanent fencing either – movable wicker panels like those that would have been used for animal pens presumably kept pigs, foxes, and badgers away, as graves do not seem to have been foraged into. Enough cemeteries are of sufficient size to be useful for statistical analysis; 224 were considered in a recent radiocarbon survey; 103 were large enough to permit a study of internal groupings; and many small ones make a total count impossible. Because inhumations take up more ground than cremations unless graves cut into each other, which was largely avoided, and because of the absence of identifiable boundaries, it is not usually possible to say with any certainty how many bodies were in a particular cemetery, but it does seem that many were quite small, serving a limited area, perhaps no more than the nearest settlement and no more than a single farmstead.[1]

When scrutinized in detail, no two cemeteries seem identical, but broad patterns can be discerned. The most frequently found grave-goods are gender-related; skeletons that can be identified as biologically female may have brooches or beads, biological males may have weapons – usually a spear, sometimes a shield, occasionally a sword (Illus. 2.1) – but other things such as glass vessels, small stave-built buckets, and copper-alloy bowls are less gender-exclusive. As the graves with the largest number or most eye-catching goods are not usually clustered together in a cemetery, burial in family groups was probably the norm, although many of the dead, especially males, had no grave-goods, suggesting that different social grades were recognized, even if people had performed broadly similar tasks in life. Neonates, babies, and infants are under-represented in most cemeteries, as though they had not lived long enough to be accepted as full members of a kin-group. A few exceptions occur: a very high proportion of infants in Great Chesterford, Essex; in Croydon, Sussex, a biological female with a shield and a spear, which could suggest that she had lived a masculine lifestyle; a biological male at Portway, Hampshire, who

DOI: 10.4324/9781003007432-3

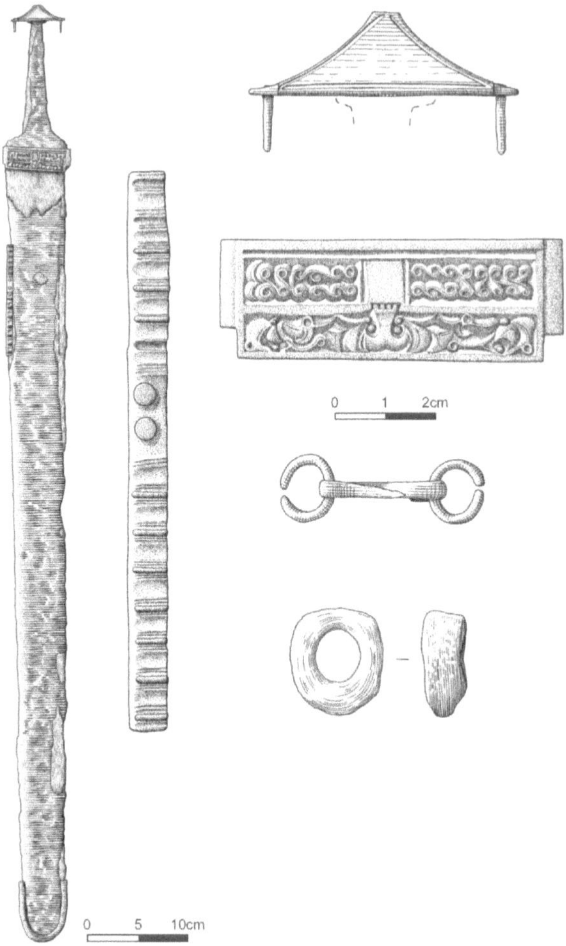

Illustration 2.1 Sword and scabbard fitting from an elderly man's grave at Pewsey, Wiltshire, dated to the first half or middle of the sixth century. The gilt copper-alloy plate is from the mouth of the scabbard; it has 'Style I' ornament, with a recognizable mask in the centre, but 'hidden' animal heads and bodies on either side. The sides of the scabbard, which had been repaired, were bounded by gilt copper-alloy strips, and there was an iron chape at the bottom. The blade of the sword is pattern-welded, hidden by corrosion (cf. Illus. 5.1). The 'cocked hat' pommel is a copper-alloy sheet, coated with white metal so that it would catch the light over a wooden core; the projecting rivets suggest that it was fitted to a short wooden upper guard, no longer surviving. Probably attached to it was an antler ring; bead-rings were attached to, or cast into, some pommel guards, seemingly as protective amulets. The copper-alloy chain may have been linked to straps at the mouth of the scabbard; poems refer to 'peace-bands' that held a sword in its scabbard, so untying them was a challenge to fight. The man was fully equipped as a warrior, with shield, spear, and knife. His was one of four swords in the cemetery, out of twenty-two male burials, an above-average ratio (Annable and Eagles 2010, 8–11 (contribution by H. Härke), 113 (contribution by C. Stuckert), and 199–204; Egging Dinwiddy and Stoodley 2016, 104; Hines and Bayliss (eds) 2013, 187; although included in the seriation, p. 260, it did not feature in the probability distributions of dates).

was buried with female-related objects. Grave-goods may not directly reflect a person's activity before death. Weapons may not mean that someone had taken part in conflict, but that they were 'spear-worthy' and of high enough status to be called on to protect their homeland if it were threatened, but they may never have gone outside it on a raiding expedition with their lord.[2]

Because the number of examples is so high, painstaking accumulation of data has revealed broad patterns, such as a correlation between a male's age and the length of knife buried with him; older men getting too weak to be effective in battle tend not to have weapons; women mostly have the most elaborate grave-goods between about 16 and 30 years of age, when they were most likely to be child-rearing. Other patterns include keys and weaving equipment with females, suggestive of a domestic role; yet men do not have tools like plough parts, wood-workers' chisels, or foresters' axes, although those must have been their working equipment. 'Frontier societies' do not have the capacity to make rigid divisions between the work that people have to undertake, so positive signalling of maleness by weapons or femaleness by ornaments may have been intended to re-establish in death gender distinctions that were seen as appropriate but could not always be maintained in life. Variations seen even in cemeteries that are not far apart, such as two analysed in detail in Cambridgeshire and Suffolk, show that no rigid rules applied generally, however. Grave-goods might have been gifts to give the dead person a status that they had not enjoyed in life, or given as signs to the dead that compensation had been paid for an injury done to them that they had not been compensated for before dying. Failure to furnish the dead in a manner that they would have considered appropriate might have been seen as likely to provoke a feud with their spirit, with malign consequences.[3]

The distribution of sixth-century cemeteries with furnished graves is not greatly different from that of the fifth, with a slight expansion westwards, for instance into Worcestershire. Association with earlier sites, particularly Bronze Age round barrows, may have been a way of claiming ancestral rights over a territory. Cemeteries tend to be in easily dug ground: gravels, chalk, and sand. That is true also of settlement sites with 'sunken-featured buildings', though with exceptions as in Northamptonshire's Raunds area, which is mostly clay. Settlements were usually close to running water, in stream and river valleys; cemeteries were usually on higher ground. Because of their locations, many settlements are now under thick build-ups of alluvium or colluvium, so are less likely to be found than lightly covered cemeteries. The two types of site are often not as far apart as used to be thought; the dead were not isolated from the living. Presumably people lived close to the fields where they worked and did not begrudge the spirits of their kin a portion of land even though it was workable with light ploughs, or at least on which animals could graze.[4]

Whether with or without objects, most burials were done with adequate decency; slight trends to larger or deeper graves for those with the most objects can sometimes be discerned, but deviancy from the standard supine position is so unusual as to create discussion. An extreme case is that of a young woman in a cemetery at Sewerby, Yorkshire, well-provided for in terms of grave-goods and in an orthodox position, but with an older woman above her, prone and with her limbs sprawled, and a large piece of quernstone over her body; had she been buried alive? Some females had bags or pouches at their waist, containing a mixed assortment of what look like mere trinkets, but include tiny bucket-pendants that may have been used as containers for herbs, hinting at someone with special healing – and possibly therefore also malign – powers, including fortune-telling, a 'cunning woman'. Human remains – it is not always clear if they were intentionally deposited – are also occasionally found in ditches and 'sfb' fills, the latter more likely to be the very young.[5]

Costume fittings survive in enough numbers for some general trends to be apparent. When first introduced, 'Great Square-headed' brooches were elaborate and found in a few elite female graves over most of England (Illus. 2.2), becoming simpler and regionalized, having a final life in the north-east. 'Cruciform' brooches became more elaborate but more geographically limited, no longer being found south of the Thames. Pairs of sleeve- or wrist-clasps were also only worn north of the Thames; a few single ones that have strayed to the south were not used in the same way. Wrist-clasps have close parallels with southern Scandinavia, but there they were worn by both men and women, whereas in England they are only in women's graves. In contrast to the wrist-clasp distribution, small circular 'button' brooches with humanoid masks are not found north of the Thames (Illus. 2.3). The regionalism suggested by the metal fittings compares to differences in costume styles, linen being worn only on inner garments and in veils in most of the south, except for Kent where there were finer weaves and more embroideries. North of the Thames, a wider variety of styles was worn; female dress overall suggests a higher standard of living than in the fifth century, as women were more likely to be buried in less coarsely woven woollens. More items that were neither dress-related nor weaponry were also buried, including things made far away (Illus. 2.4).[6]

Different questions arise from studies of cremation burials, not least why it was that some people were disposed of by placing their body on a pyre that had to be carefully constructed if it was to burn the corpse at a high enough temperature to reduce the bones to ash; the pyre then had to be left to cool so that most of the remains could be collected and buried, many but not all in a pottery urn. Occasional half-melted brooches and other items show that goods were placed on the pyre with the corpse, in particular combs, which are much less often found in inhumation burials; these might have been for renewing the human body in the afterlife. A cremation involved more effort and display than an inhumation; a few cemeteries contain large numbers of cremations, so the bodies had probably been brought from a distance, which would also have meant extra effort. Another form of extra expenditure seems to be that more animal parts were included than in most inhumations: at Spong Hill, mostly sheep and almost as many horses as cattle with male burials, and pig. Smaller urns tended to be used for the young, which might be practical or an intimation of their immaturity; to judge from its diameter, the lid found at Spong topped by a modelled seated figure staring out into the beyond must have been with a particularly large urn.[7]

Illustration 2.2 'Great Square-Headed' gilt copper-alloy brooch from a mature woman's grave at Pewsey, Wiltshire. This was found approximately over the middle of the chest, suggesting that it held a cloak worn over a dress held in place by two smaller 'saucer' brooches (cf. Illus. 2.3). Despite the modern name, they were usually worn with the rectangular plate at the bottom, but this one was found as though worn horizontally. It belongs in a classification that places it in the first half of the sixth century and geographically within a wide zone either side of the River Thames. The projections on the rectangular plate are recognizable humanoid bearded and moustachioed faces, but the circles projecting from the plate would not be identifiable except by someone who knew of similar masks, as on 'button' brooches (Illus. 2.3), nor would 'Style I' animal patterns be obvious either side of the mid-rib, even though beaked heads are clear on the sides. Were some elements deliberately 'hidden', or was the mould-maker not too bothered? The size of the brooch means that it took skill to cast and extra cost to gild, and the woman who was buried with it had other items including a small wooden pail that may symbolize feasting. Her status is also suggested by her location next to the grave of a man with a sword (Illus. 2.1) (Annable and Eagles 2010, 24–5 (contribution by B. Ager), 105, and 195–7; Hines 1997, 67–76 and 229–32).

Illustration 2.3 Brooches in female graves are often found in pairs at the shoulders, suggesting a dress style that has taken its name from the ancient Greek *peplos*. On the left is a 'saucer' brooch, one of a pair from a grave at Fairford, Gloucestershire; in the centre is a face mask, which is surrounded by three panels of 'Style I' creatures, identifiable but with their elements separated – in the more complex designs, the separate parts may not conform to anatomy, and other shapes begin to appear. The 'button' brooch from Hampshire on the right has a mask that seems to express the same concept as the 'saucer' but never appears north of the Thames. Both are of the sixth century, but Fairford was not one of the cemeteries analysed in the recent radiocarbon project, and the 'button' brooch was a stray find (Walton Rogers 2007, 148–54).

Many aspects of cremation are difficult to understand, such as why some urns were holed and plugged with lead, but a few had glass inserts as though to be 'windows', and why different designs were incised and stamped into them. Urns when placed in the grave would have seemed to the viewer looking down to have created a series of concentric circles surrounding the contents. In some cremation cemeteries, post-holes indicate that there were small timber buildings, usually seen as markers of particular burials, but they may possibly have had flat tops on which cremated bones were displayed (Illus. 2.5). Cremation was not practised only at the few sites that specialized in it, however, as it is found also in many of the cemeteries in which inhumation predominated, though whether the cremated people were any different in life from the others remains unresolved.[8]

As interesting as are the things that were deposited in graves are the things that were not or at least that are found as much or more in other circumstances. The gold bracteates known in the fifth century increase in number in the sixth, but many are stray finds, some probably deliberately deposited, such as in streams. Those found in England are very similar to continental ones, but dies prove that they were not all imports. One probable die was found in Norfolk close to a hoard of five bracteates that also had two bracelets, one gold, and one gilded copper-alloy; one of the bracteates had been deliberately folded. Bracteate designs change but seem particularly linked to gods and spirits, as though carrying special messages, and that may explain why so many are not from graves. No such special

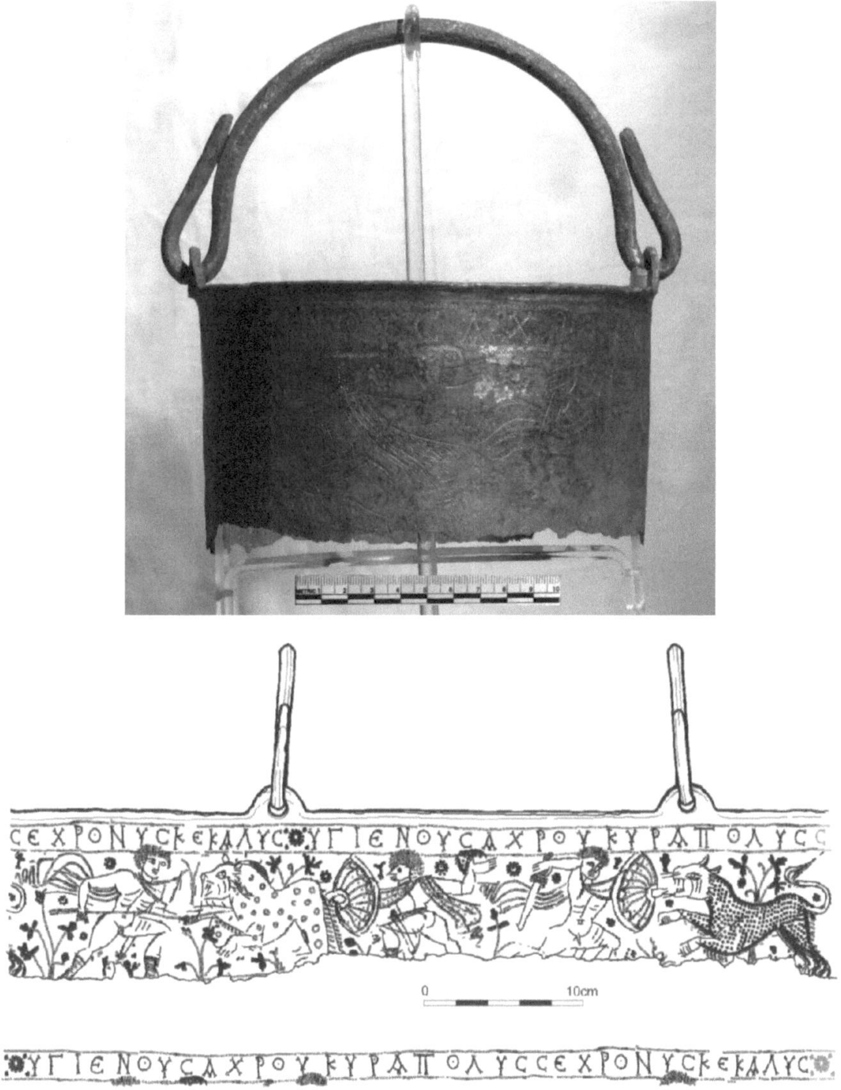

Illustration 2.4 Grave-goods other than costume fittings and weapons can often be associated with feasting, such as glass cups and beakers for drinking, and containers like this copper-alloy pail from Breamore, Hampshire, which may have been for foodstuffs. This one is exceptional; a similar one was excavated with a rich female on the Isle of Wight, another was found near the Tranmer House cemetery in Suffolk that preceded the Sutton Hoo burials, as possibly was another – they are the only four from England. It has a Greek inscription and a frieze of men fighting animals and had been made in the eastern Mediterranean, quite probably at Antioch, and was originally used for washing; the inscription reads 'Use this in good health, lady, for many happy years', though no-one in sixth-century Hampshire could have read it, and its donation to a woman had been forgotten as it was in a man's grave. How much could he have known of its origins and what could he have made of the alien, 'naturalistic', frieze (Hinton and Worrell 2017, 89–95 and 136–7, with contribution by J. Pearce and C. Roueché)?

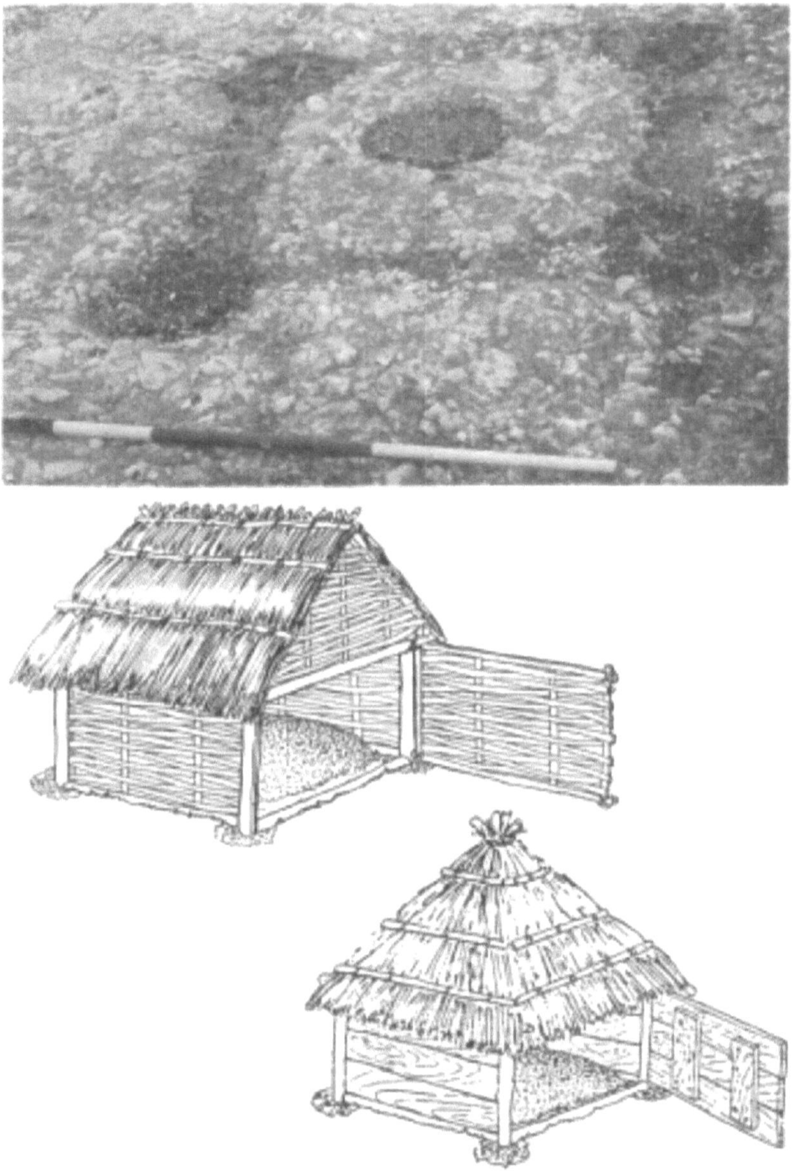

Illustration 2.5 Excavation by the late Alec Down at Compton Appledown, West Sussex, outside Chichester revealed a large cemetery dating from the end of the fifth century until well into the seventh; both cremation and inhumation burials were excavated, the two rites intermixed and contemporaneous. Some of the former were associated with four-post timber structures; the photograph shows a large pit in the centre of one, which was found to contain unurned cremated burials; many of the structures' post-holes also contained cremated remains, as though the structures were small shrines to which burials might be added. The two drawings by M. Wholey show two possible reconstructions; another possibility is that the tops were flat, for the display of remains before burial (Down and Welch 1990; Emery, K. M. and Williams 2018).

explanation is needed for the greater proportion of horse-harness fittings that are stray finds, as such items were easily lost and horse-burials were rare. Some brooch types are increasingly being found as stray finds and are accidental losses rather than deriving from graves.[9]

Settlement sites in the sixth century do not seem to have changed much: rectangular ground-level buildings and 'sfbs' were all but exclusively used, and no new structural development gave them longer lives. The problems of durability, and whether the structures had several generations of use, therefore remain; whether lack of maintenance, or because it was thought that the life of a building should end with the death of its principal occupier, meant that farmsteads were transferred regularly by a few metres to a new site is still unsettled and has major consequences for demography and the extent to which the countryside could be exploited.[10]

Demography could be discussed with greater confidence if there were better evidence about the dating of the many linear earthworks; some are certainly prehistoric, which is how Bokerley Dyke began, but others have been excavated that have produced no pre-Roman evidence; small quantities of Roman pottery and coins in banks or in ditch fills show only that those cannot predate the third century at the earliest, but the objects may already have been in the soil when the works were constructed. Even relatively short dykes, like the sequence in Cambridgeshire, would have involved considerable effort in organizing and feeding a workforce of diggers, which would have had to be even larger if the bank was revetted with timber or stone, as found in excavations at various points along West Wansdyke. That dyke runs south of the River Avon and makes some sense as a frontier to protect people in modern Somerset from whoever was living in modern Gloucestershire, later called the *Hwiccians*. West Wansdyke is linked by a Roman road to East Wansdyke on the Wiltshire downs above the Kennett valley, but whether the two were co-eval remains uncertain, and dates from every century from the fifth to the eighth have all been entertained. No historic shire or other boundary respects it. The Cambridgeshire dykes could have been in a frontier zone, and built by people in East Anglia, as their ditches are all on their south sides; a little dating evidence has the Fleam Dyke as constructed in the fifth century, with some further work done in the sixth; the Devil's Dyke to its north is late sixth century, as though the sequence shows a series of retreats.[11]

*

The vestigial evidence about the dykes does not indicate that they were built exclusively either by indigenes or by immigrants. Sixth-century graves with a wide variety of different objects in them, and 'sfbs', have still not been found in the far west and south-west of England, so the new culture was generally either unknown or resisted in those areas. Villas and towns were not reoccupied, so any stability did not lead to a return to the old norms; some hillforts stayed in use. Burial also continued in cemeteries like Cannington, with no obvious changes in burial practice and every likelihood that they were christian; the focal graves that were probably the earliest features there have comparable groupings, some with small ditched enclosures, in both Devon and Somerset, justifying the concept that they were 'managed cemeteries'. New cemeteries in Dorset were also very orderly, though not with ditched enclosures; radiocarbon dates indicate usage from the sixth to the eighth centuries. Dorset does not have any of the fifth-/sixth-century inscribed memorial stones found in Cornwall and west Devon; their precise dating remains an issue, the few personal names on them which have putative links to people named in documentary sources all being questionable. The letter forms used may have changed in the later sixth century, but that cannot be corroborated without contemporary manuscripts to show what scripts were current. The christian '*Hic iacet*', 'Here lies . . . ' formula must indicate use at burial-places, but the stones are very movable, hindering the identification of early cemeteries and churches. Such identification remains a problem even when building foundations are traced; rigorous scrutiny of the surviving records from earlier excavations at Glastonbury Abbey, Somerset, has shown that a post-built structure there can plausibly be dated by pottery to *c.* 450–550 but has not proved that it is the remains of the 'very old church of daub and wattle' that the later monks claimed to have been their founding church; its function cannot be defined, and there are no burials of that period to confirm religious use. Burials attributed to the sixth century were however excavated on Glastonbury Tor, as was the evidence of metalworking; that activity was surely not placed in such an inconvenient location for functional reasons, suggesting that some spiritual sentiment hung over it.[12]

The pottery at Glastonbury that dates the early building is the type imported from the eastern Mediterranean, as found at Tintagel and other sites. The middle of the sixth century saw a change, with north African pottery superseding it, but in smaller amounts, and with a more limited distribution, a change that makes the dating of sites even more difficult, for instance in Somerset, where some might have come into use or been abandoned or been still occupied but invisibly because there are no sherds. In Ilchester, two copper-alloy sixth-century Byzantine coins may indicate connections; a few such coins have been found in archaeological contexts, but many are later souvenirs. More difficult to understand are pilgrims' flasks from the shrine of St Menas, found in the enclave around Baldock and on the Wirrall peninsula at Meols, a site that may have been a trading place like Mothecombe and Bantham in Devon, but where Mediterranean pottery, coins, and glass have not been found. Did pilgrims go from Britain to Egypt, or were the flasks diplomatic gifts from the Byzantine court, trying to keep links with the west? Even the limited ties with the Mediterranean that the pottery indicates ceased by the end of the sixth century, though not to leave Devon and Cornwall completely isolated, as a network of south-western French connections was strengthening.[13]

At South Cadbury, two pieces of anglo-saxon metalwork are anomalous – did they arrive as loot or in a tribute payment? Or were they brought by an unfortunate anglo-saxon girl who had to live as a bride-hostage among the British to seal an alliance? One of the two bits of metalwork was a 'button' brooch, not otherwise found so far west (cf. Illus. 2.3). A few other such things are known in areas where they would not be expected but are not enough to make a pattern; a small group of weapons and other metal items, some demonstrably anglo-saxon, found as far west as Hardown, Dorset, has been reconsidered and shown not to be from burials, as had usually been assumed, but might have been taken from a raiding party; raiding may have been endemic, although not normally on the scale or with the disastrous consequences of the expedition from the north that met its doom at *Catraeth*, probably Catterick in Yorkshire, on Dere Street. The fort there may not have been the target, or even defensible, although there was occupation within and around it, including 'sfbs' and furnished burials; the raiders met an army of some sort that came together to resist its incursion. The occupied hillforts like South Cadbury mostly overlook Roman roads and other routeways (cf. Illus. 2.6).[14]

Illustration 2.6 Although no post-Roman occupation evidence has been found within it, the Iron Age ramparts of the Old Sarum hillfort in Wiltshire might have sheltered an army when the *Anglo-Saxon Chronicles* recorded that 'Cynric fought against the Britons at the place which is called *Searoburh*', purportedly in 552 – but Cynric, if he existed, was a king of Wessex, and by then anglo-saxon burials were taking place in the area; was the fight, if it took place, actually between two groups who were anglo-saxon, not British – or had a British army risked a raid along a road from the west? There is a road up into the side of the hillfort on the left in this photograph, which excavation by the Universities of Southampton and Swansea is showing to have been much used later in the Middle Ages; on the right is a north-south Roman road and a ridgeway joined it from the east, not shown in the photograph; Old Sarum may simply have been near where two armies came together.

Not only were a few bits of metalwork from the east reaching South Cadbury and elsewhere, but small penannular brooches made in the west, or in western style, and a few hanging-bowls are found in eastern graves; they could all have been loot or tribute, but more peaceful exchanges and blurring of boundaries are more likely. They do not necessarily signify an acceptance of western culture, however, as many of the brooches were not being worn but were being carried in small bags with other seemingly miscellaneous items, which could have been collected as scraps to recycle or have been amuletic. None of the many earthwork dykes can be assigned definitively to the sixth century and to attempts to keep alien cultures apart. In the south-west, a fairly clear separation can be seen, but the west Midlands and the north are more problematic; in the former, from Herefordshire up to Lancashire, there is not much evidence from burials and settlements, but Droitwich salt production seems to have increased; several stone-lined rectangular hearths have been excavated on which lead pans would have sat in which the brine was boiled. Bits of lead sheet and melted fragments are all that survived of the pans, but they must have been up to 2.3 metres long and 0.5 metres wide, so large quantities of the metal were needed, much more than could have been scrabbled together from old Roman scrap. Fresh supplies would presumably have come from Derbyshire, throwing light on another form of production otherwise not known until the next century. Also being brought into the site was pottery, including some with stamped decoration.[15]

In the north-east, cemeteries both furnished and unfurnished and 'sfbs' have been excavated, although without revealing a clear division between British and 'anglo-saxon' culture. As far north as central Northumberland, fragments of a sword, a shield, and two square-headed brooches were found that indicate a small burial group practising furnished inhumation at Eslington, and two small groups of graves at Milfield, also in Northumberland, included a girdle pendant and the remains of a sword. Yet close by in the Milfield Basin, a settlement had rectangular timber buildings but no 'sfbs'. Further south, however, Ripon, North Yorkshire, has some evidence of a group of unfurnished burials in an area which has many cemeteries with grave-goods and cremations. In the north, prehistoric monuments such as stone circles seem to have influenced the choice of cemetery and settlement locations, as though to claim ancestral rights, and may have resulted in the first phase of use at Yeavering, Northumberland. Burials have also been found at Bamburgh on the coast; both those places developed into important centres, possibly replacing the use of the forts on Hadrian's Wall.[16]

*

One factor that is very hard to assess is the possible impact on England of two worldwide crises. In the 530s, a cataclysmic event smothered the earth's atmosphere, blanketing out the sun and inevitably affecting crop growth; this had visible effects in northern lands, but in England no direct consequences have been recognized. A pandemic outbreak in the Mediterranean from 541 onwards caused heavy population loss in southern Europe, but even if it reached England, it would not have had the same effect – without towns, people were not constantly jostling with strangers, rats, and fleas, and second-hand clothing was probably not being peddled. Cemeteries do not suggest a sudden surge in burials in the 530s and 540s, and if there were changes to artefact design in efforts to assuage the gods and spirits, they have not been clearly identified. If anyone succumbed to the Justinian Plague it is hidden among the many other infections that were prevalent, and if food was particularly scarce in the later 530s and affected children's growth, rickets and other signals of malnutrition in adult skeletons do not seem to peak subsequently. Nevertheless, demographic growth may have been prevented, even if decline cannot be proven. If great international events cannot be discerned in the archaeological record, local battles and skirmishes are no more likely to be recognized; an inverse relationship between the numbers of weapons found and the recorded battles has been suggested, but dating of the latter in the sixth century is open to the uncertainty of the records.[17]

Until recently, dating of graves depended almost entirely upon the style of any brooches or other artefacts found in them, and those dates depended upon continental parallels and typological sequences with no fixed points. Many years ago, a historian sceptical of any chronology constructed upon that methodology wrote that he could never understand why an elderly lady of conservative tastes should not have chosen to be buried with her grandmother's jewellery, but at least for the second half of the sixth century, his objection has now been countered by the new precision brought by a combination of radiocarbon dating and statistics applied to inhumation graves, bringing greater confidence to sequences and date ranges proposed for many types of common artefact. Glass beads are particularly susceptible to change, but most of the sequences – of brooches, swords, shield-bosses, and so on – are developments of earlier ones, so no sudden changes indicating new peoples arriving are evident. International contacts can be seen, however, in the introduction of a new way of using animal images, long sinuous intertwined creatures replacing the ambiguities of the shape-shifting creatures of earlier work.[18]

Another indication of continental connections is that slightly more coins seem to have entered England during the course of the sixth century. Gold *solidi* like those in the fifth-century Patching hoard were minted in Byzantium and in Gaul, as were coins one-third of the size and weight called *trientes* or in the vernacular tremisses. A few people might have understood that their imperial imagery gave them authority, but they are too few and too valuable to have been used as everyday currency. Some might have crossed the Channel in trade payments, others as subsidies sent by Frankish rulers to people whom they wanted to have as dependent clients, whose raids supplied slaves and who could prevent young men from England causing trouble by joining war-bands abroad. In turn, the gold might be passed to favoured supporters, some to be mounted in rings or pendants, others to be melted down to turn into jewellery. Near whatever survived of the Roman amphitheatre in Canterbury, a *triens* with jeweller's rouge stuck to it was in the process of being pared down when it was lost, and nearby were two scraps of sheet gold also being worked. People, including chiefs, perhaps visited the old city for assembly meetings, and on such occasions a smith might be called upon to create a valuable gift to cement the loyalty of a subject. The amphitheatre area was coming back into use in sixth-century Canterbury, with buildings and signs of organization, unseen for certain yet in any other Roman town or city, although anglo-saxon objects in Winchester may suggest activity, and there are 'sfbs' in Leicester and Colchester.[19]

The smith working on gold in Canterbury may have been filing the coin down to provide powder for gilding copper-alloy and other objects. This must have been standard practice, helping to account for sets of weights found in a few sixth-century graves, as at Watchfield, Oxfordshire, which show ability to measure the precise value of anything in gold in both Byzantine and Frankish units. Whether smiths working on gold, silver, and copper alloys were also ironworkers is a moot point, but the pattern-welded sword blades show the very high quality of work achieved (cf. Illus. 5.1), and spears, shields, and knives all required iron. Burying such things involved a loss of useful commodities, arguably a greater sacrifice than represented by copper-alloy brooches or glass and amber beads. Many iron items were probably recycled, though the evidence for the practice is of later times, and it can be argued that billets of new iron were easily obtainable; ore was extracted from Rockingham Forest, Northamptonshire, and surface deposits were exploited in Essex and East Anglia, and though smelting in the Weald has not been demonstrated, some iron may have come from the British areas.[20]

The mechanisms by which bulky goods travelled may not entirely have depended upon high-status gift exchanges; pottery made as early as the sixth century in Leicestershire has been identified at sites 50 miles away, including possibly some of the urns at Cleatham. If pots could journey 50 miles or more, so could other goods like textiles, although in that case the raw materials, such as sheep's wool for woollens and flax and hemp for linens, can be reared or grown too widely for a specific locality to be postulated. Quernstones, however, which everyone needed, had to be able to reach sites a long way from the quarries and those made of lava had to be imported from the Rhineland, an example of overseas trade, and showing that there must have been places where sea-going vessels beached, which are very hard to find; the two Devon sites partly survived because of sand inundation, but any traces of most would have been eroded away.[21]

Canterbury may have re-emerged because it is in east Kent, the area closest to the continent and therefore to the Franks, and also where most of the gold coins have been found. That gold coins were sought after is understandable; much less obviously desirable would surely have been any in base metal, yet a few from the eastern Mediterranean have been found, mainly with a different distribution along the south coast. Some may be modern souvenirs, but one sixth-century specimen was lost in the eighth century in Southampton, and although none has come from a site with eastern Mediterranean pottery or glass, recent finds from Rendlesham in Suffolk confirm sixth- and seventh-century importing.[22]

Rendlesham is one of the places named in the seventh century as having royal connections which begin to emerge towards the end of the sixth. Recent work there is suggesting that there was an inhumation and cremation cemetery and perhaps a settlement with 'sfbs' of the fifth/sixth centuries, prosperous and possibly already different from others in south Suffolk, objects there including bracteates and a small gold bucket-shaped pendant, perhaps an amulet. That cemetery may have been superseded by one a little further down the River Deben, at Tranmer House, and a residential complex took over Rendlesham on a promontory overlooking the river. At present, this is only known from surface finds, so what buildings were there remains to be discovered, but metalworking took place in one zone. Tranmer House has been excavated, and also had both inhumations and cremations, with more weapons in the graves than the national norm and other rich objects. In its turn, it overlapped with and was superseded by barrow-burials a little further down the River Deben at Sutton Hoo. Those were an exclusive group; the earliest, from *c*. 580–90, were cremations in copper-alloy bowls, one of which, in Mound 5, was complete enough to show a weapon injury. Another area in south Suffolk, up the River Gipping at Coddenham, has a cemetery with rich occupants, and at a little distance, two sites have produced metalwork comparable to that at Rendlesham.[23]

Until recently, the only high-status complex known was Yeavering, which also began to become a distinctive place towards the end of the sixth century. Like Rendlesham, others have now been or are being investigated, such as Sutton Courtenay, Oxfordshire, another area where earlier and apparently unexceptional ‘sfbs’ and cemeteries are known, but which is close to the small Roman town of Dorchester-on-Thames and has ‘sfbs’ inside and unusual early burials outside. Lyminge and Eastry, both in Kent, are others: the former has two long rectangular halls, one over 20 metres long, and the latter has rich graves but as yet no discovery of grand buildings. Also in Kent, a site in Dover with ‘sfbs’ had a sequence of occupation that included buildings re-interpreted as being secular rather than ecclesiastical. Canterbury was not the only ‘central place’, therefore, in East Kent by the end of the sixth century. At the same time, a few personal names occur in reasonably reliable sources, some with the title ‘King of ’ or ‘Queen’, ‘of’ then being followed by the name of a distinct group of people, such as ‘of the East Saxons’. They had the titles, but their roles were those that anthropologists would term chiefs, holding power over people rather than over boundary-defined territories. Their lifestyle was probably peripatetic.[24]

The evidence from burials is largely consistent with the settlements’ indications of the emergence of special places for those of the highest rank; a few exceptions occur, such as the late fifth- to early sixth-century dating of a young man with a horse at Eriswell, Suffolk, but otherwise it is at the end of the sixth century that graves of special character begin to appear. The outstanding example was found in 2003 on the edge of an established cemetery at Prittlewell, Essex; a large, wood-lined chamber was hung with spears, an arrow, a shield, copper-alloy and other large vessels, and probably textiles (Illus. 2.7). On the floor were more textiles and large vessels, a maplewood box containing various items, arrays of drinking horns, glass beakers, and small wooden cups; a silver Byzantine spoon, which had had previous owners, probably also reflected feasting, as might joints of meat and what looks like a scythe blade and therefore a provider of harvest products – the large tub in which it was found might have been a water-bucket to symbolize a horse, as no trace of one was found. A lyre suggests a musical accompaniment to

Illustration 2.7 Reconstruction of the wood-lined burial chamber at Prittlewell by Faith Vardy for Museum of London Archaeological Service. It shows the final view that the burial party would have had before the roof was put over it, perhaps with a lamp burning in the stand on the coffin, which had been draped with a textile, and candles set in the upright iron object on the right. The placing of the sword at a right angle to the body is dramatic but not understandable. The lyre was placed in a bag on the opposite side (Blackmore, L. *et al*. 2019).

stories told in halls to celebrate the great deeds of the ancestors. A set of counters, two antler dice, and the remains of a wooden board show that the chamber's occupant was the sort of person who would have had the leisure to play games, because others supplied his maintenance needs. An iron stand that might have been a candelabrum and an iron lamp with organic residues may show that lights had been left burning when the chamber was roofed over, soon to dwindle away just as the body was to fade away – the burial party was not to know how complete that fading was to be, as acid soil conditions had completely eroded almost all traces of bones and teeth. The weapons indicate a young male; they include a sword, not in the usual position alongside the body in a scabbard but laid out at right angles to it on the floor. The symbolism of that is beyond certain interpretation.[25]

Two Merovingian tremisses help to provide dating evidence for the Prittlewell burial and are consistent with radiocarbon dating that gives a strong probability that the burial occurred in the 580s or 590s. That was unexpected, as placed over where the dead person's eyes would have been were two roughly made gold crosses, suggesting christianity at a time before St Augustine reached Canterbury in 597 and began to establish bishoprics. The coins were in positions where the dead person's hands might have gripped them; as a cross appears on their designs, they too might be indicative of christianity. A gold but entirely plain buckle might have been made specially for the burial to replace one that was perceived as having pagan overtones. It is possible that the man's mother was a princess sent to England as part of an alliance deal with the christian Franks, but in any case hostility to the religion may not have been deeply felt. Hanging-bowls like the one at Prittlewell show contacts with the British, at least at fairly high social levels, and cast copper-alloy vessels, again as at Prittlewell, show indirect contacts with Byzantium, just as the gold coins show contact with christian Merovingia just the other side of the Channel. From there also came red garnets, sourced from central Europe or the Far East, probably Sri Lanka, which were not entirely unknown before but were now supplied in some quantity.[26]

Only one other sixth-century cemetery has been found to contain a single burial that stands far above the rest in terms of the effort that went into it: a boat large enough to have been sea-going at Snape, Suffolk. A trend towards singling out a few people for special treatment was to become more extreme in the seventh century, but already in the later sixth, fewer people were buried with a wide range of objects than before. Other changes in the late sixth century may have been influenced directly or indirectly by developments overseas, but clear evidence is hard to find. In particular, the large cemeteries dominated by cremation burial, as at Spong Hill and Cleatham, seem to have gone out of use except for inhumation well before they could have been affected by the Augustinian mission. In the south-coast counties, however, cremation seems to have lasted longer; a mixed-rite cemetery in west Sussex, near Chichester, is the largest known. Whether 597 was a turning point is therefore a major topic for the seventh century.[27]

Notes

1 Although now ageing a little, the best introduction to cemeteries is Lucy 2000. Fences: Crawford 2009, 98; Wasperton is unusual in this as in other ways, being affected by an earlier enclosure: see Ch. 1. Radiocarbon survey: Hines and Bayliss (eds) 2013. Statistics: Sayer 2020, Introduction. Occasional finds of badger or fox bones and teeth have been made, but they were included as amulets or furs; no case of a burrow seems to have been reported: Poole 2015, 397. Beavers were also native suppliers of furs and amulets, and bear parts were imported: Spriggs 1998. Many graves have been excavated where they are revealed by metal-detecting, and there are doubtless many others unexcavated both where reports have been made of object concentrations and where they have not. An example of a 'small' site is autobiographical: a man, two women, and a baby or child disturbed on the line of a motorway might have been outliers to a larger number to the south, but not in other directions or the stripping for construction would have revealed them: Hinton 1973.

2 Age structures and gender representation: Stoodley 1999; 2000; Härke 2011. Male graves with punches are known and a hammer-head in a Spong urn, Grave 2291/1, but other tools seem all but excluded – a broken mattock in the side of a grave at Buckland, Dover, had probably broken during digging, left because it had become 'unlucky' but unassociated with the occupant: Evison 1987, 17; Parfitt and Anderson 2012, 22. Babies and infants (in both inhumations and cremations): Squires 2012,

331–5. Croydon: McKinley 2003, 108; Stoodley 1999, 29–30 showed that several other claims were unlikely or wrong. Portway: Knüsel and Ripley 2000. Weapons in general: Underwood 1999. Buckles were not gender-related; they occur in very nearly equal numbers in male and female graves: Marzinzik 2003, ch. 8. Stave-built buckets: Cook 2004. Association of documentary evidence with archaeological makes 'spear-worthy' meaningful – but was such a man also *heord-fæst*, implying someone with their own hearth and home: Faith 2019, 58–9?

3 Knife length: age correlation: Härke 1989; Gilchrist 1999, 43–51. Analysis: Pader 1982. Compensation and gifts: King, J. M. 2004 (a law-code refers to payment at the grave-side, which makes token inclusion within a grave credible). Potentially malevolent spirits living in a world parallel to the human, but in which they might interfere, are likely to have been more important to most non-christian people than belief in Woden or Tîw (whose name occurs in runes on some cremation urns, but at such an early date may have referred to gods generically: Griffiths, B. 1996, 2–3) and other gods named in later sources, although place-names indicate specific sacred places: Semple 2010; interplay with animal spirits is another consideration: Pluskowski 2010.

4 Monument reuse and effect on grave positioning: Lucy 2000, 124–30. Petts 2009, 220 warned against assuming that furnished graves are necessarily 'anglo-saxon', pointing to Cannington: see Ch. 1 (The term 'furnished' for graves with any surviving items is not very appropriate, but I can think of no satisfactory alternative). Settlement:cemetery association: Hirst and Clark 2009, 760–2, on Mucking and south Essex; Sofield 2015, 152; Saunders, P. and Algar 2020, 208, on Wiltshire. Raunds survey area: Parry 2006, 93–4. Another factor militating against the recognition of settlements is that they are much less likely to contain objects that will respond to metal-detection.

5 Sewerby: Hirst 1985, 38–43; Lucy 2000, 78–80; Sayer 2020, Introduction – discussed in relation to a woman with a child at Oakington, Cambridgeshire; Frantzen 2014, 83–5 discussed differing interpretations of the quern fragment – was it deliberately included, indicating that the woman had been a grinding-slave as mentioned in a law-code, or a woman in charge of such slaves? He cited examples from West Stow, p. 89, which seems exceptional in having so many. 'Cunning women': Dickinson 1999; a young male in Lechlade, Gloucestershire, buried with a crow might have been associated with fortune-telling using ornithomancy: Hinton 2005, 70. See Sofield 2015, 354–5 for a summary of baby/infant/child burial to which another autobiographical note would add a child at the feet of two males, with a shield placed over its body: Hinton and Worrell 2017, 86.

6 Cruciform brooches: Martin, T. F. 2015, 126–7. Wrist-clasps: Hines 1984; 1997, 132 for the singletons. Button brooches: Dickinson 1993. Great square-headed brooches: Hines 1997. Costume variety: Walton Rogers 2007, 232–4; weave quality: ibid., 107.

7 Combs: Williams, H. 2003a; hairstyles and combs: Crawford 2009, 121–4. Spong: Hills and Lucy 2013, 259–64; at Cleatham, and also Elsham, more than one third but fewer than a half of the burials contained animal bones, but the species could not be stated: Squires 2013, 162–3. Urn sizes: Hills and Lucy 2013, 235–9. Colour plate of the Spong figure and of an urn incised with a runic text: Breay and Story (eds) 2018, 66–7.

8 Urn plugging: Leahy 2007, 82; stamps: Briscoe 2011. (An argument that the holed urns had been 'killed' to symbolize weaponry that could not be included in them seems to overlook the infilling.) Urns viewed from above: Richards 1987. Structures: Emery, K. M. and Williams 2018.

9 Bracteates: Behr 2010; Binham, Norfolk, hoard: Behr and Pestell 2014, and colour plate in Breay and Story (eds) 2018, 72; a small number in silver and even copper-alloy seem to have been gilded, so were probably not expressing something different from those in gold. Richardson, A. 2011, 74–6 pointed out that the dies might themselves be imports. Horse-harness and brooches: Geake 2011 – the greater number of horse bones found in cremation graves is not matched by harness equipment in them: Hills and Lucy 2013, 59; Fern 2007 for horse burials. Brooch losses: Lewis, M. *et al.* 2011, 242–7.

10 Settlements: Hamerow 2012, 70–2.
11 Bokerley Dyke: see Ch. 1. West Wansdyke: Erskine 2007. East Wansdyke: Hinton 2021, 11–13. Cambridgeshire: Malim 1996; Rippon 2018, 321–8. See Ch. 4 for Offa's and Wats Dykes.
12 Cemeteries: Webster, C. J. 2008, 182–5; Petts 2009, 213–17. Dorset, Worth Matravers: Ladle 2018, 78–94; Toldpuddle Ball: Hearne and Birbeck 1999, 58–70 (radiocarbon dating gave one grave a date more than a century earlier than the others, so I have discounted it); Ulwell: Cox 1988. Stones: Okasha 1993; inscriptions: Handley 2001; scripts: Tedeschi 2001; locations: Turner, S. 2006, 140–3. Glastonbury: Abbey, Gilchrist and Green 2015, 384–5; Tor summary of excavation by Philip Rahtz: Wright, D. W. 2019, 277–8 and 286.
13 Pottery imports: Campbell, E. 2007, 44–6 for the 'Atlantic' trade. Baldock: Fitzpatrick-Matthews 2014, 50. Meols: Griffiths, D. *et al.* 2007, 58–61, with a contribution on the flask by S. Bangert. The St Menas cult was based in Egypt – not one of the areas from which the eastern Mediterranean pottery derived: Campbell, E. 2007, 74; coins ibid. 73–5. See Ch. 1 for Mothecombe etc. Political implications: Harris, A. 2003, 144–65. Byzantine copper-alloy coins have recently been reported from sites in Lancashire and Cumbria: Naylor 2015, 291, so perhaps they were coming through Meols after all.
14 South Cadbury: Alcock, L. 1995, 68–72. Hardown: Austin, M. 2014. Catterick: Wilson, P. R. *et al.* 1996; Cramp 1999, 2–5; a poem describes the fate of warriors who feasted, rode south, and were cut down at Catraeth: Rowland 1995 for a sobering account.
15 Penannular brooches: Dickinson 1982; hanging-bowls: Bruce-Mitford 2005. Dykes are controversial, and different opinions depend upon the views of different periods rather than on very solid evidence: Higham, N. J. and Ryan 2013, 53–4; Rippon 2018, 325 for analysis of the Fleam Dyke in Cambridgeshire that may be sixth-, or fifth-, century but did not separate native from alien culture. Droitwich: Hurst, J. D. (ed.) 1997, 17–27 and 150; the excavated area was subject to flooding, which may have terminated its use for a while, but production is documented from the seventh century onward, so continued at other sites: ibid. 27–32.
16 Eslington: Collins and Turner 2018. Milfield burials: Scull and Harding 1990. Milfield Basin (Cheviot Quarry): Johnson, B. and Waddington 2008. Ripon: Hall, R. A. and Whyman 1996, 118–19. Burial survey: Lucy 1999. For Yeavering background: Frodsham, 13–64 and see Ch. 3.
17 The reality of an event recorded in chronicles was long advocated by Baillie on the basis of his dendrochronological research, but he thought in terms of a comet strike, for example 1999, 65–6, 74, whereas a volcano may have been to blame: Gräslund and Price 2012 for the northern consequences. Justinian Plague rats: Rackham 1979; 'companion animals' such as cats and dogs also have fleas that can spread the disease, but it is not likely that many lived as pets and were therefore in close proximity; fleas in second-hand clothing spread by vendors is blamed in Egypt, etc. Disease summary: Lee 2011, 709–14. Weapons and battles: Härke 1990, 28–33; 1997, 24; more weapons might have been buried during relatively peaceful times than when warfare was recorded as taking place, because they could not then be spared. Another autobiographical note is the possible connection between a small group of graves at Breamore, Hampshire, with an exceptionally high ratio of spears and shields (but no swords) and a notional battle site nearby: Hinton and Worrell 2017, 134–6 and 138–9.
18 I have forgotten the name of the historian; although it could have been pointed out to him that the burial party might not have chosen to follow the deceased's wishes, and the age of objects when buried remains a factor to consider, as for instance by Hirst and Clark 2009, 693–5 – older females tend to have well-worn brooches, but there are many exceptions; radiocarbon dating is done of the bones, so it gives the approximate age of the burial: Hines and Bayliss (eds) 2013, 459–64 for dating and phases, 525 for the project's exclusion of earlier cemeteries, 237 for some of the problems of

contamination; the amount of sea fish that a person might have eaten is another factor to be allowed for: contribution by N. Beavan and S. Mays, 101–32. The biggest change identified for the second half of the sixth century, until its final years, is an increasing number of items that were not dress-fittings in female graves: ibid. 520. Statistics can also be used for considering groups and their significance for families and status: Sayer 2020, ch. 2. Animal forms and Style II: Webster, L. 2012, 60–7. See Ch. 3 for the seventh century.

19 The Canterbury coin was probably struck in the 480s: Kent 1995, 948. It would presumably have taken a little time at least to reach Kent and to be passed to the smith; sheet fragments: Oddy 1995; for the jeweller's rouge: Blockley, K., *et al.* 1995, 335; and for the context: Macpherson-Grant 1995, 882–4. Winchester: Ottaway 2017, 193–4.

20 Weights: Scull 1990; Hines 2010. Iron ores: Blackmore, H. L. *et al.* 2019, 316; see Ch 1 for western England.

21 Pottery: Willams, D. F. and Vince 1997 identified granodiorites (biotite granite) from Charnwood Forest, Leicestershire, and suggested its distribution, though with many cautions about other sources, which have made commentators reluctant to accept, or even discuss, the possibility of such a centre having existed, an honourable exception being Leahy 2007, 84–5 and 263; see also Spoerry 2016, 8: glacial erratics may account for some granitic inclusions but not in the same quantity. Plants for linen: Walton Rogers 2007, 14–15. Quernstones: Frantzen 2014, 89 drew attention to the excavator's suggestion that those at West Stow were reused Roman items, but it is unlikely that enough usable ones would have survived; an up-to-date review of all quern pieces from 'sfbs' would be welcome.

22 Kent and its Frankish connections: Harrington and Welch 2014, 174–82 and 183–95 for distribution of coins and other Frankish items in the south of England. Byzantine coins: Naismith 2017, 36–7; Naylor 2017, 401 for summaries (see also Ilchester, above).

23 Rendleshaam: Scull *et al.* 2016. The bucket-shaped pendant may have been an amulet, cf. Bidford-on-Avon. Tranmer House: Fern 2015. Sutton Hoo Mound 5: Carver 2005, 71–90; 2019, 333–4. Gipping valley sites: Penn 2011, 104; one has traces of buildings, including possibly a hall.

24 Yeavering: Hope-Taylor 1977; Carver 2019, 158–60. Sutton Courtenay complex: Brennan and Hamerow 2015; Dorchester-on-Thames: Booth *et al.* 2010. Lyminge: Thomas, G. 2013a. Eastry: Dickinson *et al.* 2011. Dover: Brookes and Harrington 2010, 115; Thomas, G. 2018, 274–9 – the sequence included what are argued to be halls like Lyminge's and others, perhaps beginning in the seventh century rather than the sixth; Eynsford is another: ibid. 286–8. Kingdoms: Yorke 1990. See Ch. 1 for peripatetic rulership.

25 Eriswell (Lakenheath): Hines and Bayliss (eds) 2013, 234, 237, 241, and 250; the horse and the human gave reassuringly consistent dates. A single male buried with a sword, two copper-alloy vessels, a glass cone-beaker, and other items on a hill overlooking the Thames near Marlow, Buckinghamshire, excavated in 2020, is another exceptional case, provisionally radiocarbon-dated to 450–530: G. Thomas, on-line lecture to CBA Wessex, April 2021. Prittlewell: Blackmore, L. *et al.* 2019; meticulous excavation, conservation, research, and publication by Museum of London staff make discussion possible at a level far above what a group of objects alone would permit. There were no 'sand-casts' of the body, unlike at Sutton Hoo. Dice, and presumably games, generally, involved chance and fate, so they might have been used as fortune-tellers. Radiocarbon summary by A. Bayliss *et al.*, 290–5 in Hines and Bayliss (eds) 2013.

26 One coin was found in the head region, so if hand-held the burial must have had one arm bent at the elbow; the other was in the thigh area, so that arm would have been extended in the usual way: Blackmore, L. *et al.* 2019, 112 and figs. 95–6; coins: Williams, G., 146–50 – the gold buckle weighed between the equivalent of 36–38 tremisses, added to which the two coins make a representation of 40 look very deliberate,

as suggested for Sutton Hoo: Hines 2010, 166–9; Blackmore *et al.* 2019, 325. Some kingdoms tolerated christian priests from the west. Garnet sources: contribution by J. Ambers and C. Higgitt to Fern *et al.* (eds) 2019, 129–31.

27 Snape: Filmer-Sankey and Pestell 2001; the cemetery was investigated in the nineteenth century, so records are sparse – a gold ring also came from it. Decline in grave-good quantities: Hines and Bayliss (eds) 2013, 529. Spong: Hills and Lucy 2013, 208, 'around A.D. 530–550 . . . probably marks the point at which Spong Hill went out of use'; Cleatham: Leahy 2007, 227, 263; this is consistent with inhumation dating: Hines and Bayliss (eds) 2013, 517–18 and 526. Chichester, Apple Down: Down and Welch 1990, 108; overall summary: Hills and Lucy 2013, 324–8. Cremation was also used for a very few elite seventh-century burials: see Ch. 3.

3 The Seventh Century

Kings, Christianity, and Commerce

Study of the seventh century is dominated by the ways in which privileged people lived and died; the majority of the population had to support a small number of kings and their families, and christian priests and their churches. They had to do this by supplying food renders and work services, with no noticeable improvement to their living conditions in return. Enough reasonably reliable documents survive from and about the seventh century for basic political history to be written, though it is inevitably slanted to what churchmen, who were the scribes, knew, or thought that they knew, or wanted people to believe. A little information about estates and ownership begins to come from surviving charters, and a few law-codes allow deductions about how rulership operated within a socially graded society, but no ink was wasted on recording people's standards of living or modes of behaviour.[1]

Settlements continued to be fluid, with some farmhouses abandoned, some new ones appearing, but with more signs of organization in the creation of ditched and fenced enclosures. The use of 'sunken-featured buildings' not only declined, but also spread northwards into Cumbria; no changes to weaving techniques, pig-keeping, or conditions of slavery explain why 'sfbs' became less frequent, but if they were predominantly for grain storage, a change to above-ground barns and granaries with greater capacities may be the reason. That would be consistent with early indications of changes in demand; a seventh-century tide-mill at Northfleet, Kent, would have processed wheat into flour more quickly than by hand-querns, and an iron plough-coulter found at Lyminge, Kent, may have been for use on heavy clay soils to increase arable output.[2]

That the first evidence of law-codes, charters, tide-mills, and heavy ploughs is all from Kent is not a coincidence; the pre-eminence of that kingdom, as its rulers would have wanted it to be termed, derived from its proximity and possibly subservience to the Franks on the other side of the Channel, through whom came status-enhancing gold and garnets. The first surviving coins with inscriptions relating to England were found, presumably in graves, outside Canterbury; one is inscribed '*Leudardus Ep*' for Bishop Liudhard, who accompanied the christian Frankish princess who married the king of Kent towards the end of the sixth century; another has on one side the Greek name Eusebius and '*Dorovernis Civitas*', the Latin name and title for Canterbury. The assumption is that Eusebius was a moneyer working in the city, and the gold tremissis and scraps from near the

DOI: 10.4324/9781003007432-4

old amphitheatre show that smiths were already operating there. A little later in date are coins with variations of 'London' on them, and others could have been produced in York, which acquired an archbishop and was favoured by the king of Northumbria with his baptism in 626. Blank gold discs found at Rendlesham could show that moneyers were working there. The designs on the gold coins are a mixture of imperial and christian imagery, both of which suggest anglo-saxon kings wishing to see themselves as part of the new Rome-inspired religion and on a par with continental monarchs who issued coins.[3]

Christianity brought political problems – a king who accepted it might be seen as having had it forced upon him by a superior power. Augustine brought craftsmen who knew how to build stone churches, and the anglo-saxons might have marvelled at the sight of his cathedral in, and monastery just outside, Canterbury, but the buildings were modest in size, no bigger than a farmhouse. Accepting christianity was a risk to any dynasty that gained some of its hold over its subjects from the mystique of descent from a god-like figure. Burial of a king or queen in a church or churchyard, rather than in an earthen barrow, either isolated or, like Prittlewell, on the edge of an existing cemetery, was a bold step for an heir. The opportunity to impress observers by a great display of goods in the burial was lost – however elaborate the funeral ceremony and the subsequent feast may have been. Even in Kent, the old ways were not immediately abandoned just because the king and queen had been buried in Canterbury's abbey church; most cemeteries remained in use for a while, with grave-goods still deposited in them, although the already noticeable decline in their quantities continued, particularly in male graves, with the number of swords found – nationally, not in Kent alone – declining to zero before the 670s/80s. Although a dancing warrior on a buckle from Finglesham, Kent, may not allude to the supernatural, as used to be thought, it certainly suggests reluctance to abandon old customs. On the other hand, it was made of base metal, gilded, but not pure gold; possibly people who were not close enough to the kings to receive the best gifts were less likely to believe that eternal life would be any better than their earthly one.[4]

Pagan kingship is probably seen at its height at Sutton Hoo, where the late sixth-century barrow-grave cremations were succeeded by inhumations, notably of a young man and a horse, in separate grave-pits but under the same mound. The young man was well provided for, though the horse seems to have been elderly and lame. Next, the two great ship burials took place – the extraordinary array of weapons, containers, gold, and textiles within Mound 1 outstrips what had been seen earlier at Prittlewell. No human bone had survived, but dating was obtained from beeswax in an iron lamp. This pointed to a date consistent with the coins found there, all continental tremisses; the only names struck on them that are identifiable historically show that the hoard was assembled after 595, but the beeswax almost precludes a date in the sixth century. Although some coins could date to *c*. 640, all could have been minted by the mid 620s nevertheless. The ship burial could therefore have taken place in or soon after *c*. 624, which is when the notorious King Rædwald of the East Angles disappears from the record. Certainly the riches buried and the extravagant waste of a serviceable ship would have pleased someone who had only a dim understanding of christianity, having set up an altar to the new god alongside those to the old at Rendlesham. But the robbed and wrecked Mound 2 also had remains of weapons signifying a male, so the body in the chamber below that ship, which was at ground level, could just as well have been Redwald, and parity between the two burials might possibly indicate joint rule. The queen who persuaded Redwald to maintain his traditions could have been in the chamber below Mound 14, laid out on a bed-like structure. After her, or very soon afterwards, the Sutton Hoo cemetery was disused but remembered and perhaps at first revered, then feared, until executions took place there.[5]

With three blank gold discs to bring the number up to forty and two gold ingots, making the value of fifty *scillingas* in weight, the Sutton Hoo purse-group looks like a compensation payment, or *wergild*, and not a random amount. Similarly, the other large group known, an isolated hoard at Crondall, Hampshire, had ninety-eight coins and three blanks – even though that totals 101, it is difficult not to associate it with a *wergild* of a hundred *scillingas*. But seventh-century gold coins are now being found so widely that their role in trade has to be reconsidered, and that they were not valued only as compensation payments and prestige gifts. They were also well enough known to spawn imitations, like a plated copy found recently in Watton, Norfolk.[6]

A plated copy of a Merovingian gold coin was one of the very few pieces of metalwork found at Yeavering, which developed at the beginning of the seventh century into what is clearly identifiable as a major focus of Northumbrian kingship (Illus. 3.1). Its buildings were all of timber, and perhaps initially not very distinctive, but something of the activities taking place at the site was shown by the discovery of quantities of ox-skulls and bones, suggestive of sacrificing and feasting; they had been brought to the site either as tribute or loot and probably were kept in a large circular corral before slaughter. A cemetery with graves arranged radially inside a ring-ditch with standing stones was another early feature. A structure with concentric foundation trenches is identified as a segment of an amphitheatre, unlike anything at any other site. After a fire, caused either by an accident or by an unrecorded raid by rivals, the site was redeveloped, with an even bigger hall, and the concentric structure was enlarged. Burials took place at various locations within the complex, arranged in ways that seem more obviously christian than the earlier ones; the corral was filled in, and a church was built over part of it. As no doubt has been raised about the veracity of a later account of a missionary baptizing people at the site and of a christian princess from Kent marrying one of Northumbria's kings, a process of development that included the arrival of the Roman church probably pertained, but not to the extent of including a stone structure like those at Canterbury. One grave close to the hall contained someone buried with a goat's skull – 'Yeavering' was *ad Gefrin*, 'goat hill' in Celtic – a spear and an implement identified as a surveyor's *groma* of Roman type, so perhaps one of the princess's companions persuaded the king to lay out the post-fire buildings in an orderly manner, conforming to measured units of a 'short pole' of 15 modern feet (4.59 metres), a unit that might have been introduced to England by Augustine at his arrival in Canterbury in 597.[7]

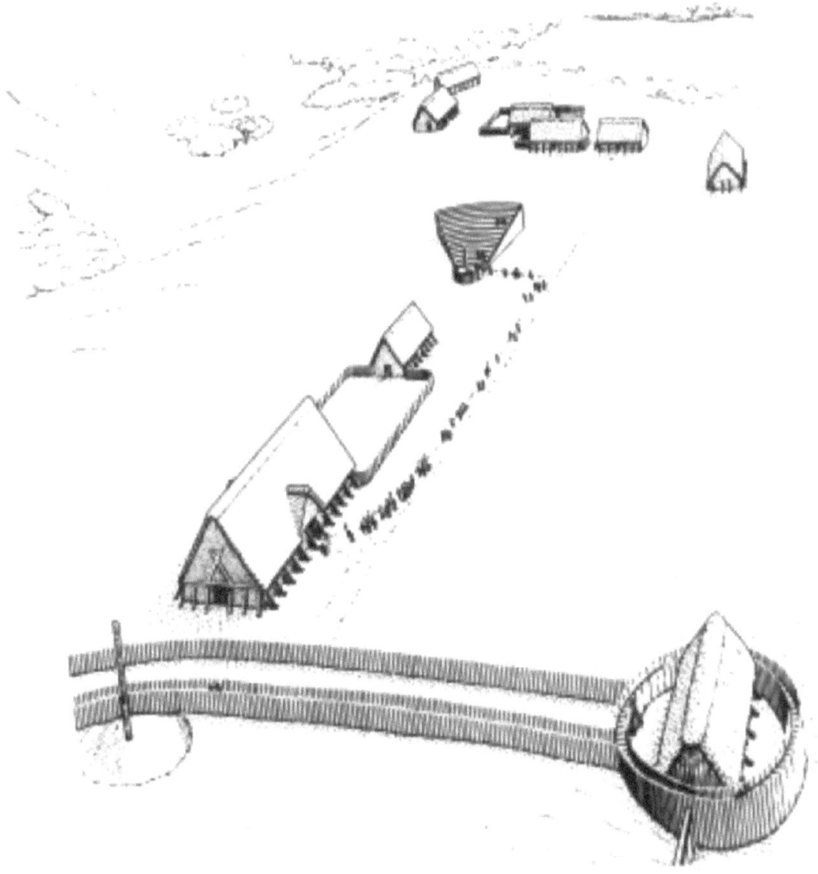

Illustration 3.1 Reconstruction by S. James of the Yeavering complex in the early seventh century. In the foreground is the 'great enclosure', perhaps used as a cattle corral despite the internal features. The great hall is about to host a feast to be enjoyed by the procession of people who are shown leaving the staged structure where assemblies were held. In the distance are other buildings, one of which may have been a temple, as it had human burials and large deposits of ox skulls and bones associated with it, the latter at least suggesting ritual slaughter. Before the site was abandoned, a christian church had been built in the foreground, over the ditch of the corral (Hope-Taylor 1977).

Yeavering is not the only site where larger buildings appeared in the seventh century. Documentary records sometimes indicate that these were royal centres, *villae regales*, like Yeavering, but most are better seen as 'headman's houses' or 'great hall complexes', symptomatic of growing social stratification. Many had rectangular buildings, often with annexes at one or both ends, of the same width as or narrower than the main 'hall'; the latter may have incorporated shrines and certainly seem too small for most other purposes. Their sites were not defended by earthwork banks and ditches, so their owners felt secure in the knowledge that no one would dare to raid them – but were also probably making sure that their overlords did not see them as a challenge. At Yeavering, a church was probably added to the site, as might have happened at Cowage Farm, near Malmesbury, Wiltshire. Two sites in prominent positions on the Hampshire Downs, Cowdery's Down and Chalton (Illus. 3.2), did not have a church nearby.[8]

Illustration 3.2 Plan of the excavated site on the Hampshire Downs at Chalton. There were only two 'sunken-featured buildings', the others being rectangular, some with annexes of uncertain purpose, also found at various other sites. The building at the top, known as AZ1, was clearly attached to a large central compound and was probably laid out disregarding the original, very rectilinear, layout of the site around an open space, unlike the sprawling sites of earlier centuries. The site was not used for long if at all after the late seventh century, and despite the likelihood that a high-status family owned such a substantial complex, no church or graveyard was included within or, so far as is known, adjacent to it.

Although many sixth-century cemeteries remained in use for a while into the seventh, new ones also appeared, often larger than those of previous centuries. Burials in them contained fewer grave-goods, with many more graves unfurnished than before. These 'Final Phase' cemeteries need not indicate christianity, though west-east burial is another reason for thinking its influence to have been spreading; a small cluster of unfurnished west-east graves near the inhumation/cremation cemetery at Apple Down suggests people who might have accepted christianity but did not want total separation from their forebears. Apple Down exemplifies another point about many of the excavated 'Final Phase' cemeteries in having no known building within or adjacent to it. Practice began to vary, however; a surprising case is Carlton Colville, where burial took place among the already existing settlement buildings, a practice that did not last long. A slightly different case is Bamburgh, Northumberland, where burials in the sand-dunes, radiocarbon-dated to the mid seventh to mid eighth century, may have been there because of the difficulty of digging into the rock of the recorded stronghold, where stone buildings of the general period have been seen in excavation: presumably by that time, there would have been a church. Isotopes indicate that many of the people in the dunes had come from a distance, including Scandinavia, suggesting continuation of connections that in earlier times had brought bracteates and wrist-clasps; others had come from much further south.[9]

The 'Final Phase' cemeteries were not necessarily much influenced by christianity when founded, although christianity may have been imposed on many of them as the seventh century developed, so that by its end all the anglo-saxon kings had willingly or otherwise accepted it. A few people were picked out for special and separate burial, usually in barrows, some remote but highly visible; these special people indicate the same emergence of overt social stratification seen in the 'great hall complexes'. They cannot be allocated even putative names from historical records, so their relationship to known kings depends upon the sources of objects found with them. Taplow, Buckinghamshire, close to the River Thames, contained glass vessels and gold dress fittings sufficiently like those found in Kent as to suggest a 'client-king', holding power in a rich area but unable to act independently of his patron. A cremation within a large round barrow at Asthall in the Oxfordshire Cotswolds may have been of the chief of a tribal people, buried with at least one Byzantine vessel and other items including gaming-pieces; his level of independence from an overlord cannot be assessed from what survived. In the Peak District, a cluster can be explained as the graves of people who grew rich from their control of lead production. No particular local circumstances explain the lone male with a helmet, sword, and hanging-bowl at Wollaston, Northamptonshire.[10]

Even more difficult to characterize are various burials of females, often placed on raised frames like the Prittlewell 'prince', wearing necklaces and pairs of pins of gold and silver, and with glass vessels and a range of other items not always now understood. Some were isolated, or in small groups, and others in quite large cemeteries. Why they were picked out for special treatment may not have been a simple matter of family status; one, a mature female, in a group of seven excavated at Westbury, Buckinghamshire, had been buried prone, yet had a necklace with a large gold pendant, silver rings, and beads, and a bag containing two iron knives and a pair of shears. At

Westfield Farm, Ely, a burial under a barrow of a child aged 10–12 years has to be assumed to have been female from the grave-goods, notably a necklace with gold and silver pendants, and, inside a wooden box, two glass vessels and a comb. This burial had fifteen or more burials around it, respecting the barrow but not otherwise very orderly. A frame burial excavated at Coddenham, Suffolk, was in a row of graves, not obviously more special than others, but in contrast, extreme regimentation was identified at Street House, Loftus, Yorkshire, where most of the burials formed a rectangle surrounding a barrow burial, again identifiable as of a female from the accompanying necklace and other objects. At Harford Farm, south of Norwich, forty-six graves were excavated, but they showed no obvious focus or traces of a barrow and included four graves with boxes, pendants, and a large brooch.[11]

The Harford Farm brooch has a cross on it picked out in small garnets. Christian imagery appears on many items, a particularly fine example being a gold and garnet pendant from a female burial on the outskirts of Canterbury. A helmet at Benty Grange in the Peak District has a silver cross set in the nasal, either because its owner believed in christianity or simply saw the cross as a protective amulet. The reverse side of the Eusebius coin has a cross, flanked on both sides by smaller crosses; despite its small size, it was clearly rendering an image of the scene at Golgotha where Christ was crucified between two thieves. This story of rejection by one thief and redemption through acceptance by the other may have resonated with the newly converted, because it occurs again in an entirely different medium, a gold sword pommel set with red garnets, found in Dinham, Shropshire. That object suggests the westward spread of anglo-saxon influence, although no new cemeteries have been found in the west Midlands. In the south-west, however, expansion is clearly shown by a cemetery outside Dorchester, Dorset, and by the appearance of anglo-saxon objects in existing cemeteries in north Somerset, like Camerton. Changes to settlement form may be another marker of developing anglo-saxon control and overlordship. Enclaves without anglo-saxon objects or cemeteries could indicate resistance to the culture even if political domination was inevitable; in Wareham, south-east Dorset, grave-markers and inscribed stones strongly suggest that the local version of christianity was derived from France, not from Canterbury. The possible enclaves in eastern England succumbed, however; even St Albans had a cemetery with furnished graves in it.[12]

*

Some kings were probably like Redwald, unwilling to reject old gods completely but not dismissive of christianity either. His ambivalence is known only because it scandalized a later writer; ecclesiastics may generally have exaggerated the paganism of any king who resisted their religion and killed some of their patrons. They saw conflicts between rival kings as being battles for or against christianity, and not as land-grabs and bounty-taking. Such fighting may have caused the burial to be considered for safe-keeping, probably intended to be temporary, of the Staffordshire hoard, discovered in 2009, close to Roman roads and to Lichfield. If they had been found on their own, antagonism towards christianity would have been offered as the explanation of the rough treatment meted out to two crosses found bent and folded up (Illus. 3.3a), but so too was a large gold

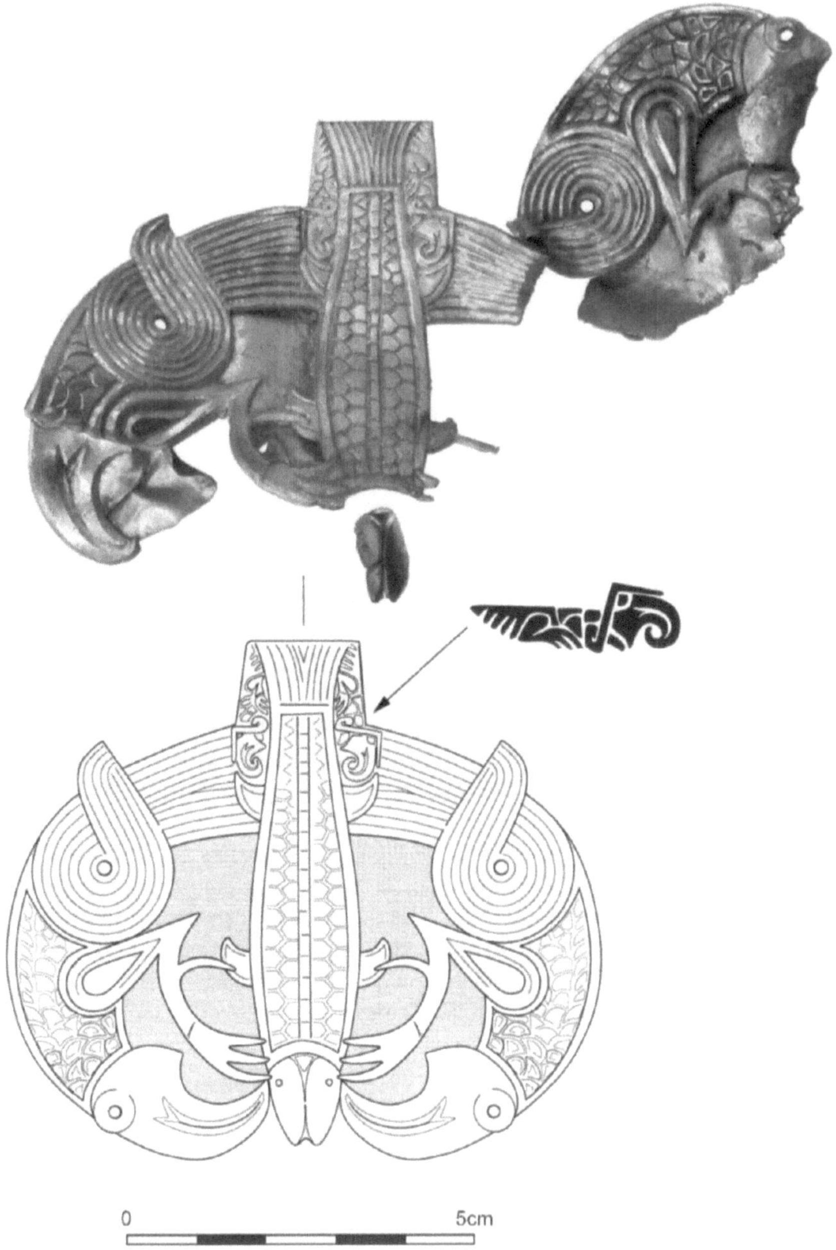

Illustration 3.3a The magnificent gold mount in the Staffordshire hoard had been bent without regard to its design or the possibility of reuse. The drawing shows the original design of sea-eagles – or of one sea-eagle 'split' – tearing at a fish. The 'helmeted' Style I creature is a development of those on earlier items, e.g. Illus. 2,3 (Fern *et al*. 2019; identification as a sea-eagle by Dale Serjeantson, personal communication).

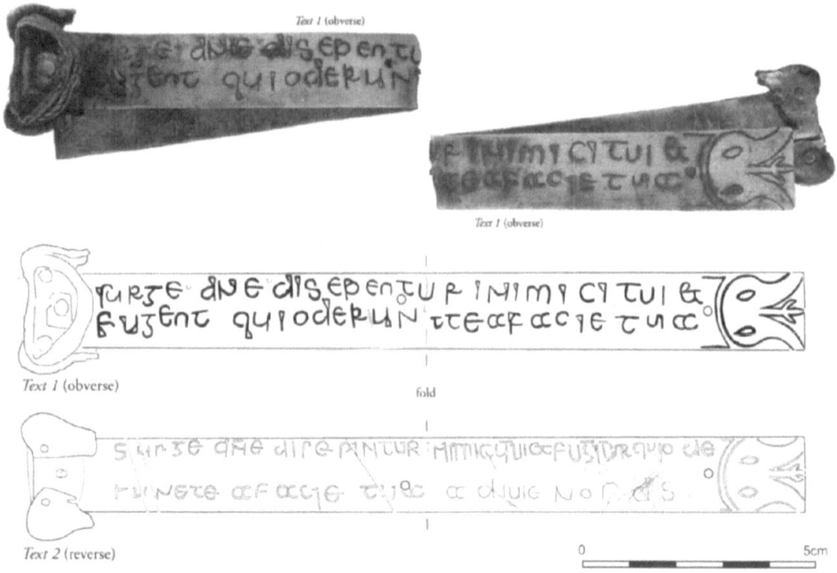

Illustration 3.3b Gold strip inscribed on both sides with Latin texts.

mount having two sea-eagles tearing at a fish that has no clear-cut christian meaning; these pieces may have been folded up to fit into a bag (Illus. 3.3b). Many of the other objects had also been roughly treated, showing where a smith's tongs had gripped them to dismantle them. Two large gilt-silver panels with die-stamped patterns of interlaced creatures had been wrenched off a helmet, and other objects had been sliced and scratched by knives. Most of the hoard's content was from weaponry, particularly pommels and other sword fittings; gold and garnets look likely to have come from horse harness, and the eagles-and-fish mount may have come from a shield if it were not from a saddle. Another object may have been part of a christian priest's headdress, and there were small pendant crosses, one with a cavity that could have contained a relic. The garnets are set in various geometric patterns and may 'hide' crosses. An overt display of a cross occurs on a remarkable ring found subsequent to the hoard in Essex; a full-length figure is shown holding a processional cross in one hand and a bird of prey in the other, while another bird flies overhead. Its motifs are comparable to some on hoard objects and at Sutton Hoo.[13]

Also bent over is a gold strip that would have been nailed to one arm of a large cross (Illus. 3.3b). It is inscribed on both sides with Latin texts, the side that would have been visible having its letters filled with black niello. The reverse side may therefore have been a trial to see how the letters should be placed, but they are in a different style, so were written by scribes with different training, even if copied and cut by the same craftworker; neither can be assigned to a specific date by comparisons with stone carvings or books. The text is from one of the psalms, slightly adapted: 'Arise, O Lord, and may your enemies be torn apart . . . ', a sentiment that would appeal to anyone going into battle. The crudely cut serpents with forked tongues must have had significance as they are on both sides despite taking up space.

The earliest objects in the Staffordshire hoard are sixth-century sword pommels, mostly silver and one certainly Scandinavian. The date when it was all buried cannot be stated precisely: despite much speculation, no known historical event gives either a precise date or a particular reason for the concealment of some 600 items, including at least seventy-four sword pommels, in total weighing over half a kilogram; that so much, and of such diverse character, should ever have been assembled still seems unthinkable, as it does that such carefully made things should have been so maltreated. The objects with the least signs of wear or repair are from well into the seventh century; the styles of lettering used for the inscriptions on one of the cross-arms were formerly thought to provide the best evidence for a terminal date near the end of the seventh century but cannot be tied down so precisely (Illus. 3.3b); an approximate burial date of between 630 and 660 is suggested on the basis of comparisons with other objects. Although traces of beeswax were found used as glues and fillers, they are too few to be tested for radiocarbon dating, and the other organics – white shells and bone inlay that gave colour contrasts to the red garnets and gold, and wood surviving in the cores of some of the pommels – are not suitable either.[14]

One reason for dating the Staffordshire hoard to the middle part of the seventh century is that most of the gold objects in it are of fairly pure gold, which became much scarcer as supplies into western Europe ended with the cessation of subsidies sent from Byzantium, following Arab invasions. The supply of garnets and other precious stones was also affected, as the invasions cut off trade with the Far East, and if garnets had also been coming from central Europe, Avar invasions would have removed that source. Those developments would have diminished the flow of prestige goods into Kent and reduced that kingdom's ability to subsidize dependent rulers in other territories. The lack of new gold is seen in the anglo-saxon coins, with silver increasingly added into the alloys; the ratios fluctuated, but in general gold descended from over 90% down to 50%/70%, dropping to as low as 22% probably in the 640s, dwindling away altogether by the mid 670s; those debased coins are now referred to as 'pale gold'. It was not a steady decline – presumably a moneyer who had a small supply of purer gold to use would have put some into his new products, so dating of individual coins cannot be exact; the coins in the Crondall hoard are more debased than those at Sutton Hoo, so they are later in date, but exactly how much later is uncertain. Smiths also had to add more silver to eke out supplies for jewellery, and the intricate garnet cutting seen at Sutton Hoo and in the Staffordshire hoard came to an end, even in Kent (Illus. 3.4). The Harford Farm brooch exemplifies the latter process, as it only had small garnets, which could be chipped down from larger ones to eke out supplies; it had been repaired, however, by someone who could not get replacement stones for some that had been lost; the smith was also unable to match the

Illustration 3.4 Two 'composite disc' brooches from Kent. On the left, the Amherst brooch, named from its previous owner but probably from a cemetery at Sarre, is of 83% fine gold and is set with well-cut red garnets, blue and green glass, and white shell – the best shells came from the Indian Ocean – in gold cells. On the right, the Monkton brooch is only 55% fine gold and has smaller, less well-cut garnets in copper-alloy cells, gilded to simulate gold, differences that might be present because its owner was less well off, but is more likely to reflect increasing difficulty of getting gold and other overseas exotica, with the Amherst brooch perhaps dating to the 620s or a little earlier, and the Monkton to the 650s. The former has a cross emanating from the central boss, 'disguised' by the intermediate triangles and circles; the gold panels on the latter make a bolder round-armed cross (MacGregor and Bolick 1993, 79–80; construction of such composites: Coatsworth and Pinder 2002, 174).

earlier gold filigree. Nevertheless, he had put his name, Luda, on the back and had incised two Style II animals.[15]

Luda is the first anglo-saxon smith whose name is recorded, but nothing else is known about him. He may have been an itinerant, finding patronage where he could, or he might have been tied to a particular king. As Norfolk was almost certainly part of the kingdom of the East Angles, he might even have worked at Rendlesham, where metalworking evidence has been found, as it has at Coddenham. The great hall complexes at Sutton Courtenay and Yeavering have also produced metalworking evidence, in the latter's case not close to the hall. This distance might have been for safety, to keep sparks from furnaces away from thatched roofs, but the risks of that are quite low with the small hearths that the smiths would have needed, and they may have been kept away because their skills involved the 'magic' of changing one thing into another. In Lincolnshire at Tattershall Thorpe, a collection of metalworkers' tools (Illus. 3.5a) and scrap that was presumably destined for reuse was excavated in an area with no other trace of activity; among the objects awaiting recycling were garnets, some skilfully cut, others roughly chipped – the former would probably have ended up like the latter (Illus. 3.5b). Graves with rich but sometimes unfinished objects in 'King's Field'

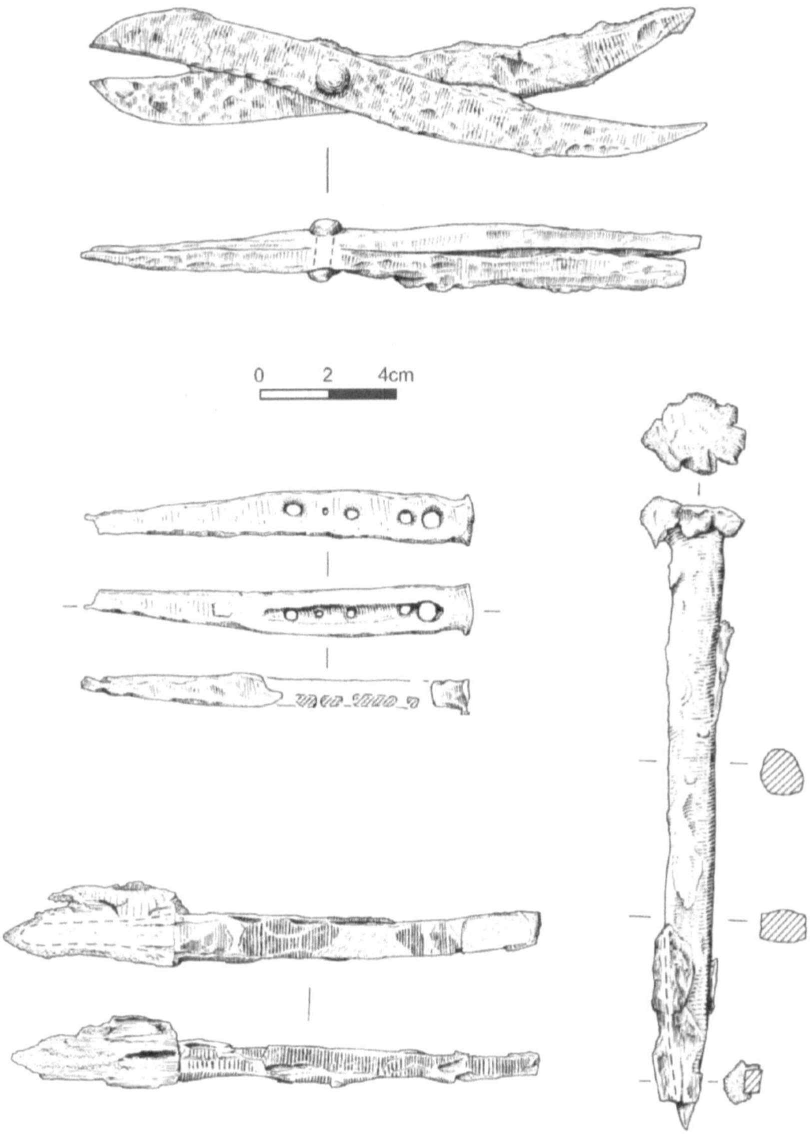

Illustration 3.5a The smith's grave at Tattershall Thorpe, Lincolnshire, included a variety of metalworker's tools, including snips for cutting sheet metal (top), a nail-making tool (and/or a draw-plate for wire-making – if that was practicable), a file with very fine teeth and part of its wooden handle surviving, and a punch, the top suggesting considerable use (Hinton 1999).

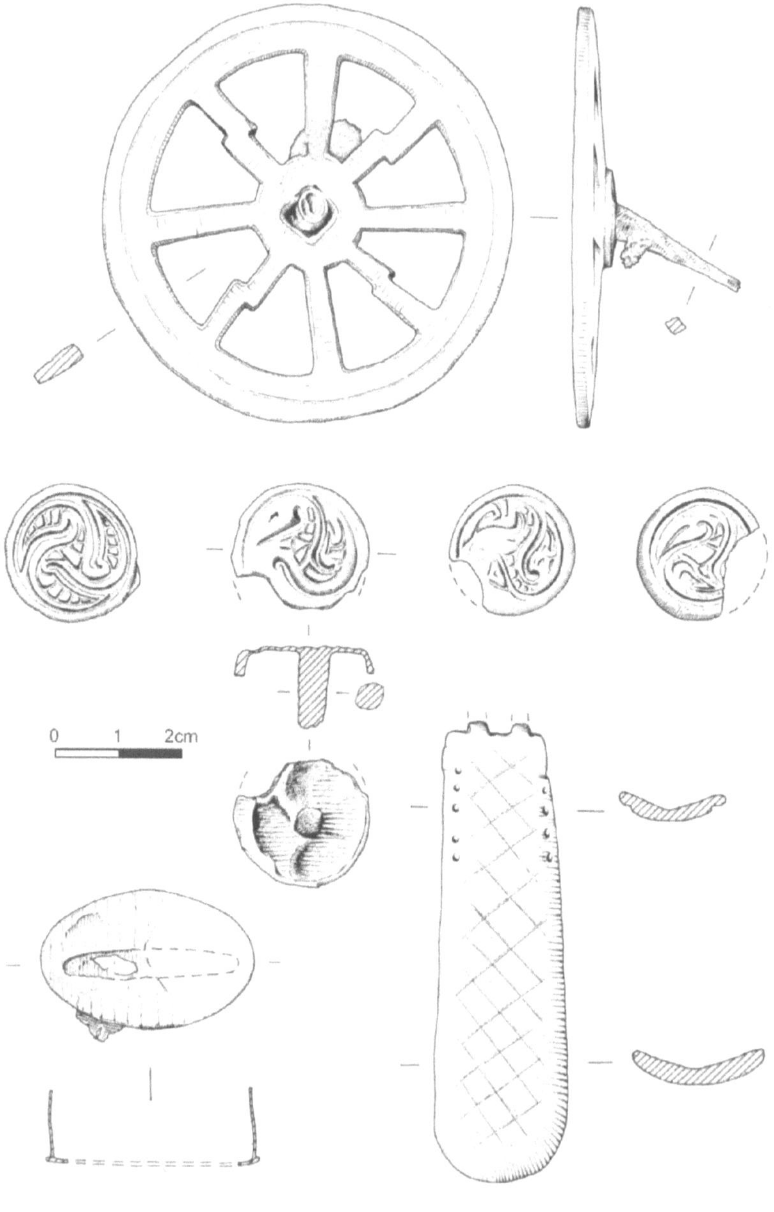

Illustration 3.5b The smith had various things which he presumably hoped to reuse rather than melt down; the copper-alloy 'wheel' was originally worn as a pendant and probably originated in the Upper Rhine during the sixth century; below it are studs with Style II animals, very similar to those from the *Hamwic* and *Gippeswic* cemeteries and probably also continental; the slot in the object bottom left suggests that it was a hilt fitting for a small seax or knife; the other object is unidentified, although if the two projections at the top are broken-off hinge fittings, it could have been a handle (Hinton 1999, contribution on the studs by C. Scull, p. 58).

at Faversham, Kent, may be those of smiths dependent on Kentish kings. Their cemetery may have kept them slightly apart even in death.[16]

*

One of the most significant arguments of the radiocarbon sequencing project was that the practice of burying objects with the dead all but ended by *c*. 670, some 20 years earlier than previously thought. That redating had considerable impact on ideas about both religious and about commercial developments and directly challenged the accepted numismatic chronology. The difficulty of maintaining even the pretence of gold coinage led perhaps directly to the production of small silver coins usually called 'sceattas'; some of the 'pale gold' coins have designs almost exactly the same as on the first sceattas, which are otherwise so rarely struck with identifiable names and vary so widely in design that establishing their chronology is difficult. The assumption was that their introduction followed trends on the continent, and that they did not appear until the 690s. A few have been found in graves, however, so the radiocarbon project required a revision of that date, with silver sceattas being minted in England some time before *c*. 670: continental dating has been revised but still regards the introduction of silver coins to be *c*. 675. Furthermore, analyses of ice-cores from Swiss glaciers show lead pollution brought by wind from France as peaking after 660, and the lead would have derived from Melle, where silver was mined and had to be separated from the lead that occurs in the same veins; increased silver output probably made the continental silver coins possible.[17]

Revision of the dating of coins in the seventh century affects consideration of commerce and the emergence of places which existed primarily for trading purposes, as opposed to settlements where other activities predominated but which traders may have visited. Leading the way was probably London. Various settlements, cemeteries, and objects have been found close to and a little inland from the Thames in the London area generally, but there was nothing to suggest anything distinctive before the placing of a bishop within the old Roman walls in 604; the early seventh-century church or churches presumably underlie St Paul's Cathedral. The bishops were supposed to serve the East Saxon people but initially depended on the support of the king of Kent, whose domination of the London area came to be disputed by various other warlords. Place-names suggest that the bishops were not the only ones to acquire properties in the City in the seventh century, but very little contemporaneous archaeological material has been found in it. Instead, archaeology has shown that trading was taking place up-river in the area of the Strand, its name referring to the shoreline on which boats were beached but with activity extending some way back from the river itself.[18]

The new London trading area was soon joined by others, at modern Southampton, Ipswich, and York, all places with the element *wic* in their names; others may now be lost to the sea. Burials around the core of new London suggest a strong elite interest: at the fifth-century tile-kiln site, where there may have been occupation also in the sixth century, graves with glass vessels and a hanging-bowl have been excavated; a disc-brooch with gold and garnets in a woman's grave was excavated in the Covent Garden area; and in Whitehall traces were found of a wide building that looks comparable to those at 'great hall complexes'. London cemeteries were not included in the radiocarbon dating project, but both Ipswich and Southampton had suitable material and both had graves containing sceattas, which had previously placed the graves towards the end of the seventh century; the revised dating moves them back probably to 650–70, which therefore takes the foundation of those two *wic* sites back as well. Just outside Ipswich was the grave of a woman with a disc-brooch comparable to that in London, and gold pendants and other rich objects; inside were two graves with exceptional contents, males with belt fittings and long knives in scabbards decorated with studs otherwise found on the continent, in northern France and the Low Countries. The only comparable set found in England is from a north-south double-burial grave on the edge of the Southampton *wic*, but a silver-coated iron buckle with copper-alloy inlay from London is also an import; no disc-brooch was found in the Southampton cemetery, but one woman had been buried with a very distinctive small gold crescentic pendant, otherwise found only at a royal site in Frisia, and another had a gold and garnet pendant that might also be from Frisia. Both the London and Southampton cemeteries had cremations as well as burials with grave-goods, which suggests that christianity was not practised uniformly, and their acceptability to people from overseas could mean that some were from unconverted Frisia; the London buckle has a long-shafted cross motif, however. York has no burials of comparable types, but a hanging-bowl found in the nineteenth century may show the seventh-century interest of well-to-do people in the new *wic*.[19]

The *wic* sites could all be reached by ships, though York and London are well inland, while Ipswich and Southampton are at river mouths but sheltered from open water. No single explanation obviously accounts for their emergence, although all may have become possible as Kent's domination through its control of gold and garnets from the Franks fell away. Trading-places would have needed the approval of whoever ruled the territories in which they were established, but that does not mean that kings necessarily founded them: Ipswich could have been fostered by the Wuffinga dynasty; it is close to Rendlesham but on a different river and may have had more to do with Coddenham; York was central to a prosperous part of Northumbria; but Southampton was in an unstable area, and London did not clearly belong to anyone. The exceptional burials at Ipswich and Southampton seem to have been of people from overseas, but that they were brought in to get the places going and oversee them like later port-reeves suggests an unlikely degree of advance planning. York had an archbishop, London a bishop, and Southampton was at the mouth of the river that ran past the bishop's base at Winchester, but the East Angles' see had no obvious connection with Ipswich, so direct involvement by the Church does not present a common thread, although it benefited from commerce generally. Kings benefited by extracting tolls from merchants and may have acquired goods from them, particularly wine. York may not have been on the same scale as the other three *wic*s; two sites on the east side of the River Foss are some way apart and might not have been linked; no inland streets have been found, as they have been at the others.[20]

Uncertainties over the stimulus for the trading sites are a consequence of the convoluted narratives of dynasties, overlords, peoples, and the progress of christianity in the seventh century. The radiocarbon dating project has made it likely that pagan practices had all but disappeared by soon after 670, and church institutions were by then well established, notably in Northumbria with the disciplined arrangements of stone buildings at Wearmouth and Jarrow, Hexham, and probably Ripon. The mid seventh-century church in Winchester and the cathedral and abbey at Canterbury were others; one now identified at Glastonbury may well have been built during the long late seventh-/early eighth-century reign of King Ine, as tradition had it; a glass furnace there shows that it had windows, as had Jarrow. They contrast with the timber structures at the nunnery at Hartlepool, which look more like a concentration of ordinary domestic buildings. Elsewhere, timber buildings and a cemetery excavated at Nazeingbury, Essex, were probably part of a recorded nunnery; eighty-six of the 113 adult burials that could be identified were female, twenty-nine aged over 45 years. Only one had clear signs of having borne a child, and few had obvious signs of having done heavy labour. There were burials of a few children and adolescents also, who had perhaps died while being schooled by the nuns.[21]

The relatively sheltered life that the women at Nazeingbury were able to lead shows how a 'princess-minster' could thrive, provided that it had substantial royal or other support. An advantage may have been that even if the minster had to be endowed, the need for the property of someone who died to be divided among a wide kinship that included a family into which a daughter or niece had married was reduced. Some of the very rich female burials are in cemeteries close to nunneries, as at Ely, or within town walls close to a church, as in Winchester. Elite men also increasingly sought burial near churches; a male with spun-gold thread around his neck, probably part of an embroidered braid from a tunic or a priest's stole, was found near the bishop's church at Worcester, founded in the 670s. Bishops were probably placed within old Roman towns because they gave authority, but the enclosure of their surviving walls was probably another attraction, not for cathedrals alone; a late seventh-century minster recorded at Exeter attracted burials, the beginning of the city's revival. Any 'minster' – the term was used of churches of all kinds – needed to be supported by production surpluses, drawn from their endowed estates and gifts, and needed the protection of patrons to whose residences many were attached, making archaeological recognition of them difficult. A major church site at Lyminge, Kent, was immediately adjacent to a secular royal hall, but others may not have maintained any clear separation.[22]

The burials at Nazeingbury and the records from many other monasteries show that a proportion of the population could be withdrawn from secular society without having any adverse effect on its ability to support and protect itself. That the population was already growing in the seventh century is also indicated by the peopling of London and the other *wics*. Although Bede wrote that his monastery had been nearly wiped out by plague, it may not have been quite as bad as his boyhood memory recalled, although it is true that people living close together in a monastic community would have been more vulnerable to infection and contagion than most of the population. If the earthwork dykes were more securely dated, it would be possible to argue about the amount of labour available, but that none is certainly of seventh-century date might be a pointer to a lack of people who could be spared even in the slacker agricultural seasons, particularly as they probably faced heavier demands to produce surpluses for lords and churches. Some of them were, however, diverted to other forms of earthwork and construction: dendrochronology showed that oak piles in a causeway at Mersea, Essex, were felled between 693 and 699, possibly to serve a minster. Although several occupation sites were thought, when first excavated, to have been totally abandoned during the seventh century, later work has shown that pottery at West Stow proves that it stayed in use well into the eighth century; the process of shift to adjacent land probably continued elsewhere, so large-scale desertion is unlikely.[23]

Producing the resources needed to sustain major church institutions would have been a reason for intensifying agricultural output and tying people to their farms. One of the best demonstrations of the scale required in the second half of the seventh century comes from the production of manuscripts: three of the largest each needed over 500 vellum quires, skins carefully prepared from young cattle. It is unlikely that more than one quire of suitable quality could have been cut from the hide of any one beast, and sometimes the scribes had to get the books written in only two or three years if they were intended for presentation. That a monastery's own estates and the renders of its tenants could yield so many animals for slaughter in a fairly short time may have been a strain, but it was done. Ink was produced from lamp-black, gall from locally grown oaks, or from iron, but the painted decoration in such works as the Lindisfarne Gospels involved some dangerous mixtures of materials such as arsenic, white lead, mercury, and copper carbonate, as well as more harmless plant and whelk dyes. If gold or silver was applied, the costs became even greater. The books are a physical testament to the resources of the great churches, as well as to their scholarship; carved stone crosses with intricate iconography like those at Ruthwell and Bewcastle are another, as are what little survives of the altars, reliquaries, and other fittings, including window glass, and ironwork. Monasteries like Jarrow and Wearmouth were on navigable rivers, easing their problems of supply, but so far as can be told, they were not producing surpluses for commercial sale, unlike later medieval houses.[24]

Apart perhaps from Kent's Reculver cross, the great seventh-century survivals are nearly all Northumbrian, a testimony to that kingdom's wealth and prestige; it was not a supremacy that would last long into the eighth century. Although the great minsters needed peaceful conditions if they were to thrive, the Church could do little to bring them about.[25]

Notes

1 The earliest law-code survives in a twelfth-century copy but seems accurate; the earliest surviving charter is from the 670s–80s: Breay and Story (eds) 2018, 89–90 and 96–7.

2 Cumbrian site: Oliver *et al.* 1996, 132–45. Granaries: Hamerow 2012, 152. Northfleet mill reconstruction: Blair 2018, ill. 41. Enclosures: Reynolds 2003. Coulter: Thomas, G. *et al.* 2016.

3 See Naismith 2017, 50–5. York: Mainman 2019, 35–46. Rendlesham blanks: Scull *et al.* 2016.

4 Baptism by a priest from Rome may have circumvented King Ethelbert's reluctance to be seen taking it from a Frank, which might have implied subordination to another monarch. Dynastic descent from gods: Yorke 1990, 15–16. Finglesham buckle (from grave 95: Hines and Bayliss (eds) 2013, 264): Brookes and Harrington 2010, 79; the Wilmington chalk-cut figure with two staffs looks surprisingly similar but is much later in date. Kent had several very rich burials in barrows, frustratingly robbed or wrecked.

5 Sutton Hoo radiocarbon dating: Hines and Bayliss (eds) 2013, 502; sequence summary and Mound 2 possibility: Carver 2019, 331–43; coins: Williams, G. 2019, 149–50; executions: see Ch. 7; joint kingship: Yorke 1990., 48–9 – kings ruling in tandem brought conflict not concord; that it was not recorded in East Anglia does not mean that it did not happen there. Mound 14 was not included in the radiocarbon sequencing, Hines and Bayliss (eds) 2013, so its dating is uncertain; it could be as late as *c.* 650, by which time Redwald's queen would have been a very old lady.

6 See Hines (2010) on the wergild equivalences and whether the buckle should be taken into consideration; Williams, G. 2019, 149–50 saw the assemblage rather as a sign of wealth and of the use of coins and coin-equivalents in commerce. Outline: Naismith 2017, 44, 52, and 61. Plated copy and examples of other finds: Naylor 2015, 291. (A scattered hoard of over 130 continental gold *solidi* and *trientes*, a gold ingot, and some scrap gold has now been reported from Norfolk.)

7 Yeavering excavation: Hope-Taylor 1977; review: Frodsham and O'Brien (eds) 2005. Cattle slaughter may have been a ritual act, using an axe-hammer like the one found at Sutton Hoo. Raids: cf. Catterick, Ch. 2. The ring-ditch of the 'western cemetery' was presumably prehistoric, like others in the area. Critique of amphitheatre, suggesting that its focus was a totem-like pole: Barnwell 2005. A very experienced excavator of difficult conditions like Yeavering's, Martin Carver, reviewed but largely accepted Hope-Taylor's interpretations of the sequence, though not of the site's origins as British rather than Anglian anglo-saxon: 2019, 369–76. 'Short pole': Huggins 1991; Blair 2018, 71–2; also Blair *et al.* 2020.

8 Yeavering christianity: Carver 2019, 370–5. 'Great hall complexes': Blair 2018, 114–23, and for shrines, Blair 1995. Cowdery's Down: Millett and James 1983. Chalton: Addyman and Leigh 1973; Champion 1977. The 'rectilinearity' is comparable to that at the Street House cemetery: Sherlock 2012. Other such complexes were discussed by McBride 2020, 1–21; he distinguished 'great' from 'minor' hall complexes but recognized the difficulty of differentiating between sites with different investigation records.

9 'Final Phase' cemeteries: Geake 1997; 2002. Apple Down: Down and Welch 1990, 14–15, 109, and 122. Carlton Colville: Lucy *et al.* 2009. Bamburgh cemetery: Turner, J. 2020; Inner Ward excavations: Kirton and Young 2017, 161–3, 166–72, and 199–202; earlier work discovered a very fine gold Style II plaque, thought to be from a reliquary or shrine: Webster, L. and Backhouse (eds) 1991, 58–9.

10 'Final Phase' burials: Geake 1992, 84–5; Hines and Bayliss (eds) 2013, 537. Taplow: Webster 2012, 61–5. Asthall: Dickinson and Speake 1992. The Peak District might have yielded silver as well as lead. Wollaston: Meadows 2019.

11 Westbury: Ivens *et al.* 1995, 71–5, with contributions by J. Mills and other specialists; the hands and arms were missing but perhaps because of the conditions in the grave. Females in isolated barrows feature particularly in Wiltshire, for example see Speake (1988). Westfield Road: Lucy *et al.* 2009, 83–91. Coddenham: Penn 2011, grave 30, 24–59; a Merovingian gold coin of Dagobert I, mounted as a pendant, was found in a bag with her, pp. 26–7 (so not 'unpublished', as Hines and Bayliss (eds) 2013, table 7.6;

the grave was excluded from the sequence, p. 418, but reinstated on p. 505, median date 653, and see pp. 507 and 509. Another possible coin was also in the grave, apparently a sceat or a counterfeit of one). Street House: Sherlock 2012; Carver 2019 for further discussion (frame-burials are of sixth- as well as seventh-century): Hines and Bayliss (eds) 2013, 370. Harford Farm: Penn 2000.

12 Dinham pommel: Webster, L. 2012, 31; the gold or silver of pommels is not normally solid pure metal but a cap over a base metal or wooden core. Canterbury pendant: contribution by L. Webster to Frere *et al.* 1987, 282–4. Somerset cemeteries: Costen 2011, 23–4 and 144–5. The Bradford Peveril cemetery is unpublished, but items from it are in the Dorset County Museum. Settlements in the south-west: Rippon 2008, 132–6. Wareham: Cramp 2006, 116–24, 117 for the Gallic link; also Charles-Edwards 2013, 22, 189, and 428. St Albans: Niblett 2010, 129–30.

13 See Fern *et al.* (eds) 2019 for all details and discussions; the publication is a testimony to the determination of those involved to ensure that the hoard received detailed conservation and analysis; one unexpected discovery, by E. Blakelock, was that some of the pommels had enamelling, also now recognized on one from north Leicestershire: Scott and Sharp 2019. Initial recording was by Kevin Leahy, who first proposed that the hoard had been contained in a bag. Damage: pp. 195–204 – some resulted from recent ploughing. 'Hidden' crosses: pp. 252–5 (there does not seem to be an equivalent to the two scabbard roundels at Sutton Hoo, where darker garnets were selected to pick out the crosses). Essex ring: Wallis, R. J. 2020 pointed out that hawks and falcons are prey providers, analogous to a leader's responsibility to provide for his people; falconry may have become increasingly an elite occupation, evidenced also by the game birds consumed at elite residential sites: Sykes 2004.

14 See Fern *et al.* 2019. Detailed analyses of the casting, beaded-wire making, niello inlaying, cell setting – even the recognition that some of the gold surfaces had been treated to remove silver from them to enhance the colour – were led by E. Blakelock: pp. 124–81. Inscriptions: contribution by R. Gameson, pp. 102–8; the texts are on both sides of the arm, in different scripts, both rendering a version of a passage from a psalm imploring the Lord to help scatter enemies, which would have appealed to a warlord who knew that turning the other cheek would lead to personal disaster. Beeswax (there was also some in a block of soil), shells and inlay: analyses by P. Mc Elhinney: 137–8. Deposition date: pp. 269–71.

15 Most of the gold objects in the Staffordshire hoard were at least 66% pure, but two were only about 50%; as is said in the report, smiths were likely to rely on supplies from patrons and may have had older objects to recycle, so the compositions of jewellery are less likely to reflect dwindling supplies as directly as coins: contribution by E. Blakelock, pp. 126–7. Harford Farm brooch: Penn 2000, 76–82, with contribution on the inscription by J. Hines.

16 Rendlesham: Scull *et al.* 2016. Hall complexes: Blair 2018, 111–31; he treated a timber 'hall' in Northampton as being of eighth-century date, p. 185, as did McBride 2020, 145, although a seventh-century one seems as plausible, because the radiocarbon dating comes from its demolition, not construction: Williams, J. H. *et al.* 1985. Tattershall Thorpe: Hinton 1999; that the objects were in a grave has been questioned (Willmott, H. and Daubney 2020, 350–2), but they were in a rectangular grave-sized feature in which the excavators recorded human bone (1999, 4–5): Willmott and Daubney reported interesting details of metalworking at a Lincolnshire site, producing iron bells brazed with copper; another site with no known royal connection but with metalworking is Carlton Colville: Lucy *et al.* 2009. Faversham is *Fefresham* in an Old English charter, originating from *faefre*, a loan-word from Latin *faber*, smith, + *hām*, homestead: Mills 2011, 185; MacGregor and Bolick 1993, 77–9 for examples of objects. Ethelbert's law-code gave smiths a high value but implies that they were servile.

17 Dating: Hines and Bayliss (eds) 2013, 473, '99% probability of end by *c.* 670'. The numismatic case was argued strongly by the late Marion Archibald, ibid. 493–512; Naismith 2017, 67–85 for the problems of typology and sequences (he advocated using the term 'early pennies' for the new silver currency, but 'sceat' is well-established and avoids confusion with the different coinage introduced in the eighth century, see Ch. 4). For an excellent illustration of the gold–silver transition, see Webster, L. and Backhouse (eds) 1991, 65. Sceattas in graves and groups: Scull and Naylor 2016; these early ones are the 'Primary series'. One law-code stipulated that a wergild compensation should be paid at the grave's mouth, so both gold-plated copies of coins and some of the sceattas in graves might be to show that the relatives had received what compensation was owing for the dead person's death, retaining the rest of the person's possessions. The Harford Farm brooch might also have been selected for burial specifically because it was no longer of top quality: Hines and Bayliss (eds) 2013, 548. Ice-cores: Loveluck *et al.* 2018; the differences may not be irreconcilable, as both have to allow something for the ranges of radiocarbon dating. It is also possible that silver as well as lead was produced in Derbyshire and other English sources in temporary quantity if a new vein was chanced upon and affected the ice-cores: see Ch. 8.

18 Greater London area: Cowie and Blackmore 2008, 129–48. Basinghall Street alludes to the *Basingas*, presumably from the peoples around modern Basingstoke, Hampshire; Steyning, Buckinghamshire, seems to account for *Stæningahaga*, both south of the river but outside Kent – no names indicate an Essex connection despite the geography. Lothbury is probably named after Hlothere, king of Kent, 673–85 (another Hlothere was a bishop of the West Saxons), whose law-code made provision for the oversight of trading through a port-reeve; but by then kings of both Mercia and Wessex were claiming rights in London: Cowie 2004, 202–3 for the issue of a royal 'palace' of some sort. The interior of Roman York was also being parcelled up in the late seventh century: Mainman 2019, 56. *Lundenwic*: Cowie and Blackmore 2012; early use may not have involved dense occupation, but streets were being laid out, pp. 202–3; also Leary 2004.

19 London was *Lundenwic*, Southampton *Hamwic*, Ipswich *Gippeswic*, and York *Eoforwic*; the *wic* element is therefore common to all of them and occurs also in various coastal places like Dunwich, Harwich, or Sandwich; but those have not produced significant amounts of seventh- to ninth-century material (the word can also mean 'dairy-farm' and other things). London, St Martin-in-the Fields graves: Telfer 2010; disc-brooch: Cowie and Blackmore 2012, 188–9; it has a round-armed cross pattern formed by the gold panels (cf. Illus. 3,4); belt-buckle: ibid. 284–6, contribution by C. Scull; Whitehall: Cowie 2004, 205–9. Radiocarbon dating: Hines and Bayliss (eds) 2013, 505–9. Ipswich: Scull 2009, 80–91, 293–4, and 317–18. Southampton: Birbeck 2005, 28–9, 34, and 43 (the Tattershall Thorpe smith had similar studs with him (Illus. 3,5b), and a single one was found at Coddenham: Penn 2011, 109, 1c); Hines and Bayliss (eds) 2013, 551, note 7: the case for 'the assertive practice of a non-christian enclave' is 'far from sufficiently substantial to be sustained' but is 'tantalizing'. York: Mainman 2019, 29–30 and 59–71; there are unfurnished graves of the period.

20 For the complex overlordship of the Southampton area, see Yorke 2021; the revised dating affects the assumption that foundation was by Ine, the powerful and long-lived king of Wessex (the bishops of Winchester later had a property in the old Roman fort on the shore opposite Hamwic, but when it was acquired is not known. The Frisians at both Ipswich and Southampton might possibly have been imposed by King Wulfhere of Mercia, exercising overlordship.) On the River Stour outside Canterbury is Fordwich, which could have served its cathedral and monastery, but very little archaeological material has been found there. Blair's reservations about the scale of *Eoforwic*, 2018, 257, are not out of line with Mainman 2019, 88–92, but parts of the west side of the river may have been used as well: ibid. 105–8.

21 Implications for christianity of the radiocarbon dating: Hines and Bayliss (eds) 2013, 551–4. Wearmouth and Jarrow: Cramp 2005; 2006; 2017, 33–7. Hartlepool: Daniels 2007 (and see Willmott, T. 2017 for Hild's Whitby). Winchester: Ottaway 2017, 191–3 – stone was carted to it from the Bath area, over 40 miles away: Canterbury: Blockley, K. *et al*. 1997. Glastonbury: Gilchrist and Green 2015, 101–5 and 388, and contribution by H. Willmott and K. Welham, 218–239; also Bayley 2000. Nazeingbury: Huggins 1978 (charters referring to Nazeingbury were only identified after publication).

22 Female religious: Yorke 2017. Winchester: Ottaway 2017, 193. Worcester: Barker, P. A. *et al.* 1974 (radiocarbon dates centred on the sixth century but need adjusting to allow for later refinements). Exeter: Bidwell 1979. Lyminge: Thomas, G. 2017 and contributors. Overall summaries: Blair 2018, 131–8 and 155–7 (focused on central England): Carver 2019, 218–50. Artefactual evidence for 'minsters': see Ch. 4.

23 Disease: Lee 2014, 22–4; Maddicott 1997 argued that plague outbreaks recorded in 664–6 and 684–7 may account not only for deaths of various kings and others thought worthy of notice in chronicles, but also for site desertion. Mersea: Crummy, P. *et al.* 1982; Secker 2019. West Stow: Crabtree 2018, 60–1. Raunds is another example: Parry 2006, 223. Reconsideration of Catholme, Staffordshire, and its use as an ordinary agricultural settlement from the sixth through to the eleventh century by Hines 2018 contrasts with Blair's view of it as being 'exceptional', partly because he discerned that it had gridded layouts in two of its phases: 2018, 158–9.

24 Quire quantities: Breay and Story (eds) 2018, 125–6. Manuscript preparation and colours: Hamel 2018; also Biggam 2006. The excavation of a vellum workshop at Portmahomack is unique within Britain: Carver 2019, 151 and 579. Introduction to stone sculptures: Bailey 1996; dating is not precise – Ruthwell and Bewcastle may be of the eighth century. Jarrow production: Cramp 2005, 230–41 and 344–6; 2006, 470–81.

25 Reculver: Tweddle 1995, 151–61. Christianity did not bring an end to territorial ambitions and violence, laconically recorded in the *Anglo-Saxon Chronicles'* account (Swanton trans. and ed. 1996, 38–40) of the process of subordination of Kent: 686: '[King] Caedwalla [of Wessex] and Mul his [?half-]brother ravaged Kent . . . 687: Mul was burnt in Kent and twelve other men with him [Mul was probably trying to establish Kent as a dependency of Wessex, and was captured and eradicated by the locals] and Caedwalla again ravaged in Kent [for revenge] . . . 694: the inhabitants of Kent came to terms with Ine [successor to Caedwalla, who had left Wessex to go to Rome, where he died; the record is totally and unusually silent about Ine's lineage and 'throne-worthiness', so he had probably seized power by violence] and granted him 30,000 . . .' [unspecified in the earliest version; later ones fill the gap with 'pounds', but the original may have been *solidi*, i.e. in gold, or 'shillings' of either four or five silver 'sceats', depending on whether the reckoning was by Wessex's or Kent's system: Hines 2011, 397. The actual sum is therefore irrecoverable, but clearly a memorably high compensation was extorted, or was claimed by Wessex to have been extorted . . . at least though for a while Wessex left Kent alone]. As well as such sources as the *Anglo-Saxon Chronicles*, which are ninth-century in the form that they have survived, and the great history written by Bede in the early eighth century, charters give information on church estates, and which kings approved land transfers in different areas; the document now called the *Tribal Hidage* names various peoples and the number of 'hides' attributed to them and gives endless scope for speculation.

4 The Eighth Century

Surpluses and Subjections

With the doctrine of Roman christianity firmly established throughout England, and with no incursions from overseas to be faced until its very end, the eighth century can be seen as a period in which agricultural output intensified while rival kingdoms competed, and commerce fluctuated.

With 'sunken-featured buildings' having all but ceased to be constructed except in east Yorkshire, rural sites are a little more difficult to trace in the eighth century. Unless excavated on a relatively large scale, their usage can be hard to judge; whether some of the 'sfb' sites in Yorkshire were summer shielings for communities practising transhumance or were in permanent occupation is one issue. Another is the extent to which a settlement might specialize in the production of a particular crop or animal. Within the dictates of their environment, peasant farmers prefer to spread their risks by growing and raising a range of products, so that if one fails, they can live off another. By the eighth century, however, documents reveal large estates owned by churches; royal and thegns' lands also increasingly superseded notions of folk and family land. On those estates, tenants were likely to be required to go beyond farming for subsistence with enough surplus to pay renders in mixed parcels, and to put most of their effort into whatever their lords thought to be most beneficial to their own interests, not only what they could consume themselves but also what they could market.[1]

Most large estates were made up of a scatter of farming units, because a single centre from which people and animals had to walk long distances to get to outlying fields was not generally cost-effective. They were therefore usually polyfocal, though with a home farm working its own 'inland' with slave or other tied labour. Nucleation of settlement ran counter to the polyfocal norm, however, as mould-board ploughs would make long furrows economical to avoid wasting time and space turning the long team of up to eight oxen needed; how widely this was practised during the eighth century is much debated, but by suppressing weeds when it turns the soil, the mould-board plough is useful on light as well as on heavy soils. Occasional signs of specialization are recognized in the faunal remains data: a high ratio of pigs at Wickham Bonhunt, Essex, suggests advantage being taken of wide areas of clay with woodland providing pannage; older sheep bones at Carlton Colville suggest animals grazing on local heathlands with limited arable potential, retained for their wool long after they

DOI: 10.4324/9781003007432-5

were at their prime for eating. Yarnton, Oxfordshire, one of the few settlements excavated on a wide scale, was not an estate centre with a 'great hall' but was probably a subsidiary of one; it showed the increasing importance of the hay crop and the management of water meadows to supply it, so that more animals could overwinter. Ditches were dug to improve drainage and to create enclosure, so labour input was considerable. Buildings there were identified as barns, with posts for platforms to raise ricks above ground level. More difficult to assess generally is the extent of plough-lands, what crops were grown on them, and how they were managed.[2]

Increasing output of cereals probably accounts for landlords being increasingly likely to invest in processing methods. Water-mills involving leats, as at Barking, Essex, may have become a common sight; one at Old Windsor may have had a double wheel, as might that at Tamworth; Barking was the site of an abbey, Old Windsor and Tamworth were both royal estates. If landlords were to construct leats and otherwise affect water flow, they had to be able to exert rights over streams and rivers. This in turn led to rights over fish, with mills later recorded to be paying tolls in eels and fish that were more easily netted within their upstream pools. Traps dating to the eighth century in rivers like the Thames and the Trent, on the foreshore in Norfolk, or the edge of the New Forest near Southampton show that catching eels and fish was increasingly important.[3]

Earth-moving projects to improve transport were also undertaken more widely in the eighth century. Causeways across river floodplains and marshes are very difficult to date precisely, but road facilities that were improved probably include one leading into Oxford from the south and one in the Somerset marshes between Street and Glastonbury, where a canal was dug to bring boats up from the River Brue.[4]

Iron production had probably increased in the seventh century and continued to do so in the eighth. Radiocarbon dating of charcoal at smelting sites shows its importance in Devon, now controlled by the kings of Wessex, who also in the eighth century controlled the area around Wareham and its continuing iron production (Illus. 4.1). At Ramsbury, Wiltshire, both bowl furnaces and the more complex tapping furnaces have been excavated. Some of the iron ore was brought there from 30 kilometres away, a testimony to carting ability, as there were no direct water routes. The work took place within 200 metres of a major church, assuming that the present building is on the same site; its importance is shown by the survival of carved cross-shafts and grave-covers. Ramsbury was later given by the king to a bishop to set up a new see, so it was presumably a royal estate when iron-working took place, although no residence has been found. The present street plan is distinctly oval and may perpetuate a perimeter.[5]

Water-mills allowed labour to be diverted from hand-grinding to other tasks such as threshing and winnowing. If barns were replacing roof storage and 'sfbs', those jobs could be done in batches throughout the autumn and winter and did not need to be done out in the fields at harvest time. Grain-dryers also reappeared (Illus. 4.2), 'parching' the wheat so that it would grind better and cutting off the germination process in barley, so that it could be malted for ale. The dryers were

Illustration 4.1 The association of these waterlogged timbers excavated near Wareham, Dorset, with iron production was shown by deposits of slag found with the feature. It could have been a quenching pit, but the known furnaces are too far away, and its capacity seems too great and its timbers too substantial for such use, and it is probably the base of a watermill, used with a trip hammer to break up the iron-bearing heathstone before smelting; if it was a labour-saving investment, it suggests considerable output, perhaps not only from the Bestwall sites, but elsewhere on Purbeck also. It could probably have been adapted for grain milling when required. Dendrochronology dated one of the timbers to a felling date of after 664 and before 709 (Maynard 1988, contribution on the iron by C. Salter; Hinton 1992; Bestwall: Ladle 2012, 75–95; mills: Watts, M. 2017).

not as uniform in design as they had been in late Roman Britain (Ill. 1.1); one at Higham Ferrers, Northamptonshire, was stone-lined and had a very long flue, as though the technology was not trusted to prevent flames from reaching the oven-pit and setting light to the suspended floor within it. The oven had a domed wattle and daub roof. The residues within it contained mostly barley, which had sprouted and germinated, so it was used for malting ale. The dryer was outside an enclosure that contained a number of good-quality buildings, two identified as barns, and was probably the main centre of a polyfocal estate that took its name from the nearby Iron Age hillfort at Irthlingborough. Attached to the enclosure was an outer one very comparable to the 'corral' at Yeavering, so animals may have been brought there for slaughter.[6]

*

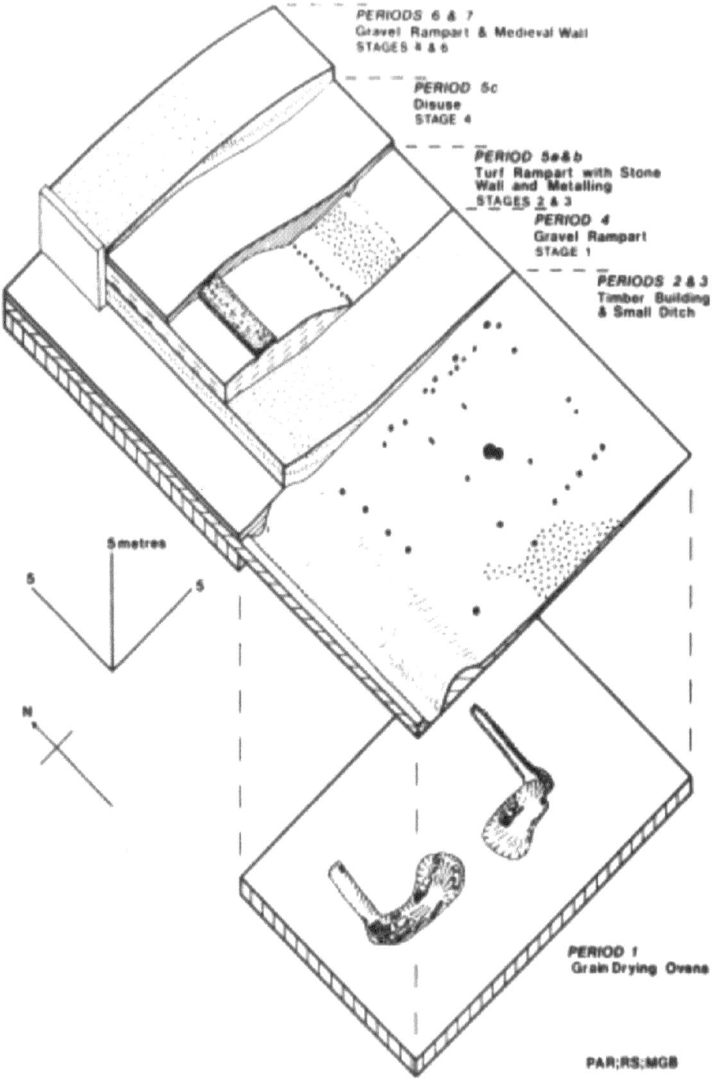

Illustration 4.2 The excavation of the defences at Hereford showed a sequence that began with grain-drying ovens utilizing some Roman stones, which suggest large-scale processing, possibly for the bishop's household. They were replaced by timber buildings, before the defensive bank covered them (Shoesmith 1982).

Unlike Yeavering, the Higham Ferrers complex does not seem to have included a church or cemetery, something that many other high-status centres had. Although usually called 'minsters', such churches would not have had the independence of a monastery or cathedral but remained family-owned, often with a family member formally in charge of the community of clerics serving it. Cloisters cannot be expected, although graveyards might appear in them. Buildings recognizable as churches, with naves and chancels, might be provided, as at Brandon, Suffolk, where several of the artefacts found such as a gold plaque with an Evangelist symbol show an ecclesiastical presence, without proving that the place was exclusively used by clerics. Styli, for writing on wax tablets, are an indication of literacy and therefore of Church training, but increased use of documents for secular purposes meant that scribes were needed to serve the laity as well as the Lord. Brandon was on an island linked by a causeway to the mainland, so was enclosed by water; other minster complexes had perimeters marked by earth banks and ditches, or fences, which may be identifiable in topographical survivals such as oval or circular streets and lanes. In a few cases, stone was used in buildings and may survive in part; more often surviving sculptures in seemingly ordinary later churches may indicate earlier superiority.[7]

Graveyards and churches might seem inevitable companions, but even in the eighth century there were probably many that started as open, or 'field', cemeteries, even if a church or chapel was added later. Some were abandoned before that happened; a graveyard with west-east, unfurnished burials recently excavated at Great Ryburgh, Norfolk, may be typical of many. It had a small space in the centre which could possibly have had a shrine, but there is no church or settlement nearby. Many of the graves there contained wooden coffins, preserved because of damp conditions; most were hollowed-out oak logs, which would have taken some four days each to make. Burials inside penannular ditches, possibly with barrows over them, have been found in *Hamwic*, and barrow burials in Ipswich, so some people were marked out in special ways. In a few cases elsewhere, boat timbers seem to have been used as grave-covers, perhaps symbolizing the soul's journey. Sometimes, coffins show evidence of iron locks, which might reference St Peter's key to the lock of Hell – they were certainly not to protect wealthy objects placed with the dead, as the uniformity of unfurnished burials is testimony to the acceptance of orthodox christianity at all social levels. Some older beliefs and practices may have survived, however; swords and other weapons found in streams and rivers might have been lost in skirmishes at fords – always likely places for such encounters – and not retrieved by the victors, but their numbers suggest that they had been deliberately deposited, perhaps because its owner's death meant that an object had come to be perceived as unlucky and dangerous to use. Groups of iron tools in lead containers hint at some other belief. Smiths retained an aura of otherworldliness, as the story of Weland shows.[8]

*

Unless silver as well as lead was being mined in England – and the sculptures at Wirksworth and Bakewell suggest that the Peak District was no less wealthy in the eighth century than is attested for the seventh by burials – commercial development was dependent primarily upon the import of silver exchanged for commodities that are archaeologically invisible, such as wool, cloth, hides, and slaves, probably lead, and possibly hunting-dogs. Some gold arrived, unless existing stocks were sufficient for sword pommels and other luxury items, of which fewer are known partly because they were no longer placed in graves and partly because gold was so much scarcer than it had been in the first part of the seventh century. Weapons may still have been the principal material reward that a king could give his followers, but donations of land were perhaps more important. Kings presumably wanted wine and silk to display their social superiority and now also wanted to show their largesse to churches within their sphere of influence, such as gold for their chalices and reliquaries and silk and gold thread for their priests' vestments, as well as estates to maintain them.[9]

Gifts and counter-gifts were important at the highest social level, but the numbers of the early eighth-century Secondary Series silver 'sceat' coins now being found show that those must have been the mainstay of a more basic commercial exchange system. They are found not only at the *wic* sites that had been established in the seventh century, but also as many stray finds in a few hoards and in places where concentrations of coins, strap-ends, and other items suggest that trading was taking place. Some of those have been found when excavated to have had occupation, but others may have been seasonal fairs where people with goods to sell would know that at a certain time of the year buyers would congregate. The majority have been found in East Anglia and Essex, but most counties in eastern and southern England have evidence suggestive of such focal places.[10]

The only sceattas with names struck on them are for a king of Northumbria who died in 705 and another who reigned 737–58; no other direct evidence of royal involvement in minting is known, but the sizes and weights of the coins seem to have been regulated, despite the very wide range of designs. Quantities of particular designs found in the *wic* sites of Ipswich and *Hamwic* must indicate production in those; the evidence from London and York is less clear-cut. A silver flan found in a grave at Carlton Colville could indicate minting there at an undocumented but substantial site, so some moneyers may have been itinerant, even though their output would have been more difficult to control than if, as later, they were tied to particular places. Many of the designs are much subtler than they seem at first glance, having christian iconography, but evidence of minting at church sites has not been found. Churches may have benefited because coins were a negotiable means of receiving alms, as well as facilitating their involvement with trade through their estates.[11]

Coins may indicate that a site was involved in trading even if that was not its main purpose. At Flixborough, Lincolnshire, the absence of gold coins and of the early 'Primary' sceattas is the best evidence that that site came into use after about 700; sixteen of the twenty-nine sceattas excavated there were continental, including some from Quentovic, on the Seine. That trading was taking place at Flixborough is clear, but the other things found there are less definitive about the whole range of activities. A lead plaque inscribed with names and crosses may have been a reminder to pray for their souls, there are styli used for writing on wax tablets, and other signs of literacy such as a gold ring with the first letters of the alphabet on it; but literacy need not mean that the site had a minster. Other objects indicate craft activity at Flixborough but not its scale. Gilt copper-alloy brooches and pins indicate moderately well-off people, but this fact does not prove that they were secular, as nothing indicates that priests or nuns eschewed secular costume and display. Other sites where trading was ongoing on a more limited scale than the four *wic* sites include Sandtun, Kent, which may have been typical of many coastal places where fishing and salt-making were the main occupations, augmented by occasional cross-channel ventures or visits by overseas merchants, accounting for imported pottery. Whether such places avoided toll payments is unknowable.[12]

Many sceattas found in England were minted on the continent, from the Low Countries northwards up to Denmark; the Merovingians in France issued silver coins of similar size, but usually closer in design to the old Roman currency and known as *deniers*. In England, therefore, the preponderance of sceattas indicates that trade was mostly across the North Sea, especially from Ipswich, London, and York, particularly to the Rhine, and probably using continental *wic* sites, such as Wijk-by-Dorestat. In France there were also *wics*, notably Quentovic on the River Seine, *Hamwic's* natural trading-partner, but even there only two French coins have been recorded, from a total of seventy-four throughout England – with no obvious bias to the south coast. Sceattas number in thousands, but even so their distribution peters out westwards, with none reported from Devon and Cornwall and only two to west of the Pennines. They are also a guide to where embryonic *wic* sites may have begun to develop, such as on the north bank of the River Wensum where Norwich was later to become Norfolk's leading town. Beverley, on the River Hull in Yorkshire, where a minster took advantage of a patch of dry ground, and where many coins have been recorded, may have inhibited the growth of *Eoforwic*. On the other side of the Pennines, reoccupation within Carlisle is shown by the excavation of over a hundred skeletons of the seventh to ninth centuries, although the many coins found in it are of the ninth century.[13]

The find-spots of coins minted in *Hamwic* and Ipswich are not found evenly radiating out from those centres: Southampton coins are found mainly in Hampshire, Wiltshire, and Dorset, but with very few on the Isle of Wight and in Sussex, despite their being integrated within the kingdom of Wessex; memories of brutal seventh-century take-overs might have lingered, as Wight in particular has a large number of coins generally, so perhaps its people avoided too much direct contact with an old enemy. Ipswich-minted coins have been found mostly in Suffolk and Norfolk, spreading out westwards and northwards, but with many fewer to the south. In that instance, it may have been because the East Saxon people were in a different kingdom from the East Angles; toll barriers may have been in place, but political and cultural circumstances may have been at least as important. That sceattas have not been found in Devon and Cornwall is an indication that trade with south-west France had fallen away. In the north-west, at Meols in the Wirrall, only two were recorded, so any trade with Ireland was negotiated without coins.[14]

The distribution of the Ipswich-minted coins can be compared to that of a distinctive type of pottery made in the *wic*, coil-built on a slow-turned *tournette* and fired in an updraught kiln (cf. Illus. 6.1), a technology used in Frisia. It was quite often finished with stamping, again like Frisian pottery, but something hardly seen in England since the cremation urns had finally passed out of use. It seems very likely that Frisians set up the craft, following the lead given by those who had been involved in establishing the *wic*. Ipswich ware is found mostly in Norfolk and Suffolk, spreading eastwards and northwards, but again with very little in Essex, only a few sherds at coastal sites. Whereas a king with an eye to his prestige might seek to forbid the use of a neighbour's coins within his kingdom, it is unlikely that any such proscription would have applied to domestic pottery. Instead, Ipswich ware can be seen as being part of an East Anglian identity, displacing native hand-formed, bonfire-fired Maxey types and others. Lipid analyses showed that many Ipswich pots had absorbed animal fats, and external sooting shows that some were used for cooking, but storage may have been their main role; perhaps they were for salt as they would have been a convenient size into which to ladle a measure from a wooden barrel brought from coastal salterns or from Droitwich. Wax residues in a few suggest honey and beeswax.[15]

Small amounts of Ipswich ware went as far inland as Northamptonshire and Gloucestershire, perhaps because it was perceived as special; nothing can have been carried in it – the pots were not large enough to transport substantial quantities of produce such as grain, and the wide-rimmed Ipswich ware jars were unsuitable for anything liquid. That some of it went eastwards, against the flows of the rivers on which its transport probably partly relied, might show that it was a cheap return cargo for those who had brought more essential commodities such as grain, downstream. They may also have taken home with them the imported lava querns and millstones from the Rhine, which have been found as far west as Herefordshire, so were worth carrying further than the pots. Although Ipswich ware is the only pottery known to have been turned and kiln-fired, other types, such as Maxey wares, were perfectly adequate for most everyday purposes, and in general it seems that chaff-tempered pottery that could be made by anybody with clay and a bonfire was giving way to more specialized products, even if the potters spent some of their time in agriculture.[16]

Continental coins and pottery at the *wic* sites show their role in overseas trading and some of the goods coming into them. Ipswich ware is the only product made in one of them that can be shown to have been distributed into the place's hinterland, and therefore whether they were integrated into the economic structures of their localities or not is hard to judge. Animal bones show that the meat eaten in them generally came from older cattle and sheep, suggesting that they were culled from rural breeding stocks, and one interpretation is that the beasts were the surplus from big estates and their renders, not freely traded piece-meal. On the other hand, apart from Ipswich, most of their pots also came from their surrounding areas, and estate control of that minor product seems unlikely. Whether any of the craft items produced in them were intended to be sold to outsiders is another matter. Bone and antler were worked, but the quantity of debris is substantial rather than enormous, and production may have been aimed only at the residents and seamen. Glass was probably made, but not much of it went out into the areas around, as not many broken fragments have been found; differences between the types of vessel mainly found in the *wic* sites and those in monasteries suggest that the latter were not getting theirs from the ports; Glastonbury in the late seventh century and Barking Abbey in the eighth were making at least some of their own. In *Hamwic*, some of the combs were probably specifically made for use in the place itself, as the teeth are more widely spaced than usual, an indication that they were needed to remove nits from hair; nits thrive when people live close together and in numbers. A few metalworkers' moulds have been found, of both clay and antler, but concentrations of metal waste are not enough to suggest a major focus of production.[17]

*

Any stimulus to trade that the sceattas provided would have been adversely affected by their increasing scarcity from the 730s onwards. The Northumbrian kings managed to maintain their currency more or less unchanged, but the rest of England eventually followed the Frankish model, a short-lived series issued by a king of East Anglia around 749 being succeeded in Mercia and Wessex, so that the second half of the eighth century had a broad-flan silver coinage, establishing the pennies that were to be the basis of medieval coinage thereafter. Markedly fewer of them are found, however, than of the earlier sceattas; they were heavier, so more valuable if their silver content was maintained, and perhaps also easier to handle and did not get lost as much, but their numbers suggest that they really were in much less use. Some 'prolific sites' do not have any pennies, and no new sites like those seem to appear. Lack of coins may have impeded the growth of the *wic* sites, though ebbs and flows in those are hard to establish from the necessarily piece-meal excavation record. A few continental *deniers* have been found, for instance one at Flixborough, but they are many fewer in number than, and less in ratio to, the native coinage than the sceattas had been. They also had kings' names on them, suggesting that, whether for prestige or profit, kings were more aware of coins than before.[18]

A downturn in commercial trade would be more possible to discuss if Ipswich pottery had changed significantly, but no new types of vessel or decoration seem to have appeared, so its distribution cannot be linked to a chronological sequence. Strap-ends, brooches, sculptures, and weapons cannot be very closely dated either; some comparisons with decoration in manuscripts can be made, but the dating of those is not always beyond argument. Within the *wic* sites, very little of the eighth-century metalwork is even of precious metal, although a silver-gilt sword pommel and grip from Fetter Lane in London are outstanding exceptions, and the helmet made for Oshere found in Coppergate, York, was made in the eighth century, although deposited in the early ninth. Even metal-detection has not added significantly to the numbers of eighth-century secular objects known; a silver-gilt sword pommel from Oxfordshire shows that complex openwork could be achieved but is one of very few newly discovered objects of precious metal attributable to the eighth century.[19]

Even the Franks Casket, almost certainly a Northumbrian work, can only be ascribed to the eighth century by comparison with other objects, despite all the information that it gives in its inscriptions; one tells how a whale caused its own doom by beaching itself – the casket is made of whalebone. Causing one's own fate was a favourite idiom; one of the Casket's scenes shows Weland the smith taking his revenge on the king who had hamstrung and imprisoned him, keeping him isolated from normal society. The smith is shown offering a potion to the king's daughter from a cup made from the skull of one of her brothers, whom he had recently killed, before seducing her and making a magic cloak of feathers and escaping the king, who is shown frantically strangling birds hoping that one of them is the man who has become his persecutor. The king who brought his suffering upon himself could transmute into a moral story when applied to Christ at his crucifixion, embracing his death to save mankind; he was a 'powerful king', as the runic text on the Ruthwell cross calls him, not a suffering victim, a theme still too far from anglo-saxon comprehension.[20]

Although the Franks Casket is ascribed to Northumbria, and sculptures like the great crosses may be of the eighth century also, the kingdom's 'Golden Age' was coming to an end; no new monastic foundations like Jarrow and Wearmouth were made, and the Lindisfarne Gospels are the last known major product of a Northumbrian scriptorium. Instead, decorated books are mostly ascribed to Canterbury or to Mercia. The largest standing anglo-saxon building, the church at Brixworth, Northamptonshire, is a testimony to Mercian wealth at the end of the eighth century. Its side chapels, or *porticuses*, have gone, and its east end semi-sunken crypt has been filled in, but its nave and rows of arches, reusing Roman brick, remain. Another Mercian church with a crypt which partly survives is Repton, Derbyshire, a royal burial-place (Illus. 4.3), where part of a sculpture shows a mounted, moustachioed figure wearing armour, with a long seax at his waist and brandishing a shield, an image of kingship. The discovery of a stone panel from a shrine, delicately carved with an angel and with some of its original paint surviving, shows that Lichfield was another well-patronized Mercian church. Northampton was probably also a major Mercian centre. The timber hall there was replaced by a stone building; the mortar mixer used in its construction was also excavated. Nearby is St Peter's church, so the complex may have combined a minster and a royal hall.[21]

The name of King Offa looms over the second half of the eighth century. The silver pennies tentatively introduced in East Anglia became the established currency during his reign, except in Northumbria. His prestige was declared by a gold coin with his name on it, the earliest of a very few anglo-saxon special issues. It is the weight of three silver pennies, was probably found in Rome, and was therefore probably a gift to the pope; it has an Arabic inscription, so it copied a *dinar*, and presented Offa as the equal of other European rulers who could mint prestigious coins. The Arabic inscription praised Allah, but neither king nor pope would have understood that. Offa's understanding of the role of imagery on coinage is shown by his use of Roman imperial imagery and the issuing of pennies in the name of his queen, Cynethryth, in the same way as Roman emperors had placed their consorts' names on coins.[22]

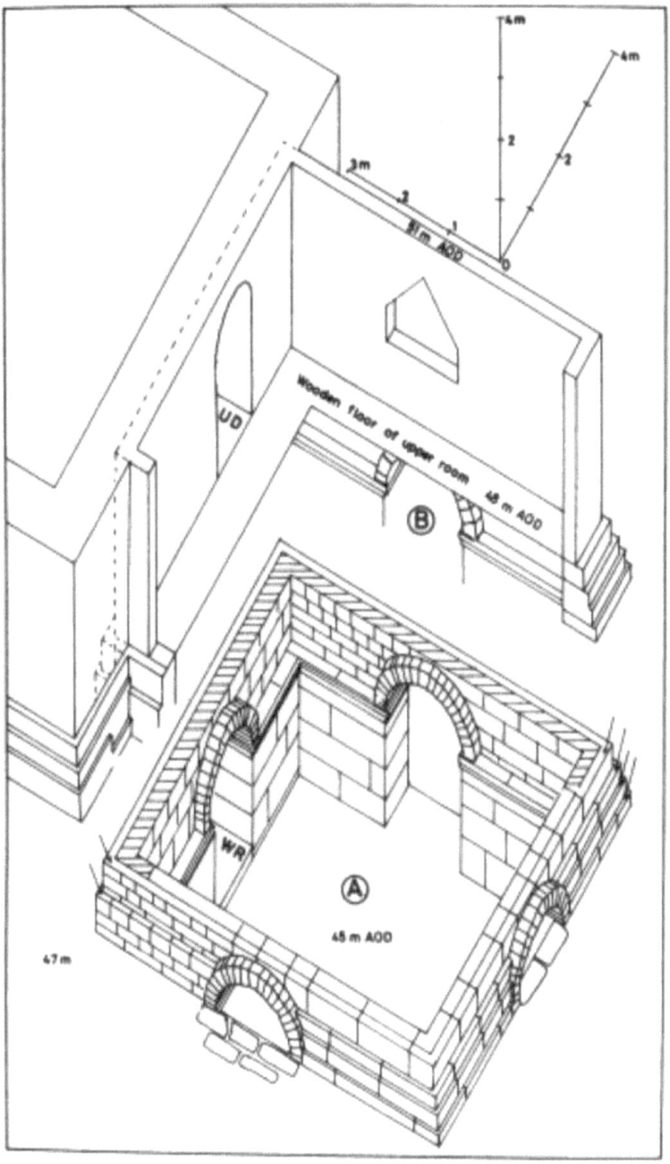

Illustration 4.3a Isometric drawings by H. M. Taylor of the crypt, phase A, and the room added above it, phase B, now attached to the east end of the church at Repton, Derbyshire. The plinth was probably at the original ground level, so that three of the arches would have been open at the top to throw a little day-light into the space, which would probably have sheltered relics, altars, and tombs of members of the Mercian royal family, some of whom are recorded as being buried at Repton. The fourth arch, marked WR, was probably the entrance, reached down using outside steps. In a later phase, not shown, four elaborate columns were added to the interior.

Illustration 4.3b The crypt was heightened and created a chancel for a church, which may have been a smaller, previously detached building to the east, extended to create a monumental structure on the scale of Brixworth. This was done in the pre-Norman period – the upright projecting pilaster strips and horizontal string-course are typical – but whether that was done in the ninth century, before the viking takeover in 874 or subsequently remains in doubt (Taylor, H. M. 1971; Parsons and Sutherland 2013, 211).

Offa is also known for the linear earthwork between England and Wales, called Offa's Dyke since at least the late ninth century, and there is no reason to doubt the ascription. Whether it ran all the way down to the River Severn or whether discontinuous dykes in that southern end were constructed at different times has been disputed, and it is unclear why it stopped short at the north end before reaching the coast, only to be replaced, early in the ninth century, by Wat's Dyke parallel to it to the east and running up to the sea. Even with a stone or timber facade, Offa's Dyke would not have been difficult for Welsh raiders to cross, as it could not have been permanently garrisoned along its whole length. Military obligations owed by Offa's subjects may have meant that mounted men patrolled along it or in the lands in front of it; the Dyke may have been a warning to the Welsh that if they crossed it they would pay the consequences, so the earthwork was making a statement about the English king's power and authority and was another way in which Offa showed himself as the equal of continental kings.[23]

Linear earthworks may not have been the only defensive structures that landholders had an obligation to send men to work on; even before the first record of viking raids, from the last decade of the eighth century, charters refer to the three inescapable obligations: military service, bridgework, and *burhbot*, the last implying a fortified enclosure. Deciding whether any were constructed is problematic; dating of sites like Hereford where a substantial bank has been excavated (Illus. 4.2) is very difficult. Hereford was the centre of a bishopric, so the church there would probably have had a perimeter bank and ditch already, but as the bank overlay grain-dryers and buildings, it was not on the same line. In that place, an army base might have been thought necessary, as protection against the Welsh or to provide an army-base from which to launch raids or counter-raids. Other churches, like Brixworth, surrounded by such earthworks had ditches up to 4 metres wide, so they were substantial, more than enough for a spiritual barrier and sufficient to deter a small band of raiders but not to withstand a determined assault: Scandinavian seamen were not to be put off so easily.[24]

Notes

1 East Yorkshire 'sfb' sites and the shieling issue: Richards 2013, 237–8, 242, and 257–8. They may still have been used at Yarnton, Oxfordshire: Hey 2004, 43–6.

2 'Polyfocal' is now preferred to 'multiple'. 'Home-farms' or 'inland': Faith 1999,9, 38–50. Place-names like Barton (*bere*, 'barley' + *tūn*) or Shipton (*sceap* or *sciep*, 'sheep') become significant but should not be taken to imply monoculture rather than specialization, for example Crabtree 2018, 96; see also McKerracher 2018, 51–68 for others, and for problems of analysis. See Yarnton: Hey 2004, 45–6 and 219–23 for the annual allocation by lot of strips within it, a nineteenth-century practice of unknown antiquity but possibly identifiable in Domesday Book: contribution by J. Munby; strip-field ploughland could have originated by such communal decisions: Banham and Faith 2014, 283–4; Williamson, T. 2013 also advocated local decision-making rather than direct 'top-down' imposition; landlords' increasing demands may have led to as much pressure as an increasing population to be fed nevertheless. 'Open fields', see also Ch. 5.

3 Intensification: Hamerow 2012, 147–8; Rippon *et al.* 2015, 305–7; Blair 2018, 247–9. Mills: Watts, M. 2017; cf. Ill. 4.1 and the plan of one with eighth- and tenth-century radiocarbon dates at Corbridge, Northumberland: *Medieval Archaeology* 40 (1996), 276–7; Snape 2003. Fish-traps: Thames: Cowie and Blackmore 2008, 115–24, Cohen 2011; Trent, Salisbury 1981; Norfolk, Robertson and Ames 2010 (they augmented the radiocarbon dates with a catalogue of local coin finds, p. 343); New Forest: Cooper, J. P. *et al.* 2017. Reynolds, R. 2017 for species, fish hooks, and net sinkers; also Rippon

2017, 101–3, noting the need for strong nets and investment in hurdles and basketry, and Blair 2018, 249–51. Appropriately, chewed eels were found on a site in Ely: Mudd and Webster 2011, 93.

4 Oxford: Dodd 2020, 55–6. Glastonbury: Hollinrake and Hollinrake 2007; Brunning, R. 2010.

5 Devon: Smart 2018: table of sites, 37–49. Ramsbury: Haslam 1980; production may have been entirely during the ninth century, but the radiocarbon dating was very wide (contribution by R. T. Otlet); ore: contribution by S. Fells; the sculptures are attributed to the ninth century: Cramp 2006, 228–34. Furnaces in Ashdown Forest, Sussex, gave ninth-century dates but are another sign of expansion: Tebbutt 1982. See also Ch. 5.

6 Grain-dryers: McKerracher 2018, 121–2: Higham Ferrers: Hardy *et al*. 2007, 48–54 and 136–40; contribution on barley by L. Moffett, p. 163. A seventh-century Kent law refers to a female grinding-slave, the last time that the role is mentioned, implying that the work was done by mills thereafter on royal properties, although hand-querns remained standard household items; cf. Fleming 2010, 285. Winnowing was usually a female task later in the Middle Ages, so could have been earlier. Irthlingborough and the polyfocal estate: Hardy *et al.* 2007, 192–208; King Offa signed a charter there in 786.

7 Because minster priests were expected to serve polyfocal estates, their *parochiae* were much larger than later parishes, and enough evidence in the form of later medieval tithe payments and other links has enabled many to be identified and mapped: Blair 2005, 100–7 and 183–291; place-names with *minster* are an obvious clue, but both *-stow* and *-bury* were also used, the latter especially for houses led by females. Brandon: Tester *et al.* 2014; see also Flixborough, note 12. Titchfield, Hampshire, provides a fine example of how a large late seventh-/eighth-century minster has been identified: Hare, M. 1992. Pre-existing enclosures may have influenced the siting of some minsters, such as the Iron Age hillfort defences at Breedon, Leicestershire, and Aylesbury, Buckinghamshire; at Brixworth, a perimeter ditch preceded the extant church: Parsons and Sutherland 2–13, 141–2: Cramp 2017, 30–2. Recent work at Ely may have located the ditch surrounding Aetheldreda's nunnery, but the authors noted that it would have been exceptionally large if so: Woolhouse *et al.* 2019, 170–9. The Anglo-Saxon Sculpture Corpus has many examples of high-quality sculptures in unpretentious surroundings.

8 Great Ryburgh: Fairclough and Sloane 2017. *Hamwic* burials: Garner 2001, 176–81. Ipswich: Brown, R. and Shelley 2014, 375. Clench-nails from clinker-planking on boats have been found in graves at York, Barton-upon-Humber, and other sites, though not in Kent where their deposition occurred in earlier furnished graves: Brookes 2007. The Old English *Charms* show the importance of what are usually termed folk-beliefs: see Jolly 1985; Griffiths, B. 1996 for how some transmogrified into christian practice, particularly if they involved agriculture. Water deposition: Reynolds and Semple 2011; a fitting perhaps from a scabbard with a runic inscription and a snarling beast's head terminal dredged from the Thames may be an example: Breay and Story (eds) 2018, 223. Iron deposits: Leahy 2013; a group of tools inside a lead container in York may indicate that the practice went on well beyond the eighth century: Hall (ed.) 2004, 466.

9 Peak District sculptures: Hawkes and Sidebottom 2018 – the complex iconography of the late eighth-century coped slab at Wirksworth, emphasizing humility and obedience leading to everlasting life, pp. 240–50, makes an interesting contrast to the warrior imagery of the Repton stone, and themes of Christ as heroic leader. Documentation on exports is sparse, with occasional letters referring to gifts justifying the inclusion of lead in the list; tin is more arguable, and hunting-dogs were listed much earlier as a *Britannia* product; their bones have been identified on anglo-saxon sites: Holmes 2018, 197–9. Charlemagne's letter to King Offa demanding that the *saga* the latter was sending should be full-length refers to high-quality English textiles, the 'black stones' that he would send in exchange being marble; these were high-status gift exchanges, not

everyday trade items: Peacock 1997; Maddicott 2002; see further below. Vestments, for example the Maaseik embroideries: Budny and Tweddle 1985.

10 Most of the 'prolific sites' (a term which I prefer to the more usual 'productive' as it has fewer overtones; Carver 2019, 246 advocated 'scatter sites' – his stress on ideology as the main driving force, rather than economic or environmental ones, for example p. 634, gives a different perspective) have been found by metal-detector users, so pottery, bone, and even iron are not picked up, leaving an unbalanced view of the range of material. They have rightly led to much discussion since their recognition in the 1980s, for example Anderton (ed.) 1999 (a combative essay by R. Samson remains worth reading); Hill, D. and Cowie (eds) 2001; Pestell and Ulmschneider (eds) 2003; Crabtree 2018, ch. 3; unreliable recording remains a problem, though the Portable Antiquities Scheme has greatly reduced it. See Rippon 2018, 305–14 for a synopsis of the eastern evidence. The *wic* sites are called *emporia* and *mercimonia* in documents.

11 Overall review: Naismith 2017, 80–1 and 93–114 (I have not been able yet to see the most recent sylloge, but it is appropriate to mention its author, T. Abramson, for his work on elucidating the sceattas generally; others have been the late Michael Metcalf and the late Mark Blackburn). Carlton Colville: Lucy *et al.* 2009, contribution by M. Blackburn; the grave also contained a silver bar (sceattas continue to occur in a few graves: Scull and Naylor 2016); no silver blanks have been reported from Rendlesham: Scull *et al.* 2016. Iconography: Gannon 2003 (her suggestion on p. 167 that Series K could represent the Five Senses is now supported by the discovery of brooches in the Galloway hoard that clearly represent the same theme, so it was better known than the Fuller brooch alone might suggest); 2011; Karkov 2011. Church involvement in trade is shown by toll remissions on some of their ships: Kelly 1992.

12 Flixborough: Evans, D. H. and Loveluck 2009, coin contribution by M. M. Archibald, 402–13 and 418–20; see Blair 2011 for a discussion of whether such sites can be termed 'minsters'; contribution by S. Foot to Loveluck 2007, 135–6. Sandtun: Gardiner *et al.* 2001; the discussion of trade, including consideration of the king's reeve in Dorset who was killed when trying to oversee what was probably an unruly group of overseas seamen, on pp. 275–8, remains valuable.

13 French *deniers* totalled 74 on the Cambridge Early Medieval Coin Corpus, accessed Aug. 26, 2021. Distribution map: Blair 2018, 29. Continental sites and contacts: Loveluck 2013, 191–212. Norwich: Ayers 2011, 'pre-urban settlement' section. Lincoln may have been another, though no sceattas are recorded from there. Beverley: Armstrong *et al.* 1991, 243 and 246; the Cambridge EMC records 30 eighth- and ninth-century coins as from Beverley (accessed Aug. 31, 2021), including a purse-hoard of 23: Pirie 1986b, 76. Carlisle: McCarthy 1990. That the *wics* did not have a monopoly is suggested by the scatter of non-*Hamwic* coins in Somerset and Dorset, counties that it might have dominated: Costen and Costen 2016.

14 Coin data from the Cambridge EMC, accessed August 26–7, 2021. Isle of Wight: Ulmschneider 2010. E-wares disappear from the south-western records: Campbell, E. 2007, 138–9; evidence of tin production is ambivalent, with one record suggesting that it dwindled and another that it prospered: Reed *et al.* 2011, 130; Rippon and Holbrook (eds) 2021, 247. Meols: Griffiths, D. *et al.* 2007, 304, contribution by S. C. Bean.

15 Ipswich pottery: Blinkhorn 2012; his major study suggested introduction *c.* 720, but the radiocarbon dating project subsequently published might take the date a little earlier: see Ch. 3; lipid analysis was by R. Evershed. His results did not show traces of vegetable matter, which is found on later pottery; possibly it was cooked differently, as some must surely have been eaten: pp. 47–51; storage and identity discussion, pp. 87–98. Frantzen 2014, 108–26 made an interesting discussion of Ipswich pottery and *habitus*. Lipid analysis of Maxey-type vessels at Flixborough has shown one use to have been for boiling fowl bones: Colonese *et al.* 2017. Another kiln, slightly different and away

from the others, was discovered after Blinkhorn's publication: Brown, R. and Shelley 2014, 375 (interim note: the full report has since been published).

16 Ipswich pottery distribution: Blinkhorn 2012, 89–90. Both pottery and sceattas seem to pay more respect to the county/kingdom boundary than to the 'Gipping Divide' which in such ways as farming regions appears to have been a 'frontier', for example Martin, E. 2012, 229–31. Lava quernstones: Parkhouse 2014; the Herefordshire example was a later discovery from a water-mill near Marden: Ray 2015, 221; it had not necessarily come through Ipswich, of course. Blair 2007, 14 made the general point about pottery as an up-river return cargo.

17 Animal bones: O'Connor 2001; Crabtree 2018, 104–5 and 113–14. Bone and antler: Riddler and Trzaska-Nartowski 2013a; 2013b. Glass: Broadley 2019, 79–81 for the church/*wic* differences and for various sites where a few glass sherds have been found; *Hamwic* glass: Hunter, J. R. and Heyworth 1998. Metalworking: contributions by J. Bayley *et al.* to Hinton 1996, 66–92. London: Cowie and Blackmore 2012, 159–69. York: Mainman 2019, 82.

18 Naismith 2017, 108–9 attributed the decline to Frankish conquest of Frisia, rather than to exhaustion of European silver mines; also Naismith 2012, 94–101, for example on royal control. Northumbria might have been getting some silver from the Cumberland deposits: Maddicott 2002, 61. Flixborough had 29 sceattas, but only one English penny: M. M. Archibald in Evans, D. H. and Loveluck 2009, 402–13 and 418–20; Middle Harling, where a hoard established the chronology of Beonna's coins, yielded no subsequent eighth-century pennies: Archibald 1995; a very rapid search through the Cambridge EMC list of 460 pennies of King Offa yielded only eight findspots that I recognized as 'prolific sites' – including two from Bidford-on-Avon, Warwickshire, one of the westernmost (accessed Aug. 29, 2021; the site has now been published by Sue Hirst and Tania Dickinson.). Over 1000 different dies are known to have been used for Offa's pennies, however, so the numbers issued may have been in the millions: Metcalf 2007. Downturn issue, for example *Lundenwic*: Malcolm and Bowsher 2003, Period 6; Cowie and Blackmore 2012, 110.

19 *Lundenwic* finds review: Cowie and Blackmore 2012, 191–9; Fetter Lane: Webster 2012, 145–6; the scabbard fitting was from the river in the *wic* area. *Hamwic*: Hinton 1996, contribution on gold-working by D. R. Hook, M. S. Tite, and W. A. Oddy, 80–2. York helmet: Tweddle 1992; Mainman 2019, 124–7. Oxfordshire pommel: Webster, L. 2012, 36; 2017.

20 Franks Casket: Webster, L. 2012, 91–7; Wright, D. W. 2019, 274–5 on Weland. The scene is juxtaposed with the Three Magi, who also had special powers but they were offering their gifts to Christ. (In another reference, Weland is said to be tormented by *wyrmas*, an indication of how the sinuous creatures of Style II had transmuted into christian warnings: Thompson 2004, 164–6). Ruthwell Cross: Breay and Story (eds) 2018; a theory that the runic texts were added later into panels conveniently left vacant seems to me to make no allowance for the difficulty of cutting neatly into a tall shaft once it is vertical.

21 Brixworth: Parsons and Sutherland 2013, 141–2, refuting the traditional claim that it was the largest seventh-century church north of the Alps. Blair 2013, 24 identified its nave as having 4 × 4 short-pole dimensions. Brixworth is an example of settlement nucleation, probably because the church provided a centre. Repton sculpture: Biddle and Kjølbye-Biddle 1985. Lichfield: Gem *et al.* 2008a; Breay and Story (eds) 2018, 144–5, contribution by J. Hawkes. Other Mercian sculptures include the cross-shafts at Sandbach, Cheshire, and Wolverhampton, Staffordshire: Hawkes 2001 for overview. Northampton: Williams, J. H. *et al.* 1985; a St Gregory's is also nearby, and names like Kingsthorpe in the area suggest a royal estate. Blair 2018, 185–6 attributed the stone building to the ninth century, but an eighth-century coin indirectly associated justifies the earlier dating.

22 Offa's *dinar* and Cynethryth coins: Naismith 2012, 62–4, 113–14, and 151: Breay and Story (eds), 150–1, contributions by G. Williams. Offa's awareness of continental kings is also shown by Charlemagne's letter. Charlemagne sent treasures from his plunder of the Avars, but Offa may have died before he received them. Continental *solidi* are occasionally found in England, but nearly all are from the ninth century.

23 Offa's Dyke: Ray and Bapty 2014 gives the most recent full-length description. Wat's Dyke: see Ch. 5. The Danewirke along the base of the Jutland peninsula, dated to *c.* 737 by dendrochronology, may have been known to Offa.

24 Obligations: Brooks 1996, 129. Hereford: Shoesmith 1982; forts and problems of recognition: Bassett 2008 and see Ch. 5. Bristol has been mooted but lacks evidence: Baker, N. *et al.* 2018, 10 and 79–80.

5 The Ninth Century

Kings and Vikings

Viking raids and settlements dominate narrative accounts such as the *Anglo-Saxon Chronicles* about the ninth century, but for those who lived in Britain at the time, other preoccupations probably meant that only episodically did the vikings impact directly on them, as they tried to feed their families, to serve the Church if they were in the small minority devoted to a religious life, or to pursue self-aggrandisement if they aspired to rulership. The everyday business of making a living was nevertheless liable to be violently disrupted, and the effect of the vikings can be explored through the buried hoards of precious metal which they hid or which were hidden from them, the defences erected by and against them, what they wore and used in life and how they were buried, the changes to settlements and churches that they may have caused, and their numbers.

Because many churches were near the east coast and contained gold and silver altar vessels and other treasures, they were very vulnerable to viking raids. Destruction of sacred places caused horror, which may have led to an exaggeration of the impact; the record that a raid in 793 'miserably destroyed God's church on Lindisfarne' – an event presaged by dramatic storms and fiery dragons in the sky – seems like hyperbole because both the famous Gospels and the relics of St Cuthbert survived, as did enough of the community to look after them. Cross-shafts and grave-markers that were an important part of the memorial landscape on Lindisfarne were still occasionally produced. A grave-marker that shows on one side the Cross with the sun and moon and two praying figures, and on the other a line of armed men with raised weaponry, is no longer thought to be a direct reference to the 793 raid and is interpreted as having a theme of the Last Judgement at Doomsday; from its style it might even post-date 875, when the Lindisfarne community left their coastal monastery, taking the relics of St Cuthbert with them. Occupation at a small settlement close to the shore in the same area seems to have ceased at much the same time; until then, ninth-century coins and cattle bones suggest that it was not a totally isolated and impoverished community. Whether it was owned by or supplied Lindisfarne is unknown, but the abandonment dates are suggestive.[1]

What happened to the other monastic communities in northern Northumbria is not recorded: at Jarrow and Monkwearmouth, a few stone structures survived, and both sites were later to come back into church use. The great Northumbrian

DOI: 10.4324/9781003007432-6

tradition of illuminated manuscript production had already ended, although a book of remembrance produced around 840 still used gold and silver leaf in its text and, like the inscribed stone grave-markers, shows the importance of perpetuating memory. Coins at Jarrow show the workshops there as being still in operation well into the ninth century. None of the sites has revealed the sort of occupation that indicates use by vikings, although some of the Lindisfarne sculptures seem to indicate Scottish connections. On the other side of the Pennines, Carlisle might have been vulnerable to raids launched from the Western Isles and Ireland but shows no obvious signs of disruption, and, although objects of 'Hiberno-Norse' type appeared they did not displace contacts with the south.[2]

In southern Northumbria, a church probably survived at York, as did the archbishopric, and use of the cemetery there continued, but sculptural fragments excavated below the eleventh-century cathedral and attributed to the ninth century are few, and some suggest a distinct decline in quality and quantity in its middle years. The burial in a wood-lined pit in the early to mid ninth century at Coppergate of a helmet indicates activity – was it to hide a valuable item from raiders or was it ritually deposited? Its fittings included metal strips with embossed texts, asking for prayers for Oshere, presumably its first owner, and whose family may have decided that it should not be used after his death. Elsewhere, a cemetery at Ripon stayed in use, but its nature changed, from being predominantly for men to a more communal mix of men, women, and children. The minster at Beverley seems to have been abandoned in the middle of the century, its surrounding ditch becoming overgrown, and someone losing or hiding a small purse.[3]

South of the River Humber, the ecclesiastical record seems less dismal, but that may be partly because there were fewer large coastal monasteries to be raided. The decline evidenced by archaeology was more gradual, spread across the whole of the ninth century, and in any case lesser minsters were more dependent upon their founders and were more vulnerable to the vicissitudes of family fortunes than were churches with large endowed estates. Several decorated manuscripts are attributed to Kent's early ninth-century churches, and Archbishop Wulfred (805–32) had a reputation as a builder – so he may have been responsible for the replacement of the original cathedral by something more on the scale of Brixworth. Control of the mint by Mercian kings in the early years of the century is shown by the very fine gold coin struck by a Canterbury moneyer for King Coenwulf, presumably for prestige reasons; on one side, the inscription '*De Vico Lundoniae*' may not refer specifically to the trading area but to a royal estate encompassing London more widely, emphasizing Mercian control. A few other gold coins, imitating *solidi* of the Frankish Emperor Louis the Pious (814–40), have been found, not in Kent alone, which were presumably regarded as 'prestige valuables' and not intended for use as currency. Kent suffered raids in 839 and 842; Minster-on-Thanet was especially vulnerable but was not abandoned until later in the century. Canterbury, which was inland but accessible up the River Stour, is not known to have been raided: documentary evidence implies that urban life continued there, but archaeology suggests that it may have been on a reduced scale – locally made eighth-century pottery is not readily distinguished from ninth-, and coins are few; minting, however, continued there.[4]

Agricultural settlements without treasuries to loot were not viking targets, and the greater emphasis upon cereal growing seen in the eighth century may have continued in the ninth, although developments are hard to pin down; for that reason, 'the long eighth century' is a term often used. The earliest phase of a water-mill at Tamworth, Staffordshire, was probably built quite early in the ninth century, with rebuilding in the 850s; enough of its timbers survived for dendrochronological dating. The dating at Higham Ferrers is less precise but certainly does not indicate abandonment very early in the century. Radiocarbon dates from a grain-drying complex at Fladbury, Worcestershire, neatly straddle the turn of the eighth/ninth centuries. Those places were all well inland and away from viking raids on the coast and probably safe from Welsh depredations – and fostered by lords protected by the enduring power of Mercia.[5]

The only large surviving church ascribed to the earlier part of the ninth century is in western Mercia, at Deerhurst, Gloucestershire, where the nave and west porch-tower survive, as does some of the painted sculpture that included figural carvings and snarling beasts' heads, as well as a highly decorative stone font, emblematic of the building's pastoral role, although nothing is known of the community of priests based there. A little documentation survives for another Mercian church with a remarkable array of sculptures datable to the same period, though set in a later building, at Breedon-on-the-Hill, Leicestershire. Excavation at Cirencester, Gloucestershire, revealed part of the foundations of a church of much the same plan and scale as Brixworth; it had a similar crypt, but neither it nor Deerhurst used the 4.6 m pole.[6]

In the early part of the ninth century, the Welsh were a greater concern to Mercia than the vikings; Offa's Dyke, left incomplete at its north end, was replaced by a bank and ditch a little further east, running up to the Dee estuary. Instead of long linear earthworks, resources began to go into the construction of bank-and-ditch enclosures, large enough to be thought of as 'forts' rather than as the surrounds of a substantial building complex such as a church precinct. Mercia may have had the earliest in England; at Hereford, a complete section across the western side of the medieval city found a ditch and earth bank (Illus. 4.2) of which traces have also been found on the north side, so it was probably an enclosure, but with the south side open to the River Wye. Its aim may have been not only to protect the cathedral there, but also to provide a base for armed men to raid into Wales. Dating is not precise; it 'could have been earlier' than the middle of the ninth century. Elsewhere, Tamworth, Staffordshire, had what may have been a ditch below, and therefore earlier than, probably early tenth-century work, and a similar pattern has been found at Winchcombe, Gloucestershire. Gloucester itself has sculptures showing burials in the area, but enclosures other than any provided by still-standing Roman walls have not been located, around Kingsholm, for instance. All these are too far west to have been needed against vikings until the second half of the ninth century. They were also minsters, around which enclosures were probably the norm.[7]

Southern England apart from Kent was also able to develop untroubled by vikings until the 840s. A king of Wessex who was heavily dependent upon Mercia for support was buried in Wareham, Dorset, early in the ninth century, where he had built a church that was nearly as large as that at Brixworth and emulated its style, possibly even including the use of the 'short-pole' module. Probably another example of West Saxon royal patronage in the first half of the ninth century are the elaborate sculptures in the church at Britford, Wiltshire. The Wessex kings expanded their territorial influence and probably brought in treasure as a result. A gold ring found in Wiltshire near Salisbury shows royal interest, as it is inscribed with the name of King Aethelwulf (839–58). It has a christian image of baptism, with two peacocks taking nourishment from the Tree of Life. Another royal gold ring has the name of Queen Aethelswyth inscribed inside its hoop, with the Lamb of God on the outside. The peacocks are in what is known as the Trewhiddle style, named from a hoard found in Cornwall in the eighteenth century, datable by coins to the end of the 860s. Although hoards like that may indicate trouble in the second half of the ninth century, they are nevertheless evidence of English wealth. A hoard with a curious mixture of silver and copper-alloy objects, with coins that show deposition after about 850, was found long ago in Sevington, Wiltshire, and undecorated strap-ends in it suggest that it belonged to an itinerant metalworker. He would not have been in that area if there had not been patrons.[8]

*

Viking raids began again in the 830s, intensifying and therefore becoming an increasing threat not only to churches but also to trading-places like *Hamwic*, recorded as targeted in 840, or London in 842, when their equivalents on the other side of the North Sea and the Channel were also attacked. The effect can be seen in coin losses, which fell right away. Even if the ports could recover physically, commerce would have diminished from the loss of confidence in being able to trade in safety. The 'prolific sites' seem either to have gone out of use altogether or to have become no different from other settlements. In Northumbria, desertions and abandonments seem likely to have been more extreme than in other kingdoms. Nevertheless, that kingdom maintained a currency, remarkably moving into a phase in which the amount of silver in each coin became less and less, until by the 850s it was effectively a base-metal series; what are now generally known as 'stycas' were unlike other kingdoms' pennies in size and design as well. Who would have used them and for what sort of transactions? Their distribution is widespread in the north, but few are found to the south of the River Humber, so unsurprisingly they were probably not acceptable outside Northumbria.[9]

Rural settlements in central Mercia may not have suffered much disruption from viking raids; work in the Raunds area hints at changes after the mid ninth century, with many settlements abandoned and the expansion of a few. Catholme survived, as did Yarnton, where a graveyard developed. At Higham Ferrers, the malting kiln was demolished and the enclosure ditch filled in, among its contents being partial human remains including the headless corpse of a woman and dismembered dogs; they may have come from a gallows, indicating that the site was a royal centre where justice was performed; the filling of the ditch may signal a functional change of the site, which stayed in use for a while, with a few scattered buildings. Many settlement sites occupied today have provided pottery evidence that they were lived in during the mid Saxon period and so perhaps continued from the eighth or ninth century in an unbroken sequence. That seems to have been the case at North Elmham, Norfolk, where the earliest buildings excavated do not suggest a settlement of more than agricultural significance, although it was later to be an episcopal centre, so might already have had a minster nearby. The earliest seal-die known from England belonged to Ethilwald, the bishop of East Anglia 845–70; perhaps his see was increasingly using documents for administration, another indication of stability at least through the mid century period.[10]

Mercian kings could not protect Flixborough, however, where objects and animal bones indicate a dramatic switch from an elite lifestyle to something closer to basic farming; no viking raid is known to have taken place, but if indeed it was a minster it could have been a target. So could Bardney, its wealth shown by the gold and niello plaque excavated there, with an apocalyptic image of an eagle-headed St John with a pen and book, probably of the ninth century. A site with no known ecclesiastical connection, Maxey, Cambridgeshire, also disappeared towards the end of the ninth century, however, and raiders can hardly be blamed for that. The nunnery at Nazeingbury, Essex, has radiocarbon dates that cease after *c*.870, but is well inland, so may have suffered from the lack of patronage rather than directly from vikings. On the Thames estuary, however, the demise of the excavated settlement at Mucking seems to have taken place long before vikings could be blamed and may simply have been part of a general process of settlement shift at no particularly obvious single moment in time; the same seems true of West Stow. England may even have been perceived to be safer than the continent; a pottery at Stamford, Lincolnshire, may have started production before the 870s viking domination of Mercia; its red-painted decoration was unlike anything previously made in England, so the potter or potters had almost certainly come from the Rhineland and might have been refugees.[11]

Forts of various sorts are the most obvious sign of viking activity. They are not always readily datable; within the *wic* in London, excavation of a very deep ditch implies a substantial bank. Fifty-seven metres of it were recognized, with other traces 160 metres away as well as perhaps at other sites, and it was more substantial than a church perimeter would have been. If completed, it enclosed 30–40 hectares, and it was cut through some existing properties, which could imply haste to get it built, perhaps to confront vikings like those known to have raided in 842 and 851, built by the king to protect the traders, or even by a civic authority if London was already able to take such action on its own behalf. A hoard of Northumbrian stycas found in an upper level and datable to 850–1 seems to preclude an earthwork by the vikings who wintered in London in 872–3 and indicates an action taken in or soon after the 851 raid. But who in London would have owned coins that were almost valueless for their metal and therefore not very negotiable as money, even if legally acceptable despite emanating from another kingdom?

Refugees in the 860s is another possibility, but would they have thought that their little treasure was still usable?[12]

That the vikings constructed defences at least after 850 is unsurprising, although no tangible evidence has been found at many of the places recorded in chronicles. York's Roman walls may have been used, just as the English may have tried unsuccessfully to shelter behind those in Winchester between 860 and 865. In Nottingham, there were no such predecessors to press into service. One viking work has been excavated at Repton, where the army 'took up *wintersetl*' in 874 not only because it was on the River Trent but also because its church was a mausoleum for Mercian kings (Illus. 4.3), and ousting them was a symbol of ambition to create a dynasty to rule a captive kingdom. The significance of the church building was not lost on the newcomers, as they buried one of their leaders close to its north wall, giving him a sword, knives, and other items, notably a Thor's hammer, presumably a declaration of his origins and possibly of his claimed ancestry. He had died violently, as his skull had been pierced by spears, and a sword blow to his thigh had emasculated him; a wild boar's tusk had been placed where his sexual organs would have been. Alongside him was a younger man, shown by DNA to have been a close relation. Other burials included a woman with a gold ring and five silver pennies minted in 872–4. The vikings presumably dug the D-shaped ditch, partly excavated and partly traced by geophysics, with the river on one side and using the church building to guard a gateway. Outside that enclosure were features that included the mass burial of the bones of over 250 people, mostly but not all males aged eighteen and over, around a skeleton excavated in the seventeenth century and no longer extant. They were below a mound which overlay a stone building, interpreted as an early mortuary chapel; they have been variously interpreted as sacrifices, battle victims, or earlier burials redeposited – radiocarbon dates seemed to favour the last possibility until adjustments were made. Many show weapon injuries, and isotopes indicate non-local origins, suggesting burial of army members in the 870s – though that does not explain why some of the skeletons were disarticulated and their bones stacked.[13]

The likelihood is that Repton's excavated ditch was an inner enclosure, with an undiscovered outer defence not only sheltering the mass grave but also probably necessary to protect an army of the size likely to have been operating in the 870s; it may already have existed in the form of a boundary around the royal complex and its mortuary chapels. A recently discovered site a mile away at Foremark may also have been an active camp. A few miles down the River Trent at Ingleby, Derbyshire, viking burials of a very different kind from those at Repton include cremations and inhumations, some under barrows, and with no christian church anywhere near. A different element within the viking army is indicated. That the armies were composed of different groups, and could split up, is known from what happened in 870–1, when men led by Guthrum left Mercia to raid Wessex. They camped at Reading, where one account credits them with building a defence. A ditch has not been found, but a location between the Rivers Thames and Kennett could easily have been protected by a land-bank across the peninsula. A sword with a very worn ninth-century hilt with Scandinavian decoration was recorded as found with the skeletons of a man and a horse, suggesting a viking leader buried in full gear near the Thames; a small hoard of pennies, dated to the 870s, was found in the churchyard, perhaps buried there in the hope that they would be given spiritual protection of some sort, if not actually of christianity. That is on the assumption that a church already existed at Reading; none is documented, but the place is called a royal vill, the sort of establishment where a church would be expected. It may already have had at least a perimeter, therefore, which the vikings perhaps enlarged.[14]

That Reading was a royal and church centre before it became a viking camp is made more likely by what happened at Wareham, Dorset, in 876; King Brihtric's burial there probably made the site symbolically important for Wessex, as Repton was for Mercia. Like Reading it was between two rivers, one navigable by the longships, so it was a good base for riding on horseback. Earth banks still surround it on three sides, the only one giving access by dry land having a deep ditch in front. As in Reading, the church may have had some perimeter boundary to be used or enlarged, but that is speculative, as is the possibility that the vikings constructed the bank between the two rivers, the other two sides being given protection later. Some sort of truce was made with King Alfred, its significance apparently symbolized by an oath sworn by the vikings on their *armilla sacra*, which is usually taken to mean 'holy ring', but sacred items included brooches in the Scandinavian world. The vikings left some material evidence of their brief occupation: a gilt-silver mount found just outside the town is almost certainly a piece of loot from the continent, and two lead weights topped with silver pennies found nearby look like the evidence of the distribution of booty.[15]

The viking penchant for loot is shown by several hoards with coins, many deriving from the continent and even Arabia, silver ingots, and rather crude rings, mostly found in places where army passage is recorded; one found recently near Watlington, Oxfordshire, was close to a ridgeway and could have been hidden by a viking loser after the Battle of Edington in 879, which established King Alfred's place in history. Another newly discovered hoard seems out of place at Eye in Herefordshire. As well as silver ingots and rings, both those hoards had some gold items and large numbers of a type of penny previously thought to be rare. On one side is a copy of a Roman 'Two Emperors' design and on the other is a helmeted bust, some with Alfred's name and others with that of Ceolwulf of Mercia, suggesting a cooperation between the two kings that is very different from the tale told in the *Anglo-Saxon Chronicles*. Two brooches in a hoard at Beeston Tor, Staffordshire, coin-dated to the mid 870s, show that such things were not confined to the south, and although its provenance is not known for certain, the splendid Strickland brooch, named after a previous owner, may have come from Whitby. A strange hoard of six brooches, without coins but stylistically well into the ninth century, except for one that was probably made in the eighth, was found in a churchyard at Pentney, Norfolk; who could have owned such a strange collection? If the church there already existed, it might have been thought to give the hoard spiritual protection. Another sort of deposition practice that involved 'burying' weapons in watery places may have continued (Illus. 5.1); a sword found in a river

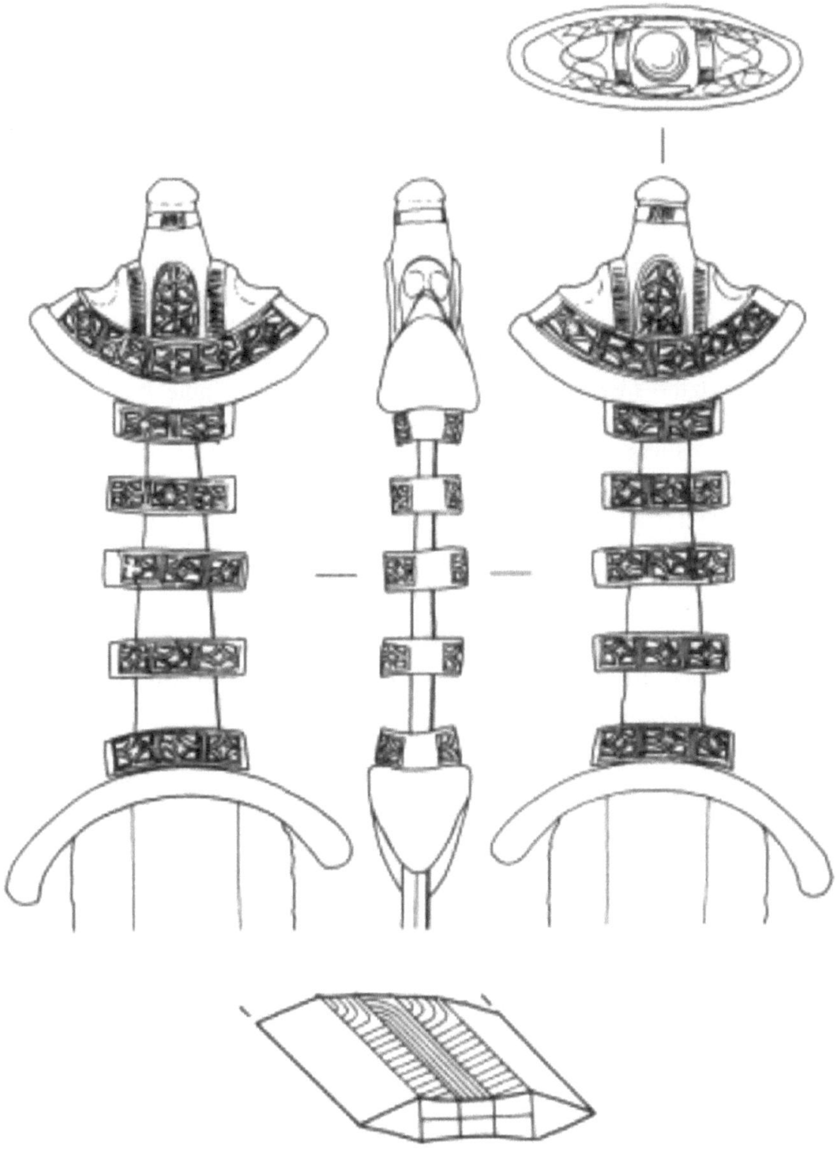

Illustration 5.1 A ninth-/early tenth-century sword found in a stream at Gilling West, North Yorkshire, drawn by H. Humphries. The hilt has silver bands, wider than the iron because they would have been set over a wooden or horn grip. They are decorated with 'Trewhiddle-type' ornament, picked out in niello, as on the upper guard and pommel. The animal heads on the ends of the pommel may be a reference to the creatures that would feed off the weapon's victims, a familiar poetic idiom. The blade is pattern-welded; separate iron rods alternately twisted and straight were welded together and etched after grinding and polishing to show up the pattern. The edge strips may have been rods with higher carbon content, for sharpness. Width of pommel: 838 mm.

at Abingdon, Oxfordshire, shows christian imagery, including an eagle very similar to the birds on the Aethelwulf ring and may be a testimony to a Mercian or West Saxon leader expressing his different ideology from that of viking opponents.[16]

The Abingdon sword may have seen service in some of the many battles and skirmishes against the vikings that are recorded but leave no direct trace, unlike some visible or excavated defensive works. These raise the much-discussed issue of the reconciliation of a documentary record with the archaeological; one version of a list of forts or *burhs* concludes with a 'formula' that seems to set down how the works were to be maintained and defended: every 'pole' required four men, each of whom was to be supplied, or paid for, by a 'hide'. This implies that landholders had to send men, whether they held a single 'hide', implying a substantial farm, or had large estates with many 'hides'. Furthermore, the list says how many 'hides' 'belong' to each fort. On the face of it, therefore, the length of each fort's walls can be deduced, if the length of a 'pole' is known; Winchester was credited with 2,400 hides, so its defences should be 9,900 feet long if the pole used was what became the standard 16½ feet – and its Roman walls are actually 9,954 feet (Illus. 5.2). At Portchester, however, the Roman walls are 2,440 feet long (Illus. 1.2), but the 500 hides attributed to it would provide for only 2,060 feet; sleight of hand can make some reconciliation by taking the outer ditch on the three land sides, which measures approximately 2,000 feet. Many of the listed forts were not Roman sites reused, although some were similar in layout, with rectangular enclosures and central gates; substantial remains of earth banks and outer ditches survive at Wallingford (Illus. 5.3), Oxfordshire, and at Wareham. Just as the coinage copied Roman designs, so there may have been a deliberate suggestion of an imperial past in those new works. They did not conform to the same formula as Winchester, however; Wareham, for instance, can only show the 6,600 feet that its 1,600 'hides' should have provided for it if the side facing the River Frome, which has no trace of a bank, is assumed not to be included. Wallingford, like Winchester, had 2,400 'hides' belonging to it, but even if the long river frontage there is included, the total comes to a mere 9,157 feet, using the parish boundary as the line. Light dawned, however, when it was realized that the Northern pole of 15¼ feet produced an allowance of 9,150 feet.[17]

The various 'Burghal Hidage' texts list only places in King Alfred's Wessex, with Buckingham an anomaly, and Worcester and Warwick probably later additions; unincluded names are just as interesting, such as both the two Dorchesters, Dorset's and Oxfordshire's, the former having serviceable Roman walls and the latter a major minster with Roman defences that could have been brought back into use. The list includes some small places, like Burpham, Sussex, and some of uncertain location, such as *Brydian*, either Bridport, Dorset, or Bredy, a nearby Iron Age hillfort. The texts imply attempts at efficient organization, probably therefore the king's, but which king, Alfred or his son Edward, and how much the administration could draw on earlier systems, and whether work was ever actually done at some of the named places, are all arguable. The effort involved in new construction was considerable in creating the deep ditches and wide earth ramparts; if these were faced with timber and not just turves, even more time and

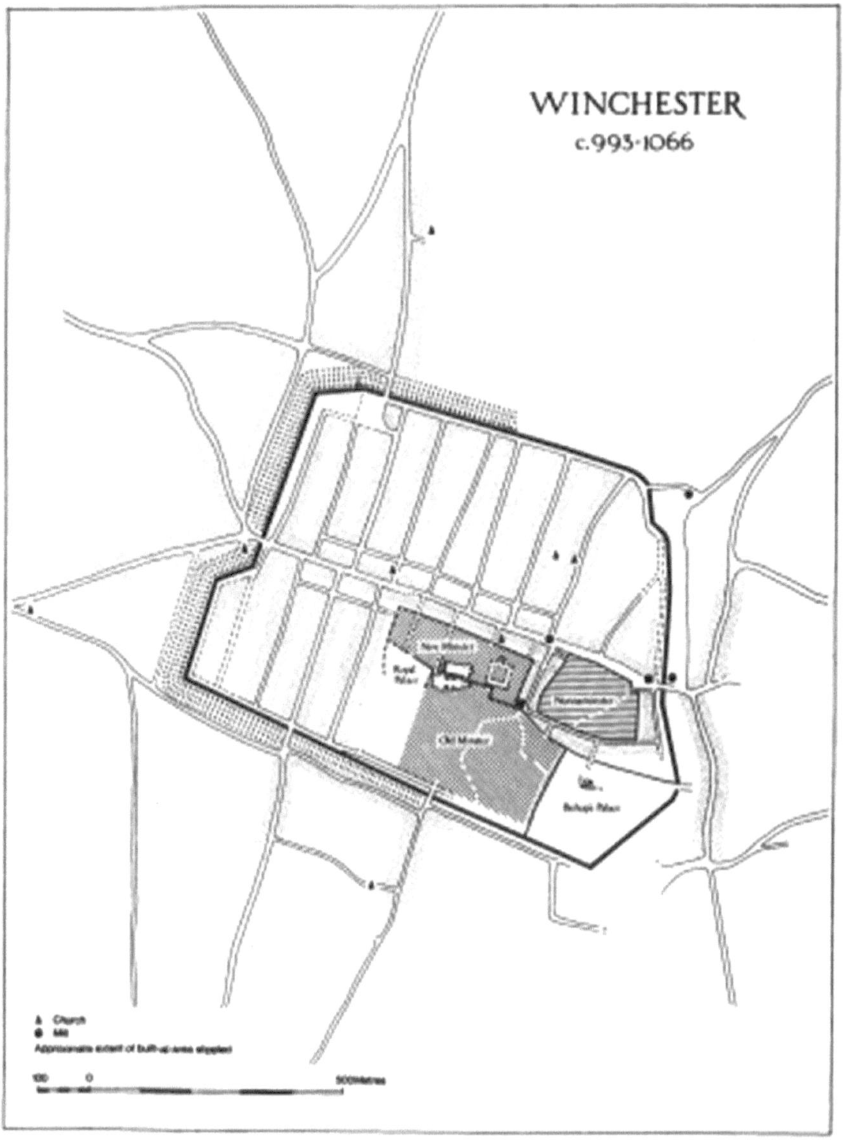

Illustration 5.2 Plan of Winchester, by M. Biddle, showing the Roman walls and the location of the bishop's church, later called the Old Minster, to distinguish it from Edward the Elder's New Minster, placed immediately adjacent to it in the early tenth century, with a nunnery to the east, next to the river crossing where a bridge may have given the city much of its new ninth-century impetus, when the regular pattern of the streets was created (Ottaway 2017).

Illustration 5.3 Wallingford in the 1930s. The trees mark the outer line of the defences, an earth bank and ditch, with gates in the centre of each as though based on the Roman plans of Winchester and others, although it had no such antecedents. On the right, the River Thames probably had a bridge-head work on the opposite bank, marked by the line of ditches (which were followed by the parish boundary). In the north-east quadrant, a Norman castle was imposed, later expanded over the earth bank and ditch, and forcing the north road to swing round it. The wide market street was later encroached upon (Christie and Creighton 2013).

logistics were needed. Excavations on the north side of Oxford – probably only recently under Wessex control – found post-holes that showed that oak posts had been used, and horizontal reinforcing timbers had gone back from them into the bank; those would have been difficult to drive into the earth, so were probably laid as the bank was constructed. Oxford has the advantage of having had very many more excavations than most places, but even so the size of the original burh is not certain: an original near-square may have been extended both to the east and to the west. Oxford went on to become a major town, as did Winchester and others, but the smaller places remained small, so urban development was presumably not part of the planning behind the 'Burghal Hidage', although it was thought important enough to be copied out in various ways at various times; not all the listed places had become mints – by the 930s, for instance, unlike some that were not included, like Dorchester, Dorset.[18]

Although the *burh* defences on the south coast and in the interior of Wessex were probably entirely protective, those on the kingdom's northern border, from Bath to Southwark, may have been chosen with an eye to its possible expansion. After the deposition of King Ceolwulf, of whom nothing is heard after 879, and Alfred's success in driving the vikings away from western Mercia, his daughter Aethelflaed was married to a Mercian leader, who may have depended upon his father-in-law for support, so the taking of territory in the Midlands further east may already have been a possibility. Certainly, Alfred took London out of viking or anyone else's control; that event is dated in the *Chronicles* to 886, but coins with Alfred's name and '*Londinium*' in a monogram on the other appear from the purity level of their silver content to be a little earlier than that. From that time onwards, activity within the *wic* area finally died away, to be replaced, if only slowly, with the use of the Thames foreshore within the Roman city, its riverside wall having crumbled to the point where it was no longer a serious obstacle. Two burials, both of women, on the water's edge seem likely to predate commercial activity; one of them was in a grave, and the other had been wrapped in cloth and placed in a bark container, so they were decently treated despite not being in a formal cemetery. Evidence of subsequent trading activity includes two stycas, three 'London monogram' half-pennies, and a quantity of base-metal brooches and other items; charters of 889 and 898 concern properties at the market and 'trading shore'. Those are significantly different from the property given in 857 'near the west gates' – implying an inland site between the old *wic* and the Roman wall but involved in trade as there was mention of weights and scales in what was called a 'profitable little estate'.[19]

'New' London may have had streets leading north from the Thames up to St Paul's and Cheapside, but initially, at least in the ninth century, no further. Whatever ambitions there were for it to replace the trade of the old *wic*, progress was slow, not least because commercial networks across the Channel and North Sea took time to re-establish, upset by further viking raids. Ipswich and Southampton's *wic* activities also died away; the latter retained a church but lost urban activity and was in time replaced for commerce by a site to its west. Ipswich remained on the same site, so the overlay makes progress there even harder to measure. The fourth *wic*, York, was different, retained by vikings after their take-over in 866, an event marked by several hoards of the base-metal styca coins, which ceased to be minted thereafter. The landing area on the east bank of the River Ouse was abandoned, and like London the focus moved back into the Roman areas, not only the walled fortress but also the *colonia* on the River Fosse. Anything done to make the old walls serviceable cannot be recognized, though a sequence of bank heightening and extension, swallowing up the base of a stone tower-like building in the process, probably began. A few silver coins show late ninth-century activity but may have been struck mints like Lincoln to the south. Some strap-ends and other objects are also derivative, having Trewhiddle-style ornament that is more usually found in southern England. Small-scale artisan works of iron, textiles, and other products have been found in the earliest, ninth-century levels at Coppergate, outside the walls but close to the river – a source of water as well as for water-borne trade; a hearth made from reused Roman tiles and used for melting glass was dated by archaeomagnetism to within 20 years of 860.[20]

York raises a particular later ninth-century issue, the extent to which vikings 'proceeded to plough and support themselves' in northern Britain, as the *Chronicles* have it. 'New' York became a permanent site, but the quantity of ninth-century objects excavated within it is much less than has been found by metal-detection at Aldwark, further north, or Torksey, to the south on the River Trent. The objects include weights and gaming-pieces – the latter can be used for fortune-telling as well as competitively, because they involve luck. These sites may have been army camps, with Torksey going on to become a town, though smaller than York and not a power-base for viking kings. That army members would have turned themselves into farmers after 876 seems unlikely, but some at least may have stayed to become estate-owners; abandonments and contractions of many rural settlements in the Danelaw show the scale of disruption, but there may also have been survival, as in the uplands at the evocatively named Gauber High Pasture; in Ribblehead, Yorkshire, is a site that may have started as a summer shieling from which grazing flocks could be supervised some time before the 870s – four coins provide the evidence. A site in a similar upland location, Simy Folds, Co. Durham, was possibly used because iron ore was being extracted in the locality, but may also have had a farming role. Transhumance is a practice likely to survive political and other upheavals, as it was an essential element in many agricultural economies, only recognizable in uplands where huts were built with drystone walls; shelters of turf and peat were probably much more widespread but lost to archaeology. Similarities of drystone buildings with sites in Norway are because of a similar terrain and are not evidence of Norse identity; Danish agricultural and settlement practice may not have been noticeably different from English, and place-names with Scandinavian elements may reflect landholders' speech rather than everyday speech.[21]

Whether large numbers of Scandinavians, including women, settled in England remains disputed; in York, amber and glass festoons of beads may suggest different display styles, but textile weaving shows English production methods and was presumably primarily a female domestic occupation. A knitted woollen sock appears to be Scandinavian but was probably an import. Two different cutting and seam-constructing methods have been identified in shoes and could indicate two different traditions, but as the finished products were no different in style, the evidence is not conclusive. Although soapstone from Norway or the Shetland Isles might suggest Scandinavians' preference for food cooked in the material that they had used at home, there are not many pieces, not all in the earliest levels, and, as soapstone was also used for metalworkers' moulds, not necessarily arriving to be cooked in. Norwegian honestones may have been introduced by migrants, but they remained popular for so long that they became everyday trade items.[22]

Away from York, even fewer pieces of soapstone have been found, far fewer than pottery sherds from English kilns. The cross-shaft at Middleton, Yorkshire, that seems to show a warrior laid out in full array of sword, spear, axe, seax, shield, and helmet seems to proclaim a proud viking and was long thought to belong to the first generation of settler/landowners, but one who had already chosen christianity for his religion; it is unlikely to predate *c.* 920, however. Other tokens of belief may be indicated by finds of Thor's hammers, like that in the grave at Repton; more of them are now known because of metal-detecting, but they are still few in number. The same is true of the very distinctive oval brooches worn by women in Scandinavia and found in a few graves as well as very occasionally as stray finds; they do not suggest that many women wore them. One pair in South Yorkshire was found in the burial of a woman whose teeth, when analysed for isotopes, indicated that she had probably been brought up in Norway. Another piece of evidence pointing towards the presence of at least a few Scandinavian women in England is a seemingly everyday domestic item, a spindle-whorl found at Scrivensby, Lincolnshire, with a runic inscription that invokes the aid of two Scandinavian gods and alludes to a saga, perhaps indicating deeply held pagan beliefs.[23]

A degree of integration may be shown by penny coins minted in the viking-dominated zones that were 'imitatives' of King Alfred's. After his defeat by Alfred at Edington, the army leader Guthrum established himself in East Anglia and issued coins which bore the anglo-saxon name he had been given at the baptism forced upon him in 878. He may have seen that christianity was the Truth – or he may have thought that espousing an English name made him seem more authoritative and international. The East Anglian coins may be a tribute to King Alfred's prestige, but his record goes far beyond that of a successful warrior. Surprisingly early in his reign, he was rich enough to raise the silver content in his coins; he also used his treasure to reward his followers, as all early kings had to do, but he did more than that with it. London's re-establishment and the creation of new mints at Oxford, Winchester, Exeter, and Gloucester, as well as the continuation of Rochester and Canterbury, suggest ambition to foster exchange and were practical steps; Exeter may have been chosen because it was close to the kingdom of Cornwall that Wessex had only recently come to dominate, and Oxford was on the Thames borderland with Mercia, but Gloucester was well outside Alfred's ancestral kingdom, and the mint may have been one way of asserting his authority over west Mercia after 878–9. The mints were probably chosen so that Alfred could make a statement of his authority. Although he entrusted west Mercia to Aethelred and Aethelflaed, they were never allowed to put their names on coins.[24]

The new mints were not prolific, a sign perhaps that Alfred's ambitions were not fulfilled. One of his two church foundations, Athelney, Somerset, was also far from being a total success, with some of the monks attempting to murder their abbot. What was built there is known only from a twelfth-century description of the church as having four *postes*, which might imply timber pillars not stone columns and also implies a structure that was not a straightforward rectangle; perhaps it was an octagon modelled on Charlemagne's great chapel at Aachen. Alfred's other foundation was a nunnery at Shaftesbury, Dorset, where only a few broken bits of sculpture indicate the presence of a ninth-century church. Gloucester and Exeter, like Winchester and London, already had minsters, but no evidence of Alfred's patronage has been found in them. A new minster at Gloucester is attributed to Aethelred and Aethelflaed, however; standing Roman walls were incorporated into the new building, which not only had a nave, chancel, and two side porticuses, which were unexceptional, but it also had a semi-circular western apse of unknown function (Illus. 6.6).[25]

The books associated with King Alfred show a different form of church patronage; they include various works produced at his instigation, though the only survival with decoration suggests that the standard of illumination had sunk to a very low ebb. Other court works may have included the complex gold, rock crystal, and enamel object inscribed '*Aelfred mec heht gewyrcan*', 'Alfred ordered me to be made', which by not giving a title frustratingly leaves an element of doubt over its patronage – although no-one of lesser status than a king seems likely to have had the resources to commission it (Illus. 5.4). Not only are the materials

Illustration 5.4 The Alfred Jewel is probably the best-known single object in England; made of gold enclosing a large piece of rock crystal that covers an enamel figure, the Old English inscription round the side reads '*Ælfred mec heht gewyrcan*', 'Alfred ordered me to be made'. It was found in Somerset at North Petherton in 1693 and has been associated with King Alfred of Wessex (871–99), although the royal title is not used. The enamel figure might be Christ, personifying Wisdom. The rock crystal is a reused Roman mount, so its shape may have dictated the shape of the jewel overall. The beast's head at the end, which is comparable to ninth-century sculptures, may symbolize Satan's threat to christian teaching; it holds a short tube. The suggestion that that held a short rod so that the object could be used as an *aestel*, apparently a pointer for use in reading or copying books, may be correct, but it may have been intended for suspension on a shrine or reliquary.

and the craftsmanship exceptional – the crystal may have been a gift from the Pope – but also the iconography, such as the enamel figure, fits with the teaching shown in books associated with the king. A word in one of Alfred's letters about valuable objects that were pointers of some sort might explain its use but does not certainly explain the short tube of gold held by a beast's head, nor with the proliferation of comparable though less splendid objects. Other courtly objects might include the large silver brooch, named Fuller after a former owner, that shows the Five Senses; it does not have an inscription, so neither its patron nor its maker are known, nor where it was made, but it seems to belong to the same sophisticated imagery as the Alfred Jewel. A different but high-value craft was embroidery, and the fine textile found in the damp conditions of Llangors Crannog near Brecon in Wales might have been a gift from Alfred to a Welsh king.[26]

With so few monasteries and major minsters still fully functioning, treasures like the Alfred Jewel cannot be attributed to a particular centre, and despite the high value of the materials, the king probably travelled round his kingdom with craftsmen, expecting them to set up forges wherever he happened to be. This might not have been possible when he was living in tents, as he is recorded as doing at times, but, when in London and elsewhere, he surely had permanent buildings and facilities at his disposal. Archaeologically, the evidence is slim; a complex at Cheddar, Somerset, that was confidently published as his palace has had both its dating and its status called in question, but the coins found there suggest that indeed the site was active in the ninth century, and it needs to be seen in relation to the whole estate around it, including a minster and a *burh* at Axbridge, not only giving protection but providing a landing-place on the River Yeo that led down to the Bristol Channel. It was also close to hunting grounds, where tradition grew that one of Alfred's successors had nearly killed himself by riding his horse into Cheddar Gorge. The long angle-sided building, substantial enough to have had an upper floor, is a type that is generally of tenth-century date, but it may be an early example. The site had a long history, so dating of some of the artefacts is not precise, but certainly in its earlier phases copper-alloy objects were being produced there, and crucibles were found. Craft activities have been found at other 'magnate' sites, such as Faccombe Netherton, Hampshire.[27]

Another substantial magnate complex was excavated at Bishopstone, Sussex, which as its name suggests became a property of the bishops of Selsey, where they would have stayed when visiting their estate and the surrounding part of their diocese. A cemetery already existed there, and graves on its south side had buildings constructed around them, notably a cellared structure, probably with a tower above. Particularly striking is the apparently deliberate concealment in one of the cellar's post-holes of a cache of iron objects. This can only have been votive, perhaps symbolizing the equipment that a well-run estate needed, including agricultural tools that helped to produce the food-renders that provisioned the owner and provided a marketable surplus – a little comparable to the elaborate blessing of the fields in which priests took part even if some of the rituals had pre-christian origins. The complex had a courtyard plan, as had some other magnate establishments, and the church was rebuilt, although a century after the estate centre's heyday; its buildings were abandoned, possibly for a new site to the south, which could account for the later date of the church. Although no crucibles were found, a copper-alloy ingot was presumably a metalworker's, though absence of iron slag suggests that smithing took place elsewhere. Another 'magnate farm' might have been the iron-smelting complex at Ramsbury. Another metal, tin, was being extracted, presumably in Devon and Cornwall, as it was a significant element in southern English coins of the 860s; the Trewhiddle hoard was found in an old tin working. Zinc, probably from Alston, Cumbria, featured in the Northumbrian stycas. Lead was probably still produced in the Peak District.[28]

*

Over the next centuries, production even of weapons was to move from estate centres into towns, where markets provided outlets and different crafts and skills could be concentrated, organized by the dictates of commerce not of lords, though their buying power remained crucial for many products. Urban development in the late ninth century because of royal protection and stimulus in the south and viking settlement in the Danelaw may have been limited, but in a few places as well as London becomes visible. In Winchester, a new river crossing meant that the main east-west road veered slightly away from the Roman line, and repositioning of the south gate meant an adjustment of the other principal axis (Illus. 5.2). Two coins of King Alfred suggest that other streets were laid out during his reign, or possibly that of his son, and their regular spacing and the earliest, well-laid flint-packed surfaces of those that have been excavated suggest an overall plan. Winchester also became a mint, and a rapid increase in pottery quantities as well as some structures are attributed to the late ninth century. In York, the focus of occupation moved from the *wic* on the east bank of the River Fosse to its west side, but how much had been achieved by the end of the ninth century seems stubbornly hard to determine; 'York ware' is attributed to the mid ninth to mid tenth centuries and is widespread across the city – but how much can be attributed to its early years? As in Winchester, one of the main roads, Micklegate, was laid out by 900, but how much early occupation flanked it remains uncertain. Another well-studied town, Oxford, like Winchester became a mint and has a grid of streets of which the earliest surfaces are much better laid than the later, indicating uniformity, but a coin pressed into one of them may show that all the work was done after 900.[29]

Other places that were to become urban during the late Saxon period had a variety of different trajectories, but growth specifically in the late ninth century is hard to pin down. In the Danelaw, Lincoln with its established ecclesiastical presence may already have had some marketing activity before viking settlement, so a triangular space on the north bank of the River Witham may already have been in use. Late ninth-century activity is marked by artefacts in Carolingian and southern English rather than in Anglo-Scandinavian styles, and 'Lincoln Gritty Ware' did not have a Scandinavian origin. The other 'boroughs' that were 'army centres', like Nottingham, have even less evidence. Also in the Danelaw, Norwich did not get underway until the mid tenth century despite the slight evidence of trading there in the eighth century, and whether Ipswich survived continuously as a trading-place or not remains to be revealed; its formerly thriving pottery industry ceased.[30]

Further west, Worcester is particularly interesting because the small enclosure around the Cathedral was added to northwards, and the works found in excavation tie in with one of the few surviving documents about trade: a charter issued in King Alfred's time sets out how the bishop and the powerful Ealdorman Aethelred and his wife, Alfred's daughter Aethelflaed, had jointly built a *burh* and now wanted to divide their rights to the market-place and streets. Special mention is made of carts and pack-horse loads of salt coming from Droitwich. *Ceap-stowe*, later called the High Street, indicates that the main market street ran close to the east wall and not immediately adjacent to the River Severn, where Aethelred and Aethelflaed acquired a large *haga*, presumably to use commercially as a landing-space. Further north, Aethelflaed after her husband's death made use of Stafford as a base, where radiocarbon dates are variously interpreted as showing either a ninth-century or a tenth-century origin for a pottery industry that must have fed into a local economic system.[31]

Viking raiders returned in the 890s but had no obvious impact on the archaeological record. When Alfred died in 899, his son had to fight for the Wessex crown against a cousin, both being 'throne-worthy'; without primogeniture, a king's death could still be a time of uncertainty and weakness, until a new king had established himself. The episode is also interesting for the way that one army used a *burh*, the other a hillfort, and for the hint that a minster church may also have been thought to be defensible, but again that story could not be reconstructed from archaeology. What the physical evidence does show clearly is that differences between kingdoms and regions at the start of the ninth century were more accentuated by its end, but whereas the south and west continued to seem part of the cultural world of the Franks and the Mediterranean, the north and east were teetering on the brink of joining the northern North Sea nexus of Scandinavia, Ireland, and the islands of Scotland. The tenth century was to see how this contrast played out.

Notes

1 See Cramp 1977, for full details of all the Lindisfarne and other Northumbrian sculptures, pp. 206–7 for the 'raid' stone in particular. (For the effects of raids, not necessarily by vikings, elsewhere, see Carver 2016 for the remarkable sequence at Portmahomack, and Campbell, E. 2019 for evaluation of Iona based on artefactual survival.) Green Shiel settlement: O'Sullivan and Young 1991.

2 Carver 2019, 220 saw evidence of recycling at Jarrow as perhaps indicating secular later ninth-century and subsequent activity. Remembrance book: Breay and Story (eds) 2018, 154–5, ascribed to either Lindisfarne or Wearmouth-Jarrow. Carlisle: McCarthy 2014.

3 York: Lang 1991, 59–69; the Coppergate helmet: Tweddle 1992. Ripon: Carver 2019, 254–5. Beverley: Armstrong *et al*. 1991, 5–14; E. Pirie, 164-7 for the coins in the purse. Durham *Liber Vitae*: Breay and Story (eds) 2018, 154–5.

4 Manuscripts: for example the 'Royal Bible': Breay and Story (eds) 2018, 166–7 and the *Codex Aureus*, 174–5, a book so revered that later in the ninth century the ealdorman

of Kent and his wife ransomed it from a viking raider and gave it to St Augustine's on condition that every month a prayer should be offered for their souls and that of their daughter: see also Crick 2000. Canterbury Cathedral: Parsons and Sutherland 2013, 199–200; Blockley, K. *et al.* 1997; Blockley, P. 1988, 72–3 for a Canterbury structure occupied in the first half of the ninth century and an 843–8 penny, and Blockley, K. *et al.* 1995, 329–50 for others; Naismith 2017, 149–53 for minting, and 2012, 112–17 for the gold coin. Louis the Pious gold coins and fragments are found widely, but many were probably loot from the continent brought by vikings; 22 of the 49 recorded by the Cambridge EMC are copies; only one coin had been drilled for suspension (accessed Sept. 14, 2021). The fate of Lyminge is shown by its anglo-saxon church not being on the site of its successor: Thomas, G. 2017, 99.

5 See Rippon 2008, 27 for the phrase 'long eighth century'. Tamworth: Rahtz and Meeson 1992, 14 and 122; reconsideration by Watts, M. 2017 suggested that it housed a pair of wheels. Higham Ferrers: Hardy *et al.* 2007, 53–4. Fladbury: contribution by A. Bayliss to Hinton and Peacock 2020, 38–40 (a similar feature at Stafford called a bread oven may also have been a grain-dryer: Carver 2019, 273). Raid developments: maps in Hill, D. 1981, 37–40.

6 Deerhurst: Gem *et al.* 2008b; Hare, M. 2009, 38; Bryant *et al.* 2012, 163–85 (and in a forthcoming article, they show that the porticuses on the south side of the nave were added at different times, and were not in the original building as at Brixworth: Parsons and Sutherland 2013, 161–8). Cirencester: Wilkinson and McWhirr 1998. Breedon: Jewell 1986.

7 Wat's Dyke: Malim and Hayes 2008, 164–5 for dating by Optically Stimulated Luminescence, a promising new technique, and 173–8 for interpretation. Hereford: Shoesmith 1982, 24–35 for the western defence, 77 for the dating; Craddock-Bennett *et al.* 2013, 295 for a comparable bank on the north side; Bassett 2008, 188 and 191, reviewed the evidence, recalibrating the radiocarbon dates but not proposing a more precise date than before 903 for the first phase. Gloucester, Tamworth, and Winchcombe: Bassett 2008, 180, 192–3, and 231. Gloucester minster: Baker, N. and Holt 2004, 18–19. Minster enclosures: Blair 2018, 237–41 and see Ch. 3.

8 Wareham: Hinton 2021, 17; the church was destroyed in the early nineteenth century (it could have had a crypt, but the existing one is later and not on the main alignment, so probably does not have an anglo-saxon origin). Britford: Cramp 2006, 206–9. Webster, L. 2012, 147–59 for the Trewhiddle style and other objects, 150–1 for the rings. Sevington: Wilson, D. M. 1964, 167–71 – another could be the small later group found in Sussex at Plumpton: Thomas, G. 2013b.

9 Northern Danelaw summary: Richards and Haldenby 2018, 327–36. Coinage: Naismith 2017, 119–26 and 367. The Beverley purse contained stycas: Armstrong *et al.* 1991, contribution by E. Pirie, 164–7.

10 Raunds: Parry 2006, 126–7 and 220. Catholme: Losco-Bradley and Kinsley 2002; Hines 2018. Yarnton: Hey 2004, 88 and 161–5. Higham Ferrers: Hardy *et al.* 2007, 54–5, 206–9, and pl. 3.6. Settlement survey: Wright, D. W. 2015 (mostly involving Mercian areas, but also inland Wiltshire). Fields: Hall 2014, 141. North Elmham: Wade-Martins 1980. Ethilwald seal: Wilson 1964, no. 18, and Heslop 1980, 2–3.

11 Bardney plaque: Webster 2012, 136. Maxey: Addyman 1964. Nazeingbury: Huggins 1978. Mucking: Hamerow 1993. West Stow: Crabtree 2018, 90. Stamford ware: Kilmurry 1980, but for reinterpretation of the start-date see Blinkhorn 2013, 160–5, disputed by Perry 2016, 104.

12 Malcolm and Bowsher 2003, 118–20 and 129, with a contribution on the coins by E. Pirie, pp. 278–84. The location of the hoard was not dissimilar to that of the smaller one in Beverley, see note 3.

13 Biddle and Kjølbye-Biddle 1992; Jarman *et al.* 2018; Jarman 2019.

14 Foremark: Jarman 2019, 24–5. Ingleby: Richards 2004. Reading: Astill 1978, 75–86, remains the best overall synopsis; the area where the viking was buried was known as the Vastern, meaning fortress.

15 Excavated long ago: RCHM 1959; mount: Webster and Backhouse (eds) 1991, no. 256; weights: Archibald 1998.

16 The Watlington hoard was properly recorded: Williams, G. and Naylor 2016; the Eye hoard was not reported, and various men went to prison for the crime of theft and concealment: Hoverd *et al.* 2020. Beeston Tor: Wilson, D. M. 1964, nos. 2–7. Strickland brooch: named from the Strickland family who owned the site of Whitby Abbey, where a number of high-quality objects have been found: Wilson, D. M. 1964, no. 152 and nos. 105–30 (summary of more recent excavations: Willmott, T. 2017). Pentney: Webster, L. 2012, 149–50; a seventh brooch, although from a different Norfolk village, is surely from the same hoard: *British Archaeology* 172 (2020), 4–5. Abingdon sword: Hinton 2008, 52–8 and Webster, L. 2012, 157–8.

17 The 'Burghal Hidage' texts, measurements, dates, and significance continue to be debated: see Hill, D. and Rumble (eds) 1996 for translations and commentaries; also Lavelle 2010, 58–60 and 209–14; Blair 2018, 233–9. Molyneaux 2015, 87–90, questioned how the assessments were arrived at, suggesting that some landowners owed army service, and others provided the labour for the defences. The Wallingford revelation was by Huggins 1991 and is credited by Blair for inspiring his search for the use of the 4.59 m 'short' pole in the seventh century and later (see Ch. 3).

18 Oxford: Dodd (ed.) 2003, 143–7 and 151 for reconstruction. Subsequent excavation of the west bank did not produce timbering evidence: Munby *et al.* 2019, 25–6; a 1960s excavation augmented by work in 2014 and 2016 makes an earlier western ditch possible; to the east, radiocarbon dating justifies a late ninth-century claim for the area usually thought to be an extension to be part of the original *burh*, but if an early surface was a road, it ran obliquely across the later grid of streets, which is unlikely: Teague and Brown 2020, 143–5 and 148–50; discussion of the excavated evidence: Dodd 2020, 56–7 (documentary evidence about mural mansions and the properties owned by Abingdon Abbey both point to differences between the west and east parts). Identification of some sites in the Burghal Hidage with places mentioned in other documents can cause confusion, as recently pointed out in a demonstration, particularly valuable for its use of LiDAR imaging, that the first place named in the list is more probably modern Rye than other claimants: Haslam 2020.

19 Ayre and Wroe-Brown 2015a, 130–59 and 162–4; the surviving grants were all to ecclesiastics, including the bishops of Worcester. The two females are in marked contrast to the broadly contemporary mutilation and isolated disposal of a young woman near a probable execution site near Basingstoke: Cole *et al.* 2020, and to the Higham Ferrers case. See Zeigler 2019 for the site transition.

20 See Hall, R. A. *et al.* 2004; Mainman 2019, 46–7 and 129–41 for discussions and summaries; see Hall, R. A. 2014, 547–8 for the hearth.

21 Torksey: Hadley and Richards 2016 - 26–7 for Aldwark, about which now see also Williams, G. (ed.) 2020, assuming that 'ARSNY' is the same site: see review by J. Richards in *Current Archaeology* 364 (2020), 56. Rural settlement: Richards and Haldenby 2018. Ribblehead: King, A. 1978. Simy Folds: Coggins *et al.* 1983; Coggins 2004. Northern upland synopsis: Wrathmell 2012b, 258–9. Transhumance: Banham and Faith 2014, 156–7. Place-names: Abrams and Parsons 2004.

22 York artefacts: Mainman and Rogers 2004 – manufacturing evidence does not seem to come from the earliest levels, pp. 472–3 – and pottery distribution 461–3; textiles: Walton 1989; Walton Rogers 1997; shoes: Cameron and Mould 2011, 111; soapstone: Sindbaek 2015; hones: Ottaway and Rogers 2002, 2794–6. Soapstone moulds: ten Harkel 2018, 5–6. See Ch. 6 for further discussion.

23 Middleton Cross: Lang 1991, 182–3, and see Ch. 6; Thor's hammers and oval brooches: Kershaw 2013, 169–70 and 157–70 (I think that our views differ on the significance of the numbers); see Parsons, A. J. *et al.* 2014 for a small group of graves at Cumwhitton, Cumberland, including one with a pair of oval brooches; see Speed and Walton Rogers 2004 for the south Yorkshire pair, with isotopic analysis by J. Langston. Scrivensby spindle-whorl: Hines 2017; the object might be as late as the early eleventh century and therefore not indicative of a Scandinavian woman of the 'first' viking period.

24 Blackburn 1998; Naismith 2017, 283–94; Blackburn 2003, 214 stressed the 'political propaganda' aspect of Alfred's coin designs. The vikings defeated at Edington retreated to Cirencester, where they may have made a fort out of the old Roman walls, before deciding that no reinforcements were going to come to their aid and moving on to East Anglia.

25 The sources on Alfred were translated and explained by Keynes and Lapidge (trans.) 1983. Books on him and his reign continue to proliferate. Attempts to locate his church at Athelney using geophysical techniques have not been conclusive. For the Shaftesbury sculptures, see Cramp 2006, 109–13. Exeter: J. Allan in Rippon and Holbrook (eds) 2021, 222–5. Gloucester: Heighway and Bryant 1999.

26 Some of the coloured images in the surviving 'Pastoral Care' text look like enamels; others are contorted beasts; Backhouse *et al.* 1984, 201–2. For the Alfred Jewel and its putative associates, see Hinton 2008: references therein include D. Howlett's exposition of the iconography and its stress on Wisdom (something associated with the Virgin Mary as well as Christ: Boss 2009), and G. Kornbluth's proposal that the crystal was from the Vatican treasury. England's close contacts with Rome are demonstrated by the large 940s hoard found in Rome in a purse, probably a payment of Peter's Pence: Graham-Campbell and Okasha 1991. Comparable gold objects with beasts' heads holding nozzles with rivets through them, though without the enamel or rock crystal, have been reported for example in *Medieval Archaeology*, 61 (2017), 408–9. (Two in the Galloway hoard have been reported as containing thread in the nozzles, perhaps favouring interpretation as pendants on reliquaries, cf. Hinton 2008, 37–9.) Fuller brooch: Webster, L. 2012, 153–4 and Coatsworth and Pinder 2011; an argument that one of the figures represents dancing did not seem to me to explain the rest of the iconography: Bayless 2016. Llangors textile: Owen-Crocker 2012.

27 Alfred's biographer, Asser, recorded the 'craftsmen, who were skilled in every earthly craft, and whom he had assembled and commissioned in almost countless quantity from many races': Keynes and Lapidge (trans.) 1983, 106. Tents: Blair 2018, 109–11; very commodious and colourful examples are shown in later manuscripts such as BL MS Cotton Claudius B.iv. The 1960s excavations were published by Rahtz 1979; a minster at Cheddar was mentioned in Alfred's will, implying particular interest in the area: Keynes and Lapidge (trans.) 1983, 175. Blair 1996, 114–16 and 119; 2018, 355–64, questioned the original dating, arguing that pre-900 coins and objects at the site may have been brought in from another site, which to me seems unlikely; the site was categorized as a 'magnate farm' by Carver 2019, 263. Faccombe Netherton: Fairbrother 1990. Textile working is also attested at these sites, perhaps but not necessarily including high-quality embroidery, for example Weikert 2018, 62.

28 Bishopstone: Thomas, G. 2010; contributions were made to discussion of the hoard and other ironwork by P. Ottaway (Alfred's writings contain a mention of the worker's need for tools, but for use not for deposition; nevertheless, awareness of their importance might be shown by both the text and the deposit), of the church by J. Blair, of the textile manufacturing by L. Keys, and of the pottery by B. Jervis. Radiocarbon dating suggests that the cellar was backfilled in the later eighth or first half of the ninth century, p. 202, although 'late ninth to early tenth' is proposed on p. 62. The estate was sometimes in royal hands: Blair 2018, 186–7. For the charm used to bless the fields, Ward 2019. Ramsbury: Haslam 1980, see Ch. 4. Coin metals: Metcalf and Northover 1985. Tin:

Fox 1999, 322. Peak District: see Ch. 4. Alfred also referred to children playing with coins and being trained, a rare reference in the period to the young except as martyrs: Crawford 1999, 32–8.

29 Winchester: Ottaway 2017, 215–19, 243, and 248; York: Hall, R. A. 2004, 495; Mainman and Rogers 2004, 459–61. Oxford: Dodd (ed.) 2003, 26–30.

30 Lincoln: Jones *et al.* 2003, 143–4 and 156; ten Harkel 2018, exclusively on metalwork. Norwich: Ayers 2011. Ipswich pottery: see Ch. 4.

31 Worcester: charter translation, Lavelle 2010, 214–15; topography: Baker, N. and Holt 2004, 133–4 and 348–9; Blair 2018, 259–60. Excavation in Droitwich found minor traces of production and a coin of King Alfred: Hurst, J. D. (ed.) 1997, 27, 79, and 96. Stafford: Blair 2018, 263–6 attributed the pottery kilns there to the ninth century, but Carver 2010; 2019, 269–74 placed them in the tenth, which is consistent with a pot containing 960s coins at Chester, see Ch. 6. Carver's reconstruction of the *burh*, fig. 3.109, put the road to the ford just inside the eastern wall, not down the centre as in most examples, though perhaps justified by Worcester's *ceap-stowe*; Blair did not address that issue.

6 The Tenth Century

Towns and Trade in Troubled Times

The decision by King Alfred's descendants to expand their kingdom northwards and eastwards disrupted the rule of the various viking leaders and whatever administrations were in place, which is reflected in the different coinage issues. Guthrum's East Anglian pennies were replaced by a series that carried the name of St Edmund, a 'memorial' of the last anglo-saxon ruler of that kingdom, but which was probably produced by leaders based in the former Mercia, such as in the 'Five Boroughs' and in Northampton, where the old stone hall may have made an appropriate headquarters. Conquest of most of Mercia meant that the Wessex kings' coinages would have replaced the 'memorial' series by *c.* 920.[1]

The mints at York and Lincoln took a different route: the latter produced pennies that cleverly achieved a recognizable form of the name by imitating the 'London monogram'; others had the name of St Martin on them, to whom the minster there was dedicated. North of the Humber, coins with the name of St Peter associated them with the minster at York and replaced the late ninth-century 'imitatives' at the turn of the century. This suggests deliberate differentiation by various kings and leaders from the Wessex dynasty's coinage, and also from each others' – the viking kings in York were Norse, not Danish. The York series is ambivalent about christianity; some had images: of a hand, which could be the Hand of God, or Thor's glove; a T shape that might be a Tau Cross or a Thor's hammer; a bird that might be Thor's or St Oswald's raven, or Noah's dove; a sword that might be St Peter's or a warrior's – even a bow and arrow might suggest the archer who appeared on the Ruthwell cross, so whether the archbishops had any part in these designs and whether they were meant to be ambiguous to satisfy both sides of any theological debate between paganism and christianity remain open questions.[2]

York has produced more evidence about coin production than is provided by its surviving coins alone, as excavations in Coppergate produced two examples of the iron dies used to strike the designs. One of them, which has a long shaft showing that it was to be fitted into the moneyer's anvil, was for the St Peter and sword issue; the other was the cap from a later issue, defaced so that it could not be used. There were also lead sheets with coin designs stamped on them, possibly used to check the progress of the die during its cutting, or to clean it while in use, possibly tokens to show that a tax or toll had been paid. The workshops where the dies were

DOI: 10.4324/9781003007432-7

made was not necessarily where the coins were struck, although the excavations found evidence of other metals being worked on the Coppergate sites; usually, the die-cutter was not the moneyer, who had to travel from his minting-place to buy the dies, paying a commission to the king for his licence.[3]

At the same time as coin production was developing in the Danelaw, tenth-century hoards north of the Humber show that silver was also in demand as bullion. The biggest of all the known hoards, found at Cuerdale in Lancashire in the 1840s, might have been put together to help to reward a king's followers (Illus. 6.1). Deposited around 904, it is the archetypal 'bullion' hoard, a mix of coins not only from England but also from continental Europe and Arabia; it also had ingots, rings, ornaments such as an anglo-saxon silver strap-end, and Scottish/Irish brooches. One result of metal-detecting has been a proliferation of hoard discoveries in the north, though none on the scale of Cuerdale, and some without coins. The 'Vale of York' hoard contained a silver-gilt cup, so similar to one found in a hoard at Halton Moor, also in Yorkshire, that it is very likely that they were taken in a raid from the same Carolingian church – yet the former was deposited in the late 920s to judge from the coins, the Halton Moor hoard a hundred years later, so the cup had been treasured for a long time. A sword hilt with gold bands round the grip and gold plates on the pommel in a hoard from Bedale, Yorkshire,

Illustration 6.1 Part of the hoard of silver ingots, coins, rings, and fragments found at Cuerdale, Lancashire, in 1840. Less than a tenth of what was discovered still survives. Deposited in *c*. 905, it might have been gathered together in York and been in transit to pay a viking army for a raid on Dublin. The deep gashes visible on one of the ingots result from someone testing to see if it was made of pure silver, not just a piece of base metal given a silver coating. About half the coins are anglo-saxon, the rest mostly Frankish and Arabian, probably acquired during viking raids in the 890s (Graham-Campbell (ed.) 1992).

may have been a prize taken from an anglo-saxon, as the central roundel has a Trewhiddle-style animal. Silver ingots and simply made gold and silver rings of various sizes are found where there is no evidence that they were part of hoards, so may have circulated alongside coins; larger ones seem to be related to a weight pattern, so were not just made from whatever someone happened to have collected together. Very different is a hoard containing various elaborate gold rings and scrap pieces found in 'Leeds District', again in Yorkshire, though why that it is so unlike any other remains unclear.[4]

The distribution of tenth- to eleventh-century bullion hoards has some similarity to that of the northern sculptures attributed to the period. They include a few crosses which look like the 'preaching' crosses of earlier Northumbria, except for the Scandinavian character of much of their decoration, and the depiction on a few of figures from Scandinavian sagas. They are, however, adaptations into christian teaching, not assertions of paganism. Much more numerous are grave-covers, also best described as Anglo-Scandinavian. Most distinctive are what have become known as 'hog-back' monuments, though it is now generally agreed that their shape mirrors a house-shaped form of reliquary – or possibly an actual house if the grave was thought of as a house for the dead. Some are carved with the heads and upper paws of bears gripping their ends, which are unlike anything anywhere else, and show that new modes were able to find patrons. Those people may have been new landowners, some claiming Scandinavian ancestry; a fragment of a copper-alloy chape of a type otherwise known only in Scandinavia suggests a weapon-owner with close ties to a homeland and was found in Ryedale, Yorkshire, an area with a number of stone sculptures. They do not extend throughout the Danelaw, although there is a group in north Lincolnshire. Otherwise, like the bullion hoards, they suggest that the River Humber was something of a frontier.[5]

The distributions of several different types of small copper-alloy brooches, which have proliferated through metal-detecting, contrast to those of the sculptures and bullion hoards, as they focus not only on East Anglia, especially Norfolk, but are also found in Lincolnshire, south-east Yorkshire, and the east Midlands. Some are clearly of types current in Scandinavia, though the argument that they were worn in England by women who were, or wanted to be thought to be, of recent Scandinavian descent is weakened by the relative lack of them in Lancashire or most of Yorkshire, where viking ancestry would be most expected: Norse predominance in the north-west might be a factor. Where most of the brooches were made remains unknown, as moulds have not been found; a Scandinavian connection shows not only in the decoration on their fronts but also in the attachment provision on their backs, but that could result from slavish copying in England by native craftsmen. Metal-working in York, Norwich, and other Danelaw centres may indicate manufacture in those but does not preclude itinerant workers. Their products, however, could have been distributed within the same networks that took pots from kilns in several of the emerging towns into the countryside.[6]

In the south of England, a small group of silver items from Plumpton, Sussex, would have been dated on the basis of their Trewhiddle-style decoration to the ninth century but for six coins showing that deposition was no earlier than 939; a difference between the north and the south of the Thames is that few hoards of any kind are found in the latter. The tenth century also saw a decline in highly ornamented gold and silver objects generally; there are very few silver brooches, and rings were not distinguished with complex iconography like King Aethelwulf's, but were twisted strands probably valued for their weight not their symbolism. Sword hilts were no longer embellished with gold and silver fittings, like those from Gilling West (Illus. 5.1) and Bedale; copper alloy, very thin silver-plating, or silver wires being used instead. Sword blades were less likely to be pattern-welded, perhaps because better-quality iron blooms were available. Most swords are still recovered from rivers or other watery locations, suggesting continued beliefs about appropriate disposal. An iron helmet found in Yarm, Yorkshire, recently identified as ninth to eleventh century, was also plainer than the known earlier ones like that found at Coppergate; a competent though not highly skilled smith was needed to manufacture the iron plates and bands. It appears to have been deliberately deposited in a pit, as Coppergate's had been. With larger armies and more archers, head protection from showers of arrows would have been more necessary.[7]

Discontinuation of the viking series of coins and the circulation of those issued in the names of the West Saxon dynasty throughout England suggest administrative and commercial integration, although some differences persisted. The tenth century saw the proliferation of potteries within the old Danelaw area, using a fast-rotating wheel and 'updraught' kilns with perforated floors through which hot air circulated from below (Illus. 6.2). Some of the 'first-generation' potters at Thetford may have come from Ipswich, but at Stamford, Torksey, Northampton, and Lincoln, some were almost certainly immigrants from the Rhineland or northern France, but not from Scandinavia, as no pottery tradition of the sort existed there. By the second half of the tenth century, when new production centres were created at Norwich and Newark-on-Trent, their descendants would have been native-born – but the methods of manufacture remained the same and were not adopted in the south. Westwards, kilns at Stafford are controversial as radiocarbon indicates origins in the ninth century, but they were certainly active in the tenth, and it is questionable whether production would have survived the turmoil of the viking-period upheavals, and whether the pots look more like Thetford-type forms and decoration than like earlier Ipswich types.[8]

Were all these potters entrepreneurs or employees? The scale of production certainly suggests large workshop operations, producing much more than was required by their immediate hinterlands. By the middle of the tenth century, for instance, Thetford-type wares predominated in York; transport would have been by boat down the Trent and then across the Humber estuary and up the Ouse; the Roman Foss Dyke may have been reopened, taking pots south to Lincoln. At Stamford, a particular type of clay produced a white fabric which could be used to make a thinner-walled vessel than others, and which had properties that made it especially suitable for use in crucibles for melting metals. Its early products included red-painted decoration, similar to continental products; later, lead glaze was added to the exteriors of pitchers, the first example of the practice in medieval

Illustration 6.2 A pottery kiln at Thetford, Norfolk, excavated in the 1950s. The ranging-rod spans the flue through which heat from the stoke-pit was drawn into the chamber to circulate under the platform on which the pots had been stacked. The platform was pierced to allow hot air to circulate round the pots. The sides and roof of the kiln are missing; the latter would have been removed after the kiln had cooled down to remove the pots and to get the next firing ready.

England. Large quantities of the metal were needed; one calculation is that 200 pots would have required forty-four pounds of lead, too much to have come from scavenged scrap or by gift-exchange with the archbishop of Canterbury, assuming that he still owned the Wirksworth estate in the lead-producing area of Derbyshire acquired in 835. Stamford ware has been found in Derby, suggesting overland links and a commercial operation run by someone who was wealthier than an everyday artisan. Stamford ware is found more widely than Thetford and other wares (Illus. 6.3), although by and large it did not penetrate their markets by travelling as much northwards as it did in other directions; much of it probably

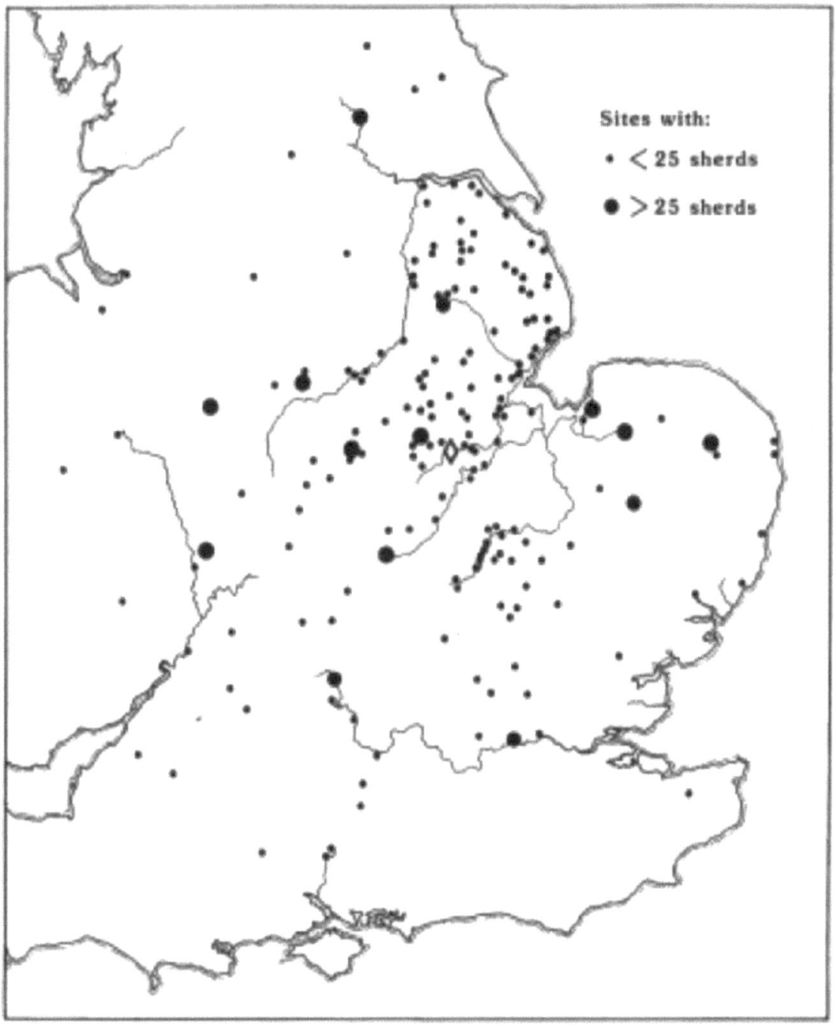

Illustration 6.3 Distribution map of pottery made in Stamford, Lincolnshire, shown by the open diamond. Use of rivers and the coast is clear, but much also went overland, presumably mainly on carts, as packhorses and people could not have carried as much as the quantities suggest (Kilmurry 1980).

went down the Welland and then round the coast to other rivers, but westwards and southwards it must have gone partly at least by land. Some has been found as far away as Oxford, including two almost complete glazed pitchers, one in a thirteenth-century context which suggests that they were very carefully looked after. Stamford ware's distribution is not unlike that of the coins from the Stamford mint, although slightly more of the coins crossed the River Thames.[9]

The Thames may have facilitated the wide distribution of a type of pottery distinctive for a high quantity of terrestrial shell in its fabric; some reached London, and it is plentiful in Oxford, but it may have been made as far away as Cambridgeshire – the kilns producing it have not been located, its common name 'St Neots ware' being misleading. In southern England generally, pottery remained a rural craft, without the technological innovations seen in the Danelaw area, although wheel-throwing was practised alongside hand-forming within Gloucester, and glazed ware was being produced in or near Winchester, though with very limited distribution. This presumably reflected not only the less severe disruption caused to existing networks by the vikings, but also the slower development of urban centres. The pottery travelling on streams and rivers may have been carried by log-boats, as probably it had been for many centuries, but increasing in number in the tenth and eleventh, to judge from recorded discoveries in rivers and estuaries. The very big storage jars made in Thetford must have presented a particular challenge; they might have carried grain or flour, but that would have made them very heavy and unwieldy, so they were probably traded in their own right for domestic use. Stone would also have travelled by water whenever feasible; Barnack, a limestone source in Northamptonshire, was well placed to use the Nene and Welland, but other quarries would have needed longer overland transport to reach a transshipment point; those who could afford stone memorials and churches could afford the extra cost. Salt was another commodity moved on both road and waterways; the late ninth-century charter that referred to tolls on salt from Droitwich reaching Worcester specified both cart-loads and pack-horse loads. Place-names such as *hyth* and *laed*, rather than direct archaeological evidence, reveal the communication networks involved.[10]

*

Coastal and sea-going vessels with sails and oars are known only from a sunken boat at Graveney, Kent, and now parts of others in London. The Graveney boat (Illus. 6.4) was abandoned in the early tenth century in marshland; she was sturdy, with a central keel and overlapping, 'clinker', planks, into which cross-frames were fitted, details of which suggest that she had been built in England. Still on board were quernstones from the Rhineland and traces of hops; the Kent marshes are known to have been producing salt, but if that was being carried, it had dissolved. The London fragments are from embankments on the waterfronts, so were from dismantled boats, mostly constructed in the same way as Graveney and viking-type 'long-ships', but including a round-bottomed clinker-built vessel, a type seemingly illustrated on continental coins and thought to be Frisian but not previously recognized in England. It could be beached easily and unloaded over the side – not that that hindered the keeled ships, but its shape may have given it a greater cargo capacity.[11]

The London foreshore development shows how facilities developed to improve cargo handling; at first, baulks and wattling held in place by posts were laid down to prevent boats from sinking into the mud and making access to them easier for horses and carts; it was even possible to erect small buildings. Then, from the later

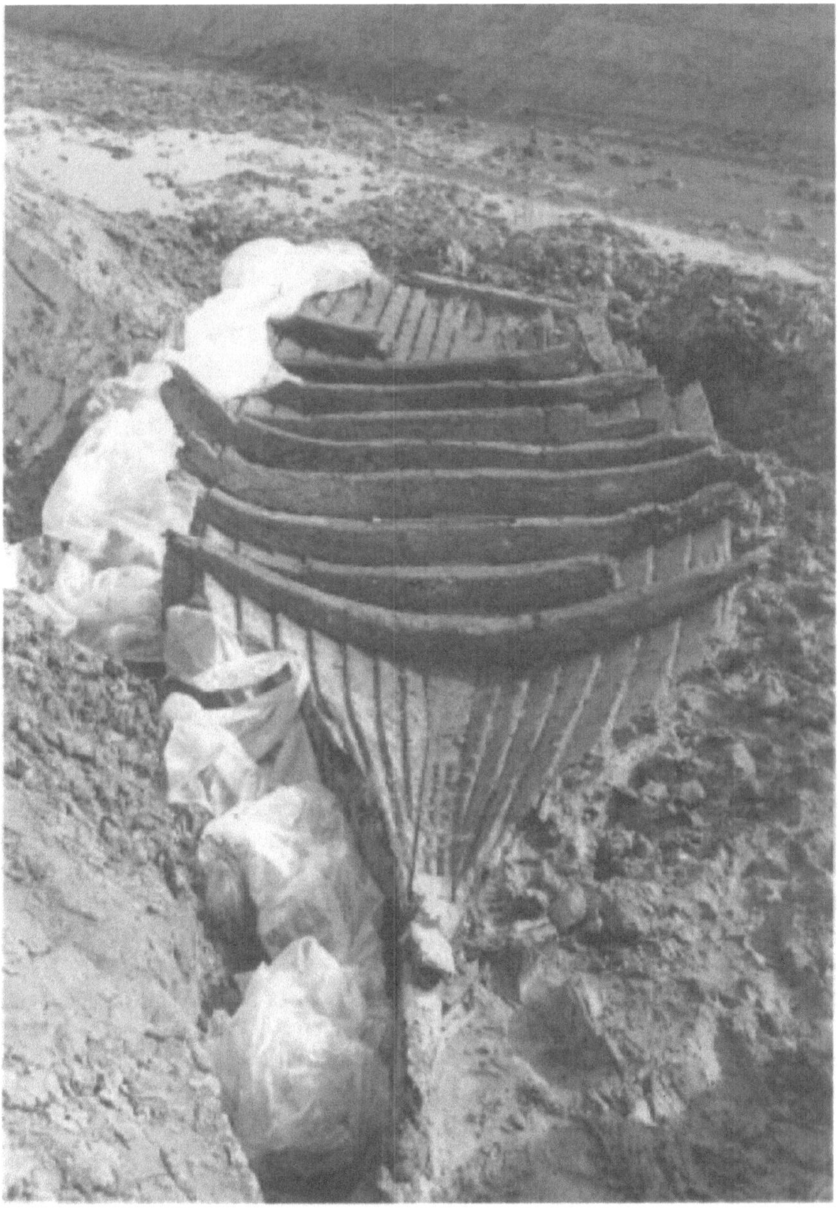

Illustration 6.4 The boat found in the marshes near Graveney, Kent, before being lifted and removed to the National Maritime Museum. Construction would have started with the keel, the overlapping planks were then fitted to it, and the stout cross-frames inserted afterwards. Dendrochronology dated her timbers to the 880s, but she was tied to a post that gave a tenth-century date, so she probably had more than half a century of use. Hops, quernstones from the Rhine, and a sherd of north French pottery were found in her, so she had presumably crossed the Channel as well as being used for coastal work, demonstrating that not all trade was carried out at the major ports (Fenwick (ed.) 1978).

tenth century onwards, the shoreline began to be embanked to form quays, and piled jetties extended from them out into the water; both allowed unloading on to dry surfaces. These developments were piece-meal, not planned in a single episode, indicating investment by individual property owners. A public landing-place was maintained but became an inlet because no one developed it. If the waterfront had previously fronted open ground where goods were viewed and exchanged in a 'beach-market', it was superseded by distribution up the slope to Cheapside to be sold from booths, although later documentation about grain being marketed at the public landing-places, Queenhithe and Billingsgate, may indicate continued trading in at least one essential foodstuff at those. These developments did not simply mean that the sort of activities seen at the earlier *wic* were replicated, however; high-quality glass and other imports were fewer and craft activity less intensive.[12]

London and Graveney show transport across the Channel and the southern part of the North Sea, from the mouth of the Rhine and modern France; no large vessel parts survive from northern England, but it was presumably served by viking-type ships witnessed by survivals in Scandinavian burials and Baltic sinkings. Trade with Ireland was important, particularly in the tenth century for the north-west, initially fostered by political ties between Dublin and York, but not severed by West Saxon expansion. In particular, Chester became a mint after 907, initially with a very distinctive design of a tower or reliquary on one side of its coins, and at times thereafter it may have been the most active mint in England, probably buoyed by processing tribute payments from the north Welsh to the English kings as well as by commerce. Nevertheless, it remained part of the 'bullion economy' of the north, as a pot of a type that has now been recognized as having been made in Stafford contained a hoard of silver ingots as well as coins dated up to the mid 960s. The Roman walls may have been extended down to the River Dee, and a rectilinear street pattern that does not exactly overlie the Roman one has been observed, but there were also buildings outside the walls. Sculptures in one of its churches, not the minster, have designs that suggest that they are memorials of Anglo-Scandinavian merchants involved in trade with Ireland who were using the foreshore upstream of the walls and were not part of the settled population. As in York, Lincoln, and London, cellared buildings indicate storage needs, and removal of Roman stonework shows space being cleared. A problem with Chester, as with any port, is to know the tidal range and the average sea level; the probability that the latter had risen by over a metre since the Roman period would have made any harbour facilities unusable, and a new landing-place might therefore be expected, but Chester's role has to be viewed in the light of the exceptional site on the Wirral at Meols, where numerous objects dating to the tenth and eleventh centuries have been found, but where a landing-place may not have fostered a permanent port.[13]

Exactly when Chester and other places developed from ecclesiastical and administrative centres into towns with markets, streets, and permanent populations involved in manufacturing as well as trading remains problematical, but excavation in York's Coppergate has provided the best evidence of streets lined by long but narrow rectangular tenements, as was to become the medieval urban norm (Illus. 6.5). The ninth-century glass-working hearth implied no great restrictions

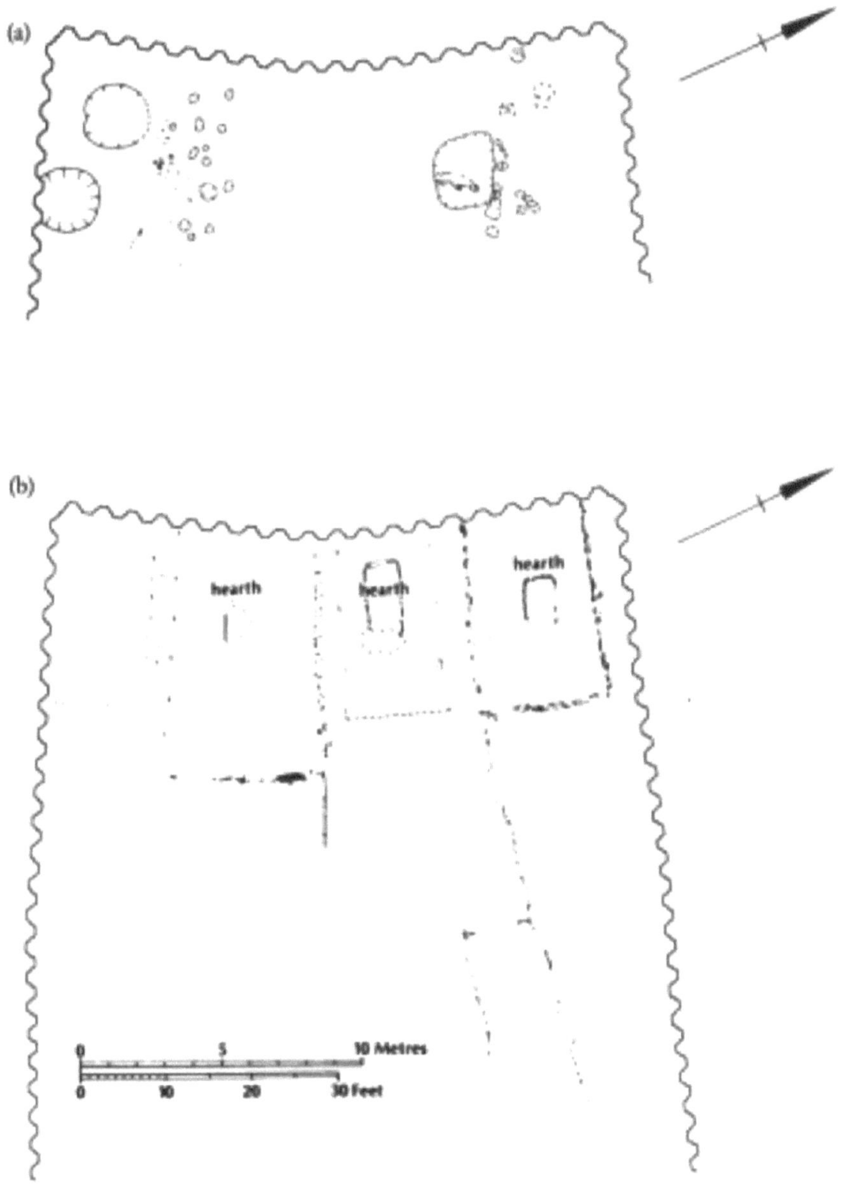

Illustration 6.5 Two of the early phases of use of Coppergate, York, excavated by the York Archaeological Trust. In the second half of the ninth century (a), features included a glass-working furnace, later abandoned and partly destroyed by a pit in which a male skeleton was found. In the early tenth century (b), the site was divided into separate tenements, each with a domestic hearth, and post-and-wattle buildings. The boundaries of the tenements were to last for a thousand years, even though the site was cleared and reconstructed in the 950s (Hall, R. A. 2014).

of space, but in the early tenth century subdivision was marked out by wattle fencing, with houses and workshops built of daub and wattle, with lice, fleas, and food debris indicating what living conditions were like; outside, the ground fell away to the River Foss and became increasingly wet. Rubbish pits were not kept separate from wells, which are only identifiable from their depth and because their contents were less foul. Because of the exceptional, waterlogged conditions, dendrochronology dates the sequence, showing that it was between 955 and 960 that the whole area was reconstructed, implying single ownership, perhaps changing because of the consequences of Eric Bloodaxe's removal in 954. Nevertheless, the tenement lines were after an interval more or less reinstated, and, from the 960s, buildings lined with solid posts and horizontal planking below ground level were constructed. One interpretation is that they had roofs not much above street level, but practicality suggests that they were floored over within a superstructure and accessed by ladder.[14]

'Coppergate', first recorded in the twelfth century, means 'the street of the cup-makers', although the cup-makers were not the only craftworkers in it; their products were probably wooden vessels and other objects, usually underrepresented in the archaeological record partly because they only survive in anaerobic deposits, which in England normally means that they were waterlogged, and partly because their final destination was the fire in the hearth not the rubbish-pit or midden like broken ceramics. Other working was in metals generally, not just the production of coin dies, in textiles, in glass, in leather, and in bone and antler, including combs, which raise the issue of whether their makers were itinerants or permanent occupants. Allied to that craft was butchery, which raises the same issue of the degree to which even York was fully urbanized, as the methods used to cut up the bones indicate every household doing its own, not yet dependent on a meat market for its joints. The affiliations of those households may have varied, some having more Scandinavian connections than others; an isolated grave contained the body of an elderly woman who had not grown up locally but either in Scotland or northern Scandinavia. As she died after the middle of the century, she could not have arrived with the ninth-century armies. A woollen sock was knitted in a technique known to have been practised in Scandinavia and not in England, but most of the other textiles were woven in patterns that were traditional in England but not in northern lands. Silks were imported and, like the occasional Arabic coin, had probably arrived through Scandinavia rather than from Italy and the Mediterranean. A silk cap or headdress found in Coppergate has Scandinavian parallels and may have been worn by someone claiming viking descent – or by someone showing off a piece of finery and unconcerned about its associations. A silk bag is thought to have been a container for a christian relic, as it had a cross stitched on to the front.[15]

As in Chester, so in York, the Roman walls were probably extended down to the river in this period. In all former Roman towns, wall circuits remained a constraint on topography, particularly if the gates remained in the same locations. In York, Coppergate was not within the Roman walls, so part of its line was sinuous, following dry ground above the river. Most towns had developed rectangular grids of streets, but Lincoln and York both had intra-mural roads that ran directly from one gate to another, cutting diagonally across the Roman grid. Lincoln's Flaxengate developed tenements set at right angles to it and cellared buildings. In all these towns, activity levels increased, but not uniformly, and there are still many unanswered questions – where in York was the cathedral since it has been shown that it did not underlie the present building? Were the sculptures found there memorials of viking leaders and their descendants with properties within the Roman walls, and what efforts went into reconstructing those? York's circuit has an excellent sequence, but its precise dating remains arguable, and the documented 'earl's burh' was outside them.[16]

The wholesale clearance and redevelopment at Coppergate suggest single ownership and control of the site. The buildings do not vary enough to indicate any social distinction between the individual tenements, so the owner and other richer people probably lived elsewhere. In Lincoln, the upper city may have been where the churchmen and wealthiest citizens, later called 'lawmen', lived; in the lower town, the axial road led down to the developing waterfront. The numbers of stone sculptures found south of the river in Wigford suggest that that was where most of the merchants who commissioned them lived by the end of the tenth century, patronizing the churches, next to which were markets that could be seen as blessing the commerce. Something of their connections can be seen in the silk headdresses found, which are very similar to York's, as are other silks. As in York, artisan activity such as metalworking was abundant. Other markets took place in corner plots and near the gates, and there may have been a larger open space which was later the hay market, fronting Brayford Pool. This became more commercial when the Foss Dyke was reopened, giving water access to the Trent, and must have represented a considerable investment of labour. Chester's postulated Anglo-Scandinavian merchants might have been investors in the urban infrastructure there; moneyers had to handle large quantities of silver, like the contents of the 960s pot, and such men were presumably capable of banding together to undertake joint projects. Another town becoming established in eastern England was Norwich, from the second half of the tenth century; its 'Tombland' does not indicate a cemetery but derives from the Norse word for 'empty/open', a space for market stalls.[17]

The quickening pace of urban development north of the Thames must have depended upon a robust agricultural economy, able to feed the townspeople. The meat component of their diet can be assessed in part from the animal bones, although how much any one townsperson consumed in a year is unknown. The bones show the ratios of the different species consumed, and also that the sheep and cows were mostly not young animals, but were not elderly either, so they were slaughtered after they had had a few years producing milk, wool, and, in the case of the cattle, doing haulage work, as stresses on their bones showed. They were not therefore animals raised only for meat, unlike the pigs which were killed once fully grown, except for a few kept for breeding. If the eleventh-century Domesday Book record of Lincoln is taken as an indicator of a population of about 4000, and assuming that meat was about the same proportion of its people's food as in modern non-European societies, something like 500 cows, 700 sheep and 400 pigs would have been slaughtered in an average year. Many of the pigs – and chickens – could have been raised in the town's backyards, and a few cows could have grazed in its back areas and adjacent meadows, but sheep need open grassland, and for 700 to be culled, a flock of about 5000 is needed, with each sheep needing 1–2 acres annually to feed on. If a larger town needed a hinterland of 5000 to 10,0000 acres just for the mutton that it was consuming, the arable area required for its grain would surely have been no less extensive. It is likely, though hard to prove, that exports of agricultural products, particularly wool but also cloth, leather, cheese, and possibly grain, were more important than metals and slaves.[18]

In the south, evidence of urban growth in the middle part of the tenth century is limited. The late ninth-century charter evidence of the property blocs created near the Thames in London for church leaders may have led to those being developed, but the archaeological record is sparse until well into the tenth century. The foreshore developments show a need to handle heavy goods, however. The pace of development in towns lacking water-frontage evidence is even harder to assess. Winchester's main street was already called *ceap streat* by the beginning of the tenth century, but despite its new grid of streets and its important mint, coin evidence of occupation activity at the end of the ninth and beginning of the tenth centuries does not show continued expansion over the next 50 to 70 years. Although tenements seem to have been maintained in the principal streets, some having cellars added to them, there was enough open space for the bishop's palace to expand, and although there were artisans at work, the extent to which they were marketing their products or directly serving the three great minsters and the bishop's palace – and the king's if there already was one – is uncertain. In the Southampton area, *Hamwic* seems to have remained largely deserted but for St Mary's church, which suggests no great volumes of trade going up to Winchester. A new site to the west developed only slowly; it seems to have had a ditched enclosure much smaller in area than the *wic* and was later expanded northwards. In Canterbury, contraction seems indicated by the abandonment of an extra-mural area, and Exeter has little tenth-century evidence, despite its mint. Other minting-places, whether former Burghal Hidage *burhs* like Chichester or centres like Dorchester or Ilchester, also do not have definite evidence of substantial activity in the first half of the tenth century.[19]

*

Expansion may have come in the later tenth century. A warming climate might have lengthened the growing season and benefited marginal areas previously too cold for confidence that crops would grow. Falling sea-levels helped to bring fens and marshland into use for grazing, some protected by artificial sea-banks. New and expanding rural settlements are to be expected but can be very hard to pin down to a particular point; a 990s coin excavated at Mawgan Porth in Cornwall is unlikely to have been very old when lost, but is one of the very few sites where there is more than a general ascription to 'late Saxon' origins, and is still the only one published that gives a coherent indication of housing at this period – untypically, because stone was used, at least for the wall footings, and its small courtyard arrangements may not be typical either. Stock-rearing is likely to have been more important there than growing grain, and the some of the buildings and yards look suitable for sheltering young animals during the winter.[20]

In most of England, earlier settlements may have remained, with many expanding and with new ones being added, but change may have been more marked in the areas of the north where viking leaders had longer to establish their grip, so that the abandonment of sites and development of new ones may have been more frequent than in other areas; Cottam has shown how new zones came into use, replacing older ones. Also in Yorkshire, Wharram Percy's nature changed, with basic material like pottery predominating over anything faintly luxurious, two parts of a belt-set with Anglo-Scandinavian Borre ornament being the last costly items found there, perhaps the property of a new owner claiming viking descent. In general, rural sites show differences from earlier periods in that they do not produce so many small costume and other traded items as earlier ones, so most would not have served as markets, although they may have been visited by itinerant tinkers and petty vendors.[21]

Wharram Percy illustrates another major issue of the period, the development of the 'typical' village with rows of houses fronting a street or a green. Even though it has been so much studied, disagreement remains over how and when it evolved into a 'nucleated' settlement with two manor-houses, one of which was subsequently abandoned. A key factor is the partly surviving church, under which traces of a timber building were found, which was of unknown size and date, leaving open the question whether it served more than the immediate population as a 'minster' or was never more than a typical village church and churchyard; the former view might account for its unusual location away from either of the manor-houses and the rest of the village. One interpretation puts the church as the earliest element and allows for a large green; another suggests that at least some of the tenements preceded the church. Neither can be supported by an unchallengeable date, and they depend largely upon reading backwards from the visible and excavated remains. What can be said with some confidence is that even if the plan developed only slowly and not in a single episode, control must have been exerted to achieve relative uniformity of plot size and position. This may have been dictated by the estate owners without the tenants having any choice in the matter, but they might have welcomed it as being beneficial because it facilitated communal activities and agreements. A current debate about rural settlement plans takes the identification of regular croft sizes a stage further by arguing for the use of a grid for planning developments; Wharram is not used in this argument, at Raunds it is suggested that an original grid may have been replaced by a much larger one, but at Mawgan Porth it looks much more credible.[22]

Wharram shows some of the problems in finding patterns in the creation or development of rural settlement within the welter of different environmental, topographical, commercial, and legal opportunities and constraints. At almost the opposite end of the country, a long-term survey of Shapwick, Somerset, presented a not dissimilar question about the status of a demolished church, forgotten but for the name 'Church Field'. The estate was owned by Glastonbury Abbey, which probably maintained an administrative centre nearby. Excavation showed that pottery became densely distributed within the present village during the tenth and eleventh centuries, strongly suggesting that outlying farms were abandoned and tenants moved into a nucleated site with tofts along a village street at a slight distance from the church.[23]

Allied to uniform tenement shapes and sizes is likely to have been the arrangement of fields, increasingly made up of large blocs of land divided into strips of fairly uniform widths. These facilitated the work of plough-teams of six or eight oxen dragging mould-boards as well as coulters through heavy but productive soils, suppressing weeds and improving drainage. Grouping people together to share beasts and equipment may have been happening as early as the eighth century in some areas but probably became more widespread as the population grew. The demand to plough, harrow, sow, weed, and harvest creates a workforce that is tied to the soil without even the limited flexibility that pastoralists have. The arable regime also suited the growing of wheat rather than barley and oats, reflecting the preference for bread made from wheat flour. Pressures like those did not make 'open fields' universal, as even within zones where they became the norm there were also places where different regimes were more profitable, particularly where sheep could be grazed in quantity. Large flocks could be maintained in areas like the brecklands in Norfolk, the chalk downlands in the south, and the emerging salt-marshes in the Fens and the Somerset Levels.[24]

The Church is likely to have been the most rigorous land manager, as its estate surveys and charters indicate – though that may only be because written texts survive whereas oral agreements do not. Even a single institution may not have had a single concept of what size or shape their farms should take, as decisions would have to take into account local conditions and customs, as they did in later centuries. Unless they lost royal support, churches could expect to hold their land in perpetuity, whereas charters show large royal and aristocratic estates being broken up into smaller units; sometimes this may have led to new farms and settlements being created, but often the farms would have been existing units of a 'polyfocal' estate. Nevertheless, the Church had interests that differed from those of the kings and other large landholders; major churches were at fixed locations, and their priests and servants had to be fed at them as they could not rely on itinerancy as practised by kings.[25]

*

At the start of the tenth century, royal patronage led to a 'New Minster' and a nunnery at Winchester. The late ninth-century church at Gloucester was extended, with an east crypt probably intended to be the mausoleum of Aethelred and Aethelflaed (Illus. 6.6); the relics of St Oswald were transferred, demonstrating West Saxon domination over Lincolnshire, where they had formerly rested. When he had gained control in the north, King Athelstan went to pay his respects to the shrine of St Cuthbert, but he and his successors left the relics there undisturbed. The presentation of gifts is shown in the earliest manuscript painting of

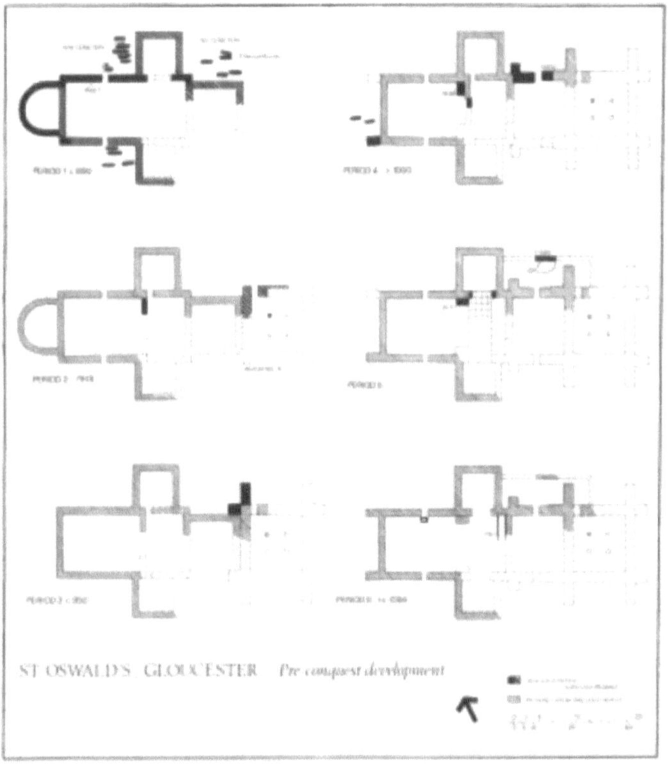

Illustration 6.6 St Oswald's, Gloucester. In the first, late ninth-century phase, a church with side porticuses and a western apse was built and extended in the early tenth with a crypt comparable to that at Repton (Illus. 4.3), and in the same way that that church was for Mercian kings, so St Oswald's may have been intended as the burial-place of Aethelflaed and her husband, rulers of west Mercia. The model shows the church as it might have appeared in the second phase; some of the wall still stands. St Oswald's body was brought to the new church from Bardney in Lincolnshire; he was the seventh-century king of Northumbria who had been praised by Bede for his success in fighting for christianity, but his bones had been taken into Lindsey (Lincolnshire), reputedly by a queen, and symbolized Mercia's domination. Other such translations to enhance one minster at the expense of another are known (Heighway and Bryant 1999; Bintley 2015).

an anglo-saxon king; one donation was the vestments taken to the shrine after the death of Bishop Frithestan of Winchester in 932, embroidered with silk and gold thread for him by Aelfflaed, possibly a wife of King Edward the Elder, and possibly commissioned from the new nunnery.[26]

The existing cathedrals, minsters, and the very few surviving monasteries like St Augustine's at Canterbury had staffs of unknown size, who had to be fed, educated, and housed – how much new building was involved is uncertain. But in the second half of the tenth century, the 'Reform' movement saw the property-holding secular clergy of some cathedral chapters turned into monks who owned nothing of their own, and in the south a few abbeys were 'Reformed', and some new nunneries were established. This led to new buildings, high-quality sculptures, and a proliferation of manuscripts, some decorated and very expensive to produce. Most of the 'Reform' churches were removed or reconstructed almost beyond recognition in subsequent centuries, but painstaking excavation and analysis allow some to be visualized, not as vast, open, Romanesque interiors but as complexities of chapels (porticuses), crypts, shrines, and towers, exemplified by the Old Minster at Winchester. Upper storeys allowed two choirs to sing responsions on either side or at either end of the church; the west end might have a tower with windows and even balconies allowing a priest to view and take part in services in the nave.[27]

The other major ecclesiastical development was occurring at the other end of the Church hierarchy. Although much of the evidence is later, the tenth century was beginning to see the proliferation of local churches, often close to manor-houses and as likely to serve as their private chapels as to have a public function: Raunds, Northamptonshire, has provided an example, and the subsequent closure of the churchyard there certainly suggests an owner's control. That provides another of the Wharram Percy conundrums; why did neither of the owners who at some stage built manor-houses there not provide a church or chapel with a graveyard for their households? If an independent minster was already there, it might have resisted such infringement on its rights – and income from burial fees.[28]

Landholders may have wanted their own churches or chapels because of a growing feeling of confidence in their position, and also because estates were becoming more important as sources of wealth and expressions of status than were royal gifts of treasure. They could express themselves through their residences, with new 'angle-sided' rather than rectangular halls, grouped with other chambers into long ranges in locally prominent but not isolated positions, such as on low ridges. Although of timber not stone, they were not necessarily drab: they may have been painted and have had decorative roof finials, but above all they would have stood out. Single-span halls like Cheddar's began to be replaced or augmented by wider buildings using internal aisles: the remains of aisle-posts and arches dated by dendrochronology to the second half of the tenth century reused in London's embankments show that halls could have been up to 11 metres high. The social status that these locations and structures imply is echoed in the bone evidence from their excavations; hunting-dogs show their owners' right to pursue game across their land, regardless of the effect on their tenantry's farming, and deer bones indicate venison. Wild birds were caught by falcons and hawks.[29]

Prosperity, at least for some, was promoted by a reliable silver currency enabling exchanges to be made in a more precise way than by barter, and between people who were strangers to each other. A development of the 970s was that all coins were struck with a mint name, as well as the king's and the moneyer's. The designs were changed frequently, though not necessarily after a fixed term of years as used to be thought. The opportunities of cheating the royal administration were even further reduced therefore, as any questionable coin could be traced back to where it was issued, as well as revealing who was responsible either for producing one that was seriously underweight or contained less than 90% silver. Coins become a little more commonly found on excavations, accidental losses reflecting their more frequent use. Before the 970s, a few round half-pennies were minted, but most small-change units were pennies cut in half, or even quarters, 'four-things' being farthings. Because of the names, the relative volume produced by each mint can be assessed, and distribution can be plotted; many coins stayed in the region close to where they were issued, but none was excluded from other parts of the kingdom – hence the comparison that can be made between Stamford's coins and its pots. At the time, Stamford had the status of a shire town; north of the Thames, most shires had a single mint, but in the south there were a larger number of smaller ones, a regional difference perhaps reflecting where the Wessex kings had estates as well as political control. Coins could be minted in increasing numbers because new silver mines were found on the continent in the Harz mountains, and England's exports brought in enough of the metal to sustain the coinage. Another imported metal, copper, also came from the Harz area. Small amounts of gold were imported either from southern France, or from Spain, as well as from the Arab world though the Baltic; a small hoard of English coins in the Pass of Roncesvalles indicates trade through the Alps.[30]

Doubts about the extent to which towns in the south of England matched the development of those in the north in the earlier part of the tenth century do not apply to its end. Not only is that shown by the output of the mints, but also by increasing quantities of pottery evidence and of occupation. A few demonstrate expansion more graphically: the earlier settlement area within Worcester was probably remodelled, and it expanded beyond its walls, having a *suthan byrig*, now Sidbury, by 963, where excavation showed an extensive use of the area. It is even possible that a new town, Bristol, had appeared before the end of the tenth century; if so, it was the harbinger of many in the next centuries.[31]

The tenth century did not end well for England, however; viking raiders returned, were not repelled, came in increasing numbers, and developed political ambitions. The sources indicate that they targeted the '*burhs*' in the first instance, presumably to break down resistance. A response may have been to strengthen existing fortifications; recent work at Oxford has shown that the bank there was heightened, and the dating fits with the second period of viking raids. The outside face of that rampart was given a stone revetment, but whether that was part of the original defence or a later replacement of a timber or turf revetment was not conclusively established. Stone walls have been seen at other burhs but with no better dating evidence. They could have been built very soon after the banks were thrown up, even in the later years of the ninth century, or a century later in King Ethelred's reign, ordered by the king and his officials in response to the renewed raids, but might have been done piece-meal by towns which saw the use of stone as giving a more prestigious appearance. Even the lines of some late Saxon defences are not certain; a recent excavation in Bedford found a wide ditch some distance to the south of what had been thought to be the defensive line.[32]

The effects of the raids are witnessed by the enormous hoards of silver found in Scandinavia which include large numbers of English coins, along with bullion and other currencies, an indication of the very heavy impositions levied by King Ethelred to raise 'Danegeld'. From the 970s onwards, the number of hoards in England increases; one or two have a few ornaments like brooches and rings that may have been valued for their weight rather than their decoration, but not ingots, so the 'bullion economy' had largely come to an end. The disruption was not as severe as in the ninth century, however; villages, towns, and churches do not seem to have been abandoned or forced to relocate, so the underlying system that had evolved survived despite the increasing inability of the administration to offer protection.[33]

Notes

1 Naismith 2017, 290–301. Northampton excavations produced enough 'memorial' coins to justify claims of a mint there: for example Williams, J. H. 1979, 244; pottery was also made in or very near the town.

2 See Gannon 2003, 96–7 on ravens and 105–6 on archers featuring on earlier coins. St Peter coinage: Gooch 2014; Woods 2016 for debate.

3 See Blackburn 2011, 593–5 for the York and other dies, 2004 for a general survey of York's coins; also see Pirie 1986a. Details about moneyers' payments are given in later documents such as Domesday Book. Eleventh-century dies have been found in London, a die-cutting centre: Archibald *et al.* 1995.

4 Cuerdale: Graham-Campbell (ed.) 1992. Rings: Kershaw 2017; 2018. Stray finds are of course very difficult to date, so the length of time that bullion circulated alongside coins is hard to estimate. (I note wryly that researchers now have portable XRF machines and electronic scales, which puts exercises like Kershaw's on a very different footing from my own early effort: Hinton 1978, 140–1.) Vale of York (also known as 'Harrogate'): Williams, G. 2013; Ager 2020 (the cups could have been diplomatic gifts to the West Saxon kings, acquired by vikings in much the same way as was the Codex Aureus, see Ch. 5). Bedale: on-line images. 'Leeds District': Marzinzik 2014. A coinless hoard found in Galloway in 2014 had what was thought also to be a Carolingian pot, but conservation has shown it to be from (modern) Iran or further east: *Current Archaeology* 378 (Sept. 2021), 16–17; other items include anglo-saxon silver brooches: National Museum of Scotland on-line.

5 Sculpture summary: Carver 2019, 544–58 (and see Ch. 5 for the Middleton cross and others). The hog-backs are particularly difficult to date, but their numbers suggest a fairly long currency. Chape: PAS SWYOR-97EOE5 (I owe this reference to a student essay). Sculptures are described in detail in the Corpus of Anglo-Saxon Sculpture volumes.

6 For a very clear explanation by H. Geake of the rather bewildering range of different types of early medieval brooches generally, undertaken for the use of Finds Liaison Officers of the Portable Antiquities Scheme, see www.finds.org.uk (accessed April 2020), using a University of Reading Ph. D. thesis by R. Weetch submitted in 2013 for

the 'Anglo-Scandinavian' ones; the identity issue proposed by Kershaw 2013, 246–9, was questioned – q.v. 134–43 for manufacture. Geake rightly challenged an earlier assumption that I made about markets, though they may have been one method of distribution. Another aspect of Scandinavian settlement involves reconsideration of place-names; that those ending in *-by* were larger than those ending in *-thorp* and that the latter showed newcomers fitting themselves into English niches has to be reconsidered by a demonstration that *-thorps* were particularly associated with arable farming and perhaps the spread of open fields, planned and established by estate-holders: Cullen *et al.* 2012, esp. 136–53.

7 Plumpton: Thomas 2013; discussion of the coins by M. M. Archibald on pp. 428–34. Swords: Wilson 1965; Evison 1967. Yarm helmet: Caple 2020, 42–5, 53–60, and metallurgical analysis by G. McDonnell. Whether bows and arrows were much used by English warriors remains debatable: only one is shown in the Bayeux Tapestry (see Ch. 7).

8 Summaries: McCarthy and Brooks 1989a; Blinkhorn 2013. Stamford: Kilmurry 1980. Lincoln: Jones *et al.* 2003, 276–82. Norwich: Ayers 2011, 84. Newark-on-Trent: Perry 2019. Stafford: Carver 2010, 76–93; Dodd 2014 – I accept Carver's tenth-century dating, not least because of the coin-dated pot at Chester, but not his idea of Roman-derived inspiration and find Perry 2016 more in line with ninth-and tenth-century distribution probabilities than other constructs. The kilns producing a pottery called 'York ware' have not been found: Mainman and Rogers 2004, 459–60.

9 Distribution map of Stamford ware: Kilmurry 1980; Stamford coins distribution from Cambridge EMC, accessed April 2020 (this is slightly at variance with the distribution of coins minted in East Anglia, which Fairbairn 2019 showed to be more likely to stay within their local hinterland than for example London's). Discovery of a kiln in Pontefract, Yorkshire, making pottery similar to Stamford ware makes the northern distribution more uncertain: Cumberpatch and Roberts 2013, and there is also a risk of confusion with Northampton products, though those were cruder: Blinkhorn 2013; Perry 2019 for distributions. Oxford: Mellor 1997, 23–4; Hassall *et al.* 1989, 205 and 208.

10 London pot sources: Vince 1985, 30–4. Gloucester; Heighway *et al.* 1979, 169 and 171–9. Winchester ware: contribution by K. Barclay and J. Allan to Gilchrist and Green 2015, 254–6. Log-boats were used for burials at Snape, Suffolk, in the late sixth/seventh centuries; tenth-/eleventh-century examples, dated by dendrochronology, include one from the River Lea near London: Marsden (ed.) 1989; Thier 2011, 55–8 – punts may also have been used, especially for ferries, but none has been found. Salt distribution: Hooke 2007; the River Salwarp was later recorded as being navigable down to the River Severn, so may also have been used: Woodiwiss (ed.) 1992, 48. Place-names: Cole 2007.

11 Graveney: Fenwick (ed.) 1978. London: Goodburn 2015a; Marsden 1994 remains useful, despite more recent finds.

12 Waterfront development: Ayre and Wroe-Brown 2015a, 134–44 and 184–6. Zeigler 2019 for very interesting contrasts between the *wic* and the new London.

13 Chester coins: Naismith 2017, 186 and 192; walls: Creighton and Higham 2005, 269; sculptures: Everson and Stocker 2017; cellared buildings: Mason 1985 (and see Blair 2018, 339–41 for further discussion). Meols: Griffiths *et al.* 2007, 61–77, 364–9, and 402–6. Meols does not fit neatly with any model of urban trajectory and is usually left undiscussed in consequence.

14 Coppergate: Hall, R. A. 2014, 605, 611–12, and 711: the 955–60 dating is a revision of the previous *c.* 975 and creates the Eric Bloodaxe effect possibility; interpretations of the cellar structures: contribution by S. J. Allen, 794–6. See Blair 2018, 339–41 for the usage of below-ground structures and other examples.

15 Wood: Morris, C. A. 2000. Urban conditions: Hall, A. and Kenward 2004. Crafts: Mainman and Rogers 2004; itinerants are discussed by Ashby 2013, but their use of workshops is clear: Riddler and Trzaska-Nartowski 2011. Butchery: O'Connor 2004.

Burial: Hall, R. A. 2014, 682–3. Textiles: Walton 1989; sock, 341–5; silks, 360–82, with contribution on the reliquary by D. Tweddle (see also Ch. 7 for textile production).

16 Lincoln Flaxengate: Perring 1981. York: Phillips 1985 for excavations finding no trace of the late Saxon minster in York, 44–5 for sculptures and graves; Coppergate street line: Hall, R. A. 2014, 709; diagonal roads: Tweddle *et al.* 1999, 153–4.

17 Lincoln: Jones *et al.* 2003, 166–70; Stocker 2013; metalworking: ten Harkel 2013; 2018; silks: Walton 1989, 374–5. Norwich: Ayers 2011, 81.

18 Lincoln animals: O'Connor 1982, 47–8 for the hinterland calculation; also 2011, 370–1.

19 London: Horsman *et al.* 1988; Steadman *et al.* 1992; Schofield 1995, 27–9. Winchester: Ottaway 2017, 215–19 and 232–7 – the documentary evidence of ownership is later so may not have applied in the early stages of development (*ceap* means 'market'; it occurs in London as modern Cheapside). 'New' Southampton: Holdsworth 1984, 338–40. Exeter: Allan *et al.* 1984, 400–5, with little increase in tenth-century evidence subsequently; its streets, which show no overlap with the Roman ones despite using the same gateways, may be of the eleventh century: J. Allan in Rippon and Holbrook (eds) 2021, 221, 225, and 231.

20 Fens and marshes: Rippon 2017 (a summary of his many valuable surveys). Mawgan Porth: Bruce-Mitford 1997, 85; it is the only site mentioned in the summaries published in Christie and Stamper (eds) 2012 to which such a precise date was attributed. The houses have been called 'long-houses' because one end may have been for humans, and the other for animals, but they do not look robust enough to have housed large animals, as suggested by the reconstruction drawing on the cover (see further Ch. 9 for 'long-houses').

21 Wright, D. W. 2015 for continuity of locations; Richards and Haldenby 2018 for disruption in Yorkshire; Wharram strap-fittings: Goodall, I. H. and Paterson 2000, 126–31; Riddler and Trzaska-Nartowski 2011 for those and other artefacts; settlement: Wrathmell 2012a.

22 Wharram: Wrathmell 2012a – his words on pp. 204 and 208 are crucial; the alternative view is put by Everson and Stocker 2012a, 208–12. I have tried to summarize a very complex argument fairly, but the location of the church suggests that the site was anyway not typical; although quite close to one of the two manor-house sites, it was not attached to it, being at the bottom of a considerable slope down from the houses, and it is not clear when either manor-house was established. Blair 2018, 317–37 for the possibility of planning and a grid system applying to farmhouses and yards, augmented by Blair *et al.* 2019.

23 Shapwick: Gerrard and Aston 2007, 29–30 and 974–9.

24 Banham and Faith 2014, 44–57 stressed the uncertainty that hangs over assumptions about population growth and urban demand and gave a clear explanation of the mouldboard plough; see also Ch. 4. They explored the different regions and regimes in chapters 6–11. See Hall 2014 for useful debate and also Jupiter 2020, 70 for reasons for their introduction and stressing that they would not have lasted for so many centuries if they had not been perceived as being practicable and desirable. See Banham 2010 for increasing demand for wheat. Marshes and fens: Rippon 2017.

25 See Blair 2018, 329–37 for discussion of charter and place-name evidence.

26 Winchester: Ottaway 2017, 220–7. Gloucester: Heighway and Bryant 1999. Aethelstan portrait: Breay and Story (eds) 2018, no. 68. Frithestan: Coatsworth 2001; Weikert 2018, 62.

27 'Reform' buildings: Fernie 1983, 93–111; Winchester Old Minster reconstruction by S. Hayfield in Biddle 2018, 55, based on the work of M. Biddle and B. Kjølbye-Biddle. West towers, for example Deerhurst and Brixworth. Manuscripts and other works of art: Webster, L. 2012, 175–207; Breay and Story (eds) 2018, nos. 85–153. At the opposite end of the artistic scale is the Cerne Abbas chalk figure of a man with a club, which in 2020–1 was reported as falling within the Reform period by Optically Stimulated

Luminescence dating of four quartz samples: Papworth 2021b, 51–3; as one of those, dated 1100–1560, is shown as in a layer cut by the trench for the figure, further research is needed before the interpretation can be accepted.

28 Raunds: Boddington 1996; see Ch. 7 for further discussion. Wharram's church had become 'proprietorial' by the later Middle Ages, as a manorial younger son became its priest.

29 Gardiner 2000, 169–78; 2013, 51–9 and 64–70; Blair 2018, 355–64 (but see the previous chapter for the Cheddar dating issue). London: Goodburn 2015b. Bones: Serjeantson 2006, 138. Bird bones in early Saxon graves indicate some falconry then, increasing in the mid period: Wallis, R. J. 2017.

30 Naismith 2017, 221, 227–8, 236, and 246–52. Molyneaux 2015, 113 argued that administrative changes in the mid tenth century aimed to make 'a neat or uniform administrative system' based on shires, hundreds, and meeting-places in which minting played a role. See Piercy 2019, 147 for moneyers' operation in family groups, maintaining 'hereditary control' and 11–12 for Edgar's reform. Harz copper was identified by antimony at Faccombe Netherton, Hampshire: contribution by L. Webster *et al.* to Fairbrother 1990, 244–72. Trade with Spain: Nightingale 1985; steel may also have begun to be imported.

31 Worcester: Carver 1980; Baker, N. and Holt 2004, 187; Haslam 2017, 9–11. Bristol: Leech 1997, 23–4; Baker, N. *et al.* 2018, 81 – the evidence amounts to no more than a couple of ditches and their fills.

32 Oxford: Munby *et al.* 2019, 26 and 56–7; Dodd (ed.) 2003, 50–1; Haslam 2011, 211–14. Bedford: Edgeworth 2004. See Astill 2009 for an overall assessment. Although not certainly part of the urban circuit, the parapet still visible within a stretch of wall at Exeter gives an idea of a late Saxon wall's appearance: Rippon and Holbrook (eds) 2021, 229.

33 For hoards, see Thompson 1956, now augmented by the Cambridge EMC check-list and Andrews, M. 2019.

7 The Eleventh Century

Conquests and their Consequences

The eleventh century began with worsening viking raids, leading to the accession of a Dane, Cnut, to the English throne in 1016, followed exactly 50 years later by that of a Norman, William. The extent to which the raids and wars affected the social and economic structure of England may be exaggerated by chronicle accounts of the political upheavals, although war and its consequences, whether by devastation or by enhanced tax and service demands, would have affected everyone. Attempts at defence continued; the old hillfort at South Cadbury, Somerset, was provided with new stone walls and a gateway, and inside it a new building thought to have been intended to become a church was begun but seems to have been abandoned. The hillfort is close to a major route through the south-west, now the A303, so it was well placed for distribution as well as for control, perhaps a further reason for its use as a mint from *c.*1009. In Wiltshire, late Saxon objects including a spur indicate that the prehistoric mound Silbury Hill was used as a look-out post overseeing the principal east-west route that is now the A4. South Cadbury was not the only new mint opened at a hillfort: Sarum, Wiltshire, was also defensible and also close to major routeways (Illus. 2.6). Unlike South Cadbury, it developed into a town. Cissbury, a hillfort in Sussex, was probably another 'emergency mint', but none was set up elsewhere.[1]

The sufferings of the English in the early years of the eleventh century probably explain an exceptional issue of silver pennies in Ethelred's reign that did not show the usual bust of a king on the obverse and some version of a cross on the reverse but had the Lamb of God on one side and on the other what is either a dove to represent the Holy Spirit or an eagle to reference forgiveness of sins – as if a prayer for divine intervention. The message was understood well enough for some of the coins to be adapted into brooches, but the design was soon abandoned for more traditional ones. The first coinage issued by Ethelred's Danish successor Cnut retained the king's head and cross motifs, perhaps deliberately to show that his rule was legitimate although it had been achieved by conquest.[2]

The viking wars were brutal, as has probably been exemplified by the recent discovery near Weymouth, Dorset, of a pit filled with sprawled corpses, many piled one on top of another, with some of the fifty-one skulls separated from their bodies and grouped together. Almost all were definitely males aged over 16 years, and none was identifiable as female – two were too young to be sexed. Many had

DOI: 10.4324/9781003007432-8

wounds, including sword cuts, and hand wounds suggested that they had tried desperately to defend themselves but were unarmed. Isotope analyses revealed that they had not been born and brought up in England but had come from various northern lands; radiocarbon dating gave a probable range of A.D. 975–1020, so the most likely explanation is that they were members of an unrecorded viking raiding-party, perhaps the crew of a single ship, who had been captured, taken up to a high point on the Dorset Ridgeway, and savagely killed.[3]

Another mass burial, on the outskirts of Oxford, consisted of at least thirty-two young men and two juveniles too young for their sex to be determined. Many had recent blade and other injuries, inflicted more often from behind than from in front, as though the victims were trying to escape their attackers (Illus. 7.1). The

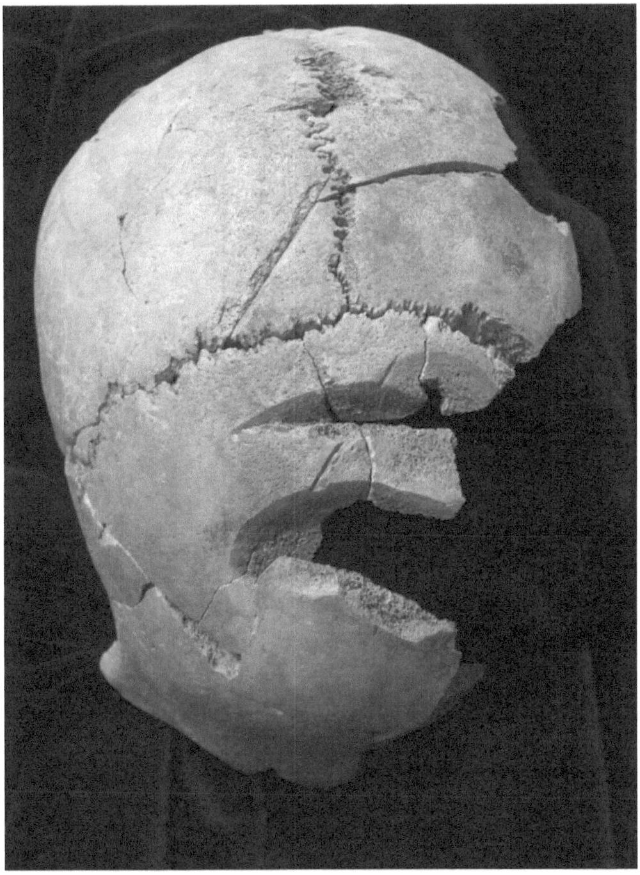

Illustration 7.1 The skull of a male found in a mass burial outside Oxford shows the brutality with which the dead had been slaughtered. The top of the skull has two straight incisions (the zig-zag lines are natural) and much deeper blows on the back of the head. These are blade injuries, inflicted with swords, axes, or seaxes; he had probably also been hit by projectiles – arrows, spears, or stones (Wallis, S. 2014; analysis by C. Falys, pp. 43 and 121–4).

bodies had not been beheaded but had been thrown into the partly filled-in ditch of a henge, one of several prehistoric earthworks quite close to the north wall of the town which may have been visible and thought of as liminal places of the ancient dead. Documents recount that in 1002 King Ethelred ordered a massacre of Danes living in England, and a charter records that some in Oxford took shelter in a church which was then burnt down; some of the bones in the ditch were charred. Most were taller by a couple of inches than average; but would there have been such a large and distinctive group of Danish people with homes in the central Midlands, and if they were living in Oxford, would there not have been women and children slaughtered with them? Radiocarbon dating did not confirm the early eleventh-century date that the documents would suggest as the explanation for the slaughter, so an element of doubt remains about the interpretation; isotopes did not reveal their origin, except that one had come from Scandinavia or Denmark. A very different burial was reported in the late nineteenth century on the east side of Oxford near the crossing of the River Cherwell, with stirrups (Illus. 7.2), a

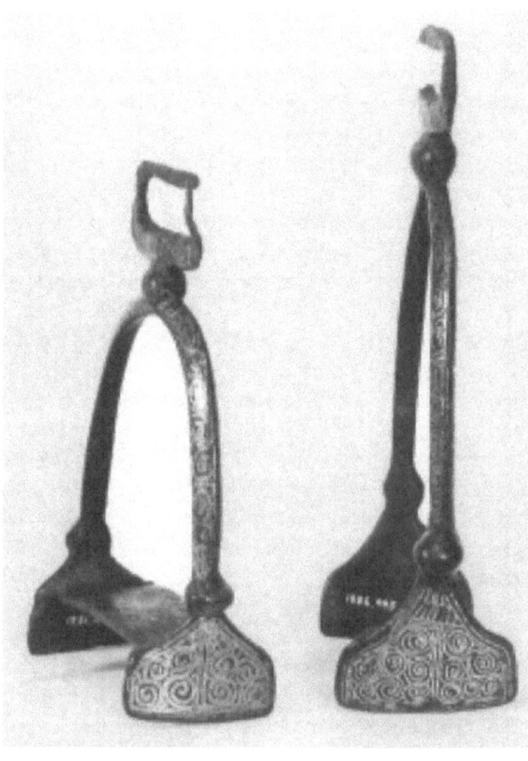

Illustration 7.2 Two stirrups, both decorated with overlaid brass wire. Although not a matching pair, they were found together on the bank of the River Cherwell in Oxford and may have been buried with a leader of the viking raid on the town in 1009. Use of stirrups may have increased because of viking raids, but they became widely used during the late Saxon period.

spur, and horse bones. That looks more like the formal burial of a viking leader, probably a member of a garrison under Cnut with no connection to the massacre, though just possibly part of an avenging army.[4]

The two massacres took place unconstrained by social norms, and the bodies were condemned to unconsecrated ground. Other discoveries of human body parts not in churchyards include two heads in a pottery kiln at Stafford which suggest people who were disposed of illicitly, unlike the seemingly public burials of earlier date on the London foreshore or the 'almost furtive' disposal of the adult woman in York's Coppergate. Certainly public were the deaths and burials of many groups of people in isolated but visible locations, often near roads and boundaries. There may be proximity to barrows because those too were thought of as housing the unremembered dead – and probably not to give extra height to the gibbets from which the people, mostly male but with some females, were hanged, often with their wrists and ankles bound, some in chains. Although some of these burials may date to the ninth century, the majority seem to be of the eleventh; one was found with a little hoard of Edward the Confessor pennies, presumably which the man had managed to hide from his executioners, and other coins recovered from these sites are all of the late tenth or the eleventh century. The bodies were not buried in neat rows with their heads to the west; many were simply thrown into pits.[5]

Most of the execution sites are in the south of England, suggesting a difference between legal systems despite the unification indicated by mints and coin distribution and the intention of law-codes. It may only be a coincidence that the pre-1066 seal matrixes that have been found, made of copper alloy or ivory, all come from the south of England, as though it was in that area that justice was more dependent upon a formal, impersonal system; family control of feuds may have continued to predominate elsewhere. An ivory matrix found in Wallingford shows a bearded, cloaked figure with a sword and *Sigillum Godwini ministri* inscribed in reverse letters; Godwin was too common a name for identification of a specific person, but the image and the title show his status, as *minister* can be translated as 'thegn'. Its handle has a finely detailed carving of God the Father and God the Son enthroned, with their feet on a prostrate, seemingly naked figure, not only illustrating a verse in Psalm 109, but also suggesting that they were giving judgement in heaven, as Godwin may have been on earth. The other side of the matrix shows a robed figure with a book in one hand and the other hand raised as though in blessing, a pose often shown in illustrations of Christ or one of the apostles, but there is no nimbus, so the figure is secular. The inscription translates as 'The seal of Godgytha a nun (*monache*) given to God'. Possibly Godwin's widow, Godgytha needed to conduct business, even though living in religious seclusion as is known to have been a late anglo-saxon practice for the high-born.[6]

Whoever ruled, Danegeld still had to be paid, so pennies continued to be needed for tax, but perhaps even more for rent, which took people into markets to sell produce in return for cash. By this time, therefore, towns had become an essential element in most people's lives and were indispensable to rural economies; they were not just serving the interests of long-distance traders and high-level purchasers. A hoard of over 5,200 silver pennies of Ethelred and Cnut found in 2014 at

Lenborough, Buckinghamshire, gives an idea of the quantities of coins available and also the degree to which whoever owned the hoard was operating within a 'monetized economy', as no gold, precious metal objects, hack-silver, or ingots were included in it. It contained only a single cut half-penny, confirming how those were generally excluded from stores of wealth despite their use in the marketplace. The spread of coinage into everyday business may have been reduced in the 1040s and later, as the mines in the Harz mountains ran out, affecting the supply of silver, but this is not easily recognized in England; there are fewer hoards until the 1060s, but that may reflect slightly more peaceful conditions.[7]

A few of the eleventh-century hoards contain twisted rings, though not bullion, and only two have brooches – one in London is probably a continental import, the other from Cambridgeshire is a very large silver one with crudely incised Ringerike-style decoration, more interesting for the inscription on the back showing its one-time ownership by a woman called Aedwen, cursing anyone who tried to steal it, suggestive of female vulnerability to loss of property. Renewed Danish influence at a high social level, resulting from Cnut's donations of estates to his followers, probably accounts for the use of styles like Ringerike derived from or shared with Scandinavia and found as much in the south of England as in the north. A grave-stone with runes commemorated two people with Scandinavian names at St Paul's in London, and part of a sculptured frieze in Winchester illustrates a Scandinavian saga and suggests strong aristocratic pride in northern ancestry. Documents that refer to 'housecarls' show that differences existed; 'fifteen acres where the housecarls stayed' in Wallingford seems to suggest a distinct enclave, which might just possibly account for a deep ditch found within the burh there; if indeed an enclosure, part of it verged on what is now the marketplace and interrupted the street pattern, which in other respects looks much like others (Illus. 5.3).[8]

*

Eleventh-century rural development was probably little affected by the changes in landownership that followed Cnut's conquest. The development of sites like Cottam in the tenth century is likely to have continued, perhaps fostered by a slight warming of the climate which would have impacted on areas where the growing season was short, making them less 'marginal'. Sites that may have started as shielings for shelter during summer grazing of the uplands may have become used all year round, as at Simy Folds in Northumberland; dry-stone wall footings allow survival to be identified more positively than post-hole and turf construction such as may have characterized Dartmoor and other 'marginal' zones. A comparable process was taking place in totally contrasting environments: coastal marshlands, such the Fens of East Anglia or the north Somerset Levels, with sea-banks and drainage channels. Coastal reclamation in Lincolnshire, however, seems to have been a less organized process, resulting from the build-up of sand from salt production. Slightly falling sea-levels may have facilitated this process, but fewer storms causing sudden surges were probably more important.[9]

The north of England may have suffered badly from William I's 'harrying', which could account for restructuring and planned villages, but the archaeological evidence is not precise and may often have resulted from landowners' later decisions, with or without their tenants' agreement. Conditions varied throughout England, and changes to field systems may have been undertaken because peasants perceived the benefits to themselves as well as to their landlords from operating more intensively. Areas where 'dispersed' settlement was the norm may have resulted from shielings becoming permanent, as in the uplands, but in other zones with less potential for increased arable output may have resulted from expansion of earlier but permanent sites, as in parts of Whittlewood. Many excavated sites throughout England have produced pottery attributed to the eleventh century, but traces of early buildings have disappeared under later developments. Against the general trend, Cornwall's Mawgan Porth was abandoned, a victim of coastal sand-blow. Its dry-stone houses with dairies or byres and ancillary buildings around 'courtyards' and its very distinctive bar-lug pottery are all unlike anything elsewhere.[10]

When the occupants of Mawgan Porth abandoned their settlement, they also left behind an adjacent cemetery which presumably contained their predecessors. It was not completely excavated, so the high proportion of children's graves in it is probably not significant; more interesting is that they were buried with the same care as the adults in graves lined and in surviving cases covered with thin stone slabs. Those cists were probably not so much a mark of status as a reflection of the lack of locally available wood for coffins. Some of the graves contained white or mottled quartz stones, which have been recognized in Barnstaple and other western cemeteries, perhaps as purity signifiers – the practice probably does not indicate different regional creeds but a different local custom resulting from the availability of appropriate pebbles. Other such variations are probably no more significant; no grave at North Elmham, Norfolk, was provided with a stone cist or a 'pillow' under the head, yet in nearby Norwich flint 'pillows' occurred frequently, especially for children. Traces of organics at some sites indicate that real pillows might have been provided, and heads were often supported on either side by stone uprights. Protection for the head implies belief in its particularly important place as the recipient of the senses – especially Sight – and provision for the body may reflect ideas about resurrection as a physical act. Another widely practised but occasional rite was charcoal burial, the corpse being placed on, or even surrounded by, ashes, which may have symbolized penitence.[11]

If there were a chapel or church associated with the Mawgan Porth cemetery, it was not discovered, but would, by the eleventh century, be expected; in Midland England, the sequence at Raunds Furnells provides an example of a church and graveyard that started in the late Saxon period, and a new settlement site developing as the large estate that included Higham Ferrers was broken up into smaller units; charters show that this often happened. In many cases, this process was concomitant with the subdivision of the large *parochiae* that were served by priests based at a minster; as this potentially meant loss of income from burial and baptism fees, tithes, and other payments, the minsters usually negotiated an arrangement, but it was not politic to attempt to resist a powerful lord altogether if he wanted his own church and priest. The minster might manage to retain some of its rights, so that the lord's building was in effect a chapel. The distinction is not always clear, but larger buildings not known to have been monasteries are likely to have been served by colleges of priests, even if supporting documentation is slight; nineteenth-century evidence of large parishes may provide a clue. Often, as at Raunds, the manor-house was adjacent to the new church.[12]

Outside the church at Raunds was a male burial under an elaborately carved stone cover, perhaps the grave of the founder, though he might have demanded a location closer to the church and on its west-east axis, so the burial may be that of one of his kin. A few of the other Raunds graves had carved stones; one included broken pieces of a cross-shaft, which might originally have marked the 'founder's grave'. There were also a few stone coffins. Raunds is on limestone, so readily available material meant that many of the graves could be provided with rubble linings. Family plots in rows have been suggested, and demand for space was not yet so great that most new graves had to disturb others, before burial was discontinued, seemingly and with a few exceptions when a larger church was built during the twelfth century. Because of that, the site has provided the best evidence available about a late Saxon rural population. Mortality was high in infancy and childhood, but anyone getting beyond the age of seventeen had a decent chance of reaching thrity-five, despite tuberculosis, by which time they would probably already have begun to feel arthritic and to have fractured some bone or other in a fall, or perhaps in a brawl, but only two seemed to have been killed by weapons. Those two were not separated from the other graves as 'evil'; nor were two people whose leprosy may already have been visible, though one was at the end of a row. Also at the end of a row was a man crippled by tuberculosis or poliomyelitis, who was the only one with a stone deliberately placed in his mouth. A development during the use of the graveyard was the burial of many infants next to the walls of the church, where the water from the eaves would fall on them to bless them by the holiness of something that had been in contact with the sacred building.[13]

The sequence of building at Raunds Furnells church was probably typical of many. It started as a small rectangle and was extended with a chancel in perhaps the eleventh century; it was then rebuilt completely with a larger nave and chancel, with a tower added at the west end not long before the complex was abandoned, presumably – and this was not typical – because the owner no longer wanted it. Its single-cell origin would have placed priest and people in close proximity; the later addition of a small chancel would have enhanced the sense that the man of God was set slightly apart. The excavation did not show where the main altar was placed, but elsewhere in two-cell churches it was at the east end of the nave, not backed against the chancel wall. Parish churches, but not chapels, provided baptism, and fonts therefore became a distinctive feature. Raunds did not provide evidence of a font but had one most unusual feature – a pot previously used for melting wax had been buried, despite being broken, in the middle of the nave floor; it may have been part of a foundation ceremony, becoming used as a soak-away for water made sacred from washing communion vessels. Presumably it was not walked on by the congregation, so it indicates that even fewer people were accommodated within the nave than its small size anyway indicates; the need for later expansion here and at most other churches is understandable.[14]

Because of the readily available limestone, the Raunds Furnells church was not originally built of timber, unlike most, but the sole survivor is the stave-constructed nave at Greensted, Essex, dated by dendrochronology to between 1063 and before 1100. Enough examples of long-and-short masonry corners, double-splay windows, and other early features survive elsewhere to show that much investment was going into ecclesiastical provision. Dating is often difficult: the chancel-arch in the church by the gate at Wareham, for instance, has features comparable to those in some larger churches generally accepted as anglo-saxon but might nevertheless be quite late in the eleventh century. Most churches did not have towers, though timber superstructures for bells may have been fitted on to the roofs of more naves than can be known. Pits in which copper-alloy bells had been cast have been found at some churches, but most may have had much less expensive but less sonorous brazed iron bells.[15]

The only still-standing ecclesiastical building with documentary evidence for its probable foundation is at Bradford-on-Avon, Wiltshire; a charter ascribing the donation of the estate there by King Ethelred to the nunnery of Shaftesbury Abbey in 1001, specifically to be a refuge for the relics of Edward the Martyr, accounts for the surviving high-walled, narrow, and multi-chambered chapel with its prominent stonework. Only one church, Sherborne, Dorset, has standing masonry from an anglo-saxon cathedral, with the possible exception of North Elmham, Norfolk; nor do any of the major monastery buildings survive above ground. A few have been excavated and show what might have been achieved: the octagonal two-storey 'rotunda' at St Augustine's, Canterbury, is an example. Gold and silver crosses and reliquaries, set with delicate ivories, and silk and gold-embroidered vestments, embellished their interiors, though few survive even in part. Many of these treasures were gifts, from kings to shrines and from families to their own foundations.[16]

*

Building churches was costly. The Lenborough and other big hoards show the wealth that some people owned, but the pennies found at some of the execution sites indicate their accessibility even to those whose crimes may have put them at the bottom of society. Less dramatic is the little group of ten or more pennies excavated at a disused kiln site in Norwich, a hoard that could be much more representative of what ordinary people owned than the eye-catching thousands in bigger hoards. An estimate made many years ago on the basis of Domesday Book suggested an average of 4d to 6d per head of a population of about 2 million; obviously many owned more than that, and some may have owned less, but allowing for a household to have averaged 4.5 people of all ages becomes some 20d and still looks credible. Another measure of coins' availability is the number that were turned into brooches, usually gilded and showing the cross side to the public gaze. The great majority of them are coins of Edward the Confessor and

William. Small enamel brooches are also quite widespread, and there are many cheaply made copper-alloy, tin, and lead-alloy brooches; a group of brooches, beads, and other pewter items found in Cheapside, London, were probably from a maker's workshop.[17]

Urban markets developed partly because landholders increasingly required some rent to be paid in cash, so that rural people had to sell produce in order to acquire pennies. The small open spaces next to churches, on street corners, and near entrance points presumably allowed them to bring in carts from which to sell or to unload into small wooden booths. The other open spaces were in wide 'high streets' rather than squares or triangles, which seem generally to be developments from the end of the century and later. Some stalls would have been for butchers, evidenced by the bone record: studies at Exeter, Lincoln, and other towns show growing ability to acquire meat that was generally from fully grown but not elderly animals killed when past their working lives. Butchery methods became more specialized, notably by cleaving the carcase, which involved suspending it on a strong and high post, after the skins had been removed for tanning to meet the demand for leather. Tanning was particularly noxious and was usually kept to urban fringes, low-lying because of the need for water to soak cow and horse hides for up to two years; in Chester, pits were dug where there had previously been buildings. In Winchester, tanning pits have been excavated in the part of the city through which streams could be diverted – and which then passed into the precincts of the nuns' and the other minsters. Tanning pits have also been found in central parts of some towns, despite the smells from them.[18]

Leather was needed primarily for boots, shoes, and knife-sheaths, which only survive in special, usually water-logged, conditions, as do wooden objects such as turned bowls; York's Coppergate means 'cup-makers' street', though rubbish concentrations do not show exclusive use by any one craft or trade there, nor in other towns in which side streets acquired craftworking names. Bone, antler, and horn were a by-product of butchery, used for combs, skates, and other items. Crucibles, ingots, and droplets are evidence of copper-alloy working, but recycling probably reduces the number of surviving objects. Stamford had iron-smelting furnaces, but otherwise production in towns was less economic than rural working, as at Burlesombe, Devon, and the blooms were transported to blacksmiths. Smelters' furnaces were a fire risk, and even the noisy smiths' forges were a danger and began to be located in suburbs of larger towns on the main roads where they were well placed to pick up business from shoeing travellers' horses. Quality varied because blacksmiths recycled objects, mixing metals. Even in Gloucester, close to the Forest of Dean, a Roman shield boss was found with a variety of other scrap items in pre-castle levels, but there were also bars, appropriately as the town was recorded in Domesday Book as having to supply annually 'one hundred rods of ductile iron for the nails of the king's ships'. Other groups of iron objects look more like deposited hoards than Gloucester's scatter and may not have been awaiting reforging; they include plough parts, tools, and weapons – one at Nazeing, Essex, included a Roman axe-head that had had a new edge welded on to it – and may represent some unrecorded and unofficial rite.[19]

Another craft that involved a fire-risk was pot-making; kilns in the central parts of Norwich and Stamford were abandoned, though increasing pressure on internal space was probably at least as significant, as potters were probably less able to pay higher rents than metalworkers. Change in demand for more basic pots is hinted at in Lincoln during the eleventh century, with wheel-throwing and updraught kilns no longer used, but production continuing on a large scale for a while. In the south, urban pot-making seems to have been an occasional exception, as at Exeter and Chichester; instead, rural potters who did not use updraught kilns or wheel-throwing may have become specialist but perhaps part-time workers in particular places, like Michelmersh, Hampshire. By the end of the eleventh century, only Stamford seems to have maintained even suburban production; was the advantage of proximity to markets outweighed by the cost of transporting clay and fuel, and by high rents, or were the fire hazard, smoke, and clay-digging deemed too anti-social? Successful towns developed extra-mural suburbs whose inhabitants may have had more tolerance of nuisance, but their rubbish does not indicate that they had lower standards of living than did those inside the walls.[20]

A reliable water supply was not only needed for tanning, but also for fulling and dyeing, the final stages of the production of the highest quality cloths. The scale of textile manufacture is impossible to judge (Illus. 7.3); clay loomweights used on vertical weaving looms are still sometimes found, but changes in bone tools probably indicate an increasing use of vertical looms which used a roller rather than weights at the bottom. Even less direct trace is left by the horizontal loom, which requires more space and is a machine that requires regular use if it is to pay for itself. This changed weaving from an everyday household activity into a full-time, specialized craft that lent itself to concentration in towns and meant that most weavers were male. Spinning remained household work, however, as it could be done intermittently, and whorls remain frequent finds. The vertical loom produced a heavier cloth which could be fulled and teaselled to produce a desirably warm, compressed fabric that could be coloured with bright dyes for the best effect. It had to be made from good-quality wool, which came from English sheep; much was exported, but towns like Stamford and Lincoln could get it from their immediate hinterlands, and their products acquired European recognition. One dye came from imported beetles' eggs, kermes, which when seen in bulk looked like grain, hence the name which became corrupted to 'Lincoln green', although the colour was scarlet red, brighter than the native madder. The cloth merchants needed capital to buy the best wool and dyes, but the profits could be enormous.[21]

The process seen in tenth-century York of the development of long narrow tenements fronting on to a street became the norm in most towns, often, as again like York, with below-ground cellars, usually wood-lined and -roofed, but some perhaps already with stone vaults; those indicate storage needs for merchants trading in bulk, and not for peasant produce. In Winchester as in York, streets and tenements initiated at the end of the ninth and in the tenth centuries continued in occupation; the king and the major local churches held blocs of land within the walls, which they could parcel up for renting out. Metalled street surfaces were maintained, as in most cases were surrounding wall circuits. Crowded conditions

Illustration 7.3 Three different types of loom. The drawing on the top left is based on a vertical loom photographed in traditional use in twentieth-century Norway; the clay weights are of the sort found on many early medieval settlement sites. The second is redrawn from a manuscript and shows ladies at a beam-tensioned vertical loom, which would leave little trace in the archaeological record. Two of the ladies (the painting is twelfth-century but shows costume similar to that in earlier books illustrating the high-born, including nuns) hold cutting shears, the third seems to have a comb in her right hand, and the fourth holds a skein of wool. The lower picture is redrawn from a thirteenth-century manuscript and shows a horizontal-tensioned loom with foot-operated treadles. Longer lengths of cloth could be produced, and male weavers had taken over the craft.

encouraged the spread of infections, including leprosy; smoke from open fires and hearths would have caused sinusitis; and a diet with sufficient vitamins may have been even more difficult to achieve in towns than in the countryside, where a greater variety and quantity of foodstuffs might have been available than in urban markets – although open spaces within urban walls might have been ploughed, as happened in Winchester, they could not have made a town self-sufficient, and although burgesses had their own extra-mural fields, later records show that they were largely for grazing animals and were not suitable for grain production. Tuberculosis was probably more of a rural problem, but even so the countryside must have been healthy enough to provide a surplus population to migrate into towns, as urban populations are rarely self-sustaining; disappearance of sensitive fish species from the rivers in York indicates pollution on a scale that the humans causing it could not have escaped. One sign of conditions is the return of rats to England, which thrive in warm conditions such as urban hearths and jostling people provided; concomitantly, a rise in dog and cat bones has been observed.[22]

Some mitigation of food problems was provided by increased availability of sea-fish, particularly cod and herring, shown by bone evidence in York, London, and Southampton. Herring may even have been an addition to the list of English exports and would certainly have led to increased salt production for inland distribution. Many ports depended as much upon fishing as upon importing and exporting. Fresh fish also remained important. Mills involved dams and sluices, which could be used in particular to catch eels, if rents recorded in Domesday Book are to be believed.[23]

One measure of a late Saxon town's growth and success is the number of small churches in it; they proliferated in London, York, and elsewhere, often as in Winchester without graveyards if an existing minster managed to hold on to its burial rights and their income. Some churches were at gates, sometimes actually part of the gate structure, although only Oxford's St Michael's has survived as direct evidence; Oxford's other extant late Saxon tower on the wall circuit, St George's, may have been alongside another of the gates. They are strikingly different in appearance, the former high and with belfry openings, doors, and windows, the latter much thicker-walled and looking much more like a part of the defences. The church to have survived at Wareham is just inside the defences by the north entrance but had no tower and was not part of a gate structure. Many gate-churches first recorded in the twelfth century may have had eleventh-century origins, as in Bristol, emerging as a new port. Another new port in the eleventh century was Sandwich, Kent, possibly replacing an earlier landing-place further up the Wantsum Channel and perhaps affected by silting.[24]

*

Evidence of basic prosperity does not signal a social system moving towards egalitarianism but may result from a fundamentally stable period of government after Cnut's accession and despite the political machinations of his various successors. Excavations at several sites have shown that aristocratic residences continued to display status, although the 'long ranges' seem to have lost favour, with free-standing double-aisled halls being preferred. Those had smaller floor areas, at least in the open spaces between the internal posts, which could indicate a move away from emphasis on the feasting that cemented loyalty at large communal gatherings, dependence instead becoming much more a factor of land tenure in return for service of various sorts. Halls may have been smaller, but aisled construction gave greater height, so lords' expression of status through their residential complexes was still important; confidence in their social position meant that deep ditches and high banks were not needed, many boundaries being no more than a fence with a gateway.[25]

Declining importance of gift-giving at feasts might help to explain the absence of highly decorated weapons and jewellery: swords decorated with gold and silver plates on pommels and guards almost disappear, though a few have wire twisted round the grips; elaborate finger-rings and large brooches are almost unknown, Aedwen's being one of the very few. Sword blades were no longer pattern-welded but were still prestigious – makers' names were important enough to be beaten into some – but they were more widely accessible. A few at least were still viewed as living; the hilt of a sword from the river at Wareham has an Old English text 'Athel . . . owns me', the owner's name not fully legible, but 'Athel' denotes someone of high standing. A lower guard from Exeter also uses 'me' in an inscription, with its maker's name. The Bayeux Tapestry shows Harold at his coronation being offered a sword by the aristocracy to signify their acceptance of his rule, the first indication of the 'sword of justice' being part of royal regalia.[26]

Men were still expected to fight when called upon, and other services were also demanded. Domesday Book reveals that many shires had large numbers of 'riding-men', whose duties presumably required them to have horses. The proliferation of discoveries of stirrups and their fittings and a slight increase in spurs show that travel on horseback was much more common. People could get from one end of the country to the other in just a few days, all that it took Harold's army to reach Hastings from Yorkshire in 1066. They could also get to market more quickly. Pack-horses could travel faster and over worse surfaces than carts, although carrying less.[27]

Discussion about the late Saxon residences has been given more focus by recent work on free-standing towers, most of which were to be churches later in their history, but perhaps not originally solely religious and to be seen as a symbol of lordship. Earls Barton, Northamptonshire, generally ascribed to the middle of the eleventh century, is famous for the very prominent stonework that adorns it – some of which seems likely to have copied the wooden beams and struts that would presumably have been familiar from timber towers (Illus. 7.4). At the top are rows of narrow openings showing that it was a *belhus*, something that a contemporary text said was appropriate for a thegn to have. The first stage has windows and other features carved with crosses, suggesting that it was a chapel; whether the spaces above that were chambers for the lord himself, or for a chaplain or some other member of the household is not obvious. Door openings at upper levels might have been to allow external access by timber stairs, decluttering interior spaces, but may have provided access to balconies and frames in which the lord or priest

Illustration 7.4 The tower of the church at Earls Barton, Northamptonshire, has many anglo-saxon features – long-and-short corner quoins, round- and triangular-headed openings, 'arcading', pilaster strips, string-courses, strip-work, baluster shafts – only the crenellated parapet is an addition. The air photograph shows a different aspect of the tower – its location on a spur dominating the nucleated village and the remains of an earthwork enclosure on the far side. The tower was probably originally free-standing, not attached to the church; at Portchester (Illus. 1.2), excavation found the foundations of a stone tower of similar date, within a thegn's residence.

could make an appearance to people below. The tower at Barton-on-Humber is also notable for its stripwork and also seems to have been a proprietary church, not a minster. The stone footings excavated at Portchester, Hampshire, also indicate a tower with functions that were ecclesiastical, as there were burials close to it, though so few as to suggest that they may all have been members of the owner's household.[28]

Edward the Confessor is credited with introducing new ideas to England, such as by rebuilding Westminster Abbey in the Romanesque style, with a long nave, round-headed arches, and wide transepts. Some of the senior churchmen in pre-Conquest England had come from the continent and may have influenced other developments such as a coin design used by Edward that was unlike anything before or after, derived from continental coins and showing him as an emperor, with orb and sceptre; it was an image of kingship that Edward showed also in his personal costume display. He used an imperial image on his seal, thought to have been cut by a craftsman from overseas, another sign of the king's wider connections. Neither of his successors in 1066 made major alterations to the coinage, however, Harold's having '*Pax*', 'peace', not a cry for help but an adaptation of one of Edward's first issues; William's first was an adaptation of Edward's last, as though to imply that Harold had had no right to the throne, unlike himself. Later, he showed a more martial side, a bust with helmet and sword.[29]

*

The extent of the disruption caused by William's invasion in 1066 and its aftermath that can be seen in the archaeological record has been a major issue ever since medieval archaeologists stopped focusing solely on great buildings and became interested in all facets of social and economic life. Castles, cathedrals, and abbeys of course remain important, because they enabled the Normans to consolidate their hold on England both physically and symbolically. Although some of Edward the Confessor's continental friends may have begun to build castles of the kind that they were used to at home, they do not seem to have had much influence on English ideas, even though church buildings show some awareness of continental trends. William and his supporters were not going to let English precedents deter them from creating strongholds from which to control their new estates, though in the case of any one motte or ringwork precise dating may not be possible, and mention of a castle in a document does not mean that what exists on or in the ground is that particular structure. To read that a castle was 'built' in a particular year may mean no more than that was when it was started; completion may have taken years and the work been discontinuous, so the end-product may not be that which was envisaged at the start. That is certainly true of palatial towers, notably the 'White Tower' in London, which has some elements planned from the start in 1075–9, such as the four corner turrets, but after a pause in 1079–83 was completed in another 10 years with one more storey than originally intended, and by then under William II not his father, who may have had different ideas. The plan allowed for a projecting semi-circular apse for a chapel, a design followed at Colchester where the castle overlay a Roman temple, but nowhere else. There was no single pattern for the great towers, although some others may have been like Chepstow or London in providing an impressive hall with controlled access by stairs and ante-chambers for subjects coming for audience with their king. Elsewhere, at Exeter, Richmond, and Ludlow, a tower was part of the gatehouse. Chepstow, incorporating Roman tiles within its stonework, may have deliberate echoes of Roman imperialism. White limestone from Caen in Normandy was admired, becoming known as the 'royal stone' because of kings' use of it.[30]

The White Tower occupied one corner of the defences of London, controlling passage upstream of ships on the Thames. The city's importance was demonstrated by its being further overseen by another large enclosure straddling the west wall of the city, effectively two separate castles; a third followed. York had two, on either side of the River Ouse, one of which also oversaw access to the Fosse, which was dammed to create the King's Fishpool; this probably caused flooding in neighbouring properties such as the back areas of Coppergate, where dumping was accelerated. Most other urban castles were built next to the wall circuits of their towns, many blocking existing streets and sweeping away people's houses, churches, and graveyards, as excavations in Norwich recently demonstrated; in Oxford, more than 1.5 metres build-up of successive surfaces of a street was abruptly terminated by the castle. For Norwich, there was some compensation in the form of the 'new borough', but people evicted from their houses may have been forced to set themselves up in suburban areas, which could give a false impression that an expanding town was thriving. At Lincoln, the 'Newport' northern suburb may be an example; it rapidly developed an extra-mural market area and acquired a church. Domesday Book attributed the 'waste' of 166 houses to the castle – and another seventy-four to fire – but excavation suggests that the Upper Bail in which the castle was inserted was not so densely occupied as that implies, so eviction may not have been as much involved as the record suggests.[31]

Even when built, urban castles might be moved to a different site. Gloucester's first castle was replaced by one nearer the River Severn, presumably for control of shipping and the crossing, and Stafford's was relocated to a site well outside the town, probably because its holder wanted a quieter and more expansive environment. No obvious reason presents itself for Canterbury's relocation; the original one used a Roman burial mound as a motte, an appropriation of an earlier monument that may have been mere expediency, but examples elsewhere have suggested that it might indicate awareness of previous use, if a site was still strategically useful. Apart from Durham's which was part of the bishop's palatinate established by William for control of the north, urban castles were royal, although administered by sheriffs. Their presence should not be taken to mean that towns were perceived as a particular threat, being outside the 'feudal' social structure that depended upon landholding not the accumulation of money, although citizens might have acted independently on a few occasions, as London's certainly did.[32]

Many castles were built by William's followers to control their new landholdings, with choice of locations varying, some because of pre-existing estate centres, some to be at a central point within a large compact land-holding, and others where scattered estates could be accessed quickly. Castles were more than defensible residences but gave physical expression to the military obligations which underpinned the 'feudal' system. Some areas were more problematic, of course: the Welsh border necessitated many small castles, in addition to Chepstow; Hen Domen was an important base but never had a stone tower. In the north, the problem was partly the threat of Scottish raids, but also that a northern earldom that had remained independent of the Norse kingdom of York was difficult to govern from the south, hence the 'palatinate'. Also in the north, the Baliol family acquired large areas of upland and lowland, which they ruled from Barnard Castle, Co. Durham, where the two resources met. Newcastle upon Tyne was not begun until 1080, following a particularly ambitious long-distance Scottish raid. In the north-west, Carlisle received a castle after 1092 when William II ousted its native ruler, giving him a base from which to oversee Cumbrian silver extraction. He is recorded as moving peasant farmers into the area; unfortunately it is not said how many were moved or where they came from, but they were probably used to introduce nucleated settlements with fenced strips for houses along a village street, widening into a green area, and surrounded by open fields.[33]

Eastern England had fewer castles, but high rental incomes meant that they could be on a grand scale. Building on the least profitable land was sensible: Castle Rising, Norfolk, is on heath, not ploughland. Competition between neighbours was sometimes a factor, perhaps accounting for the way that the Warenne family began with a relatively small tower at Castle Acre but soon enlarged it when they saw what de Albini was constructing nearby at Castle Rising early in the twelfth century. Norfolk was on the coast, so these lords could claim that their castles aided the king to repel any threatened invasion. The transfer of the bishopric of Elmham to Torksey in 1074 may have been mainly to place it in a bigger centre, but security could have been a motive; estate management and population pressure may be indicated by the manner in which the former precinct was laid out in narrow fenced strips for peasant tenements. Some sites were chosen for their control of communications, with approaches to them manipulated to give an impressive effect; some were seemingly at a distance from roads, for privacy. Some were less concerned about that, founding towns, as at Castle Rising, which were probably at least as much to have at hand traders and artisans to supply the castle as to benefit from their rents; a few used the outer bailey to encircle a new settlement, such as the town and market at Launceston, Cornwall, presumably to offer protection to traders and craftworkers who could be useful in supplying what the castle's inhabitants needed.[34]

Another frequent consideration in the choice of site for a castle was that it should be a convenient base for hunting, as quantities of deer bones found in excavations usually demonstrate – other bones also indicate rich foodstuffs such as game-birds. No Norman lord had a greater passion than their king for hunting; William I may have been attracted to Corfe in Dorset because of the potential of the chase on the Purbeck hills, for instance, acquiring a hillock from the abbess of Shaftesbury in order to construct a castle despite only a minor road passing near-by. The great tower there may have been begun by him and completed by his son or even grandson. It probably had a large window and balcony to give him a commanding view; similar provision was made at Richmond, Yorkshire, where one of William's cousins built a castle with a first-floor hall and attached chamber block, with a tower over the gatehouse. Elsewhere, at castles such as Newcastle upon Tyne and Chepstow, are 'appearance doors' that allowed the king to present himself framed in splendour to his people below. Rather like Chepstow, Richmond was built on a cliff edge, because such towers were meant to be seen and to assert their owners' authority: many, like Corfe and Richmond, had their walls carried up beyond the roof level of the upper chambers to give them the appearance of greater height.[35]

Anyone wanting extra height where no natural advantages were offered had to make do with a timber tower on an artificial motte. Until the earth had settled, the weight of stone would lead to its collapse, graphically seen at Norwich, where the first motte was enlarged and a stone tower built on it, probably in the 1090s. Even while the building was in progress, subsidence led to one wall giving way, and another had to be shored up with buttresses. Why did the king take such risks? Perhaps to ensure that his castle would overtop the cathedral, as the former see of Elmham was transferred yet again, this time from Torksey to Norwich in 1094, with the effect that it blocked off access to the developing landing-place, which had to be moved upstream. Similar competition may have affected Lincoln, to which the see was moved from the much smaller Oxfordshire town of Dorchester.[36]

The existing church of St Mary at Lincoln was rebuilt into a great Romanesque cathedral, a change made by most bishops and abbots whether or not on new sites. The discovery at Lincoln of the seal-die of a papal official, a *Legatio* recorded as being active in England between 1072 and 1080, shows the pope's concern that the see's transfer should be carried out properly and more broadly that the Church in England should conform to Hildebrandine reforms. Little of Bishop Remigius's work at Lincoln survives, but its great length is known; similarly lengthy is Winchester, where the Norman nave is larger than the whole of the Old Minster that it replaced and partly overlay. The cathedral at York was built over an existing cemetery, replacing a building that has not been located; excavation revealed an impressive foundation of carefully laid oak logs for stability. Lower in the ecclesiastical hierarchy, 'minsters' were often converted into houses of Augustinian canons living communally, not in individual houses.[37]

Some late Saxon aristocratic residences became the sites of castles for their new Norman owners, although the distinction is often blurred. The tower at Earls Barton, for instance, is surrounded by the remains of ditches, banks, and a small earth mound, none definitively dated. It may have had a ditched enclosure around it, with the 'motte' added later – but were the ditches deepened and widened and when was the work done – soon after 1066 to make the new Norman-backed lord feel more secure, or later – to protect one of his successors from the twelfth-century Anarchy? Maintaining continuity of estate administration from an established centre was often sensible, but a more compact, visibly defensible site might be desirable. At Sulgrave, Northamptonshire, a bank and ditch reduced the internal area and was thrown up over stone buildings, still rare on secular sites before the Conquest.[38]

An excavated late anglo-saxon complex at Goltho, Lincolnshire, had various buildings at right angles to each other forming three sides of a courtyard, some perhaps used for craft production, surrounded by a shallow ditch that would not have been useful against an army's attack but would have sufficed to control animals and deter thieves. The construction of a motte, with a deep ditch and high bank, destroyed many of the traces of anglo-saxon timber buildings in the twelfth century, and Goltho is now interpreted as an outpost with a timber tower, not a castle in which the lord lived; it can no longer be seen as a straightforward case of continuity, therefore, but the much smaller area enclosed for the bailey is still instructive. Crafts other than blacksmithing had no role within the much more restricted space of a castle bailey; the near-absence of spindle-whorls from them is evidence that women rarely had households within castles. On Goltho's periphery was a church, the same juxtaposition with the anglo-saxon manorial centre seen at Sulgrave, Faccombe Netherton, and Raunds. Neither of the latter two showed overt sign of dramatic change from residence into castle, and that was probably true of most. Even when a castle was created, some continuity might be permitted; at Newcastle and Trowbridge, existing cemeteries were allowed to remain in use within the castles' outer baileys, allowing some public access.[39]

As well as abbeys, cathedrals, and castles, three of England's other greatest artefacts come from the later part of the eleventh century: William II's hall at Westminster, Domesday Book, and the Bayeux Tapestry. The first, of great length and unaisled despite its width, was for ceremonial occasions when 'the king wore his crown', an important event recorded as taking place on major seasonal festivals like Christmas or Easter, as William I did at Winchester and Westminster in 1086. That was the year after he had been in Gloucester in midwinter, after which he held a council and probably put in train the survey of the whole country – never quite completed – that led to the composition of the second of the three great artefacts, Domesday Book. Whether the collection of data had been completed before his death in 1087, let alone whether the final version had been collated from all the returns, is arguable, but 'Great Domesday' at over 400 leaves of both sheepskin and calfskin – a mixture that perhaps indicates the haste used to bring together the materials needed for it – and containing information on over 13,000 different manors was a great achievement; what is now called 'Little Domesday' contains information on three eastern counties, and 'Exon Domesday' is the sole survivor of the documents sent from various groups of counties to be condensed into the central record. 'Exon' not only shows that the complaint of a chronicler that the king had demeaned himself by requiring to know every detail down to the farm animals was true – but also shows how much information is hidden, as only the stock held by the manor's lord was counted, not what his tenants and labourers owned, and although it lists the plough oxen, it does not include the milking herds.[40]

Because Domesday Book recorded manors, it is not a reliable guide to settlements – a large manor might be a polyfocal estate containing farms, hamlets, and even villages that were scattered around a wide area. Villages might be nucleated, around greens for instance, but Domesday was not concerned with such matters, nor whether open-field agriculture had been introduced. Nor is it precise in locating such resources as the mills that manors owned, which may have been on streams and rivers that ran through the estate but in some instances would have been rented at somewhere with a more reliable flow. Without Domesday, however, milling's importance would scarcely be recognizable, as few sites have been excavated; at West Cotton, Northamptonshire, timber-lined channels directed water on to a wheel, originally vertical, but subsequently horizontal, like the earlier one at Tamworth, but whereas Tamworth had been part of a royal estate and was probably therefore exceptional, West Cotton exemplifies what over 5000 mills recorded by Domesday on manorial estates would have been like. Pottery kilns known archaeologically, like those at Stamford or Michelmersh, are not included among resources in Domesday, which recorded three groups of potters, all on rural manors, in places where no kilns have been found.[41]

The three potteries mentioned in Domesday all added usefully to the income of the manors on which they were recorded, so must have been producing quite large quantities; none of the three was near a navigable river, so the pots must have gone by road, as must most of those from Michelmersh. That road transport was viable is shown also by records of food renders, still owed to many estate owners, but particularly useful to kings and churches as they could have loads carted to long-distant residences and monasteries at no expense to themselves. Because of land-carriage needs, it may have been in the eleventh century that a new form of bridge construction was introduced; excavation of a sequence at Hemington, Leicestershire, showed that the River Trent had been crossed by a bridge that was not supported on posts pile-driven into the river bed but on posts that were set on rubble-filled wooden diamond-shaped boxes, or 'caissons', which became the standard method for longer bridges, whether with wooden posts or stone piers; dendrochronology gave dates in the 1090s.[42]

Lay owners maintaining households at their manorial centres could get their food by using labour services on their own land, while renting out the parts of the estate not needed for their own supplies. Domesday Book reveals how much a lord had 'in demesne' and how much was rented out. It also shows that King William's agents were sensitive to the differences that weights and metal purity could make to the real value of a large number of pennies and legislated for it. Unlike the English earls and other major landholders, the native moneyers were not ousted, and they maintained a stable currency. An upturn in hoard deposition, some small like that in Norwich, some very large, may reflect English anxiety to disguise wealth from extortionate demands.[43]

Domesday Book also reveals a distinction between towns that had borough status and a large number of smaller places where there were already markets and a few people who were not agricultural peasants. Some of the big towns seem to have been expanded by immigrants, with distinct areas known as 'French' boroughs or by similar terms, like Nottingham and Northampton, but excavations have not shown any obvious cultural differences. Although not listed as a borough, Bury St Edmunds is revealed as a town 'enclosed in a larger circuit' since 1066, with 342 new houses; a list of bakers, brewers, tailors, and others gives some idea of the range of crafts practised in such places, although it is not complete as it only includes those who served the abbey – presumably they were not paid employees, but people who had to sell produce to it as well as maintain their own workshops and stalls; none would be easy to locate by excavation, nor probably would any distinction between the thirty-four men-at-arms there who were both French and English. Restructuring was by a French abbot appointed by Edward the Confessor, and the largely extant grid of streets is usually attributed to him, particularly a street that is aligned directly on the abbey church, seen through the 'Norman Gate'; but there is doubt over where and how much late Saxon occupation affected any overall plan and where the market-place was; parish churches were relocated in the twelfth century, so how much of any early intention was actually achieved is not clear. A better indication of the different occupations in a small town is from another new foundation, Battle, Sussex, where just after the end of the eleventh century, thirty-one rent-payers included not only some who were primarily agriculturalists, such as an ox-herd and a reed-cutter, but also bakers and cooks. The plan of Battle was more typical of small ventures than Bury, as it had a triangular market-place and streets leading into each corner, not a grid, but had the abbey gate as the focal short side.[44]

A slightly different new venture was the port at Lynn, Norfolk, where the market-place formalized an open space fronting the shoreline of the River Wensum on which boats were already beaching and paying tolls; a new priory church was established in 1095 to oversee, bless, and profit from it. Perhaps partly because of the proximity of Castle Acre, Lynn never had a castle imposed upon it, nor did Battle or Bury St Edmunds. They had no royal or aristocratic presence, and the abbots of Bury and Battle could stay inside their precinct houses and rely on the King's Peace – and favour. The Harrying of the North showed what happened to those in disfavour but seems not to have discouraged efforts at Beverley to reclaim marshy land north of the minster, with ditches and diverted watercourses, so that urban development could take place.[45]

No less extraordinary for its size than Domesday Book is the Bayeux Tapestry, with strips of linen sewn together to make a length of over 230 feet and embroidered with coloured wools. No single interpretation of it is generally agreed, nor who commissioned it, who designed it, where the work was done, or where it was displayed. Because it was at Bayeux in the fifteenth century, where William the Conqueror's half-brother Odo was bishop, he has always seemed the most likely to have been its patron, but although he is shown in some of the scenes, his role in the events is not given much emphasis. He became earl of Kent, however, and some of the images look as if they were adapted from manuscripts known to have been produced in Canterbury. The abbot of Mont St Michel in Normandy became abbot of Canterbury's St Augustine's, so he too may have had a part in the creation of the work; he might be the seated cleric in the border vignette where Harold is shown on expedition with Duke William, rescuing men from quicksands, a display of the Englishman's courage. Harold is not denigrated as though an unworthy adversary to William, but the Tapestry seems to focus on the way that he brought his doom upon himself by going back on his oath to the duke and taking the crown for himself. William is neither praised nor belittled, and he does not appear in triumph at the end, unless final scenes are missing, and his coronation was shown. His action is justified, however, by the blessing of the Pope, whose gift of a banner flies on one of the invading fleet, implying that God's will had been done; at least, trial by battle had ended decisively in William's favour. Perhaps the interpretation of the Tapestry differed from occasion to occasion, depending upon someone explaining it to an audience, in a hall or cathedral, where it was hung around the building so that it could all be seen at once.[46]

*

The Bayeux Tapestry shows a complete rout of the English but not its long-term consequences; William ruthlessly exploited the opportunity that he had created and established a dynasty that lasted much longer than Cnut's. His followers were rewarded with estates, and French and Flemish settlers are recorded in a few towns, which led to expansion – though few came to till the land, so that migration has not caused the same debate about their numbers as for the late ninth and early tenth centuries. Village plans and field lay-outs were not drastically forced into sudden changes, although William's 'Harrying of the North' may have led to resettlement. Although Norman French was to become the language of the law courts, and the administration made more use of writs and of Latin, only a few loan-words affected the everyday vernacular. Changes in the sooting found on the exteriors of some vessels could indicate immigrants cooking in pots suspended over a hearth rather than placed directly on to it, but none with pierced lugs has been found in England comparable to some in Normandy – indeed, Cornwall's integration into English culture generally is marked by the cessation of the distinctive bar-lug pottery which made provision for suspension. Any new modes of behaviour visible through the pottery and other everyday items therefore are not necessarily linked directly to immigrants – shoes and other leather goods became more decorative, but those are fashion changes that cannot be ascribed directly to Norman influence. What they do show is considerable recovery in expendable income not long after the most severe of the Conqueror's taxations.[47]

Norman lords' passion for the chase is notorious, but aristocratic hunting was far from new to England; new modes of hunting are recognizable in bone evidence, but fallow deer, long thought a Norman (re)introduction, have now been traced in pre-Conquest contexts. Butchery in general developed in line with towns and market demand, but it is possible that pig meat and chicken were favoured more by incomers. The observable changes are as likely to be due to growing demands from the native population as from immigrants, however. A more benign side of the newcomers is shown by the first hospital foundation in England, at Canterbury, some time after 1070, to relieve the sick and to offer shelter to pilgrims and other travellers; a religious community was appended to it, as became the usual practice. Also like nearly all its successors, it was on a main road just outside the city walls, where travellers could be expected to make an offering for or after a safe journey. There was also more space for new buildings. Its cemetery contained one exceptionally well-dressed priest, who had gold thread on his lower arms, probably from wrist-cuffs, so was presumably buried in vestments; he also had a chalice and paten in his grave. Although the scourge of leprosy had already arrived before 1066, the hospital was not intended for its sufferers, for whom specific provision was to come in the next century.[48]

Notes

1 Cadbury: Alcock, L. 1995. Silbury: Leary *et al.* 2013, 284–302, including contributions by N. Hembrey and V. Crosby. (Old) Sarum has become controversial, with the suggestion that a 'burh' was outside the hillfort: Langlands 2014; but that would not have overseen all the roads that focus on the fort. Cissbury: Naismith 2017, 339. No reuse of hillforts in the eleventh century has been found anywhere else, which suggests that Ethelred had no overall vision. Blair 2018, 395–6 discussed the importance of route-ways in the placing of defensible sites in the period generally.

2 Naismith 2017, 266–70; Leyser 2017, 147; Woods 2013. A religious note had been struck earlier, with the Hand of God in lieu of the Cross, but that was a token of God's blessing rather than a plea for succour.

3 Boyle *et al.* 2014.

4 Oxford St John's: Wallis, S. 2014, with contributions on the human bone by C. Falys and on the isotopes by A. M. Pollard *et al.* A subsequent analysis reported in *Nature* 585 (2020), 390–6 on one skeleton confirmed a genetic link to people in Denmark, which supports the Danish origin of the group, but not whether its members had been living in England for any length of time. *Current Archaeology* 368 (Nov. 2020) reported a case of smallpox in an Oxford mass burial, presumably the henge site (I was unable to penetrate the arcane procedures to access the original paper), which points to a viking origin as others have been found in Scandinavia. Magdalen Bridge: Blair and Crawford 1997; Oxford suffered a viking attack in 1009 (there might have been more than a single burial).

5 Reynolds 2009a for the evidence and discussion of these sites, not all of which are well dated: p. 178 for the coins; also now Russel 2016; Walker *et al.* 2020; Cole *et al.* 2020. Andrew 2019, 204 suggested in a different context that coins in burials might result from 'deliberate intent of removing dangerous or tainted objects from the world of the living', which could be apposite to execution burials as well as plague victims. Stafford skulls: Carver 2010, 78–9. London: Ayre and Wroe-Brown 2015a, 130–2.

6 Reynolds 2009a, 152–3. Matrices: Kershaw and Naismith 2013; contributions by Simon Keynes to Breay and Story (eds) 2018, 384–5. The surviving gild regulations, which provided non-family obligations, are also all from the south of England apart from Cambridge – presumably not the Cambridge in Gloucestershire. Differences between regions partly reflect the older kingdoms.

7 The Lenborough hoard is still being studied, and online reports have been used here. The list of tolls to be charged at London's Billingsgate belongs to this period and provides not only for overseas merchants bringing high-value commodities and luxuries, but even for the women who sold dairy produce and eggs, local people bringing their produce to market – such low-value foodstuffs must have changed hands for halfpennies and farthings. Fairbairn 2019 addressed this issue: fig. 5, showing the distribution of coin fractions, is telling evidence of greater use of low-value coinage in the south-east (the execution site evidence was not included in the discussion of the extent to which coins were available, but would have made little difference to the interesting conclusions). Minting of round halfpennies was probably abandoned because moneyers could not control their weights as finely as they could the larger pennies.

8 Webster, L. 2012, 208 and 223–7; Kershaw 2013, 32 and 118–25; Biddle and Kjølbye-Biddle 1995, 314–22; see Williams, A. 2008, 15–18 for bequests in wills that include 'brooches', 'rings' and so on, but such things seem to have been valued for their family associations, or for their gold and silver content, rather than for ornament or explicit symbolism. Housecarls: Lavelle 2010, 107–10 and 244; Wallingford: Pine 2012, 8–12 and 35–6.

9 Simy Folds: Coggins *et al.* 1983; Coggins 2004 – the buildings at such sites have been characterized as 'Norse', but drystone construction is concomitant with rounded corners, as at Mawgan Porth: Bruce-Mitford 1997. Fens: Rippon 2017. Somerset Levels: Rippon 2006, 97–105; 2017. Lincolnshire coast: Simmons 2015. Sea levels and climate are both still very hard to measure with precision.

10 Northern England summary: Wrathmell 2012b, 261 for devastations. One of the very few open-field systems to have remained in use, at Braunton, Devon, albeit much changed, survived because it was very profitable land but depended upon communal responsibility for a sea-wall; enclosure would have been hampered because the field was owned by three different manors, their strips intermingled – notably, and perhaps in consequence, decisions are taken by agreement, without a formal court, in contrast to the system at Laxton, Nottinghamshire: Weddell 2000. Whittlewood: Jones, R. and Page 2006, 86–7. Mawgan Porth: Bruce-Mitford 1997.

11 Mawgan Porth cemetery: Bruce-Mitford 1997, 63–70; Hadley 2009 suggested that the pebbles may reference a Revelations text. See Thompson 2004, 122–6; Hadley 2009, 475–6 for head protection and the recognition of other rites; see Soden 2018, 72–4 for examples of both charcoal and 'ear-muff' burials at an urban parish church – despite the extra elaboration, charcoal burial was not confined to major churches; Gilchrist and Sloane 2005, 120–1 traced charcoal burials into the early twelfth century, after which charcoal is sometimes found within coffins but not otherwise in graves.

12 Raunds Furnells: Boddington 1996, with contributions by R. Cramp, P. Woodfield. D. Parsons, and F. Powell; amended dating by Audouy and Chapman (eds) 2009, see Ch. 4 for Higham Ferrers. Fonts: Blair 2010. Parish churches and minsters: Blair 2005, 383–63 and 514–19; see also Ch. 5. The association between manor-houses and churches/graveyards has been questioned on statistical grounds, but where there is no association, the manor may be a later medieval creation, or the house may have been relocated to a new site: Kilby 2020, 25 and 45 for three case studies.

13 'Excluded' burials include one underneath the cemetery wall at North Elmham, a male who had been killed by a blade. *Sub stigillatio* burial may have been for neonates and babies who had not been baptized, so that the eaves-drip water gave them the blessing that they had not had in life; Crawford suggested that the practice might have echoes of earlier belief that those who died very young might hold a 'grudge' against the living and needed to be assuaged: 1993, 86–8. At Bishopstone, neonate bones were found in several rubbish pits and the cellar backfill: Thomas, G. 2010, contribution by L. Schoss and M. Lewis, 79–80, who interpreted them as stillbirths, not regarded as members of society. See Gilchrist 2012, 255 for age profiles at parish church excavations and next chapter for infant burials after the eleventh century. Stone grave-covers, including some reused Roman slabs, at Wharram may also have marked founder's kin. Raunds also had evidence of wooden coffins, though whether any of the stone-lined graves had them and whether wood was more highly regarded is not known. Population ratios in rural cemeteries are not a guide to overall mortality, as some people probably migrated into towns, although the direct evidence is slight: seven men were recorded as having moved from one of Shaftesbury Abbey's twelfth-century estates into the nearby town, yet no such record was made for any of its many other estates: Stacy (ed.) 2006, 140.

14 Fonts: Blair 2010. Parsons, D. 1996 for the Raunds pot.

15 Churches: Fernie 1983, 137–53 and 162–73 – 165–7 for Wareham; Gem 1988; Taylor and Taylor 1965 for the many partial survivals. Greensted: Tyers *et al.* 1997, 142. An

example of the difficulties in dating is provided by the round towers of East Anglia: Shapland 2019, 141, n. 40. Bell-making: Blair, C. and Blair 1991, 87, 90.

16 Bradford-on-Avon: Royal Archaeological Institute/publications (relics of royal boy-saints were especially venerated); Hinton 2009. Sherborne: Keen and Ellis 2005, 137–40. Church treasures: Webster, L. 2012, 197–206.

17 Coin numbers: Bolton 2004, 10–11, citing work by M. Dolley; see also Fairbairn 2019; the question is whether the economy was 'monetized', that is using money but not as the principal means of exchange, barter and service being other forms of payment. I would estimate the Domesday population rather higher, perhaps 2.5 million, which would be even greater if the per-household average was 5 people not 4.5 and higher still if there were accurate figures for towns: Hinton 2013, 24–5. Norwich hoard: Clough 1973, and Ayers 2011 for the kiln. Costen 2011, 138 noted an Edward penny in the hearth of a 'humble dwelling' in Somerset as evidence of widespread coin use. Coin-brooches: Naylor 2015. Enamel brooches were first recognized by Buckton 1986. Lead-alloy, etc., brooches: Egan and Blackmore 2015, 241–5; Weetch 2017; survival of lead examples is heavily biased to certain types of damp environment. London Cheapside hoard: Egan 2009, 291, for discussion of its cultural implications; illus. Homer 1991, 75.

18 Small spaces suitable for carts and booths have been identified in Lincoln: Stocker 2013, 125–9; and in pre-Conquest Barnstaple: Haslam 2016, 60–1 and post-Conquest Bridgnorth: Haslam 2017, 6–8 (market usage is my assumption). Market-places: Palliser *et al.* 2000, 167–9. Tanning: Chester: Mason 1985, period 5; Winchester: Ottaway 2017, 249–51; overview: Cherry 1991, 295–8 (smaller skins, of sheep, cats, and dogs are usually dry-tanned, or 'whittawed'). Lincoln butchery: O'Connor 1982, and see Ch. 6; Exeter: Maltby 1979.

19 Woodworking: Morris, C. A. 2000. Leather: Cameron and Mould 2011; York: Mainman and Rogers 2004. Horse-shoes may have first appeared in the ninth century, numbers increasing only slowly: Clark 1995, 91–5. Gloucester iron: contribution by C. Morris in Darvill 1988, 35–9 (use of the word 'ductile' suggests recognition of different grades of ore). Burlescombe: Reed *et al.* 2006, who argued that the three pits excavated, with rather broad radiocarbon dating, might indicate itinerant workers. Hoards: Leahy 2013; Nazeing: Morris 1983. See also Ch. 6.

20 Pottery: McCarthy and Brooks 1989a, 62–8 – a new overview would be welcome. Exeter: Allan 1984, 27–34 and contribution to Rippon and Holbrook (eds) 2021, 235–6. Chichester: Jervis 2017a. Lincoln: Jones, M. J. *et al.* 2003, 99–127. Technologies: Leahy 2003. Suburban assemblages are exemplified by Winchester: Rees *et al.* 2008; Serjeantson and Rees (eds) 2009. Michelmersh: Mepham and Brown 2007.

21 Weaving: Leahy 2003, 61–74; the waterlogged remains of pieces of what were interpreted as being parts of horizontal looms were found in ninth-/tenth-century contexts in Gloucester: contribution by J. Hedges to Heighway *et al.* 1979, 191. Gender implications: Gilchrist 1999, 50–1. (The word 'heirloom' seems to associate looms with family and property descent but is a later hybrid term, part Old English, part French.) The twelfth century has more detailed records, but it seems likely that English cloth was an export before then. Colours would have come from plants: madder, bedstraw, woad, weld, and lichen; kermes may not have been imported before the twelfth century; clubmoss was used as a mordant to fix the colours: Uzzell 2012.

22 Disease and living conditions: Rawcliffe 2011 and Roberts, C. A. *et al.* 2018. Winchester cultivation: Ottaway 2017, 228; town meadows are recorded in Domesday Book, and names like Port Meadow are presumably much earlier than their first mention. Rats: Holmes 2018, 187–9.

23 Fish: Barrett 2018, 128–30; Williams, A. 2008, 136–9; and see Ch. 6. Dam complex: Clay and Salisbury 1990.

24 Graveyards: Barrow, J. 2000 (London, York, and Lincoln had many more small urban graveyards than most towns). Winchester: Ottaway 2017, 208–9 and 219–25. Urban

churches: Morris 1989, 168–226. Wareham: Keen 1984, 239. Bristol: Leech 2014, 13–16; Baker, N. *et al.* 2018, 91–108; Leech argued that the new town was so successful that it was extended before the Conquest, an interesting point of comparison with the Oxford extension possibility. Sandwich: Clarke *et al.* 2010, 22–38.

25 Buildings: Gardiner 2013; Blair 2018, 265–70 and 372–5 for enclosures, including gateways. Ch. 6 for the big aisle-post reused in the London waterfront. Eleventh-century references to feasting and oath-swearing seem few: Williams, A. 2008, 133–4 for examples.

26 Paucity of socially expressive weapons and jewellery: Hinton 2005, 168–9 (the Bedale pommel, Ch. 6, may be the last with gold plates). The *Rectitudines Singularum Personarum* has been much studied, and different translations have been made: Harvey 1993; Williams, A. 2008, 79. Swords: Brunning 2019, 139–48. Other items that 'speak' include Aedwen's brooch: Page 1964, 84–7.

27 'Riding-men': Williams, A. 2008, 79–80. Stirrups: Seaby and Woodfield 1980; stirrup-mounts: Williams, D. 1997 (riding equipment is not of course confined to the shires in which 'riding-men' are recorded). The salt tolls are the best evidence of pack-horses and carts (see Ch. 6), augmented in mind-boggling detail in Domesday Book, which adds pack-men to the distribution methods but does not mention carriage by water: Thorn and Thorn (eds) 1982, 268b.

28 Shapland 2017; 2019 introduced the concept of 'towers of lordship', giving discussion a new dimension; see 2019, 46–8 for the possibility of the lord's chamber at Earls Barton; he pointed out that the owner at Domesday held only four hides, not the five that a thegn should have had before the Conquest – so the suggestion of appearance may be attributing too high a status to him. Barton-on-Humber: Rodwell and Atkins 2012. Portchester: Cunliffe 1976, 49–52 and contribution on the burials by B. Hooper, 235–61; one of the young adult males had been killed by a blade injury. Deep or stone foundations could have supported towers at other sites, such as Sulgrave and Bishop's Waltham.

29 Tyler 1999; 2000; an indication of the king's fine clothing is given by the fragments of imported silk found in his tomb: Coatsworth and Owen-Crocker 2007, 10–11. Imperial design: Naismith 2017, 274; perhaps it was too difficult to cut such a detailed image into the small circle of a coin-die for the type to be suitable for mass production. The earliest wax seal to survive is from Edward's reign: contribution by A. Hudson to Breay and Story (eds) 2018, 382. Edward appointed a number of Lotharingian clerics to his bishoprics.

30 A prehistorian, Stuart Piggott, may have been the first to refer to 1066 as an archaeological problem. Pre-Conquest politics: Leyser 2017, 168–73; see Guy 2016–17 for Richard's Castle, the most positive example. Mottes may not have been used in the first two years of the Conquest: Higham, R. and Barker 1992, 60 – and for timber towers in general; see also Kenyon 1990, 20–38. Tower of London interpretation: Harris, R. D. 2016; the dating is by stylistic analysis of changes in the masonry, because thermoluminescence of different mortars is not yet fine enough for this chronological level, while radiocarbon dating depends upon retrieving fragments of charcoal from the fuel used in their mixing, and has the same proviso. Colchester: Berridge 2016; Marshall 2016, 167–9. Chepstow has benefited from complete reconsideration by Turner, R. C. 2004, 225–60. Access control: Marshall 2016, 164–6. Lewis. C. P. 2018 for a general discussion of the scale of the Norman conquerors' creations.

31 The Thames was navigable far upstream from London; a new cut made by Abingdon Abbey facilitated passage. Both York castles had mottes: see Addyman and Priestley 1977 for excavation of one of them; see Hall, R. A. 2014, 685–94 and 714–15 for Coppergate, 701 for the castle; intermittent building continued in Coppergate but seems likely to have been at a reduced level, not necessarily as a result of the Conquest's effects. Lewes, Sussex, also has two Norman-period mottes, but a third has recently

been shown to be a much later garden feature: University of Reading Mounds Project. Norwich: papers in Davies, J. A. *et al.* (eds) 2016; Domesday records that 32 townspeople had fled the city to avoid taxation. Oxford: Hassall *et al.* 1989, 121–9, reproduced and discussed in Dodd (ed.) 2003, 26–7. Castles recorded in Domesday: Harfield 1991. Lincoln Newport suburb: Spence 2013, 297; castle (and cathedral): Stocker and Vince 1997.

32 Gloucester: Darvill 1988. Canterbury: Renn 1982, 72–4; Bennett *et al.* 1982; Frere *et al.* 1987, 161–8. Stafford's second site: Creighton 2002, 11–13. Fradley 2017; Lilley, K. D. 2017 for overviews. See Swallow 2016 on 'continuity of purpose' and 'power of place'. At Marlborough, Wiltshire, and Skipsea, Yorkshire, recent coring has shown that the mottes reused prehistoric mounds: Jamieson 2019. See Butler 1998 for the castle's role as the centre of a new 'Honour'. The complex terminology of 'feudalism' formulates a stratified social system expecting but often not getting loyalty to the king, in which birth was foremost but not overriding as the path to high status, with control of land and resources more important than family and kin; land tenure gave rights that overrode personal obligation: See Faith 2019, 151–64 for recent discussion.

33 Hen Domen: Higham, R. and Barker 1992, 326–50. Barnard: Austin, D. 1984, 73–5. Cumbria: Roberts, B. K. 1996, 24 for the quotation.

34 Castle Rising: Morley and Gurney 1997; Creighton 2002, 192–3. Castle Acre: Coad and Streeten 1982. Also Liddiard 2000. North Elmham: Wade-Martins 1980. Launceston: Saunders, A. D. 2006, 28–9. See Lilley, K. D. 2017 for an overview.

35 Castle sitings were studied using GIS by Lowerre 2005; see also Mathieu 1999. Corfe: Goodall, J. 2011, 109–10, Hulme 2014–15 for debate about strategic locations. Richmond: Hill, N. and Gardiner 2016, 179–80 for balconies. 'Appearance doors': Marshall 2012 and for Newcastle: Guy 2017–18. Renn 2016–17 for the pre-Conquest upper opening at Earls Barton. Tower heights: Marshall 2016, 161–2.

36 Studies of Norwich by E. Popescu, B. Ayers, and T. A. Heslop are in Davies, J. A. *et al.* (eds) 2016.

37 Romanesque buildings: Fernie 2000; cathedrals: Tatton-Brown and Crook 2002, 55–6 for Lincoln; 21–5 for Winchester, where the Old Minster foundations were excavated by Martin Biddle and Birthe Kjølbye-Biddle: Ottaway 2017, 297–303. Lincoln seal: Heslop 1986. York: Phillips 1985, 45–76 and 176. See O'Sullivan 2011 on different trajectories in different regions. See Blair 2005, 406–29 and 452–63 for 'minsters'.

38 Earls Barton: Shapland 2019, 46–8. Sulgrave: Davison 1977. Still being excavated is Hornby Castle, North Yorkshire, where a stave-built structure and late Saxon artefacts underlie Norman work: Matthews 2020–21, 232, and 234.

39 For Goltho's church, see Beresford 1987, 2; his interpretation of the Goltho sequence has not been challenged but dating and function have been. Spindle-whorls: Standley 2016, 273. Newcastle: Harbottle et al. 2010. Trowbridge is a twelfth-century example, where church and graveyard were permitted even within the inner bailey: Graham and Davies 1993, 66–71.

40 Westminster: Harris, R. D. and Miles 2015. See Harvey, S. 2014 for a clear guide to Domesday's contents, problems, and debates. Social stratification was made very evident, but the differences of servitude, for instance, among agricultural workers, are not elucidated by the archaeological record; slaves could own property, so their access to commodities may have been no less than that of their free but poor neighbours; for slavery, Pelteret 1995.

41 West Cotton: Chapman 2010, 113–16. Pottery: Le Patourel 1968, 103–6.

42 Carting services are scarcely mentioned in Domesday, but early twelfth-century records imply that they were probably already enforced in the eleventh: Stacy (ed.) 2006, 21–2 for the example of Shaftesbury Abbey. Hemington bridge complex: Ripper and Cooper 2009; Harrison 2007, 103–4.

43 Coinage: Metcalf 1987 remains a very useful survey of the intricacies and of the not inconsiderable but not enormous profits made by the Crown and others. See Piercy 2019, 147 for moneyer families and their post-Conquest continuity; on p. 33 he drew attention to reattribution of what had been thought William I's final issue, another PAXS variant, to his son, a demonstration not only of continuity but also of elements of uncertainty in monetary history. Andrews 2019, 53–7 expressed doubt about a rise in direct consequence of the events of the 1060s, but the hoard deposition rate shown on p. 29 shows a distinct 1066–1100 peak.

44 Bury: Fernie 1998; Gauthiez 1998; Statham 1998. Battle and other urban occupations: Britnell 2001.

45 Lynn: Hutcheson 2006; Parker 1971, 19–24; Clarke and Carter 1977, 411–13. Beverley: Evans and Tomlinson 1992, 5–16 and 271, with contribution by Rosemary Horrox, p. 269.

46 Work on the Bayeux Tapestry is legion; Hicks 2006 is a very good guide. For its manufacture, see Owen-Crocker 2009. Claims that it was made to fit a particular building and no other, for example Norton 2019, depend on assumptions about its length.

47 Village plans and layouts: Creighton and Rippon 2017. Language: Chibnall 2003; Short 2003 argued that French was not used for 'polite' words such as beef/*boeuf* for cow-meat alone; its impact was not immediate but long-term. Bar-lug pottery: Bruce-Mitford: 1997, 71–80. Sooting: Brown, D. H. 2002, 136. Leather: Mould and Cameron 2015.

48 Hunting: Flight 2016 argued against new modes being an introduction, but bone evidence indicates their increased practice: Sykes 2007, 75–6, 93–6. Fallow deer and livestock changes: McClain and Sykes 2019, 93–7. Pre-Conquest hunting and hawking references: Williams, A. 2008, 123–33; note also the image in calendars of a lord entering his woodland to hunt boar. Norman legislation and creation of the New Forest extended existing practice: Langton and Jones 2010. Food-style changes: Jervis *et al.* 2017. Canterbury hospital: Hicks and Hicks 2001, 284–6 and 343 for the special burial (see further Ch. 9 for chalices and patens); as silver-gilt rather than pure gold was more usual after the late eleventh century, this was an early burial and could have been a senior canon, despite not being in the chapter-house. The community might have incorporated the guild of priests recorded in Domesday Book, which later became a formal Augustinian house dedicated to St Gregory: Sparks 1998. Leprosy: Roffey 2012; 2017.

8 The Twelfth Century

Community and Constraint

The population growth that was probable in the eleventh century becomes more visible in the twelfth, particularly in the expansion of many towns and the creation of new ones. With growing demand for land, peasants faced rent rises and increased service requirements; wages were low; and migration to work in towns might not be permitted by landholders whose priorities were to increase incomes from their estates. Their predominance is shown most obviously in the Church's ability to rebuild existing institutions and to establish new ones, the best-known being the Cistercians. At parish level, the enlargement of church naves can be attributed at least in part to the need to provide for larger numbers in the congregations. The Crusades and the attempts to secure a christian kingdom based on Jerusalem were a drain on the nation's wealth, with the costs of men, their equipment, and transport: access to Arabic scholarship was a small compensation for all the royal expenditure. Danegeld taxation ceased to suffice, so feudal 'aids' and 'reliefs' were added, and taxes on the laity's revenues and movables were introduced; the last would have had the effect of developing a more material awareness of the value of commodities. Civil war was disruptive, especially the 'Anarchy' of 1138–48, but the overall pattern is of economic and social development, particularly noticeable in the century's later part.[1]

Developments in the countryside can rarely be closely dated. Population growth would have led to the expansion of existing sites and the creation of new ones, the latter usually referred to as assarts if they also involved creating new fields and referred to as 'squatter occupation' if they were merely labourers' houses. Productivity per person would not have increased, as the technology of production, such as manuring, marling, spreading seaweed, and weeding the crops was labour-intensive, and although horses may have begun to replace oxen for some purposes such as ploughing, the extra costs involved in their breeding and their winter oats would have reduced any benefit of faster movement and lighter weights on the ground. If ploughland was increased at the expense of pasture, fewer animals grazing and manuring the stubble would have reduced its fertility. The Cistercians in northern England had the most visible impact, creating granges for sheep wherever moorland permitted, sometimes moving existing settlements to create isolation for themselves, a demonstration of landlords' power. Elsewhere, marshland drainage continued, characterized by long parallel fields, to the loss of common grazing but apparently done by agreement. Common land that was grazed but not ploughed,

DOI: 10.4324/9781003007432-9

and was often wooded, was widespread and valued; 'stints' were the number of animals each village or farm was permitted to have on it.[2]

Disputes over furlong boundaries in common fields, stints, damage to trees, and so on inevitably arose but show underlying agreement of the principle of regulation, a concept that may have helped to produce what seem in many cases to be uniform sizes of village tenements, usually rectangular and often in rows. Behind the house, usually fronting the street, would be outhouses and gardens – vegetables were an important but inestimable part of peasants' diet. Such arrangements suited a 'stem' family, which might have to provide accommodation for an elderly parent, or a servant, but was a distinct household, not sharing facilities with siblings' and cousins' families. Clear property demarcation by hedges, ditches, or fences gave the household a sense of itself as a discrete unit. That was probably what both the landlord, for better oversight, and the Church, for doctrinal reasons, also wanted. The development of nucleated villages with rows of tofts, as at Wharram Percy, probably continued in a large swathe of what is called the 'Central Belt' of England, running from the south coast to the north, and which has been identified by working back from nineteenth-century maps; within it were many variations, as settlements in the undulating plains and wide valleys of some zones were more likely to be compacted into neat and uniform rows than hillier country where occupation sites had to follow the lines of stream valleys. Often, villages developed from the linking up of originally discrete settlements, perhaps as at Raunds grouped around manorial sites. In the more wooded areas, intermittent clearance was another factor, leading to small individual farms as well as to some larger villages.[3]

Outside the 'Central Belt', agriculture and settlement form varied even more widely. In East Anglia, many small farms around greens may have been created where heavier clay soils made new settlements focusing on grazing more viable – they rarely have parish churches because they were offshoots of existing villages, and the established church resisted any encroachment on its rights. Falling sea-level and fewer storm surges meant that some of the growing population numbers could be used to dig channels and build walls to drain wetlands. In Cornwall and much of Devon, the terrain meant that large open fields and with them cooperative arable farming from nucleated villages were not viable; instead, scattered hamlets and farms operated 'convertible husbandry', ploughing outfields only in patches each year and focusing on grazing. This gave the soil time to recover, but even here the arable seems to have been divided into strips – but was it for drainage or because the outfield was held in common? Far from a landlord's overview, hamlets like the excavated site at Hound Tor on Dartmoor do not look as if they were formally arranged (Illus. 10.1), but in Durham and Northumberland 'regular two-row villages' are frequent, regimented planning perhaps made possible by reorganization after Scottish incursions. In Kent, 'gavelkind' was practised, dividing a tenement equally between heirs, a practice resisted by landlords elsewhere, as the small scattered holdings that resulted were much less easily controlled. Most of the wide range of different plan-forms are easier to recognize than to date, however.[4]

Where excavations have taken place, the difficulties of establishing what was happening in rural England in the twelfth century can be seen. Buildings are hard to trace, for two main reasons: one is that they generally had little in the way of foundations and the other that such traces were usually obliterated by later development. They were not necessarily flimsy 'huts with rotten timbers and old, fallen-down walls', as earth-material walls such as cob can be substantial, high enough to give adults headroom inside and capable of bearing the weight of a thatched roof; but they did not need substantial wooden posts or deep foundations and are not recognizable unless built round a framework of stakes that, if they leave any trace at all, look irregular and insignificant, although internal floor areas could be as large as those of later medieval houses. It is impossible to equate different sizes and construction methods with the gradations of peasant landholders and labourers whose existence is increasingly documented.[5]

Social differentiation within rural settlements cannot be recognized in surviving artefacts, either. Many sites produce quantities of pottery sherds, but they are usually from pits or dumps, not directly associated with specific buildings – and of course do not fit into neat century-by-century divisions. The range of pottery need not directly represent growth or reduction in populations, as usage would have varied, and alternatives such as wood and leather infrequently survive, while metal was likely to get recycled. Apart from use for scraping bottoms in the absence of bits of rag, sherds have no secondary use. An increase in ceramics during the twelfth century is easier to assume than to prove, but what survives is predominantly from vessels used for cooking and kitchen storage in coarse fabrics. Most have slightly rounded bases to reduce thermal shock and to allow them to sit in the embers of a hearth to boil slowly, breaking coarse foodstuffs down into edible condition (Illus. 8.1). At West Cotton, Northamptonshire, residue analysis

Illustration 8.1 A large cooking-pot from Oxford. The lower part is blackened from soot through sitting on the hearth. Such vessels would have been used to simmer pottage composed of whatever was available. Height is 225 cm.

has shown that a proportion of about 10% was used predominantly for keeping, or cooking with, lard from pigs; in others, meat and vegetables were stewed. Unfortunately, cereal grains have insufficient lipids to be identifiable, so the proportions and nutritional values of the various contents of the peasant pottages cannot be established, let alone how many people they fed. Few tabulations have been attempted, but one for the earliest phase of use at Westbury, Buckinghamshire, shows only unglazed cooking-pots and bowls made from clays into which were mixed large quantities of crushed shell and stone; tellingly, no jugs appear until the next phase. Twelfth-century glazed jugs are known at other rural sites, though they seem less common than in towns. Large globular tripod pitchers, often with a short spout and ribbons of applied clay down the sides, are particularly distinctive, presumably used for ale and cider (Illus. 8.2); the feet would have helped to tilt them forward for pouring when full, which would imply hard surfaces, presumably tables, if only made of planks and trestles, and use of smaller wooden bowls for drinking. At the same time, games like Nine Men's Morris and music on bone pipes might be played.[6]

Most pottery in the twelfth century was made in the countryside, with any urban production likely to be extra-mural, reducing the fire risk and paying less in rent; one set up inside Canterbury probably by a migrant did not last long, unable to

Illustration 8.2 Tripod pitcher from Oxford. The upper part is patchily glazed. Height is 315 mm.

supplant one already established outside the walls, but that in turn lost out to one a little further away at Tyler Hill. Even in suburbs, clay digging would have been anti-social, and fuel expensive to acquire, offsetting any saving made from not having so far to cart the finished product to market – a pottery on the edge of Ely was able to make more use of water transport than most. Elsewhere, 'potting villages' were usually close to woodland for fuel, at which individual households within the crofts of the settlement probably combined the craft with farming, as at Grimston, Norfolk, which largely supplanted Thetford, Hanley Castle, Worcestershire, or Chilvers Coton, Warwickshire. Potters may have combined for some purposes such as loading carts but acted individually when making payments to a landlord for clay-digging rights; they were probably not employers on the same scale as those at Stamford or Lincoln are likely to have been. Their kilns did not have raised oven floors but were ground-level clamps or sub-surface platforms, and they rarely used a wheel to throw a pot. Country people's access to markets is shown by the pots made at different kilns found in most rural excavations; a visiting carrier would have brought the products only of a single kiln.[7]

Pottery sherds are also found in significant numbers at a distance from settlements, as far as a mile away, because they had been thrown on to domestic middens and spread as dung on to arable fields. The impression of peasant poverty indicated by pottery seems borne out by a dearth of personal ornaments, the earlier coin-brooches all but vanishing and having no obvious replacements. Excavation sites may not give a complete record, however, as few twelfth-century coins are found at them: three, all cut farthings, at Westbury, none at Shapwick, and four at Wharram. That may reflect how careful people were not to lose such valuable items, but it is increasingly at variance with reports of metal-detected finds in fields away from settlements, which show a steady increase from forty for 1100–35, eighty-three for 1138–53, despite the 'Anarchy', and 210 for 1154–1180; after that, there is a huge jump in the total to 3152, but because the next phase runs up to 1247 the average annual loss rate is more illustrative, rising from 9.6 to 47. As it had been in the 960s/70s, this growth was made possible by new discoveries of veins of silver in Germany – small amounts may have come from Cumberland.[8]

If coins show peasants increasingly using the market-place, it was because they were meeting not only increased demand for cash rent and to supply food, but also for yarn; iron tines from wool-combs, and stone, metal, and clay spindle-whorls are frequently found on rural sites. As the product had to be kept clean and dry, spinning and carding were indoor domestic work and therefore essentially women's, as were food preparation and cooking. The latter was done at ground level on open hearths, with so much time spent stirring the pots that many female skeletons at Wharram Percy exhibit squatting facets. Dairying and ale-brewing were also primarily female occupations, but because women also worked in the fields during harvest, and in the barns winnowing, their skeletons show evidence of heavy labour. Their work therefore brought cash into households, facilitating rent payment. It may have been because an estate steward at Castle Acre felt the need to check that tenants were handing over good-quality coins that a bone tumbrel for weighing pennies was found there, even though its private use was supposedly prohibited so that all checking would be done at a mint.[9]

*

Even if peasants used money to pay the rent and to make market purchases, their use of it for investment in new stock or building was probably limited because they could make only small surpluses, if any; the small and insubstantial outbuildings found in excavations contrast with the large storage facilities that some great Church estates thought worthwhile to build. They had commercial opportunities in mind, not just the need to ensure a flow of foodstuffs for their own communities. Documentary evidence from St Paul's, London, shows how in the twelfth century the cathedral chapter built barns, the different sizes of each one carefully stated because the bays between the aisle-posts were used to measure the amounts and values of different crops inside them, necessary to know because the farms were rented out, and the stock was part of the lease. Those barns do not survive, but two at Cressing Temple, Essex, show how solidly built a big aisled barn could be. Landlords' outlay on such buildings was facilitated because they could use labour services and the resources of their estates for timber and other materials, with little payment in cash.[10]

The Church is generally better known for its expenditure on abbeys and cathedrals than on estate infrastructure. The early twelfth century saw continued replacement, as at Hereford where the extension of the cathedral encroached on the cemetery; some 5000 bodies were relocated to a charnel pit. The Cistercians did not indulge in the same displays of sculpture as most Romanesque churches contained, but the grand scale of their work can still be seen in roofless ruins like those at Fountains or Tintern, isolated locations from which it was not worth the effort of carting away the stone in the sixteenth century despite the valuable lead having been stripped off. Other new Orders, such as the Cluniacs, have left much less evidence; Reading and Faversham were established so as to become royal burial-places, for Henry I and Stephen respectively, but ground plans and sculpture are almost the only relics of their grandiose ambitions: Westminster had not yet come to be the quintessential setting for kingship, despite the growing prestige of its patron, Edward the Confessor. Church and state were sometimes at odds, as Archbishop Becket's murder in 1170 showed, but no-one questioned the need for devotion, and many castle builders created priories to serve within their walls, not always with happy results. An extreme case of tension was at Old Sarum (Illus. 2.6), where the noise of the garrison disturbed the prayers in the adjacent cathedral.[11]

Many priories were Augustinian refoundations of anglo-saxon minsters, which might retain spiritual duties for the local populace, but increasingly were separate from parish churches, which took over most of their parochial income. Chapels might in their turn threaten the rights of the parish church, but usually those threats were resisted. Ownership of parish churches still largely rested with manorial lords, so rebuilding and enlarging in stone reflected their prestige and control; bell-towers at west ends were frequent additions, for large cast bells whose tolling reminded everyone of their spiritual duty but indirectly also of their place in the social hierarchy. In many cases, side-aisles provided more internal space. A change in memorial practice was the use by later twelfth-century abbots and bishops of carved figures showing them in their full canonicals with their staffs of office; lesser ecclesiastics and richer laity might have an engraved or relief cross on a stone slab in the same tradition as in earlier centuries. In northern England, rings and chalices were added to the cross. As well as regional variation, there are some odd quirks: some monks at Bury St Edmunds were buried with lead crosses, incised with texts, a practice rarely discovered anywhere else, yet in an Order that was highly regularized and whose senior members were transferred between houses, so that uniformity would be expected.[12]

*

As well as in its barns, St Paul's invested in its property in London, building a new quay on the Thames. Waterfront development there continued piecemeal, the dumped reclamation deposits now stable enough to support stone buildings. Some of the surviving timbers of the revetments show stave-building construction, like that at Greensted church but very rarely identified elsewhere. London Bridge created problems for navigation, however, perhaps especially after 1176 when work began on replacing its timber structure with stone piers and arches; larger boats had difficulty getting through it, so that the downstream eastern waterfront became more important, with Billingsgate serving as the public quay. Parts of boats were still sometimes built into the London waterfronts; a barge-like vessel at the Customs House dated by dendrochronology to 1160–90 was relatively wide and flat-bottomed, and quite short at about 10 metres, so was probably for river work only. Direct evidence of sea-going ships is lacking.[13]

Barges like the one at Customs House were needed to bring foodstuffs to the London market, which was by now large enough to affect what was grown in surrounding areas: apple and pear pips, celery and brassica (cabbage) seeds indicate plentiful market gardening, and some plants hint at a herb garden for medicinal use. Markets were needed, and buildings and alleyways in front of the Guildhall were cleared to create open space. Guilds for specific trades and products began to exert influence, but did not yet establish their own premises.[14]

Urban standards of living are hard to judge; frequent fires caused changes to buildings, with stone cellars replacing timber and tiles replacing thatch, but this extra security may have been at the expense of warmth in winter. Poor living conditions may have caused high levels of anaemia from iron deficiency, but most Londoners probably had enough to eat, though they had to put up with appalling tooth and gum decay. They could live well beyond forty, and their heights were slightly above average. Their skeletons show that many recovered from heavy falls and violence, though one or two were killed by weapons. Vanity led some to have deformed feet from wearing tight shoes. The number of different sources of pottery declined, but glazed wares were more frequent, adding a touch of colour; in London particularly, but also in other towns, demand for unglazed cooking-pots should have declined, as many people relied on buying in any hot food that they could afford from the many cooks recorded. The difficulty of paying for low-value things like pies and sausages, eggs, pottery, and base-metal ornaments with silver coins seems to have led to the use of lead tokens in twelfth-century London, an earlier date than previously thought.[15]

London was the only town where waterfront development took place on such a large scale in the twelfth century, though hards were laid over several shorelines elsewhere, and reclamation by dumping was probably deliberate, not merely a by-product of rubbish disposal. Boosted by the trade with Ireland, which it was drawing away from Chester, Bristol had a stone quay on the River Frome by the end of the twelfth century. At Gloucester, a new bridge across the Severn caused silting, so the waterfront had to be pushed out to reach a deeper channel. In Lincoln, bridges prevented larger vessels from getting up to Brayford Pool where earlier development had taken place, but although its commerce was threatened by the development of Boston much nearer the sea, the waterfront remained very active, with further land reclamation in Wigford and side alleys off the High Street. Further north, York and Beverley were both some distance from the open sea and vulnerable to competition from ports at the mouth of the Humber, including Hedon, nowadays well inland but a twelfth-century port foundation with a grid-plan and artificial watercourses draining into a small river; pottery indicates its use from the early twelfth century and steady subsequent development. By contrast, flooding and coastal changes reduced Wyke's viability, and by the end of the twelfth century Hull was developing, exporting wool from Meaux Abbey, one of the Yorkshire Cistercian foundations.[16]

Hull and other new towns might attract merchants, but any without streams providing running fresh water could not develop textile and leather industries to rival the older places. Excavation in Beverley has revealed a dye-working complex on low-lying land close to the Walkerbeck, a name strongly suggesting that it was used for fulling, by 'walking' on the soaking cloth. The dyeing began in the mid twelfth century, dated by dendrochronology because the area was damp and preserved the timbers of buildings, drains, and vats. The fulled cloths and dyes were soaked over ovens; the dyes were madder, weld, and woad, and not the costly kermes.[17]

Population growth stimulated sea-fishing: Yarmouth was already landing and, presumably, also salting and curing boatloads of herrings when a priory church was founded there, within a few years of that at Lynn, and probably with the same motive of profiting from the growing market, which an eleventh-century coin and Thetford-ware sherds indicate was in operation. On a sand-spit by the River Yare, which gave access to Norwich, Yarmouth was unstable except for a small area around the church, but even there excavation found only insubstantial remains of buildings but quantities of fish bones of various species; 'four or five little houses' on the shore were presumably for fishermen, perhaps especially busy during the herring season. Wisbech on the edge of the fens struggled with sand-blow and could not compete against Lynn's more secure waterfront on the estuary of the River Ouse. Lynn's success was marked by the extension of the town with a second, larger market-place. In the north-east, Newcastle was becoming more than just a small new castle-borough, with industrial use including a pottery kiln, the beginnings of coal shipping, and probably some reclamation of the shoreline below the castle.[18]

On the south coast, ports like Rye and Old Winchelsea benefited from reclamation of Romney Marsh, and also, like Sandwich, Dover, Hastings, and Hythe benefited from increased traffic across the Channel to France. Another port well-placed for the crossing to France was Southampton; the journey was longer, but it was closer to the king's lands in France, at first Normandy, later Anjou, and then Bordeaux. Its waterfront probably needed little improvement and had the Isle of Wight to thank for the low ebb and flow of the long inlet which meant that even the largest ships could reach it irrespective of the tide. The port was so far inland that despite not having navigable rivers to access its hinterland, carting was very practicable, and it had the advantage of royal desire for French wine. The king's supplies were unloaded straight into large stone-vaulted cellars at the castle, for distribution not only to his own residences, but also to those to whom he wished to show favour: gift-giving of a new sort. Portsmouth became a rival towards the end of the twelfth century, as it was closer to France and provided a shorter voyage, more important for the transport of people than of goods. Nearby Portchester Castle continued to be the centre for the administration of kings' overseas ventures, but its harbour was not as good as Portsmouth's; nevertheless, the tower was strengthened by thickening the walls as well as raising its height (Illus. 1.2).[19]

To the west, Poole's waterfront developed above massive dumps of oyster shells, evidence of earlier activity on a large scale; large shell-fish middens elsewhere on the south coast, on the Isle of Wight and at Braunton Burrows, Devon, did not lead to ports developing, as they did not have Poole's advantage of a good natural harbour, with easier sailing access than its two rivals, Christchurch and Wareham, and although both those were better-placed for inland distribution, Poole had the advantage as ships with deeper draughts came into use. Further west, Exeter avoided competition by having an outport a little down-river at Topsham, with better access from the sea but not a rival for distribution into the prosperous Devon hinterland.[20]

Inland towns often found their markets challenged by nearby rivals, so good access to their hinterlands was essential, and investment in roads and bridges was needed. A new bridge over the Trent at Newark, Nottinghamshire, was perceived as a threat to both Lincoln and Nottingham, as it might draw traffic and trade away from them. Upkeep was expensive, because frequent repairs were needed, as the sequence at Hemington, also on the Trent, shows. One town that went against the general trend was Thetford, Norfolk; although in the late eleventh century it had been important enough to have a castle, and briefly a bishopric, excavations have shown that whole areas were abandoned, and the thriving pottery industry came to an end. Changes to the Little Ouse River may have made it inaccessible from the sea, but it was on good road routes, and not so close to Norwich that its market could not compete, especially since it was on a classic interface location between geographical zones where meat, fish, and salt from the Fens to the west could be exchanged for grain from the common-field areas to the east. The abbots of Bury

St Edmunds, to the south, may have played a malign part by asserting rights over a wide area.[21]

Political factors also might affect towns: Winchester suffered badly in the Civil War and, then in its aftermath, lost the royal treasury to Westminster and with it a major role in the kingdom's affairs: magnate interest and purchasing declined, and its local trade was challenged by smaller towns, some new foundations and some expansions of existing places by estate owners who saw a profit in the rents and tolls that they could charge. Hampshire was not alone in this proliferation, usually characterized by cigar-shaped streets or small open squares that gave space for market stalls, fronted by long narrow tenements if the new town thrived. A few were distinctive because their shapes were dictated by adjacent castles, as at Devizes, Wiltshire, where the streets are still crescentic. Many were places with abbeys or minsters, where trading was already taking place: Stratford-upon-Avon, Warwickshire, provides an example of a town attached to but not surrounding an existing church; a surviving document shows where its inhabitants came from – most from the immediate hinterland with which Stratford would have had close ties through its everyday marketing, a few from a greater distance, and one from London. Established towns countered with attempts to create new spaces for market stalls in peripheral areas if any were available, but those might be too tangential for success. More usual was to permit markets outside the gates; they were more difficult to supervise but had the advantage of keeping large animals and carts outside where they were less likely to do damage. Reclaimed land at Beverley allowed the establishment of a new, large market-place well to the north of the minster church. Outside the walls of Bristol, landowners developed a new market to the east that obviated the need to take the difficult road round the castle to get into the town, and others developed Redcliffe on the other side of the River Avon, and Broadmead to the north, all with tenements and streets. Development of suburbs was usually more piecemeal but is a good indication of a town's success. Small open spaces on street corners and at churches may have become more profitable as permanent shops rather than spaces for carts, which could also account for what seems like encroachment on to a street.[22]

Occasional instances of markets within castle baileys continued to be established, but they were a minority and not always successful, as recent excavation in Oversley, Warwickshire, showed. At Saffron Walden, Essex, Geoffrey de Mandeville obtained a charter in 1141 to enable roads to be diverted into the new market in the bailey, where a new church was also built, but the venture was not a success, and the townspeople were relocated again in the following century. New towns did not require the interference of castles and may have deliberately eschewed a military display, having an earth bank and ditch perimeter if anything, not stone walls, which were expensive; older towns might still be able to call upon the shires around them to help with maintenance. Stone walls were therefore becoming a claim to venerable antiquity and a status symbol; the first known town seal is Oxford's, dated to 1191, and shows a town encircled by stone walls. The surviving leaded gunmetal 'moot horn' at Winchester may have been commissioned at the same time in the late twelfth century as the city's common seal and mayoralty were established.[23]

As well as marketing and trading, manufacturing of various sorts continued to be practised in towns, with the cloth industry now certainly the most profitable. The care with which the most expensive dyes were handled is shown by the deposits of vermilion found on oyster shells, used as palettes in London, although this may have been used in manuscript and wall-painting, and not in textiles. The physical evidence of the many crafts practised is the same in nature as in the previous century, as there were no significant technological changes, but quantities would have been greater, with more pressure on the principal streets for workshops and booths; tailors and cooks had greater need of frequent customer access than potters and woodturners. What is not so visible in the archaeological record is a change in craft organization, from using raw materials to make a range of different things to production of a specific item, whatever it was made of; the belt-maker bought metal buckles and strap-ends from a copper-alloy workshop to fit on to the leather that he had acquired from the tanner, and did not make sheaths and scabbards; the sheath-maker sold to the cutler, who bought iron knives from a smith and bone handles from a hafter, before assembling them to sell; a Londoner limited his production to a single item, rings, but made them in both bone and shale; guilds were now for trades, and not general fellowships like their anglo-saxon predecessors. Formalization is indicated by the increasing use of seals for individual trade-guilds.[24]

One product dependent upon localized sources was salt from inland brine springs, those in Cheshire now being exploited, as well as those in Droitwich. Excavations at Nantwich, Cheshire, revealed 'wich houses' containing long, narrow clay-lined troughs where the brine was stored before being boiled in lead vats – the lead would have needed capital outlay to acquire, so the industry was on a commercial scale (Illus. 8.3). Nantwich is the only new medieval town founded because of a specific industry. Metals such as lead did not encourage urban specialization in products made from the raw material because extraction was dependent on veins which were quickly worked out, forcing production to cease or at least move to a new location.[25]

A potential threat to trading in towns was the development of large annual fairs, difficult to recognize archaeologically because of their transient nature, but complex institutions with streets and rows designated for particular trades. Nearby towns might be prohibited from having markets while a fair was being held. Some of the great magnates bought luxuries such as wines and expensive textiles at fairs rather than in towns in which they were increasingly likely not to maintain residences, except in London because of the growing importance of the king's and other courts there; still visible despite being roofless is the bishops of Winchester's hall on the opposite side of the Thames which gave convenient access by water on land bought in the 1140s in Southwark because 'we have no house of our own in that city', an example followed by others despite the area's damp surroundings. Another exception was St Mary's Guildhall at the south end of Lincoln's Wigford, which was built in the late twelfth century as a royal palace with a first-floor hall,

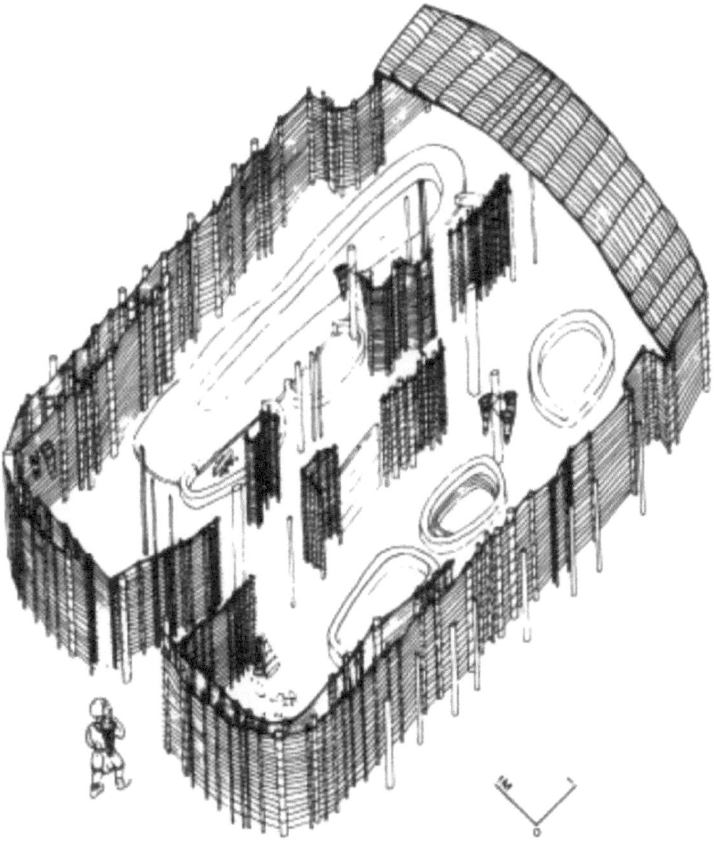

Illustration 8.3 Isometric reconstruction of one of the twelfth-century 'wich' houses excavated at Nantwich, Cheshire. It has a variety of vats for storing the brine, which was then boiled to extract the salt. This was stored and carried in the wicker baskets, known as 'barrows' (McNeil 1983).

the king perhaps responding to the bishops' relocation and rebuilding of their own palace, stretching out over the old Roman walls. A grandiose gatehouse leading into the cathedral precinct completed in about 1140 had already created a 'processional way' which the king could not match at the nearby castle. The gatehouse was more than just a facade and public spectacle but contained a chamber where the bishop or his representative held court, suitors having to ascend a grand staircase comparable to that at the Tower of London.[26]

Merchants and other rich citizens in many towns constructed stone-built houses with first-floor halls and chambers over ground-level storage. In Southampton, they lined the waterfront, so that goods could be unloaded and taken straight into an undercroft, with the merchant's living quarters above, the hall marked by an opulent fireplace and chimney, and windows with carvings as fine as any church could boast. Variations accorded to local need and topography: those in Lincoln show that the wealthy lived on the steep hill of the upper city, not near the waterfront. In towns where the water table was low enough and the ground not too hard to dig, vaulted cellars may have had timber-framed houses above them.[27]

Among the occupants of the wealthy areas in Lincoln and other towns were Jews, but no town had a ghetto, 'Jewry' being a commonly used term for an area in which rich citizens lived. Some Jews were important financiers, partly because their religion did not forbid lending money for profit, but their ownership of secure stone houses in Lincoln and elsewhere would not be known but for documentary evidence or even from a name, like the Music Hall in Norwich. Their other differences included burial customs, and they were licensed to have graveyards in specific towns. The largest excavated was on the outskirts of York, with orderly, often coffined graves laid out in rows with spaces in between, suggesting that the site had been planted to make it like a garden, conforming to the ideology of the *hortus Iudeorum*. The skeletons generally showed a good standard of living, with a higher proportion of older females than usual. In Winchester, the Jewish cemetery had a high proportion of infants, but that may have been because only part of the site was available for excavation; that cemetery was close to the castle, indicating a need for royal oversight and protection. York's was probably discretely hidden behind a high wall, just as synagogues were usually out of sight behind street-frontage ranges. Seven metres back from the road, an ornate undercroft with columns and benches in Guildford, Surrey, may well have been a synagogue. Distinctive ritual baths have been found in London and outside Bristol where the natural springs were adapted. Other material evidence is more elusive: seals, 'sabbath lamps', and a large copper-alloy bowl (Illus. 9.1). Some coin hoards may have been Jewish, but none can be proven so. Jewish diet included a ban on eating pork, and analysis by gas chromatography and carbon isotopes of some sherds in an area known to have had Jewish occupants in Oxford showed that pig fat had not been used in cooking – unlike sherds from other parts of the town. In appearance, Jews may have had swarthier skin tones, and possibly a distinctive smell, but they could if they wished disguise such differences by wearing the same clothing as gentiles.[28]

The wealthiest Jewish community was in London, where the cemetery and its garden were located outside Cripplegate. Extra-mural developments generally were a mark of London's growing size and wealth, seen in the number of its suburban hospitals: St Mary Spital took over an established extra-parochial cemetery, the need for which shows that already by the twelfth century the city was overcrowded, with internal space at a premium. The vulnerability of the poorer citizens to famine when harvests were bad probably accounts for the first example of 'catastrophe' burials, with up to eight bodies in a single pit, not individual graves; their radiocarbon dating is consistent with the record of extreme dearth in 1162. Most hospitals were not tucked away, but flanked a road leading into a town, to encourage travellers' donations and in some cases forming part of a sacred ring around it, augmented by prominently located chapels. They also had access to cleaner water, needed for cleanliness and for absolution; some religious institutions inside walled towns provided themselves with piped supplies – pieces of Purbeck marble columns and capitals from a late twelfth-century *lavabo* have been found at a priory within Exeter. Some healing measures were undertaken; various plants and herbal mixtures at least relieved pain, and some were specially cultivated, like those found in residues from the prior's garden at St Mary Spital, but dill, traced at an isolated hospital site in Yorkshire, was probably imported and used as oil extract. Roman samian sherds were presumably valued for their red colour and were closer to 'magic'. Surgical intervention was very rare, although occasional trepanation has been identified. At a priory in York with a reputation for healing, an attempt to ease a twist-fracture simply involved binding copper-alloy plates on both sides of the knee. The copper would have inhibited sepsis and may have been used knowingly. The cemetery there had a higher than normal proportion of young men with traumas, interpreted as battle wounds.[29]

Hospitals for lepers echoed the sufferers' liminal position, partly in the present world and suffering for their perceived 'sin' but partly already in the next and receiving absolution through their suffering. Anyone disfigured, and not from leprosy alone, was regarded as physically manifesting that their soul was impure. There was no cure except through prayer, so the hospitals were religious institutions, nearly always with their own chapels. A chapel was an essential element of any hospital, so that it could provide equally for spiritual and physical needs, and many were attached to priories or other religious institutions so that the clergy could minister to the sick. As there was no understanding of how the disease spread, lepers were allowed inside towns to collect alms and not only to remind the citizens of their duty to relieve the afflicted but also to remind them of the perils of sin. Some may have remained in their communities, at least until the disease became too noticeable, not only visibly but also by the smell; two buried at Raunds were among other burials, not isolated.[30]

*

Large and successful towns like London and Lincoln were affected by pressures on space that did not apply in most situations. A stately presence could be achieved within a castle enclosure by having a large, aisled ground-floor hall for dining and entertaining such as within Oakham and Leicester castles, the former with stone columns and the latter timber. Chamber blocks were usually separate structures, having a ground-floor undercroft for storage and food preparation, with a smaller and more private hall for less formal family use and a chamber on the upper floor. Apart from the different use of the undercrofts, these blocks are no different from those in towns, and whether one copied the other is a moot point. They were not confined to castles; Boothby Pagnell had one at a manor-house, and the excavated one at Wharram Percy is different only in that its undercroft was half-sunken; as it had three central columns, it probably supported floors above.[31]

Although large halls may seem to revive earlier anglo-saxon modes, social practices were different, without the oath-swearing and gift-giving of weapons and treasure that needed frequent reiteration when lordship had no permanence;

Norman lords ruled primarily through land tenure. Increasingly complex and theoretically God-devoted knighthood ceremonies developed, which initially involved girding with a sword and fostered a concept of honour, setting knights further apart from other social ranks. What had probably been no more than occasional family emblems on shields and banners were becoming formalized into heraldry, more necessary as armour encased the knight beyond recognition. Free-for-all and dangerous *mêlées* became controlled 'hastiludes' or tournaments, with select spectators but not open to vulgar scrutiny.[32]

Building of castles continued throughout the twelfth century, the scale dependent on the owner's purse and political ambitions, the last including kings' aspirations to conquer first Wales and then Ireland. Appearance also mattered, not only impressive height, but also in the quality of stonework, notably associated with a bishop of Salisbury and his early twelfth-century courtyard blocks within the walls of Sarum (Illus. 2.6) and Sherborne castles. Some magnates had the power to manipulate approaches by road so that everyone viewed their power: the bishop of Durham even cleared houses away from the space between his castle and the cathedral to improve the appearance of both, creating the Green that still exists. Elsewhere in Durham, Bishop Flambard is credited with building Framwell gate and a stone bridge, purportedly to benefit the town, but really also to be a reminder of his magnificence as well as his munificence; the bridge is one of the earliest to have had a stone span or vault, rather than a timber trestle. Excavation of three tenements in the town has been redated to this period on the basis of the artefacts.[33]

The bishops of Durham had a particular role, controlling the 'Palatinate'; the threat from Scotland made a particular need. King David took advantage of King Stephen's weakness to annexe Carlisle and Cumbria, acquiring silver mines that enabled him to establish a currency to emulate England's. Territorial blocs like those became an aspiration for rebellious barons during the 'Anarchy', their control symbolized by issuing their own coins; Matilda used western mints, reflecting her power base, as did her main supporter Robert of Gloucester, but even a few quite minor barons issued coins in defiance of King Stephen. The most notorious of them, Geoffrey de Mandeville, did not do that, despite his obvious desire to rule Essex, using a new castle at Walden as his main base. Other new castles in the Anarchy included one at Trowbridge, Wiltshire, which replaced a manorial enclosure, just as had happened frequently in the years after 1066; unusually, continued use of an existing burial ground was permitted there, the graves becoming more and more intercut and overlaid, with charnel from older ones being placed in the new ones (Illus. 8.4).[34]

Direct capture of a castle was difficult; stone-throwing machines were not very effective against stout walls nor probably accurate enough to be sure of targeting a weak point such as a gate, and mining was usually impractical, in view of the time needed to dig through solid ground and deep enough to go below a defensive ditch. In the 'Anarchy', hastily dug ditches and banks sheltered a few soldiers to prevent supplies or reinforcements getting into a targeted castle; some of these siegeworks were just beyond arrow or crossbow range from it, others blockaded it

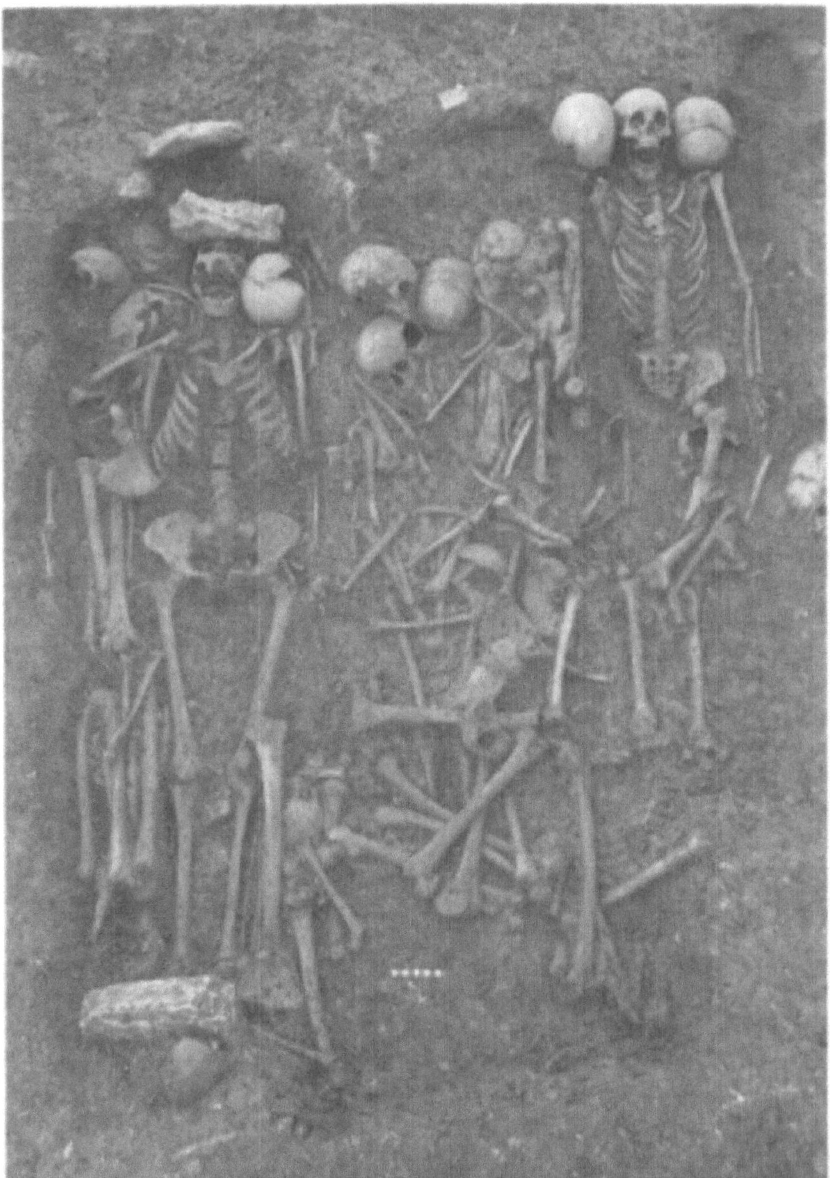

Illustration 8.4 Intercutting graves at Trowbridge, Wiltshire, within the outer bailey of an Anarchy castle, show how pressure on space mounted. Some of the skulls and bones from earlier graves were redeposited as charnel, some of the skulls being placed so as to prop the new corpse's head upright, in the way that stones were often used. On the right and left, long bones were quite carefully placed, but in the middle they were merely thrown in randomly. Stone slabs had been carefully positioned at the head and foot of the burial on the left (Graham and Davies 1993, 67–9).

from a distance, but they were not intended to be permanent and only a few have left visible traces. Crossbows were detested by knights because the bolts were so penetrative, but they took so long to rewind that they had limited use, though occasional 'nuts' deriving from them are found; the earliest known slits specifically for their use are in the late twelfth-century Avranches Tower at Dover. Those without the resources of a king, baron, or bishop of a wealthy see had increasing difficulty in maintaining a martial appearance, in buildings, or in person; for a knight, the costs of a horse bred and trained to fight with the weight of an armed man on its back, of weapons and armour, and of the retinue needed to maintain it all necessitated service in someone else's army, good fortune in the tournament, or a rich heiress to marry. A suit of mail could take 140 hours of a craftsman's time, a sword up to 200. No wonder that they resented the high wages that a mere crossbow-man could get.[35]

Kings also spent lavishly on undefended palaces and houses. Clarendon, Wiltshire, probably originated as a hunting-lodge for William I and was expanded by Henry I; by then, it may have been more than a quiet refuge from the noise and bustle of Old Sarum but a reminder as well that the king did not need to rule from a castle because he had the whole country under his control; important legislation was enacted there. Also undefended was the royal palace at Woodstock, where Henry I had a zoo, and Henry II later had a pleasure garden for Rosamund's Bower. Another palace that remained in use was Kingsholm, just outside Gloucester, which was preferred to the intra-mural castle for meetings. Henry I's rule saw new accounting methods introduced, using the abacus and checked cloth, leading to a new office of government.[36]

Settings like Clarendon's influenced contemporary writers who began to express appreciation of landscapes for their beauty, enhanced by pheasants, partridges, and deer; peacocks and doves ornamented courtyards, with dovecotes as physical expressions of lordly ability to enjoy a luxury food in the summer and adding the appearance of a tower to the precinct. Rabbits were introduced but did not become a pest because they were confined to warrens, artificial mounds that would have become another landscape feature to enjoy and exploit during the second half of the twelfth century. Fish-ponds supplied another luxury food, permissible to eat on days of fast when meat was forbidden; they took up meadowland especially valuable for hay-making. Much more land, though not necessarily the most fertile, was taken up by parks, provided especially for fallow deer; these enclosures were attached to one side or were even separate from the courtyards of the houses, but unlike later landscape developments did not entirely surround them, isolating and hiding them from the view of the tenantry and passers-by: medieval owners wanted to be seen and admired, their use of their land showing their ability to disregard economic restraints. It may have been to admire the view from its top rather than from any intention of using it for defence that a bishop of Winchester built a tower at Witney, Oxfordshire, thick-walled but with ground-floor windows, and only 11 metres by six internally. At Little Downham, Cambridgeshire, the bishops of Ely had wide views across the fens to enjoy, and the cathedral could be seen on higher ground to the south-east.[37]

An important feature of many house complexes was an enclosed garden, where sweet-smelling and colourful plants could be grown and enjoyed. On warm summer days, men and women could sit outside, demonstrating that they had leisure and did not do manual work. They might pass the time playing board games, which had a long history; 'nine men's morris' and others that did not need costly equipment were popular, and dice could be thrown to foretell the future as well as for bets. More complex was a tables game similar to backgammon, which needs a special board, though coloured bone discs could serve as counters; few would have been able to afford the elaborately carved set found virtually complete with remains of a board in a pit at Gloucester Castle – were they thrown down in a fit of rage by a bad loser (Illus. 8.5)? Above all, chess began to be played widely in the twelfth century; its pieces mirror feudal society. The skill needed to play it well could only be achieved by those with the time to learn it and to take part in long games, which could be between men and women. Some skilfully carved pieces could be admired, but there were also much simpler versions, found in contexts that suggest that chess was played by some townspeople as well as in castles and manor-houses.[38]

*

After the 'Anarchy', Henry II enforced his authority by having many castles removed or rendered defenceless, which probably enhanced the status of those allowed to remain. At each end of his kingdom, at Newcastle-upon-Tyne and Dover, he added great rectangular towers which look little different from those built a hundred years earlier and were perhaps deliberate statements of ancient power and authority as well as for defence against Scots and French, respectively; yet at Orford, Suffolk, he built a tower that must have surprised all who saw it by its unusual design of a circle with three projecting rectangular turrets, though how many would have understood either the geometry or its possible Trinity symbolism? The local great family, the Bigods, certainly understood the main message that the king's work overtopped theirs at Framlingham, which they reconstructed with a high curtain wall and twelve mural towers including the gate – Christ and the apostles? At Colchester, the name associated the castle with the legend of King Cole, and thus back to the real Constantine the Great, and to the cult of Mary that developed at Constantinople. Helmsley, Yorkshire, made more allowance for comfort, and round towers, such as at Barnard, introduced a new visual statement.[39]

Henry II also spent heavily on Clarendon Palace, though all that survives from his period is a large subterranean wine-cellar. Less than a day's ride away he had another cellar, recently excavated at Tidgrove, Hampshire, a small complex on one side of a valley, to which a public road on the other side gave easy access; the surrounding ditch and bank were for privacy rather than defence. A stream ran down the valley, dammed for fish-ponds. Just as Clarendon provided hunting in its adjacent Forest, so Tidgrove provided it on open downland. Another, larger, royal house at Clipstone, Nottinghamshire, was convenient for getting into Sherwood Forest and from the late 1170s had a deer-park attached to it. It also had a

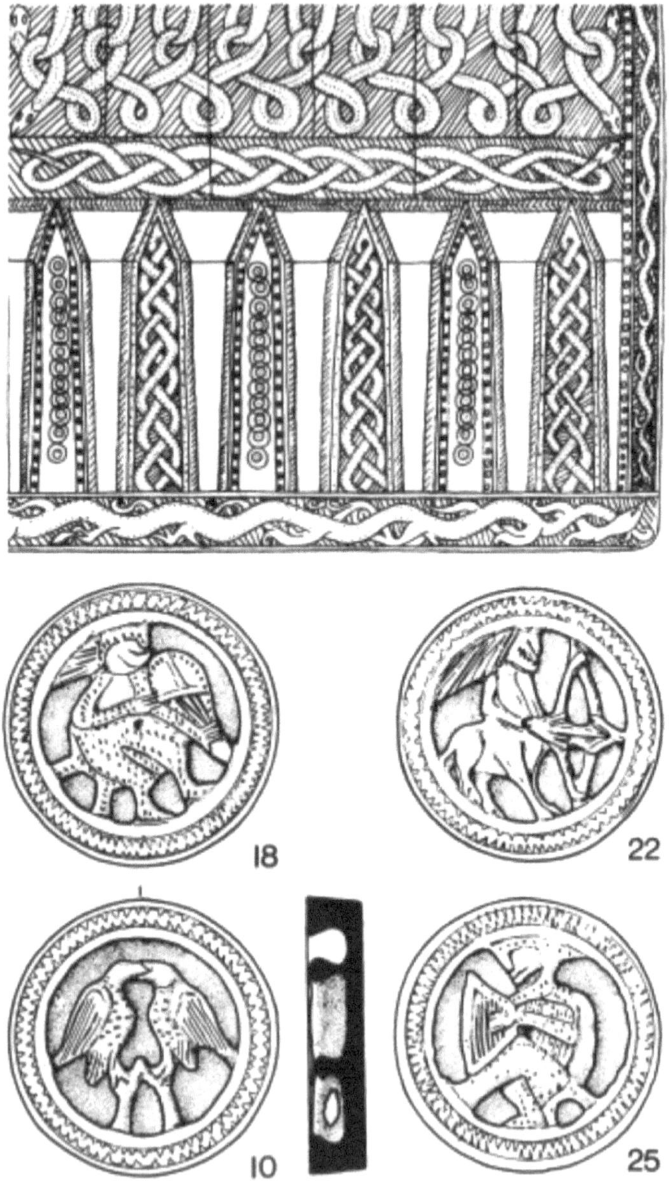

Illustration 8.5 A set of the game Tables was excavated in a pit at Gloucester Castle, apparently with a complete board and pieces. Although they had been used together, the styles of the two elements were very different – the board with its interlace and (at the bottom) undulating animal patterns is Anglo-Scandinavian, but the circular counters are Romanesque. Presumably they were painted or stained to create two opposing sets. Drawings by J. Knappe and P. Moss.

Illustration 8.5 (Continued)

fish-pond. Like wine, venison and fresh fish were useful as gifts as well as for the royal table.[40]

Henry II was not only a builder; he also instituted new legal procedures, so that the royal court was the supreme arbiter, supported at county and local level through sheriffs and travelling judges. This took the administration of justice other than of petty crimes and disputes away from the open-air hundred meeting places, and most of the late anglo-saxon execution burial sites were phased out. Presumably the gallows at most were replaced as well, with new sites for them on roads leading out of towns – if Norwich is typical. There, just inside the walls, was a church 'where the hanged are buried', and excavation revealed a number of bodies, dumped rather than placed, some prone and some with their wrists clearly bound, and in pits rather than individual graves; as might be expected of people rightly or wrongly condemned, the majority were males in their late teens and twenties, who had a little more evidence of violence on their bones than the norm. According to documentary records, the gallows were just outside the gate. Where trials took place seems not to be recorded; royal castles may have been used, and some have small rooms accessible only by ladders, but whether those were dungeons or strong-rooms is a moot point. Prisoners were not retained as punishment but were confined until the justices arrived. Only Lydford, Devon, has a record of specific adaptation for the administration of justice, in the particular circumstances of Dartmoor. A strong tower was heightened there, and earth piled up around it so that it has the appearance of a motte; the entombed space could have been where prisoners were held. Such features as 'ordeal pits' referred to in documents have not been recognized, and other forms of trial by ordeal would not leave an archaeological trace.[41]

Early in his reign, Henry II regained the Carlisle region from the Scots, stabilizing the north and allowing development. Lead production from there increased, as it did in the Peak District; this has been dramatically shown recently by an analysis of a Swiss ice core. Peveril Castle oversaw the Derbyshire mines – but the site was perhaps selected with an eye to the picturesque cavern out of which hot air came, known as the 'Devil's arse' and listed as one of Britain's seven great marvels. As important as the lead was the silver that occurs in the same strata, although English production was much less significant for the increase in coinage – and perhaps concomitant inflation – than imports. Henry re-established royal control over the mints, reducing their number, although not improving quality.[42]

In the same way as he strengthened Peveril Castle near the lead mines, Henry II added a tower to St Briavel's, Gloucestershire, in the Forest of Dean; it helped his control over the Welsh March and was a base for hunting expeditions, but probably most important was its oversight of the local iron production. Gloucester was another castle able to oversee the Forest; kings were not only interested in the profits that iron could make, but also in its use for their swords and arrows, as well as horseshoes and nails. No evidence that Gloucester smiths had special skills has been found, despite their access to ores. A very significant indicator of the increasing demand for the metal by the end of the twelfth century was found in excavation at Bordesley Abbey, Worcestershire, where a water-mill was used to operate a tilt-hammer to break up iron ore and to power the bellows to smelt it. Evidence of the process of manufacture of weapons was found there, so presumably the monks were leasing out the mill rather than selling the products themselves.[43]

By the end of the twelfth century, vertical mill-wheels, like those at Bordesley, had generally replaced the low-energy horizontal wheels. A few tide-mills were built, but potentially more significant were windmills, making grain production more viable in areas with only slow-moving water-courses. They needed substantial foundation timbers laid out cross-wise to support a massive vertical post that had to turn the whole superstructure, including the sails which by their weight pulled away from the vertical; such structures were costly both to build and to maintain, therefore. Vertical wheels were also larger and more expensive than horizontal ones and needed a greater 'head' of water and so were more likely to have to be fed by leats, also excavated at Bordesley, controlled by weirs; obstruction to inland navigation became a common complaint, but the landowner had legal right to the water flow. An advantage of weirs and mill leats was that they facilitated the catching of fish, particularly eels, which may sometimes have been at least as valuable as the mill. A complex excavated at Castle Donington, Leicestershire, has shown how dams were constructed to direct the water from the River Trent, and wattle fish-traps may have preceded the waterwheels there. Fish were also caught in nets, attested by stone sinkers, which may show regional variation. Hooks were also used to take fish from ponds as well as larger sea fish.[44]

Running water was also important spiritually, as a reminder of God's blessing. Some urban cathedrals and monasteries constructed aqueducts to bring clean supplies from extra-mural springs and wells; in Exeter, lead pipes sealed in clay to reduce leakage were laid in deep trenches from an extra-mural well outside the city to a conduit in the cathedral precinct, an operation which involved a tunnel under the city wall (Illus. 9.5). Many shrines had holy wells, where votive and other offerings were made. Attention has been drawn to the number of weapons found in the River Witham in Lincolnshire, perhaps maintaining the late anglo-saxon practice. A bowl found in an early twelfth-century construction context in the Hemington bridge sequence was made of burr alder, the burr giving a prized spotted effect. It may have been accidentally lost, but there is a possibility of deliberate deposition of a prestigious item. Other river finds include a metal 'Hanse' bowl found in the River Nene.[45]

Stone bridges were taking advantage of new understanding of vaulting, as 'Gothic' architecture replaced Norman, for instance at Wells Cathedral in Somerset. Other new learning was needed for accounting, as kings were changing tax systems, including levying customs duty on exports, and landholders were more likely to farm their estates themselves than to rent them out, needing stewards to keep records of income and expenditure. The university at Oxford reflected new emphasis on training and learning, not least of accounting methods. The murder of Becket in 1170 led to a cult centre for a new English saint at Canterbury, much more accessible to southern pilgrims than Durham's Cuthbert or Bury's Edmund, more meaningful than Shaftesbury's Edward or Gloucester's Oswald.

Etiquette books were advocating more genteel behaviour with all but the lord being exhorted not to piss in the hall; the hall was to be seen as a special space, where everyday work should not take place, and which only horses, dogs, and hawks should enter – not pigs. Social differentiation is shown by admonishments not to 'spit like a rustic' or 'eat like a ploughman'.[46]

Difference in costume was being joined by slowly increasing displays of personal jewellery, with gems filtering into the secular from the ecclesiastical world, and items such as a gold brooch with a rampant lion, an early use of a heraldic emblem. Personal jewellery now included wedding and betrothal rings, often showing clasped hands, and in various metals. Gemstones and some fossils were valued for their 'properties', such as protecting from poison. As with deposition in rivers, beliefs and practices are not always explained in texts, and objects in burials may have been deliberately included as amulets as well as to symbolize a pilgrim or some other distinctive characteristic. As the corpse was prepared for burial in the person's home, whether they were buried clothed as well as shrouded, and whether a token was placed with them or a pebble in their mouth would not have been known to the priest, but he would certainly have witnessed the inclusion of staffs or wands, as well as the multiplicity of arrangements of stones, crushed chalk, charcoal, and so on, but none of these was proscribed. When found in a domestic context, it is more difficult to know if an object had been deliberately concealed as a good luck or other token, but bent coins are certainly significant. A fragment of gilded glass from an Arabian vase found at Seacourt, Oxfordshire, may have been much more than a curiosity or a memento of a crusade but an object of wonder.[47]

Social and economic changes in the 1180s and 90s were played out in the following decades, and the term 'the long thirteenth century' is often used to show the continuum. Politically, the death of Richard II in 1199 was momentous by bringing John to the throne, but how much long-term effect do the actions of monarchs have? Henry I had given stability, but not enough to prevent the 'Anarchy'; Henry II had restored order, but John was to fail to maintain it. Aristocratic machinations brought strife, taxation, and destruction, affecting everyone's lives and aspirations, but they have to be set against famine, disease, and climatic changes to see the whole picture.

Notes

1 Taxation: Jurkowski *et al.* 1998, xiii–xxiii. 'Development' is not synonymous with 'improvement'.
2 Muck-spreading: Jones, R. 2004.
3 Roberts and Wrathmell 2000 mapped the 'provinces'; their details have been much debated, but a broad pattern remains; see O'Donnell 2018 for a recent overall survey. Wharram is symptomatic of the difficulty of dating village tenement rows: Everson and Stocker 2012b, 266 postulated 'possible – even probable' expansion along one side of the green, its regularity due 'perhaps . . . even to a twelfth-century replanning'. Villages developing from discrete units: Taylor, C. 1983, 131–3; a linear example was recently shown at the aptly named The Street in Old Basing, Hampshire: Pringle 2020, 316–17.

Vegetables such as 'worts' (cabbages), leeks, onions, turnips, and carrots, and a range of herbs, were garden products; peas and beans were field crops also: Dyer 2006a; Stone, D. 2005, 62–4; see Pounds 1989, 176 for a poem by the aptly named John Gardener; see Dunne *et al.* 2019 for brassica identification in lipid residues; because vegetables are eaten before they seed, they do not reveal themselves in pollen analyses. The importance of the tenement unit is shown by measures to protect 'hamsocn', for instance in the heavy penalties for 'eavesdropping': Müller 2005.

4 An element of similar problems occurs with East Anglian greens, as dating to the twelfth century often depends upon the absence of Thetford-type wares from them, rather than more positive data: Martin, E. 2012, 235–8. For country-wide surveys, see Christie and Stamper (eds) 2012. Like the Cistercians, hermits also sought solitude – woodland clearance is evidenced by complaints that they had less chance of finding it: Golding 2001, 114–15.

5 Cob walling was explained very clearly by Beresford 1975, 36–40; the Westbury, Buckinghamshire, site gives several examples of the evidence and its problems: Ivens *et al.* 1995, 93–4 and 136–8; a survival was excavated immured in castle earthworks at Wallingford: Creighton 2018, 361–2; see Dyer 2008 for the documentary record. The quotation is from *c.* 1180 about Witham, Lincolnshire, when peasants were being relocated: Bartlett 2000, 301; *bordelli* was a term used on Glastonbury estates for 'sub-cottagers'' houses: Fox, H. S. A. 1996, 536–8. Lords' control over people is shown by this, but legal changes put greater stress on control of land and of its tenants' dues than on individuals' personal obligations, be it to kin or community (effected by tithing and pledging): Kilby 2015, 74; Schofield, P. 1996. Peasants/husbandmen represented the feet of the body politic to John of Salisbury; they 'always cleave to the soil', but could not be replaced by 'brute animals', so were at the bottom of the social order, below those who fought and those who prayed, graphically shown in Henry I's nightmare as boorish figures with scythe, pitchfork, and spade, basic instruments of their toil: Hinton 2005, 173. Merchants and townspeople did not fit into the concept of the Three Orders; John saw them as society's arms.

6 West Cotton residue analysis: Dunne *et al.* 2019; the brassicas were probably cabbages and leeks (stews can be dipped into at any time, so fixed meal times would not necessarily have structured peasant life routines). Westbury: Ivens *et al.* 1995, 290–1. Tripod pitchers: Mellor 1997, 25–6. Small pottery bowls seem less frequent than in the eleventh century, so wooden ones seem likely (see also Ch. 9). A range of gaming counters and chess pieces, a board, and bone pipes (capable of a good tone and if used with a reed for pitch) were found at the Raunds sites: Auduoy and Chapman (eds) 2009; Chapman 2010.

7 Canterbury potter: Cotter 1997; Diack 2005. Ely: Spoerry 2016. Potting: Mellor 2005; 2018, 444–5. Grimston: Leah 1994; Hanley Castle, where six tenants paid 8d each per year and two pots per week to the bishop, their landlord, in 1187: Hurst, J. 1994; Chilvers Coton: Mayes and Scott 1984. The eleventh-century potters in Domesday Book were also working near extensive woodlands and were perhaps living in 'potting villages': see Ch. 7. Some cooperation would have reduced what are known as 'transaction costs'.

8 Dung: Jones, R. 2004, 165–9 – he pointed out that this does not mean that large open fields were necessarily created in the twelfth century, as they might previously have been manured exclusively by animals grazing on the fallow. Coins: Kelleher 2018, 520–1; a search for 'Richard I coin' on the PAS database produces too many that are not attributed to his reign for easy assessment. Wharram: Barclay 2007, 301.

9 See Dyer 2012, 326 for Wharram textile evidence. An illustration in the Holkham Bible clearly shows women indoors combing and spinning, while men are shown digging and pruning outside: MS BL Add MS 47682. Archaeology cannot detect gender differentiation in dairying and brewing, but the word for a servant involved in the former was the

female *daia*, and 'ale-wives' was already standard terminology when the documentary record opens. Spindle-whorls: Standley 2016. Skeletal data: Mays *et al.* 2007, 125–7. Women were already less likely to prepare and cook food in larger towns: Carlin 1998, and urban malting ovens, which involved considerable below-ground stonework, may have been operated by either gender: see Atkins 2021, 25–6 for a recent example. Castle Acre tumbrel: Margeson 1982, 244–5.

10 St Paul's: Hale (ed.) 1888; Faith 1994. Cressing Temple dendrochronology: Tyers and Hibberd 1993, 50–2. See Brady 2018 for a recent survey.

11 Fernie 2000 is the best architectural guide. Hereford: Stone, R. and Appleton-Fox 1996, 22–3; Leicester had another. On a much smaller scale is a recently excavated charnel pit at Poulton, Cheshire: Cootes *et al.* 2019, 38. Owen 1971, 5 cited a new church being built on a new site to replace a wooden one before 1180, to which 'the bodies buried in [the old church] shall be taken to the new church.'

12 For minsters, see Chs 6 and 7. Even a 'great' minster like St Oswald's, Gloucester, might be regularized into the Augustinian Order. Chapels: Orme 1996. Bell-towers were not invariably at the west end: Fawcett 2018, 598; and many churches had a bell-cote set above the roof for a couple of bells if they could not afford a tower; see Mileson 2018, 718–25 for the significance of bells. Slabs: Badham 2005, 165–6 and Butler 1987; the regional implications were explored further by McClain 2012, 149–51. Bury: Gilchrist and Sloane 2005, 91–2; Gittos 2017.

13 London Bridge: Harrison 2007, 115 and 123–4; waterfront excavations: Ayre and Wroe-Brown 2015b, 212–14 and 220–1; Schofield 2019; boats: Marsden 1996.

14 London fruit and vegetables: Jones, G. *et al.* 1991 – grain deposits were also considered in detail. Guilds: Nightingale 1985; Ramsay 1991, xx–xxii.

15 London skeletons: White 1988; pottery: Vince and Jenner 1991, 44–7 and Pearce 2015, 265–6; tokens: Bowsher and Egan 2015, 238–40; metalwork: Egan and Blackmore 2015. Urban cooks: Carlin 1998; pies and sausages were notorious and doubtlessly added to urban ill-health.

16 Bristol: Jones, R. H. 1991; Baker, N. *et al.* 2018, 103–4. Lincoln: Jones, M. J. *et al.* 2003, 239–41 – the Foss Dyke reopening is attributed to the later tenth century on the basis of pottery from Torksey arriving in Lincoln then; Wigford reclamation: Glover *et al.* 2014. Boston: Rigby 2017. York: Hall, R. A. 1992, 182; York was transitioning from national to regional centre. Hull: see Ch. 9.

17 Beverley: Evans, D. H. and Tomlinson 1992, 18–61.

18 Yarmouth: Rogerson 1976; Potter 2008; herring fishing was practised by most east coast ports: Barrett 2018, 132. Wisbech: Spoerry 2005, 102–5. Lynn: Parker 1971, 26–7. Newcastle: O'Brien *et al.* 1988; O'Brien 1991; Kermode 2000b, 69–70.

19 Old Winchelsea and Rye: Eddison 2004, 2–4. Southampton: Platt 1973, 21–2. Portsmouth: Fox, R. and Barton 1986, 37–41. Portchester: for the development of the keep, see Cunliffe and Munby 1985, contribution by D. Renn and J. Munby, 72–87; also Chibnall 1986, 125. Fishing would have been important for the south coast ports as well as those on the east; see Ch. 9 for evidence at Dover.

20 Coastal middens: Dunning 1937; Smith *et al.* 1983; marine shells have been found far inland at Oxford and Leicester. Poole: Horsey 1992, 4–8, with report on the oysters by J. M. Winder, 194–200. Exeter: Kowaleski 1993.

21 The Newark bridge evidence is documentary: Harrison 2007, 44. Hemington: Ripper and Cooper 2009. Thetford: Rogerson and Dallas 1984; Dunmore and Carr 1976; the arid breckland may have been a negative factor but did not stop the town from growing in the first place; the abbot of Bury once sent 600 armed men to destroy a rival market: Smith, R. M. 1996, 460. Common fields: Martin, E. 2012, 230–5.

22 Street markets and market-places: Schofield and Vince 1994, 46–52; shops: Antrobus 2018, 319. Oxford's Cornmarket had frontage occupation moved backwards on one side of the street as though to widen it, but the opposite occurred on the other side,

perhaps because tenements originally had empty spaces in front of buildings, used for temporary booths: Sturdy and Munby 1984; Dodd (ed.) 2003, 201. Winchester's market development is complicated because extra space became available after the mid twelfth century with the removal of the royal palace from part of the High Street: Ottaway 2017, 219, 297, and 301. For new towns generally, see Beresford, M. W. 1967; Britnell 2006. Expansion can sometimes be recognized through identification of 'plan-units', blocs of tenements and streets: Lilley 2018, 276–80. Devizes has been much discussed because one of its market-places is within what seems to have been the outer bailey of the castle, as is a church, but there is another market-place and another church in an outer circuit: Royal Archaeological Institute/Publications: 'Devizes' (online); a recent excavation has suggested a third ditch closer to the motte: Robinson and Cox 2020, 224–5. Stratford-upon-Avon: Carus-Wilson 1965, data from a mid thirteenth-century rental for 234 tenants with surnames nearly all showing their place of origin or their occupation – most were in the leather or textile trades, a few in building, a few in smithing, barrel-making, and other specialist occupations that a village probably would not have accommodated – there was even a juggler to keep people entertained; plan: Slater and Wilson 1977, the grid 'distorted' to fit the river. Beverley: Evans and Tomlinson 1992, 271–3. Bristol: Leech 2014, 17–20; Baker, N. *et al.* 2018, 101–8. Domesday Book reveals small-scale trading in some eleventh-century places that became identifiable as towns in the twelfth. Market-places in general: Keene 2000b, 85–6 (see also Ch. 7).

23 Oversley: Jones, C. *et al.* 1997. Walden: Bassett 1982. Town walls: Creighton and Higham 2005, 166–8 and 179–80. Oxford seal: Davis, R. H. C. 1968 (although ostensibly the result of a dispute with the main church in the town, the citizens may have had an eye to corporate identity against the growing university). Winchester moot-horn: Crummy, N. *et al.* 2008. Horns became symbols of authority more widely, for example hereditary wardenships of forests: Bathe 2012.

24 The range of objects found is well demonstrated by publications from York: Ottaway and Rogers 2002; MacGregor *et al.* 1999; from Winchester: Biddle (ed.) 1990; and the series of monographs from London, mostly masterminded by the late Geoff Egan. Oyster shells with vermilion: Pritchard 1991, 170 (Uzzell 2012 did not discuss vermilion as a textile dye). Knives and cutlers: Goodall, I. H. 2011, 111; other examples include combs: Riddler *et al.* 2012, 417. Ring specialization: Riddler and Trzaska-Nartowski 2011, 132. Craft specialization in the guilds involved a degree of fluidity: Swanson, H. 1988, 40–3. Linen-weaving and rural flax-retting to obtain the fibres both may be underestimated in the archaeological record.

25 Nantwich: McNeil 1983.

26 Fairs: Moore, E. W. 1985; Epstein 1994. de Blois's Southwark: Carlin 1996; the bishop's purchase came *cum portu navium* for the landing place; the rose window that survives is in the gable of the early thirteenth-century first-floor hall: Hare 2021, 83. Lincoln: Stocker 1991 (who noted Oxford and Gloucester as other towns where the king had a castle but built a separate 'palace', probably for greater privacy and space); Guy 2019–20, 123–5. The present west end of the cathedral might have started as a separate residential defensive block, with the cathedral added later; for a summary of the problem, see Fernie 2000, 108–10.

27 Stone houses: Quiney 2003, 143–7 and 166–81. Southampton: Faulkner 1975, 83–94. Lincoln: Jones *et al.* 1996; Johnson, C. and Jones 2016. See Ch. 13 for cellars.

28 Lincoln: Johnson, C. and Jones 2016. Norwich: Grenville 1997, 177; 'Music' seems a corruption from 'Moses'. York cemetery: Lilley *et al.* 1994. My paper on Jews' archaeological representation (Hinton 2003) has been superseded in parts by Hillaby and Hillaby 2013, by Watson 2014 on lamps, and on matters such as clothing by Lipton 2016. Oxford: Teague *et al.* 2020, 79–80, with residue analyses by J. Dunn and R. P. Evershed on pp. 100–1; there were also no eel bones, another forbidden food, so household rubbish in stone-lined pits was not so intermixed as to prevent the identification of

specifically Jewish rubbish deposits – contrary to what I said in 2003! Money lending by Christians was generally frowned upon if it made more than a small return, anything more being usurious, an abuse of God-given time by making a profit from it using non-natural means; circumvention, for example buying next year's crop in the hope of getting higher prices after harvest, was frequent. The late twelfth-century saw the first 'blood-libel' accusations and boy-saint shrines at Lincoln and Norwich, leading to the first massacre of Jews in York in 1189.

29 Harward *et al.* 2019; extra-parochial cemetery 15–18; map on p. 7 for hospital locations. See Gilchrist 1999, 112–13 for discussion of ideas of cleanliness primarily involving fear of 'bad' odour, ritual purity, and that proscription on drinking from communal vessels could indicate awareness of contagion; Golding 2001, 150–4; Huggon 2018, 846–51. Exeter: Stoyle 2014, 17–21. Medical plants: contribution by A. Davis to Harward *et al.* 2019, 172–3; dill: Cardwell *et al.* 1995, 227 and 232, samian pottery sherds: 238 (either amuletic or to be ground up as a powder). York: Daniell 2001; knee: Knüsel *et al.* 1995; also Huggon 2018, 838–9.

30 Leprosy: Lee 2011; Roffey 2012; Rawcliffe 2005; Jeanne 2014; Roberts, C. A. *et al.* 2018, 829–30; Huggon 2018, 843–6. Disfigurement: Woodcock 2005, 18. Because they smelt foul, lepers might be given foul meat, following medieval notions of 'sympathetic' practice: Woolgar 2006, 127. Raunds: Boddington 1996, 69.

31 See Blair 2015, who was able to cite the further evidence of the surviving timbers reused in the London waterfront, see Ch. 6; Campbell, J.[a] 2018, 243–6. Leicester re-assessment: Hill, N. 2019a. First-floor halls: Hill, N. and Gardiner 2018, noting Richmond, Yorkshire, as a distinguished exception. Christchurch had a long first-floor room heated by a side chimney, has space within the precinct for a separate and more public ground-floor hall. Wharram Percy (South Manor): Wrathmell 2012a, 232–4 (a ground-level hall may also have existed, but the evidence is inconclusive).

32 Knighting ceremonial became more and more elaborate: Pilbrow 2002. Tournaments: Barber and Barker 1989.

33 Old Sarum and Sherborne: White, P. and Cook 2015, 17–9. Durham bridge: Britnell 2006, 137; Harrison 2007, 112; excavation reanalysis: Vince and Mould 2007. Invisible archaeologically is that despite their general stench and noise, towns might be perceived as places to admire and enjoy: for example see Clarke, C. A. M. 2006, 90–105, on London and Chester.

34 King David and silver: Blanchard 1996; Allen, M. 2011, 115–16 and 121–4 – output was probably small but useful; Allen, M. 2017; Scottish coins maintained the same standard as English, and circulated in England, until the mid fourteenth century. The Border region: Barrow, G. 1989. Anarchy coins and regionalism: Chibnall 1986, 98–9; Green 1997, 48–60 – Henry I had reduced the number of mints, but his successor could not exercise the same level of control. Trowbridge: Graham and Davies 1993, 57–77.

35 See Hulme 2019–20, a valuable critique of various different views of the extent and reality of the 'War of Stephen and Matilda'. Examples of siegeworks: Laban 2013; Stamper 1984. Cross-bow 'nuts' and other evidence: Kenyon 1990, 172. Mail: Peirce 1986.

36 Clarendon: James and Robinson 1988, 1–7. Exchequer: Church 2012. The checked cloth gave us the Exchequer and its Chancellor, just as other governmental changes have given us different Courts, all ultimately from the king's household: Chibnall 1986, 124–5. Although the abacus and Arabic numerals were both coming into use, the checked cloth was retained because it enabled business calculations to be seen and followed: Evans, G. R. 1979.

37 Landscape: Creighton 2002. New species: Sykes 2007, 76–85; rabbits: Standley 2018. Witney: Allen, T. G. 2002, 20–2 and 206–8; few later medieval bishops visited Witney, but it was maintained to demonstrate their local role: Hare, J. 2021, 88. Little Downham: Taylor, C. 2010. Doves were not a relief to winter famine, as was once thought,

although rabbits were: Dyer 2006b, 206. Peacocks and other birds consumed: Serjeantson 2006. Parks: Mileson 2009 (dating of their introduction, increase, and decline is difficult – p. 6); Williamson, T. 2010, 164–5 – Restormel was encircled by its park, but its location on Cornish moorland may have been unrestrained by agricultural or access needs. Dovecotes: Hansson 2009, 449.

38 See Ch. 3 for early anglo-saxon game-playing. 'Tables' were found in Anglo-Scandinavian York, as were dice: MacGregor *et al.* 1999, 1981–5. Typical examples of dice and counters: Margeson 1982, 252–4 and 260–1 for 'nine men's morris' boards cut into flat stone. Gloucester backgammon: Stewart and Watkins 1984; Stewart 1988. Chess: Eales 1985; Hall, M. A. 2018b, 532–3 (part of a set found at Witchampton, Dorset, was from a manor-house site: I accepted an early date for it too readily in Hinton 1998, 75); the debris of bone and antler from the workshop of someone making the simpler pieces has now been reported from Northampton, underlining the game's widespread popularity: Atkins 2021.

39 Newcastle-upon-Tyne: Guy 2017–18; Dixon 2018, 382–5; Dover 385–90; Scarborough is another in the north-east on a prominent headland and looking as much like William I's work as Henry II's: Goodall, J. 2011, pl. 103; baronial Bungay is another: Guy (ed.) 2011–12, 87–90, as is Middleham, though less martial in appearance if its doors and windows are original: Kenyon 2018, 141–6. Orford: Goodall, J. 2011, 126–30, who pointed out that the full effect cannot be judged because the surrounding bailey walls are lost and may have had turrets to match those of the tower. See Wheatley 2004, 39–43 for Colchester, and for symbolism generally. Arrow-slits: Renn 2011–12. Helmsley: Kenyon 2018, 146–53. Barnard: Davis, P. 2012–13; Hislop 2018.

40 Tidgrove: Kris Strutt, University of Southampton, personal communication. Clipstone: Wright, J. and Gaunt 2013–14.

41 Legal procedures: Hudson 2011, 121–2. The only 'execution cemetery' with evidence of use into the thirteenth century is outside Andover: Walker *et al.* 2020; the others do not necessarily extend even into the twelfth century, and churchyard burial replaced them: Reynolds 2009a, 245–7. Norwich: Stirland 2009, and see Ch. 9; two probable execution burials have been recorded at Cambridge. Prisons in castles: Kenyon 1990, 136–7; Brears 2008, 17–20. Lydford: Saunders, A. D. 1980. Hudson 2011, n. 19 cited a Pipe Roll record of expenditure on a gaol in Oxford, presumably at the castle, but the excavations did not show what work was done: Munby *et al.* 2019. There are later records of gaols within town gates: Creighton and Higham 2005, 179–80.

42 Northern England: Britnell 1996a. Peveril Castle: Goodall, J. 2011, 139; Marsall 2016, 163; Loveluck *et al.* 2020, 482; that article introduced a new dimension to medieval studies by correlating the layers in the ice-core to documented events, but I have doubts about the dramatic falls suggested when a king died – it seems more likely that production continued but the royal 'farm' was retained by its collectors. Nor do I see that the seventh-century cores necessarily witness production at Melle, if those in the twelfth attest English production: see Ch. 3.

43 St Briavel's: English Heritage web-site, accessed June 2020. Bordesley mill: Astill *et al.* 2004, 126–38, augmenting Astill 1993.

44 Mills: Rynne 2018, 493–6 and 503–6; also see Holt 1988 (landlords who invested in windmills insisted on their right of 'multure', forcing tenants to grind their grain at their lord's mill and paying a fee; this had probably not been enforced previously if the lord did not have a water-mill); Watts, M. 2017 for anglo-saxon mills, see Chs 3, 4, and 7. Castle Donington: Clay and Salisbury 1990; also Wharram Percy: Treen and Atkin 2005. Windmill foundation excavations: for example Ocklynge Hill, Sussex: Stevens 1982; Strixton, Northamptonshire: Hall, D. 1973; Great Linford, Buckinghamshire: Mynard and Zeepvat 1992, 104–7; they were often built on low mounds, so sometimes reused prehistoric barrows, though no-one has claimed those as attempts to reconnect with the past. Net sinkers and hooks: White, A. J. 1988, 31–2; Goodall, I. H. 2011, 299,

and also for eels: Reynolds, R. 2017, 159–60. Angling only became a leisure activity at the very end of the Middle Ages, if then.

45 Exeter: Stoyle 2014, 17–25. Hemington bowl: Morris, C. A. 2009. River Witham: Everson and Stocker 2011, 394–5. 'Hanse' bowl: *Northamptonshire Archaeology* 17 (1982), 102 – its rarity is shown by its auction price in the 1980s of £11,000.

46 Bridges: Harrison 2007, 112. Vaults and pointed arches: Fernie 2000, 139. Swanson, R. N. 1999 for a review of education and culture. Etiquette: Bartlett 2000, 575–6 and 582–8.

47 Rings and gem-stone lore: Hinton 2005, 187–93 ('hand-fasting' was used for the exchange of vows; the ring was worn on the third finger of the left hand as its vein ran straight to the heart) and Woolgar 2006, 51–4. Folkingham brooch: Cherry, J. and Goodall 1985. 'Magic': Gilchrist 2008. Corpse preparation: Gilchrist 2012, 191; example of range of burial linings: White, W. J. 1988; see also following chapters. Bent coins: Hall 2018a, 616; Gilchrist and Sloane 2005, 101. Seacourt glass: Hinton 2010, 91–2; black-painted and blue-glazed Raqqa pot sherds from Syria may also be rare relics of Crusader veterans, but may alternatively have arrived as fruit containers: Hurst, J. G. 2002.

9 The Thirteenth Century

Magnates, Money, and Obligations

For medievalists, the thirteenth is the most abundant century. For archaeologists, there are more coins, more pottery, and more metalwork; many great buildings were created or enlarged; and by the century's end there are even survivals of peasant houses. For social and economic historians, documents provide often voluminous evidence about the running of estates and households, with information about all ranks of society; the written records about the peasantry nearly all detail the work that they were supposed to do or the payments that they had to make if they wanted to do almost anything other than to work for their lord, but even for them a little record of what they owned survives. Population increase is likely to have continued through at least the first half of the thirteenth century, though actual numbers are impossible to state with confidence from tax records because of exemptions and cheating. Constitutional change ranged from Magna Carta in 1215 – and its more significant successors like the *Carta Forestum* – to the first meetings of Parliament. These and Henry III's works at Westminster cemented London's pre-eminence as England's political as well as commercial centre. The century began badly with King John and ended with England nearly bankrupted by Edward I's military campaigns as well as facing agricultural and inflationary problems, but the general picture is of expansion at least until 1258.[1]

King John not only had to strengthen his own castles and to lay siege to others in his attempts to subdue his barons and resist French invasion, but he also had new ideas about comfort; at Corfe, he built not only defensive walls and towers, but also a thin-walled courtyard block so that he and his guests had more attractive accommodation than the old great tower offered; later, the courtyard was called *la gloriette* in acknowledgement of its alien but seductive appeal. John's successor Henry III also suffered rebellion, but his main concern was to make the castles that he used himself more suitable for his self-image, building within Winchester's a great aisled hall with Purbeck marble columns.[2]

The worst conflict was in the 1260s, but it differed from that of the mid twelfth century in being a struggle for control of the government and the whole kingdom, not a series of attempts to carve out separate autonomous territorial blocs. Decisions were taken by battles to see which side could muster the most support, not by sieges to take castles. The stone-throwing trebuchet had become a much more powerful weapon, and castle walls could not withstand a sustained onslaught. An

DOI: 10.4324/9781003007432-10

outer wall to keep the machines further away was sometimes added, as to London's Tower, but were expensive to build and needed far more men to defend, although moats, wall-towers, and gateways could make a statement of strength and enhance a castle's appearance. An external barbican was another occasional addition; at Sandal Castle, Yorkshire, one was built between the existing motte and the bailey, as though the Warenne family thought of their tower on the top of the motte as showing the height of their power. Sandal was well to the south of the border with Scotland, but raids had to be considered; Brougham, 20 miles south of Carlisle, was more obviously for defence than to provide a suitable 'caput' for the Cliffords' baronial honour.[3]

Edward I is best known for the castles that he built in Wales, to hold his conquests against the hostility of the kings he had not managed to subdue, but he also added an imposing twin-towered gate-house to St Briavel's, specifically to oversee the Forest of Dean's iron production, noted for its crossbow bolts. Kings' brothers and sons maintained castles appropriate to their social positions, as did the great barons; a castle was still the centre of an 'honour'.[4]

For the knights and their relations, a motte and bailey or a ringwork was by now neither appropriate nor desirable, a manor-house giving all the status that they required. This could be enhanced by the setting; after 1254, Wharram Percy's tenants were physically dominated by a manor-house, with a barn and other buildings within a fenced enclosure, on the highest point of occupation overlooking all the other properties. It has not been excavated, but the earthworks suggest that at its centre there was a long range that, if it followed the pattern that became standard in the thirteenth century, did not consist of a hall with separate chamber-blocks but had the hall at the centre of a long integral range that had service-rooms for buttery and pantry at the 'low' end, probably separated by a passage that led through to the outbuildings, including the kitchen. The main door was at the 'low' end of the hall, leading into a screens passage, a practical feature that kept the interior warmer but which also hid the everyday comings and goings from the lord and his family; anyone entering to see the lord had to approach him respectfully up the length of the hall. The lord's food was brought to his table at the 'high' end in a formal procession. Direct access from the high end into the family's chambers completed the standard arrangement. Tradition required that the hall should still be open to the full height of the building, with a central hearth even when in later centuries a side fireplace was provided for the high end; it is not certain when this was first embellished with a raised dais, although Henry III certainly had one in his hall at Westminster, with a throne and a long table of Purbeck marble. A development which stressed the central place of the hall was to set the service rooms and chambers in wings at right angles to it and projecting slightly forward as though to frame it.[5]

Another feature of thirteenth-century manorial and other residences was that many of them were on islands within a wet moat, fed by streams or springs. The reasons for these are debated: social separation, security from roaming brigands by those who could not afford a castle, a wish to have some sort of enclosure at no great cost, emulation of higher-status palaces, drainage, and a desire for gardens and for fresh fish, swans, and other wildfowl are all possible factors, and probably no single one accounts for any one decision. They were only practical in low-lying locations – rock-cut ditches surrounding castle baileys were usually dry and much harder and more expensive to dig out than a shallow feature on clay or lighter soil. Castle enclosures would have been familiar to everyone, but great royal palaces like Clarendon and Woodstock were not moated; new ideas may have been promoted by low-lying sites like Odiham Castle, where King John 'for his enjoyment' constructed a double moat, one with an octagonal tower inside, and the new early thirteenth-century palace for the bishop of Wells next to the Cathedral. Water could be used for boating parties, and 'pleasances' created by damming a small river were a feature of Woodstock and others; they had gender implications, allowing dalliance. Gardens with sweet-smelling flowers and herbs in the most exclusive settings were seen as female spaces, and great houses and castles increasingly provided separate accommodation for queens and ladies.[6]

Moated sites can be very hard to date with precision; excavations have often found occupation evidence below the upcast soil from the digging of the moat, but whether that was associated with an earlier manor-house is usually uncertain; one excavated at Northolt, Middlesex, certainly overlay several peasant tofts. An Oxfordshire village, Chalgrove, had two manorial sites, both set well back from the village street; the more extensively excavated had two islands, the smaller one without buildings and perhaps therefore a pleasure garden. A large moat at Wintringham, Huntingdonshire, also had a smaller one adjacent. Such complexes were estate centres as well as residences, needing storage facilities like barns and processing facilities such as stone-lined malting ovens. They were therefore work-places, one use of barns being to have ridged floors inside on which grain and pulses could be flailed to remove husks, a service demanded of villeins throughout the winter, followed by winnowing in sieves to clean the crop, an arduous but less heavy labour, often carried out by women.[7]

Many moats were not the residences of a manor's owner. Some were probably constructed for younger sons, but the majority were 'non-seigneurial', though the names and status of their builders are rarely known. Many 'homestead' moats belonged to better-off peasants who saw no advantage in living among their fellows, and were farming small patches of land, probably assarts reclaimed from wasteland on the clays and gravels, perhaps recently improved by drainage. Very occasionally they were constructed in towns, like the one behind the High Street in Eccleshall, Staffordshire, which is known to have been robbed, when goods claimed as worth £10 were taken – a useful indicator of an owner's wealth if it could be relied upon. A few owners were granted 'licences to crenellate', an acknowledgement that they had a right to self-defence provided that it was in the interests of the kingdom, but neither moated nor unmoated houses and towers routinely acquired a licence, and existing castles did not need them; several Church institutions had them, as did a few towns, but again there is no clear pattern.[8]

Other new ideas about houses were affected by developments in carpentry. Because oak timbers of many later medieval standing buildings survive, dendrochronology often permits them to be closely dated. Some in the thirteenth century used naturally curved, paired timbers, known as crucks; they take various forms, but there seems a clear distinction between 'base-crucks' which were built into masonry walls and were linked by a horizontal timber that supported the upper roof structure, and 'full' or 'true' crucks which were paired timbers rising from ground level up to the ridge of the roof where their ends were jointed together. Both kinds needed long and thick timbers, which were expensive, and skilled carpentry for their shaping and jointing. By a small and perhaps insignificant margin, base-crucks have the earlier date, 1245–7, in a barn at Siddington, Gloucestershire, in which they were used together with aisle-posts. Another barn that blends base-crucks and aisle-posts is at Great Coxwell, Berkshire, built by Beaulieu Abbey and dated to 1291–2, a little later than used to be thought. Those very large and substantial barns are both on estates then owned by church institutions, like the earlier ones at Cressing Temple and most others surviving from the thirteenth and fourteenth centuries, as few other owners had the same attitude to long-term investment. Private individuals were prepared to invest in their houses, however, and some used base-crucks in their halls in later thirteenth-century manor-houses such as West Bromwich, Staffordshire, of *c.* 1279. Base-crucks did not mean that halls could be wider, but they cleared the internal space and, in some cases, were inserted to replace existing aisle-posts. This was not universal, however; the possession of a large aisled hall may already have been seen as a prestigious marker of ancient lineage.[9]

A few base-crucks occur in houses below manorial level, but 'full' crucks were used almost exclusively in farmhouses and barns. None has yet been found earlier than 1262, in Northamptonshire, causing a debate on whether they were a development from the base-crucks or were a separate tradition not surviving in its earliest forms. Like base-crucks, full crucks required skilled carpentry for their shaping and jointing, but unlike them the main frames had to be pegged together on the ground and hauled up into place by rope. They would have needed large, carefully shaped post-holes equally spaced along the length of both side-walls of a building if their feet were set into the ground, and those have not been found in excavations. The crucks' feet must therefore have rested on the ground surface or on low walls or padstones; as they would quickly have begun to rot if in contact with the ground, they would soon have needed underpinning if they were to survive, an expense well worth making as their lengths made them a considerable investment, and low stone walls or padstones became widespread in peasant buildings during the thirteenth century.[10]

The alternative to cruck construction was 'post-and-truss' ('box-frame') buildings constructed with strong, straight vertical posts able to take the weight of horizontal tie-beams and principal rafters to carry longitudinal purlins for the support of lesser rafters – needing jointed carpentry if a house was to be wider than most daub or cob buildings but without the need of rearing. In some areas, stone walls were used, but in Northumberland, excavation at West Whelpington suggested that timber framing was preferred despite the availability of stone and the lack of tall trees locally. These differences raise the issue of the significance of regional variation: whereas base-crucks are recorded throughout most of the country, and have continental antecedents, full crucks do not occur in Lincolnshire, East Anglia, and the south-east, even after the thirteenth century when many more survive, a distribution that does not clearly fit with any other, be it physical like pottery or cultural like dialect. The earliest so far found are in the West Midlands, where they might have originated – the continent has few and not of high quality. Furthermore, full crucks were essentially rural; a few urban examples have been found, but mostly in outer zones.[11]

Full-cruck and box-frame buildings both create a rhythm of 'bays' between their principal upright timbers so were likely to be where internal partitions would be placed; the difference between the two systems may not have been significant for their occupants, particularly since both allowed for a room with a central hearth open to the roof, not crossed by joists for a first floor. Such halls were the norm in houses of all social levels but the poorest, both in town and country. The more substantial ones occupied two bays, so a central truss could dispense with a tie-beam and create the effect of an arch if the collar-beam was supported with a curved brace. In Essex, where survival is good, many small halls are in houses of sub-manorial level, often in dispersed settlements where farmers had better opportunities; the earlier thirteenth-century ones are aisled, but base-crucks came into use in its second half. The only manor-house recorded with full crucks is said not to have been used as a residence by its owner and that is in south Oxfordshire, another area with many wealthy peasant holdings and farmhouses with base-crucks, sometimes converted from aisles. Did full crucks rarely get used in higher-status contexts because of the practicalities of height and width, or because full crucks had the wrong social connotation? Perhaps not, as some high-status buildings used 'raised crucks' with the feet imbedded quite high up a masonry wall but meeting at the apex of the roof.[12]

Both cruck and box-frame systems allowed for expansion by adding extra bays at the end of a building, so cross-wings at right angles were not needed for service-rooms for farmhouses. In theory, both systems could be used for 'long-houses' in which farm animals are sheltered – at least in winter – at one end of the building. Like crucks, long-houses used to be considered to be a very ancient tradition only becoming identifiable when extant examples first seemed to appear in the thirteenth century or even later, but excavations have now shown that such arrangements hardly if at all pertained any earlier; identification used to be made simply on the basis that an end-bay had a drain running through it, but that would also have been needed for dairying, brewing, and other activities. Only by evidence of stalls, or of a substantial phosphate element in the floor caused by animal dung, can a 'long-house' be claimed.[13]

Identification of other buildings on peasants' tenements, such as barns, byres, pig-styes, granaries, detached kitchens, and bakehouses, is difficult because so many would not have been substantially built; malting-kilns which involved some digging out of a below-ground flue are more recognizable. Even a round feature, usually interpreted as a dove-cote, may in fact have been the base for a hay-rick; only a significant quantity of pigeon bones can verify the attribution. The importance of dairying, especially cheese-making, is shown by the numbers of sherds of large bowls; gas chromatography is now able to identify milk residues in such vessels. At some sites, rectangular buildings with one end having a substantial drain, as at Raddon, Wiltshire, were replaced by houses with separate buildings for dairying, and barns, creating a courtyard complex. Raddon was high up on chalk downland and was probably an offshoot of a village some distance away, created to expand the estate's output of sheep and grain; documents indicate that the landowner originally leased out the new farm but after *c*. 1248 took it over to farm directly, using tied labour. Sheep-rearing was probably the main focus on many rural manors, but a few specialized in rearing cattle in large enclosures called vaccaries.[14]

*

An aspect of the long-house debate is its implications about living conditions, particularly in causing exposure to tuberculosis, and opens up the possibility of exploring ideas about human/animal distinctions, attitudes to cleanliness, and understanding of disease. The more plentiful evidence of the thirteenth century allows questions about social behaviour and beliefs to be pursued through both archaeological and documentary evidence. Christian teaching that mankind was made in God's image meant that anyone who deviated from the norm in outward appearance was likely to be thought to be showing inner possession by devils. Lepers were marginalized for this reason, as were others who were regarded as disfigured. They had been tormented in life and might therefore come back to torment the living. Belief in 'revenants' was more than merely a way of discouraging bad behaviour in churchyards at night; the extremes that might have been gone through to 'quieten' them may have been revealed recently at Wharram Percy, where a quantity of human skull and bone fragments showed signs of burning and cutting, unlike anything previously recorded. The charring had certainly taken place after death, as it was on breaks as well as on surfaces, so the cut-marks were presumably also post-mortem. The bones were found in pits, some way from the churchyard, but they were not complete bodies. Were they people who had been marginalized in life, buried originally on the margins of the churchyard, subsequently disinterred and their corpses damaged to remove Satan from them? The preaching manuals did not advocate such extremes, but unofficial beliefs and practices probably existed unrecorded by any learned cleric, or manorial or royal agent. The inclusion of fossils – thought generally to ward off thunder and lightning – in a few graves may be the surviving residues of more widespread inclusion of good-luck symbols not now identifiable.[15]

Another unofficial but occasional practice was more widespread, which was the burial within houses of babies, some perhaps unborn, some who might have died not only during or within a couple of weeks of birth, but also very occasionally a little older; some might have been unwanted, but most seem too carefully treated for that. Some might have died before they could be baptized, buried where they could at least be within the living household. The most recent to be reported is the first from a manorial site and also the first found within a pottery vessel, a large cooking-pot, but several others have things with or near them that suggest apotropaic belief, as does their frequent positioning near a door or hearth. More formally, the practice of burying neonates and infants under the eaves of a church may have been replaced by locating them in the graveyard but near the west end, where the font was usually placed on the inside, which was near the main door to show baptism as entry into christianity. Entry into marriage was symbolized by the formal exchanges of vows and confirmation of legal agreements taking place in the church porch, before going inside for the blessing. In some cases, this probably led to larger porches with side-seating being built and perhaps encouraged entry being provided on the south side near the west end rather than through the west wall, for extra warmth; bell-towers and bell-cotes at the west end would also have made a new access point desirable to avoid the dangling ropes and the ringers. A person's last journey would be through the same door for the funeral service and out again for burial. The west end was therefore the congregation's entry-point, so it became generally accepted that the nave and its ancillaries were the congregation's responsibility.[16]

The chancel was the responsibility of the priest or whoever owned his 'living' and usually had a separate door. New doctrinal practice meant that the main altar was moved from inside the nave to the east end of the chancel, so that when the priest elevated the host during Mass he was facing east, with his back to the people in the congregation and further from them, setting him apart and making him more of an authority figure. In many cases the chancel was enlarged and aligned more closely to 'true' east than the earlier structure. The mystical experience of the supernatural transformation of bread and wine was also less directly experienced by the congregation. Confession of sins to the priest gave him new authority, and he could expect to be buried within the chancel, his part of the church, often with a chalice and paten to show his role. Preaching became more standardized through manuals and education, the parish clergy probably having to improve their performance because of the friars' competition.[17]

The concept of Purgatory was formalized, teaching that human life only partly ended in death, and by heightening awareness of Resurrection probably increased sensitivity to the human skeleton because the body would be reunited with the soul in the next world. When old graves were disturbed as new ones were dug, the skull and long bones might be replaced (Illus. 8.4) or put in a special pit with others, or transferred to a charnel-house, such as the crypt at Rothwell, Northamptonshire, which even had a small window so that the living could pray for the souls whose remains they could see inside and help them through Purgatory; in return, the dead would plead for those who prayed for them. Most people had to accept that they would be forgotten as individuals, but would join a new family, the community of the dead; richer people increasingly followed the example of the clergy, wanting internal burial and monuments so that their names would be remembered either at an abbey or priory that they patronized or in the nave or side chapels of their parish church. From the 1270s, incised brasses became an alternative to stone carvings, and cast letters made inscriptions with names more available, so that those who could read might include them in their prayers. Particularly in the north of England, floor-slabs and grave-covers with crosses carved in relief were often anonymous but might have symbols to show someone's occupation in life: priests might have books, chalices, and patens; swords may have indicated social rank; but shears, keys, and other everyday objects are ambivalent.[18]

Prayers for the help of saints meant that space had to be provided for more altars, and for processions to each in turn, another reason for side-aisles. Internal private seating was beginning to both interfere with space and to cause disharmony as only richer people could afford it. Their monuments also took up space, especially if they were raised on a plinth, like the full-size effigies of knights in their armour. Building went on at all the great cathedrals and abbeys, and a proliferation of chapels in prominent places meant that the christian message was a constant visible presence. This perhaps provided a further reason for antipathy to the small number of Jews (Illus. 9.1), who were increasingly persecuted and finally expelled in the 1290s.[19]

Illustration 9.1 The Bodleian bowl is one of the few tangible records of Jewry; it has a Jewish inscription round it that says, 'The gift of Joseph, son of the holy Rabbi Yechiel . . . '. Yechiel could be the same man as Yehiel, a Talmudic scholar in thirteenth-century Paris, where the bowl may have been cast. He might also be Jehiel whose sons had associations with Colchester. The bowl was not found in the town, but somewhere in East Anglia, so it might well have come to England in the thirteenth century (Hillaby and Hillaby 2013, 55–7).

The extent to which orthodox or unofficial beliefs may have affected everyday lives as well as deaths can sometimes be seen; horse-meat was not supposed to be eaten by humans, for instance, although at times when food was scarce it may have happened – very few horse bones show the sort of butchery marks that cattle bones display, but at West Cotton some had been smashed open to extract the marrow, which suggests human consumption. Horse carcases were usually skinned and then dumped, occasionally and probably illicitly in ditches, more often in dumps away from human dwellings – for practical reasons or because animals were 'unclean' spiritually? How rigidly fast-days were observed in great households can be measured through records of expenditure, but did a rural or urban housewife sieve any meat residues out of a bowl of pottage before serving it? Medical treatises placed great stress on the balance in the body of the four humours, so cooks were expected to produce dishes that were hot, cold, wet, or dry according to what was required – but how widely was such teaching put into practice? Fish were supposed to be eaten on meat-free days, and again records suggest that this was generally observed among the religious orders and the aristocracy, but unlike most people they had access to freshwater species from ponds and through their reserved fishing rights in streams and rivers. Bones of cod and other marine fish far inland at towns like Northampton show that some were available, but that the range was less than that nearer the coast. Isotopic studies of the human bone at Wharram Percy show that the people there ate less fish than those in York, but that may have been a factor of the distance from a reliable market supply rather than deliberate flouting of religious instruction. Getting to market was made easier and faster by increasing use of carts, facilitated by more efficient harnessing, so horses were also used more often in farm-work generally. Only an increase in the numbers of bones of slightly larger horses and a visible switch to a heavier shoe attest this archaeologically.[20]

Villagers who could not get access to fish may unwittingly have made up for the lack of Vitamins A and D that they would have derived from it by eating more eggs, notably a food of the poor. Their gardens provided vegetables, which were not seen as desirable in higher society and which would have lost some of their food value through constant boiling. Some meat was available to the peasants, as bones show from butchery that not all animals were driven to market to be sold; even some cows were slaughtered on site, although a cow or ox produces such a large amount of meat that it presents storage problems if not quickly distributed, because of the quantities of salt needed to preserve it. The balance between meat and cereal in people's food cannot be measured, but sites like Barton-on-Humber and Wharram Percy provide data on some of the consequences, such as rickets caused by undernourishment in childhood. Although those who reached adulthood were not much shorter on average than today, they took longer to get to maturity. Periostitis and osteoarthritis show that most adults had a hard working life, and their worn or missing teeth show that they ate and chewed coarse food. Few lived for more than 50 years.[21]

Most cemeteries have examples of bone fractures, which may be from falls or other accidents, or from casual violence, or from injuries sustained in battle. Even if not immediately fatal, wounds would often have led to death from septicaemia. Only a few skulls show evidence of injuries from swords or other bladed weapons that would have killed immediately; rib bones rarely have evidence of knife stabbings, but those may not leave much if any trace. Cemeteries with exceptional skeletal records may have particular causes: St Andrew's, York, may have served a hospital with an exceptional reputation for healing, whereas most hospitals only offered respite care. The high ratio of males with traumas there is suggested not to result from a single-incident battle, but because men injured in tournaments were taken there – their burial locations hint at high social status, and stable isotope analysis has shown that they had a different diet from the norm. Also extreme is the survival of iron arrow-heads in five male skeletons at Poulton, Cheshire; they may have been killed in Welsh raids, but bow-and-arrow deaths are not uncommon in the records. Another exceptional case is St Margaret's just outside the walls of Norwich near the gallows and 'where the hanged are buried'; over three-quarters of the 368 identifiable skeletons were male, and ten cranial injuries were recorded, as well as others with old but healed wounds; most of them were probably from the medieval underworld, but rather different were two cases of cerebral palsy, who would have needed care in life. Many of the studies of human skeletons are from hospital sites, which have the problem of typicality; people in them were likely to have been relatively elderly when admitted or privileged in some way. Large numbers at Wharram Percy or London's St Nicholas Shambles are probably more representative but less likely to be chronologically defined.[22]

The fine line between dearth and famine was demonstrated at St Mary Spital, where pits were dug and used as mass graves for several thousand bodies. Their radiocarbon dating correlates with documentary accounts of starving people coming into the city in 1257–8 desperately searching for food, so not all were citizens, perhaps unlike the burials in the smaller twelfth- and earlier thirteenth-century mass pits. The bodies were treated with respect, as they had at least been placed in the orthodox west-east alignment, not merely thrown in – some children were placed north-south, as though to take up empty space. They were almost certainly victims of a natural disaster caused by a massive volcanic eruption in Indonesia in 1257, which blotted out sunlight around the whole world, so that crops did not grow, and introduced a period of unstable weather conditions that would have made agriculture in many 'marginal' areas unviable.[23]

*

The Wharram Percy villagers may not have eaten as much fish as townspeople, or as much meat as they would have wished, but they had access to various commodities, either through markets or from pedlars. What survives of peasants' material culture may be unrepresentative; did they aspire to have special clothes for Sundays and holy-days, for instance? Their pottery was a little more varied than in the twelfth century, with a few more glazed jugs, which may have been appreciated for their colour, but perhaps also for their gloss, since 'sheen' was appreciated at higher social levels; some copper-alloy items were given a white-metal coating perhaps for the same reason, and not only to make them look like silver. Awareness of appearance is indicated by attempts to control nuns' and priests' dress and fittings, and taxation levies and exemptions by the end of the century indicate growing ideas about what was appropriate to the different ranks of the laity. Taxes on movable goods did not include items like earthenware pots that were too cheap to be worth valuing, and only a few detailed records survive, mostly from towns; a few court records listed what peasants owned, although how much was omitted is never clear, creating the general impression that many people owned virtually nothing, but that a few were well-to-do. Awareness of material possessions as a measure of someone's place in society must have become ingrained. Inventories do not explain usage, such as the occasional discovery of whole or nearly whole pots buried in the interior of houses; if close to a hearth and upright, they may have been to hold water for use in cooking, but a few upside down are more suggestive of foundation or other rituals.[24]

Documents sometimes reveal a village seeming to act communally, but was that community only the wealthier element, excluding those who had no direct stake in the land? The use of base-metal seals spread widely, some with names, some with devices, some showing sexual inuendo, but all showing involvement in legal proceedings and a sense of individual responsibility. The disharmony felt inside parish naves may have expressed deeper currents. Records of estate administration laid emphasis on the different obligations of the free and the unfree and show the wide disparity of the acreages that people in the same vill held. These differences do not show clearly in the archaeological record; occasionally a village plan suggests that a tenement had been divided in half, like one at the north end of Wharram Percy's west row, but cottars' dwellings are not clearly differentiated from a virgate-holder's. Although a nuclear family was the norm, servants and labourers may have had accommodation within their employer's barns and lofts, as did elderly relatives who had passed on their land to an heir.[25]

Wharram's apparent uniformity is not invariable; much less formality existed at Westbury, for instance, where the crofts were irregular circles rather than rectangles, and the houses did not use substantial posts, so were only identifiable from spreads of stone taken to have been floors. Very basic housing for the rural poor, within a croft or even on a village green, is even more difficult to recognize. The size of a house may not be an indicator of status; the smallest building excavated at Seacourt, Berkshire, had stone foundations and may well have had an upper floor reached by a staircase in a semi-circular annexe, an interpretation strengthened by a subsequent excavation nearby at Fringford, where up to five courses of dry-stone walls survived; that building went through various phases, with an internal partition and the strong possibility of having had an upper floor added to it. The Seacourt building was originally interpreted as being an ale-house or a priest's, both of which could be true, but Fringford may show that it was not as exceptional as once thought.[26]

The records of estate administration do not emanate from the peasants themselves and do not express their ideas and aspirations, nor whether if they prospered they sought to acquire more land or farmstock rather than more consumables or leisure-time. Certainly their engagement with the market that was becoming more evident in the twelfth century continued into the thirteenth. Metal-detected, rather than excavated, coin-finds remain a better gauge of the availability of money in the countryside, but the high ratio of halfpennies and farthings to whole pennies at peasant house sites such as Westbury, or at a probable ferry crossing of the Humber, suggests that small-scale transactions using coins were more frequent than used to be thought. The coins are mostly not from local mints, which shows that they were circulating, not being hoarded. Whole pennies as well as cut are found at churches, suggesting mislaid offerings and payments of dues, but some are folded and may have been deliberately placed when a private vow was made. A group of 40 coins found in front of the chapel altar at a hospital in Sandwich might be thank-offerings for a successful naval enterprise; there were nine pennies, but twenty-four half-pennies, and six farthings, which might represent the individual donations of relatively poor sailors. Even the landless servile labourers received paltry cash wages, though for them food-allowances for tasks performed were at least as important, and beyond what can be recognized archaeologically, as is the contribution of female and child labour in the fields or in domestic work. What the coins suggest, however, is that commerce played a part in everyone's lives, and documents occasionally reveal peasant housewives selling the produce of their gardens in town markets. The priority of landlords who farmed their demesne lands was to ensure supplies to their own households rather than to sell, and their manorial courts controlled most land transfers, which limited the scope for commercial development, and rising population kept wages low and rents high.[27]

A few other employment opportunities were offered by iron-ore collection and smelting wherever deposits existed, the Forest of Dean helping to make Gloucester famous and prosperous, but smaller operations are sometimes found, like the small furnace excavated at Waterley, Northamptonshire. The first record of production in the Weald in south-eastern England is a 1242 royal order for 20,000 nails and 8000 horseshoes; the first located furnace was excavated at Alsted, Surrey; although only a bowl, not providing for slag-tapping, even the king's large order could have been supplied by a mere six such furnaces working for eighteen days. Nevertheless, water power was applied elsewhere; at Bordesley Abbey, Worcestershire, one use of a mill was for hammers to break up iron ore into pieces that were small enough to allow air to circulate around them in the furnace, and high temperatures could be maintained in it by using the wheel also to operate bellows. The wheels at Bordesley were vertical, as probably were most by the thirteenth century. In the south-west, tin-streaming may have been a useful additional income for farmers, not yet a full-time occupation, as at St Neot, Cornwall; an attempt to extract silver at Bere Ferrers, Devon, involved more capital. These operations still involved surface working, not underground galleries, although some were created in stone quarries. Lead in Derbyshire and the Mendips and coal around Newcastle were extracted by digging pits from the surface.[28]

Another industry that involved extraction by digging was salt production around Droitwich, where excavation at one site has located a deep brine-well, with lifting-gear, called a *rydhok*, possibly a winch; dendrochronological dating of 1264 from the timber lining of the well-shaft exactly equated with a documentary record of

1264–5 about the well needing repair and 'houses' having to be removed to make space. Two workshops were found in the excavation, with barrels set into their floors, presumably for storing brine before it was boiled in lead vats, like those found in the earlier excavation at Nantwich (Illus. 8.3).[29]

Demand for lead and tin was stimulated by increased use of pewter, 'saucers' as tableware being a much cheaper but quite glossy alternative to silver (Illus. 9.2). Typical of London's dominance is that the craftsmen were based there, and not in the provinces; they were sufficiently organized to be able to control

Illustration 9.2 Late thirteenth-century pewter saucer from Southampton, found in a pit with other items from the household of a wealthy merchant. The letter 'P' stamped on the rim is probably the maker's mark; a similar one has been found at a site near Birmingham. Pewter is a soft metal, and knife-marks scored into the saucer show that it had been much used (Platt and Coleman-Smith 1975, 250–1; Brown, D. H. 2018).

quality, and therefore prices. London braziers also dominated the manufacture of memorial brasses, which were not only sought by the aristocracy, but also were acquiring a clientele of lesser knights and better-off farmers, whom it was becoming appropriate to call yeomen. Further from London, transport costs put brasses beyond their reach. A few ecclesiastical centres were far enough from London to support brass-makers, but metallurgical analysis has shown that those were likely to be of poorer metal, with a higher proportion of tin, confirming what stylistic analysis had suggested. Another use of brass was for the outer casing of lead steelyard weights, which usually bore a coat of arms; a few had a higher proportion of zinc, giving them a shinier and crisper appearance, and the combination of the armorial devices on those suggests a form of quality control, which is most likely to have been achieved in London.[30]

A new industry that could not be practised in London was glass production, which needed supplies of potash from trees and plants, as well as charcoal for furnaces. The craft began in the Weald during the thirteenth century, though the earliest sites have not been located. 'Forest' glass includes iron oxides that gave it a green tinge; its documented use was in windows, but it was probably also used for hanging-lamps and for urinals, flasks used by doctors and most often was found in monasteries and hospitals. The few fragments of drinking glasses found at high-status sites, at monasteries, and in towns where they had presumably been discarded by merchants were imports from the Mediterranean. They were probably significant as items for display on wealthy tables when guests were entertained. A few enamelled and gilded vessels came from Byzantium and the Near East, using techniques that were copied in Italy and led to the importing of very distinctive beakers with Latin texts naming makers. A few of those were imported into London at the end of the thirteenth century or a little later and do not seem to have been traded on to castles and other aristocratic houses; the merchants may have kept them as particular markers of their international commercial links.[31]

Involvement in commerce meant use of urban markets, augmented by fairs. Itinerant pedlars brought some goods to villages, though a cache of unfinished brooches found at Hambleden, Buckinghamshire, is the only evidence of an itinerant metalworker. That potters took laden carts around, as they did in the nineteenth century, could account for many of the locally made vessels at excavated villages, but occasional references to tolls paid for stalls in urban markets show that potters or their agents found it worth their while to travel as much as 50 miles, particularly with the glazed jugs that required a little more skill and investment than everyday cooking-pots and which also reached rural sites in greater quantities than in the twelfth century (Illus. 9.3). Most potters still worked in 'potting villages', their kilns still not the updraught type, but usually made with a central platform on which the pots were stacked, hot air being drawn in from the firing-pit, usually with a flue on the opposite side to create a flow. Occasionally a potter set up on the edge of a town, usually a small one, presumably in the hope of cutting transaction costs by being close to a market, but other expenses, in carting fuel and clay, and paying rent, usually made the enterprise unviable, even if neighbours would

Illustration 9.3 Two thirteenth-/early fourteenth-century glazed jugs from Oxford, both probably made in kilns at Brill or Boarstall, 'potting villages', some 15 miles away and involving overland transport for much of the way. The small one on the left in shape and decoration imitates contemporary imports from south-west France. The elaborate puzzle jug on the right has two separate compartments, the lower filled through the hollow handle. The stag's head is the spout, so that an unwary drinker gets drenched when tipping up the pot. Jugs like these involved more work and more glaze than the twelfth-century tripod pitchers (Illus. 8.2), which suggests that many people had at least a little more spending money. Heights of the jugs are 205 mm and 330 mm.

put up with the fire risk. A few found a wider national, even international, market, such as the group working in Scarborough, Yorkshire, a small port that could take their wares over a much greater distance by sea than most potters could achieve overland.[32]

Although found in much lower numbers than unglazed vessels, jugs may have been more carefully looked after; at an isolated farmhouse at Dinna Clerks on Dartmoor, Devon, which was destroyed by fire and only partly cleared out, an inner room contained two of the three fairly complete jugs found inside it, so they may have been kept away from where they were most likely to get broken. A few pottery vessels were more elaborate, with modelled faces, sometimes arms, and sometimes other anatomical features. Some jugs were ornamented with figures of knights riding aimlessly round the rims or chains of dancers or with different compartments so that anyone who did not know the trick would be drenched from a hidden spout (Illus. 9.3). These might have been used in ale-houses and on occasions like Plough Monday in early January, or May Day; cheap metal badges show that those were celebrated. Bone pipes survive often enough to show that melodic music was played as well as instruments that could keep a beat and others that merely made a noise. Jew's harps, found in London and Westbury among others, involve holding the metal instrument in the mouth to achieve resonance, and a modicum of pitch can be achieved. Stringed instruments are known from bone tuning-pegs, but both the cost of the instrument and the training to play it presumably required skill and expense.[33]

Another occasional pottery vessel is in the form of an animal with four short stumpy legs and heads acting as spouts. These are clearly based on much more expensive metal 'aquamaniles', used in great households for hand-washing, an elaborate ritual before a meal. The diners' hands were then dried with a towel. Was that how they were used in peasant households, emulating behaviour observed in higher social circles? Records show that towels and occasional basins were owned but do not reveal their specific functions. Possibly, therefore, the pottery aquamaniles were used as an amusing form of jug. Possibly, though, they had another meaning; the metal vessels are in the form of lions, griffins, and other noble creatures, and some are mounted knights in full armour. The pottery animals are nearly all farmyard creatures, however, and any with a mounted knight look more like Don Quixote than a resplendent hero. Were the potters and their patrons subtly mocking rather than emulating their lords?[34]

Jugs and their meanings lead on to another question about peasant behaviour more generally: how much formality was practised in their households? Meagre records of tables and 'forms' (i.e. benches) do not reveal where they were positioned and whether in a rural hall there was the same arrangement of seating as in a lord's, with an 'upper end' where family and guests sat with their backs to the wall so that they could be served from in front of the table and where they could be clearly seen by lesser members of the household who might be sitting at right angles to them in the lower part of the hall. Did peasant households take their meals with anything like that formality – if indeed there were meals in the sense of communal eating at a regular time? Noble lords with dishes that needed to be served soon after their preparation were not necessarily the model for peasants eating pottage from a stew-pot that was constantly simmering and could be dipped into at any time. Behaviour patterns probably varied widely among the peasantry, those who cooked on the open hearth within the hall having less space for formality than those with a detached kitchen.[35]

Pottery sherds are the most frequently found artefact at rural sites, over 100,000 at the extensively excavated West Cotton, Northamptonshire. Other vessels are underrepresented, such as two wooden bowls or cups that survived in the special conditions at Dinna Clerks; were they used for drinking, suggesting that small amounts were poured into them from a jug, or were they used to serve salt or chopped herbs? Either interpretation implies elements of formal etiquette. Wood-turning was a skilled craft, but its raw material was cheap, so its products vied with pottery but still had to be purchased. Also purchased were whetstones, the preferred ones of imported Norwegian schist, as were stone mortars and querns. All men carried an iron knife, the blades of varying quality, but all cost money. Gold and silver finger-rings are more common than might be expected, and brooches are more frequent finds than of the eleventh or twelfth centuries, although precise dating can be problematic. Very occasionally, something exceptional is found at a rural site, which in most cases can be explained away as detritus from a manor-house but not always: a recent report of a gold strip, only 2 mm wide, excavated at what appears to have been an entirely unexceptional rural farmstead at Kimmeridge, Dorset, seems unprecedented – had a peasant owned it or stolen it?[36]

Wharram Percy had one element in its archaeology that throws light on the importance of ownership, for one of its two manors bought out the other in 1254, and the manor-house in the centre of one of the tenement rows became redundant. Much of the building material from it ended up in the foundations of peasant houses; one interpretation is that this was stealing, done as a deliberate act of subversion, but it is just as likely that the builders made small payments to the lord for a conveniently accessible material. In this instance, documents do not help, as there are no manorial accounts. Other examples of the consequence of manorial decisions include Raunds, with the abandonment of the graveyard and church by one of the two owners in the vill, and at West Cotton, where the manor-house was removed, and the settlement rearranged with half a dozen farmsteads around the existing triangular green. At Broadfield, Hertfordshire, a church was built over existing occupation, though as one of the buildings may have been manorial, the action may not have been as high-handed as it would have been if the displacement was of peasant tenements.[37]

*

Greens like those at Wharram or West Cotton could be used for grazing, penning stray animals, village festivities, and for small-scale markets and fairs if nearby licensed towns could not prevent them, although licences were more often acquired to prevent a neighbouring town from usurping its rival's established weekly market-day. Control of competition is a sign that the urban network was effectively complete by the beginning of the thirteenth century. As in the twelfth century, archaeological evidence consists primarily of intra-mural densities and suburbs (Illus. 9.4) – new towns were many fewer. The most famous exception, Wiltshire's New Salisbury, is really a case in point, as it came at the expense of Old Sarum (Illus. 2.6) and, after the building of a new bridge in 1264 that diverted traffic, Wilton. Very occasional failures have been found, as in Warwickshire at Oversley, where the market that had been set up adjacent to a castle in the twelfth century was abandoned in the early thirteenth as the castle had been slighted, and,

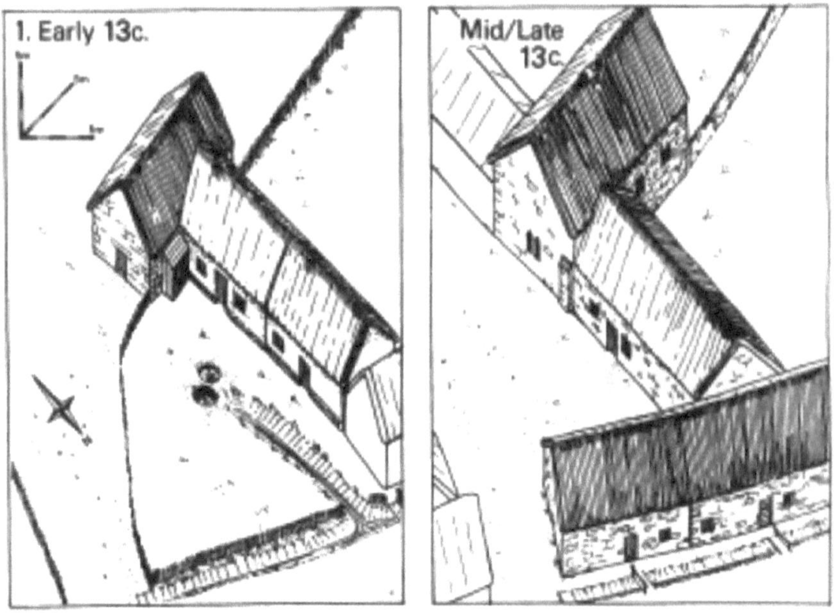

Illustration 9.4 Reconstruction of the development of a suburb in west Oxford, where excavation showed development starting *c.* 1200 on land near the river, where drainage ditches showed that floods were a hazard. The first phase involved a short terrace of cottages, with a slightly larger house at right angles to it. Pressure on space continued, and the site was redeveloped during the course of the thirteenth century with more cottages, but one larger house was still included, so a range of occupants was provided for. A seal-die of 'Adam the Chaplain' may have belonged to the owner or tenant of the larger house (Palmer 1980).

although a road had been diverted to run through it, the market could not compete with one at Alcester, only about a mile away – nearly all the pottery at Oversley came from a kiln in Alcester, which suggests how the larger town dominated. A malting-kiln and high-quality blacksmithing may have been to produce ale and ironwork for the castle rather than the market. Most towns expanded, however, one measure of their growth being the arrival of the new preaching order, the friars, and the provision for their churches, which were often initially small and central but were resited to marginal areas and built much bigger when they successfully attracted large congregations.[38]

The market-place was not a commercial free-for-all; proscriptions on selling shoddy goods and price controls were in place, as were regulations to ensure that goods came to markets where all could buy what they needed, not least the itinerant royal households. The major cash-producing craft was still textiles, though England suffered from Low Countries competition, and the most expensive cloths such as Stamford red or Lincoln green ceased production. Demand for slightly cheaper products remained high, however, and were still mostly woven in towns – the fulling-mill may have replaced 'walking' in troughs, but their introduction did not lead to wholesale shift to rural production as used to be thought. Another late thirteenth-century innovation was the introduction of the spinning-wheel, which produces a more irregular yarn that fulling disguised. Despite the machine, the craft remained a female one, unlike the earlier weaving change.[39]

Weavers needed good light, which may have been one reason for increased urban use of upstairs space, avoiding the shadows and dirt thrown by passing traffic and the buildings opposite. An urban origin can be claimed for one highly visible trend in thirteenth-century carpentry, the use of 'jettying' to project an upper floor over the ground floor, usually over the street. This is recorded in London in 1246, when it was already common enough to be causing a nuisance and began to appear in rural houses in the 1280s. Jetties were possible because the increased use of timber-framing made more substantial and investment-worthy properties possible for those who could not afford stone; they show that upstairs space not only mattered, but also looked good; the projecting beam-ends could be painted or even carved. They may have been a factor in causing complaints about neighbours building over what should have been narrow open spaces.[40]

Another 'origin' issue is whether rural buildings and behaviour were influenced by what was happening in towns or if rural experience shaped the urban. As rich merchants conducting business with manor-house owners would have seen base-crucks, they might be expected in towns, but the only ones known are in guildhalls, not private houses. In towns, various expedients for making the best use of space were practised by burgesses, such as having a full-height open hall at right angles to the two-, or later three-, storey street frontage block. Another way to make maximum use of space was to build in rows parallel to a street, which might also allow for a bigger house behind a frontage of shops if the houses were deprived of any back yard. The rich merchants' twelfth-century stone houses with first-floor halls on the street frontage were no longer so fashionable, and ground-floor halls set further back from the frontage for seclusion were preferred – a trend which may have been influenced by rural manor-houses. A few urban halls were aisled, despite width constraints. 'Full' crucks were unsuitable in towns, as the natural curve of the blade encroached on upstairs space, which townspeople needed to use. At the other end of the urban social scale, one- or two-room and probably single-storey rows of cottages appeared in back alleys leading off side-streets, cheek-by-jowl with many of the industrial activities, among which stone houses lived in presumably by their owners were included.[41]

Close-set buildings, the range of crafts and products on sale, and the concentration of both noise and smell – shouting, metalworkers' hammerings, church bells, and rumbling carts on metalled streets, together with smells of cooking, charcoal fumes and hot metal, dye-boiling, tanning, and rubbish rotting in shallow pits if not actually in the streets – might have made towns alien to rural people, especially larger ones encircled by stone walls; but peasants went into the markets, and most would have had relatives to visit. Debate continues on whether townspeople had significantly different ambitions, opportunities, and sense of self-identity from those of their rural cousins. Certainly burgesses were not legally servile, had no restrictions on property sales, and lived a different experience within much more enclosed spaces within their houses and streets. They were likely to live within the central part of a town, however, for business reasons, rather than in one of the suburbs that successful places continued to develop (Illus. 9.4). In general, the things that townspeople other than the richest merchants owned and lost, such as their knives and dress fittings, were not noticeably different from what peasants had. Their meat was more likely to be from butchered carcases of older but not worn-out animals, and was more likely to be beef than mutton, but nothing in their pottery suggests that their food was cooked differently.[42]

Towns and markets fostered the use of coins, but the high value of the official silver issues led to the use of imported Low Countries' coins of lower weight than the English, and probably of base-metal tokens, especially after the weight of the penny was increased after 1279, a reform which caused the export of many English coins as they were desirable on the continent. The same reform attempted to address the problem of shortage of small change by again introducing a round half-penny, but an opposite effect was to introduce a coin worth 4d, presumably to facilitate larger transactions, but actually taking silver out of circulation as the groats and half-groats were more likely to be hoarded. Hoards could be very large; one of two specially made lead canisters found in Colchester held over 14,000 pennies, although other hoards might consist of just a few coins hidden in a pot. Criminals, rural or urban, rarely show up archaeologically, but a corroded lump of several hundred counterfeit coins copying Henry III pennies, the metal half copper, would have made spectacular profits if they had been launched successfully on to the market.[43]

Wine continued to be a major import but from a different source after the English kings lost control of Normandy but acquired Bordeaux in the thirteenth century. Imported with it was a distinctive type of pottery from Saintonge, in particular skilfully thrown jugs of white clay painted with exotic birds and plants. Quantities have been found in Southampton, and the merchants there may have used it to show their position in society. Very little has been found inland, and most of that in castles and the sort of high-status sites to which wine was going to be served. It may be that the merchants were not importing it to sell but made gifts of it to their clients.

One pit in Southampton had large amounts of Saintonge pottery, mostly whole jugs as though from a house clearance, and some lustrous pottery from Spain; it also contained such finery as a pewter saucer (Illus. 9.2) and vessel glass, the former a new fashion, the latter almost certainly an expensive import. A boxwood gaming-piece indicated that the owner had leisure time – chess in particular was a signifier of time to spare and of education to understand the moves. The animal and fish bones included hunted species, and the merchant also owned a sword. He was living an aristocratic lifestyle; although few went to the extreme of buying an estate and building a castle, as Laurence of Ludlow did when he purchased

Stokesay in 1284, the implication is that the richest merchants aspired to join the barony, not to undermine it.[44]

Laurence gave himself an elegant but cruck-framed hall, with tall windows and two towers, one of which is the only example in England with projecting timber-work, 'hoarding'. The walls were not very thick, and one of the towers had to be buttressed as it was collapsing, so was more military at first sight than on closer inspection, possibly because Laurence did not want local barons to see him as a challenge but to feel secure against Welsh raids. That might also have applied to a neighbouring castle, Acton Burnell, Herefordshire, built at his birthplace by a bishop of Wells, which was effectively a large square hall with chambers and low towers at each corner, a less traditional arrangement than at Stokesay. Acton's appearance was made more striking by the use of red sandstone, and it is probably not a coincidence that another 'new man' used brick when building a tower at Little Wenham, Suffolk.[45]

*

The dominance of London in the urban hierarchy was bolstered as meetings of the new parliament became more established at Westminster, and as the royal courts of justice met there rather than travelling with the kings, bringing more people to London for business. London continued to be the main source of credit – used to buy luxuries in Cheapside and to finance lifestyles in the country rather than to invest in property or mills. Londoners continued to develop their waterfront, extending jetties out into the Thames, and began to use bricks in their buildings. Their main overseas links were with the Low Countries, the Rhineland, and up to Scandinavia, as imported and exported pottery shows, and their internal hinterland was extensive, with grain coming down the Thames from the transshipment point at Henley. Most of the boat parts reused in the waterfront jetties were from the inland craft that would have been used for such transport.[46]

Direct evidence of the vessels used to transport goods, armies, and pilgrims overseas is lacking. Images of ships, particularly those on the seals of ports where observation is likely to have been more accurate than on anything produced inland, show vessels with timbers protruding through the sides so that the planking would not rub against a quay. Mostly they show that steering was still by a side-rudder, needing a massive timber like one dredged from the Channel and radiocarbon-dated to the thirteenth century. Single mainsails were beginning to be augmented by bowsprits, so sailing could be more precisely adjusted to the wind, which rear rudders facilitated. 'Castles' at both ends provided fighting platforms to ward off pirates, but their height endangered stability.[47]

The most complete thirteenth-century wreck discovered, at Magor Pill on the Welsh side of the River Severn, had probably been built to a traditional regional design suitable for the Severn and its tributaries, where tides, currents, winds, and shoals make navigation especially problematic. The boat was not unlike the basic design of viking ships, equal-ended with a single mast. Such vessels do not need formal harbours, though some lords invested in waterfront installations to improve landing-places, as Tintern Abbey did on the Severn, at Wolaston, Gloucestershire, where timber piles have been found. Iron ore from south Wales found with the Magor Pill boat was probably destined for Bristol, a tortuous journey up the narrow Avon. Despite that, Bristol was flourishing, helped by a new road bridge and by the digging in the 1240s of a new channel for the River Frome to allow marshland to be drained and improving the landing-places along the Avon. Excavation showed the sequence of one development, with a stone-based slipway in front of the twelfth-century river wall, and thereafter a series of extensions and larger buildings; as in London, this was the work of the tenement owner, not a communal enterprise, and also as in London, dye-boiling vats had contained madder, woad, weld, and greenweed.[48]

The church of St Mary with a steeple to rival Salisbury cathedral's remains as testimony to the wealth of the Bristol's Redcliffe suburb. Like most new churches in the thirteenth century and later, it did not have a graveyard, as established ones resisted the loss of income, but as Bristol had three monasteries, four friaries, at least sixteen other churches, and up to a dozen hospitals at some of which burial took place, the citizens may have thought that they were sufficiently provided for. Bristol's nearest rival, Exeter, was too far up-river for access by larger boats and used an outport at Topsham; a new stone road bridge with causeways leading to it improved hinterland access. Excavations at several other ports have shown sequences of waterfront reclamation, notably those on the east coast which could hope to take some of the Low Countries and Scandinavian trade from London, as well as to supply it, as Newcastle was doing with coal, mainly for lime-burning.[49]

Newcastle was a supply-base for Edward I's Scottish campaigns in the 1290s, as was Hartlepool, where a stone and timber dock may belong to the period; further north, Berwick was fortified with stone walls, their circuit enclosing a smaller and more defensible area than an older bank and ditch that Edward's army had overwhelmed. Another north-east coastal town developed by the king was at the mouth of the Humber and was to develop as Kingston-upon-Hull. The River Hull may have been canalised, making a waterfront viable, and a market was already developing in opposition to Hedon and Ravenserodd by the 1270s. A street with houses had been established, and an aisled building founded on post-pads could have been Meaux Abbey's warehouse, from which they exported wool.[50]

As a Cistercian house, Meaux used its own wool to provide it with all the cloth that it needed – the great religious institutions did not shun commerce, but their ideal was self-sufficiency with a surplus to sell, not to produce as much as they could of a saleable product and to use the cash income from it to buy all their needs. The wool-house at Fountains where stone fulling-tubs were excavated shows that the estate was well organized, but at less than 2 metres in diameter, the tubs were quite small: enough for the cloth that the house needed for itself but not enough to produce a worthwhile amount to market. Abbeys and priories would borrow money by selling their surpluses in advance, but spent it on their buildings and upkeep; they were not involved in capitalist ventures, a limitation on economic development. The same principle applied to secular households, advocated by manuals, so that although there was investment in infrastructure projects, such as bridges or river diversions, they were seen as communal benefits, not as profit-making; tolls were charged for upkeep, not for redistribution.[51]

Hull was on land liable to flood, but Hedon gradually shrank as it lost its access to the sea, and Ravenserodd disappeared from the shifting sands on which it had been built. Further south, new artificial channels redirected the flow into the River Ouse to the further detriment of Wisbech and the gain of Lynn, where reclamation meant that its two market-places no longer had boats landing on their open beaches, which were built over; inland expansion was marked by 'Newlands' and building along the principal road eastwards. Despite excavated evidence of sand-blow, Yarmouth apparently stabilized, with the narrow alleys leading to the waterfront known as the Rows attributed to the thirteenth century, and the town walls were probably begun after a murage grant of 1265, though the ground's instability required them to have timber footings. The most notorious casualty of the sea was not far to the south at Dunwich, where from the 1280s a sequence of high tides and gales blocked the harbour and eventually eroded the shoreline.[52]

The storm surges of the later thirteenth century may have led to the construction of a wall at Dover, which would have blocked off access to the shore from what had been a densely used area dominated by evidence of sea-fishing; not only were quantities of iron hooks and net weights found, but also the bases of large ovens where curing could have taken place. The buildings were small and probably insubstantial, with successions of floors. Nevertheless, they were probably lived in, not simply huts and storage sheds, and other crafts such as antler- and bone-working took place; gaming counters show that some occupants had leisure time.[53]

Further west on the south coast, (Old) Winchelsea also became inaccessible, but in that case the shingle on which it is thought to have been built was being swept away from the 1250s onwards, to be replaced in the 1280s by a new hilltop site overlooking a harbour and waterfront on the river below. A new town planned for Poole Harbour despite the established port at Poole came to nothing, indicative of an end to expansion generally, although ironically giving a very clear expression of what was expected, with a market, church, and 'plots for merchants and others'. Poole itself has evidence of its prosperity in the very long warehouse now called the Town Cellars, built at the turn of the thirteenth century.[54]

New Winchelsea was built on a grid-plan, more regular than New Salisbury's as it was less affected by pre-existing roads, streams, and churches. Its square market-place was smaller and was blessed by a friary rather than a parish church. Stone-covered drains ran below many of the streets, but a high water-table probably meant that fresh water from wells was easily obtained. Many established towns found greater difficulty with getting drinkable water as their populations increased, and some, like Exeter, negotiated for the cathedral's piped supply to be extended to a well at the lower end of the town for public use, but that cannot have been enough to meet demand (Illus. 9.5). The Blackfriars there provided themselves with a separate supply; the vaulted stone chamber which took the pipe under the city wall survives. London created its own supply, using lead pipes to

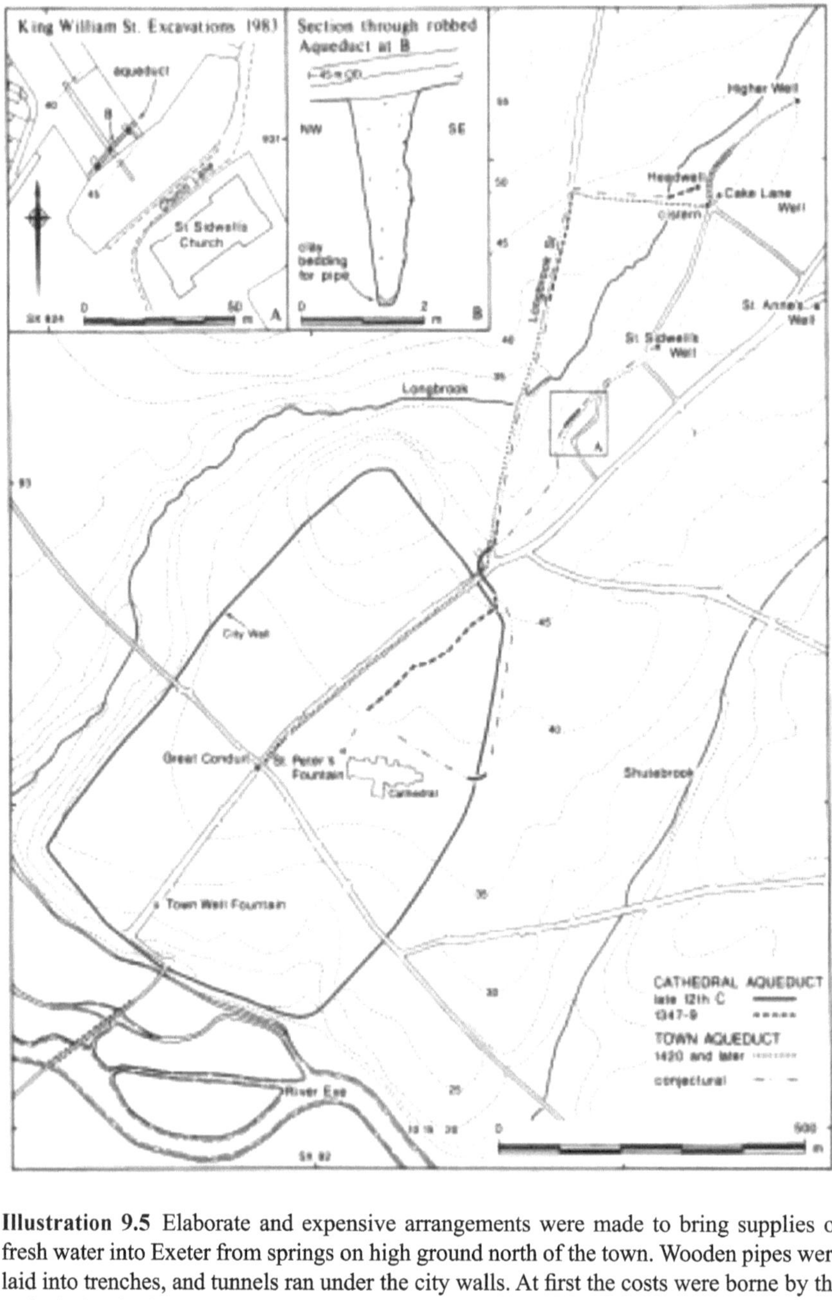

Illustration 9.5 Elaborate and expensive arrangements were made to bring supplies of fresh water into Exeter from springs on high ground north of the town. Wooden pipes were laid into trenches, and tunnels ran under the city walls. At first the costs were borne by the cathedral and Blackfriars for their own benefits; later, arrangements were made to supply the townspeople (Stoyle 2014).

feed conduit houses in the city; a lead trough was supported on an arched base at one site.[55]

Like most new inland towns, Salisbury did not have stone walls, though it was surrounded by a bank and ditch where rivers were not natural barriers. Coastal New Winchelsea had to have stone walls and gates; these defences had by now become the responsibility of the towns themselves, not of the local areas or aristocrats, a sign of urban self-government and civic responsibility, but a huge expense. Winchelsea traffic had to make a steep climb up from the river to pass through a gate where tolls could be extracted if they were due. The gradient does not seem to have been the deterrent to trade that it might have been, as the town was largely filled with houses, many with vaulted stone cellars. These were not linked directly to the houses above them but were entered from the street down stone steps; some had windows and other features, so they were completely self-contained and could be let out separately. Such a convenient and profitable arrangement featured in several ports where secure storage was required, along streets leading from the landing-places, as in Southampton, Bristol, and perhaps London, where the wide range of different types may have included the earliest in England. Later documents suggest that some were wine-taverns, and merchants may have used them to entertain bulk-buying customers, away from the throngs who used the shops at street level. Something similar appears in the Rows at Chester, but there the upper-level properties are linked by walkways, which no other town favoured. The street sides of the walkways are still lined with sloping boards on which the owners would have displayed their wares. Shops were not only for retail use but also were workshops where the goods for sale were produced – visibly, as a control on cheating.[56]

*

Henry III's work at Westminster included reconstructing the abbey church to make it his equivalent of Paris's Notre Dame, but he also looked beyond France, bringing Italians, members of the Cosmati family, to create mosaic pavements and monuments of patterns and colours not seen before in northern Europe; those craftsmen were probably the first from south of the Alps to work in medieval England. Henry's interests seem to have been shared by his queen, Eleanor of Provence; she maintained her own household, a physical separation taken to extremes at Clarendon where not only separate sets of chambers were provided, but also separate halls. Although not as polychromatic as the Cosmatis' work, red-clay tiles stamped with patterns that were then filled with white clay gave a colour contrast on the floors, made by French tilers who had worked first at Westminster. Thereafter they moved on to other contracts; English craftworkers learnt the technique, and in modified form decorated tiles spread widely, though mostly used in churches, with workshops becoming established as demand grew.[57]

Henry III is known also to have had wall-paintings in his houses, not only at Clarendon; a convenient distance away, a day's journey, at Ludgershall, Wiltshire, he built a castle in a countryside setting, where evidence of wall-paintings has been excavated. A Jesse tree, showing the lineage of Jesus, was a favourite with those who used their own family trees to demonstrate their claim to long ancestral rights. A Wheel of Fortune reminded such people that their lives were precarious, however, as did a sensitive carving of a young man with a fashionable hairstyle to indicate his high social status but suffering the disfigurement of leprosy. The parable of Dives and Lazarus showed them their duty to relieve the poor. Edward the Confessor giving a gold ring to a beggar was a particular role model for kings, and Henry III favoured Westminster because of its connection to Edward. Henry also used gift-giving in a different way, however, bestowing belts, brooches, and cups on foreign visitors and his own subjects, to cement alliances and create bonds.[58]

Edward I is best-known for his castles in Wales, but the crosses that he ordered when his queen, Eleanor of Castile, died on her travels in 1290 were pinnacles of Gothic architecture. As was still usually the case, the king was not with her at the time. Older people tended to become less mobile, unsurprisingly, but demanded a high standard of accommodation, like Joan de Valence at Goodrich Castle, notable as much for its garderobes as for its impregnable appearance. Queen Eleanor was given Leeds Castle in the 1270s, a moated site to which she added a large tower block, close enough to the water to be reflected in it in the right light, perhaps an effect achieved already by the moat at the Tower of London. Edward I used the Arthurian legends to bolster his claim to Wales, and his tournament at Winchester in 1290 may have been when the great Round Table now in the castle hall was constructed. A feast at it would have given the illusion of equality, but of course only amongst the privileged few with invitations, who would be well aware who was the principal. Edward's reign also saw a new coinage, under the control of a new official, the Master of the Mint, who had sole responsibility for its standard, so that the names of individual moneyers no longer appeared on the royal pennies.[59]

The thirteenth century did not end well; bad storms were recorded even before the 1257 volcano, which may have had a long-term effect on weather patterns; floods recorded as swamping fens and marshlands would not only have caused immediate drownings but longer-term damage from salt seeping into the soil as well. Wool production suffered because sheep suffered from scab. Civil war in the 1260s created social instability, and Edward I's campaigns and castle-building in Wales in the 1280s followed by his raids into Scotland demanded heavy taxation, at a time when silver mines in Europe were being worked out, affecting money supplies and causing inflation. Although Edward's armies were an unwitting form of job creation, taking surplus men out of production and possibly therefore easing a little of the strain on communities, they came at a heavy cost. The French raided the south coast, testing New Winchelsea's walls. Much worse was to come.[60]

Notes

1 Households: Woolgar (ed.) 1993; Woolgar 1999.

2 Corfe: Brown, R. A. *et al.* 1963, 617–22; Henry III and Edward I subsequently walled, towered, and gated the lower bailey. The summary by Brown, R. A. *et al.* of Henry III's castle works remains unsurpassed: 1963, 110–19. Winchester hall: Guy 2020–21, 250–72. Gloriet: Ashbee 2004, associating the term, also used at Leeds (see Ch. 10), with heroic poetry. Swallow 2014, 293–8 for possible Crusader influence.

3 London: Goodall, J. 2011, 190–1; Ashbee 2021 showed how Henry III's works reconfigured the Tower with moats and wall circuits, and Edward I altered it again with a new water gate. Siege engines: Purton 2018, on the counterweight-using trebuchet, p. 180 for the first mention of it in England, in 1216–17. Winchester hall: Biddle and Clayre 2006. Barbicans, and dramatic photograph of Sandal excavation: Kenyon 1990, 78–81. Brougham: Summerson *et al.* 1998; Guy 2013–14.

4 St Briavel's: Goodall, J. 2011, 236. Dean iron: Meredith 2006, 62–4 for estimates of the number of smiths required to meet the royal orders, for example 14 in 1257, with ancillary workers, making a work-force of around 50. 'Tough Gloucester iron' was used for ties and hooks in Westminster Abbey: Steane 1993, 169.

5 Wharram Percy: Wrathmell (ed.) 2012, 26–31 and 71–2; manor-houses generally: Campbell, J. [a] 2018, 243–9. Westminster hall fittings: Collins, M. *et al.* 2012, 207–12.

6 General discussion of moats: Campbell, J. [a] 2018, 252–4; Platt 2010 (further discussion in *Medieval Archaeology* 56); see Johnson, E. D. 2015 for the over 300 in the Weald of Kent and Sussex. Odiham: Allen, D. and Stoodley 2010; Wells: Emery, A. 2006, 669; Witney's moat may date to the thirteenth century also: Allen, T. G. 2002, 217–18 (but Salisbury despite being on a new site and low-lying was not moated, nor was Ely's Little Downham: Taylor, C. 2010, see Ch. 8). Aristocratic spatial divisions: Gilchrist 1999, ch. 6. Gardens might have Arthurian overtones, as well as promoting the language of flowers and purity.

7 Northolt: Hurst, J. G. 1961, 232–9. Chalgrove: Page *et al.* 2005. Wintringham: Beresford 1977, 194–225. See Kilby 2020, 45 for manorial relocations and stabilities in eastern England. Malting ovens may have had dual functions as dryers to parch grain before it was ground. Winnowing: see also Ch. 8.

8 Licences: Davis, P. 2006–07; 2011–12; licences have become part of the debate over lawlessness, status, and so on (see further Ch. 10). Sydenham, Warwickshire, may be an example of a younger son's moat, perhaps resulting from a grant of 1240; the house within it had a hall and service-wing: Smith, L. 1989–90. Eccleshall: Hawke-Smith 1984. Over 5,000 moated sites have been recorded in England, including some too small for residential use but were for mills, haystacks etc.

9 Crucks: Alcock, N. 2019a. See Meeson 2012 for a review of carpentry developments. Base-crucks: Meeson 2019; Alcock, N. and Miles 2013, 151–2; Pearson 1994, 56. Great Coxwell: Miles, D. H. *et al.* 2014, 123. Stable isotopes are starting to give an alternative dating method for timbers without enough rings to fit into a dendrochronological sequence and are less likely to be affected by soot deposits and other factors than radiocarbon: Miles, D. H. *et al.* 2019; elm, more widely used than once thought, resists dendrochronological analysis: Bridge 2020. To ensure that the pre-cut timbers were assembled in the right order, they were often numbered; Roman numerals are easier to cut, but Arabic began to be used in the thirteenth century, an indication of their spreading acceptance: Pacey 2005. Large barns are usually now called 'tithe barns', but they were nearly all built on estates where there was produce from the ecclesiastical owners' demesne land also to be stored and processed; tithes were, however, increasingly acquired by abbeys and priories as rights to them were a frequent pious donation from a church's owner – the parish priest then received a stipend and/or some 'glebe-land' but usually far from the equivalent value.

10 Pre-1200 buildings: Gardiner 2000 found a few possible uses in the excavation evidence but noted that rearing would have required a distinctive type of post-hole and that therefore the feet of the earliest crucks may have rested on the ground surface. For the cruck origin debate, see Alcock, N. 2019b; Hill, N. 2019b; a few documentary mentions of *furcae* may indicate cruck usage a century or more before their first physical appearance, but the contexts are not conclusive about precise meanings. See Hill, N. 2019b for the possible East Midlands origin. Distribution issues include different apex types and the use of 'jointed' crucks, mostly in the south-west and presumably to give the appearance of crucks without the use of such long timbers – so the general form must have been seen as the norm.

11 Barnwell 2019 suggested that different woodland management and higher demand for fuel as well as for building timber may have been a factor; he also noted that the 'non-cruck' area was the most commercially advanced – which leads back to an old argument that curved timbers were in demand for ship construction (see Milne 2004), and the wrights could outbid the carpenters for them. Granite blocks packed with soil were estimated to have allowed for a wall 6 feet wide at the base to have been at least 4 feet high, at Old Lanyon, Cornwall: Beresford 1974, 138–42. West Whelpington: Evans, D. H. and Wrathmell 1987. Dialect and word-use: Lass 1992, 35; Hogg 2006, 362–5; distributions indicate inter-regional contact as much as localism. Distributions of pots from different kilns reflect marketing opportunities, but in the thirteenth century have only slight variations in form, not type, apart from some continued use of 'West Country' dishes: McCarthy and Brooks 1989a, 125. Another and similarly unexplained regional variation is the alignment of rural church chancels, which varies progressively from Kent to Cornwall: Hinton, I. D. 2012. A recently identified type of buckle, attributed to a southern French fourteenth-century origin, is instructive because examples have been found throughout England, although possibly mostly worn by traders: Thaudet and Webley 2019, 299–300.

12 Essex: Stenning 2003, 1–19; south Oxfordshire: Currie 1992, 97–8 – there are examples of sub-manorial base-crucks in Hampshire also: Roberts, E. 1993. Full crucks were used in some Welsh manor-houses: Suggett 2013, 8–9, and to span the hall at Stokesay in the 1290s: below. Bays make discussion of spatial arrangement and social norms possible: summary in Grenville 1997, 17–22.

13 Gardiner 2000, 163–8; the reconstruction as a long-house of a building excavated at Mawgan Porth seems dubious, as it has a large beast dangerously close to a post supporting the roof: Bruce-Mitford 1997, 8 and front cover; see Ch. 6. The discussion of Seacourt (Biddle 1961–62, 121–2) was fundamental in changing the view that long-houses were universal; it was also one of the first sites where peasant use of low stone walls, suitable for timber-framing, was recognized.

14 Excavated farm buildings: Dyer 2019a, 37–48; granaries raised on staddle-stones to thwart vermin are even more difficult to trace, though documents suggest that they had been introduced by the fourteenth century: Dyer 1984. Great Linford, Buckinghamshire, excavations found two malting-kilns within peasant crofts and one in the manor-house complex: Mynard and Zeepvat 1992. Dairy bowls: Mellor 1994b, 353–4 (a Leicestershire priory spent 2d on two earthen pots for milking in 1414 × 18, the only time that ceramic rather than wood or metal was specified: Johnson, D. (trans.) 2013, 237). Gas chromatography on lipids has been developed by R. Evershed, for example 197–9 in Connor and Buckley 1999. Raddon: Fowler and Blackwell 1998, 79–93; Hare, J. 2011, 19–21. Vaccaries: Margetts 2017, with references on pp. 120–1; also Campbell, B. M. S. *et al.* 1996, 36.

15 Wharram 'revenants': Mays *et al.* 2017; one individual had had Paget's disease, so may have been disfigured by it, but if there were other Paget's cases in the Wharram churchyard they had not apparently been ostracized: Mays *et al.* 2007, 329–30. Formal teaching was that revenants were souls waiting in Purgatory, returning to earth to warn the living rather than evil spirits sent to torment them; it is probably a mere coincidence that beliefs in substantial ghosts were recorded in Yorkshire: Horrox 1999, 95–7. Woodcock 2005, 13–14 showed that beliefs were folkloric but not pagan survivals; see Dyer 2012, 338 for other evidence of 'unofficial' belief. The extraordinary carvings and other features in the Royston, Nottinghamshire, cave can also be called 'unofficial', but if associated with the Knights Templar, are unlikely to represent serious deviation: English Heritage online entry; human skulls in it, if original, might be interpreted as charnel. See Daniell 1997, 149–71 for a wide range of burial practices such as plant-filled pillows and stone head supports.

16 Infant burial: Gilchrist 2012, 220–2 and 284–5; Crawford 2018, 779–80; midwives could baptize a baby, but in remoter settlements none may have been available in time;

that would not have been a problem in towns, but there is no greater evidence of malpractice, two in Dover having been carefully placed, one of them upright: Parfitt *et al.* 2006, 319–21. See Randall 2020, 28, 31–2, and 117–20 for the manorial example (the context was inside a stone building, but one which might have been a first-floor hall over an undercroft, presumably a working area, so the baby seems likely not to have been placed there by a member of the owning family); Randall drew attention to other 'threshold' deposits. At Wharram, infants tended to be on the north side, so there was no canonical decree: Mays *et al.* 2007, 189 and 330. A neonatal burial within a locked box on the edge of the cemetery at Poulton is so far unique: Cootes *et al.* 2019, 39–40.

17 The Eucharist: Gilchrist 1999, 83–5; 2006 for 'tolerated' beliefs generally; 'magic' was not because of underlying pagan survival. Chancel alignment: Hinton, I. D. 2012. Chalice-and-paten burials: Gilchrist and Sloane 2005, 160–5; Gilchrist 2009, 206–7; Rogers, N. 2005. Even abbots and archbishops were normally buried in chapter-houses not inside 'their' churches until the thirteenth century: Bertram 2007. Friaries: O'Sullivan 2013

18 Purgatory: Horrox 1999; Duffy, E. 2006, 309–10 – corporeal resurrection was not formal teaching, but 'unofficial'. Charnel-houses: Gilchrist and Sloane 2005, 41–3 (the anglo-saxon chapel at Bradford-on-Avon was known as 'the old skull house' before it became a school); St Mary Spital had a fourteenth-century charnel crypt: Harward *et al.* 2019, 68–71. The practice of dividing a dead body so that the heart could be buried in one place, the disembowelled corpse in another, was increasingly frowned upon: Binski 1996, 60–2; Horrox 1999. Burial as remembrance: Binski 1996, 33–4; Williams, H. 2003b. Internal burial: Bertram 2007. Funeral monuments and brasses: Badham 2005; Binski 1987, 70–2; Blair 1987, 133–44; tomb-chests: Rogers, N. J. 1987, 20; Brieger 1957, 104–5 (where the association with crusaders was discussed and denied; it seems to have been an English custom for representations to suggest that the dead person was actively ready for the Resurrection: Bertram 2007). Slabs and covers: Butler 1987.

19 Seating: Steane 2001, 141; Byng 2017. Chapels: Orme 1996. Jews' maltreatment and expulsion: Mundill 2003.

20 Horses: Clark 1995, 25–7 and 30–1, and contribution by D. J. Rackham, 19–22; horse bones butchered much like cow bones at a few sites may indicate human consumption, not just food for pigs and dogs: Woolgar *et al.* 2006, 271; West Cotton: Dunne *et al.* 2019, 13 (humans may also have eaten horsemeat unwittingly in pies and sausages; at Bury St Edmunds in 1258, a chronicler recorded that famine forced people to eat horsemeat, but that was an expression of clerical outrage, not a sociological examination: Marvin 1998; famine-foods included wild berries, but the truth is hard to disentangle). Horse increase: Dyer 2012, 320; Claridge 2017. Langdon 1986 remains the classic study. Humoral theory and cooking: Sykes 2006, 70; Woolgar 2006, 198. Fish bones: Serjeantson and Woolgar 2006, 105–23; Parfitt *et al.* 2006, 353–69. Isotopes: Müldner and Richards 2006, 230–1 (the Wharram Percy data might seem at variance with records of rural labourers' food allowances, but those may be slanted to particular seasons (Serjeantson and Woolgar 2006, 122). Analysis by S. Mileson of people who paid an annual fee to use the market in thirteenth-century Wallingford shows that more journeys of 5 or 6 miles were made that could only have used roads than could have used the Thames: Christie and Creighton 2013, 383 (an alternative, though probably only occasional, was for an agent to go into a town and negotiate with a buyer, who would then collect the goods – and hope to dodge toll payments: Britnell 1996b, 382.

21 Skeletal summary: Roberts, C. A. *et al.* 2018.

22 At Wharram, slightly less than 20% of adults had fractures, but only an elderly male had injuries that would certainly have caused death, and a male in his 20s also may not have survived an attack, as his skull had an unhealed blade injury: Mays *et al.* 2007, 143–5. Only one of over 200 skeletons in a London cemetery had been struck on the head and probably killed by a blade blow; two other skulls had penetrating injuries,

probably caused by a knife or arrow: White, W. J. 1988, 4; one male at East Smithfield had three head wounds that had had time to heal before he suffered a blow that would have killed him: Walker, D. 2006. St Andrew's, York: Daniell 2001; isotopes: Müldner 2009, 340–1; the Gilbertines' surgery attempts included strapping copper plates on either side of an elderly male's knee to allow his leg to bear some weight, though he needed to use a crutch: Knüsel *et al.* 1995; metal plates to support legs/knees were also found at St Mary Spital; Harward *et al.* 2019, 174. Poulton: Cootes *et al.* 2019, 41. Arrow injury has been identified in an Exeter friary cemetery: Creighton *et al.* 2020. Norwich: Stirland 2009, 19 for wounds, 31–3 for cerebral palsy, and see Ch. 8. A male at Hulton Abbey, Staffordshire, who had been mutilated and violently killed was identified as possibly Sir William Audley, killed by the Welsh in 1282: Klemperer and Boothroyd 2004, 133, and a man in a pitch-soaked shroud within a lead container at a priory in Cumbria who had died a violent death and had been mutilated may have been Anthony de Lucy, who died on crusade in Prussia in 1368: Knüsel *et al.* 2010, 288–91 and 300–1. A few injuries were reported in other cemeteries by Gilchrist and Sloane 2005, 72–3. Of the 240 cases of homicide recorded in Northamptonshire, 93 involved knives, compared to 49 sticks and staffs, 15 swords, 9 bows and arrows, and a miscellany of tools etc. snatched up in anger: Thornton 2014.

23 Pounds 1989, 176–81 raised many of the issues; Albarella 1997 made an interesting contrast between archaeological evidence of bones and documentary records of sales and pointed out the preservation issue. Cooking: Willmott, H. 2018, 698–700. Human bone and diet: Waldron 2006 – the difficulty of identifying anaemia from iron deficiency is a particular problem, pp. 259–60; Roberts, C. A. *et al.* 2018, 822–3. St Mary Spital: Harward *et al.* 2019, 30 and 66–7; the records of alms-giving at Westminster, if reliable, would have led people to expect relief in the capital: Dixon-Smith 1999, 87–9. 'Marginal' agricultural areas are those where even a slight change makes arable farming untenable, such as on moorland; grazing may still be possible and was valuable, for example the 'stints' on Otterburn, Northumberland pasture in 1245 allowed for 1140 sheep, 1400 cows, and some horses: Fraser (ed. and trans.) 1968, viii–ix. Volcano: Campbell, B. M. S. 2017.

24 Jug increase, for example Westbury: Ivens *et al.* 1995, 290. 'Sheen': Woolgar 2006, 150–1. Dress codes: Lachaud 2002, 107–15. Lay subsidies, that is taxes on movable goods: Nightingale 2004, defending their overall reliability. Some peasant inventories were drawn up for lords who owned the *principalia,* that is things that belonged with the tenement and were not deemed personal property, for example Field 1965; others were also drawn up for lords, if a peasant's whole property was claimed because they had become felons etc. and in theory were more complete: Briggs forthcoming. Seals: Heslop 1988; Cherry, J. 2018. Hearth-pots: Moorhouse 1978; upside-down pots: Ivens *et al.* 1995, 272–5 (an earlier example, although later in date than the rest of the occupation, was found at Bishopstone next to a post-hole and interpreted as a cistern: Thomas 2010, 64 and 94–5; but as it would have been hard to access, it might be another example of a foundation deposit).

25 Wharram Percy tenement plan: Everson and Stocker 2012b, 266. See Dyer 2012, 329–30, 338, and 337–8 for communal activities; Heslop 1988, illus. 2 for a document witnessing a communal agreement laden with peasant seals. See Dyer 1989, 109–18 for the differences in rural wealth and land-holding.

26 See Ivens *et al.* 1995, 85 for Westbury plan, and Smith, S. V. 2010 for a penetrating analysis (see also next chapter). Buildings on greens etc. called *bordelli*: Fox, H. S. A. 1996. Seacourt: Biddle 1961–62, 110–11. Fringford: Blinkhorn *et al.* 2000. An example of problems of interpretation of such structures comes from what is described as a one-room cottage at a grange, which might have shown the living conditions of a farm servant but had a drain, a trough, and an oven and looks to me much more like one of the out-buildings: Allen, T. G. 1994, 257–72.

27 Coins: annual loss rates rise from 47 to 81, Kelleher 2018, 521 (15 years earlier, an estimate gave nine and thirty respectively: Hinton 2005, 197); Westbury had nine excavated coins, none being whole pennies: Ivens *et al.* 1995, 332; Humber crossing: Cook, B. J. 1998; although distribution mapping is so affected by detection and recording rates, some detailed geographical patterns are interesting, for example the decline in numbers around a site in Wiltshire may indicate the reality of competition from rival markets: Oksanen and Lewis 2020, 125–9. Church finds: Gilchrist 2008, 133–5; at Wharram, five of the eleven thirteenth-/fourteenth-century coins were from the church or churchyard: Barclay 2007, 301. Folded coins: Naylor 2015, 296. Sandwich: Wanostrocht 1992. Peasant inventories rarely mentioned cash, but the few exceptions suggest that there was quite a lot of it, for example a Norfolk widow who in 1271 held less than 2 acres nevertheless had 2s 6d in silver: Briggs forthcoming, no. 12. The role of commerce and investment as factors changing the whole structure of society was hotly debated in the 1990s and 2000s: for exampleBailey, M. 1989; Langdon and Masschaele 2006. By-employment: Britnell 2001, 5–7 and 10; peasant marketing: Dyer 2002, 163–5.

28 For summaries of all extractive industries: Parsons, D. 2018; Waterley: Hall, D. 1983; other small-scale operations have been found recently near Melksham, Wiltshire: Hardy and Dungworth 2014, and near Basingstoke, Hampshire: Pringle 2020, 300–1 and 317; Alsted: Ketteringham 1976; Bordesley: Astill 1993. Mills: Holt 1988 for the history, Rynne 2018 for the archaeology; vertical wheels are more powerful if fed from a chute above, as shown in the Luttrell Psalter: Camille 1998, pl. 89. Devon silver: Allen, M. 2011. St Neot tin-streaming perhaps associated with a mid thirteenth-century long-house: Austin, D. 1989.

29 Hurst, J. D. (ed.) 1997, 32–41 and 151; dendrochronology by C. Grove and J. Hillam, 112.

30 Marks: Ramsay 1991, xxvi–xxvii. Pewter: Brownsword and Pitt 1985; Homer 1991, 67–79. Tin: Hatcher 1972; Greeves 1981. Brasses: Badham 2005; Blair 1987, with Lincoln analysis by R. Brownsword; see also above. Steelyard weights: Brownsword and Pitt 1983.

31 Tyson 2000. London enamelled glasses: Clark 1983. See Ch. 8 for an enamelled fragment from Seacourt.

32 Wine, spices, textiles, and so on were the principal goods traded from fairs and do not survive; lesser products such as pots were sold at them but would not have come from far away, nor travelled far afterwards: Moore, E. W. 1985; Epstein 1994. Hambleden: Babb 1997. Pedlars and 'bag-men' generally: Nightingale 1995, 365–6; 'chapmen' might imply the same occupation: Britnell 2001, 10–11. See Mellor 1994a, 94–5 for an example of pottery distribution into a region rather than just from an individual kiln site; she also made the point that distribution would have been affected not only by distance, but by avoidance of tolls and by service dues that forced tenants to take goods to a lord's household, so that they may have used the market nearest to that even if there were others nearer their home; see also Mellor 2005, 155–6. Itinerant households account for many of the vessels found a long way from where they were made: Moorhouse 1983. Scarborough: McCarthy and Brooks 1989a, 94–6. Short-lived enterprises recently investigated include one in a ribbon development growing from Hitchin, Hertfordshire: Ashworth 1998, and one just inside the boundary of Salisbury, which seems to have been an off-shoot of the 'potting village' at Laverstock a mile away: Algar and Saunders 2014.

33 Dinna Clerks: Hinton 2010, 97–8, citing work by S. Moorhouse and J. Allan. Few peasant inventories specified earthen pots and then not necessarily their size or function, for example Briggs forthcoming no. 8, dated 1416, *olla terrea*. Rural ceremonies and badges: Gilchrist 2012, 106–9; Duffy, E. 1992, 13–15. The use of jugs with bearded images in coming-of-age rituals has been suggested, which raises an issue

over recognition of 'unofficial' behaviour; many societies have the practice, so it might have been expected in the Middle Ages, but could it have escaped documentary notice (see e.g. Hanawalt 1986 for absence of deaths arising from it)? Music: Gilchrist 2012, 108 and 152; Mileson 2018, 715; instruments: Egan 1998, and further on bone pipes: Chapman 2010, 351–5; bagpipes may not have appeared until the fourteenth century: Hooke 2020, 41–3.

34 Hand-washing: Woolgar 2016, 160–1 and 174. Emulation: Dyer 2002, 6. Aquamaniles: Hinton 2010, 104.

35 Peasant formality and eating: Pounds 1989, 206–8; Dyer 2013, 20 and 24; Woolgar 2016, 26–41 and 239 (much of what is known about peasant cooking comes from coroners' inquests into deaths caused by accidents during it). Detached kitchens: Gardiner 2000, 162–3. Inventoried tables: Briggs forthcoming.

36 West Cotton pottery: Chapman 2010, contribution by P. Blinkhorn. For other references: Hinton 2010; small black hones were perforated for suspension, and so were carried visibly, presumably so that their glossy sheen could be admired. Mortars and querns are discussed in Ch. 10. Knives: Goodall 2011, 105–11. Gold strip: Robinson *et al.* 2018, 188 (its intended function is unclear; for embroidery, silver-gilt was usual by this time).

37 Wharram South manor-house excavation: Stamper and Croft 2000; revised interpretation of the North Manor: Everson and Stocker 2012b, 270–2; peasant use of the redundant manor-house materials: Smith 2009, 404–7. Raunds: Auduoy and Chapman (eds) 2009; West Cotton: Chapman 2010. Broadfield: Klingelhöfer 1974, 8, 30, and 34–5.

38 New Salisbury: Royal Archaeological Institute/Publications, Wiltshire; the 'chequers' and the huge market-place look like overall planning but were probably not laid out at the beginning, and occupation within them developed piece-meal: Harding 2020. Oversley: Jones, C. *et al.* 1997, 32–3, 60–3, and 92–4. Large stone-lined malting-ovens with long flues to reduce fire-risk occur in various contexts, like the presumably commercial one found in Reigate, Surrey: Williams, D. 1983. A typical peasant's oven was less than a metre long, for example Ivens *et al.* 1995, 186–7. Smaller towns: Dyer 2003. Friaries: O'Sullivan 2013; an example is the Dominicans of Beverley, able to acquire quite a large site but on wet land; urban tenements only reached it later: Foreman 1996, 231–2. Suburbs: London's, McDonnell 1978; Oxford's The Hamel remains one of the best sequences, because the frontages were available for excavation, not the back yards only: Palmer 1980; Winchester's are being studied in detail, for example Serjeantson and Rees (eds) 2009.

39 Fulling-mills: Munro 1998, 195. Spinning and spinning-wheel: Standley 2016, 285; Gilchrist 1999, 50–1; yarn: Childs 1996.

40 Jettying: Quiney 2003, 119–22; Pearson 2005, 50–1.

41 Urban building: Quiney 2003; Pearson 2009, 2–3. Remains of row buildings on the outskirts of Winchester have been dated to 1253–4 and 1292–3: Bridge *et al.* 2010, 107. Winchester also has one of the best examples of the excavation of one-room back-street rows: Ottaway 2017, 323–5.

42 Town–country relationships and the experience of townscapes have become foci of discussion, for example Giles and Dyer (eds) 2005; Dugan 2018. Various metals were worked on in towns, notably London: Egan 1996; Keene 2000a, but have been investigated in Coventry, Nottingham, and elsewhere – summaries by Bayley 1996; Bayley noted that as crafts and trades were increasingly grouped together, so the nature of urban deposits changes, metalworking debris not being found so widely distributed, for instance. See Swanson, H. 1989 for documentary evidence of the various metalworking crafts and their practices. Urban immigration: Galloway 2005, 114–19. Diet: Albarella 2005; the numbers of cooks and so on suggest that many townspeople did not cook their own food: Carlin 1998. Sausage-makers were forbidden to use the scraps thrown out by butchers, so must have been doing so; pie-makers had just as bad a reputation.

43 Half-pence: Cook, B. J. 1998. The 4d coins became known as groats: Allen, M. 2013; their introduction was not very successful (unintended consequences still occur; new coins like the 50p or the £2 may be minted in their millions, but their circulation is initially restricted because adults save them up for children's money-boxes). Colchester and other hoards: Archibald and Cook 2001; another hoard found in Colchester had over 11,000 pennies; Jewish financiers might have amassed them, but there is no direct evidence: Brooks, Crummy, and Archibald 2004. Handling such large quantities was difficult, but Treasury officials were used to collecting taxation, and Richard I's ransom in 1193 would have involved amassing over 24 million silver pennies together if it had been fully paid in coin. Southwark counterfeits: Egan 1996, 192–3; also involving Henry III's coinage was evidence of counterfeiting cut half-pence in Nottingham: MacCormick 1996, 109–10.

44 The Southampton pit has been re-assessed by Brown, D. H. 2018; *q.v.* for Saintonge pottery (the barbary ape skull found in that pit may not, as originally interpreted, have been the merchant's living pet but a dried head kept as a curio). The pit attributed to Jews in Oxford, see Ch. 8, supports Brown's contention that I was incorrect to argue that the Southampton one came from more than one household as rubbish would have become intermixed. Surviving inventories, such as from Lynn, indicate that richer people also owned silver, notably spoons. Pewter: Homer 1991. Although glass was being made in Kent from early in the thirteenth century, it was probably not for tableware: Tyson 2000, 7. Stokesay: Emery, A. 2000, 574–6; Goodall 2011, 157 and 234–5 (the military appearance is enhanced by the adjacent church tower), and Vernacular Architecture Group data-base for dendrochronology.

45 Acton Burnell: Emery, A. 2000, 502–4; Goodall 2011, 231–2 (where he used Acton as the basis for discussion of 'the Real Castle'). Little Wenham: Emery, A. 2000, 119–22; Goodall, J. 2011, 233. Contrasting colours in masonry were used by royal builders, for example at the Tower of London in the 1240s: Keevill 2004.

46 Parliament: Maddicott 1999 (it did not always meet in London; Acton Burnell hosted it, for instance, in 1283). Law courts in Westminster hall: Collins *et al.* 2012, 216–17; the courts still occasionally met elsewhere but permanence was expected and stipulated in Magna Carta: Ormrod 2000b. London: magnate involvement: Keene 2000a; city and port: Milne 2003; Schofield, J. 2019; hinterland: Galloway 2000; Keene 2000a; boats: Marsden 1996. Estimates based on payments made for royal purveyancing indicate that barge transport cost about 1½d per ton mile, half the cost of carts, but more than twice that of longer sea journeys; private households had to pay about twice those rates: Woolgar 1999, 186 (pack-horses, punts, and dug-outs are beyond estimation, and very little survives of the last two in the archaeological record: Hutchinson 1994, 122–5). Light two-wheeled carts would have been quicker than four-wheeled wagons but less commodious; household accounts show that wheeled baggage vehicles could cover as much as 30 miles on an exceptional day, but might average 20–26 miles, and only 11 miles if a steep hill was involved, for which plodding oxen might be engaged: Woolgar 1999, 187); Langdon 1986 (in which the use of oxen and horses as plough animals was also reviewed); Masschaele 1993.

47 Shipping generally: Unger 1980; Hutchinson 1994, 10–20; Friel 1995; Marsden 1997, 65–6, illus. 51 for the massive side rudder; McGrail 2001, 230–43; and for images and their interpretation: Flatman 2007 – illus. 27 and 29 for ships with stern castles and bowsprits, but still using a massive side-rudder; Pevensey's and Winchelsea's thirteenth-century seals show forecastles and rear castles but not bowsprits, Ipswich's is much higher-sided and has a rear rudder: Pedrick 1904, pl. 2, 4, and 10. The investment involved is shown by a Lynn merchant's inventory valuing his cog at £40, a quarter-share in another at £10, and a hulk (a distinct type of vessel, with a more rounded keel than a cog) at £13 6s 8d: Owen (ed.) 1984, 247. Shipping was one of the few enterprises which allowed for joint capital but not for insurance or limited liability, essential for

capitalism to thrive (capitalism also involves control of production, difficult to achieve when most producers were self-employed).

48 Magor Pill wreck: Nayling 1998. Planks found at Doncaster, Yorkshire, may indicate another regional design: Allen, S. J. *et al.* 2005, with a contribution on caulking using tar, cattle hair, and wool by P. Walton Rogers. Wolaston: Fulford 1992. Bristol: Leech 1997; 2014, 20–1; Jones, R. 1991; Baker, N. *et al.* 2018, 136–46. Summaries of other ports: Good *et al.* 1991.

49 Exeter bridge: Harrison 2007, 177–8; Brown, S. 2019; hinterland: Kowaleski 1995, 41–53; Topsham customs records give an exceptionally detailed record of coastal and overseas importing, made very accessible by Kowaleski 1993. Newcastle and sea-coal: O'Brien 1991, 40–2; it was difficult for metalworkers to use, and I know of no instance of its use in drying sea-salt, despite the ease of landing it – presumably it fouled the taste, although there is some evidence of its use in Droitwich: Hurst, J. D. (ed.) 1997, 151; it was not suitable for open hearths, and Queen Eleanor of Provence objected to the smell of it, so it was not used in royal fireplaces; nevertheless enough was brought into London for 'Seacole Lane' to be named: Galloway *et al.* 1996, 447–9.

50 Berwick: Hunter 1982. Hartlepool: Daniels 1991. Hull: Evans, D. H. 2018, 87–90. Hedon: Hayfield and Slater 1984.

51 Fountains Abbey wool-house: Coppack 1986. Secular households: Woolgar 1999, 111–14.

52 Wisbech: Spoerry 2005, 102–5; Stone, D. 2005, 29. Lynn: Parker 1971, 25–7; Clarke, H. M. and Carter 1977. Great Yarmouth: Potter 2008. Dunwich: D. Sear, University of Southampton, online information.

53 Dover: Parfitt *et al.* 2006, 25–9, 32–95, and 417, with contributions by I. Riddler and R. Nicholson; the buildings are probably what the earlier 'little houses' at Yarmouth were like: see Ch. 8.

54 Old and New Winchelsea: contribution by J. Eddison in Martin and Martin 2004, 1–6. *Nova Villa* in Poole Harbour: Cox and Hearne 1991, 19 and 91–3. Poole: Horsey 1992, 34–48; it was probably a communal not a private enterprise (photographs do not do it justice, as a road was driven through it in the eighteenth century, so one end is separate from the rest).

55 Salisbury water-courses: Chandler 2001, 27. Exeter: Stoyle 2014, 28–33. New Winchelsea: Martin and Martin 2004–27–36 for the plan. In Norwich, the open 'cockeys' were notably foul – in a town in which stray pigs were blamed for the deaths of children: Rawcliffe 2004.

56 New Winchelsea cellars and functions: Martin and Martin 2004, 105–27. Town walls and gates: Creighton and Higham 2005. London: Schofield, J. 1995, 70–81. Bristol: Leech 2014, 150–60. Chester: Brown, A. *et al.* 2000, arguing that Roman debris cleared back from the streets was partly responsible, p. 7, and pp. 2 and 20–2 for 'stallboards'. House plans generally: Pearson 2005, 47–51. Shops: Antrobus 2018. Walls and gates: Creighton and Higham 2005, 84–5 and 180–4 for murage grants, which involved towns keeping parts of the toll income owed to the Crown; the system mostly phased out during the fourteenth century. Urban heroes included King Col of Colchester, Brutus of London: Wheatley 2004, 54–8, and Bevis of Southampton: Rance 1986; they were used as opportunities for pageants (see also Chs 8 and 11).

57 Cosmati work: Rodwell and Neal 2019; Henry III's close personal interest in Westminster, intending it to be his burial-place: Payne and Foster 2020, 242–5. Clarendon: James, T. B. and Robinson 1988, 18–22, and contribution on the tiles by E. Eames, pp. 127–67. The first off-site tile manufactories are difficult to pin down, for example Mellor 2018, 93–8; later ones include Penn, Buckinghamshire; Chilvers Coton, Warwickshire; Tyler Hill, Kent; and Danbury, Essex.

58 Clarendon: James, T. B. and Robinson 1988: little wall-painting survived, but preserved work at Rochester shows what it would have been like; for the head, 246 and

frontispiece. Ludgershall: Ellis (ed.) 2000, 13 and 233–4. The cult of Edward the Confessor: Dixon-Smith 1999, 79–85; Edward's gift-giving is shown on Richard II's Wilton Diptych. Henry III's gift-giving: Wild 2010 (the first record of New Year's Day gifts, which remained the tradition for many centuries). The gender issues involved in such élite establishments, with different levels of accessibility, were explored by Richardson, A.[a] 2003. Summary of work by Henry II, Edward I, their queens, and their contemporaries: James, T. B. 1990: 48–101.

59 Itinerant households: Woolgar 1999, 181–93; Wilkinson, L. J. 2018 for the extraordinary journeys made by Eleanor de Montfort in 1265 from Odiham to Portchester and on to Dover in 1265, trying all the while to maintain political support by gifts of venison and entertainment. Leeds: Goodall, J. 2011, 236–7. Moat at Tower of London: Keevill 2004. Gardens: Steane 1993, 121–2. Winchester Round Table: Biddle and Clayre 2006; Edward's uncle Richard of Cornwall had also tried to associate himself with the Arthurian legends, building a castle at remote Tintagel.

60 Volcano: Campbell, B. M. S. 2017. Storms: Griffiths, D. 2015, 104–5; in 1250, no one in Tydd St Giles in the Cambridgeshire fens could pay any rent because its land had been 'totally destroyed by the sea': Willmoth and Oosthuizen (eds) 2015, 161. Sheep scab: Slavin 2020. A consequence of the French raids was trade disruption and the decline of the fair of St Giles, Winchester, from international to local significance: Arthur 2021, 103. Wider general questions are raised by the later thirteenth-century downturn: was arbitrary taxation a disincentive to investment? Were institutional landlords more conservative than the laity, prioritizing their own consumption needs over the opportunities offered by the market? Could arable output have increased further and sustained an even higher population, especially in towns? Could 'transaction costs' such as the movement of goods have been reduced or were they a significant restraint? Edward I's taxation has been said to have moved England from being a 'domain state' with kings deriving less of their incomes from taxation than from their lands, from the profits of justice, and from their colonialist expansions into Wales, Ireland, and France to being a 'tax state' with subsidies and tolls on imports more important and the 'colonies' requiring more expenditure to protect than they yielded in profits: Ormrod 2000a.

10 The Fourteenth Century

Dearth and Death

The Black Death entered England in 1348 and is estimated to have killed at least half the population in the next 18 months. Study of the fourteenth century is dominated by consideration of the effects of its impact, and its further outbreaks in 1361, 1369, and thereafter, but it was preceded by famines in 1315–18, which may have slowed if not halted demographic growth. At that time, there was also heavy loss of sheep to murrain, followed by the mortality of over half the cattle. Agricultural stability was not only threatened by weather fluctuations, but also by a colder climate; the latter would not have been perceptible to those living with it but is shown by glaciers and ice-cores. Economic and social stabilities were further threatened by Scottish raids in the north and by French raids on the south coast. Edward III initially had success in France, but his expeditions are reckoned to have cost England over £1 million; feudal levies serving for forty days in defence of the kingdom were insufficient for long campaigns overseas, and waged soldiers had to be relied upon. Those who could enter contracts to raise such troops might make large profits, but the Poll Taxes levied to meet the costs were a major cause of the Revolt in 1381, which threatened the whole social fabric.[1]

Edward II's defeat at Bannockburn in 1314 opened Northumberland to destructive raids by the Scots and may have been the direct cause of the abandonment of a house at West Whelpington, in which half-a-dozen coins were found hidden in a cavity in the wall: the earliest was a halfpenny from King John's reign, and others were Edward II pennies; it seems more likely that an early thirteenth-century coin was still in circulation a hundred years later than that the coins were added to the little hoard one at a time, so probably someone hid their purse and never came back for it. If that is correct, it shows how even seemingly isolated peasants were operating in a money-using economy and had small reserves. A silver lace-end was also found at West Whelpington, an indication that people there could afford small precious items, in that case probably a costume fitting, so even villagers were aware of new, closer-fitting dress modes. A small silver brooch was excavated at another subsequently deserted north-eastern site, West Hartburn, Northumberland. Brooches increased in number generally, suggesting both greater awareness of personal display and a belief in the effectiveness of christian talismans, as they often had religious inscriptions.[2]

DOI: 10.4324/9781003007432-11

Occasional abandonments were caused by lords extending their parks, evicting tenants whose powers of resistance were limited. An example is Okehampton, Devon, where the earls of Devon renovated their castle, providing lodgings for guests to view their newly extended park and enjoy the hunting. Bones show that the venison served came from fallow deer kept in the park rather than from red deer hunted across the open spaces of Dartmoor; arrow-heads, barbed to cut their hamstrings and bring them down, show how they were killed. Magnates increasingly needed to provide comfortable accommodation and suitable recreation for visitors, as they were less able to rely upon old, feudal ties of loyalty created by land-holding but needed 'affinities' of supporters who would serve them in the courts and in their other power struggles.[3]

Six or seven houses had been within the Okehampton park, but whether their occupants were compensated by new, perhaps better, holdings elsewhere, or left to their own devices, is unrecorded. Higher up on Dartmoor, the farmhouse at Dinna Clerks seems to have been left to rot after a fire, without all its contents being removed. As had become standard by then, entry was through central doors protected by small porches, but was that a gesture towards enhancing the appearance or just to give a little more protection from the rain? Despite their isolation, the Dinna Clerks occupants had maintained a lifestyle that other peasants would not have sneered at; they might have augmented their incomes by streaming for tin, as demand for pewter was increasing, as well as for bell metal – though the profits mostly went to the merchants who traded in it, as the producers had little choice but to sell what they found to middlemen who could process it and take it to market. No metal items were found at Dinna Clerks, but that need not mean that the occupants were too poor to have any, as anything of value – the sorts of item that feature in peasant inventories – may have been removed. Elsewhere, the remains of iron implements that survived recycling suggest a limited range of basic farm equipment – sickles, an occasional bill-hook, or pitchfork – without any evidence of regional or craft specialization.[4]

Mortality in 1315–21 was high, nearly one-fifth of the labour force on two of the very few manors from which there are reliable records; it does not seem to have caused an acute shortage of workers but meant that there was no superfluity of them for lords to exploit. Ownership and agricultural practice continued to vary across the country, and documents reveal widely different conditions of tenure and strategy, even by a single landlord. Surviving houses suggest that only a few peasants were able to build substantially, using either crucks or box-frame construction, in the years before the Black Death. Wiltshire is an exception, with three crucks dated to the 1320s/30s, but Surrey, close to London and therefore likely to have benefited from supplying its markets, has none. This general impression of peasant stagnation is borne out by coin finds, as the Portable Antiquities Scheme shows that the average annual loss between 1279 and 1351 is almost exactly the same as for the previous period, so the increase had come to an end. Pottery seems no different, as decorated jugs did not develop exciting new forms and styles and are mostly difficult to distinguish from thirteenth-century wares; nor do early fourteenth-century unglazed vessels suggest new cooking methods or a wider choice of foodstuffs. Whether the more expensive metal vessels were making further inroads into the ceramics market before the Black Death is not known; recycling means that few survive complete, though legs, spouts, and handles were brazed on and therefore easily knocked off and are quite often found, indicating a general late medieval increase. Makers' marks were not required on them, unlike the assay marks by then demanded on gold and silver plate. Even iron knives began to have a maker's mark, if made in London by a member of the Cutlers' Company.[5]

An upsurge in mass burials at London's St Mary Spital shows that towns were as vulnerable as the countryside to the early fourteenth-century mortality. Generally, however, towns seem to have been more buoyant, at least insofar as buildings can be used as an indicator. At Chester, the Water Tower was built in the 1320s in the river, joined to the rest of the walls by a spur; although it had royal support, the city had to find most of the cost. At York, the Water Tower was built by St Mary's Abbey, but the city built the Lendal Tower, which was paired with another on the opposite bank, so that a chain could be stretched between them to control the passage of ships.[6]

York's prosperity is shown by the timber-framed terraced row of 'renters', for craft-workers and artisans, still standing in Goodramgate, testimony to good building by the vicar who provided for the edge of his church's cemetery to be used for it in 1315–16, a date now confirmed by dendrochronology. Each cottage consisted of a single ground-floor room, with a jettied upper storey; the vicar did not permit further encroachment on the graveyard to allow for back-yards. Nearby is a row in Stonegate, constructed in much the same way and probably therefore of similar date but having two upper storeys, presumably for slightly richer townspeople. York had other such terraces, and they were probably also built in London, as streets named 'row' are recorded from early in the fourteenth century, but do not survive. Small 'renters' did not have the traditional open hall with an open hearth – heating must have been by braziers – the beginning of a social revolution. Their occupants may not have been leading citizens, setting an example, but similarly constricted houses were allowed to encroach into market-places, presumably with ground-floor shops ousting movable stalls, and with no space for an open hall.[7]

Another new type of building that has now been shown probably to have begun in towns just before the Black Death is the 'Wealden' house, so-called because it was first identified in Kent, but is more widespread as well as less rural than its name suggests; the earliest examples so far recorded are in East Grinstead, dated to 1325–40, and in Winchester, dated to 1340. The plan gave an open hall with jettied end-blocks. Jettying became more pronounced, with three-storey buildings like Stonegate's in various towns; if extended too far, the jetties had to be supported by pillars, obstructing the street.[8]

A dramatic feature of some towns was wealthy citizens' towers. Only one survives, at Lynn, which is of the sixteenth century, but London had several, the earliest certainly known owned by William Servat, *civis et mercator*, in 1305. Although he obtained a royal licence to crenellate it, he was probably following continental practice rather than trying to express equality with rural knights and barons. Rich merchants might marry their offspring into noble families, but most seem to have preferred to remain in their familiar urban environment, not to follow the example of Laurence of Ludlow at Stokesay. A seeming exception, Sir John Pulteney, a London alderman who bought a manor at Penshurst, Kent, in 1337 where he built a house, had a landed background. His full-height hall was entered from a two-storey porch at one end, giving entry into a passage with service-rooms on the other side. The roofs were battlemented, justifying his purchase of a licence, but nothing else about the site seems to have been defensive. Pulteney also co-founded a Carmelite priory in Coventry, where his coat of arms was prominently displayed.[9]

Some rich merchants acquired urban blocs on which to construct courtyard houses, variously planned, but always giving them an open hall, which for the larger properties was placed away from the street frontage. Despite that gesture towards seclusion, the houses were not in quieter streets or suburbs, but amidst the noise and smells of craftworking and trades of various kinds. One excavated in Winchester had the only pieces found in the town of the painted Saintonge pottery that features so prominently in Southampton, testimony to mercantile contacts and self-identity. Such merchants had their own warehouses, like one in Southampton recorded as 'newly built' in 1407, a date consistent with its dendrochronological range of 1370–1420.[10]

One Saintonge jug found in Exeter is modelled with two bishops, apparently naked apart from mitres and croziers, surrounded by figures that suggest that they were in a bawdy-house. This elaborate object may have been expressive of a particular situation in Exeter, where the citizens resented the control over the town's business that the Church held by ancient right. In 1326, the bishop of Exeter was murdered, but in London and because he was a royal official, by rioting citizens whose assembly in the Guildhall may have been a significant indication of the way that such buildings were socially important to townspeople. This seems to have been the first time that a mob behaved quite so violently, but in 1327 at Bury St Edmunds, where resentment of the abbot's exceptional hold over the town and adjoining area had caused a riot in the thirteenth century, a far worse episode led to most of the abbey buildings being burnt and the abbot seized, though not killed. In Exeter, some resolution between the cathedral and the citizens seems to have been achieved, as in the 1340s an agreement was reached to share a new water supply system, which involved an underground passage within the walls, with man-hole vents to allow access for repairs to the lead pipe (Illus. 9.5). The system no longer relied entirely on a steady gradient fall; technological understanding that pressure can make water flow uphill had developed.[11]

A consequence of the Bury riot was rebuilding, notably of a new tower-gateway. The pronounced vertical lines of its buttresses and niches are examples of the new Perpendicular style of architecture that dominated church building for the next two centuries. Gates were important for monasteries not only for control of access and defence, but also because it was at them that alms were usually distributed to the poor, an important ritual. In any circumstances, throwing the doors wide for an important visitor was a gesture of deference as well as of welcome. Towns might greet important visitors by escorting them through one of the gates in the hope of gaining favours and privileges.[12]

Rural resentment was slower than urban to break into violence; thirteenth-century labourers had had few legal means to challenge their lords' demands, but occasional bouts of slow working, or even refusal to work at all, showed lords that it was generally politic to observe the customs of their estates and not to be too oppressive. From the 1320s, reflecting the shift in the availability of labour, some lords tried to extort more services or to supply less food, leading to more records of peasant resistance, a few of which involved physical damage to property. Archaeological evidence of peasant attitudes towards authority is not clear-cut. The decoration of a few earthenware pots may have been intended as derisory, and there are some cheaply made badges that could be mocking the clergy and others, but who wore them and when are unknown. 'Cocking a snook' at lords by challenging their hunting rights could have been a motive for poaching; one part of the petition drawn up during the 1381 Revolt was for the right to hunt, so resentment may have been felt, and poaching may have been an expression of social defiance. Deer bones are a very small element in most rural village assemblages, so venison was not a significant part of peasant diet but may have been an occasional treat enjoyed all the more for being illicit, although some may have come from unwanted carcases or those found by foresters, half-eaten by wild animals. Arrowheads have been used to suggest that villagers went poaching but are more likely to result from archery practice to train men for war, made compulsory by an Act of 1363. To make arrows effective against plate armour, steel heads became mandatory.[13]

Peasant beliefs and behaviour are often difficult to identify, and there can be conflicting views on whether they were significantly different from christian orthodoxy or were 'unofficial' but still not outside the christian mainstream. The carved saltire cross at West Hartburn and a figure with crossed arms at West Cotton may be protective, and objects with inscriptions may be deliberate deposits of things with formulaic prayers – but none need mean more than blessing of the home. The way that different interpretations can be placed on the same evidence is exemplified by a strange discovery at Avebury, Wiltshire, of a skeleton underneath a buried sarsen stone with three coins of *c.*1320–50, iron scissors, and a long iron probe that were used to identify him when first found as a barber who also practised surgery, a slightly suspect occupation because it permitted the drawing of blood to heal wounds and was therefore 'dirty'; surgery interfered with the human body, which was supposedly perfect. Doctors used herbs and potions, knew astrology and how to balance the humours, and were therefore 'clean' as well as learned. It was suggested that the dead man had been trapped under a falling stone while helping to dismantle the 'fearful silent array' of the stone circle, under Church orders. But although many of the stones have indeed been buried or broken up, there is no reason to think that the Church was involved, and all would have been removed if they had been a cause for christian concern. Besides, barber-surgeons were not all that common, and it seems more likely that the unfortunate man was a shepherd, whose equipment would have included a long probe to use as a trocar to pierce a sheep's stomach to let out the gas if it swelled up, a frequent problem. His scissors would have been used to cut off the tangled ends of a fleece. He might have been murdered, or found dead, and the villagers concealed him where he would not be found by the sheriff's men, to avoid having to pay a fine.[14]

A shepherd needed expertise to look after his flocks, which were carefully managed by the larger, documented estates. Traces of sheepcotes in open country show how they were sheltered in the winter. The later Middle Ages saw a shift in the balance of the economy from export of wool to the Low Countries to domestic cloth production of lower value than the earlier Stamford russets and Lincoln greens, and this affected the distribution of wealth; parts of Suffolk, Kent, Wiltshire and Somerset, the Cotswolds, and Shropshire had the advantage of being the best sheep-rearing areas, bringing weavers and merchants to them. Even so, they were not spared the bad weather which at the end of the thirteenth century and in the fourteenth made sheep more liable to diseases such as scab; poor feed caused them to produce coarser wool. The weather also affected grain production, and population loss throughout Europe meant that there was also less demand for English supplies in the Low Countries and Norway, affecting trade through the east coast ports. Baltic timber was an increasingly significant import and is recognizable in the dendrochronological record, particularly in oak chests.[15]

*

Many ecclesiastical landlords continued to provide for the processing and storage of the large amounts of produce that they were getting from their estates, but in some cases in ways that suggest that security against robbery that amounted to more than petty pilfering was of concern. Shaftesbury Abbey built a complex at Bradford-on-Avon which included the cruck-framed barn, dendrochronologically dated to 1334–79, that still stands, with another at right angles to it, forming two sides of a large enclosed yard, or *curia*, with a granary on the third side; this was raised on posts to keep the grain cool as well as to deter vermin. It too was cruck-built, dated to 1370–90. The fourth side had a steward's house, not particularly grand because so far as is known the abbess never visited. Nevertheless, the scale of the complex, entered by a gatehouse, must have served as an impressive reminder of her status as the landlord and must have been difficult for a mob to break into. The same security seems to have been a motive for a *curia* at Tisbury, with a great barn and in that case a manor-house, as the abbess occasionally stayed there. Many abbots and bishops used some of their estates as country retreats, although a surrounding wall may have been enough for most, like the complex that Glastonbury owned at Meare, Somerset, where much of the house survives, as does a building nearby possibly used partly as a salting and smoking house for preserving the fish caught in the profitable open water of the Somerset Levels. Glastonbury Abbey's control over its estates enabled a surprising development at Shapwick, where a new church was built in the centre of the village, replacing the existing one next to the original *curia* which had been moved to a new moated site prominently placed at the end of the village.[16]

Kings also had to be builders, though none showed quite the same level of detailed interest as Henry III had done. Edward II's major building work was the new tower at Knaresborough, Yorkshire, soon after 1307, perhaps intending it for his widely resented favourite Piers Gaveston. Knaresborough was even provided with a throne room in which may have been England's first example of a projecting oriel window, but the tower was not merely for show, as the king must have been aware of the dangers from Scotland, and work was done on other northern royal castles. His main rival for power, Earl Thomas of Lancaster, built a completely new castle at Dunstanburh, Northumberland, from 1312, although it was not a centre of his honour. He may have wanted a coastal stronghold to challenge the king's use of the sea. The coastal setting and the landscaping made the new building look impressive, with the main emphasis being on the gate-tower and perimeter walls – there was no great central tower. Whatever may have been the earl's motive, the fiasco of Bannockburn in 1314 made the Scots even more of a threat but did not end the factional fighting that was to lead to Thomas's execution and improbable reputation for sanctity, justifiable only by his foundation of a college of priests at Kenilworth Castle. That was an early example of a trend for the very rich to create a chantry separate from any other church and to maintain priests at it to pray for the founder and his family's souls, and which obviated restrictions on founding new priories.[17]

Kenilworth's proximity of the castle to Warwick meant that it was a permanent challenge to the regional authority of the Beauchamp family, with a parvenu earl adding to the mix with a new castle at Maxstoke. The Beauchamp response may have been the complete restructuring of Warwick, with a palatial suite overlooking the river and elaborate towers, one lobed in plan and the other octagonal for extra effect, named Caesar's and Guy's in homage to the Beauchamps' claimed ancestry. Ominously, they included lodgings for visitors, with separate and well-appointed individual chambers increasingly required as the different factions built up their affinities of people who would support them and who relied on them for protection.[18]

The status that came with the holding of a castle may be distantly reflected by licences to crenellate, but their proliferation does not show particular peaks and troughs, or regional variation, as might for instance have been expected in the north after Bannockburn. Edward III held family rivalries in check during most of his long reign, his hold over them the result of the patronage that he could bestow after successes in France brought huge sums in ransom money, though only after a succession of damaging raids by the French on the south coast in the 1330s, which led to new work at various castles, including Portchester where a small courtyard complex had already improved the accommodation (Illus. 1.2). To provide a suitably martial setting for the Knights of the Garter, a new order created by the king for those who had fought with him at Crécy in 1346, he used Windsor Castle, where he established a new college for priests to serve the chapel and built a new great hall. The king also spent large sums on Westminster and Sheen, which was close to London – his sons, the Black Prince and John of Gaunt, also built palaces close to London, Kennington and Savoy respectively – and the distance from the centre of government meant that he and his successors showed little interest in the great palaces at Woodstock and Clarendon. John of Gaunt, however, had works done at Kenilworth that made it more like the king's Windsor, including a great hall raised on an undercroft.[19]

Kings could raise the status of their adherents, some of whom 'rose' spectacularly; when an early fourteenth-century Hull merchant moved to London and became rich, he seems to have changed the family name from 'Rottenherring' to 'de la Pole'; a loan of £100,000 to the king in 1337 led to royal favour, and the son became a banneret, a new title senior to a knight; the grandson in turn became earl of Suffolk in 1385, and the great grandson a duke, another new title. The grandson acquired a base at Wingfield, Suffolk, through marriage; his father-in-law had already established a college there and might have at least started to build the large moated courtyard castle with corner towers and tall gate-house, though it was the earl who acquired the crenellation licence. To emphasize their status, the de la Poles endowed more new church institutions than did longer-established families – a priory for Carthusian monks at Hull, with associated hospital and three other hospitals. The Carthusians were a new Order, their members living in almost total seclusion in their cells; this austerity freed them from the taint of indulgent living that diminished the reputations of the established Benedictines and others, including by now the friars, but like the Brigettine nuns who were also noted for austerity, the Carthusians were never numerous.[20]

The importance of family and marriage is shown graphically in the great painted psalter prepared for a Suffolk knight, Sir Geoffrey Luttrell, in the 1320s–40s, in which the frontispiece image shows him mounted and in full armour, with his wife ostentatiously handing him a shield displaying his coat-of-arms, while next to her is his daughter-in-law with a shield displaying her own, more illustrious lineage. The book is well-known for the many everyday scenes painted in it that show Sir Geoffrey's labourers and servants maintaining his estates and social position. Some details are accurate to a remarkable degree; a poor woman's hen has a white lobe on its neck that is known to be a feature of a good egg-layer. The Luttrell Psalter is one of several illustrated books produced in East Anglia in the first half of the fourteenth century, a regional grouping that is not explained simply by the wealth of the area's cloth industry, which was to peak later. Sir Geoffrey himself was not a great landholder, so his commissioning of the Psalter is surprising. So is the painting of a different sort in the same part of the world, at Longthorpe Tower, built by a contemporary of much the same status who embellished his walls with a variety of images, some biblical or showing morality scenes as those at Clarendon had done, including a more complex Wheel of the Five Senses. It also has East Anglian birds, coats of arms, and a grotesque, as does the Luttrell Psalter.[21]

As well as his Psalter, Sir Geoffrey Luttrell's will has survived; his bequests included provision for his funeral, including the huge sum of £200 to be distributed to the poor and £20 for candles to be lit in the church – beeswax was expensive, and hives are among the rural property shown in the Psalter; bees were symbolic of chastity as well as of estate ownership. He wished to be buried in the chancel of Irnham church 'next to the high altar' – the church was part of his estate, next door to his manor-house, and he wanted to be remembered there in its most sacred location, where his forebears awaited him. To ensure that a physical monument kept him in people's view and minds, he almost certainly commissioned the partly surviving and very ornately carved Easter Sepulchre. His bequests included jewels for the shrines at Canterbury, Walsingham, and St Paul's; silver basins and jewels given to Lincoln were to be 'firmly placed over the said altar . . . remaining there in perpetuity'. Visitors would in the future see his gifts and think of the donor even if they knew nothing about him. It seems to have been generally accepted that in due course bequests to churches of such items as marriage rings would be melted down and turned into plate, keeping the association if not the object in the place. Because of named memorials, a very few instances of known people have been recovered, such as Sir Hugh de Hastyngs, who was buried at Elsing, Norfolk, in 1347.[22]

Sir Geoffrey left sums of cash and robes to many of his relatives and servants, and kitchen utensils and vessels to the cook and the porter; there was nothing exceptional in those distributions, although the bequests of so much cash may seem surprising in view of the currency problems of the fourteenth century. Silver was scarcer, and lack of small change hindered everyday marketing; lower-quality continental 'lusshebournes' succeeded the pollards and crockards of the previous century but reduced confidence in money as a medium of exchange. Base-metal jettons were permitted to have coin-like designs and may have been used for some everyday transactions, although supposedly were only meant as reckoning counters. A lighter penny coin was issued from 1351, but that meant that fixed cash rents were devalued, so Parliament resisted any further debasement attempts by the kings. Other monetary innovations of the mid century were the reintroduction of the silver groat, worth four pennies, half-groats, and gold coins, initially a 'florin' worth 3 shillings derived from the Italian *fiorini*, soon replaced by a 'noble' worth 6s 8d, which thus gave physical reality to the half-mark, a division much used in accounting. Also called a 'leopard' from its design, the gold coin was deliberately regal because one motive for its introduction was to show that King Edward was the equal of continental monarchs and Italian dukes who had been issuing gold coins for some time and were known in England; a few from Spain may have resulted from the Black Prince's attempts at peninsula conquest.[23]

High-value coins were not for everyday use but were more flexible wealth reserves than gold and silver plate, although there was plenty of that. Most of the surviving gold coins are from hoards, and only one, a quarter-noble, has been found on a rural excavation, although a weight found at Wharram shows that people were sufficiently familiar with them to feel the need to make sure of their value before accepting them, as people were tempted into cheating despite harsh penalties; clipped and forged coins are known, and two iron dies for counterfeiting gold nobles and half-nobles and a coin weight were found in an Exeter pit. A hoard found in a wooden box outside Cambridge shows the complexities of hoarding: it contained nine gold and 1,805 silver coins, mostly datable to before 1345, with none later than 1351–2; the gold coins were all of 1353–6, however. The interpretation is that most of the hoard was assembled in the mid 1340s, was added to in 1351–2, and again in *c.* 1356 – and how much silver might then have been taken out, as the nine gold coins were together worth more than one-third of all the silver, so the more gold, the less the quantity and problems of handling and hiding? With fewer pennies and halfpennies in circulation, and groats and half-groats more likely to be carefully looked after, the numbers of individual stray finds fall away and are not comparable to the earlier records.[24]

*

The immediate consequences of the Black Death on settlements after 1348 have proved no easier to demonstrate in the archaeological record than those of 1315–21, although the very many deserted and shrunken late medieval sites show longer-term consequences. Despite the deaths of probably at least half the population, rural society managed to maintain some basic order; the churchyard at Wharram did not provide evidence of a sudden surge in burials, and the settlement does not show a major phase of abandonment; a house whose tenant died might lie empty for a while, but such an interlude need not show archaeologically. Superficially, nucleated settlements like Wharram retained their appearance of well-regulated tenements, though the decay of buildings and the abandonment of outlying cottages might have presented a different impression to visitors; amalgamations might not even have led to the infilling of boundary ditches if they were still needed for drainage. Dispersed sites like Westbury had crofts going out of use, but new ones being established, as in previous centuries. Very few lowland sites seem to have been deserted immediately after 1349, and those were usually on poorer soils; Hatch Warren, Hampshire, has a document recording that in 1378 no-one was living in the parish – but even there a few sherds of later pottery were found, probably from a sheep-farm built where once there had been a manor-house. Change of ownership in 1311 may have been as significant as poor soil and mortality for the hamlet's disappearance.[25]

Upland sites were more vulnerable, but West Whelpington seems not to have been totally abandoned, though reconstruction in the following century obscured much of the earlier evidence. A little further south, in County Durham, Thrislington apparently had an uninterrupted sequence, though with no indication of rebuilding and prosperity. On Dartmoor, the isolated Dinna Clerks house and the Hound Tor hamlet were abandoned (Illus. 10.1), but whether the occupants died during the Black Death, moved out after it to take advantage of lower rents or higher wages elsewhere, perhaps finding that cereal farming high on the moors became even more unviable as the colder climate shortened the growing season, or were evicted by their landlord who wanted their cultivated land as sheep pasture, cannot be known. Hound Tor had stone buildings with ovens, originally identified as needed for desperate attempts to dry wheat, but they are as likely to have been for dairy and domestic use. Oats and rye were found in one, but those are not grains that usually need drying – the former are needed for horses as well as humans, so might possibly indicate increased use of those even in the uplands. Nevertheless, labour-intensive ploughlands, even if suitable for oats on wetter land and rye on drier, were more likely to be abandoned than where wheat and

Illustration 10.1 High on Dartmoor, Hound Tor was a hamlet probably abandoned during the second half of the fourteenth century. The four longest buildings were presumably the principal houses; their ends were assumed to have been used to shelter animals during the winter, but they may have been dairies – or both. Smaller buildings were barns and stables, lived in sometimes by elderly parents or by servants. On the right, the three buildings with ovens were thought to have been grain-dryers, constructed in a desperate attempt to dry wheat which became more and more unviable to grow as the weather deteriorated, but they may have been baking ovens. Small garden plots would have been for cultivating vegetables and keeping hens.

barley were grown. Conversion to grazing was more profitable; sites like Raddon, Wiltshire, were removed so that the land could be used for sheep and cattle and also for rabbits, valuable for their meat and fur, and kept in artificial warrens, low mounds often mistaken for prehistoric long barrows; as well as the southern downs, the dry and infertile Norfolk brecklands were major producers.[26]

Open-field ploughlands seem to have been maintained if humanly possible, as probably happened at Wharram. Grassed-over ridge-and-furrow and hillside strip lynchets that show the earlier need to plough as much land as possible demonstrate the abandonment of medieval systems but not the dates when this happened. Lack of manpower led to sea-walls not being maintained, and farmland flooded. A novel way of showing the longer-term consequences of the Black Death has been from interpretation of some 2000 metre-square test-pits excavated in 'Continuously Occupied Rural Settlements' in eastern England, which has shown a significant decline in the number of pottery sherds found in over half of them, more than can be accounted for by changes in ceramic usage or in manuring practice. Furthermore, a few pits show the opposite evidence of increased use, consistent with the prosperity of a few places because of the area's cloth trade, a trade that gave employment to many who could therefore avoid agricultural work, driving up wages.[27]

Direct evidence of the immediate and appalling impact of the Black Death in eastern England has been found at Thornton Abbey, Lincolnshire, with the discovery of a large pit containing at least fifty bodies of children, young men and women, and a few older people. Radiocarbon dates and two Edward III pennies are consistent with 1348–9, although not precluding the later 1361–2 or 1368–9 outbreaks. The last two are less likely to have overwhelmed the burial resources of parish churches, however, as is suggested for the Thornton Abbey burials because of the children. The corpses there were not merely thrown into the pit but had been shrouded and buried with their heads to the west, so although they did not have the individual grave that was generally regarded as essential, some decency was observed.[28]

Excavation of the East Smithfield cemetery on the fringe of medieval London has shown how the parish graveyards in the city could not cope. As at Thornton, the analysis showed that the plague was caused by the *Yersinia pestis* bacterium, probably a new strain to which humans had no stored resistance; its rapid spread could have been caused by a pneumonic element, and not just flea bites. Three large pits showed how individual graves became impossible, and mass burial had to be practised. Even so, nearly all the bodies had been laid out with their heads to the west, a few exceptions with heads to the east probably resulting from misidentification of shrouded corpses. Only infants and children, perhaps neglected orphans, were buried wherever there was space, regardless of orientation. Haste and fear of contagion are shown by the pennies and farthings found with one woman, whose coins would surely have been removed in normal circumstances. Unlike the people buried in London in 1257–9, who may have been outsiders seeking food, the Smithfield cemeteries would have been townsfolk, many of them weakened by childhood and adolescence during the famine years of 1315–22. No cure was known, so prayer had to be resorted to, though a more practical attempt to find one might be shown by the building at St Mary Spital of a pharmacy with tiled hearths, special-purpose glass and pottery vessels, and some dangerous metals such as arsenic and mercury suggesting attempts at alchemy. One effect of the Black Death seems to have been a dearth of memorial brass engravers in London, as an influx of Flemish imports indicates. Otherwise, the recognition of the immediate effects of the plague is no easier to trace in the archaeological record in towns than in rural settlements.[29]

The Black Death largely spared the royal family and courtiers, those who suffered it often having suffered poor nutrition earlier in life. After initial panic, government was maintained; the first reaction was to try to prevent labourers from demanding higher wages or from escaping from their servile status. Many lords who had been operating demesne farming turned to leasing so as to get a guaranteed rental income, even if the profits were less than they had been. Consequently, many serfs left their homes and took up land on estates where they were free of bond labour, with no questions asked. Sumptuary laws sought to restrict aristocratic overindulgence but were more concerned with what people generally spent on foodstuffs and clothing; their increasing stringency is a sure sign that the Three Orders were under threat: 'outrageous and excessive apparel of divers people against their estate and degree, to the great destruction and impoverishment of the land' meant that 'people of handicraft and yeomen' should not own precious stones or things made of gold and silver – if they did, they would be using material objects to boost their social aspirations; the number of finds shows that such things were quite common, so restrictions may have had the opposite effect to the one intended. 'Carters, ploughmen . . . ' were only to wear woollen cloth not linen or anything finer; despite the law, however, their demands for higher wages or better food allowances were hard to resist, as in practice labour mobility was more possible. A 1388 Statute required itinerant labourers to have passes; a die for sealing them was found recently in Sussex. Complaints about labourers' laziness almost certainly mean that they could work fewer hours and still earn as much money as they wanted, so that they could spend more time in ale-houses. An analysis of children's skeletons has suggested that they were better fed immediately after the Black Death but may have had to begin adult work earlier.[30]

Peasant demands for better food such as wheat bread may be reflected by changes in pottery, with more evidence of flat dishes to catch fat from roasting meat and small bottles used for sauces. Labour shortages may have meant that less time and effort went into decorating jugs, for which demand may anyway have been waning because more people could afford metal vessels and preferred them for both cooking and serving. Absence of copper-alloy and pewter mugs indicates that wooden vessels were probably used in most households for drinking, but with pottery becoming more acceptable. Drinking vessels of glass may have become more unobtainable. A trend towards smaller drinking vessels already visible before the Black Death may have developed partly because of a developing taste for stronger drink, hopped beer rather than ale; small jugs facilitated individual measures. Communally, what are now called lobed cups, usually two-handled, could be passed from hand to hand, each drinker using a separate lobe; the wood-turner had difficulty in matching those or the distinctive shape of many small, handled jugs which swell out at the waist, keeping the liquid cooler and making them easier to drink from than from an open bowl or dish.[31]

London remained a strong market for pottery, though with fluctuations of supply sources that might have been affected by the Black Death, perhaps accounting for the disappearance of vessels made in Mill Green, Essex, and the growth of Kingston on the River Thames. The clay used there was white, perhaps an attempt to imitate the French Saintonge wares, which comprised not only the painted jugs, but green-glazed wares also. White clay was not available at Kingston, so had to be carted there; presumably transporting the raw material rather than the finished product by road was thought to have a cost benefit, but Kingston was to be supplanted in turn by supplies from Cheam and the Surrey–Hampshire border. Elsewhere, production continued at some of the 'potting villages' such as Hanley Castle and Grimston, though the latter suggests a period of disruption; some combined their pot-making with tile production, as at Chilvers Coton.[32]

Lack of people meant that monasteries could not easily recruit novices to fill vacancies; Cistercian houses had to abandon their farming system which had relied on lay-brothers for much of the work, leaving vacant the dorters on the west side of the cloisters. Farm work was not the only labour problem; masons, carpenters, tilers, metalworkers, and painters were all in short supply for cathedrals, churches, castles, houses, or books like Luttrell's. Production of decorated floor-tiles continued at various sites in the south Chilterns, but the quality was not what it had been, and higher prices may have inhibited widespread domestic use. At Winchester, remodelling of the cathedral nave to convert it into the Perpendicular style was started by a very wealthy bishop perhaps soon after his inauguration in 1345, with an interlude after 1348–9, while any available builders were transferred to work on a new foundation at Edington, Wiltshire, one of the very few projects attributable to the 1350s. Another is the Vicars' Close, Wells, a range recorded as built in 1350, a date confirmed by dendrochronology; the two rows of buildings provided individual accommodation for those who took the services in the cathedral and are significant because they show how demand now was for privacy rather than for shared dormitory accommodation, although a hall for communal eating was still provided. At a different social level, a few cruck buildings and others have been found by dendrochronology, a hint of rural ambition for investment in buildings.[33]

The Black Death did not diminish Edward III's ambitions in France, which the Black Prince extended to Spain. Wars were costly, and ceased to be successful in winning ransoms and booty, and government finances were further stretched because wool export levies fell away. In the 1360s, the Black Prince's expeditions brought Castilians and their ships to join French expeditions against England, which became increasingly expensive to resist. One completely new royal castle on the Isle of Sheppey, Kent, was built in the 1360s, presumably to guard the entrance to the Thames, although it had comfortable accommodation and was named Queenborough as though to associate it with tranquillity; nothing of it survives, but a drawing shows it as having had a revolutionary design of a great round courtyard wall interspersed with towers, inside a circular outer wall.[34]

Unfortunately, the drawing of Queenborough does not have enough detail to show whether it made provision for a new weapon, artillery using gun-powder. The earliest known gun-loops in England may be those in the 1340s walls of Norwich, threatened by attack from Flanders. Early loops were quite small, for small-bore weapons; over the next one and a half centuries, stave-built wrought iron cannons were developed. The effect can be seen at Southampton, which had suffered internal damage by a raid in 1338, evidenced by the amount of burnt rubble found in excavations. After 1360, the town was forced to complete its wall circuit to protect the waterfront; the new walls included small round gun-loops with short sighting slots above – very different from the long slits for archers. Guns fired from them would probably not have been powerful enough to bombard ships – but might have been deadly against a landing-party. The walls infilled the doors of the old Norman warehouses, so that all goods had to use the gates, making property closer to the markets more valuable than those which previously had direct access to the waterfront. A little later, in 1378–9, the new Westgate built at Canterbury also had gun-loops, but in each of the towers' three storeys (Illus. 10.2). At Portchester in 1376–85, Richard II was obliged to build Assheton's Tower and a wall-walk with gun-loops at different levels for '*iii gonnes*' and lead shot (Illus. 1.2); on the opposite side of the Solent, Quarr Abbey had a wall pierced by gun-ports facing the sea. If indeed only three guns were provided for Portchester, it may reflect their high cost, prohibitive for most people, although the upper storey of one of Warwick Castle's towers had gun-loops and other castles followed.[35]

*

The costs of war and the burdens of the Poll Taxes to pay for them were the immediate cause of the Revolt of 1381, a primary demand being the abolition of villeinage. One manorial right was that unfree peasants could be forced to use their lord's mill and pay for the privilege; they also had to make a payment if they wanted to use their own handmills. At St Albans in 1331, the abbot had removed privately owned handmills, broken them up, and used them as a pavement; during the Revolt, rioters destroyed the pavement and were said to have handed round the pieces in a gesture symbolic of the Eucharist. This episode is often said to demonstrate peasants using material culture to express their resentment, because the abbot's tenants had to walk over the broken stones when paying their rents and fines, reminding them of their servitude – but the stones were in the cloister, not where lay people entered. Moreover, St Albans was controlled by the abbey, and the abbot was going so far as to claim that the townsmen were not freemen, but villeins; it was their handmills that he had seized, and it was they who led the revolt. Rural peasants may have been involved, but seemingly in a supporting role, so how far millstones were a general issue, therefore, or whether elsewhere small fines were paid with no great sense of aggrievement, is debatable.[36]

Illustration 10.2 The West Gate, Canterbury, was built in the 1370s/80s when French raids were feared. The prominent drum towers contain several 'inverted keyhole' gun-loops, round openings for guns with small barrels, with sighting slits above. There would have been a draw-bridge in the foreground over the River Stour. The gateway is protected by machicolations projecting forwards from the top through which stones could be dropped. The rows of small square 'putlog' holes are where the ends of scaffold poles were placed during building. Although austere, the gate could have been dressed with banners and painted panels on special occasions.

When broken pieces of millstone are found in excavations of peasant tofts, it may not be because stones from the lord's mill were deliberately smashed and placed where they would give a resentful tenant quiet satisfaction; a broken piece of millstone might simply have been from one damaged beyond repair at the mill. A flat stone would have been particularly welcome in areas where the local geology creates boulders, as at West Hartburn, where one was found in a hearth; a bakestone for oat-cakes would have been one use. Furthermore, flat stones for water and windmills were not usually very large, so broken pieces found in excavations may not be separable from handmill stones; only the occasional pot-quern with upturned rim is clearly recognizable as being domestic. Handmills were expensive, so many households probably did not own one; stone mortars probably cost as much but had more general use for pounding pulses and anything fibrous, so broken pieces are a little more often found. More frequent are hand-held whetstones, for sharpening knives and tools; they were not always of local material picked up freely but came from a distance. Some black ones from Norway were eye-catching – and another thing that peasants were prepared to pay for.[37]

Many peasants who had left an estate lived under the threat of being summoned back if they could not prove that they had bought their way out of servility, and even the free-born who held their land by free tenancy feared that the courts would rule in favour of a lord who claimed that they owed service and other payments and restrictions. Manorial court records and custumals were a lord's means of arguing that they had rights over individuals and together with tax records were targeted by rebels and publicly burned. Stout oak chests like those in some Kent churches ceased to be enough for muniments, iron bands all over the wood becoming a wise precaution – a particularly fine chest in the church at Icklingham, Suffolk, is thought to have come from one of the major local abbeys, perhaps Bury St Edmunds where the Revolt was bloodier than at St Albans. Chests had to be kept secure: some castles and houses had windowless strong-rooms, reached by ladder from the chamber of the official who received the rents. Gatehouse towers might house institutional records; others were in purpose-built muniment towers, such as one at New College, Oxford, that still has its original late fourteenth-century floors, fireproofed by clay tiles stamped with the armorial device of the founder, William of Wykeham. Colleges like those in Oxford and Cambridge were partly devotional, to preserve the memory of the founder and to pray for his soul; personal mementos might be preserved, like Wykeham's gloves. But university colleges were primarily educational, training not only the next generation of priests and monks, but secular clerics who would become estate stewards and lawyers as well, increasingly needed as ownership and other disputes had to be argued out in the law courts.[38]

In some towns, uprisings were against urban oligarchies by those poorer elements who felt excluded; in Beverley, their seizure of the town seal was a symbolic gesture using material culture. That was a town that may have been experiencing decay, as the dyeing industry seems to have come to an end, so textile finishing and rich merchants may have left it. Government extortion was a particular target; the rebels destroyed John of Gaunt's Savoy Palace on the outskirts of London, and a few officials were seized and killed. One was Sir John Hales, whose property at Cressing Temple was looted, but the two great barns there were spared, although they might so easily have been resented as a symbol of peasant servility, being buildings in which labour services such as threshing and unloading carts took place. When great estates accepted that demesne farming was less reliable as a means of income than leasing, the number of great barns diminished, though a few new 'rectorial' ones were built to store tithes, such as Winchcombe Abbey's at Church Enstone, Oxfordshire, using full or raised crucks as the span did not need to be nearly as wide as would have been needed if the entire estate produce were to be stored; the barn is dated to 1382 by a Latin inscription on a stone outside recording that the abbey had responded to the request of its bailiff, an odd touch that does not make clear who paid for it – possibly the bailiff himself as a memorial.[39]

Many royal officials were killed in 1381, and fear of rebels and rioters may have been in the minds of the builders of some of the later medieval castles, although many other motives have been proposed. Gun-loops have played a part in consideration of the military effectiveness of such late fourteenth-century castles as Bodiam, Sussex, built in the 1380s by a wealthy but not enormously rich knight, where they feature near the bottom of the gatehouse. How effective would guns firing through them have been? Some could cover the drawbridge approach, but others face over the moat – are those merely for show or to allow for the possibility of attackers draining the water and getting to the walls? Who would attack – the French, as they did in the 1360s, a rival faction, or dissident peasants? Could the castle have protected the neighbourhood? Did the moat do more than create a conventional setting and a peaceful boating lake to impress approaching visitors? Were the towers of no great height so as not to excite the jealousy of the earls of Arundel, whose ancient and very prominent hill-top castle was not far away, and where the central motte crowned by a shell keep separated an upper and a lower ward, much like Windsor? Or was there greater concern about John of Gaunt, newly in charge of Pevensey? Another much-discussed castle is Cooling. Associated with it was a chantry college, attached to the parish church and still partly surviving, for five priests, choristers, and others who were to pray for the king and queen, as well as for the founder and his family.[40]

Further from London and the south coast, different circumstances prevailed. In the north, Bolton Castle in Wensleydale, Yorkshire, which was begun in 1378, is on a hilltop, with an outer curtain wall not a tranquil moat, and although like Bodiam it had a courtyard with a hall and chambers round it, the interior included stabling, so horses were perceived to need protection from raiders as well as humans; there was no separate access for them, so they had to be led through the central courtyard. The castle has four substantial corner towers but no ostentatious gatehouse and no provision for guns. A horse-mill was built inside to ensure food preparation during a siege. The builder was a knight, not an earl or a duke, so had ambitions but with circumspection. The effect of a crowded working complex would have been very different from the more private and secluded spaces achieved by Bodiam and others, where etiquette and gender separation could be practised. Not far from Bolton, another socially ambitious knight built a much less compact new castle at Sheriff Hutton, replacing one nearby; it had extensive grounds offering pleasant walks.[41]

These buildings reflect new rivalries, which came to a head in the reign of Richard II, who finally lost control in 1399. Edward III's Order of the Garter was a badge of honour and a sign of royal favour, but it stimulated the display of other badges showing loyalties and affinities. Richard II's enthusiastic use of the white hart and the broom-cod for his favourites is shown in one of the great English works of art, the Wilton Diptych; his munificence alarmed the House of Commons. Richard's architectural taste for grandeur was expressed in the restructuring with a hammer-beam roof displaying carved angels and tracery of the great hall at Westminster, where the royal courts were usually held. Ambition reflected in buildings is displayed at Dartington, Devon, built by the king's half-brother after he was granted the estate in 1388. It had two courts, the outer and larger with ranges of two-storey lodgings on two sides, arranged so that privileged guests each had a private chamber with a fireplace and a lavatory. The gate is off-centre, and seems unimpressive, perhaps so as to cause surprise when the great porch-tower entrance to the hall opposite is first seen. The hall itself was open in the traditional manner, originally with a hammer-beam roof and tall windows. Badges, including Richard II's white hart, were prominent. Remarkably, the mansion had small towers but was in no way defensible; it is as though the builder was proclaiming his security as the king's close relative by showing that no one, and in particular the earl of Devon whose power-base he was challenging, would dare to attack.[42]

For the majority of the population who survived the plagues, slight signs of improving late fourteenth-century rural conditions can be seen; two Wealden houses survive from the south-east, and full crucks also increase a little in number. Peasant houses were more likely to be built with stone foundations, making investment in solid timber worthwhile (Illus. 10.3). Bigger crofts became available, as in Caldecote, Hertfordshire, where fifteen of them, 21 feet wide, were replaced in the late fourteenth century by six of them, 70 feet wide. This was partly possible because the tenant of the manor-house had died, and St Albans Abbey, the landlord, seems to have taken the opportunity to replan the site. Keeping the estate viable would have been facilitated by its proximity to London and the still buoyant market there. Slight increases in the sizes of sheep and cattle evidenced by London bones may indicate better management generally in its hinterland; bones also indicate some changes to pig rearing, with larger animals kept in styes. Larger and heavier shoes gave better traction and may indicate slightly larger horses, presumably better fed and more selectively bred, but that was a trend begun in the thirteenth century. Although only some 5% of the recorded bones at West Cotton, this is more than on most sites and may reflect horses' use on the local light soils. No urban houses with timbers of the final 20 years of the fourteenth century have been recorded, and the evidence of abandonments, amalgamations of tenements, and rebuildings is limited. One reason for that could be changes to waste disposal, with stone-lined pits in towns more often emptied, removing archaeological dating material.[43]

Illustration 10.3 Fourteenth-century foundations for a timber-framed or earth-material superstructure, excavated at Popham, Hampshire. Stone footings meant that walls could have a longer life.

One sign of change is the increasing role of guilds, for individual crafts in some towns, and for religious fraternities in others. Most continued to meet in rooms over gates or other premises that were not purpose-built, but as early as 1356–7, York's Merchant Adventurers began the complex that developed into a hall, chapel, and hospital for themselves. The double-aisled open hall with a central hearth was on the first floor, with the high end carefully enhanced to show the guild's internal social hierarchy, and on the ground floor were beds for the sick, whom the members had to parade past as they went into the chapel, a reminder of the need for charity. Dendrochronology and thermoluminescence dating have shown that the hall of the Guild of St Mary in Boston, Lincolnshire, was constructed in the 1380s and 1390s. It maintained priests who led services in a chapel that was part of Boston's mainly fourteenth-century enormous church, famous for its 'stump', built on the prosperity of the wool trade and St Botolph's annual fair.[44]

Later fourteenth-century changes include greater use of English in literature and formal documents; Sir Geoffrey Luttrell's will had been written in Latin in the 1340s, but one in English survives from 1387. The spread of education is suggested by the translation of Wycliffe's bible in 1382, which began to make scripture accessible to anyone who could read, without the intercession of a learned priest, although heretical Lollardy has not left identifiable physical trace. Greater awareness of sudden death may have spurred on survivors to undertake even more pilgrimages than before, but the pilgrims' badges that are the best evidence of the relative popularity of the various shrines visited are not readily datable. One new shrine was that of Thomas of Lancaster at whose tomb a miracle was claimed to have been performed, enough to turn a noble villain into a potential saint. Despite the dangers of the sea voyage, many pilgrims went to Compostela in Spain; it could be that the graffiti of ships in inland churches are visible prayers for a safe journey. Many badges and ampullae became talismans, for instance nailed to a post to bless the crops. The sacred contents of the latter were sprinkled for various forms of blessing; votive deposit in water was frequent. Folded coins are records of vows or thanks, such as for a journey, but not specifically for pilgrimages. Brooches were more likely to have inscriptions such as AGLA, a formula to ward off sudden death, and gold rings with images of saints became widely worn; rosary beads also became more common.[45]

Pilgrims were able to undertake southward journeys by sea, because transport was readily available: the fleet that left England to collect wine from Bordeaux might consist of 1000 ships, carrying back an average of 250 barrels each. Salt was also imported in bulk from the same region and became cheaper than products of the English salterns, although it was coarser. Some continued production nevertheless, even the more northerly ones such as those in Lincolnshire, despite being subject to storms and floods. The Cheshire saltworks were less directly affected.[46]

Trading and raiding meant that even if they did not have guns, towns on or near the coast felt need of the protection of walls and gates, which were a financial drain that ports like Yarmouth, affected not only by war but by the Dutch challenge to its herring trade as well, could ill afford. They may also provide evidence of maritime trading contacts, as piles of stone ballast maintained at waterfronts that had come from a variety of different boats were readily available: Yarmouth has igneous rocks from Scandinavia in its walls, Lynn shows Estonian links – pottery made at Grimston, Norfolk, shows trade going the other way. East coast towns were more likely to make use of bricks, however; some at Yarmouth was probably imported from the Netherlands, but Hull had its own brickyard to build the walls added on top of the earth ramparts there after 1303. If its gates and walls were completed, over 4 million bricks would have been needed. Beverley also had a municipal works, as did Boston, where the kilns used coal, presumably a slight saving over peat and wood. Nevertheless, and despite the low cost of clay compared to stone, the labour involved in mixing larger quantities of mortar and the payment of wages to skilled workers to do the laying made the expense of brick too great for most purposes. A few high-status buildings used it in the last quarter of the fourteenth century.[47]

A few ports were active in shipbuilding and co-ordinating supplies, boosted by royal expeditions overseas and to Scotland. After Edward II's defeat at Bannockburn in 1314, however, English expeditions ceased, affecting some east coast ports adversely. In particular, Berwick-upon-Tweed sank back into the role of a small port, liable to be attacked by the Scots; excavation has shown how some of its internal space fell into disuse. By contrast, however, most of the Welsh border was safer; citizens of Shrewsbury were even allowed to build houses over the town walls. Edward III and his sons switched their attentions to France and Spain; their expeditions might account for the evidence of activity on Portsmouth's foreshore that included a rectangular, below-ground wood-lined cistern to hold fresh water, a stake-and-wattle lined dock 6 metres wide, a substantial oven, and a forge.[48]

Some signs of waterfront reclamation were found in Portsmouth, but in general this process was coming to an end, so that the always limited evidence of ship and boat parts used in jettying virtually ceases. No fourteenth-century wrecks of sea-going vessels have been found in England, but lengths of what are probably ship's planking, dated by dendrochronology to 1332–61, have been found near Sandwich, Kent, and are thought to have come from a ship of the type known as a hulk, sunk to strengthen waterfront defences after long use. A more square-ended vessel type, the cog, is best known from one raised at Bremen; capable of carrying over 150 tuns, she was clinker-built and had a single sail, which was still the norm in northern Europe. She was relatively high-sided, so a rear rudder was more practicable than a massive side-rudder like the one found off Sandwich. Images of ships on seals indicate that this navigational change was happening in England in the fourteenth century, the earliest known being Poole's of *c.* 1325. It had the potential to make navigation more precise, although geometrical aids such as the fourteenth-century *quadrans novus* recently found outside Canterbury could not be used at sea if latitude was unknown. Sea-marks, such as church towers and chapels in prominent coastal locations, were useful, though very few were fitted out with lanterns for beacons; fishermen subscribed to maintenance of the light on St Michael's Mount, Cornwall, but was that for piety or because they might get caught out at sea in the dark?[49]

The fourteenth century ended with the violent death of Richard II, whose attempts to promote the exalted status that he believed had been bestowed upon him by his god at his coronation did not save him from the Lancastrian take-over. At the time, it may have seemed that the threat of plague had passed, but it was to return in the next century, unlike leprosy which had become much less prevalent – though with tuberculosis increasing in its place. For most people, there must have seemed little cause for optimism in a new century, and they were to be proved largely right. The 1381 rebels had not achieved the social revolution that some of them sought, but imperceptibly to them the old, feudal order was giving way to a hierarchy a little more dependent upon personal achievement than birth, upon payment by contract and cash than by dues of service in return for land, and a little less manorial and more commercial. Kings did not seek to expand their influence by internal development but by conquest: Ireland in the twelfth century, Wales in the thirteenth, and France and even Spain in the fourteenth. England was still on the edge of the known world, however; although its cloth industry was beginning to take it away from a dependence upon raw materials to export in return for manufactured goods and precious metal, it was still undeveloped in comparison to the power-houses of the northern Hanse merchants and the southern Italians.[50]

Notes

1 Adverse weather conditions: Stone, D. 2014 – droughts could be as bad as floods; see Brown, A. T. 2015, 154–6; Astill 2018, 79–80 for the problem of differentiating between the evidence for short-term weather and long-term climate consequences; sheep: Slavin 2020. The events of 1381 are no longer to be called the Peasants' Revolt, as it was not only country labourers who were involved: for example Barker 2014.

2 West Whelpington: Evans, D. H. and Wrathmell 1987, 254–5 (Andrews, M. 2019 online list shows a possible termination date as late as 1351, but that was when the coins should have been withdrawn from circulation, so does not date the deposition); silver lace-end: Standley 2013, 50. West Hartburn: Standley 2013, 82–3, where she also suggested that two brooches found at one of the north-east's abbeys might have been deliberately buried as protective votives; West Hartburn also had a stone carved with a saltire cross, possibly apotropaic but certainly not something expected: Pallister and Wrathmell 1990, 64. Fewer excavations have taken place in the north-west, in Cumbria, but disruption has not been shown.

3 Okehampton castle: Higham, R. *et al.* 1982; the process began in the 1290s, the date of a complex agreement with the town's burgesses over grazing rights, which would not show in the archaeological record, unlike the clearances: Creighton 2002, 191. The barbs on hunting arrows were Y-shaped to give a wider cutting edge.

4 Dinna Clerks: see Ch. 9. Tin output: Fox, H. S. A. 1999, 323–5. Pewter: Homer 1991, 66–79 and see Ch. 9; Egan 2009, 51 noted a considerable increase in the use of pewter for costume fittings. Pottery and wood are occasionally entered in lists of peasants' goods, but usually then only as groups, not as individually valued items; an *olla terrea* was valued at 1d in 1416, but its size and function were not stated; four platters, seven dishes, and three saucers of wood were listed but unfortunately not valued (a small brass pan was 12d): Briggs forthcoming no. 8. Agricultural tools: Goodall, I. H. 2011, 77–103; Lay Subsidy records suggest a wider range of craftworkers, such as tailors, living in villages than excavations indicate.

5 Mortality on two Glastonbury Abbey estates: Farmer 1989. Ramsey Abbey ran its Huntingdonshire estate at nearby Upwood as demesne, presumably to ensure a food supply for the monks, but was already leasing out Ellington, although it was only 10 miles away from the abbey: Olson in Razi and Smith (eds) 1996. Wiltshire was beginning to develop the cloth industry which was to bring it prosperity later: Hare, J. 2011, 179. Coins: Kelleher 2018, 521. Pottery is very hard to date, and my generalization might not stand up to scrutiny; peasant inventories record metal vessels, but there are too few to show any trends: Briggs forthcoming. Assaying: Campbell, M. 1991, 140–1. Knife-blades: Goodall, I. H. 2011, 111. Cherry, J. 2018 for an overview of the proliferation of sealing.

6 St Mary Spital: Harward *et al.* 2019, 66–7. Chester Water Tower and others: Mercer 2018, 301–3; Creighton and Higham 2005, 118–20.

7 Goodramgate, York: Short, P. 1980, 86–96; Arnold *et al.* 2012, 94; Stonegate: Short, P. 1980, 96–108. London: Schofield, J. 1995, 55–6; documents indicate that they featured in Bristol: Leech 2014, 22. Overall review: Quiney 2003, 254–60, and see Ch. 9 on Winchester and Illus. 9.4. Market encroachment: Pearson 2009, 7–8.

8 'Wealdens'; urban origin: Pearson 2005, 57, and survey: Alcock, N. 2010; Winchester: James, T. B. and Roberts 2000, 189–92. Jettying: Pearson 2005, 50–1; 2009, 8–11. Pillar supports survive in Totnes, Winchester, and Southampton: Quiney 2003, 247.

9 Urban towers, Lynn: Parker 1971, 47; London: Schofield, J. 1995, 36–7 and 68–9; they were also an occasional feature of guildhall complexes: Quiney 2003, 219. Penshurst: Emery, A. 2006, 386–9; Platt 2007, 90–1; Coventry Whitefriars: Woodfield 2005; Poulteney was probably born on the eponymous family estate in Leicestershire, close to Coventry.

10 Winchester courtyard house: Scobie *et al.* 1991, 42–8; Martin and Martin 2004, 129–30 for Winchelsea; Parker 1971, 40–1 for Lynn. Southampton Woolhouse: Bridge *et al.* 2014, 120–1.

11 Exeter jug: Hinton 2005, 216 (a photograph of the jug appeared in a notice of that book in the *Church Times*, but the interpretation was passed over); a cathedral official was killed in Exeter, but some of his colleagues were implicated as well as townsfolk. London Guildhall: Schofield, J. 1995, 14–16. Urban conflicts: Prestwich 2005, 476–81. Exeter passages: Stoyle 2014, 35–46.

12 Bury St Edmunds gatehouse: Goodall, J. 2011, 275; Barker, J. 2014, illus. 18 (for an eighteenth-century print, Gransden (ed.) 1998, pl. 30). Church demand for window glass grew, with new production centres answering it, for instance in Staffordshire: Welch 1997. Gatehouse symbolism: Heal 1990, 32–3; Attreed 1994; see also Ch. 11.

13 See Bailey 1989; Campbell, B. M. S. *et al.* 1996 for pledging, tithing, villeinage, manumission, and many other complexities. See Stone, D. 2005; 2014 for the Fens and weather effects. The Robin Hood ballads may have been told in some circumstances to express peasant discontent: Coss 1985. Disputes: Birrell 2010; Watts, D. G. 1982. Badges: Gilchrist 2012, 100–1 and 105–11. Poaching: Birrell 1996; Smith, S. V. 2009, 407–8; both pointed out that peasants would have used nets and snares which would not leave an archaeological trace. Arrowheads and archery practice: Gilchrist 2012, 56, citing work by H. Wheeler; Wadge 2008 for typology.

14 Physical evidence of belief other than in churches: Gilchrist 2012, 227–32. West Cotton: Chapman 2010, 359–61 (the figure was found in the manorial kitchen, so perhaps I should not associate it with 'peasant' culture). West Hartburn: see Ch. 9. Avebury: Gillings *et al.* 2008, 118–19 (they pointed out that a tailor is an alternative. But for the coins, the burial would have been claimed as that of a man recorded as murdered in Avebury in 1289.). A pointed implement on the belt of a shepherd in a late fifteenth-century woodcut looks like a short trocar, although they seem not to have been mentioned as a tool of the medieval shepherd; Rose, S. 2017, 84–7. Barbers' skill with knives led to their practising surgery; 'Barber-surgeons' were later to be formally recognized, with a guild, but the better surgeons of this 'handy crafte' would presumably not also have done hair-cuts and shaves: see Rawcliffe 1995 for doctors, surgeons, apothecaries, and alchemists, and the many potions and treatments; surgery: Binski 1996, 64–5; Swanson, H. 1989.

15 The careful management of sheep flocks is documented for many Church estates, on which they were kept in separate groups and moved between farms; most owners would not have had that level of specialization, but shepherds needed skill whoever employed them. Sheep-cotes: Dyer 1995. Sheep and weather: Stone, D. 2005; Rose, S. 2017; Slavin 2020. Wool and cloth: Rose, S. 2017, 84–7; some Lincoln green was still produced: Childs 1996. Grain: Hybel 2002 (rye and oats were the main imports, wheat an export, although sometimes an import; barley sometimes went out as malt, e.g. pp. 226–7).

16 Farm buildings: Brady 2018, 263–9. Bradford-on-Avon: Slocombe and Slocombe 2016. Even if unvisited by the owner, appearances had to be kept up, so 'influence, patronage and bureaucracy' required a suitable presence: Hare, J. 2021, 77. Meare: Emery, A. 2006, 591–4 – see note 6 for useful questioning of the traditional assumption about the 'fish-house'; Rippon 2004 for the Somerset Levels. Fish, ponds, and nets: essays in Aston, M. (ed.) 1988; also a detailed study of Whittlesea Mere, Cambridgeshire: Lucas 1998. Shapwick: Gerrard, C. M. and Aston 2007, 72 and 983–97.

17 Knaresborough, Dunstanburh, and other northern castles: Goodall, J. 2011, 239–55; Dixon 2018, 378 for the earl's political needs (he may also have been jealous of the work at Alnwick, newly acquired by the Percy family; both were close to the Scots who had taken Berwick-on-Tweed, moving the border southwards). Chantries: Duffy, E. 2006, 309–10 ('college' was a term used widely for clerical institutions of various sorts, not necessarily educational).

18 Warwick and Maxstoke: Parkin and McNeill, 512–7; they showed that dating has to be from detailed stylistic analysis, and their 1340s–70s argument is based on the career of a particular earl.

19 The geographical and temporal distribution of licences were analysed statistically by Dean 2010–11; Davis, P. 2011–12, 288 considered that agricultural wealth and proximity to London were more important than reaction to particular events. Portchester: Cunliffe and Munby 1985, 19–23 and 124–6. Windsor and the Garter: Goodall, J. 2011, 182–91(the first recorded clock in a secular context was installed at Windsor in the 1350s). Some new priories were established, but colleges became generally preferred. Westminster and other palaces: James, T. B. 1990, 109–27. There was also a royal residence of some grandeur within the city: Schofield, J. 1995, 41 – preferable, presumably, to the old-fashioned style of accommodation in the Tower. London was further boosted by court expenditure with its merchants rather than at fairs. Kenilworth: Goodall, J. 2011, 292–5; ground-floor halls remained the norm, though like Westminster's might be remodelled or rebuilt without aisles and making a display of roof carpentry: Hare, J. 2021, 87–8.

20 Wingfield: Goodall, J. 2011, 302–3. de la Pole foundations and chantries generally: Rosenthal 1972. Excavation of a Carthusian house in Yorkshire: Coppack and Keen 2019.

21 Luttrell Psalter: Backhouse 1989; Camille 1998; Brown, M. P. 2006; its hen and chicks: Serjeantson 2006, 141. Eggs are shown on Sir Geoffrey's dining table in front of two visiting friars, whose Order prevented them from sharing the family's more elaborate foods; clerics were welcome guests as they came with well-informed gossip: Swabey 1999, 97–116. Eggs and poultry were peasant staples: Dyer 2020. The scenes of people working, the windmill, and the water-mill created a 'taskscape' like that suggested for Bodiam by Johnson 2020, 317–19; images of hunting, hawking, orchards, a rabbit warren, and a pond full of fish all emphasize the lord's rights – even the water-mill with its overshot wheel that required a leat showed his right to manipulate a water-course. Longthorpe: Rouse and Baker 1955; Emery, A. 2000, 272–4; Woolgar 2006, 25–7.

22 Sir Geoffrey's will and Irnham church: Camille 1998, 122–38; Millar 1932, 52–6 – did he really have so much to give away? Wishes were not always fulfilled: one lady admitted in her own will that she had not distributed the bequests made in her husband's, although he had died 30 years earlier: Swabey 1999, 150. The Paston letters in the next century show one family member's growing concern at the non-completion of a monument. One hopes that the wish of a fourteenth-century Lincolnshire widow that her small lead vessel should be used in the church guttering was fulfilled; presumably she wanted her object to be used in that way to keep her personal connection, and not simply sold: Foster, C. W. (ed.) 1914, *s. a.* 1327. Beeswax: Sapoznic 2019; wax was also used for votive offerings, modelling limbs that needed healing, and in time were melted down and used for candles, a final dedication; barber-surgeons used wax to bind

wounds, so some tried to become chandlers: Swanson, H. 1989. Aristocratic burial-places and endowments: Rosenthal 1972. Sir Geoffrey's son wanted to be buried in the nave, but his fine memorial brass belies any intention of humility.

23 Coinage: Allen, M. 2012, especially 354–63 for low-value coins; Naylor 2015, 293–6. See Kelleher 2018, 517 for groats and nobles (similar denominations had been attempted in the thirteenth century, see Ch. 9, but had not been sustained). Nine Spanish gold coins were found recently in Shropshire. Italian bankers were very active in the English wool trade, and a source of credit (which is documented at all social levels and may have partly compensated for the lack of coin supplies); they were bankrupted by English kings' failure to redeem their debts, which might be said to have held back the advance of capitalism. Gold became a little more available because of discoveries in Hungary. The leopard was an animal with which Edward III liked to be associated, a royal alternative to the lion: Shenton 2002.

24 Surviving examples of gold and silver plate are few, but the Lynn chalice or the Great Royal Cup show what was available. Richard II's list of valuables, mostly plate, is in small handwriting on a roll over 2 metres long: Stratford 2013; queens also had eye-watering amounts of plate, but there were significant numbers of silver cups, dishes, and saucers in baronial and knightly households as well: Woolgar 2016, 178–91. Gold problems: Allen, M. 2012, 375–6. Excavated rural gold coin: Musty and Algar 1986, 142. Wharram weight: Barclay 2007, 304, no. 36. Exeter: Shiel 1984. A coin-forger's mould has been found even in a remote part of Cumberland: Summerson *et al.* 1998, 25. Cambridge hoard: Andrews 2019 and for many others. PAS finds: Kelleher 2018, 521. Long-term hoarding reduced the amount of money available for transactions; if the West Whelpington group was built up over a long period, and not just accumulated for a short time to pay the annual rent, those coins were not circulating and if typical would have impeded the development of a money-using economy – 'velocity' of exchange is as important a factor in that as the amount of money produced: Mayhew 1995.

25 Mortality: the two Glastonbury manors that had lost 17/18% of their labour force in 1315–17 lost 57% in 1348–50: Farmer 1989; in Northamptonshire, 19 of the 51 people who should have been at a meeting of the manor court had died in the 3 weeks since the previous one. Wharram churchyard: Mays *et al.* 2007, 216–18: settlement: Wrathmell (ed.) 2012, 363–4 (documents recorded 30 peasant households in 1368 at Wharram, but perhaps only 12 in 1377, either because the latter caught a temporary decline or more probably was not assessing the same thing). Westbury: Ivens *et al.* 1995, 89–198. Hatch Warren: Fasham and Keevill 1995, 151; James, T. B. 1999 for the plague and its effects in Hampshire generally. For the Midlands, see Jones, R. and Lewis 2012, 191–3. Farming-system variety and change: Campbell, B. M. S. *et al.* 1996. See Hatcher 2008 for a very sensitive portrayal in a partly fictional account by a highly respected historian of the effects of the Black Death on a single community and the different approaches taken by different landlords in their efforts to maintain their incomes.

26 West Whelpington: Evans, D. H. and Wrathmell 1987, 354–5. Thrislington: Austin, D. 1989, 177 and 197. Raddon: Fowler and Blackwell 1998, 79 (the site was reused in the sixteenth century). Wharram: Dyer 2012, 318 and 321. Westbury: Ivens *et al.* 1995, 89–196. Campbell, B. M. S. *et al.* 1996, 135 and 137, estimated an increase in landlords' stock-keeping, especially sheep, of about 60%, but Oldland 2014 argued that overall the increase in sheep numbers only began after 1440. Rabbits: Standley 2018 – she noted how rabbit furs had become a significant export by the fifteenth century, p. 375; Bailey, M. 1989, 251–6 (their production seems not to have been taken into account by Campbell, B. M. S. *et al.* 1996).

27 Floods: Stone, D. 2005, 120 and 123 (this work also showed how fleece weights and quality deteriorated); see Bailey, M. 1990, who pointed out that the Norfolk Broads result from shrinking peat as well as inundations. 'CORS': Lewis, C. 2016; 2020 (I have tried to compare the test-pit results with those from a large and well-published

excavation with a long timespan, Westbury, but the results are presented by percentages not quantities; nevertheless, the steep decline in cooking pottery at one croft even though it was not deserted is worth noting: Ivens *et al.* 1995, 297.). A comparable pattern of later medieval pottery numbers declining has recently been published from north Hampshire: Pringle 2020, 316–17. Different degrees of contraction are shown by intensive surveys, such as on the Somerset Levels: Rippon 2006, 275. The collapse of the bishop of Winchester's income from St Giles fair 1348–9 is another example of the effect of the Black Death, with wage increases after 1364–5 indicating that casual labour had by then become less available than in the immediate aftermath of 1348–50: Arthur 2021, 98–102. International fairs like St Giles or St Ives dwindled, only Stourbridge remaining significant, but this was a trend before the Black Death, affected for instance by royal purchasing direct from Italian merchants: Moore, E. W. 1985; Ramsay 1991, xxix–xxx; Epstein 1994.

28 Willmott, H. *et al.* 2020.

29 East Smithfield: Grainger *et al.* 2008; the coins: 15–17, also Allen, M. 2011, 354; Andrews 2019, 194–5 suggested that such fear could have been spiritual because the coins were 'polluted'. The St Mary Spital cemetery showed no increase in burial, so Death victims may have been kept in isolation as much as possible: Harward *et al.* 2019, 66–7. Thornton: Willmott, H. *et al.* 2020; a 'catastrophe cemetery' has also been excavated in Hereford: Stone, R. and Appleton-Fox 1996. Overall survey: Gilchrist and Sloane 2005, 74–6 (written before the Thornton discovery). Surveys of towns include Dobson 2000, 275–8; Schofield, J. and Vince 1994, 212–14; Jervis 2017b. *Yersinia pestis*: Huggon 2018, 840–1; fleas spread by human contact with infected textiles, and by contact with animals such as dogs and cats as well as the notorious rats might have been enough on their own to have caused the rapid mortality: Lee 2014. St Mary Spital pharmacy: Harward *et al.* 2019, 83–5, with contribution on the vessels by L. Whittingham and J. Pearce, 165–72. Brasses: Badham and Norris 1999. Documentary evidence indicates that the new water supply in Exeter was completed despite the labour problems and was helped by sales of indulgences throughout the diocese, which were doubtless stimulated by fear of sudden death: Stoyle 2014, 46.

30 Poor nutrition is shown by Harris Lines: Lee 2014. Government: Ormrod 2000a. Society: Goldberg 2008, 168–88. Sumptuary laws: Lachaud 2002 for the background; the intention was not to prevent people from bettering themselves, provided that they did the service appropriate to the social position that wealth might bring them. Labourer's pass: Burnett 2009; also Cherry 2008, 15. Labourers probably adjusted their working hours to fit their expectations and preferred to have extra leisure rather than a higher standard of living, on the principle of 'task-orientation': Blanchard 1978. As well as 'top-down' attempts at social control, it was also exercised among neighbours to curb disharmony, bad neighbourliness, and eaves-dropping, for instance by raising the hue and cry: Müller 2005; McIntosh 1998, 186–90. Control measures can be seen as an aspect of 'closure theory': Rigby 1995; Hinton 1999. Children: Penny-Mason and Gowland 2014, 181–3 (their interpretation that children were less supervised and therefore more subject to trauma seems to me more likely a consequence of working than of their being abandoned orphans, though the cemeteries suggest that there was no lack of those); Lewis, M. 2016, 152 noted an increase in the number of young females found in urban cemeteries after the Black Death but a decrease in the numbers of young males – the latter perhaps more likely to remain working in agriculture; a thwarted aim of the Wharram skeletal analysis was to see whether any dietary changes could be observed: Mays *et al.* 2007, 77, but a 'Black Death moment' was not identifiable.

31 Pottery: Marter 2021 estimated a decline of about a third in the number of production centres but stressed the difficulty of associating change directly with the Black Death; Haslam 1978, 28; McCarthy and Brooks 1989a, 90. Glass: Tyson 2000, 26–31 – the decrease in archaeological survivals seems at variance with the documentary record,

but that may be because some importing continued but on a smaller scale: see Woolgar 1999, 153–4; in aristocratic and some college halls, communal drinking vessels such as wooden mazers with elaborate metal fittings were used – presumably a servant wiped these clean(er?) as they went round. Imports of beer into east coast ports: Unger 2004, 98.

32 London: Vince 1985, 50–69; Pearce and Vince 1988, 66–7 and 74–5 (the extra initial cost of transporting the clay to Kingston has led to the suggestion that the operation was someone's investment opportunity); London had a wide hinterland for its food and other supplies, for example Galloway 2005. Grimston: Leah 1994. Chilvers Coton: Mayes and Scott 1984.

33 Art and architecture: Lindley 1996. Floor- (and roof-)tiles: Mellor 2018, for example 89 and 98; in Kent, the cost of lime doubled, as did the cost of sea-coal to burn it; a tiler who was paid 10 shillings in 1347–8 was paid nothing in 1348–9 'because he was dead': Adams, M. 1996, 45–53. Winchester and Edington: Hare, J. 2012, 290–2. Vicars' colleges: Stocker 2005; practice varied, Lincoln's for instance having a dormitory block, but divided internally into *cubiculi*, each with its own fireplace and garderobe, but with access into a shared corridor; also see Quiney 2003, 232–3; the Vicars Close at Wells was remodelled in the 1460s, when chimneys were added. Dendrochronology from the invaluable databases was maintained by the Vernacular Architecture Group.

34 Queenborough: Goodall, J. 2011, 291.

35 Southampton: Platt and Coleman-Smith 1975, 294–7 (although the stone-lined pit reanalysed by Brown, D. H. 2018 contained rubble, other contents seem slightly earlier than 1338, and a house fire rather than the raid is indicated as the cause, unlike burning elsewhere in the neighbourhood). Gunpowder artillery: Purton 2009–10. Norwich Cow Tower: Saunders, A. D. 1985, Ayers *et al.* 1988. Southampton walls (the loops could be later insertions, though they do not look like it to me): Platt 1973, 123–5; Spencer, D. 2019, 176. Portchester: Cunliffe and Munby 1985 (with contribution by D. Renn), 95, 112–3, and 128; being on the south coast, Portchester – and Corfe – were royal castles where the constables were made responsible for protection of the surrounding area – coastal towns had to arrange their own defence: Alban 1981. The loops at Quarr might be later insertions. It is worth noting that the 1320s Chester Water Tower only had arrow-loops: Mercer 2018, 306–9, as did the 1340s walls at Yarmouth, the cost of which crippled the port: Turner, H. L. 1971, which shows the speed of change. See Purton 2020–21 and Spencer, D. 2019 for various examples and dates; Creighton and Higham 2005, 110–18 for a summary of town walls and provision for artillery.

36 The St Albans episode is told by a single chronicler, who may have exaggerated the symbolism of the rioters' behaviour: Aston, M. 1994; Barker, J. 2014, 279–88; fixing a live rabbit to a pillory to 'symbolize the liberty of warren' (Müller 2010, 43) sounds more like rural (mis)behaviour than handing round broken stones as Eucharist symbols. The gesture was not against rabbits *per se* but for the general right to hunt and to have parks removed. Rabbits get mentions in court records, with occasional complaints about their eating crops, for example in 1340s Sussex: Coulton 1925, 78, but were not a major bone of contention. Langdon 2004 argued that lords were primarily anxious to protect their mills from competition rather than to emphasize their seigneurial rights. Other examples of discord involved refusal to work: Birrell 2010.

37 Pot querns may have been used to refine coarse mill-ground flour: Brears 2008, 96–7. Malt was also ground for ale and mustard: Henry Mustardir of Bridport, Dorset had a pair of stones valued at 3s 4d in 1319: Dorset Record Office HMC, BTB M35, and M 36. Archaeological evidence for the use of handmills by peasants and their resistance symbolism: Smith, S. V. 2009, 408–10. West Hartburn: Pallister and Wrathmell 1990. Few lists of goods include handmills, but a Cambridgeshire peasant's 'quern for grinding malt' was valued at 2 shillings in 1361 (his ox was worth 8 shillings): Briggs forthcoming, no. 1. Several householders in Lynn had them variously valued between

12½d and 18d, and they were frequent cargoes, as they were in Ipswich: Owen (ed.) 1984, 235–47 and 357–60. (Twelfth-century legislation specifically permitted that 'any burgess may have his own . . . handmill': EHD 2, 971.) Further references in Parsons, D. 2018, 470; Rynne 2018, 502–3. Grindstones were also used. References to fines for not using the lord's oven show another manorial perquisite that might be resented at times, and at times welcomed as a saving on fuel-gathering.

38 The prior of Bury was pursued and killed, while all the St Albans clergy seem to have been left uninjured: Barker, J. 2014, 286 (there had been dangerous riots in Bury in 1328). Muniment towers: Steane 2001, 239–49; Kent chests: Pickvance 2018, with thirteenth-/early fourteenth-century tree-ring dating by M. Bridge and D. Miles; Icklingham chest: Campbell, M. 1998, 74–5. (Another problem was deciding whether documents were genuine: in 1381, the constable of Corfe Castle produced a 'customary' proving royal rights over the liberties of the town, only for the townsfolk to have the strangely good fortune to find another in 'ancient writing' 'in a missal in the parish church', which they claimed trumped the constable's: Hinton 2002, 86.) Strongrooms: Brears 2008, 18–19; Thompson, M. W. 1998. 110–15. New College tiles: Mellor 2018, 98–9. Although not the first intra-mural college, that so much space was available inside Oxford for New College is a sign of that town's stagnation; the college was allowed to straddle the walls, a breach which weakened both their defensibility and their display of civic pride: see Dodd 2020, 61–5 for the way that the university's growth affected Oxford's development.

39 Beverley seal seizure, involving butchers, tilers, fullers, and others: Kermode 1998, 27 and 57; dyeing complex: Evans, D. H. and Tomlinson 1992, 61–73. Revolt events: Harriss 2005, 228–34; Barker, J. 2014, including 196–7 for Cressing Temple. After 1369, wars in France swung against the English, and costs rose to over £1 million, hence the Poll Tax was introduced: Sherborne 1977. Urban riots and expression of discontent: Dobson 2000, 281; Rigby and Ewan 2000, 297–311; Rosser 2000, 368. Among the sufferers were 'many hundreds' of Flemings, especially brutally treated in London: Harriss 2005, 307; Barker, J. 2014, 265–6; unlike the Jews earlier, their presence is undetectable archaeologically, though the spreading taste for beer may have been influenced by them, and some may have been employed in making and laying 'Flanders tiles' as in a 1370 London contract: Schofield, J. 1995, 115. The Church Enstone inscription deserves deeper study and comparison with the better-known Cooling Castle's or New Winchelsea's gate.

40 The Bodiam debate was analysed by Johnson 2017, 193–7, stressing how human motive is not necessarily fully explained by what people say about themselves; also see Goodall, J. 2011, 314–17; both authors discussed other castles such as Cooling and Scotney, Goodall also covering Nunney, Somerset. See Johnson, M. 2020, 317–19 for viewing the estate as a 'taskscape'. Bodiam's builder had risen a long way from being a forebear's late thirteenth-century 'serjeant-forester' status: Saul 1998. Arundel Castle: Woodburn and Guy 2006, 9–24; the earl who died in 1376 had £30,000 in gold and silver in his high tower at the castle, which shows the need for a secure treasury; Holmes 1957 remains worth reading on Arundel and others, not least for phrases about magnates' 'exploits of chivalric banditry'; the dowager 'generally seems to have survived childbirth better than [the magnates] survived the battlefield', followed by a discussion of the role of such powerful ladies; '"bastard feudalism" is a misnomer which has no justification except a vague prejudice against the later Middle Ages'. The south coast had special military arrangements because of raids by swift French galleys: Alban 1981; even the Spanish joined in 1380. Nothing seems to have been done at Bramber Castle, however, perhaps because the owning Mowbrays thought it to be too close to the Howards' Arundel, and they did not want to challenge for local power. Cooling college: Gibson 2005, 83; Lord Cobham also provided brass memorials to go in the

chancel of the church, for his father and a cousin – and for himself, making provision long before his death.

41 Bolton: Hislop 1996, who showed that although the castle was carefully planned from the start, modifications were made during the building; that applies to Bodiam and others, making a single interpretation of building even more problematic: Johnson (ed.) 2017, 43–5 (it is possible but unlikely that stables were provided within the quadrangle, p. 46). See Brears 2008, 43–51; McNeill and Scott 2018, 338–46 for further insights and discussion of other northern castles, for which see also Goodall, J. 2011, 323–34. Sheriff Hutton: Creighton 2002, 211–12. Etiquette and exclusion: Cooper 2017.

42 Badges: Siddons 2009. Wilton Diptych: essays in Gordon *et al.* (eds) 1997; contemporary writers saw that Richard was deceived into thinking that those who wore his white hart would be loyal to him. Westminster hall: Emery, A. 2006, 254–5 (the present-day arrangement without hangings and furniture does not give the impression that Richard sought). Dartington Hall: Emery, A. 2006, 534–49; 2007. Devon earls: Cherry, M. 1979.

43 Caldecote: Beresford 2009, 95–123. Cattle and sheep: Thomas, R. *et al.* 2013; pigs: Hamilton and Thomas 2012. Horses and their shoes: Clark 1995, 28–32 and 96–101; West Cotton: Dunne *et al.* 2019, 12. Fleece weights and qualities show the effects of scab and poor feeding more generally, however. Wealdens and crucks: Vernacular Architecture Group data-bases. Waste disposal: Astill 2000, 226–7 (an article with valuable discussion of other recognition factors); Jervis 2014, 122–9.

44 Guildhalls: Giles 2000 (with a very clear discussion of post-processualism and other new approaches); Quiney 2003, 217–22; Boston: Giles and Clark 2011. Guilds in general: Rosser 2015; West, C. 2011, 200, 202, and 205 for their origins; McRee 1994 for their ceremonies, processions and frictions; see also Ch. 11. York's Merchant Adventurers' hall is occasionally still used for feasts; one that he prepared for an archbishop is described by Brears 2008, 9, with 'strip-cartoons' to show the elaborate serving rituals, 458–82.

45 Vernacular language: Coss 1985 (the analysis of different interpretations of the Robin Hood legends has echoes for archaeologists). Badges: Spencer 1990; 1998; Gilchrist 2012, 73–4 and 158–61; Anderson 2010; ampullae were small containers for holy water or oil, so were made of tin by 'slush casting', so that the metal would fuse instantly: Bayley and Watson 2009, 366. Even when French and Spanish raids were in abeyance, pirates were a constant maritime threat, yet large numbers of vessels took pilgrims bound for Compostela across the Channel, especially between 1370 and 1430; in some years, over a thousand people took the risk: Childs 1999. Ship graffiti are mostly in coastal churches: Champion, M. 2018, 635–7; for the large number in Winchelsea, recorded using Reflectance Transformation Imaging: Dhoop *et al.* 2016. Objects: Hinton 2005, 212–19 (numbers reported to the Portable Antiquities Scheme have increased considerably since that book was published). Texts: Gilchrist 2012, 165, and for folded coins, 243, also Naylor 2015, 296; gold 'nobles' were presumably too valuable or too much respected for this token treatment. Pilgrimage summary: Yeoman 2018.

46 Salt: Woolgar 2016, 71–3; Brears 2008, 148 for salting. Continued use of brine springs in Cheshire: Hurst (ed.) 1997, 40–1; of salterns in Lincolnshire: Simmons 2015, 16–17 and Lane, T. 2019 and in Dorset: Keen 1987, 28 (quantities may have reduced). As well as floods, storms caused sand-blow, though English sites were not much affected: see Griffiths, D. 2015, 112 for an example in Cornwall; Mawgan Porth had been abandoned for this reason much earlier.

47 Yarmouth: Potter 2008. Herrings: Barrett 2018, 134–5. Lynn: Hoare *et al.* 2003 – murage grants suggest that these were thirteenth-century. Pottery: Vince 1985; London-area products were also well represented. Hull: Evans, D. H. 2018, 100–3 (nothing survives above ground, so this article is a fine compendium from piecemeal excavations). Early use of brick: Smith, T. P. 1975, 131; Moore, N. J. 1991, 211–14.

48 Berwick-upon-Tweed: Hunter, J. R. 1982. Shrewsbury: Carver 1983. Portsmouth: Fox, R. and Barton 1986, 46–57.

49 Foreshore reclamation in London: Schofield, J. 2019, 66. A few boat planks in York are of post-1376 date: Hall, R. A. and Hunter-Mann 2002, 837–8. The River Ouse at Ely seems to have developed waterfront usage with channels dug through reclamation deposits, with wattling only at the landward ends: Cessford *et al.* 2006, 24–8. Sandwich timbers: Milne 2004. One type of vessel entirely missing from the archaeological record is the oared galley for troop carriage, used by the government, for example Friel 1986. Seals: Pedrick 1904, nos. 3–4, 7, 11, 15, 19, 31–4, 42, 65, and 69. The Bremen cog, and discussion of shipping issues such as crewing costs and risk: Unger 1980; cogs and hulks: see Hutchinson 1994, 10–20, and p. 90 for an illustration of a laden vessel carrying a mixed cargo of woolsacks and /or cloth bales, barrels for wine, herrings etc., and metal jugs and cauldrons – the sort of mixed cargo that is well documented for example for Exeter: Kowaleski (ed. and trans.) 1993. Sandwich rudder: Marsden 1997, 65–6, and see Ch. 9. The first references to quayside cranes occur in the fourteenth century, providing an alternative to unloading by swinging a ship's yard; using them incurred a fee, but the speed of unloading presumably made the payment worthwhile; the machines would only have been available at larger ports with deep-water quays and jetties, giving them an advantage over beaching, though that continued into the nineteenth century. Chapels: Orme 1996. Navigation: McGrail 1987, 199–240 and 275–80; Childs 2006, 260–1; *Quadrans Novus*: Linklater and Dekker 2010 (a small horological device suggests similar interest in scientific approaches: Geake 2004, 241–2); lighthouses: Hague and Christie 1975.

50 Leprosy and tuberculosis: Roberts, C. A. 2009.

11 The Fifteenth Century

Living in Reduced Circumstances

Although nothing as dramatic as the mortality of 1348–9 occurred in the fifteenth century, plague outbreaks were recorded in every decade except the 1440s and 1490s, curbing population growth and perhaps even causing its further decline. Some of the worst diseases associated with overcrowding may have eased, and leprosy continued to disappear – but syphilis became a threat. The weather was cold and unreliable. In 1400, the new Lancastrian dynasty had yet to establish itself, challenged not least by the Percy family in the north. Henry V's incursions into France began another huge drain on English finances. Henry VI could not govern; magnate factional intrigue, violence, and extortion led to Jack Cade's rebellion in 1450, symptomatic of the worst, mid century period. Edward IV seized, lost, and regained the Crown; Richard III became the last king of England to die on the battlefield; and although Henry VII had consolidated his position by 1500, the succession of his son – expected to be Arthur, not Henry – was not a certainty.[1]

Kings and claimants had to pay their armies in cash, and landowners continued to prefer leasing to demesne farming, wanting tenants and money rents rather than a large labour force; 'feudalism' no longer had much practical relevance, but its legal implications remained. Many people were the descendants of villeins and serfs, and even if they had bought their freedom they might still face a lord's claim that they were in bond. If wealthy, they were worth pursuing; the rich Salisbury merchant John Halle, whose fine mid fifteenth-century open hall survives in the city centre, was in dispute with a local abbey that claimed him as its serf, so that he faced both economic and social ruin.[2]

Despite political turmoil and taxation, opportunities existed for merchants like Halle, or to lease a small farm. A greater number of rural houses survive from the fifteenth century than from the fourteenth, more than can be accounted for merely by the passage of time, and survivals go against the trend by being unaffected by the mid century problems. The basic technology of building in timber did not change; crucks continued to be used except in the south-east but alongside box-framing, including Wealdens. Both systems allowed for an open hall and hearth, which remained a family's centre for social interaction, although sometimes also used for communal purposes, even as ale-houses, where business could be discussed and in which the owner could display any items that would impress

DOI: 10.4324/9781003007432-12

visitors; it was a mark of independent status to have a weapon for use in defence of the country, a useful symbol if a lord claimed the owner as a serf.[3]

A few houses were built by landlords hoping to attract tenants, but most attest ability to invest in permanence by those who lived in them, now increasingly referred to as yeomen, and who could take advantage of lower rents and sustained market demand for their produce. Labourers, however, probably did not benefit from higher wages, because of rising prices. Some of the intensively worked open-field systems continued to be abandoned and enclosed for stock-grazing and rabbit-rearing; fenced yards identified at Goltho, Barton Blount, and Low Throston show the importance of raising cattle. Some whole settlements continued to be deserted or to shrink, particularly in areas without a cloth trade, although precise dating remains problematic. The pottery record at West Cotton suggests mid fifteenth-century abandonment, even though the site had relatively recently been reconstructed. Excavations at some moated houses have shown disuse, perhaps because the owning family died or sold out.[4]

What is true of farmhouses is broadly true of barns, of which many more survive from the fifteenth century, mostly of two to four bays, sizes appropriate to the output of leased farms. Tithes were still collected even if the rest of an estate was leased; a small group of tithe barns in north Oxfordshire, preluded by Winchcombe Abbey's Church Enstone of 1382, looks as if they were competitive, especially as one of the owners involved was a college with no previous ties to the area. A few larger barns were built, as in 1407/9 by the abbey at Titchfield, Hampshire, of sixteen aisled bays to store the produce of a home farm and other supplies necessary for the monks. A commercial motive accounts for the twelve-bay aisled barn at Harmondsworth, Middlesex, where Winchester College continued demesne farming, against the general trend; surviving accounts record expenditure in the 1420s, consistent with the dendrochronological dating of 1424–6. The estate was close enough to London to supply the market there, and documents indicate that other landowners were also building large barns from which the city could be accessed easily. The tenants at Caldecote, who probably also benefited from proximity to London, had barns that were often longer than their houses, usually unaisled but probably timber-framed on padstones.[5]

London was the only town in England that could affect its hinterland to the extent seen in the barn-building around it. The problem of feeding its tightly packed inhabitants led to the building between 1439 and 1455 of the three-storey stone-built Leadenhall complex, quadrangular so that it could be locked securely against theft and pillage. London was England's only city on a European scale and was where most fortunes were made, with lawyers increasingly getting prominence as the courts focused more on Westminster and less on kings' personal presence; they made the City area their base, however, with 'inns of court'. Such people mostly lived or lodged on the north bank of the Thames but crossed the river to Southwark for much of their entertainment, so that that area was much more mixed, with not only houses for the likes of the bishops of Winchester or Sir John Fastolf, but also a variety of trades and occupations, many noisome and even worse than the new hop-brewing that focused there. Along the Thames were shipbuilding, metalworking, brick-making and lime-works, despite the risk of flooding. To the north, however, there was less support for the maintenance of St Mary Spital, where the pharmacy was dismantled, its site probably reused for metalworking.[6]

Other towns faced different problems from London. Inland, dependence on textiles meant that they were more subject to the vagaries of both internal and international demand, and although hide-tanning and metalworking offered steadier incomes, they did not have the same potential for profit. Textiles were generally the key to success or failure; York had the slightly doubtful advantage of being the seat of regional government for the north of England, and some parts of the surrounding shire benefited from new but relatively poor-quality cloth production, particularly around Halifax, where a number of distinctive houses with single, not double, aisles were built, perhaps to improve the light for weaving. Those houses tended to have end-wings at right angles to the hall, whereas farmers lucky enough to have good land in the Vale of York preferred to have end-blocks on the same axis as the hall – but most of them adopted the single-aisle mode that became a local tradition. In Beverley, the former dyeing complex was replaced by a substantial stone-footed building, suggesting a 'gentry' house replacing industry. Few other areas in the north had such favourable conditions. A few grander houses were built, like Bramall Hall, in Stockport, and Smithill's Hall outside Bolton, and a significant sign of Manchester's growth was the foundation in 1421 of the college that was later to become Chetham's Library and School. In Cumberland, Kendal's woollen industry does not seem to have produced a boost in expenditure on buildings like that in the Halifax area.[7]

No well-established town was actually deserted, though some newcomers shrank to village level; many markets and fairs disappeared from the record, and toll incomes declined. Excavations in Leicester 250 metres outside the town walls revealed how an area used for domestic building in the twelfth and thirteenth centuries first reduced in intensity, with some parts grassing over, then having pits, a water-channel and other features suggesting some sort of industrial use, and then around 1500 being used for soaking hides, with large rectangular pits. The absence of traces of oak bark and the presence of sheep and cat bones suggest that the premises were used for whittawing of the skins of smaller animals, rather than tanning of cow- and horse-hides. Northampton has produced similar evidence of a suburb being used for late-medieval leather production. But the centre of the same town also had tanning activity; one side of a street was cleared of previous buildings, and rebuilt as a terrace, apparently uniform on the frontage, but with one house considerably larger at the back than the others, yet also used for leather production; on the other side, further back from the frontage, tanning pits were also found. The fringe areas inside a town's walls became more likely to be used as well for other industries, such as metal-casting. In general, urban suburbs contracted, unless there were special circumstances (Illus. 11.1).[8]

Landlords, particularly church institutions, were prepared to invest in urban shops and houses in the hope of attracting tenants and therefore maintaining income streams, so towns might seem prosperous because of the quantity of new

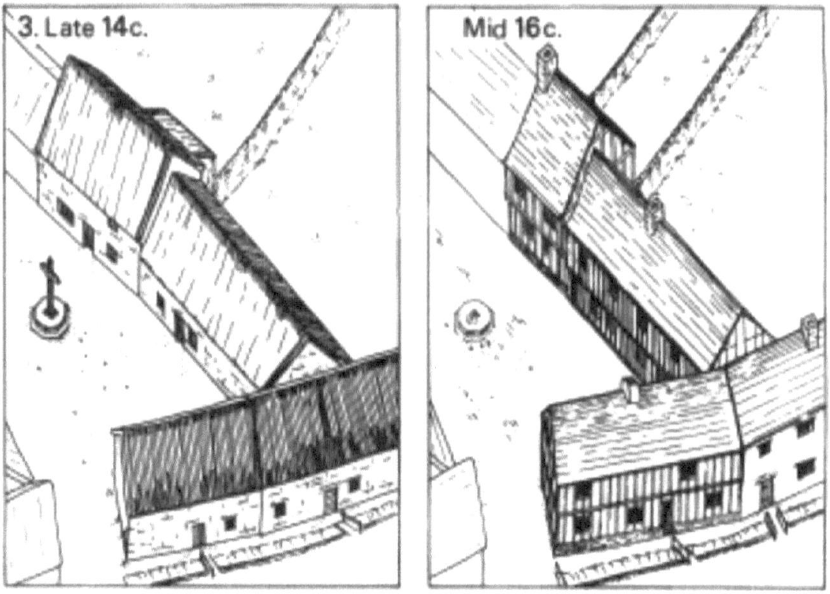

Illustration 11.1 Although most towns saw suburbs reduced or changed in use, in Oxford demand for houses was maintained because of the growth of the University, with much urban space both inside and outside the walls taken up by colleges and inns for scholars. The Hamel, therefore (see Illus. 9.4), remained buoyant, though still with small terraced housing. The late fifteenth and early sixteenth centuries saw much more substantial, timber-framed buildings (Palmer 1980).

buildings, but they may disguise underlying problems. Sandwich, for instance, has many later fifteenth-century survivals, but they became possible for less wealthy people to build or lease, as the very rich had moved out. In some towns, terraced rows continued to be built, as in Tewkesbury, where the long jettied row has now been dated by dendrochronology to 1405/8; it follows the curving boundary of the abbey precinct into which it encroached and was presumably a church investment, as York's Goodramgate had been in the previous century.[9]

Private investors seem likely to have been responsible for the terraces in Coventry, which had risen rapidly to become the leading Midlands town, thriving with metalworkers as well as cloth-makers; Black Swan Terrace, dated to 1454/5, comprises very small units with flat facades, while Upper Spon Street has a row of 'half-Wealdens', slightly larger and with jettied fronts. Elsewhere in the town, fifteenth-century rebuilding has been found in excavation on a site that had had a period of disuse and at a site near the fourteenth-century walls there were even stone cellars, by this time an unusual new investment; also found was evidence of iron-smelting, copper-alloy working, cloth and leather production, pottery- and tile-making, and even mixing of ink for manuscript painting. In Battle, Sussex, a row of 'half-Wealdens' was probably an investment by the abbey there. Jettying involved substantial timbers, so such houses were worth adapting to new circumstances without total replacement; Coventry's Black Swan Terrace was also quite well built, but in general it was easier to demolish and rebuild such very small housing, and that row probably only survives because the city went into steep decline as its textile workers failed to adapt to new demands, outpaced by smaller towns and even large villages which benefited from improved conditions in the last third of the fifteenth century.[10]

These urban houses all allowed for small individual shops and workshops; they were not only fitted out to provide for specific trades, which maintained flexibility, but also showed that the medieval standard that each person was responsible for their own work still applied. Of course there were apprentices and servants, but even in the cloth trade the normal practice was for spun yarn to be acquired by a weaver, who sold the product to a clothier, who might pass it on to a fuller and a dyer, perhaps finally buying the finished product back to sell; hints of change are that some clothiers bought pastures and fulling-mills and supplied weavers with yarn.[11]

Travellers like clothiers needed accommodation, so inns were another major building investment in the fifteenth century. Monasteries were less willing to cover the cost of guest-houses for pilgrims and other visitors, and rich merchants and gentry travelling on business needed the security of private chambers that could be locked, though the less well-off still had to sleep communally. Gloucester's New Inn, built round a courtyard with galleries for access to the rooms, was an investment by the abbey attributed to a monk who had left it by 1441, consistent with two dendrochronological dates of or immediately after 1432; in the same town, the Fleece Inn has two ranges dated by dendrochronology to the 1470s. Glastonbury Abbey built one with a gate-like stone facade in the town's main street for its many visitors to the supposed tomb of King Arthur. At Canterbury, the appeal of Becket's shrine was waning slightly, but pilgrims could stay at one of several inns, some known from documentary evidence and some partly surviving, like 'The Bull', reconstructed over twelfth-century cellars on the street frontage, with a courtyard behind. Inns were not all at pilgrimage centres or in large towns but wherever roads meant long-distance travellers. Consequently, they were often in quite small towns like Andover, Hampshire, where one that was the subject of a building contract in 1445 partly survives; stone for its foundations came from as far away as Beer, Devon, and 20,000 bricks were bought specifically for use in its frontage. In Somerset at Norton St Philip, the local monastery preferred in the 1430s to have a timber-framed, jettied range facing the road, although the ranges around the courtyard behind were of stone (Illus. 11.2). That inn was licensed for the storing and selling of cloth, unusually because local markets generally resisted competition.[12]

Also increasingly part of the urban scene were guildhalls. Although some, particularly in London, were for individual trades, most had religious dedications and served the wealthier townspeople generally; a large town, like York or Lynn, might have several guilds, smaller towns a single one, like Stratford-upon-Avon's,

Illustration 11.2 Late medieval investment in inns by ecclesiastical institutions is typified by the George, Norton St Philip, Somerset. The facade has a stone ground floor, with two jettied storeys above. The arrangement of windows suggests that the first floor had the best guest rooms. A doorway led into a courtyard, with other ranges. On the extreme left can be seen the sign for the Fleur de Lys, now an inn, but probably before that one of the licensed village ale-houses that also proliferated in the later Middle Ages.

dedicated to the Holy Cross, where the hall was described as 'new' in 1417/18, which is consistent with the dating of its timbers to between 1410 and 1435; Stratford was a twelfth-century new town where the pre-existing parish church was well outside the street grid, so the guild members provided themselves with an impressive chapel on one side of their hall, with a school on the other, a charitable foundation. Despite this expenditure, the town had its problems, with vacant properties; a merchant who built himself a good 'Wealden' house in the 1480s was able to do so because he could amalgamate two earlier tenements. Elsewhere, guilds supported their local church by maintaining lights as well as contributing to its upkeep and building. Another charity was to support almshouses for the poor and hospitals for the sick and aged. The Stratford guild had a clock-house, showing how mechanical measuring of time rather than judgement of hours by length of day-light was permeating society.[13]

York's Merchant Adventurers' hospital was in the undercroft below the great hall through which members had to pass on their way to the chapel, a reminder of their obligation and of their own mortality. The halls, of which York's Merchant Taylors had two, a great hall of 1412/13 augmented by a 'little' one of 1425/26, were important as settings for carefully prepared and orchestrated feasts, placing the masters at the head table with the senior member presiding like the head of a family. Coventry's Trinity Guild has preserved a carved Guild Chair, almost a throne for the Master. Indeed, one reason for guild membership was that its members provided an alternative 'family', at a time when sons and daughters were even less likely to survive than before 1348–9. To have one's soul prayed for was a reason for charitable bequests generally; Stratford benefited from the will of Sir Hugh Clopton, who had made his fortune in London, but, like many, saw fit to provide a visual reminder of himself in his birthplace, in his case by providing it with a stone replacement for its timber bridge. Such gestures towards a town's infrastructure were rarely on such a scale, and towns had major burdens to sustain, such as maintenance of their walls and gates. Guild membership brought people together in 'good unity, concord and charity' and probably made cooperative working easier for mayors and corporations. Several towns negotiated to draw off fresh water from the pipes that supplied religious houses, and Exeter went so far as to organize its own separate supply.[14]

One indication of stress is parish churches, with many abandonments recorded both in town and country. A few towns, like Wallingford, were already unable to support all their small churches in the thirteenth century, but the process accelerated. Lincoln's problems in the fifteenth century led to several parish churches being lost and suburbs being turned into pasture; some substantial stone buildings in Newport were demolished, and although its church was not abandoned until the following century, it had few parishioners. Although part of the Wigford suburb near the commercial waterfront was not abandoned, its use for a large bakery rather than housing may indicate retraction. Pottery was also made in the suburb; two moulds for impressing clay faces on to glazed jugs are very early finds. Along Wigford's main road, tenement amalgamation enabled a few large houses to be built, and the city had three inns, so a visitor might not have been aware of the losses. The desperate pleas by many towns that they had lost so many people and so much trade that they could not survive without help from the king were usually exaggerated but were not utterly unfounded; Winchester claimed in 1418 that a third of the town was desolate and later that a thousand of its houses were empty and that seventeen of its churches had no priest to serve them. Many churches were indeed redundant, yet all three that have been excavated had some work done on them in the fifteenth century. Outside the walls, one suburb remained in use for substantial buildings, while use of others fell away, a contrast seen also in the range of artefacts.[15]

Also indicative of urban problems are urban castles; they were not well placed for royal hunting parties, and centralized government meant that their legal role was diminishing, and even if they housed local law courts and gaols, needed much less space. They do not seem to have been used as mustering places for royal armies, and few of them were used for storing weaponry. A few had been sold off in the fourteenth century, but outer baileys were not built over in Bedford or Gloucester despite being recorded as 'void' and 'bareland'. Because sheriffdoms had become virtually hereditary, a few urban castles were in aristocratic hands, notably the Nevilles' Warwick until the 'king-maker' was killed at Barnet in 1471. Warwick Castle was therefore retained in good condition because it was the family's power-base, but the impression is that the king's urban castles were fairly ruinous, except for London's Tower, Dover, and some others with a strategic role, and would have done little to improve a town's standing.[16]

Even worse problems were faced by ports than by inland towns, as they were vulnerable to raids when kings were weak, as well as to trade fluctuations. A few merchants flourished in them, like the unknown owner of the surviving Hampton Court in Lynn, which had a range of shops along the street, with a gated cart passage giving access to a yard with an open hall along one side and a brick-built storage range at right angles to it, which has an open arcade facing the quay. The buildings are all only two storeys high, however, unlike the blocs with three or sometimes four jettied storeys that graced many high streets, with shops at street level. Even one of the richest merchants in fifteenth-century England, William Canynges of Bristol, seems to have had a shop fronting the street, with a narrow passage beside it leading directly into his hall, yards behind – probably with separate side access to kitchens and other rooms – and a tower at the back overlooking the river and his quays and ships; most of this long but quite narrow block was built over the water frontage that had been reclaimed in earlier centuries. Canynges also had a floor with fine-quality clay tiles, like those usually found in churches, but their design was secular, with roundels centred on a rose badge.[17]

Canynges's tower does not survive, but in eastern England, some merchants built brick towers partly in emulation of castles like Tattershall and Caister, as most notably the Hussey Tower next to the River Witham at Boston in south Lincolnshire. A comparable location alongside the River Trent at Gainsborough, at the northern end of Lincolnshire, was chosen by a local notable who built a fine brick mansion, its completion dated by dendrochronology to 1469–70; it had a grand hall, open in the traditional manner, many chambers, service rooms, and guest accommodation, and a three-storey tower was added that would have given the owner oversight of shipping on the river.[18]

Canynges prospered because Bristol was a beneficiary of an upsurge in trade through the south-western ports. The fifteenth century was a period of European expansion, led by the Portuguese. England played almost no part in the expeditions to Africa and beyond but did venture across the Atlantic for Newfoundland cod. South-western fisheries benefited from their distance from the Dutch competition that Yarmouth and other eastern ports had to contend with. The reduced journey time for boats bringing salt and wine from western France gave ports like Dartmouth and Plymouth an advantage over Rye and New Winchelsea further along the Channel, which were more vulnerable to French raids. They could also challenge Exeter for tin exports, though Exeter and its Topsham outport remained dominant in Devon; significantly, its pottery imports were mostly Breton and

Spanish not northern French or Dutch. Also trading with Britanny, and the Channel Islands, was Poole, not only in fish but also in linen and hemp for ropes and nets; it was also well-positioned for ships taking pilgrims to and from Compostela in Spain and in the 1430s to take royal expeditions to France.[19]

These ports were also notorious for pirates, whose activities brought retribution to Poole in a raid of 1405, when the Town Cellars were probably severely damaged and had to be completely reroofed. Such dangers led to Poole being one of the only English towns where new walls were proposed, though they were probably never built, apart from a gate across the main road. Individual prosperity is shown by a fifteenth-century merchant's substantial courtyard complex, one range having a roof very similar to the Cellars', but Poole was too far from London to compete for the big Italian carracks and galleys with Southampton, from which overland carts distributed goods to as far away as Coventry. Many went to London, although some Italians preferred to go all the way round the Dover Straits to enter the Thames estuary. The shifting sands of estuaries were always a problem and made Sandwich more difficult to access, so that Italian vessels that used to land there deserted it, as therefore did the richest English merchants.[20]

Poole is one of the few places where direct evidence of boat-building has been found. Shaped timbers, some new and some taken from dismantled vessels, were found waterlogged on the edge of the harbour. They were probably intended for fishing-boats and small coastal vessels, although even ships that crossed the open seas were small; anything over 200 tuns was a very expensive loss if it fell victim to pirates or storms. On a different scale are two barges in the Thames that may have sunk when they collided in the late fifteenth century; the better preserved of the two was built between 1380 and 1415, so had been carrying goods up and down the Thames and its tributaries for at least 50 years. It was only a little under 15 metres long, but over 4 metres wide, and although it had a keel and provision for a mast, it was very flat-bottomed and less than a metre high – it could not have gone out to sea but could have been sailed and poled quite far up rivers and could have been hauled over weirs where they impeded passage. Evidence of shipbuilding has also been traced at Small Hythe, Kent.[21]

A sea-going ship has been excavated in Newport, south Wales, where she was being repaired, or possibly dismantled, in 1467–8 – a very precise date obtained from dendrochronology of the timbers used to shore her up in the inlet where she was abandoned. Her beech keel was over 20 metres long; embedded in it was a deliberately placed French coin minted in 1447, chosen because it bore a text invoking God's name and displaying the Cross. All the other coins were Portuguese, as were the many pottery sherds found, so she had probably been built in Iberia and had certainly taken part in Iberian trade. She had provision for pumping water out of the bilges, perhaps not very efficiently as one of the exit holes had been blocked up. Small bits of stone shot suggest that she carried light guns, and someone owned a helmet on which there was a protective text, favoured by anyone crossing the sea. Fragments that may have come from a sand-glass for telling the hours would be indicative of various new navigational aids that helped

Europeans to make their journeys across the Atlantic and round the Cape of Good Hope.[22]

The threat of raiding from overseas and Henry V's expeditions in France renewed a perceived need for royal ships, rather than reliance upon impressed merchant vessels. The lower part of the king's *Grace Dieu*, built in 1416–20, still lies enshrined in mud in the River Hamble in Hampshire, where she was laid up to save maintenance. Her keel was around 125 feet (40 metres) long, so she was bigger than most merchant ships; her strength came from triple layers of clinker planking, needing nails over 8 inches long, a major cost. Her weight probably meant loss of manoeuvrability, as well as making her too costly for commercial work, so she could not be sold off for use other than dismantling. She is thought to have had one high main mast and a smaller one, and a bowsprit, demanding many men for handling her sails and rigging. The thickness of her planking protected her from bombardment, but whether she herself carried guns is a moot point; if she did, they would have been quite light and probably mounted on her fore and stern castles, although possibly also along her top deck: port-holes were yet to be introduced.[23]

Despite his Agincourt victory, Henry V was so worried about French raids that in 1416 he ordered construction of two towers, one of which partly survives, on either side of the entrance to Portsmouth harbour so that a chain could be stretched between them 'for the safe keeping of the king's ships'. This system was an alternative to the artillery towers within or attached to town defences as at Norwich or Southampton and was followed later in the century with blockhouses to guard river entrances like those on Devon's River Dart, the south-west becoming even more vulnerable to raids from south-west France and Spain; although named castles, they were not residences and were built at public not private expense. No royal ships are known to have been built again until the late 1480s, at the same time as a royal dockyard was established at Portsmouth, but its cost of £124 was nothing compared to Henry V's expenditure of over £1000 on the towers there in 1420–1.[24]

*

Churches were under threat in rural parishes as well as in towns, though most were retained because they offered provision for the afterlife, always likely to arrive swiftly and unannounced; cooperative parochial enterprises were many, soliciting donations and bequests. Financing of churches reflects an area's prosperity, the 'wool-churches' of the Cotswolds, Somerset, and Wiltshire, and the clothiers' churches of Suffolk being the most famous. The former, often being located in valleys, tended to make their statements by the height and elaboration of their towers, the latter by the flooding of light into their heightened naves through glass windows. Noticeably less money was spent by the Church on the chancels that were its responsibility, although rood screens to separate the priest's zone from the congregation's were increasingly used, some finely carved and painted. Despite building for prestige – church towers were 'liturgically useless' but contained bells that loudly reminded everyone of the Church's presence in their lives – patrons were conservative; no fifteenth-century East Anglian church displayed brick rather than stone, even though the predominance of awkward flint and the need to bring ashlar from a distance might have encouraged change. By contrast, the prosperity of Romney Marsh was much reduced by flooding, and there two churches used brick in their rebuilding. Contributing to church building was a means of being commemorated, donors being included in prayers. Gifts and bequests of visible items such as altar cloths or pieces of communion plate were more individual reminders, as were funeral monuments, from incised stone slabs to brasses and figural tombs; the last included *transi* or 'cadaver' tombs showing the living and the dead, but expressing hope in the Resurrection. Alabaster from the west Midlands augmented the output of the limestone quarries.[25]

Expenditure incurred on church naves was partly because preaching was important and sermons well-attended; several outside preaching-crosses survive to show that some churches were not large enough to contain all who wanted to hear. In London, outdoor preaching at St Paul's and at St Mary Spital drew crowds; trenches to support the timber galleries built at the latter in 1488 have been excavated. Nevertheless, private devotion and prayer certainly became more evident, even though Lollard teaching that a priest's intervention between Man and God at the confession was unnecessary died out. Great castles and houses had always included chapels, either as separate buildings or within a tower, and this practice spread to less grand manor-houses; some even allowed the owner's family to watch services from the seclusion of their own chambers. People who were less wealthy but nevertheless substantial maintained their own pews in their local church. Many more people mumbled prayers, repeating formulaic 'Ave Marias' which were counted off with rosary beads made of gold and niello for the wealthy, of coral or bone for the rest. New devotional cults suitable for personal contemplation were fostered, such as that of Corpus Christi or more prosaically the cult of St Apollonia to relieve toothache. The downside to these trends was that private prayers could become more like incantations and charms, even leading to witchcraft. Although greater output of books and tracts by printing only began late in the century, small manuscript prayerbooks and images for private devotion became widespread. Alabaster panels carved and coloured with crucifixion and many other religious scenes were not reserved for churches but, set within painted wooden frames, could be used anywhere. Silver spoons were not merely a display of wealth but made reference to the communion service and the Last Supper with end-knops modelled with the heads of Christ, Mary, or one of the saints; it became common practice to give them as wedding and christening presents.[26]

Spoons were not the only tableware that could have religious connotations within secular contexts. Silver cups, mazers made from burr maple or other high-quality woods, often fitted with silver or silver-gilt rims and enamelled base-escutcheons, drinking-horns, and containers for salt were frequent gifts or bequests, treasured items to be displayed on tables or sideboards and therefore to bring the donor to mind; if not left to a family member, a guild or college could be the recipient, for memory in perpetuity. The richest might go much further in creating a visible legacy: Archbishop Chichele, who died in 1443, not only founded a college in Oxford, but also at Higham Ferrers, Northamptonshire, his birthplace, with a school and an alms-house, creating a 'memorial landscape' for himself.[27]

Religion permeated society in other tangible ways. Often with a cross indented on the outside are small cased mirrors, which could have a range of different meanings, not least to warn against vanity as they encouraged superficial admiration of appearance – yet for the initiated could be seen as a reminder to look beyond the physical into the soul. They could also be used at shrines to catch the light and therefore to attract the attention of the saint. They are not common but were not exclusive to richer people, as they have been found on rural sites like Westbury where badges and ampullae show the importance of pilgrimage even to people who could perhaps not afford to go further than to a local shrine. Badges are frequent finds, and there are some examples of the *ex voto* models of the body parts that people hoped to have, or to have been, healed. By the end of the century, tin-glazed Delft pottery was being imported; its white background could be painted with images like the Sacred Monogram or Marian lilies, its pure finish reflecting Mary's purity; those small vessels could therefore have been used in private devotion. A widespread introduction was the purse-bar, from which to hang a bag; many had religious inscriptions or sacred images, though not specific prayers for the protection of the contents, which does not suggest deep understanding of the religious message.[28]

*

Although purse-bars do not necessarily indicate that more people were carrying coins, as draw-string bags were probably already widespread, they do suggest everyday use. The introduction of pottery money-boxes also suggests general availability of low-value coins. This is in contrast to the international problems of bullion supply, especially in the middle of the fifteenth century. The weight of the silver pennies was reduced, first in 1411 and again in 1464. A dearth of small change was partly offset by low-value base-metal 'Galley Halfpence', brought from Italy in ships from the Mediterranean together with their more valuable cargoes of silks and wines; copper-alloy jettons and tokens might also have been used. The numbers of single finds of coins reported show a marked decrease, but that is partly because groats and half-groats were more valuable and would have been more carefully looked after. That is even more true of the gold 'nobles' and their subdivisions, but another factor with them is that some designs had religious overtones; gold 'angels' were talismanic, showing the winged St George slaying the dragon and a biblical text, and therefore became a favoured donation or bequest to a church. Also taking bullion out of circulation were jewellery and plate, another factor to consider in assessing whether there was a bullion crisis; unfortunately, few records seem to survive from the fifteenth century, but Sir John Fastolf in 1459 had 13,400 ounces of silver items and 154 ounces of gold, as well as £2,643 10s 0d in coin. Plate could be used as pledge for credit, as well as display, and might even be taken abroad if ill-fortune befell its owner.[29]

Religious connotations cannot be ascribed to all domestic items: copper-alloy and pewter spoons for ordinary domestic use had acorn or other knops, if any, and not images of saints like the silver ones; those in London are noticeably of better quality than in the provinces. The increase in their numbers is symptomatic of changing dining practices generally; fewer knife scabbards may indicate that more people were keeping table-knives at home. Fourteenth-century trends towards the greater use of sauce-bottles and of dripping-trays to catch fat from roasting meat to make gravies continued. Roasting requires less tough meat than stewing, and in towns, people were eating tender beef from cattle slaughtered while still young. Stews and vegetable pottages were still a basic foodstuff but were more likely to be cooked in metal than in clay cauldrons, affecting the taste and perhaps boiling more quickly. Their use is one reason why fewer large clay cooking-pots are found, but other factors make the role of ceramics generally hard to assess; many rural sites have been excavated because they were abandoned during the late medieval recession, and large assemblages are therefore fewer. In towns, rubbish may have been more carefully disposed of, with stone-lined pits regularly emptied. Nevertheless, some trends can be seen, such as an increase in small jugs, which may have been used for serving individual portions of wine in taverns, or more generally for ale and beer, although the practice of passing a vessel from hand to hand continued at least at feasts (Illus. 11.3). Beer was stronger than ale and was brewed with hops, which made it last longer. Consequently, it was more likely to be produced by full-time specialists, many of whom were Dutch or Flemish, rather than by part-time domestic ale-wives, and on a bigger scale. An increase in larger pottery vessels with bung-holes at the base may result from their use to draw off beer from larger barrels and to allow dregs to settle before decanting into cups.[30]

Despite competition from metalworkers, woodturners, and leather-workers, some potters did quite well for themselves; two were members of the prestigious

Illustration 11.3 A selection of fifteenth-/early sixteenth century pottery products, smaller and more delicate than earlier vessels, and for a range of different purposes. They include (left to right) a tripod pan, probably for warming food; a small drinking-jug; a lamp; a money-box with a thin slit for the coins – it had to be broken to extract them; a whistle; a drinking-beaker; and a lobed cup.

Guild of the Holy Trinity at Coventry. Several pot- and tile-making enterprises were close to the town, the long-lived 'Potterscoton' having several kilns that have been excavated; potters there were prepared to experiment, using local coal rather than wood, and therefore needing kilns with three and even four flues instead of the usual two. Some of their fifteenth-century products were glazed dark purple or black, a type misnamed in the past as 'Cistercian ware'. A few new products were made, such as tripod pipkins – part of the trend to use smaller cooking vessels for more delicate dishes, and chafing-dishes for keeping food warm, either on a table or on a sideboard; both of those copied metal. Some found in Norwich may have been made at the well-established Grimston 'potting village', but the earlier complete dominance of the prosperous city's market was lost to new competitors, a fluidity that was fairly typical. Among the competition were imports, from Spain and Portugal for shiny lustreware, from the Low Countries for redwares and a few white tin-glazed vases, and from the Rhineland for hard stoneware, imported increasingly in the later part of the fifteenth century.[31]

Pottery imports like the lustrewares are colourful enough to have been used on tables, perhaps kept on display on a sideboard when not in use, like pewter, silver plate, and copper-alloy jugs with raised inscriptions and heraldic devices; one of the last, found in west Africa, presumably went there as 'trade-goods' when European ships began to open up an alternative to the trans-Saharan route which had for so long benefited Italy. The role of vessel glass is more difficult to assess, as it is not often found or recorded – perhaps it was too fragile and impermanent to have been suitable for bequests, although textiles were very carefully listed; the colourful enamelled cups that London merchants had displayed in the fourteenth century do not seem to have had an equivalent, although some Venetian imports are known. Glass was also used by doctors and apothecaries for uroscopy and distilling; the latter included production of mercury to treat syphilis, although alchemy was probably more widely practised. Such science was the preserve of people with special knowledge, but education was becoming more available, even at village level. Villagers were being drawn into the wider trading that lustrewares, stonewares, and other imported pottery imply; at Wharram Percy, for instance, stonewares were found in some numbers, unlike the two or three imported sherds from earlier centuries. Those villagers may have been making more use of the market in York at the expense of those closer to hand, a trend possibly seen more widely.[32]

Lustrewares were a minor addition to people's widening experience of colour. Stained glass transformed the interior lighting of a church, making more visible wall-paintings, painted tombs and screens, and painted alabaster panels. Enamels, niello, and gemstones became more frequent on gold jewellery, and although coloured dyes had always been used, clothing at least for the better off became more varied, with different textile pieces sewn together into a single garment. Even bricks played a part, bringing polychromy not only to aristocratic towers, but also to a few town gates as at Lynn – although the town faced the exterior with dressed stone to present a more traditional appearance to the outside world. The painted coats of arms and panels that were added to welcome important visitors to a town were another use of colour, and pageants provided another opportunity for display, as did processions on patronal saints' days. The costume for the parade of the giant Hob-Nob survives in Salisbury Museum, as does a fire-belching dragon in Norwich Castle.[33]

*

The extraordinary list of valuables owned by Sir John Fastolf was probably beyond the means of most earls and dukes, let alone an average knight's. Whether he aspired to higher rank is not known, but his building of Caister Castle, Norfolk, from 1432 onwards gave him a setting that would have been appropriate. Although its plan was not exceptional, its use of brick was; Fastolf might have chosen the material deliberately to emphasize that he was not claiming ancient lineage and an honour. The distinction between a grand house and a castle could be a fine one: in the 1440s, Lord Cromwell had a castle at Tattershall, Lincolnshire, and a manor-house in Derbyshire at Wingfield, yet both had towers; the former's was much less traditional, being brick with stone only for the openings and machicolations, whereas the latter's used only stone. Sir Roger Fiennes acquired Herstmonceux near the Sussex coast in 1438 to show that he was worthy of a barony, enlarging it into a four-courtyard complex, also making use of brick. The gate was the central focus of the approach across the moat; the symmetrical facade was difficult to achieve without total rebuilding such as few could attempt.[34]

Those with fewer resources might be able to afford updating to enhance the appearance of their house by building a new porch and adding projecting oriel windows, for instance, as at Nevill Holt, Leicestershire, in the 1440s where the owner also displayed his coat of arms and had lions and wild men with clubs carved where they could be seen and admired. Whether Herstmonceux was built to protect the coast from French attacks rather than to impress and outrank local competition from Bodiam and others is problematic; the south was less dangerous than the border with Scotland, the whole of which was vulnerable to raids by land and where towers were certainly needed for more than just display; some, like Clifton Hall, Cumberland, even had first-floor entrances which could only be reached by ladders that could be hauled up for safety. But Clifton already had a hall, to which the tower was added, and many seemingly solitary tower-houses or pele-houses may have been like it.[35]

Towers of course gave barons and their families views over their parks and estates, and a sense of their domination over them. For many, this may have been as important as the architectural setting and other people's views of their house or castle. Only a few parks were abandoned, despite the cost of maintenance; some new ones were made and others extended – hunting became more of a spectacle, with grandstands and viewing points. Manipulation of water also remained socially significant: Herstmonceux followed Leeds, Bodiam, and others by having a moat so close to the walls that the building was reflected in its water. Water was also manipulated at Kenilworth Castle by Henry V to create a spectacularly large pleasance (Illus. 11.4); this involved much more than creating a mere by damming a stream, as had been done at Sherborne and many others in the past,

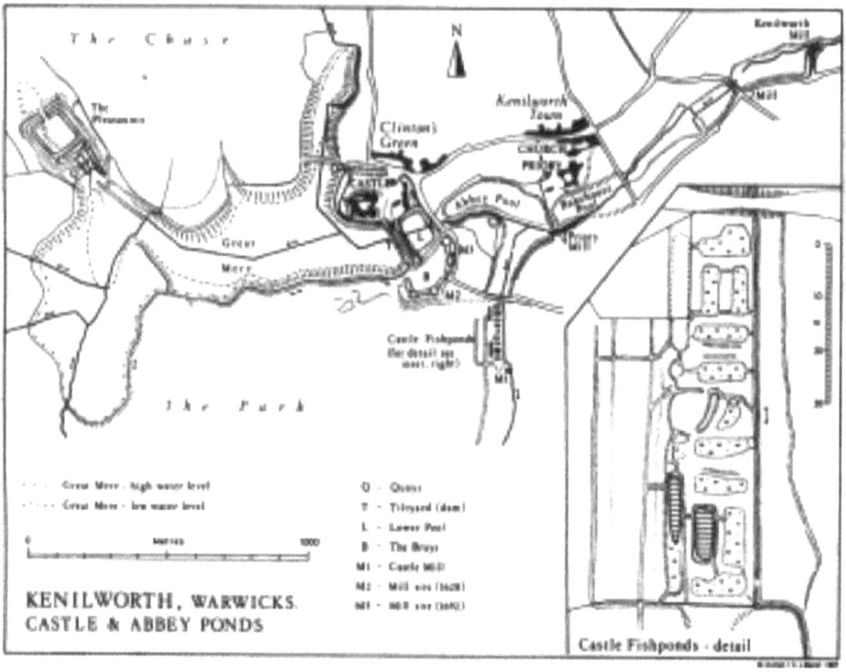

Illustration 11.4 The setting of a castle was always important, as a statement of power and control. One aspect of control was over the immediate surroundings and the views across them from the castle to the lord's deer-park, from which venison was supplied to guests. Fish-ponds not only supplied another prestigious foodstuff but attracted wildfowl that could be hunted with hawks and falcons. Streams and rivers could be dammed to create meres for boating, an extreme example being at Kenilworth where a moated platform was created that could be used for entertainment outdoors or within a tented pavilion (Plan by C. J. Bond and the late Mick Aston).

but constructing a large double-moated earth platform for a garden at one end, with a dock where pleasure boats could land. Rivalry with nearby Warwick was maintained in this, just as it had formerly been in building. Surviving earthworks at Bassingbourne, Cambridgeshire, suggest water-filled moats around a series of platforms and causeways, giving views and walks for the owner's family and his privileged guests – and the owner had spent time in Italy, so may have been influenced by what he observed there.[36]

*

The Wars of the Roses were fought to win kingship and to control the government, rather than to win territory, so sieges played little part in them; Alnwick resisted for a while, and Caister held out in 1469, as for two months did Powderham, Devon, in 1455, despite guns being used against it. After 1471, Edward IV was in a more powerful position, and castle acquisition was constrained, although Lord Hastings's Kirby Muxloe and Ashby de la Zouche were permitted exceptions; neither was completed, and the placing of gunloops below the water level in the moat at the former suggests a planning failure.[37]

Apart from castles, further evidence of the Wars of the 1460s to 1480s is in the battle injuries suffered by a group of men who were almost certainly casualties of the Battle of Towton in 1461, and in the insulting stabs inflicted on the corpse of a male buried in Leicester identified as King Richard III, buried with his wrists still bound and pushed into an underlength grave without a coffin. At least Richard was in consecrated ground, like other noblemen slain in battle; a trench or pit sufficed for the rest. The Towton group had most of their injuries on the head and neck, suggesting that they were not wearing helmets, perhaps because they were under-equipped, or because they had taken them off in order to run away more easily. Some of the wounds seem to have been inflicted when the men were already dead, perhaps done in the frenzy of battle, but perhaps their faces were deliberately disfigured so that they could not enter Purgatory in a state of human perfection.[38]

Coin hoards do not peak at the times of recorded battles, as they might if people had been panicked into hiding their wealth against sudden attack. One hoard that contained jewellery as well as over 1,200 gold coins was found at Fishpool, Nottinghamshire, and was deposited no earlier than 1461 and in or very soon after 1464, so might have been hidden at the time of the Battle of Hexham, assuming that the coins were drawn from money that was circulating at the time, not in a group that was 'closed' and not added to in a period of unknown length before deposition. Another hoard with jewellery and coins, found at Thame, Oxfordshire (Illus. 11. 5), contained silver groats of which the latest was minted in 1445–54, so is less likely to have been hidden because of a specific battle – but had been 'closed' for a very long time if, as recently suggested, it was taken from a monastery to hide it from Henry VIII's commissioners in 1538; it also had gold rings, one large enough to have been a container for a relic, concealed under an amethyst cross, but no gold coins were reported by its finders.[39]

One jewel in the Fishpool hoard was a tiny gold padlock, which contemporaries might have identified as a badge, the Yorkist 'fetterlock', but it was inscribed '*de tout mon coer*', 'with all my heart', an expression of loyalty that might have been for lovers or possibly from a retainer to a lord. French was often used for inscriptions on jewellery, although English had replaced it as the spoken language even in the highest circles; presumably it was a 'secret' between those who had the education to read it. A gold ring in the Fishpool hoard has '*de bon coer*' hidden on the inside; on the front, the bezel was deeply cut so that it could be used for sealing messages, but without the owner's name, so that the recipient was expected to recognize it from its device of a hawk's lure, presumably an aristocratic family's emblem. Badges were common in base metal and continued to play a major part in civil conflict, displaying affiliations. Even something as delicate as a gold and enamelled swan found at Dunstable – a tournament centre – would have been seen as the device of the Lancastrian party. Display of affiliation was necessary for protection, not only on the person, but also in buildings – town gates were

Illustration 11.5 The gold rings from the Thame hoard include a very large one set with an amethyst in the shape of a double-armed cross and an inscription in openwork gold letters on the top and round the sides, a prayer for remembrance. The ring has two small knobs allowing it to be opened, so it originally contained a relic. The other rings are not obviously devotional; the one on the bottom left holds a 'toadstone', thought to come from a toad's mouth but actually a fossilized tooth. The other stones are a peridot and a turquoise. The ring on the bottom right is inscribed with a love-motto in French, still the 'polite' language, *tout pour vous*, 'all for you.' The rings were found with silver coins, but their latest date, 1454, does not preclude a later date for deposition (Standley 2016).

embellished with painted badges and coats of arms of local landowners whose favour was sought by the corporation. Even churches were not exempt; stained glass roundels in the church at Tattershall, Lincolnshire, included a different version of the Yorkist fetterlock.[40]

*

Wars interrupted both internal and external trade, creating uncertainty and making sea transport dangerous. Despite the cost of importing salt from the Bay of Bourgneuf being reduced by the saving in sailing time, uncertainty over its regular supply helped to allow salt to continue to be produced in England, even as far north as the Lincolnshire coast, where excavation found a filtration unit comprising a trough filled with peat used to filter scraped-up sand so that brine water would drain into a vat ready for boiling. Inland, Droitwich saw the application of an early attempt at suction-pumping; excavation showed that the thirteenth-century lifting-gear was removed from the brine well, and two wooden pipes, supported on a massive beam across the top of the well and dated by dendrochronology to 1420–2, were lowered into it; one still had its iron piston inside. The pump mechanism did not survive but was probably hand-operated, as no water channel to power a wheel for it was found. By this time, mineral coal as well as charcoal was being used, and demand for that fuel was increasing; a remarkable complex of horizontal galleries accessed by horizontal shafts were exposed at Coleorton, Leicestershire, during modern open-cast mining. The roofs were maintained not only by leaving intermittent pillars, but also by the use of timber pit-props, which gave fifteenth-century dates.[41]

Pumping technology was inevitably of limited use because with only leather or textile valves, it would have been very difficult to make a fairly air-tight seal, but despite that it began to be applied to metal extraction; the value of silver led to the Bere Alston mines being suction-pumped by waterwheels fed by long leats that included tunnels like those used in Exeter. Silver and lead occurred together and had to be separated, with the lead then being further refined using ovens heated by bellows that were operated by water-wheels; water also powered crushing mills and blowing-houses for bellows that refined tin on Dartmoor and Bodmin Moor. A more significant introduction in the long term was the blast furnace for producing iron, first recorded in the Weald of Kent in 1496; until then, smelting seems to have been unaffected by technological changes in the fifteenth century, characterized by small-scale operations which probably only lasted until local supplies of wood for charcoal had been used up. An excavated complex at Rotherfield, Sussex, lasted long enough for the original furnaces to have been replaced by a complex that had a roasting hearth, a smelting oven within a stone-footed timber-frame building, a hut, and bins for storing charcoal. But the oven was only a metre in diameter, and water power was not applied, so breaking the ore and pumping the bellows were done by hand, limiting output. In Weardale, extraction pits show where the bishops of Durham tried unsuccessfully to establish a much larger estate industry.[42]

Blast furnaces produce cast not wrought iron, and the Crown presumably hoped to use it for making solid gun-barrels rather than the stave-built type, as the binding hoops were liable to snap under pressure; as a survival shows, a large solid cylinder breech was another construction problem. That gun had a barrel nearly 8 feet long and was over a foot wide in diameter. Firing of monsters like it meant that artillery towers would have to be almost impossibly thick-walled to withstand the recoil; Richard III, having taken control of Warwick Castle, began a gate-tower intended for guns, and, although not completed, enough of the lower part survives to show that its walls were no more massive than those of the curtain. The citizens of London were sufficiently concerned about the effect of bombardment that they strengthened the interior of the city's wall with brick arches in the 1470s, but no-one undertook the more effective but costly and very wasteful of space 'rampiring' that involved piling earth against them.[43]

Smiths may have made more kitchen equipment, such as iron griddles and trivets, but their range of products did not expand, nor did the quality of their work noticeably improve. The volume of imports of such everyday items began to worry the government; luxury goods for the wealthy were not a problem, but cheaper things that could be made in England were becoming displaced by manufactured goods from overseas, reducing people's ability to pay their taxes. Sumptuary laws began to try to restrict not only clothing and items of precious metal like brooches, but even everyday things such as 'locks, hammers, fire-tongs, dripping pans . . . ', itemized in 1473. Ten years later, 'no man under the estate of a lord shall wear any kind of woollen cloth made outside this realm', so even the most important domestic industry was perceived to be under threat.[44]

The fluctuations in the fortunes of the holders of the Crown in the second half of the fifteenth century are reflected in their stop-start building campaigns. Henry VI's Eton College and King's College chapel in Cambridge were left unfinished until the Lancastrians returned; the Yorkist Edward IV had the confidence to begin the huge new St George's Chapel at Windsor as an Arthurian setting for the Order of the Garter but did not have the time to complete his own chantry there, and the Lancastrian Henry VII was too mean to finish it for him. None of these kings tried to reverse the process of reduction in the number of royal houses that had been a trend since King John's time but focused their attention around London and Westminster and maintained much larger households than their predecessors, necessitating extensive lodgings, service provision, and stables. Only the archbishops of Canterbury aspired to anything quite so grandiose, as at their newly acquired Knole, Kent, but other bishops were constantly updating and enhancing their various residences. Henry VII's leading minister, notorious for 'Morton's fork', left his mark on Canterbury Cathedral by building 'Bell Harry', the great central crossing tower; it is harmonious because it was an entirely traditional perpendicular design, with no hint of continental ideas, although it was built in the 1490s to celebrate the archbishop's being made a cardinal by the pope.[45]

Henry VII followed tradition in building for his own commemoration, but the great chantry chapel that he added to the east end of Westminster Abbey is surrounded by a profusion of polygonal towers and windows, a striking design but not one that suggests new Renaissance ideas, unlike the monument by Torrigiano commissioned to go inside it. At Windsor Castle, an extension was added to the king's lodging suite to accommodate a new office of state, the Privy Chamber; the block echoes the Abbey in having polygonal corners with battlemented oriel windows on the third and fourth storeys, a striking but again not a Renaissance design. The well-lit first-floor long gallery that gave an internal walking-space at Richmond Palace, which was Sheen Palace renamed in honour of the king's descent from the earldom, was a more influential innovation. Henry may have been sensitive to his relatively humble origin, causing him to build at Woodstock and other places associated with earlier kingship.[46]

Signs of change in ideas about the social requirements of housing were creeping into towns. The open hall was becoming less of a requisite even for some of the well-to-do. Urban blocks with three or four shops on the frontage and chambers above might not have a traditional open hall behind, but were not therefore of poor quality, as they might have chimney stacks and fireplaces, decorative carpentry, and first-floor rooms suitable for entertaining. Some Winchelsea houses were built in the late fifteenth century without open halls, even in zones where there was plenty of ground space available; although elaborately carpentered, they did not have fireplaces. Perhaps surprisingly, those who did not have fireplaces do not seem to have adopted the Low Countries heating method using flat-backed stoves, as no fragments earlier than the sixteenth century have been found in a private house in England.[47]

Although some townsfolk were abandoning open halls, their example was not yet being followed in the countryside; both cruck and box-frame systems continued to provide for houses to have open halls. The open-hall tradition was far too established in England for gentry or aristocracy to adopt such a socially revolutionary change, despite what they experienced in France, although some smaller rooms may have been used for more private family dining, and in those fireplaces and chimneys were becoming preferred to open hearths. No one would have predicted in 1500 that such an old practice would have been abandoned by all except the highest in the land by the end of the next century. They would not have foreseen the impact on agricultural production that water meadows were to have from the few examples of streams being dammed to flood neighbouring fields, gaining nutrients and preserving early growth of grass from frosts. Nor would they have seen anything in religious practice to cause them to forecast the break with Rome, let alone Protestantism. They would probably not have placed their money on a Tudor still ruling England either, let alone a queen.[48]

Notes

1 Plague outbreaks: Hatcher 1977, 57–8. Leprosy: Huggon 2018, 845–6 (a world-wide study has been published subsequently by C. A. Roberts). Syphilis: Roberts, C. A. *et al.* 2018, 825; Harward *et al.* 2019, 164. Cade's rebellion: Harriss 2005, 619–21. The Percy family in the north had little interaction with the royal court, so were not dependent on its favours: Holmes, G. R. 1957, 50–2.

2 Mobility weakened any protection once offered by a vill's customary practices: Schofield, P. 1996. John Halle: Hare, J. 2011, 126–7 and 154–6; the hall, heavily restored by Pugin, survives within a cinema: RCHM 1980, 103–4.

3 Peasant property and display: Dyer forthcoming (a thirteenth-century statute required free men to maintain weapons; those kept in urban halls identified by Leech 2000, 17–18 is analogous). Twice as many cruck buildings survive in two Midlands counties from the 1430s–1470s (except the 1460s) than for any other decades: Alcock, N. and Miles 2013, 113, and the study by Moir *et al.* 2019 of a Shropshire village with both cruck and box-frame houses shows a peak in the 1450s. Different types of cruck, of roofing methods, and of carpentry show sometimes a bewildering range of differing regional practices.

4 See Dyer 2019b for discussion of lords/tenants building; seeAlcock, N. 2020 for a Devon example of a landlord rebuilding a three-bay house for a tenant at a cost of over £8, not including some of the timber. The theory that the fifteenth century was a 'golden age' for labourers was rejected by Hatcher 2011. Enclosure 'commodified' the landscape: Johnson, M. 1996, 71–9. Rabbits: see Ch. 10. Goltho and Barton Blount: Beresford 1975, 13–18. Low Throston: Austin, D. 1977, 21–30. West Cotton: Chapman 2010. An abandoned moated house in Warwickshire was in the wooded Arden so may have lacked agricultural potential: Smith, L. 1989–90; Penhallam, Cornwall, was collapsing

in the late fourteenth century or later (Beresford 1974; the Conclusion, p. 126, has a date of *c.* 1260, but that should have been 1360, the date of the jettons found below collapsed roofing, p. 143); its abandonment was probably because the estate was divided up (p. 97). The owner of Wintringham, Huntingdonshire, sold his estate in 1375 but negotiated a lease, so the house was probably not maintained for long afterwards and had no pottery suggesting use much after the mid fourteenth century: Beresford 1977, 196 and 246.

5 I have extrapolated the totals by decade of barns from the invaluable lists published each year in *Vernacular Architecture*: they are in the threes and fours in the first four decades, jumping to nine in the 1450s, five in the 1460s and twelve in the 1470s – but only two in the 1480s before ending with thirteen (one of which was aisled and of nine bays at Ovington, Hampshire, and cost the bishop of Winchester £47 – possibly because the lessee was a nephew: Roberts, E. 1996). A detailed contract between two carpenters and a butcher for a five-bay barn included provision of an upper room in one bay, perhaps sleeping space for a servant: Dymond 1998, 270–4. The north Oxfordshire group includes New College's Swalcliffe, dated by building records to between 1400 and 1407, the same college's Tadmarton, and Abingdon Abbey's Upper Heyford: Munby and Steane 1995, with discussion on pp. 374–5. Titchfield: Miles, D. H. and Worthington 1998, 119; many landowners retained a home farm to supply their own households, even if they leased all the rest of their estates. Harmondsworth: Impey 2017, with contributions on the dendrochronology by I. Tyers, p. 19; Harmondsworth faced refusal to work in 1450 and switched to leasing a few years later: Impey 2017, 58. Caldecote: Beresford 2009, 103–5 and 113–15. Harmondsworth barn's internal floor space is very roughly 7000 square feet, one of Caldecote's 800 – some crofts had two, some were a bit larger, but all would have been lower, so five to ten tenants would have produced the equivalent amount to Harmondsworth's tied labour . . .

6 London's Leadenhall was partly funded as a charitable endeavour by a merchant; it was not intended that grain should be given away as alms but sold at a fair price: Samuel 1989, 149. Almshouses: Huggon 2018, 850–1. The Paston letters show London's lawyers' importance to the provinces; debt records show how its capital was available throughout the country, unlike York and other provincial centres: Galloway 2005, 123–6 (and see Stevens, M. F. 2016 for how its withdrawal could affect England's economy overall); Schofield, J. 2011. Southwark: Carlin 1996; the area notably attracted immigrants. The 'East End': McDonnell 1978. St Mary Spital: Harward *et al.* 2019, 106–8 and 164–5.

7 Yorkshire houses: Hutton 1984. A few documents indicate the social significance of the hall to peasants and others for entertainment, contract agreements, and even for childbirth: Poos 1991. 84–6. Beverley: Evans, D. H. and Tomlinson 1992, 74–5; Kermode 1998, 18–20 noted a gentry element in the town. Bramall Hall dendrochronology: Arnold *et al.* 2013, 92–3. Summary of Manchester area in *Archaeological Journal* 144 (1987), 17–69. Cumbria's pottery is symptomatic of the area's relative wealth, with no imports: McCarthy and Brooks 1989b, 36.

8 See Holford 2016 for small markets and fairs. Leicester: Finn 2004, 25–41. Northampton: Williams, J. H. 1979, 145; Shaw 1996, 72–84. Copper-alloy metal casting: Saunders, P. and Algar 2017; in London, vociferous complaints were made about lead casting by nearby residents; the nuisance was not removed, but a higher chimney was demanded – 'whoever has smelt the smoke therefrom has never escaped without mischief,' so the health risk was known but little was done about it: Homer 1991, 65.

9 See Astill 2000 for urban decline. Sandwich: Clarke, H. *et al.* 2010, 165. See Jervis 2017b for discussion of issues affecting late medieval towns generally. Renters: Meeson and Alcock 2017.

10 See Ch. 10 for Wealdens; 'half-Wealdens' were an adaptation for restricted urban spaces in which the central open hall's two-bay space was divided between two prop-

erties, giving each a one-bay hall. Terraces were also appropriate for almshouses, for example perhaps two cruck-built rows in Much Wenlock, Shropshire, with fifteenth-century tree-ring dates: Moran 2010. Coventry's building: Meeson and Alcock 2017, 10; economy: Kermode 2000a, 453–4; Dyer and Slater 2000, 635–6; Bayley 1996; excavations: Wright, S. M. 1982; Miller and Radford 2020, 379–83. Textile summary: Britnell 2000, 319–20.

11 Shops and workshops: Alston 2004; Antrobus 2018; Goldberg 2019. Whether looms were more likely to be in better-lit and warmer upstairs chambers, away from the noise and dirt of the street, as they were later, is worth considering. Employment: Dyer 1991; Britnell 1992, 97; Thomas Spring of Lavenham was directly employing a workforce, but seemingly not in a centralized manufactory as was attempted at Malmesbury in the next century. As well as cloth, some linen was still produced, but it was not a major industry for England: Walton 1989, 348–52; iron flax heckles later than the thirteenth century have not been found in York: Walton Rogers 2002, 2732–4, but flax/hemp was still needed for nets, ropes, and sacking, with some places being recorded as producers, and retting pits been identified in Yorkshire and Humberside: Geary *et al.* 2005.

12 Inns for travellers provided accommodation as well as food and drink; taverns were for selling wine, often in the stone cellars built in earlier centuries, see Ch. 8; ale-houses were probably often people's homes: Hare, J. 2013; Roberts, E. 2021. Gloucester New Inn: Holt 1985, 77 (the inn was described as 'newly built' in both 1445 and 1455) and Nayling 2002, 79; Fleece Inn: Bridge and Miles 2017, 111; New Inn: Nayling 2002, 79. Canterbury, The Bull: Bennett 1984, 299–300 and 305–6; 1985, 252–3; the city owned an inn with new chambers in the 1430s: Salzman 1952, 511. Glastonbury: Grenville 2003, cat. no. 119. Norton St Philip: Williams, E. H. D. *et al.* 1987, but note revised dating by Penoyre 1998, 29–30. Andover: Roberts, E. 1991; Winchester College spent £400 on its Andover inn, for an annual rent of only £10. Road travel for individuals was hazardous if the government could not control robbery but was generally safer and quicker than by boats on rivers, or even by coastal vessels between ports, in which inns are rarely mentioned; Southampton had a 'hosting' system, so that foreign merchants mostly billeted with private citizens or fellow merchants.

13 Lynn: Parker 1971, 141–8. Stratford dendrochronology: Arnold *et al.* 2017, 100–1; almshouses were added to the guild's responsibilities at the turn of the century. A contract for the guildhall at Canterbury in 1438 specified the sizes of the structural timbers to be of heart oak, with a dais for the 'high bench' and two side benches; its two-storey 'geteyyed' frontage was to match that of a new inn on the opposite side of the street: Salzman 1952, 510–12. Stratford 'Wealden': Slater and Wilson 1977; Alcock, N. 2010, 39. Guildhall building seems to have all but ceased after about 1450, but whether that was from urban poverty or because there was no need for more is a moot point.

14 York: Giles 2000, and see Ch. 10; Merchant Taylors dendrochronology: Arnold *et al.* 2013, 95; Ormrod 2000b. Coventry: Quiney 2003, 219–20: the hall also has a tapestry, an example of the hangings that would have been in most halls. Guilds were not exclusively male, as a few widows or daughters of members were allowed to join, though not to become officials. Stratford's documents show the importance of its feasts: Woolgar 2016, 128–40. Guild hierarchy was reinforced by processions as well as in seating; see Rosser 2015 for overview. Clopton's bridge, which survives, and other fifteenth-century benefactions for bridges: Harrison 2007, 113–15, 196–8, and 204–5 for guilds' inclusion of bridge maintenance as charitable. (Bridges might be thought 'secular' and a contrast to the 'religious' foundation by an earlier London-based benefactor of the Carmelites at Coventry in the previous century, see Ch. 10). Exeter: Stoyle 2014, 47–75; Sandwich council bought a supply from the Carmelite friars, whose stone well-house sheltered a stone-lined settling tank from which the water ran partly in pipes and partly in an open ditch: Parfitt and Clarke 2016.

15 The excavated churchyard of St Martin's, Wallingford, went out of use after the collapse of the church building in 1412: Soden 2018, 7–8. Lincoln: Jones, M. J. *et al.* 2003; see Kissane 2017 for the documentary record; Spence 2013, 302 for Newport; Glover *et al.* 2014, 371–3 for Wigford. Winchester: Ottaway 2017, 357, 368–9, and 379–84; Rees *et al.* 2008, 401–2.

16 Brown, R. A. *et al.* 1963, 238–43.

17 See Quiney 2003, 235–68 for general discussion of late medieval urban housing of all types. Lynn: Parker 1971, 40, 67 and fig. 8 (the hall is attributed to the fourteenth century, the brick warehouse to the later fifteenth). Bristol: Leech 2014, 93–6; Baker, N. *et al.* 2018, 220–4 for William Canynge's house. Bristol has perhaps the earliest detailed bird's-eye vignette of an English town, drawn in the late fifteenth century; it emphasized walls, gates, churches, the central market cross, and jettied houses but ignored the ships and quays that gave the place its prosperity and fame – Edward IV had a carvel built there to use in trade with west Africa, and John Cabot's voyage to the Americas left from it in 1497: Grenville 2003, illus. 110; Baker, N. *et al.* 2018, 64–5, contribution by J. Brett.

18 Hussey Tower: Smith, T. P. 1979. See also Caister and Tattershall. Gainsborough Old Hall: Stocker 2018. It has been estimated that at least 34 towers were built in fifteenth-century England.

19 Sea-fishing methods: Hutchinson 1994, 129–34; Newfoundland could supply cod, the Channel Islands and Britanny hake and conger eel. Kowaleski 2000; Cod, hake, and conger eel bones predominate in the Exeter bone record: Maltby 1979, contribution by M. Wilkinson, 76; Exeter pottery: Allan 1984, 20–2; tin: Kowaleski 1995, 310–17. Pilgrims: Childs 1999 – Plymouth and Bristol were also major departure points.

20 Poole buildings: Horsey 1992, 34–48 and 58–9: see also Ch. 9. The south-west was also notorious for men like Harry Paye of Poole, who raided foreign shipping whether or not he was licensed by the English king: Rose, S. 2002, 82–4. Southampton carting and the Italians: Hicks (ed.) 2016, contribution by H. Bradley, pp. 65–80. Sandwich: Clarke, H. *et al.* 2010, 121–3.

21 Poole: Watkins 1994, 10–12 and contribution by G. Hutchinson, pp. 23–43; the timbers were still usable when lost, possibly flooded by rising sea-level. A useful new website developed at the University of Southampton, www.medievalandtudorships.org, has all known fifteenth- and sixteenth-century journeys recorded at every port in England; mostly they are customs accounts so do not reveal ships' sizes, but occasional entries give the tunnage, with most under a hundred tuns, a tun was a barrel, theoretically holding 240 gallons, but a ship's capacity could only be reckoned very approximately).and very few over 200. See Unger 1980, ch. 5 for European developments generally. Ships exemplify the Darwinian approach to technological change, that is primarily governed by cultural conservatism, as opposed to an adaptation of Lamarckism, defined as seeking solution to perceived problems, discussed in relation to mills by Langdon 2004, 66–8 and 131–5; he noted occasional willingness to experiment. Blackfriars barges: Marsden 1996. London tolls distinguished between a 'shout', probably like the Blackfriars barges, and boats, with half the capacity: Turner, H. L. 1971, 229. Small Hythe: Bellamy and Milne 2003.

22 Newport: Nayling and Jones 2014; dendrochronological investigation of the ship's timbers has found matches in Iberia, but a southern French origin remains possible; see also Jones, E. T. and Stone (eds) 2018. A vessel thought to date to the early sixteenth century found off Plymouth had a pump and guns that swivelled: Redknap 1984. Navigational aids: McGrail 2001, 247. England played only a late part in European long-distance ventures: Casimiro 2020.

23 Earlier royal vessels: see Ch. 9. *Grace Dieu*: Hutchinson 1994, 27–32 and 156; McGrail 2001, 244–5; she may even have had three masts. Ships' guns: Hutchinson 1994, 156–61; manuscript pictures show two forward-facing holes high in ships' bows, but as they

are empty, use for guns rather than, or as well as, for ropes is uncertain: Flatman 2007, illus. 92–3.

24 Portsmouth: Brown, R. A. *et al.* 1963, 792–3. Norwich: see Ch. 10. Southampton's God's House Tower was built in the early fifteenth century: Spencer, D. 2019, 176–7. Block-houses in the south-west: Higham, R. 1999, 141–2; Duffy, M. 1999, 158–9. Elements of Henry VII's *Sovereign* were probably found in Woolwich in 1912; although she was clinker-built, carvel building, with edge-to-edge planking and a different method of construction, was being practised in England before the end of the century: Adams, J. 2003, 50 and 65–7.

25 Overviews: Duffy, E. 2003 (the phrase 'liturgically useless' is from Duffy, E. 1992, 132); Aston, M. 2003; Wilson, C. 2003a, 113–16; see Byng 2017, 2–45 for financing and architectural styles; whether a difference can be seen between nucleated and dispersed villages' churches is an interesting question raised on p. 17; pp. 232–40 have a few examples of chancel rebuilding. Bricks' intermittent use in churches may have begun in the early fourteenth-century transepts at Hull; Smith, T. P. 1975, 130, cited early use of bricks in churches in Suffolk and Cambridge but suggested that they might have been plastered over; there is no entry for brick in Byng's index, and no churches feature in for example Moore, N. J. 1991; Romney Marsh churches: Tatton-Brown 1989, 259–64; part of the marsh was retained or reclaimed, so that its sheep could supply Kent's woollen industry: Eddison and Draper 1999. Monuments: Badham 2005. *Transi* tombs: Aston, M. 2003, 72 and illus. 105; Binski 2003, 437–8; Morgan 1999, 133–4; Andrews 2019, 1, cited a detailed instruction for one by a wealthy rector in 1448; see Rimmer 2019 for that of John Baret of Bury St Edmunds.

26 Lollardy: Bernard 2012, 206–9. St Mary Spital: Harward *et al.* 2019, 106–8 (the hospital was struggling to keep going, despite such crowds). Chapels: Platt 1990, 242–4. Rosary beads: Standley 2013, 64–9. Contemplative cults: Bernard 2012, 44. Prayer-charms: Duffy, E. 1992, 73–85; an image of St Apollonia in the Luttrell Psalter shows her garlanded with what on close inspection can be seen to be teeth – she had been tortured by having them pulled out, so understood what toothache sufferers endured: Camille 1998, 141–2. Prayer-books and panels: Foster 2003. Spoons: Goldberg 2008; Olva 2008; Gilchrist 2012, 125 and 144 (the spoon-knop tradition was so embedded that it did not succumb to Puritan bans on representation of saints); Woolgar 2016, 190–1.

27 Mazers: Woolgar 2016, 57–60; 2018, 442–3; Sweetinburh 2015; Marks and Williamson (eds) 2003, cat. no. 102 and nos. 179–94 for a range of other vessels; glass seems not to have been favoured – perhaps it did not acquire the status that came from family descent, as well as being highly breakable if a feast became rowdy. See Campbell, M. 2002 for bequests and donations to colleges. Heirlooms: Woolgar 2018. Higham Ferrers: Morgan 1999, 138–9; the men in the alms-house had to be 'clean of their bodies, without blotches, blains, or boils'; if they became physically imperfect they were expelled.

28 Mirrors: Hinton 2005, 211–2; Gilchrist 2012, 77; Standley 2013, 36–8. Pilgrimage: Yeoman 2018, including burials identified as those of pilgrims by the inclusion of scallop-shells and the like, pp. 651–5; Townsend 2003, 424–5 noted the proliferation of local shrines, often with images rather than relics; illus. 45 for wax survivals and cat. nos. 324–5 for a range of badges. Westbury: Ivens *et al.* 1995, figs. 149–57. Purse-bars: Williams, D. 2018, 4 and 11 for inscriptions and dating; also Standley 2013, 18 and 62–4.

29 Money-boxes: Mellor 1985, 75–6. Coin losses: Kelleher 2018, 521 – Period IX from 1412 to 1464/5 is the first since the twelfth century to have had such a low loss-rate; see Allen, M. 2017, tables 8 and 9, for values, which present a slightly different pattern, even more so when considered as an average per head of the much reduced population. Plate: Woolgar 2016, 177–88; Britnell 1992, 180–4. Fastolf inventory: Amyot 1827

(the gold count is my own; Sir John Paston, who compiled the inventory, could value the silver, much of which was gilt and enamelled, but not the gold). The range and quantity of metal items recorded by the Portable Antiquities Scheme broadly support the argument for consumption more generally: Oksanen and Lewis 2020, graphs on p. 128. Another indication of consumerism is that base-metal toys begin to be recorded: Forsyth 2005.

30 Base-metal spoons: for London, Egan 1998, 244–52 (this catalogue ends in the middle of the fifteenth century, because there are fewer London assemblages after that, in particular from the waterfront dumps as well as from pits: pp. 2–3, 6, and 11) and for the provinces, for example several at Meols: Griffiths, D. *et al.* 2007, 173–4. Knife scabbards: Cowgill *et al.* 1987, 34 and 61 (men still routinely carried daggers, not least the 'ballock' type: Hinton 2005, 250 and 363). Cooking and dining: Willmott, H. 2018, 699–704, and see Ch. 10. Lipid residue analysis has shown pig fat in dripping-dishes, dispelling any doubts about their identification: Evershed 1999, 197–9. Veal: Albarella 2005, 136–7; changes in the ratios of the ages at which animals died or were killed do not indicate a clear general trend to eating more tender meat from younger beasts – but relatively more people may have enjoyed the better cuts. Beer: Unger 2004 and see Ch. 10; at first imported, it was being brewed in London by 1391, predominantly by immigrants, who came to be much resented and victimized: see Ormrod *et al.* 2019 for the numbers and nationalities involved. Pottery cisterns:McCarthy and Brooks 1989a, 397–460. Leather jugs, later called 'black-jacks', were an alternative to ceramics but could not have bung-holes: Cherry, J. 1991, 312–14.

31 'Potterscoton' is now Chilvers Coton: Mayes and Scott 1984, with contribution by A. Gooder on the documentary evidence; her reference to two potters in the Coventry guild raises the issue of terminology, but by the fifteenth century a metals pot-maker was more likely to be termed a brasier. Norwich: Jennings 1981, 61. Grimston: Leah 1994, 117–18. Oxford's pottery continued to be supplied by the Brill-Boarstall potting complex but also faced new competition: Mellor 1997, 32–4. London's sequence is affected by the deposition problem (see note 30), but domestically was dominated by pottery from the Hampshire–Surrey border, which outstripped Cheam: Pearce and Vince 1988, 91; Tipton 2012; maiolica and lustreware – and even pots from north Africa and Syria or Egypt – had been reaching London from the late thirteenth century: Vince 1985, 81. Imports: Gaimster and Nenk 1997.

32 Consumables for show: Gaimster 1994, 286–92. Copper-alloy jugs: Hinton 2005, 234–5 (the jug from west Africa: Alexander and Binski (eds) 1987, cat. no. 726; it was among the 'spoils obtained at the last sacking of the Ashante capital', now within Ghana, and the British Museum 'secured it from the officer to whom it fell'; as it was looted, should it be repatriated to west Africa or remain in the country where it was made? To whose history does it belong?). Glass: Tyson 2000, 28 (the argument is very much affected by the London discard pattern, see note 30); I could find only one mention of glass in Sir John Fastolf's inventory, among all the gold, silver, other metals, and textiles – 'two little ewers of blue glass powdered with gold': Amyot 1827, 269; the only possible example in Northamptonshire wills is ambiguous – 'a red goblet' could have been stained or painted wood: Edwards (trans. and ed.) 2005, 20. Glass alembics: Tyson 2000, 168–9. Distilling was not used to produce alcohol to drink; alchemy was justified as a search for the perfect metal analogous to the search for perfection through prayer, as Tyson pointed out, but was also condemned as, like telling the future, the 'marvels of hidden things' had no basis in nature; astrology, the balance of the humours and apothecaries' spices to balance them, and charms to staunch bleeding: Rawcliffe 1995. Spices were also used to 'balance' foods: see Woolgar 2016, 336–7 for their variety. Alembics for distilling also become more frequent in the pottery record: Moorhouse 1972; Harward *et al.* 2019, 106–8 and 164–6, with contributions on the vessels used by L. Whittingham and J. Pearce, pp. 165–72. Wharram Percy imports: Hurst, J. G. 1979. Marketing: Astill 1983.

33 See Woolgar 2006, 155–78; Huxtable and O'Donnell 2018. Aristocratic transition to wearing black may have countered the more general displays of dyes, with 'sheen' still more important than colour. Coloured wall-paintings in churches and secular buildings were not new, of course: see Chs 9 and 10. Another form of display was ornamented fireplace surrounds, in carved but painted stone, as within Tattershall Castle; many abbots removed themselves from communal dormitories into their own suites, with such chimney fittings – many taken after the Dissolution for inclusion in nearby properties. Lynn: Turner, H. L. 1971, 127; James 1987; Creighton and Higham 2005, 195. Urban processions and pageants: Keene 2000b, 86–7; Barron 2000, 407–9; Kermode 2000a, 462; Wheatley 2004, 54–8; Gog and Magog challenged entry into London, as did Ascupart into Southampton: Rance 1986; Grimsby showed an image of the giant Grim on its seal: Pedrick 1904, 68–9 and pl. 3; Hob-Nob: Chandler 2001, 113. Towns also celebrated notional founders, such as Brutus of London, King Col of Colchester or King Lear of Leicester: Kermode 2000a, 462; York sent King Ebrauk out to greet Henry VII in the hope that the new Lancastrian king would overlook the town's support for his Yorkist predecessor, if it were explained to him that Ebrauk was of claimed British descent, as was Henry, from Arthur and Cadwallader: Attreed 1994.

34 Castles: Goodall, J. 2011, 351–7; Caister (despite having a castle, Fastolf stored much of his plate at a local abbey, a frequent procedure), Tattershall, and South Wingfield: Emery, A. 2005, 56–61, 308–16, and 449–59; Mercer 2020–21. Machicolation: Harris, J. 2009–10 Confidence in the possibilities of thermoluminescence dating is renewed by a result of 1453/5±15 years from a Tattershall brick: Bailiff *et al.* 2010, 168.

35 Bodiam, like Herstmonceux, was symmetrical but had been built on a new site. Clifton Hall: Fairclough 1980. Tower-houses: Dixon 1979; 1992; Ryder 1992 (terms like pele-houses and bastles are used to differentiate different types but were not used consistently by contemporaries). Nevill Holt: Hill, N. 1999, 258–9 (earlier work had included dividing the complex between four sisters; there was also a range that linked directly to the church, which was very unusual); 'wild men' were the stuff of legend, like giants. Town walls often had 'gret ymages wrought out of stone' overlooking the parapets to suggest well-manned strength: Turner, H. L. 1971, 93. See Ch. 10 for the 'Bodiam debate'.

36 Parks: Mileson 2009, 37–44 and 72–6. Kenilworth: Jamieson and Lane 2015, 264 for Warwick; see Ch. 10 for earlier competition (which might have been renewed after the king's brother Clarence was given Warwick, but for a close encounter with a barrel of wine). Sherborne's Mere was particularly extensive: White and Cook 2015, 2–3 and 124 (the castle is well-known from a fourteenth-century dispute over ownership, which the Bishop of Salisbury celebrated on his sepulchral brass as a victory won in combat – but he had actually paid large sums for it: ibid. 124). 'Pleasances' had already been used to describe features at Gloucester and Hereford. Bassingbourn: Oosthuizen and Taylor 2000.

37 Sieges: King, D. J. Cathcart 1988, 168–70; Goodall, J. 2011, 366–7; the Paston letters reveal how even a single well-armed and -trained man could be enough for stout defence. At Caister in 1459, the Paston family relative and patron Sir John Fastolf had 'three guns called serpentines'; their name suggests long, narrow barrels useful against individuals but less relied upon than crossbows and arrows: Amyot 1827, 270 and 272. Powderham: Higham, R. 1999, 141. Lord Hastings's work: Goodall, J. 2011, 374–8. The grandest new building was outside England, at Raglan, Monmouthshire, 1465–70: Goodall, J. 2011, 367–9.

38 Richard III: Morris, M. and Buckley 2013; Towton victims: Fiorato *et al.* (eds) 2007, 185–6 for the Purgatory suggestion.

39 Hoards and the Wars: Thompson, J. D. A. 1956, xlvii–xlviii. Fishpool: Cherry, J. 1973. Thame: Standley 2016, associating the coins with the cult of Henry VI, which might explain the exclusion of any subsequent Yorkist coins, p. 136, but not that of the non-inclusion of any of Henry's 1454–60 or 1470–1 ('restoration') issues; Standley's paper

would have appeared too late for consideration by Andrews 2019 (who took issue with Thompson's correlation of northern hoard deposition aligning with the earlier Scottish wars, pp. 57–60, but did not note that his general conclusions concurred with Thompson's that the fifteenth-century hoards do not directly reflect the Wars.). A processional cross, said sometimes to have been found on Bosworth Field and discarded there by one of Richard III's fleeing chaplains, is probably later in date and was found somewhere else: Hill, J. Ashdown 2004; Fosse 2013.

40 Fishpool: Cherry, J. 1973, 310–11 for the ring. Cherry, J. 1997, 260–1 noted the late medieval increase in the writing of private letters, such as survive from the Pastons and Stonors, for which seals would have been needed. Badges: Aston, M. 2003, 72–3 (cat. no. 87); Cherry, J. 2003, 204–5; Hinton 2005, 238–55.

41 Lincolnshire saltern: McAvoy 1994. Droitwich: Hurst, J. D. (ed.) 1997, 41–8, and 151 (a bad misreading of the data by Hinton 2018, 485 placed the pump into an earlier phase). Mineral coal: Parsons, D. 2018, 465–6, citing work by R. F. Hartley on Leicestershire; in Durham, extraction was pursued by the bishops on their estates, but these may not have gone beyond sinking pits, not risking shafts: see Brown, A. T. 2015 for the documentary evidence.

42 Metals: Mellor 2018, 437; Parsons, D. 2018, 461–2; Homer 1991, 60 and 63–4. Devon's silver output declined despite the technology, which had already included the 'turnbole', so that hearths could be rotated to face into the wind – but such hearths could only have been small: Allen, M. 2011, 125–6; Mayer 1990; Rippon *et al.* 2009. The output of lead increased considerably in the fifteenth century, particularly in Derbyshire and the north: Blanchard 1978, 19–21. Pumping on ships, see note 22. Blast furnaces: Geddes 1991, 173–4. Rotherfield: Money 1971. Weardale: Childs 1981; 13 tons of charcoal could have produced 24 tons of iron bloom, but the effort probably failed because demand could not justify the cost of production and transport.

43 The 1496 record is of artillery carriages, but guns soon followed: Cleere and Crossley 1985. Bombards: Blackmore 1987. Warwick: Goodall, J. 2011, 383 and 474. London: Schofield, J. 2011.

44 Iron kitchen products: Goodall, I. H. 2011, 304–12. The 1473 law listed many things that appear in peasant and artisan inventories even in Yorkshire, not the richest part of England: Dyer 2013; fifteenth-century households may have had more such 'stuff', including wooden furniture and textiles, on average than earlier, but comparability with Lay Subsidies and other records is difficult. Customs records show that manufactured iron goods really were being imported, as well as the raw material: Childs 1981; it may be that many of those imported items were cast rather than wrought and therefore harder and preferable – provided that they did not shatter. Fastolf's inventory specified that some vessels were French: Amyot 1827, 261. These 'mercantilist' protection measures seem not to have bothered about foodstuffs, unlike both earlier and later attempts at restriction.

45 See James, T. B. 1990, 144–54 and 164–5. Knole: Cohen and Parton 2019. See Hare, J. 2021 for other bishops (fifteenth-century churchmen were as involved in government as their predecessors but seem to have avoided the hatred that had led to the killing of some in the previous century, and they enjoyed more stability in the fifteenth century than secular lords who took part in battles).

46 See Wilson 2003a, illus. 70 for interior view of St George's Chapel nave and illus. 72 for the exterior of Henry VII's chapel at Westminster; Wilson 2003b, 143 and cat. nos. 3, 19 (Henry VII's badges and arms adorn King's College chapel because he paid for its completion in the 1500s), 23, 25, 28, and 29 (the monument belongs to the 1500s); see also no. 83 for the Windsor chapel and its internal provision for the Order of the Garter.

47 Winchelsea: Martin and Martin 2004, 141–5. See Dymond 1998, 274–81 for contracts spelling out new house requirements in Suffolk at Bury St Edmunds; but also in East Anglia, in Norwich, open halls seem to have remained the norm until the sixteenth

century, apart from very small one-room cottages on the outskirts and one central property with a chimney-stack providing back-to-back internal fireplaces – and which may have had a special function: King, C. 2010, 60–2. In later fifteenth-century Bristol, a clear distinction was drawn between 'hall-houses' and 'shop-houses', but the buildings themselves were not apparently different from those in other towns: Leech 2000; also see Leech 2014, chs. 5–6. A few London houses known from contracts already had first-floor halls: Pearson 2009, 7, and market-encroachment houses did not have space for anything else, ibid. 6–7 and see Ch. 10. In York, late medieval references to 'summer halls' may mean 'parlours', more intimate spaces than traditional halls: Goldberg 2019. Stove-tiles: Gaimster 1988, 316 (if any urban finds have been made since that publication, I have missed them).

48 See Barron 2002 for London. The hall was seen as having the chief role in holding a house together in 'oon formal, oon seemely, beuteful, eseful and comfortable habitacioun' in *The Reule of Crysten Religioun* by a bishop of Chichester (who was subsequently but not consequently charged with heresy): Greet 1927, 22. Lords' 'withdrawal from the hall' was a popular lament, but the use of smaller rooms is difficult to confirm from building plans: Heal 1990 has possible examples, as well as on entertainment at Christmas etc. of tenantry and the 'local poor': pp. 65–76. Stream flooding: Cooke *et al.* 2003.

References

Abdy, R. 2006. After Patching: Imported and recycled coinage in fifth- and sixth-century Britain, 75–98 in Cook and Williams (eds).

Abrams, L. and Parsons, D. N. 2004. Place-names and the history of Scandinavian settlement in England, 379–432 in Hines *et al.* (eds).

Abramson, T. (ed.) 2011. *Studies in Early Medieval Coinage 2: New Perspectives* (Woodbridge: Boydell Press).

Adams, J. 2003. *Ships, Innovation and Social Change: Aspects of Carvel Shipbuilding in Northern Europe 1450–1850*, Stockholm Studies in Archaeology 24/Stockholm Marine Archaeology Reports 3 (Stockholm: Stockholms Universitet).

Adams, M. 1996. The development of roof-tiling and tile-making on some mid-Kent manors of Christ Church Priory in the thirteenth and fourteenth centuries, *Archaeologia Cantiana* 116, 35–59.

Adams, N., Cherry, J., and Robinson, J. (eds) 2008. *Good Impressions: Image and Authority in Medieval Seals* (London: British Museum).

Addyman, P. V. 1964. A dark-age settlement at Maxey, Northamptonshire, *Medieval Archaeology* 8, 20–73.

Addyman, P. V. and Black, V. E. (eds) 1984. *Archaeological Papers from York Presented to M. W. Barley* (York: York Archaeological Trust).

Addyman, P. V. and Leigh, D. 1973. The anglo-saxon village at Chalton, Hampshire: Second interim report, *Medieval Archaeology* 17, 1–25.

Addyman, P. V. and Priestley, J. 1977. Baile Hill, York, *Archaeological Journal* 134, 115–56.

Agate, A., Duggan, M., Roskams, S., and Turner, S. 2012. Early medieval settlement at Mothecombe, Devon: The interaction of local, regional and long-distance dynamics, *Archaeological Journal* 169, 343–94.

Ager, B. 1985. The smaller variants of the anglo-saxon quoit brooch, *Anglo-Saxon Studies in Archaeology and History* 4, 1–58.

Ager, B. 2020. The Carolingian cup from the Vale of York viking Hoard: Origins of its form and decorative features, *Antiquaries Journal* 100, 86–108.

Alban, J. R. 1981. English coastal defence: Some fourteenth-century modifications within the system, 57–78 in Griffiths (ed.).

Albarella, U. 1997. Size, power, wool and veal: Zooarchaeological evidence for later medieval innovations, *Papers of the Medieval Brugge Conference* 9, 19–35.

Albarella, U. 2005. Meat production and consumption in town and country, 131–48 in Giles and Dyer (eds).

Alcock, L. 1995. *Cadbury Castle, Somerset: The Early Medieval Archaeology* (Cardiff: University of Wales Press).

Alcock, N. 2010. The distribution and dating of Wealden houses, *Vernacular Architecture* 41, 37–44.

Alcock, N. 2019a. The discovery of crucks, 1–19 in Alcock, Barnwell, and Cherry (eds).

Alcock, N. 2019b. Crucks: Dating, documents and origins, 97–134 in Alcock, Barnwell, and Cherry (eds).

Alcock, N. 2020. Building a cob house in Devon in 1461, *Vernacular Architecture* 51, 23–9.

Alcock, N. and Miles, D. 2013. *The Medieval Peasant House in Midland England* (Oxford/ Oakville: Oxbow Books).

Alcock, N., Barnwell, P. S., and Cherry, M. (eds) 2019. *Cruck Building: A Survey*, Rewley House Studies in the Historic Environment 11 (Donington: Shaun Tyas).

Alexander, J. and Binski, P. (eds) 1987. *Age of Chivalry. Art in Plantagenet England 1200-1400* (London: Royal Academy of Arts).

Algar, D. and Saunders, P. 2014. A medieval pottery kiln in Salisbury, Wiltshire, *Wiltshire Archaeological and Natural History Magazine* 107, 146–55.

Allan, J. P. 1984. *Medieval and Post-Medieval Finds from Exeter, 1971–80*, Exeter Archaeological Report 3 (Exeter: Exeter City Council/University of Exeter).

Allan, J. P., Henderson, C., and Higham, R. 1984. Saxon Exeter, 385–214 in Haslam (ed.).

Allen, D. and Stoodley, N. 2010. Odiham Castle, Hampshire: Excavations 1981–85, *Proceedings of the Hampshire Field Club and Archaeological Society* 65, 23–101.

Allen, M. 2011. Silver production and the money supply in England and Wales, 1086–c. 1500, *Economic History Review* 64i, 114–31.

Allen, M. 2012. *Mints and Money in Medieval England* (Cambridge: Cambridge University Press).

Allen, M. 2017. The first Sterling area, *Economic History Review* 701, 79–100.

Allen, M. [a] *et al.* 2017. *The Rural Economy of Roman Britain*, Britannia Monograph Series 30 (London: Society for the Promotion of Roman Studies).

Allen, S. J. *et al.* 2005. Reused boat planking from a thirteenth-century revetment in Doncaster, South Yorkshire, *Medieval Archaeology* 49, 281–304.

Allen, T. G. 1994. A medieval grange of Abingdon Abbey at Dean, Court Farm, Cumnor, Oxon, *Oxoniensia* 59, 219–447.

Allen, T. G. 2002. *The Excavation of a Medieval Manor House of the Bishops of Winchester at Mount House, Witney, Oxfordshire, 1984–92*, Thames Valley Landscapes Monograph 13 (Oxford: Oxford University School of Archaeology).

Alston, L. 2004. Late medieval workshops in East Anglia, 38–59 in Barnwell *et al.* (eds).

Amyot, T. 1827. Two rolls containing an inventory of the effects of Sir John Fastolfe, *Archaeologia* 21, 232–80.

Anderson, W. 2010. Blessing the fields? A study of late medieval ampullae from England and Wales, *Medieval Archaeology* 54, 182–203.

Anderton, M. (ed.) 1999. *Anglo-Saxon Trading Centres: Beyond the Emporia* (Glasgow: Cruithne Press).

Andrews, D. D. and Milne, J. G. (eds) 1979. *Wharram: A Study of Settlement on the Yorkshire Wolds. Volume I: Domestic Settlement, 1: Areas 10 and 6*, Society for Medieval Archaeology Monograph Series 8 (Leeds: S. M. A.).

Andrews, M. 2019. *Coin Hoarding in Medieval England and Wales,* c. *973–1544: Behaviours, Motives, and Mentalités*, British Archaeological Reports British Series 651 (Oxford: BAR Publishing).

Annable, F. K. and Eagles, B. N. 2010. *The Anglo-Saxon Cemetery at Blacknall Field, Pewsey, Wiltshire*, Wiltshire Archaeological and Natural History Society Monograph 4 (Devizes: W. A. N. H. S.).

Antrobus, A. 2018. Medieval shops, 312–24 in Gerrard and Gutiérrez (eds).

Archibald, M. M. 1995. The coins, 48–53 in Rogerson.

Archibald, M. M. 1998. Two ninth-century viking weights found near Kingston, Dorset, *British Numismatic Journal* 68, 11–20.

Archibald, M. M. and Cook, B. J. 2001. *English Medieval Coin Hoards: I. Cross and Crosslets, Short Cross and Long Cross Hoards*, British Museum Occasional Paper 87 (London: B. M.).

Archibald, M. M., Lang, J. R. S., and Milne, G. 1995. Four early medieval coin dies from the London waterfront, *Numismatic Chronicle* 155, 163–200.

Armstrong, P., Tomlinson, D., and Evans, D. H. 1991. *Excavations at Lurk Lane, Beverley, 1979–82*, Sheffield Excavation Reports 1 (Sheffield: J. R. Collis Publications).

Arnold, A., Howard, R., and Litton, C. 2012. List 244: Dates from the Nottingham Tree-Ring Dating Laboratory, *Vernacular Architecture* 43, 87–94.

Arnold, A., Howard, R., and Litton, C. 2013. List 252: Dates from the Nottingham Tree-Ring Dating Laboratory, *Vernacular Architecture* 44, 91–6.

Arnold, A., Howard, R., and Litton, C. 2017. List 292: Dates from the Nottingham Tree-Ring Dating Laboratory, *Vernacular Architecture* 48, 94–103.

Arthur, P. 2021. The effect of the Black Death of 1348–49 on the fair of St Giles, Winchester, 95–106 in Richardson, A.[a] and Allen (eds).

Ashbee, J. A. 2004. 'The chamber called *Gloriette*': Living at leisure in thirteenth- and fourteenth-century castles, *Journal of the British Archaeological Association* 157, 17–40.

Ashbee, J. A. 2021. King Edward I and the water-gate at the Tower of London, 59–74 in Richardson, A.[a] and Allen (eds).

Ashby, S. 2013. Making a good comb: Mercantile identity in ninth- to eleventh-century England, 193–208 in Hadley and ten Harkel (eds).

Ashworth, H. 1998. *Excavation of a Medieval Pottery Kiln at the Rear of 93–98 Bancroft, Hitchin, Herts* (St Albans: St Albans and Hertfordshire Archaeological Society).

Astill, G. G. 1978. *Historic Towns in Berkshire: An Archaeological Appraisal*, Publication 2 (Reading: Berkshire Archaeological Committee).

Astill, G. G. 1983. Economic change in later medieval England: An archaeological review, 217–47 in Aston (ed.).

Astill, G. G. 1993. *A Medieval Industrial Complex and Its Landscape: The Metalworking Watermills and Workshops of Bordesley Abbey*, Council for British Archaeology Research Report 92 (York: C. B. A.).

Astill, G. G. 2000. Archaeology and the late medieval urban decline, 214–34 in Slater (ed.).

Astill, G. G. 2009. Medieval towns and urbanization, 255–70 in Gilchrist and Reynolds (eds).

Astill, G. G. 2018. Overview: Geographies of Medieval Britain, 69–85 in Gerrard and Gutiérrez (eds).

Astill, G. G., Hirst, S., and Wright, S. M. 2004. The Bordesley Abbey Project reviewed, *Archaeological Journal* 161, 106–58.

Aston, M. (ed.) 1988. *Fish, Fisheries, and Fish-Ponds in Medieval England*, British Archaeological Reports British Series 182 (Oxford: B. A. R.).

Aston, M. 1994. Corpus Christi and Corpus Regni: Heresy and the Peasants' Revolt, *Past and Present* 143, 3–47.

Aston, M. 2003. The use of images, 68–75 in Marks and Williamson (eds).

Aston, T. H. (ed.) 1983. *Social Relations and Ideas: Essays in Honour of R. H. Hilton* (London: Past and Present Society).

Atkins, R. 2021. Northampton's chequered history, *Current Archaeology* 377, 20–6.
Attreed, L. 1994. The politics of welcome: Ceremonies and constitutional development in later medieval English towns, 208–31 in Hanawalt and Reyerson (eds).
Audouy, M. and Chapman, A. (eds) 2009. *Raunds: The Origins and Growth of a Midland Village A. D. 450–1500* (Oxford: Oxbow Books).
Austin, D. 1977. Low Throston II: Excavation on a deserted medieval hamlet, *Transactions of the Architectural and Archaeological Society of Durham and Northumberland* 4, 21–30.
Austin, D. 1984. The castle and the landscape: Annual lecture to the Society for Landscape Studies, May 1984, *Landscape History* 6, 69–81.
Austin, D. 1989. *The Deserted Medieval Village of Thrislington, County Durham: Excavations 1973–1974*, Society for Medieval Archaeology Monograph 12 (Leeds: S. M. A.).
Austin, M. 2014. Rethinking Hardown Hill: Our westernmost early anglo-saxon cemetery?, *Antiquaries Journal* 94, 49–69.
Ayers, B. 2011. The growth of an urban landscape: Recent research in early medieval Norwich, *Early Medieval Europe* 19, 62–90.
Ayers, B. S., Smith, R., and Tillyard, M. 1988. The Cow Tower, Norwich: A detailed survey and partial reinterpretation, *Medieval Archaeology* 32, 184–207.
Ayre, J. and Wroe-Brown, R. 2015a. The post-Roman foreshore and the origins of the late Saxon waterfront and dock of Aethelred's Hithe: Excavations at Bull Wharf, City of London, *Archaeological Journal* 172, 121–94.
Ayre, J. and Wroe-Brown, R. 2015b. The eleventh- and twelfth-century waterfront and settlement at Queenhythe: Excavations at Bull Wharf, City of London, *Archaeological Journal* 172, 195–272.
Babb, L. 1997. A thirteenth-century brooch hoard from Hambleden, Buckinghamshire, *Medieval Archaeology* 41, 23–36.
Backhouse, J. 1989. *The Luttrell Psalter* (London: British Library).
Backhouse, J., Turner, D. H., and Webster, L. (eds) 1984. *The Golden Age of Anglo-Saxon Art: 966–1066* (London: British Museum Publications).
Badham, S. 2005. Evidence for the minor funerary monument industry 1100–1500, 165–95 in Giles and Dyer (eds).
Badham, S. and Norris, M. 1999. *Early Incised Brasses from the London Marblers*, Society of Antiquaries of London Research Report 60 (London: S o. A. L.).
Bailey, M. 1989. *A Marginal Economy* (Cambridge: Cambridge University Press).
Bailey, M. 1990. Coastal fishing off south-east Suffolk in the century after the Black Death, *Proceedings of the Suffolk Institute for Archaeology and History* 37, 102–14.
Bailey, R. N. 1996. *England's Earliest Sculptors*, Publications of the Dictionary of Old English 5 (Toronto: Pontifical Institute for Medieval Studies, University of Toronto).
Bailiff, I. K. *et al.* 2010. Uses and recycling of brick in medieval and Tudor English buildings: Insights from the application of luminescence dating and new avenues for further research, *Archaeological Journal* 167, 165–96.
Baillie, M. 1999. *Exodus to Arthur: Catastrophic Encounters with Comets* (London: B. T. Batsford).
Baker, J. 2017. Old English *sæte* and the historical significance of 'folk' names, *Early Medieval Europe* 25iv, 417–42.
Baker, N. and Holt, R. 2004. *Urban Growth and the Medieval Church: Gloucester and Worcester* (Aldershot/Burlington: Ashgate).
Baker, N., Brett, J., and Jones, R. 2018. *Bristol: A Worshipful Town and Famous City: An Archaeological Assessment* (Oxford/Philadelphia: Oxbow Books).

Banham, D. 2010. 'In the sweat of thy brow shalt thou eat bread': Cereals and cereal production in the anglo-saxon landscape, 175–92 in Higham and Ryan (eds).

Banham, D. and Faith, R. 2014. *Anglo-Saxon Farms and Farming* (Oxford: Oxford University Press).

Barber, B., Bowsher, D., and Whitaker, K. 1990. Recent excavations of a cemetery of *Londinium*, *Britannia* 21, 1–12.

Barber, R. and Barker, J. 1989. *Tournaments: Jousts, Chivalry and Pageants in the Middle Ages* (Woodbridge: Boydell Press).

Barclay, C. 2007. A review of the medieval coins and jetons from Wharram Percy, 301–3 in Mays *et al.*

Barker, J. 2014. *England, Arise: The People, the King and the Great Revolt of 1381* (London: Little Brown).

Barker, P. A., Cubberley, A. L., Crowfoot, E., and Ralegh Radford, C. A. 1974. Two burials under the refectory of Worcester Cathedral, *Medieval Archaeology* 18, 146–51.

Barnwell, P. S. 2005. Anglian Yeavering: a continental perspective, 174–84 in Frodsham and O'Brien (eds).

Barnwell, P. S. 2019. Trees and crucks: A speculation, 359–76 in Alcock *et al.* (eds).

Barnwell, P. S., Palmer, M., and Airs, M. (eds) 2004. *The Vernacular Workshop: From Craft to Industry 1400–1900*, Council for British Archaeology Research Report 140 (York: C. B. A.).

Barrett, J. H. 2018. Medieval fishing and fish trade, 128–40 in Gerrard and Gutiérrez (eds).

Barrett, J. H. and Gibbon, S. J. (eds) 2015. *Maritime Societies of the Viking and Medieval Worlds*, Society for Medieval Archaeology Monograph 37 (Leeds: Maney).

Barron, C. M. 2000. London 1300–1540, 395–440 in Palliser (ed.).

Barron, C. M. 2002. Chivalry, pageantry and merchant culture in medieval London, 195–218 in Coss and Keen (eds).

Barrow, G. 1989. Frontier and settlement: Which influenced which? England and Scotland 1100–1300, 1–18 in Bartlett and MacKay (eds).

Barrow, J. 2000. Churches, education and literacy in towns, 127–52 in Palliser (ed.).

Bartholomew, P. 1982. Fifth-century facts, *Britannia* 13, 261–70.

Bartlett, R. 2000. *England under the Norman and Angevin Kings, 1075–1225* (Oxford: Clarendon Press).

Bartlett, R. and MacKay, A. (eds) 1989. *Medieval Frontier Societies* (Oxford: Clarendon Press).

Bassett, S. R. 1982. *Saffron Walden: Excavations and Research 1972–80*, Chelmsford Archaeological Trust Monograph 2/Council for British Archaeology Research Report 45 (London: Council for British Archaeology).

Bassett, S. R. 2008. The middle and late anglo-saxon defences of western Mercia, *Anglo-Saxon Studies in Archaeology and History* 15, 180–239.

Bathe, G. 2012. The Savernake horn, *Wiltshire Archaeological and Natural History Society Magazine* 105, 168–81.

Bayless, M. 2016. The Fuller brooch and anglo-saxon depictions of dance, *Anglo-Saxon England* 45, 183–201.

Bayley, J. 1996. Innovation in later medieval urban metalworking, *Journal of the Historical Metallurgy Society* 30ii, 67–71.

Bayley, J. 2000. Saxon glass working at Glastonbury Abbey, 161–8 in Price (ed.).

Bayley, J. and Watson, J. 2009. Emerging from the appendices: The contributions of scientific examination and analysis to medieval archaeology, 63–81 in Gilchrist and Reynolds (eds).

Bedos-Rezalc, B. M. (ed.) 2018. *Seals: Making and Marking Connections across the Mediterranean World* (Amsterdam: Arc Humanities Press).

Behr, C. 2010. New bracteate finds from early anglo-saxon England, *Medieval Archaeology* 54, 34–88.

Behr, C. 2011. An unusual new gold A-bracteate from Scalford, Leicestershire, 1–6 in Brookes *et al.* (eds).

Behr, C. and Pestell, T. 2014. The bracteate hoard from Binham: An early anglo-saxon Central Place?, *Medieval Archaeology* 58, 44–77.

Bellamy, P. S. and Milne, G. 2003. An archaeological evaluation of the medieval shipyard facilities at Small Hythe, *Archaeologia Cantiana* 123, 353–82.

Bennett, P. 1980. 68–69a Stour Street, *Archaeologia Cantiana* 96, 406–10.

Bennett, P. 1984. Interim report on the work in 1984 of the Canterbury Archaeological Trust, *Archaeologia Cantiana* 101, 277–312.

Bennett, P. 1985. Interim report on the work carried out in 1985 by the Canterbury Archaeological Trust, *Archaeologia Cantiana* 102, 233–56.

Bennett, P., Frere, S. S., and Stow, S. 1982. *Excavations at Canterbury Castle*, Archaeology of Canterbury 1 (Canterbury: Kent Archaeological Society).

Beresford, G. 1974. The medieval manor of Penhallam, Jacobstow, Cornwall, *Medieval Archaeology* 18, 90–145.

Beresford, G. 1975. *The Medieval Clay-Land Village: Excavations at Goltho and Barton Blount*, Society for Medieval Archaeology Monograph Series 6 (Leeds: S. M. A.).

Beresford, G. 1977. Excavations of a moated house at Wintringham, Huntingdonshire, *Archaeological Journal* 134, 194–286.

Beresford, G. 1987. *Goltho: The Development of an Early Medieval Manor* c. *850–1150* (London: Historic Monuments and Buildings Commission for England).

Beresford, G. 2009. *Caldecote: The Development and Desertion of a Hertfordshire Village*, Society for Medieval Archaeology Monograph Series 28 (Leeds: S. M. A.).

Beresford, M. W. 1967. *New Towns of the Middle Ages* (London: Lutterworth Press).

Bernard, G. W. 2012. *The Late Medieval Church: Vitality and Vulnerability before the Break with Rome* (London/New Haven: Yale University Press).

Berridge, P. 2016. Colchester Castle: 'Some tyme statelye, as the ruynes do shewe', 55–68 in Davies *et al.* (eds).

Bertram, J. 2007. From Duccius to Daubernon: Ancient antecedents of monumental brass design, 219–28 in Gilmour (ed.).

Biddick, K. (ed.) 1985. *Archaeological Approaches to Medieval Europe* (Kalamazoo: Michigan University Press).

Biddle, M. 1961–62. The deserted medieval village of Seacourt, Berkshire, *Oxoniensia* 26/27, 70–201.

Biddle, M. (ed.) 1990. *Object and Economy in Medieval Winchester*, Winchester Studies 7.ii (Oxford: Clarendon Press).

Biddle, M. 2018. Old Minster at Winchester and the Tomb of Christ, 45–56 in Jervis (ed.).

Biddle, M. and Clayre, B. 2006. *The Castle, Winchester, Great Hall and Round Table* (Winchester: Hampshire County Council).

Biddle, M. and Kjølbye-Biddle, B. 1985. The Repton stone, *Anglo-Saxon England* 14, 232–92.

Biddle, M. and Kjølbye-Biddle, B. 1992. Repton and the vikings, *Antiquity* 66, 36–51.

Biddle, M. and Kjølbye-Biddle, B. 1995. Winchester, 273–327 in Tweddle.

Bidwell, P. T. 1979. *The Legionary Bath-House and and Basilica and Forum at Exeter*, xeter Archaeological Reports 1 (Exeter: Exeter City Council/University of Exeter).

Biggam, C. P. 2006. Knowledge of whelk dyes and pigments in anglo-saxon England, *Anglo-Saxon England* 35, 23–56.
Binski, P. 1987. The stylistic sequence of London medieval figure brasses, 69–132 in Coales (ed.).
Binski, P. 1996. *Medieval Death: Ritual and Representation* (London: British Museum Press).
Binski, P. 2003. The art of death, 436–55 in Marks and Williamson (eds).
Bintley, M. D. J. 2015. The translation of St Oswald's relics to New Minster, Gloucester, *Anglo-Saxon Studies in Archaeology and History* 19, 173–83.
Bintley, M. D. J. and Shapland, M. G. (eds) 2013. *Trees and Timber in the Anglo-Saxon World* (Oxford: Oxford University Press).
Birbeck, V. 2005. *The Origins of Mid-Saxon Southampton: Excavations at the Friends Provident St Mary's Stadium 1998–2000* (Salisbury: Wessex Archaeology).
Birch, T. 2013. Does pattern-welding make anglo-saxon swords stronger?, 127–34 in Dungworth and Doonan (eds).
Birley, A. 2014. *Brigomaglos* and *Riacus*: A brave new world? The balance of power at post-Roman Vindolanda, 195–215 in Haarer (ed.).
Birrell, J. 1996. Peasant deer poachers in the medieval forest, 68–88 in Britnell and Hatcher (eds).
Birrell, J. 2010. Confrontation and negotiation in a medieval village: Alrewas before the Black Death, 197–211 in Goddard *et al.* (eds).
Blackburn, M. A. S. 1998. The London mint in the reign of Alfred, 105–24 in Blackburn and Dumville (eds).
Blackburn, M. A. S. 2003. Alfred's coinage reforms in context, 199–217 in Reuter (ed.).
Blackburn, M. A. S. 2004. The coinage of Scandinavian York, 325–49 in Hall *et al.*
Blackburn, M. A. S. 2011. Coinage in its archaeological context, 580–99 in Hamerow *et al.* (eds).
Blackburn, M. A. S. (ed.) 1986. *Anglo-Saxon Monetary History: Essays in Memory of Michael Dolley* (Leicester: Leicester University Press).
Blackmore, H. L. 1987. The Boxted bombard, *Antiquaries Journal* 67i, 86–96.
Blackmore, L., Blair, I., Hirst, S., and Scull, C. 2019. *The Prittlewell Princely Burial: Excavations at Priory Crescent, Southend-on-Sea, Essex, 2003*, Museum of London Archaeology Monograph 73 (London: Museum of London).
Blair, C. and Blair, J. 1991. Copper alloys, 81–106 in Blair and Ramsay (eds).
Blair, J. 1987. English monumental brasses before 1350: Types, patterns and workshops, 133–74 in Coales (ed.).
Blair, J. 1995. Anglo-Saxon pagan shrines and their prototypes, *Anglo-Saxon Studies in Archaeology and History* 8, 1–28.
Blair, J. 1996. Palaces or minsters? Northampton and Cheddar reconsidered, *Anglo-Saxon England* 25, 97–121.
Blair, J. 2005. *The Church in Anglo-Saxon Society* (Oxford: Oxford University Press).
Blair, J. 2007. Introduction, 1–18 in Blair (ed.).
Blair, J. 2010. The prehistory of English fonts, 149–78 in Henig and Ramsay (eds).
Blair, J. 2011. Flixborough revisited, *Anglo-Saxon Studies in Archaeology and History* 17, 10–17.
Blair, J. 2013. Grid-planning in Anglo-Saxon settlements: The short perch and the four-perch module, *Anglo-Saxon Studies in Archaeology and History* 18, 18–61.
Blair, J. 2015. The making of the English house: Domestic planning, 900–1150, *Anglo-Saxon Studies in Archaeology and History* 19, 184–206.

Blair, J. 2018. *Building Anglo-Saxon England* (Princeton/Woodstock: Princeton University Press).

Blair, J. and Crawford, B. E. 1997. A late-viking burial at Magdalen Bridge, Oxford?, *Oxoniensia* 62, 135–43.

Blair, J., Rippon, S., and Smart, C. 2020. *Planning in the Early Medieval Landscape* (Liverpool: Liverpool University Press).

Blair, J. (ed.) 1988. *Minsters and Parish Churches: The Local Church in Transition 950–1200* (Oxford: Oxford University Committee for Archaeology).

Blair, J. (ed.) 2007. *Waterways and Canal-Building in Medieval England* (Oxford: Oxford University Press).

Blair, J. and Ramsay, N. (eds) 1991. *English Medieval Industries: Craftsmen, Techniques, Products* (London/Rio Grande: Hambledon Press).

Blake, N. (ed.) 1992. *The Cambridge History of the English Language* (Cambridge: Cambridge University Press).

Blanchard, I. 1978. Labour productivity and work psychology in the English mining industry, *Economic History Review* 31i, 1–24.

Blanchard, I. 1996. Lothian and beyond: The economy of the 'English Empire' of David I, 23–45 in Britnell and Hatcher (eds).

Blaylock, S. 2008. Buckles, belts and borders, *Current Archaeology* 207, 12–19.

Blinkhorn, P. 2012. *The Ipswich Ware Project: Ceramics, Trade and Society in Middle Saxon England*, Medieval Pottery Research Group Occasional paper 7 (London: M. P. R. G.).

Blinkhorn, P. 2013. 'No pots please, we're vikings': Pottery in the southern Danelaw, 800–1100, 157–71 in Hadley and ten Harkel (eds).

Blinkhorn, P., Bloor, C., and Thomason, D. 2000. *Excavations at the Paddock, Rectory Lane, Fringford, 1999*, Occasional paper 6 (Oxford: Oxford Archaeological Unit).

Blockley, K., Sparks, M., and Tatton-Brown, T. 1997. *Canterbury Cathedral Nave: Archaeology, History and Architecture*, Archaeology of Canterbury n. s. 1 (Canterbury: Dean and Chapter of Canterbury Cathedral and Canterbury Archaeological Trust).

Blockley, K., Blockley, M., Blockley, P., Frere, S. S., and Stow, S. 1995. *Excavations in the Marlowe Car Park and Surrounding Areas*, Archaeology of Canterbury 5 (Canterbury: Canterbury Archaeological Trust).

Blockley, P. 1988. Excavations at No. 41 St George's Street, Canterbury, 1985, *Archaeologia Cantiana* 105, 59–178.

Boddington, A. 1996. *Raunds Furnells: The Anglo-Saxon Church and Churchyard*, Archaeological Report 7 (London: English Heritage).

Bolton, J. L. 2004. What is money? What is a money economy? When did a money economy emerge in medieval England?, 1–15 in Wood (ed.).

Booth, P., Gosden, C., and Hamerow, H. 2010. Dark earths in the Dorchester allotments, *Medieval Archaeology* 54, 414–16.

Boss, S. J. 2009. Alcuin of York on wisdom and Mary: Texts and buildings, 62–71 in Devlin and Holas-Clark (eds).

Bowsher, J. and Egan, G. 2015. Medieval coins and tokens, 237–40 in Ayre and Wroe-Brown.

Boyle, A., Score, D., Webb, H., and Loe, L. 2014. *'Given to the Ground': A Viking Mass Grave on Ridgeway Hill, Weymouth*, Dorset Natural History and Archaeological Society Monograph 22 (Dorchester: D. N. H. A. S.).

Brady, N. 2018. Agricultural buildings, 259–74 in Gerrard and Gutiérrez (eds).

Brears, P. 2008. *Cooking and Dining in Medieval England* (Totnes: Prospect Books).

Breay, C. and Story, J. (eds) 2018. *Anglo-Saxon Kingdoms: Art, Word, War* (London: British Library).

Brennan, N. and Hamerow, H. 2015. An anglo-saxon great hall complex at Sutton Courtenay/Drayton, Oxfordshire: A royal centre of early Wessex?, *Archaeological Journal* 172, 325–50.

Bridge, M. 2020. Elm dendrochronology, *Vernacular Architecture* 51, 94–9.

Bridge, M. and Miles, D. 2017. Tree-ring dates from the Oxford Dendrochronology Laboratory, *Vernacular Architecture* 48, 108–16.

Bridge, M., Roberts, E., and Miles, D. 2014. List 265: Hampshire Dendrochronology Project: Phase twenty, *Vernacular Architecture* 45, 120–1.

Bridge. M. and four others 2010. List 225: Hampshire Dendrochronology Project: Phase sixteen, *Vernacular Architecture* 41, 105–8.

Brieger, P. 1957. *English Art 1216–1307* (Oxford: Clarendon Press).

Briggs, C. S. forthcoming. Manorial court roll inventories as evidence for peasant consumption and living standard, *c.*1270–*c.*1420 in Furio and Garcia-Oliver (eds).

Briscoe, D. 2011. Continuity in Cambridge? Pot-stamp evidence for continuity from the fourth to fifth centuries A.D., 7–13 in Brookes *et al.* (eds).

Britnell, R. 1992. *The Commercialization of English Society, 1000–1500* (Cambridge: Cambridge University Press).

Britnell, R. 1996a. Boroughs, markets and trade in northern England, 1000–1216, 46–67 in Britnell and Hatcher (eds).

Britnell, R. 1996b. Production for the market on a small fourteenth-century estate, *Economic History Review* 19ii, 380–7.

Britnell, R. 2000. The economy of British towns 1300–1540, 313–34 in Palliser (ed.).

Britnell, R. 2001. Specialization of work in England, 1100–1300, *Economic History Review* 44i, 1–16.

Britnell, R. 2006. Town life, 134–78 in Horrox and Ormrod (eds).

Britnell, R. and Hatcher, J. (eds) 1996. *Progress and Problems in Medieval England* (Cambridge: Cambridge University Press).

Broadley, S. 2019. *The Glass Vessels of Anglo-Saxon England* c. *A.D. 650–1100* (Oxford: Oxbow Books).

Brookes, S. 2007. Boat-rivets in graves in pre-viking Kent: reassessing anglo-saxon boat-burial traditions, *Medieval Archaeology* 51, 1–18.

Brookes, S. and Harrington, S. 2010. *The Kingdom and People of Kent A.D. 400–1066: Their History and Archaeology* (Stroud: History Press).

Brookes, S., Harrington, S., and Reynolds, A. (eds) 2011. *Studies in Early Anglo-Saxon Art and Archaeology: Papers in Honour of Martin G. Welch*, British Archaeological Reports British Series 527 (Oxford: B. A. R.).

Brooks, H., Crummy, N., and Archibald, M. M. 2004. A medieval lead canister from Colchester High Street: Hoard container, or floor safe? *Medieval Archaeology* 48, 131–42.

Brooks, N. 1996. The administrative background to the Burghal Hidage, 128–50 in Hill and Rumble (eds).

Brown, A. T. 2015. *Rural Society and Economic Change in County Durham: Recession and Recovery*, c. *1400–1640* (Woodbridge: Boydell).

Brown, A. T. *et al.* 2000. *The Rows of Chester: The Chester Rows Research Project* (London: English Heritage).

Brown, D. H. 2002. *Pottery in Medieval Southampton,* c. *1066–1510*, Council for British Archaeology Research Report 133 (York: C. B. A.).

Brown, D. H. 2018. Cuckoo Lane revisited, 71–84 in Jervis (ed.).

Brown, M. P. 2006. *The World of the Luttrell Psalter* (London: British Library).

Brown, M. P. and Farr, C. A. (eds) 2001. *Mercia: An Anglo-Saxon Kingdom in Europe* (London: Continuum).

Brown, R. A. and Shelley, A. 2014. From kiln to cemetery: New data on early medieval and medieval Ipswich from excavations at South Quay, *Medieval Archaeology* 58, 373–6.

Brown, R. A. *et al.* 2019. The archaeology of Budbury, Bradford-on-Avon, *Wiltshire Archaeology and Natural History Society Magazine* 112, 85–110.

Brown, R. A., Colvin, H. M., and Taylor, A. J. 1963. *The History of the King's Works. Volumes I and II: The Middle Ages* (London: Her Majesty's Stationery Office).

Brown, S. 2019. *The Medieval Exe Bridge, St Edmund's Church and Excavation of Waterfront Houses* (Exeter: Devon Archaeological Society).

Brownsword, R. and Pitt, E. E. H. 1983. A technical note on some thirteenth-century steelyard weights, *Medieval Archaeology* 27, 158–9.

Brownsword, R. and Pitt, E. E. H. 1985. Some examples of medieval domestic flatware, *Medieval Archaeology* 29, 152–5.

Bruce-Mitford, R. 1997 (ed. R. Taylor). *Mawgan Porth: A Settlement of the Late Saxon Period on the North Cornish Coast* (London: English Heritage).

Bruce-Mitford, R. 2005. *A Corpus of Late Celtic Hanging-Bowls* (Oxford: Oxford University Press).

Brunning, R. 2010. Taming the floodplain: River canalisation and causeway formation in the middle anglo-saxon period at Glastonbury, Somerset, *Medieval Archaeology* 54, 319–29.

Brunning, S. 2019. *The Sword in Medieval Europe: Experiences, Identity, Representation*, Anglo-Saxon Studies 36 (Woodbridge: Boydell Press).

Bruns, D. 2003. *Germanic Equal Arm Brooches of the Migration Period*, British Archaeological Reports International Series 1113 (Oxford: B. A. R.).

Bryant, R., Hare, M., and Heighway, C. 2012. *Corpus of Anglo-Saxon Stone Sculpture. Volume 10: West Midlands* (Oxford: Oxford University Press).

Buckton, D. 1986. Late tenth- and eleventh-century *cloisonné* brooches, *Medieval Archaeology* 30, 8–18.

Budny, M. and Tweddle, D. 1985. The early medieval textiles at Maaseik, Belgium, *Antiquaries Journal* 65ii, 353–89.

Burnett, L. 2009. Wartling area, *Medieval Archaeology* 53, 328.

Butler, L. A. S. 1987. Symbols on medieval memorials, *Archaeological Journal* 144, 246–55.

Butler, L. A. S. 1998. The origins of the Honour of Richmond and its castles, *Château Gaillard* 15, 69–80.

Byng, G. 2017. *Church Building and Society in the Later Middle Ages* (Cambridge: Cambridge University Press).

Cambridge, E. and Hawkes, J. (eds) 2017. *Crossing Boundaries: Interdisciplinary Approaches to Art, Material Culture, Language and Literature of the Early Middle Ages: Essays Presented to Professor Emeritus Richard N. Bailey, O. B. E., on the Occasion of His Eightieth Birthday* (Oxford: Oxbow).

Cameron, E. and Mould, Q. 2004. Saxon shoes, viking sheaths? Cultural identity in Anglo-Scandinavian York, 457–66 in Hines *et al.* (eds).

Cameron, E. and Mould, Q. 2011. Devil's craft and dragons' skins? Sheaths, shoes and other leatherwork, 93–115 in Clegg Hyer and Owen-Crocker (eds).

Cameron, E. (ed.) 1998. *Leather and Fur: Aspects of Early Medieval Trade and Technology* (London: Archetype Publications).

Camille, M. 1998. *Mirror in Parchment: The Luttrell Psalter and the Making of Medieval England* (London: Reaktion Books).
Campbell, B. M. S. 2017. Global climates, the 1257 mega-eruption of Samalas volcano, Indonesia, and the English food crisis of 1258, *Transactions of the Royal Historical Society* 278, 87–121.
Campbell, B. M. S., Bartley, K. C., and Power, J. P. 1996. The demesne-farming systems of post-Black Death England: A description, *Agricultural History Review* 44ii, 131–79.
Campbell, E. 2007. *Continental and Mediterranean Imports to Atlantic Britain and Ireland, A.D. 400–800*, Council for British Archaeology Research Report 157 (York: C. B. A.).
Campbell, E. 2019. Furnishing an early medieval monastery: New evidence from Iona, *Medieval Archaeology* 63ii, 298–337.
Campbell, J. 2010. Questioning Bede, 119–27 in Henig and Ramsay (eds).
Campbell, J. [a] 2018. The medieval manor house and the moated site, 242–58 in Gerrard and Gutiérrez (eds).
Campbell, M. 1991. Gold, silver and precious stones, 107–66 in Blair and Ramsay (eds).
Campbell, M. 1998. Medieval metalworking and Bury St Edmunds, 169–81 in Gransden (ed.).
Campbell, M. 2002. Medieval founders' relics: Royal and episcopal patronage at Oxford and Cambridge colleges, 125–42 in Coss and Keen (eds).
Caple, C. 2020. The Yarm helmet, *Medieval Archaeology* 64i, 31–64.
Cardwell, P. *et al.* 1995. Excavation of the hospital of St Giles by Brompton Bridge, North Yorkshire, *Archaeological Journal* 152, 109–245.
Carlin, M. 1996. *Medieval Southwark* (London/Rio Grande: Hambledon Press).
Carlin, M. 1998. Fast food and urban living standards in medieval England, 27–51 in Carlin and Rosenthal (eds).
Carlin, M. and Rosenthal, J. T. (eds) 1998. *Food and Eating in Medieval Europe* (London/New York: Hambledon Press).
Carus-Wilson, E. M. 1965. The first half century of the borough of Stratford-upon-Avon, *Economic History Review* 18, 46–63.
Carver, M. O. H. 1980. The excavation of three medieval craftsmen's tenements in Sidbury, Worcester, 1976, *Transactions of the Worcestershire Archaeological Society* 7, 154–219.
Carver, M. O. H. 1983. Two town houses in medieval Shrewsbury, *Transactions of the Shropshire Archaeological Society* 61.
Carver, M. O. H. 2005. *Sutton Hoo. A Seventh-Century Burial Ground and its Context*, Society of Antiquaries Research Report 69 (London: Society of Antiquaries of London).
Carver, M. O. H. 2010. *The Birth of a Borough: An Archaeological Study of Anglo-Saxon Stafford* (Woodbridge: Boydell).
Carver, M. O. H. 2016. *Portmahomack: Monastery of the Picts* (Edinburgh: Edinburgh University Press).
Carver, M. O. H. 2019. *Formative Britain: An Archaeology of Britain, Fifth to Eleventh Century A. D.* (London/New York: Routledge).
Carver, M. O. H. (ed.) 1992. *The Age of Sutton Hoo: The Seventh Century in North-Western Europe* (Woodbridge: Boydell Press).
Carver, M. O. H., Sanmark, A., and Semple (eds) 2010. *Signals of Belief in Early England: Anglo-Saxon Paganism Revisited* (Oxford/Oakville: Oxbow Books).
Casey, P. J. and Hoffman, B. 1999. Excavations at the Roman temple in Lydney Park, Gloucestershire, in 1980 and 1981, *Antiquaries Journal* 79, 81–143.

Casimiro, T. M. 2020. Geoff Egan memorial lecture 2019: Globalization, trade, and material culture: Portugal's role in the making of a multicultural Europe (1415–1806), *Post-Medieval Archaeology* 54i, 1–17.

Cessford, C., Alexander, M., and Dickens, A. 2006. *Between Broad Street and the Great Ouse: Waterfront Archaeology in Ely* (Cambridge: Cambridge Archaeological Unit).

Champion, M. 2018. Medieval graffiti inscriptions, 626–40 in Gerrard and Gutiérrez (eds).

Champion, T. 1977. Chalton, *Current Archaeology* 59, 364–9.

Chandler, J. 2001. *Endless Street: A History of Salisbury and its People* (Salisbury: Hobnob Press).

Chapman, A. 2010. *West Cotton, Raunds: A Study of Medieval Settlement Dynamics: Excavation of a Deserted Medieval Hamlet in Northamptonshire 1985–9* (Oxford: Oxbow Books).

Charles-Edwards, T. M. 2013. *Wales and the Britons, 350–1064* (Oxford: Oxford University Press).

Cherry, J. 1973. The medieval jewellery from the Fishpool, Nottinghamshire, hoard, *Archaeologia* 104, 307–21.

Cherry, J. 1991. Leather, 295–318 in Blair and Ramsay (eds).

Cherry, J. 1997. Seals and heraldry, 1400–1600: Public policy and private post, 251–63 in Gaimster and Stamper (eds).

Cherry, J. 2003. Heraldic livery badges, and the Dunstable Swan Jewel, 204–5 in Marks and Williamson (eds).

Cherry, J. 2008. Heads, arms and badges: Royal representations on seals, 12–16 in Adams (ed.).

Cherry, J. 2018. The cloth seal: A mark of quality, identification or taxation?, 167–92 in Bedos-Rezalc (ed.).

Cherry, J. and Goodall, J. 1985. A twelfth-century gold brooch from Folkingham Castle, Leicestershire, *Antiquaries Journal* 77, 388–90.

Cherry, M. 1979. The Courtenay earls of Devon: The formation and disintegration of a late medieval affinity, *Southern History* 1, 71–97.

Chibnall, M. 1986. *Anglo-Norman England 1066–1166* (Oxford: Blackwell).

Chibnall, M. 2003. Feudalism and lordship, 123–34 in Harper-Bill and van Houts (eds).

Childs, W. R. 1981. England's iron trade in the fifteenth century, *Economic History Review* 34, 25–47.

Childs, W. R. 1996. The English export trade in cloth, 121–47 in Britnell and Hatcher (eds).

Childs, W. R. 1999. The perils, or otherwise, of maritime pilgrimage to Santiago de Compostela in the fifteenth century, 127–43 in Stopford (ed.).

Childs, W. R. 2006. Moving around, 266–75 in Horrox and Ormrod (eds).

Christie, N. and Creighton, O. (eds) 2013. *Transforming Townscapes: From Burh to Borough: The Archaeology of Wallingford A.D. 800–1400*, Society for Medieval Archaeology Monograph 35 (London: S. M. A.).

Christie, N. and Stamper, P. A. (eds) 2012. *Medieval Rural Settlement: Britain and Ireland, A.D. 800–1600* (Oxford: Windgather Press).

Church, S. 2012. Exchequer, 197–9 in Owen-Crocker *et al.* (eds).

Claridge, J. 2017. The role of demesnes in the trade in agricultural horses in late medieval England, *Agricultural History Review* 65, 1–19.

Clark, J. 1983. Medieval enamelled glasses from London, *Medieval Archaeology* 27, 152–6.

Clark, J. 1995. *The Medieval Horse and Its Equipment. Medieval Finds from Excavations in London* (London: Her Majesty's Stationery Office).

Clarke, C. A. M. 2006. *Literary Landscapes and the Idea of England, 700–1400* (Woodbridge: D. S. Brewer).
Clarke, H. and Carter, A. 1977. *Excavations in King's Lynn 1963–1970*, Society for Medieval Archaeology Monograph Series 7 (London: S. M. A.).
Clarke, H. *et al.* 2010. *Sandwich: 'The Completest Medieval Town in England': A Study of the Town and Port from its Origins to 1600* (Oxford: Oxbow Books).
Clay, P. and Salisbury, C. R. 1990. A Norman mill dam and other sites at Hemington Fields, Castle Donington, Leicestershire, *Archaeological Journal* 147, 276–307.
Cleere, H. and Crossley, D. 1985. *The Iron Industry of the Weald* (Leicester: Leicester University Press).
Clegg Hyer, M. and Hooke, D. (eds) 2017. *Water and Environment in the Anglo-Saxon World* (Liverpool: Liverpool University Press).
Clegg Hyer, M. and Owen-Crocker, G. (eds) 2011. *The Material Culture of Daily Living in the Anglo-Saxon World* (Exeter: Exeter University Press).
Clemoes, P. and Hughes, K. (eds) 1971. *England before the Conquest: Studies Presented to Dorothy Whitelock* (Cambridge: Cambridge University Press).
Clough, T. H. McK. 1973. A small hoard of William I Type I pennies from Norwich, *British Numismatic Journal* 43, 142–3.
Coad, J. G. and Streeten, A. D. 1982. Excavations at Castle Acre Castle, Norfolk, 1972–77: Country house and castle of the Norman Earls of Surrey, *Archaeological Journal* 139, 138–301.
Coales, J. (ed.). 1987. *The Earliest English Brasses: Patronage, Style and Workshops 1270–1350* (London: Monumental Brass Society).
Coates, R. 2007. Invisible Britons: The view from linguistics, 172–91 in Higham (ed.).
Coatsworth, E. 2001. The embroideries from the tomb of St Cuthbert, 292–306 in Higham and Hill (eds).
Coatsworth, E. and Owen-Crocker, G. R. 2007. *Medieval Textiles of the British Isles A.D. 450–1100: An Annotated Bibliography*, British Archaeological Reports British Series 445 (Oxford: B. A. R.).
Coatsworth, E. and Pinder, M. 2002. *The Art of the Anglo-Saxon Goldsmith*, Anglo-Saxon Studies 2 (Woodbridge: Boydell Press).
Coatsworth, E. and Pinder, M. 2011. Sight, insight and hand: Some reflections on the design and manufacture of the Fuller brooch, 258–74 in Clegg Hyer and Owen-Crocker (eds).
Coggins, D. 2004. Simy Folds: Twenty years on, 325–44 in Hines *et al.* (eds).
Coggins, D., Fairless, K. J., and Batey, C. E. 1983. Simy Folds: An early medieval settlement site in Upper Teesdale, *Medieval Archaeology* 27, 1–26.
Cohen, N. 2011. Early anglo-saxon fish-traps on the River Thames, 131–8 in Brookes *et al.* (eds).
Cohen, N. and Parton, F. 2019. *Knole revealed: Archaeology and Discovery at a Great Country House* (London: National Trust).
Cole, A. 2007. The place-name evidence for water transport in anglo-saxon England, 55–84 in Blair (ed.).
Cole, G. *et al.* 2020. Summary justice or the king's will? The first case of formal facial mutilation in anglo-saxon England, *Antiquity* 94, 1263–77.
Collins, M. *et al.* 2012. The king's high table at Westminster Palace, *Antiquaries Journal* 92, 197–243.
Collins, R. and Turner, S. 2018. The Eslington sword and the kingdom of Northumbria, *Medieval Archaeology* 62i, 28–52.

Collins, R. and Allason-Jones, L. (eds) 2010. *Finds from the Frontier*, Council for British Archaeology Research Report 162 (York: C. B. A.).

Colonese, A. C. *et al.* 2017. The identification of poultry processing, *Journal of Archaeological Science* 78, 179–92.

Connor, A. and Buckley, R. 1999. *Roman and Medieval Occupation in Causeway Lane, Leicester: Excavations 1980 and 1991*, Leicester Archaeology Monographs 5 (Leicester: Leicester University Archaeological Services).

Cook, B. J. 1998. Medieval and early modern coin finds from South Ferriby, Humberside, *British Numismatic Journal* 68, 95–118.

Cook, B. J. and Williams, G. (eds) 2006. *Coinage and History in the North Sea World, c. A.D. 500–1250: Essays in Honour of Marion Archibald* (Leiden/Boston: Brill).

Cook, J. M. 2004. *Early Anglo-Saxon Buckets: A Corpus of Copper-Alloy- and Iron-Bound Stave-Built Vessels*, Oxford University School of Archaeology Monograph 60 (Oxford: Institute of Archaeology).

Cooke, H., Steane, K., and Williamson, T. 2003. The origins of water meadows in England, *Agricultural History Review* 51, 155–62.

Cooper, C. 2017. Lived experience at Bodiam and Ightham, 143–7 in Johnson (ed.).

Cooper, J. P. *et al.* 2017. A Saxon fish weir and undated fish trap frames near Ashlett Creek, Hampshire, *Journal of Maritime Archaeology* 12, 33–9.

Cootes, K., Axworthy, J., Davenport, C., and Jordan, D. 2019. Living like common people: Excavating a medieval peasant farming community at Poulton, *Current Archaeology* 352, 34–41.

Coppack, G. 1986. The excavation of an outer court building, perhaps the Woolhouse, at Fountains Abbey, North Yorkshire, *Medieval Archaeology* 30, 46–87.

Coppack, G. and Keen, L. 2019. *Mount Grace Priory: Excavations of 1957–1992* (Oxford/Philadelphia: Oxbow Books).

Corney, M. 2003. *The Roman Villa at Bradford on Avon* (Bradford on Avon: Ex Libris Press).

Coss, P. R. 1985. Aspects of cultural diffusion in medieval England: The early romances, local society and Robin Hood, *Past and Present* 108, 35–79.

Coss, P. R. and Keen, M. (eds) 2002. *Heraldry, Pageantry and Social Display in Medieval England* (Woodbridge: Boydell Press).

Coss, P. R. and Lloyd, S. D. (eds) 1992. *Thirteenth-Century England IV* (Woodbridge: Boydell).

Costen, M. D. 2011. *Anglo-Saxon Somerset* (Oxford/Oakville: Oxbow Books).

Costen, M. D. and Costen, N. P. 2016. Trade and exchange in anglo-saxon Wessex, *c.* A.D. 600–780, *Medieval Archaeology* 60i, 1–26.

Cotter, J. 1997. *A Twelfth-Century Pottery Kiln at Pound Lane, Canterbury. Evidence for an Immigrant Potter in the Late Norman Period*, Canterbury Archaeological Trust Occasional Paper 1 (Canterbury: C. A. T.).

Cotton, J. (ed.) 2014. *'Hidden Histories and Records of Antiquity': Essays on Saxon and Medieval London for John Clark, Curator Emeritus, Museum of London*, London and Middlesex Archaeological Society Special Paper 17 (London: L. A. M. A. S.).

Coulton, G. G. 1925. *The Medieval Village* (Cambridge: Cambridge University Press).

Cowgill, J., de Neergard, M., and Griffiths, N. 1987. *Knives and Scabbards* (London: Her Majesty's Stationery Office).

Cowie, R. 2004. The evidence for royal sites in middle anglo-saxon London, *Medieval Archaeology* 48, 201–9.

Cowie, R. and Blackmore, L. 2008. *Early and Middle Saxon Rural Settlement in the London Region*, Museum of London Archaeology Service Monograph 41 (London: M. o. L. A. S.).

Cowie, R. and Blackmore, L. 2012. *Lundenwic: Excavations in Middle Saxon London, 1987–2000*, Museum of London Archaeology Service Monograph 63 (London: M. o. L. A. S.).

Cox, P. W. 1988. A seventh-century inhumation cemetery at Shepherd's Farm, Ulwell, near Swanage, *Proceedings of the Dorset Natural History and Archaeological Society* 110, 37–47.

Cox, P. W. and Hearne, C. M. 1991. *Redeemed from the Heath. The Archaeology of the Wytch Farm Oilfield (1987-90)*, Dorset Natural History and Archaeological Society Monograph 9 (Dorchester: D. N. H. A. S.).

Crabtree, P. J. 1985. The archaeozoology of the anglo-saxon site at West Stow, Suffolk, 223–35 in Biddick (ed.).

Crabtree, P. J. 1989. *West Stow, Suffolk: Early Anglo-Saxon Animal Husbandry*, East Anglian Archaeology Report 47 (Dereham: Suffolk Archaeological Unit).

Crabtree, P. J. 2018. *Early Medieval Britain: The Rebirth of Towns in the Post-Roman World* (Cambridge: Cambridge University Press).

Craddock-Bennett, L., Murphy, J., and Rouse, D. 2013. New windows onto Hereford's Saxon and medieval town defences, *Medieval Archaeology* 57, 291–6.

Cramp, R. 1977. *Corpus of Anglo-Saxon Stone Sculpture Volume I: County Durham and Northumberland* (Oxford: Oxford University Press).

Cramp, R. 1999. The Northumbrian identity, 1–11 in Hawkes and Mills (eds).

Cramp, R. 2005 and 2006. *Wearmouth and Jarrow Monastic Sites*, Volumes 1 and 2 (Swindon: English Heritage).

Cramp, R. 2006. *Corpus of Anglo-Saxon Stone Sculpture Volume 7: South-West England* (Oxford: Oxford University Press).

Cramp, R. 2017. New perspectives on monastic buildings and their uses, *Anglo-Saxon Studies in Archaeology and History* 20, 27–42.

Crawford, S. 1993. Children, death and the afterlife in anglo-saxon England, *Anglo-Saxon Studies in Archaeology and History* 6, 83–92.

Crawford, S. 1999. *Childhood in Anglo-Saxon England* (Stroud: Sutton Publishing).

Crawford, S. 2009. *Daily Life in Anglo-Saxon England* (Oxford/Westport: Greenwood World Publishing).

Crawford, S. 2018. Birth and childhood, 774–88 in Gerrard and Gutiérrez (eds).

Crawford, S. and Lee, C. (eds) 2014. *Social Dimensions of Disease and Disability*, British Archaeological Reports International Series 2608 (Oxford: B. A. R.).

Creighton, O. H. 2002. *Castles and Landscapes: Power, Community, and Fortification in Medieval England* (London: Equinox Publishing).

Creighton, O. H. 2018. Overview: Castles and elite landscapes, 355–70 in Gerrard and Gutiérrez (eds).

Creighton, O. H. and Higham, R. 2005. *Medieval Town Walls: An Archaeological and Social History of Urban Defences* (Stroud: Tempus).

Creighton, O. H. and Rippon, S. 2017. Conquest, colonisation and the countryside: Archaeology and the mid eleventh to mid twelfth century, 57–87 in Hadley and Dyer (eds).

Creighton, O. H. *et al.* 2020. The face of battle? Debating arrow trauma on medieval human remains from Princesshay, Exeter, *Antiquaries Journal* 100, 165–89.

Crick, J. 2000. Posthumous obligations and family identity, 193–208 in Tyrrell and Frazer (eds).

Crick, J. and van Houts, E. (eds) 2011. *A Social History of England 900–1200* (Cambridge: Cambridge University Press).

Crossley, D. (ed.) 1981. *Medieval Industries*, Council for British Archaeology Research Report 40 (London: C. B. A.).

Crummy, N., Cherry, J., and Northover, P. 2008. The Winchester Moot Horn, *Medieval Archaeology* 52, 211–30.

Crummy, P., Hillam, J., and Crossan, C. 1982. Mersea Island: The anglo-saxon causeway, *Essex Archaeology and History* 14, 77–86.

Cullen, P., Jones, R., and Parsons, D. 2012. *Thorps and the Open Fields: A New Hypothesis from England* (Hatfield: Hertfordshire University Press).

Cumberpatch, C. and Roberts, I. 2013. A Stamford ware pottery kiln in Pontefract: A geographical enigma and a dating dilemma, *Medieval Archaeology* 57, 111–50.

Cunliffe, B. 1976. *Excavations at Portchester Castle, Vol. 2, Saxon*, Report of the Society of Antiquaries of London 43 (London: S. A. L.).

Cunliffe, B. and Munby, J. 1985. *Excavations at Portchester Castle, Vol. 4, Medieval, the Inner Bailey*, Report of the Society of Antiquaries of London 43 (London: S. A. L.).

Currie, C. R. J. 1992. Larger medieval houses in the Vale of the White Horse, *Oxoniensia* 57, 81–244.

Daniell, C. 1997. *Death and Burial in Medieval England, 1066-1550* (London: Routledge).

Daniell, C. 2001. Battle and trial: Weapon injury burials of St Andrews Church, Fishergate, York, *Medieval Archaeology* 45, 220–6.

Daniels, R. 1991. Medieval Hartlepool: Evidence of and from the waterfront, 43–50 in Good *et al.* (eds).

Daniels, R. 2007. *Anglo-Saxon Hartlepool and the Foundations of English Christianity: An Archaeology of the Anglo-Saxon Monastery*, Tees Archaeology Monograph 3 (Hartlepool: Tees Archaeology).

Darvill, T. 1988. Excavations on the site of the early Norman castle at Gloucester, 1983–4, *Medieval Archaeology* 32, 1–49.

Davenport, P. 2002. *Medieval Bath Uncovered* (Stroud: Tempus Publishing).

Davenport, P., Poole, C., and Jordan, P. 2007. *Excavations at the New Royal Baths (The Spa, and Bellott's Hospital) 1998–1999*, Oxford Archaeology Monograph 3 (Oxford: Oxford Archaeology Unit).

Davies, J. A., Riley, A., Levesque, J.-M., and Lapiche, C. (eds) 2016. *Castles and the Anglo-Norman World* (Oxford: Oxbow Books).

Davies, S. M., Bellamy, P. S., Heaton, M. J., and Woodward, P. J. 2002. *Excavations at Alington Avenue, Fordington, Dorchester, Dorset, 1984–87*, Dorset Natural History and Archaeological Society Monograph 15 (Dorchester: D. N. H. A. S.).

Davis, P. 2006–07. English licences to crenellate, and list of licences to crenellate, *Castle Studies Group Journal* 20, 226–33 and 234–45.

Davis, P. 2011–12. Licences to crenellate: Additions and corrections, *Castle Studies Group Journal* 25, 287–8.

Davis, P. 2012–13. The round tower at Barnard Castle and gendered space, *Castle Studies Group Journal* 26, 282–4.

Davis, R. H. C. 1968. An Oxford charter of 1191 and the beginnings of municipal freedom, *Oxoniensia* 33, 53–65.

Davison, B. K. 1977. Excavations at Sulgrave, Northamptonshire, 1960–76, *Archaeological Journal* 134, 105–14.

Dean, J. 2010–11. Statistical analysis of licences to crenellate, *Castle Studies Group Journal* 24, 299–309.

Denison, D. and Hogg, R. (eds) 2006. *A History of the English Language* (Cambridge: Cambridge University Press).
Devlin, Z. L. and Holas-Clark, C. N. J. (eds) 2009. *Approaching Interdisciplinarity: Archaeology, History and the Study of Early Medieval Britain,* c. *400–1100*, British Archaeological Reports British Series 486 (Oxford: B. A. R.).
Dhoop, T., Cooper, C., and Copeland, P. 2016. Recording and analysis of ship graffiti in Winchelsea, East Sussex, *International Journal of Nautical Archaeology* 45ii, 296–309.
Diack, M. 2005. Archaeological investigations at Canterbury Police Station, *Archaeologia Cantiana* 125, 27–42.
Dickinson, T. M. 1982. Fowler's Type G penannular brooches reconsidered, *Medieval Archaeology* 26, 41–68.
Dickinson, T. M. 1993. Early Saxon saucer brooches: A preliminary overview, *Anglo-Saxon Studies in Archaeology and History* 6, 11–44.
Dickinson, T. M. 1999. An anglo-saxon 'cunning woman' from Bidford-on-Avon, 359–73 in Karkov (ed.).
Dickinson, T. M. and Speake, G. 1992. The seventh-century cremation burial in Asthall barrow, Oxfordshire: A reassessment, 95–127 in Carver (ed.).
Dickinson, T. M., Fern, C., and Richardson, A. 2011. Early anglo-saxon Eastry: Archaeological evidence for the beginnings of a district centre in East Kent, *Anglo-Saxon Studies in Archaeology and History* 17, 1–86.
Dixon, P. 1979. Towerhouses, pelehouses and Border society, *Archaeological Journal* 136, 240–52.
Dixon, P. 1992. From hall to tower: The change in seigneurial houses on the Anglo-Scottish border after *c.* 1250, 85–107 in Coss and Lloyd (eds).
Dixon, P. 2018. Patron and builder, 377–92 in Guy (ed.).
Dixon-Smith, S. 1999. The image and reality of alms-giving in the great halls of Henry III, *Journal of the British Archaeological Association* 152, 79–96.
Dobson, B. 2000. General survey 1300–1540, 273–90 in Palliser (ed.).
Dodd, A. 2014. Excavations at Tipping Street, Stafford, *Staffordshire Archaeological and Historical Society* 47.
Dodd, A. 2020. Overview of the excavation results, 53–70 in Dodd *et al.* (eds).
Dodd, A. (ed.) 2003. *Oxford before the University: The Late Saxon and Norman Archaeology of the Thames Crossing, the Defences and the Town*, Thames Valley Landscapes Monograph 17 (Oxford: Oxford University School of Archaeology).
Dodd, A., Mileson, S., and Webley, L. (eds) 2020. *The Archaeology of Oxford in the Twenty-First Century*, Oxfordshire Archaeological and Historical Society Occasional Paper 1 (Oxford: O. A. H. S.).
Dodds, B. and Liddy, C. D. (eds) 2011. *Commercial Activity, Markets and Entrepreneurs in the Middle Ages: Essays in Honour of Richard Britnell* (Woodbridge: Boydell).
Down, A. and Welch, M. 1990. *Chichester Excavations 7: Apple Down and the Mardens* (Chichester: Chichester District Council).
Duffy, E. 1992. *The Stripping of the Altars: Traditional Religion in England 1400–1580* (New Haven/London: Yale University Press).
Duffy, E. 2003. Late medieval religion, 56–67 in Marks and Williamson (eds).
Duffy, E. 2006. Religious belief, 293–339 in Horrox and Ormrod (eds).
Duffy, M. 1999. Coastal defences and garrisons 1480–1914, 158–65 in Kain and Ravenhill (eds).
Dugan, H. 2018. London smellwalk around 1450: smelling medieval cities, 728–41 in Gerrard and Gutiérrez (eds).

Dungworth, D. and Doonan, R. C. P. (eds) 2013. *Accidental and Experimental Archaeometallurgy*, Occasional Paper 7 (London: Historical Metallurgy Society).
Dunmore, S. and Carr, R. 1976. *The Late Saxon Town of Thetford*, East Anglian Archaeology Report 4 (Gressenhall: Norfolk Archaeological Unit).
Dunne, J. *et al.* 2019. Reconciling organic residue analysis, faunal archaeology and historical records, *Journal of Archaeological Science* 107, 58–70.
Dunning, G. C. 1937. Twelfth-century middens in the Isle of Wight, *Proceedings of the Isle of Wight Natural History and Archaeological Society* 2, 671–95.
Dyer, C. 1984. Evidence for helms in fourteenth-century Gloucestershire, *Vernacular Architecture* 15, 42–6.
Dyer, C. 1989. *Standards of Living in the Later Middle Ages. Social Change in England* c. *1200-1520* (Cambridge: Cambridge University Press).
Dyer, C. 1991. Were there any capitalists in fifteenth-century England?, 1–24 in Kermode (ed.).
Dyer, C. 1995. Sheepcotes: Evidence for medieval sheep farming, *Medieval Archaeology* 39, 136–64.
Dyer, C. 2002. *Making a Living in the Middle Ages: The People of Britain 850–1520* (London/New Haven: Yale University Press).
Dyer, C. 2003. The archaeology of medieval small towns, *Medieval Archaeology* 47, 85–114.
Dyer, C. 2006a. Gardens and garden produce in later medieval England, 27–40 in Woolgar *et al.* (eds).
Dyer, C. 2006b. Seasonal patterns in food consumption in the later Middle Ages, 201–14 in Woolgar *et al.* (eds).
Dyer, C. 2008. Building in earth in late medieval England, *Vernacular Architecture* 39, 63–70.
Dyer, C. 2012. The late medieval village of Wharram Percy: Farming the land, 312–40 in Wrathmell (ed.).
Dyer, C. 2013. Living in peasant houses in late medieval England, *Vernacular Architecture* 44, 19–27.
Dyer, C. 2019a. The housing of peasant livestock in England, 1200–1520, *Agricultural History Review* 67i, 29–50.
Dyer, C. 2019b. A comment on rural tenants and their buildings in the later Middle Ages, *Vernacular Architecture* 50, 55–6.
Dyer, C. 2020. Peasants and poultry in England, *Quaternary International* 543, 113–8.
Dyer, C. forthcoming. Furnishings of medieval English peasant houses: Investment, consumption and life style in Furio and Garcia-Oliver (eds).
Dyer, C. and Slater, T. R. 2000. The Midlands, 609–38 in Palliser (ed.).
Dyer, C. and Jones, R. (eds) 2010. *Deserted Villages Revisited*, Explorations in Local and Regional History 3 (Hatfield: University of Hertford Press).
Dymond, D. 1998. Five building contracts from fifteenth-century Suffolk, *Antiquaries Journal* 78, 269–87.
Eagles, B. N. 2001. Anglo-Saxon presence and culture, *c.* A.D. 450–*c.* 675, 199–233 in Ellis (ed.).
Eagles, B. N. 2015. 'Small shires' and *regiones* in Hampshire and the formation of the shires of eastern Wessex, *Anglo-Saxon Studies in Archaeology and History* 19, 122–52.
Eales, R. 1985. *Chess: The History of the Game* (London: Batsford).
Eddison, J. 2004. The origins of Winchelsea, 1–6 in Martin and Martin.
Eddison, J. and Draper, G. 1999. A landscape of medieval reclamation: Walland Marsh, Kent, *Landscape History* 19, 75–88.

Edgeworth, M. 2004. Recent archaeological investigations in Bedford town centre: Evidence for an early northern boundary?, *Bedfordshire Archaeology* 25, 190–200.

Edwards, D. (trans. and ed.) 2005. *Early Northampton Wills from 1467 to 1503: Preserved in the Northampton Record Office* (Northampton: Northamptonshire Record Society).

Egan, G. 1996. Some archaeological evidence for metalworking in London, *c.* 1050–*c.*1700, *Journal of the Historical Metallurgy Society* 30ii, 81–95.

Egan, G. 1998. *The Medieval Household: Daily Living* c. *1150*–c. *1450*, Medieval Finds from Excavations in London 6 (Norwich: Stationery Office).

Egan, G. 2009. Costume fittings, 46–58 in Gilchrist and Reynolds (eds).

Egan, G. and Blackmore, L. 2015. Metalwork and other finds of the eleventh and twelfth centuries, 240–53 in Ayre and Wroe-Brown b.

Egging Dinwiddy, K. and Stoodley, N. 2016. *An Anglo-Saxon Cemetery at Collingbourne Ducis, Wiltshire*, Wessex Archaeology Report 37 (Salisbury: Wessex Archaeology).

EHD 1981. *English Historical Documents, Volume 2, 1042–1189*, ed. Douglas, D. C. (Oxford: Oxford University Press).

Ellis, P. (ed.) 2000. *Ludgershall Castle: Excavations by Peter Addyman 1964–1972*, Wiltshire Natural History and Archaeological Society Monograph 2 (Devizes: Wiltshire Natural History and Archaeological Society).

Ellis, P. (ed.) 2001. *Roman Wiltshire and After: Papers in Honour of Ken Annable* (Devizes: Wiltshire Natural History and Archaeological Society).

Emery, A. 2000. *Greater Medieval Houses of England and Wales. Volume II: East Anglia, Central England and Wales* (Cambridge: Cambridge University Press).

Emery, A. 2005. Late medieval houses as an expression of social status, *British Institute of Historical Research* 78 no. 200, 140–61.

Emery, A. 2006. *Greater Medieval Houses of England and Wales*. Volume III: Southern England (Cambridge: Cambridge University Press).

Emery, A. 2007. Dartington Hall: A mirror of the nobility in later medieval Devon, *Archaeological Journal* 164, 227–48.

Emery, K. M. and Williams, H. 2018. A place to rest your (burnt) bones? Mortuary houses in early anglo-saxon England, *Archaeological Journal* 175, 55–86.

Epstein, S. R. 1994. Regional fairs, institutional innovation, and economic growth in late medieval Europe, *Economic History Review* 47iii, 459–82.

Erskine, J. G. P. 2007. The West Wansdyke: An appraisal of the dating, dimensions and construction techniques in the light of excavated evidence, *Archaeological Journal* 164, 80–108.

Esmonde Cleary, S. 2011. The ending(s) of Roman Britain, 11–29 in Hamerow *et al.* (eds).

Evans, D. H. 2018. The fortifications of Hull between 1321 and 1864, *Archaeological Journal* 175, 87–156.

Evans, D. H. and Loveluck, C. P. 2009. *Life and Economy at Early Medieval Flixborough,* c. *A.D. 600–1000: The Artefact Evidence*, Excavations at Flixborough 2 (Oxford: Oxbow Books).

Evans, D. H. and Tomlinson, D. G. 1992. *Excavations at 33–35 Eastgate, Beverley, 1983–86*, Sheffield Excavation Reports 3 (Sheffield: J. R. Collis Publications).

Evans, D. H. and Wrathmell, M. G. 1987. The deserted medieval village of West Whelpington, Northumberland: Third report, part one, *Archaeologia Aeliana* 15, 199–308.

Evans, G. R. 1979. Schools and scholars: The study of the abacus in English schools, *c.* 980–*c.* 1150, *English Historical Review* 94, 71–89.

Evershed, R. 1999. Gas chromatography, 197–9 in Connor and Buckley.

Everson, P. and Stocker, D. 2011. *Custodians of Continuity? The Premonstratensian Abbey at Barlings and the Landscape of Ritual*, Lincolnshire Archaeology and Heritage Report 11 (Lincoln: Society for Lincolnshire History and Archaeology).

Everson, P. and Stocker, D. 2012a. Why at Wharram? The foundation of the nucleated settlement, 208–20 in Wrathmell (ed.).

Everson, P. and Stocker, D. 2012b. Who at Wharram?, 262–77 in Wrathmell (ed.).

Everson, P. and Stocker, D. 2017. Transactions on the Dee: The 'exceptional' collection of early sculpture from St John's, Chester, 274–99 in Cambridge and Hawkes (eds).

Evison, V. I. 1967. A sword from the Thames at Wallingford Bridge, *Archaeological Journal* 124, 160–89.

Evison, V. I. 1987. *Dover: Buckland Anglo-Saxon Cemetery*, Historic Buildings and Monuments Commission for England Report 3 (London: H. B. M. C. E.).

Evison, V. I. 2008. *Catalogue of Anglo-Saxon Glass in the British Museum* (London: British Museum).

Fairbairn, H. 2019. Was there a money economy in late anglo-saxon and Norman England?, *English Historical Review* 134, 1081–1135.

Fairbrother, J. R. 1990. *Faccombe Netherton: Excavations of a Saxon and Medieval Manorial Complex*, British Museum Occasional Paper 74 (London: British Museum).

Fairclough, G. 1980. Clifton Hall, Cumbria: Excavations 1977–79, *Transactions of the Cumberland and Westmorland Antiquarian and Archaeological Society* 80, 45–68.

Fairclough, J. and Sloane, B. 2017. Great Ryburgh: A remarkable anglo-saxon cemetery revealed, *Current Archaeology* 322, 18–23.

Faith, R. 1994. Demesne resources and labour rent on the manors of St Paul's Cathedral, 1066–1222, *Economic History Review* 47iv, 657–78.

Faith, R. 1999. *The English Peasantry and the Growth of Lordship* (London: Leicester University Press).

Faith, R. 2019. *The Moral Economy of the Countryside* (Cambridge: Cambridge University Press).

Farmer, D. L. 1989. Two Wiltshire manors and their markets, *Agricultural History Review* 37i, 1–11.

Fasham, P. J. and Keevill, G. 1995. *Brighton Hill South (Hatch Warren): An Iron Age and Deserted Medieval Village in Hampshire*, Wessex Archaeology Report 7 (Salisbury: Trust for Wessex Archaeology).

Fawcett, R. 2018. The medieval parish church: architecture, furnishings, and fittings, 597–613 in Gerrard and Gutiérrez (eds).

Faulkner, P. A. 1975. The surviving medieval buildings, 56–124 in Platt and Coleman-Smith.

Fenwick, V. (ed.) 1978. *The Graveney Boat: A Tenth-Century Find from Kent*, British Archaeological Reports British Series 53 (Oxford: B. A. R.).

Fern, C. 2007. Early anglo-saxon horse burial of the fifth to seventh centuries A.D., *Anglo-Saxon Studies in Archaeology and History* 14, 92–109.

Fern, C. 2015. *Before Sutton Hoo: The Prehistoric Remains and Early Anglo-Saxon Cemetery at Tranmer House, Bromeswell, Suffolk*, East Anglian Archaeology Report 155 (Bury St Edmunds: Suffolk County Council Archaeology Service).

Fern, C., Dickinson, T. M., and Webster, L. (eds) 2019. *The Staffordshire Hoard: An Anglo-Saxon Treasure* (London: Society of Antiquaries of London).

Fernie, E. 1983. *The Architecture of the Anglo-Saxons* (London: B. T. Batsford).

Fernie, E. 1998. The Romanesque church of Bury St Edmunds Abbey, 1–15 in Gransden (ed.).

Fernie, E. 2000. *The Architecture of Norman England* (Oxford: Oxford University Press).
Field, R. K. 1965. Worcestershire peasant buildings, household goods, and farming equipment, *Medieval Archaeology* 9, 105–45.
Filmer-Sankey, W. and Pestell, T. 2001. *Snape Anglo-Saxon Cemetery: Excavations and Surveys 1824–1992*, East Anglian Archaeology Report 95 (Ipswich: Suffolk Archaeological Unit).
Finn, N. 2004. *The Origins of a Leicester Suburb: Roman, Anglo-Saxon, Medieval and Post-Medieval Occupation on Bonners Lane*, British Archaeological Reports British Series 372 (Oxford: B. A. R.).
Fiorato, V., Boylston, A., and Knüsel, C. (eds) 2007. *Blood Red Roses: The Archaeology of a Mass Grave from the Battle of Towton A.D. 1461* (Oxford: Oxbow Books).
Fitzpatrick-Matthews, K. 2014. The experience of 'small towns': Utter devastation, slow fading or business as usual, 43–60 in Haarer (ed.).
Flatman, J. 2007. *The Illuminated Ark: Interrogating Evidence from Manuscript Illumination and Archaeological Remains for Medieval Vessels*, British Archaeological Reports International Series 1616 (Oxford: John and Erica Hedges).
Fleming, R. 2010. *Britain and Rome: The Fall and Rise, 400–1070* (London: Allen Lane).
Flight, T. 2016. Aristocratic deer hunting in late anglo-saxon England: A reconsideration based upon the *Vita S. Dunstani*, *Anglo-Saxon England* 45, 311–31.
Ford, W. J. 1996. Anglo-saxon cemeteries along the Avon valley, *Transactions of the Birmingham and Warwickshire Archaeological Society* 100, 59–98.
Foreman, M. 1996. *Further Excavations at the Dominican Priory, Beverley, 1986–89*, Sheffield Excavation Reports 4 (Sheffield: Sheffield Academic Press).
Forsyth, H. 2005. *Toys, Trifles and Trinkets: Base-Metal Miniatures from London, 1200 to 1800* (London: Unicorn Press).
Fosse, P. 2013. Correspondence, *Transactions of the Leicestershire Archaeological Society* 87, 233–5.
Foster, C. W. (ed.) 1914. *Lincolnshire Wills 1271–1526*, Lincoln Record Society 5 (Horncastle: L. R. S.).
Foster, S. 2003. Private devotion, 334–47 in Marks and Williamson (eds).
Fowler, P. and Blackwell, I. 1998. *The Land of Lettice Sweetapple: An English Countryside Explored* (Stroud: Tempus).
Fox, H. S. A. 1996. The exploitation of the landless in early medieval England, 519–51 in Razi and Smith (eds).
Fox, H. S. A. 1999. Medieval rural industry, 322–30 in Kain and Ravenhill (eds).
Fox, R. and Barton, K. J. 1986. Excavations at Oyster Street, Portsmouth, Hampshire, 1968–71, *Post-Medieval Archaeology* 20, 31–256.
Foys, M. K., Overbey, K. E., and Terkla, D. (eds) 2009. *The Bayeux Tapestry: New Interpretations* (Woodbridge: Boydell Press).
Fradley, M. 2017. Scars on the townscape: Urban castles in Saxo-Norman England, 120–38 in Hadley and Dyer (eds).
Frantzen, A. J. 2014. *Food, Eating and Identity in Early Medieval England* (Woodbridge: Boydell Press).
Fraser, C. M. (ed. and trans.) 1968. *The Northumberland Lay Subsidy Roll of 1296* (Newcastle: Society of Antiquaries of Newcastle).
Frazer, W. O. and Tyrrell, A. (eds) 2000. *Social Identity in Early Medieval Britain* (London/New York: Leicester University Press).
Frere, S. S., Bennett, P., Rady, J., and Stow, S. 1987. *Canterbury Excavations: Intra- and Extra-Mural Sites 1949–55 and 1980–1984*, Archaeology of Canterbury 8 (Canterbury: Canterbury Archaeological Trust).

Friel, I. 1986. The building of the Lyme galley 1294-1296, *Proceedings of the Dorset Natural History and Archaeological Society* 108, 41–4.

Friel, I. 1995. *The Good Ship: Ships, Shipbuilding and Technology in England, 1200–1500* (London: British Museum Press).

Frodsham, P. 2005. 'The stronghold of its own native past': Some thoughts on the past in the past at Yeavering, 13–64 in Frodsham and O'Brien (eds).

Frodsham, P. and O'Brien, C. (eds) 2005. *Yeavering. People, Power and Place* (Stroud: Tempus Publishing).

Fulford, M., Clarke, A., and Eckhardt, H. 2006. *Life and Labour in Late Roman Silchester: Excavations in Insula IX since 1993* (London: Society for the Promotion of Roman Studies).

Fulford, M., Rippon, S., Allen, J. R. L., and Hillam, J. 1992. The medieval quay at Wolaston Grange, Gloucestershire, *Transactions of the Bristol and Gloucestershire Archaeological Society* 110, 101–22.

Fulford, M. and Holbrook, N. (eds) 2015. *The Towns of Roman Britain: The Contribution of Commercial Archaeology*, Britannia Monograph 27 (London: Society for Roman Studies).

Furio, A. and Garcia-Oliver (eds) forthcoming. *Pautes de Consumo y Niveles de Vida en el Mundo rural medieval* (Valencia: Publicacions de la Universitet de Valéncia).

Gaimster, D. R. M. 1988. Post-medieval ceramic stove-tiles bearing the Royal Arms: Evidence for their manufacture and use in southern England, *Archaeological Journal* 145, 314–43.

Gaimster, D. R. M. 1994. The archaeology of post-medieval society, *c.* 1450–1750, 283–313 in Vyner (ed.).

Gaimster, D. R. M. and Nenk, B. 1997. English households in transition, *c.* 1450–1550: The ceramic evidence, 171–95 in Gaimster and Stamper (eds).

Gaimster, D. R. M. and Redknap, M. (eds) 1992. *Everyday and Exotic Pottery from Europe: Studies in Honour of John G. Hurst* (Oxford: Oxbow Books).

Gaimster, D. R. M. and Stamper, P. A. (eds) 1997. *The Age of Transition: The Archaeology of English Culture 1400–1600*, Society for Medieval Archaeology Monograph 15 (Oxford: Oxford Books).

Galloway, J. A. 2000. One market or many? London and the grain trade of England, 23–42 in Galloway (ed.).

Galloway, J. A. 2005. Urban hinterlands in later medieval England, 111–30 in Giles and Dyer (eds).

Galloway, J. A., Keene, D., and Murphy, M. 1996. Fuelling the city: Production and distribution of firewood and fuel in London's region, 1290–1400, *Economic History Review* 49, 447–72.

Galloway, J. A. (ed.) 2000. *Trade, Urban Hinterlands and Market Integration* c. *1300–1600*, Centre for Metropolitan History Working Papers Series 3 (London: University of London).

Gannon, A. 2003. *The Iconography of Early Anglo-Saxon Coinage, Sixth to Eighth Centuries* (Oxford: Oxford University Press).

Gannon, A. 2011. Coins, images, and tales from the Holy Land: Questions of theology and orthodoxy, 88–103 in Abramson (ed.).

Gannon, A. 2015. Money, power and women: An inquiry into early anglo-saxon imagery, 211–28 in Solway (ed.).

Gardiner, M. 2000. Vernacular buildings and the development of the later medieval domestic plan in England, *Medieval Archaeology* 44, 159–79.

Gardiner, M. 2006. The transformations of marshlands in Anglo-Norman England, *Anglo-Norman Studies* 28, 35–50.

Gardiner, M. 2013. The sophistication of late anglo-saxon timber buildings, 46–77 in Bintley and Shapland (eds).

Gardiner, M., Cross, R., MacPherson-Grant, N., and Riddler, I. 2001. Continental trade and non-urban ports in mid-anglo-saxon England: Excavations at *Sandtun*, West Hythe, Kent, *Archaeological Journal* 158, 161–290.

Garner, M. F. 2001. A middle Saxon cemetery at Cook Street, Southampton (SOU 823), *Proceedings of the Hampshire Field Club and Archaeological Society* 56, 170–91.

Gauthiez, B. 1998. The planning of the town of Bury St Edmunds: A probable Norman origin, 81–97 in Gransden (ed.).

Geake, H. 1992. Burial practice in seventh- and eighth-century England, 83–94 in Carver (ed.).

Geake, H. 1997. *The Use of Grave-Goods in Conversion-Period England*, British Archaeological Reports British Series 261 (Oxford: B. A. R.).

Geake, H. 2002. Persistent problems in the study of Conversion-Period burials in England, 144–55 in Lucy and Reynolds (eds).

Geake, H. 2004. Portable Antiquities Scheme, *Medieval Archaeology* 48, 232–47.

Geake, H. 2011. Accidental losses, plough-damaged cemeteries and the occasional hoard: The Portable Antiquities Scheme and early anglo-saxon archaeology, 33–9 in Brookes *et al.* (eds).

Geary, B. R. and five others, 2005. Recent palaeoenvironmental evidence for the processing of hemp (*cannabis Sativa* L.) in eastern England during the medieval period, *Medieval Archaeology* 49, 317–22.

Geddes, J. 1991. Iron, 167–88 in Blair and Ramsay (eds).

Gem, R. 1988. The English parish church in the eleventh and early twelfth centuries: A great rebuilding?, 21–30 in Blair (ed.).

Gem, R., Howe, E., and Bryant, R. 2008a. The Lichfield angel: A spectacular anglo-saxon painted sculpture, *Antiquaries Journal* 88, 48–108.

Gem, R., Howe, E., and Bryant, R. 2008b. The ninth-century polychrome decoration at St Mary's church, Deerhurst, *Antiquaries Journal* 88, 109–64.

Gerrard, C. M. and Aston, M. 2007. *The Shapwick Project, Somerset: A Rural Landscape Explored*, Society for Medieval Archaeology Monograph 25 (Leeds: Maney).

Gerrard, C. M. and Gutiérrez, A. (eds) 2018. *The Oxford Handbook of Later Medieval Archaeology in Britain* (Oxford: Oxford University Press).

Gerrard, J. 2007. The temple of Sulis Minerva at Bath and the end of Roman Britain, *Antiquaries Journal* 87, 148–64.

Gerrard, J. 2010. Pottery from south-east Dorset, *Britannia* 41, 293–312.

Gerrard, J. 2013. *The Ruin of Roman Britain: An Archaeological Perspective* (Cambridge: Cambridge University Press).

Gerrard, J. 2014. Roman pottery in the fifth century: A review of the evidence, 89–98 in Haarer (ed.).

Gibson, J. 2005. The chantry college of Cobham, *Archaeologia Cantiana* 125, 83–118.

Gilchrist, R. 1999. *Gender and Archaeology: Contesting the Past* (London: Routledge).

Gilchrist, R. 2008. Magic for the dead? The archaeology of magic in later medieval burials, *Medieval Archaeology* 52, 119–59.

Gilchrist, R. 2009. Medieval archaeology and theory: A disciplinary leap of faith, 385–408 in Gilchrist and Reynolds (eds).

Gilchrist, R. 2012. *Medieval Life: Archaeology and the Life Course* (Woodbridge: Boydell Press).

Gilchrist, R. and Green, C. 2015. *Glastonbury Abbey: Archaeological Investigations 1904–79* (London: Society of Antiquaries of London).

Gilchrist, R. and Reynolds, A. 2009. Introduction: 'The elephant in the room' and other tales of medieval archaeology, 1–7 in Gilchrist and Reynolds (eds).

Gilchrist, R. and Sloane, B. 2005. *Requiem: The Medieval Monastic Burial in Britain* (London: Museum of London Archaeological Service).

Gilchrist, R. and Reynolds, A. (eds) 2009. *Reflections: 50 Years of Medieval Archaeology, 1957–2007*, Society for Medieval Archaeology Monograph 30 (Leeds: Maney).

Giles, K. 2000. *An Archaeology of Social Identity: Guildhalls in York,* c. *1350–1630*, British Archaeological Reports British Series 315 (Oxford: B. A. R.).

Giles, K. and Clark, J. 2011. St Mary's Guildhall, Boston, Lincolnshire: The archaeology of a medieval 'public' building, *Medieval Archaeology* 55, 220–56.

Giles, K. and Dyer, C. (eds) 2005. *Town and Country in the Middle Ages, Contrasts, Contacts and Interconnections, 1100–1500*, Society for Medieval Archaeology Monograph 22 (Leeds: Maney).

Gillings, M., Pollard, J., Wheatley, D., and Peterson, R. 2008. *Landscape of the Megaliths: Excavation and Fieldwork on the Avebury Monuments 1997–2003* (Oxford: Oxbow Books).

Gilmour, B. 2010. Ethnic identity and the origins, purpose and occurrence of pattern-welded swords in sixth-century Kent: The case of the Saltwood cemetery, 59–70 in Henig and Ramsay (eds).

Gilmour, L. A. (ed.) 2007. *Pagans and Christians: From Antiquity to the Middle Ages: Papers in Honour of Martin Henig on the Occasion of His 65th Birthday*, British Archaeological Reports International Series 1610 (Oxford: B. A. R.).

Gingell, C. J. 1975–76. The excavation of an early anglo-saxon cemetery at Collingbourne Ducis, *Wiltshire Archaeological and Natural History Magazine* 70/71, 61–98.

Gittos, H. B. 2017. Archaeological evidence for local liturgical practices: The lead plaques from Bury St Edmunds, 225–42 in Cambridge and Hawkes (eds).

Glover, G., Pürainen, M., and Oakley, E. 2014. Roads, merchants and buildings in medieval Wigford, *Medieval Archaeology* 58, 370–3.

Goddard, R., Langdon, J., and Müller, M. (eds) 2010. *Survival and Discord in Medieval Society: Essays in Honour of Christopher Dyer* (Turnhout: Brepols).

Goldberg, P. J. P. 2008. The fashioning of bourgeois domesticity in later medieval England: A material culture perspective, 124–44 in Kowaleski and Goldberg (eds).

Goldberg, P. J. P. 2019. Making the house a home in later medieval York, *Journal of Medieval History* 45ii, 162–80.

Golding, B. 2001. The Church and christian life, 135–66 in Harvey (ed.).

Gooch, M. 2014. The swordless St Peter coinage of York, *c.* 905–*c.* 919, 459–70 in Naismith *et al.* (eds).

Good, G. L., Jones, R. H., and Ponsford, M. W. (eds) 1991. *Waterfront Archaeology: Proceedings of the Third International Conference, Bristol, 1988*, Council for British Archaeology Research Report 74 (London: C. B. A.).

Goodall, I. H. 2011. *Ironwork in Medieval Britain: An Archaeological Study*, Society for Medieval Archaeology Monograph 31 (London: S. M. A.).

Goodall, I. H. and Paterson, C. 2000. Non-ferrous metal objects, 126–32 in Stamper and Croft.

Goodall, J. 2011. *The English Castle 1066–1650* (New Haven/London: Yale University Press).

Goodburn, D. 2015a. Early medieval boat- and ship-building, 165–71 in Ayre and Wroe-Brown a.

Goodburn, D. 2015b. Evidence of an arcaded tenth-century timber building, 172–9 in Ayre and Wroe-Brown a.

Gordon, D., Monnas, L., and Elan, C. (eds) 1997. *The Royal Images of Richard II and the Wilton Diptych* (London: Harvey Miller).
Gowland, R. 2007. Beyond ethnicity: Symbols of social identity from the fourth to sixth centuries in England, *Anglo-Saxon Studies in Archaeology and History* 14, 56–65.
Graham, A. H. and Davies, S. M. 1993. *Excavations in the Town Centre of Trowbridge, Wiltshire, 1977 and 1986–88*, Wessex Archaeology Report 2 (Salisbury: Wessex Archaeology).
Graham, A. H., Hinton, D. A., and Peacock, D. P. S. 2002. The excavation of an Iron Age and Romano-British settlement in Quarry Field, south of Compact Farm, Worth Matreavers, Dorset, 1–83 in Hinton (ed.).
Graham-Campbell, J. 2017. A Scandinavian gold brooch from Norfolk, 201–10 in Cambridge and Hawkes (eds).
Graham-Campbell, J. and Okasha, E. 1991. A pair of inscribed anglo-saxon hooked tags from the Rome (Forum) 1883 hoard, *Anglo-Saxon England* 20, 221–9.
Graham-Campbell, J. (ed.) 1992. *Viking Treasure from the North West: The Cuerdale Hoard in Its Context* (Liverpool: Liverpool Museum).
Graham-Campbell, J. and Williams, G. (eds) 2007. *Silver Economy in the Viking Age* (Walnut Creek: Left Coast Press).
Grainger, I. and three others 2008. *The Black Death Cemetery, East Smithfield, London*, Museum of London Archaeolgical Service Monograph 43 (London: M.o. L. A. S.).
Gransden, A. (ed.) 1998. *Bury St Edmunds: Medieval Art, Architecture, Archaeology and Economy*, British Archaeological Association Conference Transactions 20 (London: B. A. A.).
Gräslund, B. and Price, N. 2012. The catastrophic event of A.D. 536, *Antiquity* 86, 428–43.
Green, J. A. 1997. *The Aristocracy of Norman England* (Cambridge: Cambridge University Press).
Greet, W. C. (ed.) 1927. *The Reule of Crysten Religioun*, Early English Text Society 171 (Oxford: Oxford University Press).
Greeves, T. A. P. 1981. The archaeological potential of the Devon tin industry, 85–95 in Crossley (ed.).
Grenville, J. 1997. *Medieval Housing* (London/Washington: Leicester University Press).
Grenville, J. 2003. The urban landscape, 254–61 in Marks and Williamson (eds).
Griffiths, B. 1996. *Aspects of Anglo-Saxon Magic* (Hockwold-cum-Wilton: Anglo-Saxon Books).
Griffiths, D. 2015. Medieval coastal sand inundation in Britain and Ireland, *Medieval Archaeology* 59, 103–21.
Griffiths, D., Philpott, R. A., and Egan, G. 2007. *Meols: The Archaeology of the North Wirral Coast*, Oxford University School of Archaeology Monograph 68 (Oxford: Institute of Archaeology, University of Oxford).
Griffiths, R. A. (ed.) 1981. *Patronage, the Crown and the Province* (Gloucester: Alan Sutton).
Guest, P. 2014. The hoarding of metal objects in fifth-century Britain, 117–29 in Haarer (ed.).
Guy, N. 2013–14. Brougham Castle: The dating of the double-gate-house, vaulting and 'bottle dungeons', *Castle Studies Group Journal* 27, 142–80.
Guy, N. 2016–17. Richard's Castle, *Castle Studies Group Journal* 30, 66–74.
Guy, N. 2017–18. Newcastle upon Tyne Castle: Aspects of the Great Tower, *Castle Studies Group Journal* 31, 185–209.
Guy, N. 2019–20. Newark-on-Trent Castle summary, *Castle Studies Group Journal* 33, 120–5.

Guy, N. 2020–21. The art and architecture of Henry III: With a focus on Winchester: Part 1, *Castle Studies Group Journal* 34, 239–80.
Guy, N. (ed.) 2011–12. The CSG conference 'Castles of Essex and Suffolk (with the Tower of London)', *Castle Studies Group Journal* 25, 4–100.
Guy, N. (ed.) 2018. *Castles: History, Archaeology, Landscape, Architecture and Symbolism: Essays in Honour of Derek Renn* (Castle Studies Group).
Haarer, F. K. (ed.) 2014. *A.D. 410: The History and Archaeology of Late and Post-Roman Britain* (London: Society for the Promotion of Roman Studies).
Hadley, D. M. 2009. Burial, belief and identity in later anglo-saxon England, 465–88 in Gilchrist and Reynolds (eds).
Hadley, D. M. and Richards, J. D. 2016. The winter camp of the great viking army, A.D. 872–3, Torksey, Lincolnshire, *Antiquaries Journal* 96, 23–68.
Hadley, D. M. and Dyer, C. (eds) 2017. *The Archaeology of the Eleventh Century: Continuities and Transformations*, Society for Medieval Archaeology Monograph 38 (Leeds: Maney).
Hadley, D. M. and ten Harkel (eds) 2013. *Everyday Life in Viking-Age Towns: Social Approaches to Towns in England and Ireland,* c. *800–1100* (Oxford: Oxbow Books).
Hague, D. B. and Christie, R. 1975. *Lighthouses: Their Architecture, History and Archaeology* (Llandyssul: Gomer Press).
Hale, W. H. (ed.) 1888. *The Domesday of St Paul's of the Year M.CC.XXII . . . and Various Other Original Documents*, Volume 69 (London: Camden Society).
Hall, A. and Kenward, H. H. 2004. Setting people in their environment: Plant and animal remains from Anglo-Scandinavian York, 372–426 in Hall *et al.* (eds).
Hall, D. N. 1973. A thirteenth-century windmill site at Strixton, Northamptonshire, *Bedfordshire Archaeological Journal* 8, 109–35.
Hall, D. N. 1983. The excavation of an iron-smelting site at Easton Mauduit, Northamptonshire, *Bedfordshire Archaeology* 116, 65–74.
Hall, D. N. 2014. *The Open Fields of England* (Oxford: Oxford University Press).
Hall, M. A. 2018a. Approaching medieval sacrality, 614–25 in Gerrard and Gutiérrez (eds).
Hall, M. A. 2018b. Play and playfulness in late medieval Britain, 530–42 in Gerrard and Gutiérrez (eds).
Hall, R. A. 1992. The waterfront of York, 177–84 in Good *et al.* (eds).
Hall, R. A. 2004. The topography of Anglo-Scandinavian York, 408–502 in Hall *et al.*
Hall, R. A. 2014. *Anglo-Scandinavian Occupation at 16–22 Coppergate: Defining a Townscape*, Archaeology of York 8/5 (York: Council for British Archaeology).
Hall, R. A. and Hunter-Mann, K. 2002. *Medieval Urbanism in Coppergate: Refining a Townscape* (York: Council for British Archaeology).
Hall, R. A. and Whyman, M. 1996. Settlement and monasticism at Ripon, north Yorkshire, from the seventh to the eleventh centuries A.D., *Medieval Archaeology* 40, 62–150.
Hall, R. A., Rollason, D. W., Blackburn, M., Parsons, D. N., Fellows-Jensen, G., Hall, A. R., Kenward, H. K., O'Connor, T., Tweddle, D., Mainman, A., and Rogers, N. S. H. 2004. *Aspects of Anglo-Scandinavian York*, Archaeology of York 8/4 (York: Council for British Archaeology).
Hall, R. A. (ed.) 1978. *Viking Age York and the North*, Council for British Archaeology Research Report 27 (London: C. B. A.).
Halsall, G. 2013. *Worlds of Arthur: Facts and Fictions of the Dark Ages* (Oxford: Oxford University Press).
Hamel, C. de 2018. *Making Medieval Manuscripts* (Oxford: Bodleian Library).

Hamerow, H. 1993. *Excavations at Mucking. Volume 2: The Anglo-Saxon Settlement: Excavations by M. U. Jones and W. T. Jones*, English Heritage Archaeological Report 21 (London: English Heritage).

Hamerow, H. 2011. Anglo-saxon timber buildings and their social context, 128–55 in Hamerow *et al.* (eds).

Hamerow, H. 2012. *Rural Settlements and Society in Anglo-Saxon England* (Oxford: Oxford University Press).

Hamerow, H., Hinton, D. A., and Crawford, S. (eds) 2011. *The Oxford Handbook of Anglo-Saxon Archaeology* (Oxford: Oxford University Press).

Hamilton, J. and Thomas, R. 2012. Pannage, pulses and pigs: Isotopic and zooarchaeological evidence for changing pig management practices in later medieval England, *Medieval Archaeology* 56, 234–59.

Hanawalt, B. A. 1986. *The Ties That Bound: Peasant Family Life in Medieval England* (Oxford: Oxford University Press).

Hanawalt, B. A. and Reyerson, K. L. (eds) 1994. *City and Spectacle in Medieval Europe*, Medieval Studies at Minnesota 6 (Minneapolis: University of Minnesota Press).

Handley, M. A. 2001. The origins of christian commemoration in late antique Britain, *Early Medieval Europe* 10, 177–99.

Hansen, G., Ashby, S., and Bang, I. (eds) 2015. *Everyday Products in the Middle Ages: Crafts, Consumption and the Individual in Northern Europe* c. *800–1600* (Oxford: Oxbow Books).

Hansson, M. 2009. The medieval aristocracy and the social use of space, 435–52 in Gilchrist and Reynolds (eds).

Harbottle, B., Nolan, J., and Vaughan, J. 2010. The early medieval cemetery at the Castle, Newcastle-upon-Tyne, *Archaeologia Aeliana* ser. 5, 39, 147–287.

Harding, P. 2020. Forty years in the making: An amalgam of archaeological work in Salisbury, *Wiltshire Archaeological and Natural History Magazine* 113, 303–7.

Hardy, A. and Dungworth, D. 2014. A medieval iron production site at Little Snarlton Farm, East Melksham, Wiltshire: Excavations in 2010, *Wiltshire Archaeological and Natural History Society Magazine* 107, 118–45.

Hardy, A., Mair, B. M., and Williams, R. J. 2007. *Death and Taxes: The Archaeology of a Middle Saxon Estate Centre at Higham Ferrers, Northamptonshire*, Oxford Archaeology Monograph 4 (Oxford: Oxford Archaeology).

Hare, J. 2011. *A Prospering Society: Wiltshire in the Later Middle Ages*, Studies in Regional and Local History 10 (Hatfield: University of Hertfordshire Press).

Hare, J. 2012. The architectural patronage of two late medieval bishops: Edington, Wykeham and the rebuilding of Winchester Cathedral nave, *Antiquaries Journal* 92, 273–306.

Hare, J. 2013. Inns, inn-keepers and the society of later medieval England, *Journal of Medieval History* 39, 477–97.

Hare, J. 2021. The palaces and residential buildings of the medieval bishops of Winchester, *c.* 1300–*c.* 1500, 75–93 in Richardson, A.[a] and Allen (eds).

Hare, M. 1992. Investigations at the anglo-saxon church of St Peter, Titchfield, 1982–9, *Proceedings of the Hampshire Field Club and Archaeological Society* 47, 117–42.

Hare, M. 2009. The ninth-century west porch of St Mary's Church, Deerhurst, Gloucestershire: Form and function, *Medieval Archaeology* 53, 35–93.

Harfield, C. G. 1991. A hand-list of castles recorded in the Domesday Book, *English Historical Review* 106, 371–92.

Härke, H. 1989. Knives in early Saxon burials: Blade length and age at death, *Medieval Archaeology* 33, 144–8.

Härke, H. 1990. Warrior graves? The background of the anglo-saxon burial rite, *Past and Present* 126, 22–43.

Härke, H. 1997. Material culture as myth: Weapons in anglo-saxon graves, 119–27 in Jensen and Høilund Nielsen (eds).

Härke, H. 2011. Anglo-saxon immigration and ethnogenesis, *Medieval Archaeology* 55, 1–28.

Harkel, L. ten 2013. Urban identity and material culture: A case study of viking-age Lincoln, *c.* A.D. 850–1100, *Anglo-Saxon Studies in Archaeology and History* 18, 157–73.

Harkel, L. ten 2018. Ethnic identity or something else? The production and use of non-ferrous dress accessories and related items from early medieval Lincoln, *Anglo-Saxon Studies in Archaeology and History* 21, 1–27.

Harland, J. M. 2019. Memories of migration? The 'anglo-saxon' burial costume of the fifth century A.D., *Antiquity* 93, 954–69.

Harper-Bill, C. and Harvey, R. (eds) 1986. *The Ideals and Practice of Medieval Knighthood* (Woodbridge: Boydell).

Harper-Bill, C. and van Houts, E. (eds) 2003. *A Companion to the Anglo-Norman World* (Woodbridge: Boydell).

Harrington, S. and Welch, M. 2014. *The Early Anglo-Saxon Kingdoms of Southern Britain, A.D. 450–650: Beneath the Tribal Hidage* (Oxford: Oxbow Books).

Harris, A. 2003. *Byzantium, Britain and the West: The Archaeology of Cultural Identity* (Stroud: Tempus).

Harris, J. 2009–10. Machicolation: History and significance, *Castle Studies Group Journal* 23, 191–214.

Harris, R. D. 2016. Recent research on the White Tower: Reconstructing and dating the Norman building, 177–90 in Davies *et al.* (eds).

Harris, R. D. and Miles, D. 2015. Romanesque Westminster Hall and its roof, 22–71 in Rodwell and Tatton-Brown (eds).

Harrison, D. 2007 (pbk edn). *The Bridges of Medieval England: Transport and Society 400–1800* (Oxford: Clarendon Press).

Harriss, G. 2005. *Shaping the Nation: England 1360–1461* (Oxford: Clarendon Press).

Harvey, B. F. (ed.) 2001. *The Twelfth and Thirteenth Centuries* (Oxford: Oxford University Press).

Harvey, P. D. A. 1993. *Rectitudines Singularum Personarum* and *Gerefa*, *English Historical Review* 108, 1–22.

Harvey, S. 2014. *Domesday: Book of Judgement* (Oxford: Oxford University Press).

Harward, C., Holder, N., Phillpotts, C., and Thomas, C. 2019. *The Medieval Priory and Hospital of St Mary Spital and the Bishopsgate Suburb: Excavations at Spitalfields Market, London, E1, 1991–2007*, Museum of London Archaeology Monograph 59 (London: M. o. L. A.).

Haslam, J. 1978. *Medieval Pottery in Britain* (Aylesbury: Shire Publications).

Haslam, J. 1980. A middle Saxon iron smelting site at Ramsbury, Wiltshire, *Medieval Archaeology* 24, 1–68.

Haslam, J. 2011. Dawes Castle, Somerset, and civil defence measures in southern and Midland England in the ninth to eleventh century, *Archaeological Journal* 168, 195–226.

Haslam, J. 2016. The articulation of burgages and streets in early medieval towns: Part 1, the case of Bridgnorth, Staffordshire, *Landscape History* 37i, 51–68.

Haslam, J. 2017. The articulation of burgages and streets in early medieval towns: Part 2, *Landscape History* 38ii, 5–28.

Haslam, J. 2020. *Eorpeburnan* and Rye: Some aspects of late anglo-saxon settlement development in East Sussex, *Landscape History* 41ii, 5–25.
Haslam, J. (ed.) 1984. *Anglo-Saxon Towns in Southern England* (Chichester: Phillimore).
Hassall, T. G., Halpin, C. E., and Mellor, M. 1989. Excavations in St Ebbe's, Oxford, 1967–1976: Part I: Late Saxon and medieval domestic occupation and tenements, and the medieval Greyfriars, *Oxoniensia* 54, 71–277.
Hatcher, J. 1972. *English Tin Production Before 1550* (Oxford: Clarendon Press).
Hatcher, J. 1977. *Plague, Population and the English Economy 1348–1530* (London/Basingstoke: MacMillan).
Hatcher, J. 2008. *The Black Death: An Intimate History of the Plague* (London: Weidenfeld and Nicolson).
Hatcher, J. 2011. Unreal wages: Long-run living standards and the 'Golden Age' of the fifteenth century, 1–24 in Dodds and Liddy (eds).
Hawkes, J. 2001. Constructing iconographies: Questions of identity in Mercian sculpture, 221–46 in Brown and Farr (eds).
Hawkes, J. and Sidebottom, P. C. 2018. *Corpus of Anglo-Saxon Stone Sculpture Volume 18: Derbyshire and Staffordshire* (Oxford: Oxford University Press).
Hawkes, J. and Mills, S. (eds) 1999. *Northumbria's Golden Age* (Stroud: Sutton).
Hawke-Smith, C. 1984. Rescue excavations at Eyeswell Manor moated site, Eccleshall, Staffordshire, 1981–1983, *Staffordshire Archaeological Studies* 1, 7–39.
Hayfield, C. and Slater, T. 1984. *The Medieval Town of Hedon, Excavations 1975–1976*, Humberside Heritage Publication 7 (Hull: Humberside Leisure Services).
Heal, F. 1990. *Hospitality in Early Modern England* (Oxford: Clarendon Press).
Hearne, C. M. and Birbeck, V. 1999. *A35 Tolpuddle to Puddletown Bypass DBFO, Dorset, 1996–8* (Salisbury: Trust for Wessex Archaeology).
Hedges, R. 2011. Anglo-saxon migration and the molecular evidence, 79–90 in Hamerow *et al.* (eds).
Heighway, C. M. 2010. Christian origins at Gloucester: A topographical inquiry, 39–48 in Henig and Ramsay (eds).
Heighway, C. M. and Bryant, R. 1999. *The Golden Minster: The Anglo-Saxon Minster and Later Medieval Priory of St Oswald at Gloucester*, Council for British Archaeology Research Report 117 (York: C. B. A.).
Heighway, C. M., Garrod, A. P., and Vince, A. G. 1979. Excavations at 1 Westgate Street, Gloucester, 1975, *Medieval Archaeology* 23, 159–213.
Henderson, C. G. 1999. The city of Exeter from A.D. 50 to the early nineteenth century, 482–99 in Kain and Ravenhill (eds).
Henig, M. and Ramsay, N. (eds) 2010. *Intersections: The Archaeology and History of Christianity in England, 400–1200: Papers in Honour of Martin Biddle and Birthe Kjølbye-Biddle*, British Archaeological Reports British Series 505 (Oxford: B. A. R.).
Heslop, T. A. 1980. English seals from the mid ninth century to *c.* 1100, *Journal of the British Archaeological Association* 133, 1–16.
Heslop, T. A. 1986. A walrus ivory seal matrix from Lincoln, *Antiquaries Journal* 66ii, 371–2.
Heslop, T. A. 1988. Peasant seals, 214–15 in King.
Heslop, T. A. 2016. The shifting structure of Norwich Castle keep, 43–53 in Davies *et al.* (eds).
Hey, G. 2004. *Yarnton: Saxon and Medieval Settlement and Landscape*, Thames Valley Landscapes Monograph 20 (Oxford: Oxford University School of Archaeology).

Hicks, C. 2006. *The Bayeux Tapestry: The Life Story of a Masterpiece* (London: Chatto and Windus).
Hicks, M. (ed.) 2016. The Later Medieval Inquisitions *Post Mortem*: Mapping the Medieval Countryside and Rural Society (Woodbridge: Boydell).
Hicks, M. and Hicks, A. 2001. *St Gregory's Priory, Northgate, Canterbury: Excavation 1988–1991*, Archaeology of Canterbury n.s. 2 (Canterbury: Canterbury Archaeological Trust).
Higgitt, J., Forsyth, K., and Parsons, D. N. (eds) 2001. *Romans, Runes and Ogham: Medieval Inscriptions in the Insular World and on the Continent* (Donington: Shaun Tyas).
Higham, N. J. 1986. *The Northern Counties to A.D. 1000* (London: Longman).
Higham, N. J. 2002. *King Arthur: Myth-Making and History* (London/New York: Routledge).
Higham, N. J. and Ryan, M. J. 2013. *The Anglo-Saxon World* (New Haven/London: Yale University Press).
Higham, N. J. (ed.) 2007. *Britons and Anglo-Saxons in England* (Woodbridge: Boydell).
Higham, N. J. and Hill, D. (eds) 2001. *Edward the Elder 899–924* (London: Routledge).
Higham, N. J. and Ryan, M. J. (eds) 2010. *The Landscape Archaeology of Anglo-Saxon England* (Boydell: Woodbridge).
Higham, R. 1999. Castles, fortified houses and fortified towns in the Middle Ages, 136–43 in Kain and Ravenhill (eds).
Higham, R. and Barker, P. 1992. *Timber Castles* (London: B. T. Batsford).
Higham, R., Allan, J. P., and Blaylock, S. R. 1982. Excavations at Okehampton Castle, Devon, Part 2: The bailey, *Proceedings of the Devon Archaeological Society* 40, 19–151.
Hill, D. 1981. *An Atlas of Anglo-Saxon England* (Oxford: Basil Blackwell).
Hill, D. (ed.) 1978. *Ethelred the Unready: Papers from the Millenary Conference*, British Archaeological Reports British Series 59 (Oxford: B. A. R.).
Hill, D. and Cowie, R. (eds) 2001. *Wics: The Early Medieval Trading Centres of Northern Europe*, Sheffield Archaeological Monographs 14 (Sheffield: Sheffield Academic Press).
Hill, D. and Rumble, A. R. (eds) 1996. *The Defence of Wessex: The Burghal Hidage and Anglo-Saxon Fortifications* (Manchester/New York: Manchester University Press).
Hill, J. Ashdown 2004. The Bosworth Crucifix, *Transactions of the Leicestershire Archaeological Society* 78, 83–96.
Hill, N. 1999. Nevill Holt: The development of an English country house, *Archaeological Journal* 156, 246–93.
Hill, N. 2019a. The twelfth-century aisled hall at Leicester Castle: A re-assessment, *Transactions of the Leicestershire Archaeological Society* 93, 123–67.
Hill, N. 2019b. Crucks at the edge: The stone belt of the East Midlands, 135–67 in Alcock, Barnwell, and Cherry (eds).
Hill, N. and Gardiner, M. 2018. The English medieval first-floor hall: Part 1: Scolland's Hall, Richmond, Yorkshire, *Archaeological Journal* 175, 157–83; Part 2: The evidence from the eleventh to early thirteenth century, *ibid.* 315–62.
Hillaby, J. and Hillaby, C. 2013. *The Palgrave Dictionary of Anglo-Jewish History* (Basingstoke: Palgrave Macmillan).
Hills, C. and Hurst, H. 1989. A Goth at Gloucester?, *Antiquaries Journal* 69i, 154–8.
Hills, C. and Lucy, S. 2013. *Spong Hill: Part IX: Chronology and Synthesis* (Cambridge: McDonald Institute for Archaeological Research).
Hines, J. 1984. *The Scandinavian Character of Anglian England in the Pre-Viking Period*, British Archaeological Reports British Series 124 (Oxford: B. A. R.).

Hines, J. 1997. *A New Corpus of Anglo-Saxon Great Square-Headed Brooches* (Woodbridge: Boydell Press).
Hines, J. 2010. Units of account in gold and silver in seventh-century England: *Scillingas, Sceattas* and *Pænningas*, *Antiquaries Journal* 90, 153–74.
Hines, J. 2011. Units of account in gold and silver in seventh-century England: *Scillingas, Sceattas* and *Pænningas: Erratum*, *Antiquaries Journal* 91, 397–8.
Hines, J. 2017. A glimpse of the heathen Norse in Lincolnshire, 211–24 in Cambridge and Hawkes (eds).
Hines, J. 2018. The anglo-saxon settlement at Catholme, Staffordshire: A reassessment of the chronological evidence and possible reinterpretation, *Anglo-Saxon Studies in Archaeology and History* 21, 47–59.
Hines, J. and Bayliss, A. (eds) 2013. *Anglo-Saxon Graves and Grave-Goods of the Sixth and Seventh Centuries A.D.: A Chronological Framework*, Society for Medieval Archaeology Monograph 33 (London: S. M. A.).
Hines, J., Lane, A., and Redknap, M. (eds) 2004. *Land, Sea and Home*, Society for Medieval Archaeology Monograph 20 (Leeds: Maney).
Hinton, D. A. 1973. Site 7: Anglo-saxon burials at Postcombe, Lewknor, *Oxoniensia* 38, 120–3.
Hinton, D. A. 1978. Late Saxon treasure and bullion, 135–58 in Hill (ed.).
Hinton, D. A. 1990. *Archaeology, Economy and Society: England from the Fifth to the Fifteenth Century* (London: Seaby).
Hinton, D. A. 1992. Revised dating of the Worgret structure, *Proceedings of the Dorset Natural History and Archaeological Society* 114, 258–9.
Hinton, D. A. 1996. *The Gold, Silver and Other Non-Ferrous Alloy Objects from Hamwic*, Southampton Archaeology Monographs 6 (Stroud: Alan Sutton Publishing).
Hinton, D. A. 1998. *Discover Dorset: Saxons and Vikings* (Wimborne: Dovecote Press).
Hinton, D. A. 1999. 'Closing' and the later Middle Ages, *Medieval Archaeology* 43, 172–82.
Hinton, D. A. 2002. A 'marginal economy'? The Isle of Purbeck from the Norman Conquest to the Black Death, 84–117 in Hinton (ed.).
Hinton, D. A. 2003. Anglo-saxon smiths and myths, 261–82 in Scragg (ed.).
Hinton, D. A. 2005. *Gold and Gilt, Pots and Pins: People and Possessions in Medieval Britain* (Oxford: Oxford University Press).
Hinton, D. A. 2008. *The Alfred Jewel and Other Late Saxon Decorated Metalwork* (Oxford: Ashmolean Museum).
Hinton, D. A. 2009. Recent work at the chapel of St Laurence, Bradford-on-Avon, Wiltshire, *Archaeological Journal* 166, 193–209.
Hinton, D. A. 2010. Deserted medieval villages and the objects from them, 85–108 in Dyer and Jones (eds).
Hinton, D. A. 2013. Demography from Domesday and beyond, *Journal of Medieval History* 39, 146–78.
Hinton, D. A. 2018. The medieval workshop, 475–90 in Gerrard and Gutiérrez (eds).
Hinton, D. A. 2021. Early medieval defences in southern England, 7–28 in Richardson, A.[a] and Allen (eds).
Hinton, D. A. and Peacock, D. P. S. 2020. *Impinging on the Past: A Rescue Excavation at Fladbury, Worcestershire, 1967* (St Andrews: Highfield Press).
Hinton, D. A. and Worrell, S. 2017. An early anglo-saxon cemetery and archaeological survey at Breamore, Hampshire, 1999–2006, *Archaeological Journal* 174, 68–145.
Hinton, D. A. (ed.) 2002. *Purbeck Papers*, University of Southampton Department of Archaeology Monograph 4 (Oxford: Oxbow Books).

Hinton, I. D. 2012. *The Alignment and Location of Medieval Rural Churches*, British Archaeological Reports British Series 560 (Oxford: Archaeopress).
Hirst, S. M. 1985. *An Anglo-Saxon Cemetery at Sewerby, East Yorkshire*, York University Archaeological Publications 4 (York: York University).
Hirst, S. M. and Clark, D. 2009. *Excavations at Mucking: Volume 3, The Anglo-Saxon Cemetery Excavations by Tom and Margaret Jones* (London: Museum of London Archaeology).
Hislop, M. 1996. Bolton Castle and the practice of architecture in the Middle Ages, *Journal of the British Archaeological Association* 149, 10–22.
Hislop, M. 2018. The round tower of Barnard Castle, 82–104 in Guy (ed.).
Hoare, P. and three others 2002. Reused bedrock ballast in King's Lynn 'Town Wall' and the Norfolk port's trading links, *Medieval Archaeology* 46, 91–105.
Hogg, R. 2006. English in Britain, 352–83 in Denison and Hogg (eds).
Holbrook, N. 2015. Towns of South-West England, 90–116 in Fulford and Holbrook (eds).
Holdsworth, P. 1984. Saxon Southampton, 331–44 in Haslam (ed.).
Holford, M. 2016. Fairs and markets in the Inquisitions *Post Mortem*, 100–14 in Hicks, M. (ed.).
Hollinrake, C. and Hollinrake, N. 2007. The water roads of Somerset, 228–34 in Blair (ed.).
Holmes, G. R. 1957. *The Estates of the Higher Nobility in Fourteenth-Century England* (Cambridge: Cambridge University Press).
Holmes, M. 2018. Beyond food: Placing animals in the framework of social change in post-Roman England, *Archaeological Journal* 175, 184–213.
Holt, J. C. (ed.) 1987. *Domesday Studies* (Woodbridge: Boydell).
Holt, R. 1985. Gloucester in the century after the Black Death, *Transactions of the Bristol and Gloucestershire Archaeological Society* 109, 149–61.
Holt, R. 1988. *The Mills of Medieval England* (Oxford: Blackwell).
Homer, R. F. 1991. Tin, lead and pewter, 57–80 in Blair and Ramsay (eds).
Hooke, D. 1998. *The Landscape of Anglo-Saxon England* (London/Washington: Leicester University Press).
Hooke, D. 2007. Use of waterways in anglo-saxon England, 37–54 in Blair (ed.).
Hooke, D. 2020. Sound in the landscape, a study of the historical literature: Part 2: The medieval period: The eleventh to fifteenth century (and beyond), *Landscape History* 41i, 29–49.
Hooke, D. (ed.) 1988. *Anglo-Saxon Settlements* (Oxford: Blackwell).
Hooke, D. and Burnell, S. (eds) 1995. *Landscape and Settlement in Britain A.D. 400–1066* (Exeter: University of Exeter Press).
Hope-Taylor, B. 1977. *Yeavering. An Anglo-British Centre of Early Northumbria* (London: Her Majesty's Stationery Office).
Horrox, R. 1999. Purgatory, prayer and plague, 1150–1380, 90–118 in Jupp and Gittings (eds).
Horrox, R. and Ormrod, W. M. (eds) 2006. *A Social History of England, 1200–1500* (Cambridge: Cambridge University Press).
Horsey, I. P. 1992. *Excavations in Poole 1973–1983*, Dorset Natural History and Archaeological Society Monograph 10 (Dorchester: D. N. H. A. S.).
Horsman, V., Milne, C., and Milne, G. 1988. *Aspects of Saxo-Norman London: I. Building and Street Development near Billingsgate and Cheapside*, London and Middlesex Archaeological Society Special Paper 11 (London: L. A. M. A. S.).

Hoverd, T., Reavill, P., Stevenson, J., and Williams, G. 2020. The Herefordshire viking hoard, *Current Archaeology* 361, 46–51.

Hudson, J. 2011. Order and justice, 115–23 in Horrox and van Houts (eds).

Huggins, P. J. 1978. Excavation of a Belgic and Romano-British farm with middle Saxon cemetery and churches at Nazeingbury, Essex, 1975–76, *Essex Archaeology and History* 10, 29–117.

Huggins, P. J. 1991. Anglo-saxon timber measurements: Recent results, *Medieval Archaeology* 35, 6–28.

Huggon, M. 2018. Medieval medicine, public health, and the medieval hospital, 836–55 in Gerrard and Gutiérrez (eds).

Hughes, R. 2004. Wattle and dub: A technical and experimental study based on materials from the National Portrait Gallery, 115–40 in Leary (ed).

Hulme, R. 2014–15. 'Well-placed for waging war': Strategic aspects of William the Conqueror's rural castles, *Castle Studies Group Journal* 28, 225–38.

Hulme, R. 2019–20. Siege warfare in King Stephen's reign (1135–54): An introduction, *Castle Studies Group Journal* 33, 186–203.

Hunter, F. 2014. Looking over the wall: The late and post-Roman Iron Age north of Hadrian's Wall, 206–16 in Haarer (ed.).

Hunter, J. R. 1982. Medieval Berwick-upon-Tweed, *Archaeologia Aeliana* ser. 5/10, 67–124.

Hunter, J. R. and Heyworth, M. P. 1998. *The Hamwic Glass*, Council for British Archaeology Research Report 116 (York: C. B. A.).

Hurst, H. 1975. Excavations at Gloucester: Third interim report, Kingsholm 1966–75, *Antiquaries Journal* 55ii, 267–94.

Hurst, J. 1994. A medieval ceramic production siteand other medieval sites in the parish of Hanley Castle, *Transactions of the Worcestershire Archaeological Society* 14, 1–14.

Hurst, J. D. (ed.) 1997. *A Multi-Period Salt Production Site at Droitwich: Excavations at Upwich*, Council for British Archaeology Research Report 109 (York: C. B. A.).

Hurst, J. G. 1961. The kitchen area of Northolt Manor, Middlesex, *Medieval Archaeology* 5, 211–99.

Hurst, J. G. 1979. Imported pottery, 94–5 in Andrews and Milne (eds).

Hurst, J. G. 2002. Raqqa-type ware, 128–30 in Mayes.

Hutcheson, A. R. J. 2006. The origins of King's Lynn? Control of wealth on the Wash prior to the Norman Conquest, *Medieval Archaeology* 50, 71–104.

Hutchinson, G. 1994. *Medieval Ships and Shipping* (London: Leicester University Press).

Hutton, B. 1984. Aisles to outshots, 145–51 in Addyman and Black (eds).

Huxtable, M. J. and O'Donnell, R. P. 2018. Medieval colour, 742–55 in Gerrard and Gutiérrez (eds).

Hybel, N. 2002. The grain trade in northern Europe before 1350, *Economic History Review* 55ii, 219–47.

Impey, E. 2017. *The Great Barn of 1425–27 at Harmondsworth, Middlesex*, London: Historic England.

Inker, P. 2003. Technology as active material culture: The quoit brooch style, *Medieval Archaeology* 44, 25–52.

Ivens, R., Busby, P., and Shepherd, N. 1995. *Tattenhoe and Westbury: Two Deserted Medieval Settlements in Milton Keynes*, Buckinghamshire Archaeological Society Monograph Series 8 (Aylesbury: B. A. S.).

James, E. H. 1987. A fresh study of the South Gate at King's Lynn, in the light of recent restoration work, *Norfolk Archaeology* 40i, 55–72.

James, T. B. 1990. *The Palaces of Medieval England* (London: Seaby).

James, T. B. 1999. *The Black Death in Hampshire*, Hampshire Papers 18 (Winchester: Hampshire County Council).

James, T. B. and Roberts, E. 2000. Winchester and late medieval urban development, *Medieval Archaeology* 44, 181–200.

James, T. B. and Robinson, A. M. 1988. *Clarendon Palace: The History and Archaeology of a Medieval Palace and Hunting Lodge near Salisbury, Wiltshire*, Report 45 (London: Society of Antiquaries).

Jamieson, E. 2019. The siting of medieval castles and the influence of ancient places, *Medieval Archaeology* 63, 338–74.

Jamieson, E. and Lane, R. 2015. Monuments, mobility and medieval perceptions of designed landscapes: The Pleasance, Kenilworth, *Medieval Archaeology* 59, 255–71.

Jarman, C. L. 2019. Resolving Repton: A viking Great Army winter camp and beyond, *Current Archaeology* 352, 18–25.

Jarman, C. L., Biddle, M., Higham, T., and Bronk Ramsey, C. 2018. The viking Great Army in England: New dates from the Repton charnel, *Antiquity* 92i, 183–99.

Jeanne, D. 2014. Leprosy: Lepers and leper-houses: Between Human Law and God's Law, 69–82 in Crawford and Lee (eds).

Jennings, S. 1981. *Eighteen Centuries of Pottery from Norwich*, East Anglian Archaeology Report 13 (Norwich: Centre for East Anglian Studies).

Jensen, C. K. and Høilund Nielsen, K. (eds) 1997. *Burial and Society: The Chronological and Social Analysis of Archaeological Burial Data* (Aarhus: Aarhus University Press).

Jervis, B. 2014. *Pottery and Social Life in Medieval England* (Oxford: Oxbow Books).

Jervis, B. 2017a. Consumption and 'social self' in medieval southern England, *Norwegian Archaeological Review* 50i, 1–29.

Jervis, B. 2017b. Late medieval urban decline in southern England, *Archaeological Journal* 174, 211–43.

Jervis, B., Whelan, F., and Livarda, A. 2017. Cuisine and conquest: Interdisciplinary perspectives on food, continuity and change in eleventh-century England and beyond, 242–62 in Hadley and Dyer (eds).

Jervis, B. (ed.) 2018. *The Middle Ages Revisited* (Oxford: Archaeopress Archaeology).

Jewell, R. H. I. 1986. The anglo-saxon friezes at Breedon-on-the-Hill, Leicestershire, *Archaeologia* 108, 95–116.

Johnson, B. and Waddington, C. 2008. Prehistoric and dark age settlement remains from Cheviot Quarry, Milfield Basin, Northumberland, *Archaeological Journal* 165, 107–264.

Johnson, C. and Jones, S. 2016. *Steep, Strait and High: Ancient Houses of Central Lincoln* (Woodbridge: Boydell Press).

Johnson, D. (trans.) 2013. *Grace Dieu Priory, Leicestershire: The Draft Account Book of the Treasuresses 1414–18* (Ashby: Ashby-de-la-Zouch Museum).

Johnson, E. D. 2015. Moated sites and the production of authority in the eastern Weald of England, *Medieval Archaeology* 59, 233–54.

Johnson, M. 1996. *An Archaeology of Capitalism* (Oxford: Blackwell Publishers).

Johnson, M. 2020. Bodiam Castle and the *Canterbury Tales*: Some intersections, *Medieval Archaeology* 64ii, 302–29.

Johnson, M. (ed.) 2017. Lived Experience in the Later Middle Ages: Studies of Bodiam and Other Elite Landscapes in South-Eastern England (St Andrews: Highfield Press).

Jolly, K. L. 1985. Anglo-saxon charms in the context of a christian world-view, *Journal of Medieval History* 11iv, 279–93.

Jones, C., Eyre-Morgan, G., Palmer, S., and Palmer, N. 1997. Excavations in the outer enclosure of Boteler's Castle, Oversley, Alcester, 1992–3, *Transactions of the Birmingham and Warwickshire Archaeological Society* 101, 1–98.

Jones, E. T. and Stone, R. (eds) 2018. *The World of the Newport Medieval Ship: Trade, Politics, and Shipping in the Mid Fifteenth Century* (Cardiff: University of Wales Press).

Jones, G., Straker, V., and Davis, A. 1991. Early medieval plant use and ecology, 347–85 in Vince (ed.).

Jones, M. J., Stocker, D., and Vince, A. 2003. *The City by the Pool: Assessing the Archaeology of the City of Lincoln*, Lincoln Archaeological Studies 10 (Oxford: Oxbow Books).

Jones, M. J. and Dimbleby, G. (eds) 1981. *The Environment of Man: The Iron Age to the Anglo-Saxon*, British Archaeological Reports British Series 87 (Oxford: B. A. R.).

Jones, R. H. 1991. Industry and environment in medieval Bristol, 19–26 in Good, Jones, and Ponsford (eds).

Jones, R. H. 2004. Signatures in the soil: The use of pottery in manure scatters in the identification of medieval arable farming regimes, *Archaeological Journal* 161, 159–88.

Jones, R. H. and Lewis, C. 2012. The Midlands: Medieval settlements and landscapes, 186–205 in Christie and Stamper (eds).

Jones, R. H. and Page, M. 2006. *Medieval Villages in an English Landscape: Beginnings and Ends* (Macclesfield: Windgather Press).

Jones, S. R., Marks, R., and Minnis, A. J. (eds) 2000. *Courts and Regions in Medieval Europe* (York: York Medieval Press).

Jones, S. R., Major, K., Varley, J., and Johnson, C. 1996. *Houses in the Bail: Steep Hill, Castle Hill and Bailgate* (Lincoln: Lincoln Civic Trust).

Jupiter, K. 2020. The function of open-field farming: Managing time, work and space, *Landscape History* 41i, 69–98.

Jurkowski, M., Smith, C. L., and Crook, D. 1998. *Lay Taxes in England and Wales 1188-1688* (Richmond: PRO Publications).

Jupp, P. C. and Gittings, C. (eds) 1999. *Death in England: An Illustrated History* (Manchester: Manchester University Press).

Kain, R. and Ravenhill, W. (eds) 1999. *Historical Atlas of South-West England* (Exeter: Exeter University Press).

Karkov, C. E. 2011. The boat and the cross: Church and state in early anglo-saxon coinage, 47–60 in Abramson (ed.).

Karkov, C. E. (ed.) 1999. *The Archaeology of Anglo-Saxon England: Basic Readings* (New York/London: Garland Publishing).

Keen, L. 1984. The towns of Dorset, 203–47 in Haslam (ed.).

Keen, L. 1987. Medieval salt-working in Dorset, *Proceedings of the Dorset Natural History and Archaeological Society* 109, 25–9.

Keen, L. and Ellis, P. 2005. *Sherborne Abbey and School: Excavations 1972–76 and 1990*, Dorset Natural History and Archaeological Society Monograph 16 (Dorchester: D. N. H. A. S.).

Keen, L. (ed.) 1997. *'Almost the Richest City': Bristol in the Middle Ages*, British Archaeological Association Conference Transactions 19 (Leeds: Maney).

Keene, D. 2000a. London from the post-Roman period to 1300, 187–216 in Palliser (ed.).

Keene, D. 2000b. The medieval urban landscape, A. D. 900–1540, 74–98 in Waller (ed.).

Keevill, G. 2004. *The Tower of London Moat: Archaeological Excavations 1995–9* (Oxford: Oxford Archaeology).

Kelleher, R. 2018. Old money, new methods: Coins and later medieval archaeology, 511–29 in Gerrard and Gutiérrez (eds).

Kelly, S. 1992. Trading privileges from eighth-century England, *Early Medieval Europe* 2i, 3–28.

Kent, J. P. C. 1995. The tremissis, 947–8 in Blockley *et al.*

Kenyon, J. R. 1990. *Medieval Fortifications* (Leicester/London: Leicester University Press).

Kenyon, J. R. 2018. Two remarkable north Yorkshire buildings: Middleham's great tower and Helmsley's west tower, 140–54 in Guy (ed.).

Kermode, J. 1998. *Medieval Merchants: York, Beverley and Hull in the Later Middle Ages* (Cambridge: Cambridge University Press).

Kermode, J. 2000a. The greater towns, 1300–1540, 441–66 in Palliser (ed.).

Kermode, J. 2000b. Northern towns, 657–80 in Palliser (ed.).

Kermode, J. (ed.) 1991. *Enterprise and Industries in Fifteenth-Century England* (Stroud: Alan Sutton).

Kershaw, J. E. 2013. *Viking Identities: Scandinavian Jewellery in England* (Oxford: Oxford University Press).

Kershaw, J. E. 2017. An early medieval dual-currency economy: Bullion and coin in the Danelaw, *Antiquity* 91, 173–90.

Kershaw, J. E. 2018. Gold as a means of exchange in Scandinavian England (*c.* 850–1050 AD) in Kershaw and Williams (eds).

Kershaw, J. E. and Naismith, R. 2013. A new late anglo-saxon seal matrix, *Anglo-Saxon England* 42, 291–8.

Kershaw, J. E. and Williams, G. (eds) 2018. *Silver, Butter, Cloth: Monetary Economy in the Viking Age* (Oxford: Oxford University Press).

Ketteringham, L. 1976. *Alsted: Excavation of a Thirteenth-/Fourteenth Century Sub-Manor Site with Its Ironworks in Netherne Wood, Merstham, Surrey*, Surrey Archaeological Research Report 2 (Guildford: S. A. S.).

Keynes, S. and Lapidge, M. (trans.) 1983. *Alfred the Great* (Harmondsworth: Penguin Books).

Kilby, S. 2015. Mapping peasant discontent: trespassing on manorial land in fourteenth-century Walsham-le-Willows, *Landsacpe History* 36ii, 69–88.

Kilby, S. 2020. *Peasant Perspectives on the Medieval Landscape: A Study of Three Communities*, Studies in Regional and Local History 17 (Hatfield: University of Hertfordshire Press).

Kilmurry, K. 1980. *The Pottery Industry of Stamford, Lincolnshire,* c. *A.D. 850–1250*, British Archaeological Reports British Series 84 (Oxford: B. A. R.).

King, A. 1978. Gauber High Pasture, Ribblehead: An interim report, 21–5 in Hall (ed.).

King, C. 2010. 'Closure' and the urban great rebuilding in early modern Norwich, *Post-Medieval Archaeology* 44i, 54–80.

King, D. J. Cathcart 1988. *The Castle in England and Wales: An Interpretative History* (London/Sydney: Croom Helm).

King, E. 1988. *Medieval England 1066–1485* (London: Guild Publishing).

King, E. 1996. Economic development in the early twelfth century, 1–22 in Britnell and Hatcher (eds).

King, J. M. 2004. Grave-goods as gifts in early Saxon burials, *Journal of Social Archaeology* 4ii, 214–38.

Kirton, J. and Young, G. 2017. Excavations at Bamburgh: New revelations in light of recent investigations at the core of the castle complex, *Archaeological Journal* 174, 140–210.

Kissane, A. 2017. *Civic Community in Late Medieval Lincoln: Urban Society and Economy in the Age of the Black Death, 1280–1409* (Woodbridge: Boydell).

Klemperer, W. D. and Boothroyd, N. 2004. *Excavations at Hulton Abey, Staffordshire, 1987-94* (London: Routledge).

Klingelhöfer, E. C. 1974. *Broadfield Deserted Medieval Village*, British Archaeological Reports British Series 2 (Oxford: B. A. R.).

Knüsel, C. J. and Ripley, K. 2000. The *Berdache* or man-woman in anglo-saxon England and early medieval Europe, 157–91 in Frazer and Tyrrell (eds).

Knüsel, C. J., Kemp, R. L., and Budd, P. 1995. Evidence for remedial treatment of a severe knee injury from the Fishergate Gilbertine monastery in the City of York, *Journal of Archaeological Science* 22, 369–84.

Knüsel, C. J. *et al.* 2010. The identity of the St Bees lady, Cumbria: An osteobiographical approach, *Medieval Archaeology* 54, 271–311.

Kowaleski, M. 1993. *Local Customs Accounts of the Port of Exeter, 1266–1321*, Devon and Cornwall Record Society n.s. 36 (Exeter: D. C. R. S.).

Kowaleski, M. 1995. *Local Markets and Regional Trade in Medieval Exeter* (Cambridge: Cambridge University Press).

Kowaleski, M. 2000. The expansion of the south-western fisheries in late medieval England, *Economic History Review* 53iii, 429–54.

Kowaleski, M. and Goldberg, P. J. P. (eds) 2008. *Medieval Domesticity: Home, Housing and Household in Medieval England* (Cambridge: Cambridge University Press).

Laban, G. 2013. Evidence for a Stephanic siege castle at the Lister Wilder site, Crowmarsh Gifford, *Oxoniensia* 78, 189–211.

Lachaud, F. 2002. Dress and social status in England before the sumptuary laws, 105–23 in Coss and Keen (eds).

Ladle, L. 2012. *Excavations at Bestwall Quarry, Wareham 1992–2005: Volume 2: The Iron Age and Later Landscape*, Dorset Natural History and Archaeological Society Monograph Series 20 (Dorchester: D. N. H. A. S.).

Ladle, L. 2018. *Multi-Period Occupation at Football Field, Worth Matravers, Dorset: Excavations 2006–2011*, British Archaeological Reports British Series 643 (Oxford: BAR Publishing).

Lane, A. 2014. Wroxeter and the end of Roman Britain, *Antiquity* 88, 501–15.

Lane, T. 2019. *Mineral from the Marshes: Coastal Salt-Making in Lincolnshire*, Lincolnshire Archaeology and Heritage Series 12 (Lincoln: Heritage Trust of Lincolnshire).

Lang, J. 1991. *Corpus of Anglo-Saxon Stone Sculpture Volume III: York and Eastern Yorkshire* (Oxford: Oxford University Press).

Langdon, J. 1986. *Horses, Oxen and Technological Innovation* (Cambridge: Cambridge University Press).

Langdon, J. 2004. *Mills in the Medieval Economy: England 1300–1540* (Oxford: Oxford University Press).

Langdon, J. and Masschaele, J. 2006. Commercial activity and population growth in medieval England, *Past and Present* 190i, 35–81.

Langdon, J. and Jones, G. (eds) 2010. *Forests and Chases of Medieval England and Wales c. 1000–1500: Towards a Survey and Analysis* (Oxford: St Johns College Research Centre).

Langlands, A. 2014. Placing the burh in *Searobyrig*: Rethinking the urban topography of early medieval Salisbury, *Wiltshire Archaeological and Natural History Society Magazine* 107, 91–105.

Langlands, A. 2019. *The Ancient Ways of Wessex: Travel and Communication in an Early Medieval Landscape* (Oxford: Oxbow Books).

Lass, R. 1992. Phonology and morphology, 23–155 in Blake (ed.).

Lavelle, R. 2010. *Alfred's Wars: Sources and Interpretations of Anglo-Saxon Warfare in the Viking Age* (Woodbridge: Boydell and Brewer).
Leach, P. 1982. *Ilchester Volume 1: Excavations 1974–5*, Western Archaeological Trust Monograph 3 (Bristol: W. A T.).
Leach, P. 1994. *Ilchester Volume 2: Archaeology, Excavations and Fieldwork to 1984*, Sheffield Excavation Reports 2 (Sheffield: J. R. Collis Publications).
Leah, M. 1994. *The Late Saxon and Medieval Pottery Industry of Grimston, Norfolk: Excavations 1962–92*, East Anglian Archaeology Report 64 (Gressenhall: Norfolk Archaeological Unit).
Leahy, K. 2003. *Anglo-Saxon Crafts* (Stroud: Tempus).
Leahy, K. 2007. *'Interrupting the Pots': The Excavation of Cleatham Anglo-Saxon Cemetery*, Council for British Archaeology Research Report 155 (York: C. B. A.).
Leahy, K. 2013. A deposit of early medieval iron objects from Scraptoft, Leicestershire, *Medieval Archaeology* 57, 223–37.
Leary, J. 2004. *Tahtberht's* Lundenwic*: Archaeological Investigations in Middle Saxon London*, Pre-Construct Archaeology Monograph 2 (London: P.-C. A.).
Leary, J., Field, D., and Campbell, G. (eds) 2013. *Silbury Hill: The Largest Prehistoric Mound in Europe* (Swindon: English Heritage).
Lee, C. 2007. *Feasting the Dead: Food and Drink in Early Anglo-Saxon Burial Rituals*, Anglo-Saxon Studies 9 (Woodbridge: Boydell Press).
Lee, C. 2011. Disease, 704–26 in Hamerow *et al.* (eds).
Lee, C. 2014. Invisible enemies: The role of epidemics in the shaping of historical events in the early medieval period, 15–28 in Crawford and Lee (eds).
Leech, R. H. 1997. The medieval defences of Bristol revisited, 18–30 in Keen (ed.).
Leech, R. H. 2000. The symbolic hall: Historic context and merchant culture in the early modern city, *Vernacular Architecture* 31, 1–10.
Leech, R. H. 2014. *The Town House in Medieval and Early Modern Bristol* (London: English Heritage).
Le Patourel, J. 1968. Documentary evidence and the medieval pottery industry, *Medieval Archaeology* 12, 101–26.
Lewis, C. 2016. Disaster recovery: New archaeological evidence for the long-term impact of the 'calamitous' fourteenth century, *Antiquity* 90, 777–97.
Lewis, C. 2020. A thousand years of change: New perspectives on rural settlement from test pit excavations in eastern England, *Medieval Settlement Research* 35, 26–46.
Lewis, C. P. 2018. Audacity and ambition in early Norman England, *Anglo-Norman Studies* 40, 25–45.
Lewis, M. 2016. Work and the adolescent in medieval England A.D. 900–1500, *Medieval Archaeology* 60i, 138–71.
Lewis, M., Richardson, A., and Williams, D. 2011. Things of this world: Portable Antiquities and their potential, 231–51 in Clegg Hyer and Owen-Crocker (eds).
Leyser, H. 2017. *A Short History of the Anglo-Saxons* (London/New York: I. B. Taurus).
Liddiard, R. 2000. Population density and Norman castle building: Some evidence from East Anglia, *Landscape History* 22, 37–46.
Lilley, J. M., Stroud, G., Brothwell, D., and Williamson, M. H. 1994. *The Jewish Burial Ground at Jewbury*, Archaeology of York 12/3 (York: Council for British Archaeology).
Lilley, K. D. 2017. The Norman Conquest and its influence on the urban landscape, 30–56 in Hadley and Dyer (eds).
Lilley, K. D. 2018. Overview: Living in medieval towns, 275–96 in Gerrard and Gutiérrez (eds).

Lindley, P. 1996. The Black Death and English art: A debate and some assumptions, 125–46 in Ormrod and Lindley (eds).

Linklater, A. and Dekker, E. 2010. The discovery of a *quadrans novus* at the House of Agnes, St Dunstan's Street, Canterbury, *Archaeologia Cantiana* 130, 65–82.

Lipton, S. 2016. Isaac and Antichrist in the archives, *Past and Present* 232, 3–44.

Losco-Bradley, S. and Kinsley, G. 2002. *Catholme: An Anglo-Saxon Settlement on the Trent Gravels in Staffordshire* (Nottingham: University of Nottingham Department of Archaeology).

Loveluck, C. P. 2007. *Rural Settlement, Lifestyles and Social Change in the Later First Millennium A.D. Anglo-Saxon Flixborough in Its Wider Context*, Excavations at Flixborough Volume 4 (Oxford: Oxbow Books).

Loveluck, C. P. 2013. *Northwest Europe in the Early Middle Ages,* c. *A.D. 600–1150: A Comparative Archaeology* (Cambridge: Cambridge University Press).

Loveluck, C. P. *et al*. 2018. Alpine ice-core evidence for the transformation of the European monetary system, A.D. 640–70, *Antiquity* 92, 1571–85.

Loveluck, C. P. and ten others 2020. Alpine ice and the annual political economy of the Angevin Empire, from the death of Thomas à Becket to Magna Carta, *c.* 1170–1216, *Antiquity* 94 no. 374, 473–90.

Lowerre, A. 2005. *Placing Castles in the Conquest: Landscape, Lordship and Local Politics in the South-East Midlands, 1066–1100*, British Archaeological Reports British Series 385 (Oxford: B. A. R.).

Lucas, G. 1998. A medieval fishery at Whittlesea Mere, Cambridgeshire, *Medieval Archaeology* 42, 19–44.

Lucy, S. 1999. Changing burial rites in Northumbria, A.D. 500–750, 12–43 in Hawkes and Mills (eds).

Lucy, S. 2000. *The Anglo-Saxon Way of Death* (Stroud: Sutton Publishing).

Lucy, S., Newman, R., and *et al*. 2009. The burial of a princess? The later seventh-century cemetery at Westfield Farm, Ely, *Antiquaries Journal* 89, 81–142.

Lucy, S., Tipper, J., and Dickens, A. 2009. *The Anglo-Saxon Settlement and Cemetery at Bloodmoor Hill, Carlton Colville*, East Anglian Archaeology 131 (Cambridge: Cambridge Archaeological Unit).

Lucy, S. and Reynolds, A. (eds) 2002. *Burial in Early Medieval England and Wales*, Society for Medieval Archaeology Monograph 17 (London: S. M. A.).

MacCormick, A. 1996. Metalworking in medieval Nottingham 1100–1640, *Journal of the Historical Metallurgy Society* 30ii, 103–10.

MacGregor, A. 2007. The cult of Master John Schorne, 327–36 in Gilmour (ed.).

MacGregor, A. and Bolick, W. 1993. *Ashmolean Museum, Oxford: Summary Catalogue of the Anglo-Saxon Collections (Non-Ferrous Metals)*, British Archaeological Reports British Series 230 (Oxford: B. A. R.).

MacGregor, A., Mainman, A., and Rogers, N. S. H. 1999. *Craft, Industry and Everyday Life: Bone, Antler and Horn from Anglo-Scandinavian and Medieval York*, Archaeology of York 17/12 (York: Council for British Archaeology).

MacPhail, R. 1981. Soil and botanical studies of the 'Dark Earth', 309–32 in Jones and Dimbleby (eds).

Macpherson-Grant, N. 1995. 3: Chronology: The key factors, 882–91 in Blockley *et al.*

Maddicott, J. R. 1997. Plague in seventh-century England, *Past and Present* 156, 7–54.

Maddicott, J. R. 1999. 'An infinite number of nobles': Quality, quantity and politics in the pre-Reform Parliaments of Henry III, 17–46 in Prestwich *et al*. (eds).

Maddicott, J. R. 2002. Prosperity and power in the age of Bede and Beowulf, *Proceedings of the British Academy* 117, 49–71.

Maddicott, J. R. and Palliser, D. M. (eds) 2000. *The Medieval State: Essays Presented to James Campbell* (London/Rio Grande: Hambledon Press).

Mainman, A. 2019. *Anglian York* (Pickering: Blackthorn Press).

Mainman, A. and Rogers, N. 2004. Craft and economy in Anglo-Scandinavian York, 459–87 in Hall *et al.*

Malcolm, G. and Bowsher, D. 2003. *Middle Saxon London: Excavations at the Royal Opera House 1989–99*, Museum of London Archaeological Services Monograph 15 (London: Museum of London).

Malim, T. 1996. New evidence of the Cambridgeshire Dykes and Worsted Roman Road, *Proceedings of the Cambridgeshire Antiquarian Society* 85, 27–122.

Malim, T. and Hayes, L. 2008. The date and nature of Wat's Dyke: A reassessment in the light of recent investigations at Gobowen, Shropshire, *Anglo-Saxon Studies in Archaeology and History* 15, 147–79.

Maltby, M. 1979. *Faunal Studies on Urban Sites: The Animal Bones from Exeter 1971–1975*, Exeter Archaeology Reports 2 (Sheffield: Department of Prehistory and Archaeology, University of Sheffield).

Margeson, S. 1982. Worked bone, 241–55 in Coad and Streeten.

Margetts, A. 2017. The Hayworth: A lowland vaccary site in south-east England, *Medieval Archaeology* 61i, 117–48.

Marks, R. and Williamson, P. (eds) 2003. *Gothic: Art for England 1400–1547* (London: V & A Publications).

Marsden, P. (ed.) 1989. A late Saxon log-boat from Clapton, London Borough of Hackney, *International Journal of Nautical Archaeology* 18, 89–111.

Marsden, P. 1994. *Ships of the Port of London, First to Eleventh Centuries A.D.*, English Heritage Archaeological Report 3 (London: English Heritage).

Marsden, P. 1996. *Ships of the Port of London, Twelfth to Seventeenth Centuries A.D.*, English Heritage Archaeological Report 5 (London: English Heritage).

Marsden, P. 1997. *Ships and Shipwrecks* (London: Batsford/English Heritage).

Marshall, P. 2012. Making an appearance: Some thoughts on the phenomenon of multiple doorways and large upper openings in Romanesque *donjons* in western France and Britain, *Château-Gaillard* 25, 233–41.

Marshall, P. 2016. Some thoughts on the use of the Anglo-Norman *donjon*, 159–74 in Davies *et al.* (eds).

Marter, P. 2021. Catastrophe and ceramics: A preliminary assessment of the impact of the Black Death of 1348–50 on pottery production in England, 107–16 in Richardson, A.[a] and Allen (eds).

Martin, D. and Martin, B. 2004. *New Winchelsea Sussex: A Medieval Port Town* (King's Lynn: Heritage Marketing and Publications).

Martin, E. 2012. Norfolk, Suffolk, and Essex, 225–48 in Christie and Stamper (eds).

Martin, T. F. 2015. *The Cruciform Brooch and Anglo-Saxon England*, Anglo-Saxon Studies 25 (Woodbridge: Boydell).

Marvin, J. 1998. Cannibalism as an aspect of famine in two English chronicles, 73–86 in Carlin and Rosenthal (eds).

Marzinzik, S. 2003. *Early Anglo-Saxon Belt Buckles (Late Fifth to Early Eighth Century A.D.): Their Classification and Context*, British Archaeological Reports British Series 357 (Oxford: B. A. R.).

Marzinzik, S. 2014. An outstanding hoard of gold objects deposited in the late Saxon period, *Medieval Archaeology* 58, 256–68.
Mason, D. J. P. 1985. *Excavations at Chester: 26–42 Lower Bridge Street 1974–6: The Dark Age and Saxon Periods*, Grosvenor Museum Archaeological Excavation and Survey Report 3 (Chester: Chester City Council).
Masschaele, J. 1993. Transport costs in medieval England, *Economic History Review* 46ii, 266–79.
Matthews, G. 2020–21. Grandeur and decline in an élite landscape, *Castle Studies Group Journal* 34, 230–7.
Mayer, P. J. 1990. Calstock and the Bere Alston silver-lead mines in the first quarter of the fourteenth century, *Cornish Archaeology* 29, 79–95.
Mayes, P. J. and Scott, K. 1984. *Pottery Kilns at Chilvers Coton, Nuneaton*, Society for Medieval Archaeology Monograph 10 (London: S. M. A.).
Mayhew, N. J. 1995. Population, money supply, and the velocity of circulation in England, *Economic History Review* 18ii, 238–57.
Maynard, D. 1988. Excavations on a pipe-line near the River Frome, *Proceedings of the Dorset Natural History and Archaeological Society* 110, 77–98.
Mays, S., Harding, C., and Heighway, C. 2007. *The Churchyard*, Wharram: A Study of Settlement on the Yorkshire Wolds, 11/York University Archaeological Publications 13 (York: University of York).
Mays, S. *et al*. 2017. A multi-disciplinary study of a burnt and mutilated assemblage from a deserted medieval village in England, *Journal of Archaeological Science Reports* 16, 441–55.
McAvoy, F. 1994. Marine salt extraction: The excavation of salterns at Wainfleet St Mary, Lincolnshire, *Medieval Archaeology* 38, 134–63.
McBride, A. 2020. *The Role of Anglo-Saxon Great Hall Complexes in Kingdom Formation, in Comparison and in Context A.D. 500–750* (Oxford: Archaeopress Archaeology).
McCarthy, M. 1990. *A Roman, Anglian and Medieval Site at Blackfriars Street, Carlisle*, Cumberland and Westmorland Antiquarian and Archaeological Society Research Series 4 (Carlisle: C. W. A. A. S.).
McCarthy, M. 2014. A post-Roman sequence at Carlisle Cathedral, *Archaeological Journal* 171, 185–257.
McCarthy, M. 2018. Carlisle: Function and change between the first and seventh centuries A.D., *Archaeological Journal* 175, 292–314.
McCarthy, M. R. and Brooks, C. M. 1989a. *Medieval Pottery in Britain A.D. 900–1600* (Leicester University Press).
McCarthy, M. R. and Brooks, C. M. 1989b. The establishment of a medieval pottery sequence in Cumbria, England, 21–37 in Gaimster and Redknap (eds).
McClain, A. 2012. Theory, disciplinary perspectives and the archaeology of later medieval England, *Medieval Archaeology* 56, 131–70.
McClain, A. and Sykes, N. 2019. New archaeologies of the Norman Conquest, *Anglo-Norman Studies* 41, 85–101.
McDonnell, K. G. T. 1978. *Medieval London Suburbs* (Chichester: Phillimore).
McGrail, S. 1987. *Ancient Boats in North-West Europe* (London: Longman).
McGrail, S. 2001. *Boats of the World: From the Stone Age to Medieval Times* (Oxford: Oxford University Press).
McIntosh, M. K. 1998. *Controlling Misbehaviour in England, 1370–1600* (Cambridge: Cambridge University Press).

McKerracher, M. 2018. *Farming Transformed in Anglo-Saxon England: Agriculture in the Long Eighth Century* (Oxford: Windgather Press).
McKinley, J. I. 1994. *The Anglo-Saxon Cemetery at Spong Hill, North Elmham Part VIII: The Cremations*, East Anglian Archaeology Report 69 (Gressenhall: Norfolk Museums Services).
McKinley, J. I. 1999. Excavations at Tinney's Lane, Sherborne, Dorset, *Proceedings of the Dorset Natural History and Archaeological Society* 121, 53–68.
McKinley, J. I. 2003. The early Saxon cemetery at Park Lane, Croydon, *Surrey Archaeological Collections* 90, 1–116.
McNeil, R. 1983. Two twelfth-century wich houses in Nantwich, Cheshire, *Medieval Archaeology* 27, 40–88.
McNeill, T. and Scott, G. 2018. Langley Castle, Northumberland, 314–49 in Guy (ed.).
McOmish, D., Field, D., and Brown, G. 2002. *The Field Archaeology of the Salisbury Plain Training Area* (Swindon: English Heritage).
McRee, B. R. 1994. Unity or division? The social meaning of guild ceremony in urban communities, 189–207 in Hanawalt and Reyerson (eds).
Meadows, I. 2019. *The Pioneer Burial: A High-Status Burial from Wollaston, Northamptonshire* (Oxford: Archaeopress) ['Pioneer' from the name of the company operating the quarry where the burial was found, not an implied identification].
Mees, K. 2019. *Burial, Landscape and Identity in Early Medieval Wessex* (Woodbridge: Boydell and Brewer).
Meeson, B. 2012. Structural trends in English medieval buildings: new insights from dendrochronology, *Vernacular Architecture* 43, 58–75.
Meeson, B. 2019. Base crucks: Have we got to the crux?, 70–96 in Alcock *et al.* (eds).
Meeson, B. and Alcock, N. 2017. Black Swan Terrace, Upper Spon Street, Coventry: A comparison of medieval renters, *Vernacular Architecture* 47, 1–19.
Mellor, M. 1985. Pottery, 73–6 in Sturdy and Munby.
Mellor, M. 1994a. A synthesis of middle and late Saxon, medieval and early post-medieval pottery in the Oxford region, *Oxoniensia* 59, 17–218.
Mellor, M. 1994b. Early Saxon, medieval and post-medieval pottery, 325–54 in Allen, T.G.
Mellor, M. 1997. *Pots and People That Have Shaped the Heritage of Medieval and Later England* (Oxford: Ashmolean Museum).
Mellor, M. 2005. Making and using pottery in town and country, 149–64 in Giles and Dyer (eds).
Mellor, M. 2018. Overview: Medieval industry and commerce, 435–54 in Gerrard and Gutiérrez (eds).
Mepham, L. and Brown, L. 2007. The Broughton to Timsbury Pipeline, Part 1: A late Saxon pottery kiln and the production centre at Michelmersh, Hampshire, *Proceedings of the Hampshire Field Club and Archaeological Society* 62, 35–58.
Mercer, D. 2018. The Water Tower at Chester reconsidered, 295–313 in Guy (ed.).
Mercer, D. 2020–21. Review of P. Dixon, *Wingfield Manor* (London: English Heritage, 2019), *Castle Studies Group Journal* 34, 325–30.
Meredith, J. 2006. *The Iron Industry of the Forest of Dean* (Stroud: Tempus).
Metcalf, D. M. 1987. The taxation of moneyers under Edward the Confessor and in 1086, 279–93 in Holt (ed.).
Metcalf, D. M. 2007. Regions around the North Sea with a monetized economy in the pre-viking and viking ages, 1–12 in Graham-Campbell and Williams (eds).
Metcalf, D. M. and Northover, J. P. 1985. Debasement of coinage in southern England in the age of King Alfred, *Numismatic Chronicle* 145, 150–76.

Miles, D. (ed.) 1986. *Archaeology at Barton Court Farm, Abingdon, Oxfordshire: An Investigation of Late Neolithic, Iron Age, Romano-British and Saxon Settlement*, Council for British Archaeology Research Report 50/Oxford Archaeological Unit Report 3 (London: C. B. A.).

Miles, D. H. and Worthington, M. J. 1998. List 91: Hampshire Dendrochronological Project: Phase 4, *Vernacular Architecture* 29, 117–21.

Miles, D. H., Bridge, M., and Clark, D. 2014. List 266: Oxfordshire dendrochronology project, *Vernacular Architecture* 45, 121–5.

Miles, D. H. and six others 2019. Stable isotope dating of historic buildings, *Vernacular Architcture* 50, 78–87.

Mileson, S. A. 2009. *Parks in Medieval England* (Oxford: Oxford University Press).

Mileson, S. A. 2018. Royal and aristocratic landscapes of pleasure, 386–400 in Gerrard and Gutiérrez (eds).

Millar, E. G. 1932. *The Luttrell Psalter* (London: Trustees of the British Museum).

Miller, I. and Radford, A. 2020. Excavations in the northern quarter of medieval Coventry, *Medieval Archaeology* 64ii, 378–84.

Millett, M. and James, S. 1983. Excavations at Cowdery's Down, Basingstoke, Hampshire, 1978–81, *Archaeological Journal* 140, 151–279.

Mills, A. D. 2011. *A Dictionary of British Place-Names*, First Edition Revised (Oxford: Oxford University Press).

Milne, G. 2003. *The Port of Medieval London* (Stroud: Tempus).

Milne, G. 2004. The fourteenth-century merchant ship from Sandwich: A study in medieval maritime archaeology, *Archaeologia Cantiana* 124, 227–63.

Moffett, C. 2017. Slate discs at Tintagel Castle: Evidence for post-Roman mead production?, *Antiquaries Journal* 97, 119–43.

Moffett, L. 2011. Food plants on archaeological sites: The nature of the archaeobotanical record, 346–60 in Hamerow *et al.* (eds).

Moir, A., Nash, G., and Reid, A. 2019. New insights into timber-framing in Shropshire: Findings from the Tilley Timber Project, *Vernacular Architecture* 50, 40–52.

Molyneaux, G. 2015. *The Formation of the English Kingdom in the Tenth Century* (Oxford: Oxford University Press).

Money, J. H. 1971. Medieval iron-workings at Rotherfield, Sussex, *Medieval Archaeology* 15, 86–111.

Moore, E. W. 1985. *The Fairs of Medieval England: An Introductory Study* (Toronto: Pontifical Institute of Medieval Studies, University of Toronto).

Moore, N. J. 1991. Brick, 211–36 in Blair and Ramsay (eds).

Moorhead, T. S. N. 2006. Roman bronze coinage in sub-Roman and early anglo-saxon England, 99–109 in Cook and Williams (eds).

Moorhead, T. S. N. and Walton, P. 2014. Coinage at the end of Roman Britain, 99–116 in Haarer (ed.).

Moorhouse, S. 1972. Medieval distilling-apparatus of glass and pottery, *Medieval Archaeology* 16, 79–121.

Moorhouse, S. 1978. Documentary evidence for the uses of medieval pottery: An interim statement, *Medieval Ceramics* 2, 3–22.

Moorhouse, S. 1983. Documentary evidence and its potential for understanding the inland movement of medieval pottery, *Medieval Ceramics* 7, 45–87.

Moran, M. 2010. A second terrace of crucks in Much Wenlock, Shropshire, *Vernacular Architecture* 41, 45–50.

Morgan, P. 1999. Of worms and war: 1380–1555, 119–51 in Jupp and Gittings (eds).

Morgan Evans, D. 2014. Legacy hunting and Welsh identities, 173–81 in Haarer (ed.).
Morley, B. and Gurney, D. 1997. *Castle Rising Castle, Norfolk*, East Anglian Archaeology 81 (Gressenhall: East Anglian Archaeological Committee).
Morris, C. A. 1983. A late Saxon hoard of iron and copper-alloy artefacts from Nazeing, Essex, *Medieval Archaeology* 27, 27–39.
Morris, C. A. 2000. *Wood and Woodworking in Anglo-Scandinavian and Medieval York*, Archaeology of York 17/13 (York: Council for British Archaeology).
Morris, C. A. 2009. The wooden bowl, 43–4 in Ripper and Cooper.
Morris, J. and Jervis, B. 2011. What's so special? A reinterpretation of anglo-saxon 'special deposits', *Medieval Archaeology* 55, 66–81.
Morris, M. and Buckley, R. 2013. *Richard III: The King under the Car Park* (Leicester: University of Leicester School of Archaeology).
Morris, R. 1989. *Churches in the Landscape* (London: Dent).
Morrisson, C. 2014. Byzantine coins in early medieval Britain: A Byzantinist's assessment, 207–42 in Naismith *et al.* (eds).
Mould, Q. 2015. The home-made shoe, a glimpse of a hidden, but most 'affordable' craft, 125–42 in Hansen *et al.* (eds).
Mould, Q. and Cameron, E. 2015. Fashion and necessity: Anglo-Norman leatherworkers and changing markets, 143–56 in Hansen *et al.* (eds).
Mudd, A. and Webster, M. 2011. *Iron Age and Middle Saxon Settlements at West Fen Road, Ely, Cambridgeshire*, British Archaeological Reports British Series 538 (Oxford: B. A. R.).
Müldner, G. and Richards, M. P. 2006. Diet in medieval England: the evidence from stable isotopes, 228–38 in Woolgar *et al.* (eds).
Müldner, G. 2009. Investigating medieval diet and society by stable isotope analysis of human bone, 327–46 in Gilchrist and Reynolds (eds).
Müller, M. 2005. Social control and the hue and cry in two fourteenth-century villages, *Journal of Medieval History* 31, 29–53.
Müller, M. 2010. Food, hierarchy and class conflict, 231–48 in Goddard *et al.* (eds).
Munby, J. T. 1991. Wood, 379–405 in Blair and Ramsay (eds).
Munby, J. T. and Steane, J. M. 1995. Swalcliffe: A New College barn in the fifteenth century, *Oxoniensia* 60, 333–78.
Munby, J. T., Norton, A., Poore, D., and Dodd, A. 2019. *Excavations at Oxford Castle 1999–2009*, Thames Valley Landscapes Monograph 44 (Oxford: Oxford University School of Archaeology).
Mundill, R. R. 2003. Edward I and the final phase of Anglo-Jewry, 55–70 in Skinner (ed.).
Munro, J. H. 1998. The 'industrial crisis' of the English textile towns, 1290–1330, 103–42 in Prestwich *et al.* (eds).
Murphy, P. 2009. *The English Coast: A History and a Prospect* (London: Continuum).
Musty, J. and Algar, D. 1986. Excavations at the deserted medieval village of Gomeldon, near Salisbury, *Wiltshire Natural History and Archaeological Magazine* 80, 127–69.
Mynard, D. C. and Zeepvat, R. J. 1992. *Great Linford*, Buckinghamshire Archaeological Society Monograph 3 (Aylesbury: B. A. S.).
Naismith, R. 2012. *Money and Power in Anglo-Saxon England: The Southern English Kingdoms, 757–865* (Cambridge: Cambridge University Press).
Naismith, R. 2017. *Medieval European Coinage 8: Britain and Ireland* c. *400–1066* (Cambridge: Cambridge University Press).
Naismith, R., Allen, M., and Screen, A. (eds) 2014. *Early Medieval Monetary History: Studies in Memory of Mark Blackburn* (Aldershot: Ashgate).

Nayling, N. 1998. *The Magor Pill Medieval Wreck*, Council for British Archaeology Research Report 115 (York: C. B. A.).

Nayling, N. 2002. List 125: Tree-ring dates from the University of Wales Lampeter Dendrochronology Laboratory, *Vernacular Architecture* 33, 78–81.

Nayling, N. and Jones, T. 2014. The Newport medieval ship, Wales, United Kingdom, *International Journal of Nautical Archaeology* 43ii, 239–78.

Naylor, J. 2015. Portable Antiquities Scheme Report, *Medieval Archaeology* 59, 290–310.

Naylor, J. 2017. Portable Antiquities Scheme Report, *Medieval Archaeology* 61ii, 400–20.

Niblett, R. 2010. Offa's St Albans, 129–34 in Henig and Ramsay (eds).

Nightingale, P. 1985. The London Pepperers' Guild and some twelfth-century English trading links with Spain, *Bulletin of the Institute of Historical Research* 58, 123–32.

Nightingale, P. 1995. *A Medieval Mercantile Community: The Grocers' Company and the Politics and Trade of London, 1000–1485* (New Haven/London: Yale University Press).

Nightingale, P. 2004. The Lay Subsidies and the distribution of wealth in medieval England, 1275–1334, *Economic History Review* 57i, 1–32.

Norton, C. 2019. Viewing the Bayeux Tapestry, now and then, *Journal of the British Archaeological Association* 172, 52–89.

Nowakowski, J. A. and Thomas, C. 1990. *Excavations at Tintagel Parish Churchyard, Cornwall, Spring 1990* (Truro: Cornwall Archaeological Unit and Institute for Cornish Studies).

O'Brien, C. 1991. Newcastle upon Tyne and its North Sea trade, 36–42 in Good *et al.* (eds).

O'Brien, C., Brown, L., Dixon, S., and Nicholson, R. 1988. *The Origins of the Newcastle Quayside: Excavations at Queen Street and Dog Bank*, Society of Antiquaries of Newcastle-upon-Tyne Monograph 3 (Newcastle: S. A. N.).

O'Connor, T. P. 1982. *Animal Bones from Flaxengate, Lincoln* c. *870–1500*, Archaeology of Lincoln 18–1 (London: Council for British Archaeology).

O'Connor, T. P. 2001. On the interpretation of animal bone asemblages from *wic* sites, 54–60 in Hill and Cowie (eds).

O'Connor, T. P. 2004. Animal bones from Anglo-Scandinavian York, 427–43 in Hall *et al.* (eds).

O'Connor, T. P. 2011. Animal husbandry, 361–76 in Hamerow *et al.* (eds).

Oddy, W. A. 1995. Anglo-saxon, 1068 in Blockley *et al.*

O'Donnell, R. P. 2018. Field systems and the arable fields, 86–101 in Gerrard and Gutiérrez (eds).

Okasha, E. 1993. *Corpus of Early Christian Inscribed Stones of South-West Britain* (Leicester: Leicester University Press).

Oksanen, E. and Lewis, M. 2020. Medieval commercial sites: As seen through the Portable Antiquities Scheme, *Antiquaries Journal* 100, 109–40.

Oldland, J. 2014. Wool and cloth production in late medieval and Tudor England, *Economic History Review* 67i, 25–47.

Oliver, T., Howard-Davis, C., and Newman, R. 1996. A post-Roman settlement at Fremington, near Brougham, 127–69 in Lambert.

Olva, M. 2008. Nuns at home: The domesticity of sacred space, 145–61 in Kowaleski and Goldberg (eds).

Oosthuizen, S. 2017. *The Anglo-Saxon Fenland* (Oxford: Windgather Press).

Oosthuizen, S. 2019. *The Emergence of the English* (Amsterdam: Amsterdam University Press).

Oosthuizen, S. and Taylor, C. 2000. 'John O'Gaunt's House': Bassingbourn, Cambridgeshire: A fifteenth-century landscape, *Landscape History* 22, 61–76.

Orme, N. 1996. Church and chapel in medieval England, *Transactions of the Royal Historical Society* 6, 75–102.

Ormrod, W. M. 2000a. The English state and the Plantagenet Empire: A fiscal perspective, 197–214 in Maddicott and Palliser (eds).

Ormrod, W. M. 2000b. Competing capitals? York and London in the fourteenth century, 75–98 in Jones *et al.* (eds).

Ormrod, W. M., Lambert, B., and Mackman, J. 2019. *Immigrant England 1300–1500* (Manchester: Manchester University Press).

O'Sullivan, D. 2011. Normanizing the north: The evidence of anglo-saxon and Anglo-Scandinavian sculpture, *Medieval Archaeology* 55, 163–91.

O'Sullivan, D. 2013. *In the Company of Preachers: The Archaeology of Medieval Friaries in England* (London: Taylor and Francis).

O'Sullivan, D. and Young, R. 1991. The early medieval settlement at Green Shiel, Northumberland, *Archaeologia Aeliana* 19, 55–70.

Ottaway, P. 2000. Excavations on the site of the Roman signal station at Carr Naze, Filey, 1993–94, *Archaeological Journal* 157, 79–199.

Ottaway, P. 2013. 'All shapes and sizes': Anglo-saxon knives *c.* 700–1100, 111–38 in Reynolds and Webster (eds).

Ottaway, P. 2015. Commercial archaeology and the study of Roman York, 1990–2013, 20–43 in Fulford and Holbrook (eds).

Ottaway, P. 2017. *Winchester: St Swithun's 'City of Happiness and Good Fortune', an Archaeological Assessment* (Oxford/Philadelphia: Oxbow Books).

Ottaway, P. and Rogers, N. S. H. 2002. *Craft, Industry and Everyday Life: Finds from Medieval York*, Archaeology of York 17/15 (York: Council for British Archaeology).

Owen, D. M. 1971. *Church and Society in Medieval Lincolnshire*, History of Lincolnshire 5 (Lincoln: Lincolnshire Local History Society).

Owen, D. M. (ed.) 1984. *The Making of King's Lynn* (Oxford: Oxford University Press).

Owen-Crocker, G. R. 2007. British wives and slaves? Possible Romano-British techniques in 'women's work', 80–90 in Higham (ed.).

Owen-Crocker, G. R. 2009. Behind the Bayeux Tapestry, 119–29 in Foys *et al.* (eds).

Owen-Crocker, G. R. 2012. Llan-Gors decorated garment, 338–40 in Owen-Crocker *et al.* (eds).

Owen-Crocker, G. R. and Thompson, S. D. (eds) 2014. *Towns and Topography: Essays in Memory of David Hill* (Oxford: Oxbow Books).

Owen-Crocker, G. R., Coatsworth, E., and Hayward, M. (eds) 2012. *Encyclopaedia of Dress and Textiles in the British Isles,* c. *450–1450* (Leiden/Boston: Brill).

Pacey, A. 2005. Some carpenters' marks in Arabic numerals, *Vernacular Architecture* 36, 69–72.

Pader, E.-J. 1982. *Symbolism, Social Relations and the Interpretation of Mortuary Remains*, British Archaeological Reports International Series 130 (Oxford: B. A. R.).

Page, P., Atherton, K., and Hardy, A. 2005. *Barentin's Manor. Excavations of the Moated Manor at Hardings Field, Chalgrove, Oxfordshire, 1976-9* (Oxford: Oxford Archaeology).

Page, R. I. 1964. The inscriptions, 67–90 in Wilson.

Palliser, D., Slater, T. R., and Dennison, E. P. 2000. The topography of towns 600–1300, 153–86 in Palliser (ed.).

Palliser, D. (ed.) 2000. *The Cambridge Urban History of Britain. Volume I, 600–1540* (Cambridge: Cambridge University Press).

Pallister, A. and Wrathmell, S. 1990. The deserted village of West Hartburn, third report: Excavation of Site D and discussion, 59–75 in Vyner (ed.).

Palmer, N. 1980. A beaker burial and medieval tenements in The Hamel, Oxford, *Oxoniensia* 45, 124–225.

Papworth, M. 2019. Excavation and survey at Badbury Rings, Dorset, *Proceedings of the Dorset Natural History and Archaeological Society* 140, 130–71.

Papworth, M. 2021a. The case for Chedworth villa. Exploring evidence for fifth-century occupation, *Current Archaeology* 373, 18–25.

Papworth, M. 2021b. A Saxon god? Dating the Cerne Abbas giant, *British Archaeology* 179, 48–53.

Parfitt, K. and Anderson, T. 2012. *Buckland Anglo-Saxon Cemetery, Dover. Excavations 1994*, Archaeology of Canterbury n. s. 6 (Canterbury: Canterbury Archaeological Trust).

Parfitt, K. and Clarke, H. 2016. Scouring the conduit head at Wodnesborough: Investigation into the Convent Well, Sandwich, *Archaeologia Cantiana* 137, 127–48.

Parfitt, K., Corke, B., and Cotter, J. 2006. *Townwall Street, Dover: Excavations 1996*, Archaeology of Canterbury, n. s. 3 (Canterbury: Canterbury Archaeological Trust).

Parker, V. 1971. *The Making of King's Lynn* (London/Chichester: Phillimore).

Parkhouse, J. 2014. Putting lava on the map, 19–25 in Owen-Crocker and Thomson (eds).

Parry, S. 2006. *Raunds Area Survey: An Archaeological Study of the Landscape of Raunds, Northamptonshire, 1985–94* (Oxford: Oxbow Books).

Parsons, A. J. *et al.* 2014. *Shadows in the Sand. Excavation of a Viking-Age Cemetery at Cumwhitton, Cumberland* (Oxford: Oxford Archaeology).

Parsons, D. 1996. Liturgical and social aspects, 58–66 in Boddington.

Parsons, D. 2018. Quarrying and extractive industries, 455–74 in Gerrard and Gutiérrez (eds).

Parsons, D. and Sutherland, D. S. 2013. *The Anglo-Saxon Church of All Saints, Brixworth, Northamptonshire. Survey, Excavation and Analysis 1972–2010* (Oxford/Oakville: Oxbow Books).

Payne, M. and Foster, R. 2020. The medieval sacristy at Westminster Abbey, *Antiquaries Journal* 100, 240–73.

Peacock, D. P. S. 1997. Charlemagne's black stones: The reuse of Roman columns in early medieval Europe, *Antiquity* 71 no. 273, 709–15.

Pearce, J. 2015. Imported non-local and continental pottery, 263–6 in Ayre and Wroe-Brown b.

Pearce, J. and Vince, A. G. 1988. *A Dated Type-Series of London Medieval Pottery. Part 4: Surrey Whitewares* (London: London and Middlesex Archaeological Society).

Pearson, S. 1994. *The Medieval Houses of Kent: An Historical Analysis* (London: Her Majesty's Stationery Office).

Pearson, S. 2005. Rural and urban houses 1100–1500: 'urban adaptation' reconsidered, 43–64 in Giles and Dyer (eds).

Pearson, S. 2009. Medieval houses in English towns: Form and location, *Vernacular Architecture* 40, 1–22.

Pedrick, G. 1904. *Borough Seals of the Gothic Period* (London: J. M. Dent).

Peirce, I. 1986. The knight, his arms and his armour in the eleventh and twelfth centuries, 152–64 in Harper-Bill and Harvey (eds).

Pelteret, D. A. E. 1995. *Slavery in Early Medieval Europe: From the Reign of Alfred to the Early Twelfth Century* (Woodbridge: Boydell and Brewer).

Penn, K. 2000. *Norwich Southern Bypass, Part II: Anglo-Saxon Cemetery at Harford Farm, Caistor St Edmund*, East Anglian Archaeology 92 (Gressenhall: Norfolk Museums Service).

Penn, K. 2011. *The Anglo-Saxon Cemetery at Shrubland Hall Quarry, Coddenham, Suffolk*, East Anglian Archaeology 139 (Bury St Edmunds: Suffolk County Council Archaeology Service).

Penn, K. and Brugman, B. 2007. *Aspects of Anglo-Saxon Inhumation Burial: Morning Thorpe, Spong Hill, Bergh Apton and Westgarth Gardens*, East Anglian Archaeology 119 (Gressenhall: Norfolk Museums and Archaeology Service).

Penny-Mason, B. J. and Gowland, R. L. 2014. The children of the Reformation: Childhood palaeoepdemiology in Britain, AD 1000–1700, *Medieval Archaeology* 58, 162–94.

Penoyre, J. 1998. Medieval Somerset roofs, *Vernacular Architecture* 29, 22–32.

Perring, D. 1981. *Early Medieval Occupation at Flaxengate, Lincoln*, Archaeology of Lincoln 9–1 (London: Council for British Archaeology).

Perring, D. 2015. Recent advances in the understanding of Roman London, 20–47 in Fulford and Holbrook (eds).

Perry, G. J. 2016. Pottery production in Anglo-Scandinavian Torksey, Lincolnshire: Reconstructing and contextualizing the *châine opèratoire*, *Medieval Archaeology* 60, 72–114.

Perry, G. J. 2019. Situation vacant: Potter required in the newly-founded late Saxon *burh* of Newark-on-Trent, Nottinghamshire, *Antiquaries Journal* 99, 33–61.

Pestell, T. and Ulmschneider, K. (eds) 2003. *Markets in Early Medieval Europe. Trading and 'Productive' Sites* (Macclesfield: Windgather).

Petre, J. (ed.) 1985. *Richard III. Crown and People* (Stroud: Alan Sutton).

Petts, D. 2009. Variation in the British burial rite: A.D. 400–700, 207–21 in Sayer and Williams (eds).

Petts, D. 2014. Christianity and cross-Channel connectivity in late and sub-Roman Britain, 73–86 in Haarer (ed.).

Phillips, D. 1985. *The Cathedral of Thomas of Bayeux: Excavation at York Minster, Volume II* (London: Her Majesty's Stationery Office).

Pickvance, C. G. 2018. The Canterbury group of arcaded gothic early medieval chests: A dendrochronological and comparative study, *Antiquaries Journal* 98, 149–86.

Piercy, J. 2019. *The Moneyers of England, 973-1086*, British Archaeological Reports British Series 650 (Oxford: B. A. R.).

Pilbrow, F. 2002. Looking for the Knights of the Bath: Dubbing to knighthood in Lancastrian and Yorkist England, 195–218 in Coss and Keen (eds).

Pine, J. 2012. Medieval and later occupation at 51–53 St Mary's Street, 9–38 in Preston (ed.).

Pirie, E. J. E. 1986a. *Post-Roman Coins from York Excavations 1971–81*, Archaeology of York 18/1 (London: Council for British Archaeology).

Pirie, E. J. E. 1986b. Finds of 'sceattas' and 'stycas' of Northumbria, 67–90 in Blackburn (ed.).

Platt, C. 1973. *Medieval Southampton. The Port and Trading Community, A. D. 1000–1600* (London: Routledge and Kegan Paul).

Platt, C. 1990. *The Architecture of Medieval Britain* (New Haven/London: Yale University Press).

Platt, C. 2007. Revisionism in castle studies, *Medieval Archaeology* 51, 83–102.

Platt, C. 2010. The homestead moat: Security or status?, *Archaeological Journal* 167, 115–33.

Platt, C. and Coleman-Smith 1975. *Excavations in Medieval Southampton 1953–1969*, two volumes (Leicester: Leicester University Press).

Pluskowski, A. 2010. Animal magic, 103–27 in Carver *et al.* (eds).

Poole, K. 2015. Foxes and badgers in anglo-saxon life and landscape, *Archaeological Journal* 172, 389–422.

Poos, L. R. 1991. *A Rural Society after the Black Death: Essex 1350–1525* (Cambridge: Cambridge University Press).

Potter, J. F. 2008. *The Medieval Town Walls of Great Yarmouth*, British Archaeological Reports British Series 461 (Oxford: B. A. R.).

Pounds, N. 1989. *Hearth and Home* (Indiana: Indiana University Press).

Powlesland, D. 1999. The anglo-saxon settlement at West Heslerton, North Yorkshire, 55–65 in Hawkes and Mills (eds).

Powlesland, D. 2014. Reflections upon the anglo-saxon landscape and settlement of the Vale of Pickering, Yorkshire, 111–23 in Owen-Crocker and Thompson (eds).

Preston, S. (ed.) 2012. *Archaeological Investigations in Wallingford, Oxfordshire, 1992–2010*, Thames Valley Archaeological Services Monograph 10 (Reading: T. V. A. S.).

Prestwich, M. 2005. *Plantagenet England 1225–1360* (Oxford: Oxford University Press).

Prestwich, M., Britnell, R., and Frame, R. (eds) 1998. *Thirteenth-Century England, VII: Proceedings of the Durham Conference 1997* (Woodbridge: Boydell Press).

Price, E. 2000. *Frocester, a Romano-British Settlement, its Antecedents and Successors, Volume 2, The Finds* (Gloucester: Gloucester and District Archaeological Research Group).

Price, J. (ed.). 2000. *Glass in Britain and Ireland, A.D. 350–1100*, British Museum Occasional Paper 127 (London: B. M.).

Pringle, G. 2020. Settlement and social and economic patterns at Old Basing, Hampshire: The results of a community archaeology project, *Proceedings of the Hampshire Field Club and Archaeological Society* 75i, 273–322.

Pritchard, F. 1991. The small finds, 120–278 in Vince (ed.).

Purton, P. 2009–10. Guns and loops during the first half century of gunpowder artillery, *Castle Studies Group Journal* 23, 215–9.

Purton, P. 2018. A medieval wall breaker: Origins, evolution and impact of the trebuchet, 174–89 in Guy (ed.).

Purton, P. 2020–21. A lonely gun-hole – (Oxford city wall), *Castle Studies Group Journal* 34, 281–4.

Quiney, A. 2003. *Town Houses of Medieval Britain* (New Haven/London: Yale University Press).

Rackham, J. 1979. *Rattus rattus*: The introduction of the black rat into Britain, *Antiquity* 53, 112–20.

Rahtz, P. 1979. *The Saxon and Medieval Palaces at Cheddar*, British Archaeological Reports British Series 65 (Oxford: B. A. R.).

Rahtz, P. and Meeson, R. 1992. *An Anglo-Saxon Watermill at Tamworth. Excavations in the Bolebridge Street Area of Tamworth, Staffordshire, in 1971 and 1978*, Council for British Archaeology Research Report 83 (London: Council for British Archaeology).

Rahtz, P., Hirst, S., and Wright, S. M. 2000. *Cannington Cemetery*, Britannia Monograph Series 17 (London: Society for the Promotion of Roman Studies).

Rahtz, P. *et al.* 1992. *Cadbury Congresbury 1968–73. A Late/Post-Roman Hilltop Settlement in Somerset*, British Archaeological Reports British Series 223 (Oxford: Tempus Reparatum).

Ramsay, N. 1991. Introduction, i-xxxiv in Blair and Ramsay (eds).

Rance, A. B. 1986. The Bevis and Ascupart panels, Bargate Museum, Southampton, *Proceedings of the Hampshire Field Club and Archaeological Society* 42, 147–53.

Randall, C. 2020. *'Anciently a Manor'. Excavation of a Medieval Site at Lower Putton Lane, Chickerell, Dorset*, Dorset Natural History and Archaeological Society Monograph 24 (Dorchester: D. N. H. A. S.).

Rawcliffe, C. 1995. *Medicine and Society in Later Medieval England* (Stroud: Alan Sutton Publishing).

Rawcliffe, C. 2004. Sickness and health, 301–26 in Rawcliffe and Wilson (eds).

Rawcliffe, C. 2005. The earthly and spiritual topography of suburban hospitals, 251–74 in Giles and Dyer (eds).

Rawcliffe, C. 2011. Health and disease, 66–75 in Crick and van Houts (eds).

Rawcliffe, C. and Wilson, R. (eds) 2004. *Medieval Norwich* (London/New York: Hambledon Press).

Ray, K. 2015. *The Archaeology of Herefordshire* (Hereford: Logaston Press).

Ray, K. and Bapty, I. 2014. *Offa's Dyke: Landscape and Hegemony in Eighth-Century Britain* (Oxford: Windgather Press).

Razi, Z. and Smith, R. (eds) 1996. *Medieval Society and the Manor Court* (Oxford: Clarendon Press).

RCHM: Royal Commission on Historical Monuments (England) 1959. Wareham West Walls, *Medieval Archaeology*, 3, 120–38.

RCHM: Royal Commission on Historical Monuments (England) 1980. *Ancient and Historical Monuments in the City of Salisbury*, Volume 1 (London: Her Majesty's Stationery Office).

Redknap, M. 1984. *The Cattewater Wreck: The Investigation of an Armed Vessel of the Early Sixteenth Century*, British Archaeological Reports British Series 131 (Oxford: B. A. R.).

Reed, S. J., Bidwell, P., and Allan, J. 2011. Excavations at Bantham, South Devon, and post-Roman trade in south-west England, *Medieval Archaeology* 55, 82–138.

Reed, S. J., Juleff, G., and Bayer, O. J. 2006. Three late Saxon iron-smelting furnaces at Burlescombe, Devon, *Proceedings of the Devon Archaeological Society* 64, 71–122.

Rees, H., Crummy, N., and Ottaway, P. J. 2008. *Artefacts and Society in Roman and Medieval Winchester: Small Finds from the Suburbs and Defences, 1971–1986*, Winchester: Winchester Museums Service.

Renn, D. F. 1982. Canterbury Castle in the early Middle Ages, 70–5 in Bennett *et al.*

Renn, D. F. 2011–12. Arrow-loops in the Great Tower of Kenilworth Castle: Symbolism vs active/passive 'defence', *Castle Studies Group Journal* 25, 175–9.

Renn, D. F. 2016–17. A return to the burh-geat, *Castle Studies Group Journal* 30, 167.

Reuter, T. (ed.) 2003. *Alfred the Great: Papers from the Eleventh-Centenary Conferences* (Aldershot/Burlington: Ashgate).

Reynolds, A. 2003. Boundaries and settlements in later sixth- to eleventh-century England, *Anglo-Saxon Studies in Archaeology and History* 12, 98–136.

Reynolds, A. 2009a. *Anglo-Saxon Deviant Burial Customs* (Oxford: Oxford University Press).

Reynolds, A. 2009b. Medieval landscapes: An early medieval perspective, 409–34 in Gilchrist and Reynolds (eds).

Reynolds, A. and Semple, S. 2011. Anglo-saxon non-funerary weapon depositions, 40–8 in Brookes *et al.* (eds).

Reynolds, A. and Webster, L. (eds) 2013. *Early Medieval Art and Archaeology in the Northern World: Studies in Honour of James Graham-Campbell* (Leiden/Boston: Brill).

Reynolds, R. 2017. Food from the water: Fishing, 136–51 in Clegg Hyer and Hooke (eds).
Richards, J. D. 1987. *The Significance of Form and Decoration of Anglo-Saxon Cremation Urns*, British Archaeological Reports British Series 166 (Oxford: B. A. R.).
Richards, J. D. 2004. Excavations at the viking barrow cemetery at Heath Wood, Ingleby, Derbyshire, *Antiquaries Journal* 84, 23–116.
Richards, J. D. 2013. Cottam, Cowlam and environs: An anglo-saxon estate on the Yorkshire Wolds, *Archaeological Journal* 170, 201–71.
Richards, J. D. and Haldenby, D. 2018. The scale and impact of viking settlement in Northumbria, *Medieval Archaeology* 62, 322–50.
Richardson, A. 2011. The third way: Thoughts on non-Saxon identity south of the Thames, A.D. 450–600, 72–81 in Brookes *et al.* (eds).
Richardson, A.[a] 2003. Gender and space in English royal palaces *c.* 1160–*c.* 1547, *Medieval Archaeology* 47, 131–66.
Richardson, A.[a] and Allen, M. (eds) 2021. *Building on the Past: Medieval and Post-Medieval Essays in Honour of Tom Beaumont James*, British Archaeological Reports British Series 662 (Oxford: BAR Publishing).
Riddler, I. 2012. The late Saxon material culture, 196–202 in Wrathmell (ed.).
Riddler, I. and Trzaska-Nartowski, N. 2011. Chanting upon a dunghill: Working skeletal materials, 116–41 in Clegg Hyer and Owen-Crocker (eds).
Riddler, I. and Trzaska-Nartowski, N. 2013a. The Insular comb, 259–74 in Reynolds and Webster (eds).
Riddler, I. and Trzaska-Nartowski, N. 2013b. *Lundenwic* worked bone, *Anglo-Saxon Studies in Archaeology and History* 18, 75–96.
Riddler, I., Trzaska-Nartowski, N., and Soulat, J. 2012. 'Riveted mounts' reconsidered: Horn composite combs in early medieval Britain and France, *Archaeological Journal* 169, 395–421.
Rigby, S. H. 1995. *English Society in the Later Middle Ages* (Basingstoke: Macmillan).
Rigby, S. H. 2017. *Boston 1068–1225: A Medieval Boom Town* (Lincoln: Society for Lincolnshire History and Archaeology).
Rigby, S. H. and Ewan, E. 2000. Government, power and authority 1300–1540, 291–312 in Palliser (ed.).
Rimmer, M. 2019. Silver and guilt: The cadaver tomb of John Baret of Bury St Edmunds, *Journal of the British Archaeological Association* 172, 131–54.
Ripper, S. and Cooper, L. P. 2009. *The Hemington Bridges: The Excavation of Three Medieval Bridges at Hemington Quarry, near Castle Donington, Leicestershire*, Leicestershire Archaeological Monograph 16 (Leicester: University of Leicester).
Rippon, S. 2004. Making the most of a bad situation? Glastonbury Abbey, Meare, and the medieval exploitation of wetland resources in the Somerset Levels, *Medieval Archaeology* 48, 91–130.
Rippon, S. 2006. *Landscape, Community and Colonisation: The North Somerset Levels during the First to Second Millennia A.D.*, Council for British Archaeology Research Report 152 (York: C. B. A.).
Rippon, S. 2008. *Beyond the Medieval Village: The Diversification and Landscape Character of Southern Britain* (Oxford: Oxford University Press).
Rippon, S. 2017. Moorlands and other wetlands, 89–106 in Clegg Hyer and Hooke (eds).
Rippon, S. 2018. *Kingdom, Civitas and County* (Oxford: Oxford University Press).
Rippon, S., Claughton, P., and Smart, C. 2009. *Mining in a Medieval Landscape: The Royal Silver Mines in the Tamar Valley* (Exeter: Exeter University Press).

Rippon, S., Smart, C., and Pears, B. 2015. *The Fields of Britannia: Continuity and Change in the Late Roman and Early Medieval Landscape* (Oxford: Oxford University Press).

Rippon, S. and Holbrook, N. (eds) 2021. *Roman and Medieval Exeter and the Hinterlands: From* Isca *to* Escanceastre*: Exeter, a Place in Time*, Volume 1 (Oxford: Oxbow Books).

Roberts, B. K. 1996. The great plough: A hypothesis concerning village genesis and land reclamation in Cumberland, *Landscape History* 18, 17–30.

Roberts, B. K. and Wrathmell, S. 2000. *Region and Place: A Study of English Rural Settlement* (Swindon: English Heritage).

Roberts, C. A. 2009. Health and welfare in medieval England: The human remains contextualized, 307–26 in Gilchrist and Reynolds (eds).

Roberts, C. A., Bekvalac, J., and Redfern, R. 2018. Health and well-being: The contribution of human remains to understanding the late medieval period in Britain, 819–35 in Gerrard and Gutiérrez (eds).

Roberts, E. 1991. A fifteenth-century inn at Andover, *Proceedings of the Hampshire Field Club and Archaeological Society* 47, 153–70.

Roberts, E. 1993. A base-cruck house at Froxfield, *Proceedings of the Hampshire Field Club and Archaeological Society* 49, 175–94.

Roberts, E. 1996. Overton Court Farm and the late medieval farmhouses of demesne lessees in Hampshire, *Proceedings of the Hampshire Field Club and Archaeological Society* 51, 89–106.

Roberts, E. 2021. The late medieval inns of Hampshire: Their architecture and plan-forms, 123–35 in Richardson, A.[a] and Allen (eds).

Roberts, I. 2014. Re-thinking the archaeology of Elmet, 182–94 in Haarer (ed.).

Robertson, D. and Ames, J. 2010. Early medieval inter-tidal fishweirs at Holme Beach, Norfolk, *Medieval Archaeology* 54, 329–46.

Robinson, S. and Cox, P. 2020. Evidence for the outer defences of Devizes Castle at *The Beeches*, Castle Road, Devizes, *Wiltshire Archaeological and Natural History Magazine* 113, 213–25.

Robinson, S. *et al.* 2018. Excavations on the site of the Museum, Kimmeridge, Dorset, *Proceedings of the Dorst Natural History and Archaeological Society* 139, 177–96.

Rodwell, W. and Atkins, C. 2012. *St Peter's, Barton-on-Humber, Lincolnshire: A Parish Church and Its Community: Volume 1: History, Archaeology and Architecture* (Oxford: Oxbow Books).

Rodwell, W. and Neal, D. S. 2019. *The Cosmatesque Pavements of Westminster Abbey* (Oxford: Oxbow Books).

Rodwell, W. and Tatton-Brown, T. (eds) 2015. *Westminster II: The Art, Architecture and Archaeology of the Royal Palace*, British Archaeological Association Conference Transactions 39 (London: B. A. A.).

Roffey, S. 2012. Medieval leper hospitals in England: An archaeological perspective, *Medieval Archaeology* 56, 203–33.

Roffey, S. 2017. Charity and conquest: Leprosaria in Norman England, 159–76 in Hadley and Dyer (eds).

Rogers, N. J. 1987. English episcopal monuments, 1270–1350, 8–68 in Coales (ed.).

Rogers, N. J. 2005. Pewter funerary chalices from York Minster, *Medieval Archaeology* 59, 193–211.

Rogerson, A. 1976. Excavations on Fuller's Hill, Great Yarmouth, *East Anglian Archaeology* 2, 131–245.

Rogerson, A. 1995. *A Late Neolithic, Saxon and Medieval Site at Middle Harling, Norfolk*, East Anglian Archaeology 74 (Gressenhall: Norfolk Archaeological Unit).
Rogerson, A. and Dallas, C. 1984. *Excavations in Thetford 1948–59 and 1973–80*, East Anglian Archaeological Report 22 (Gressenhall: Norfolk Archaeological Unit).
Rose, P. and Preston-Jones, A. 1995. Changes in the Cornish countryside, A.D. 400–1100, 51–68 in Hooke and Burnell (eds).
Rose, S. 2002. *Medieval Naval Warfare 1000–1500* (London/New York: Routledge).
Rose, S. 2017. *The Wealth of England: The Medieval Wool Trade and Its Significance 1100–1600* (Oxford: Oxbow Books).
Rosenthal, J. T. 1972. *The Purchase of Paradise: Gift-Giving and the Aristocracy, 1308–1485* (London: Routledge Kegan Paul).
Rosser, G. 2000. Urban culture and the Church 1300–1540, 335–70 in Palliser (ed.).
Rosser, G. 2015. *The Art of Solidarity in the Middle Ages: Guilds in England 1250–1550* (Oxford: Oxford University Press).
Rouse, E. C. and Baker, A. 1955. The wall-paintings at Longthorpe Tower, near Peterborough, Northamptonshire, *Archaeologia* 96, 1–57.
Rowland, J. 1995. Warfare and horses in the *Gododdin* and the problem of Catraeth, *Cambrian Medieval Celtic Studies* 30, 13–40.
Russel, A. D. 2016. Hung in chains: A late Saxon execution cemetery at Oliver's Battery, Winchester, *Proceedings of the Hampshire Field Club and Archaeological Society* 71, 89–109.
Ryder, P. F. 1992. Bastles and bastle-like buildings in Allendale, Northumberland, *Archaeological Journal* 149, 351–79.
Rynne, C. 2018. Water and wind power, 491–510 in Gerrard and Gutiérrez (eds).
Salisbury, C. R. 1981. An anglo-saxon fish-weir at Colwick, Nottinghamshire, *Transactions of the Thoroton Society* 85, 26–36.
Salzman, L. E. 1952. *Building in England down to 1540: A Documentary History* (Oxford: Clarendon Press).
Samson, R. 1999. Illusory emporia and mad economic theories, 76–90 in Anderton (ed.).
Samuel, M. 1989. The fifteenth-century garner at Leadenhall, London, *Antiquaries Journal* 69i, 119–53.
Sapoznic, A. 2019. Bees in the medieval economy: Religious observance and the production, trade, and consumption of wax in England, *c.* 1300–1555, *Economic History Review* 72iv, 1152–74.
Sargent, A. 2013. Early medieval Lichfield: A reassessment, *Staffordshire Archaeological and Historical Society* 46, 1–37.
Saul, N. 1998. The rise of the Dallingridge family, *Sussex Archaeological Collections* 136, 123–32.
Saunders, A. D. 1980. Lydford Castle, Devon, *Medieval Archaeology* 24, 123–86.
Saunders, A. D. 1985. The Cow Tower, Norwich: An East Anglian bastille?, *Medieval Archaeology* 29, 109–19.
Saunders, A. D. 2006. *Excavations at Launceston Castle, Cornwall*, Society for Medieval Archaeology Monograph 24 (S. M. A.).
Saunders, P. and Algar, D. 2017. A medieval brazier's well in Milford Street, Salisbury, Wiltshire, *Wiltshire Archaeological and Natural History Society Magazine* 110, 191–202.
Saunders, P. and Algar, D. 2020. The anglo-saxon cemetery at Petersfield, near Salisbury: An additional grave and associated settlement, *Wiltshire Archaeological and Natural History Society Magazine* 113, 202–12.

Sayer, D. 2020. *Early Anglo-Saxon Cemeteries: Kinship, Community and Identity* (Manchester: Manchester University Press on-line).

Sayer, D. and Williams, H. (eds) 2009. *Mortuary Practices and Social Identities in the Middle Ages* (Exeter: University of Exeter Press).

Schofield, J. 1995. *Medieval London Houses* (New Haven/London: Yale University Press).

Schofield, J. 2011. *London 1100–1600: The Archaeology of a Capital City* (Sheffield/Oakville: Equinox Publishing).

Schofield, J. 2019. London's waterfront 1100–1666: Summary of the findings from four excavations that took place from 1974 to 1984, *Antiquaries Journal* 99, 63–94.

Schofield, J. and Vince, A. G. 1994. *Medieval Towns* (London: Leicester University Press).

Schofield, P. 1996. The late medieval view of frankpledge and the tithing system, 409–49 in Razi and Smith (eds).

Scobie, G. D., Zant, J. M., and Whinney, R. 1991. *The Brooks, Winchester: A Preliminary Report on the Excavations, 1987–88*, Winchester Museums Service Archaeology Report 1 (Winchester: W. M. S.).

Scott, W. and Sharp, H. 2019. The Scalford sword-pommel cap: New evidence for early medieval metalworking techniques, *Transaction of the Leicestershire Archaeological Society* 93, 115–22.

Scragg, D. (ed.) 2003. *Textual and Material Culture in Anglo-Saxon England: Thomas Northcote Toller and the Toller Memorial Lecture* (Cambridge: D. S. Brewer).

Screen, E. 2007. Anglo-saxon law and numismatics: A reassessment in the light of Patrick Wormald's *The Making of English Law*, *British Numismatic Journal* 77, 150–72.

Scull, C. J. 1990. Scales and weights in early anglo-saxon England, *Archaeological Journal* 147, 183–215.

Scull, C. J. 2009. *Early Medieval (Late Fifth-Early Eighth Centuries A.D.) Cemeteries at Boss Hall and Buttermarket, Ipswich, Suffolk*, Society for Medieval Archaeology Monograph 27 (Leeds: S. M. A.).

Scull, C. J. and Harding, A. F. 1990. Two early medieval cemeteries at Milfield, Northumberland, *Durham Archaeological Journal* 6, 1–29.

Scull, C. J. and Naylor, J. 2016. Sceattas in anglo-saxon graves, *Medieval Archaeology* 60ii, 205–41.

Scull, C. J., Minter, F., and Plouviez, J. 2016. Social and economic complexity in early anglo-saxon England: A central place complex of the East Anglian kingdom at Rendlesham, Suffolk, *Antiquity* 90, 1594–612.

Seaby, W. A. and Woodfield, P. 1980. Viking stirrups and their background, *Medieval Archaeology* 24, 87–122.

Secker, D. 2019. The Church of SS. Peter and Paul, West Mersea, Essex: An anglo-saxon minster or a major Roman villa site, *Journal of the British Archaeological Association* 14, 77–86.

Semple, S. 2010. In the open air, 21–48 in Carver *et al.* (eds).

Serjeantson, D. 2006. Birds: Food and a mark of status, 131–47 in Woolgar *et al.* (eds).

Serjeantson, D. and Woolgar, C. M. 2006. Fish consumption in medieval England, 102–30 in Woolgar *et al.* (eds).

Serjeantson, D. and Rees, H. (eds) 2009. *Food, Craft and Status in Medieval Winchester: The Plant and Animal Remains from the Suburbs and City Defences* (Winchester: Winchester Museums Service).

Shapland, M. G. 2017. Anglo-saxon towers of lordship and the origins of the castle in England, 88–119 in Hadley and Dyer (eds).

Shapland, M. G. 2019. *Anglo-Saxon Towers of Lordship* (Oxford: Oxford University Press).
Shaw, M. 1996. The excavation of a late fifteenth- to seventeenth-century tanning complex at The Green, Northampton, *Post-Medieval Archaeology* 30, 63–128.
Shenton, C. 2002. Edward III and the symbol of the leopard, 69–81 in Coss and Keen (eds).
Sherlock, S. J. 2012. *A Royal Anglo-Saxon Cemetery at Street House, Loftus, North-East Yorkshire*, Tees Archaeology Monograph 6 (Hartlepool: Tees Archaeology).
Shiel, N. 1984. A medieval coin forger's dies from Trichay Street, Exeter, 253–4 in Allan.
Shoesmith, R. 1982. *Excavations on and Close to the Defences*, Hereford City Excavations Volume 2, Council for British Archaeology Research Report 46 (London: C. B. A.).
Short, I. 2003. Language and literature, 191–213 in Harper-Bill and van Houts (eds).
Short, P. 1980. The fourteenth-century rows of York, *Archaeological Journal* 137, 86–136.
Siddons, M. P. 2009. *Heraldic Badges in England and Wales: 1. Introduction* (London: Boydell Press).
Simmonds, A. *et al.* 2020. Evidence for the anglo-saxon *burh* defences, medieval tenements, and New Inn Hall: Investigations at Linton and Chavasse Quads, 127–38 in Dodd *et al.* (eds).
Simmons, I. G. 2015. The landscape development of the Tofts of south-east Lincolnshire 1100–1650, *Landscape History* 36i, 9–24.
Sindbaek, S. 2015. Steatite vessels in Britain and Ireland, 198–218 in Barrett and Gibbon (eds).
Slater, T. R. 1998. Benedictine town planning in medieval England, 155–76 in Slater and Rosser (eds).
Slater, T. R. and Wilson, C. 1977. *Archaeology and Development in Stratford-upon-Avon* (Birmingham: University of Birmingham Department of Geography).
Slater, T. R. (ed.) 2000. *Towns in Decline, A.D. 100–1600* (Aldershot: Ashgate).
Slater, T. R. and Rosser, G. (eds) 1998. *The Church in the Medieval Town* (Aldershot: Ashgate).
Slavin, P. 2020. Mites and merchants: The crisis of the English wool and textile trade revisited, *Economic History Review* 73iv, 885–913.
Slocombe, P. M. and Slocombe, I. 2016. *The Buildings of Bradford-on-Avon* (Bradford-on-Avon: Ex Libris Press).
Smart, C. (ed.) 2018. *Industry and the Making of a Rural Landscape: Iron and Pottery Production at Churchills Farm, Hemyock, Devon*, British Archaeological Reports, British Series 636 (Oxford: B. A. R.).
Smith, L. 1989–90. Sydenham moat: A thirteenth-century moated manor-house in the Warwickshire Arden, *Transactions of the Birmingham and Warwickshire Archaeological Society* 96, 27–68.
Smith, P. D. E. *et al.* 1983. The investigation of a shell-midden in Braunton Burrows, *Devon Archaeological Society Proceedings* 41, 75–90.
Smith, R. M. 1996. A periodic market and its impact on a manorial community, 450–73 in Razi and Smith (eds).
Smith, S. V. 2009. Materializing resistant identities among the medieval peasantry: An examination of dress accessories from English rural settlement sites, *Journal of Material Culture* 14, 309–32.
Smith, S. V. 2010. Houses and communities: Archaeological evidence for variation in medieval peasant experience, 64–84 in Dyer and Jones (eds).
Smith, T. P. 1975. Rye House, Hertfordshire, and aspects of early brickwork in England, *Archaeological Journal* 132, 111–50.

Smith, T. P. 1979. Hussey Tower, Boston: A late medieval tower-house of brick, *Lincolnshire History and Archaeology* 14, 31–7.

Snape, M. E. 2003. A horizontal-wheeled watermill of the Anglo-Saxon period at Corbridge, Northumberland, and its river environment, *Archaeologia Aeliana* 32, 37–72.

Soden, I. 2018. *Excavation of the Late Saxon and Medieval Churchyard of St Martin's, Wallingford, Oxfordshire* (Oxford: Archaeopress).

Sofield, C. M. 2015. Living with the dead: Human burials in anglo-saxon settlement contexts, *Archaeological Journal* 172, 351–88.

Solway, S. (ed.) 2015. *Medieval Coins and Seals: Constructing Identity, Signifying Power* (Turnhout: Brepols).

Sparks, M. 1998. St Gregory's Priory, Canterbury: A reassessment, *Archaeologia Cantiana* 118, 77–90.

Speake, G. 1988. *A Saxon Bed-Burial on Swallowcliffe Down: Excavations by F. de M. Vatcher* (London: Historic Building and Monuments Commission for England).

Speed, G. 2014. *Towns in the Dark? Urban Transformations from Late Roman Britain to Anglo-Saxon England* (Oxford: Archaeopress).

Speed, G. and Walton Rogers, P. 2004. A burial of a viking woman at Adwick-le-Street, South Yorkshire, *Medieval Archaeology* 48, 51–90.

Spence, C. 2013. The rise and fall of medieval Lincoln's northern suburb of Newport, *Medieval Archaeology* 57, 296–302.

Spencer, B. 1990. *Pilgrim Souvenirs and Secular Badges*, Salisbury and South Wiltshire Museum Medieval Catalogue Part 2 (Salisbury: Salisbury and South Wiltshire Museum).

Spencer, B. 1998. *Pilgrim Souvenirs and Secular Badges*, Medieval Finds from Excavations in London 7 (Norwich: Stationery Office).

Spencer, D. 2019. *Royal and Urban Gunpowder Weapons in Late Medieval England* (Woodbridge: Boydell Press).

Spoerry, P. 2005. Town and country in the medieval Fenland, 85–110 in Giles and Dyer (eds).

Spoerry, P. 2016. *The Production and Distribution of Medieval Pottery in Cambridgeshire*, East Anglian Archaeology 159 (Cambridge: Oxford Archaeology East).

Spriggs, J. A. 1998. The British beaver – fur, fact and fantasy, 91–101 in Cameron (ed.).

Squires, K. E. 2012. Populating the pots: the demography of the early anglo-saxon cemeteries at Elsham and Cleatham, North Lincolnshire, *Archaeological Journal* 169, 312–42.

Squires, K. E. 2013. Piecing together identity: A social investigation of early anglo-saxon cremation practices, *Archaeological Journal* 170, 154–200.

Stacy, N. E. (ed.) 2006. *Charters and Custumals of Shaftesbury Abbey 1089–1216*, Records of Social and Economic History n. s. 39 (Oxford: Oxford University Press).

Stamper, P. A. 1984. Excavations of a mid twelfth-century siege castle at Bentley, Hampshire, *Proceedings of the Hampshire Field Club and Archaeological Society* 40, 81–9.

Stamper, P. A. and Croft, R. A. 2000. *Wharram: A Study of Settlement on the Yorkshire Wolds, 8: The South Manor Area*, York University Archaeological Publications 10 (York: University of York).

Standley, E. R. 2013. *Trinkets & Charms: The Use, Meaning and Significance of Dress Accessories*, Oxford University School of Archaeology Monograph 78 (Oxford: Institute of Archaeology, University of Oxford).

Standley, E. R. 2016. Hid in the earth and secret places: A reassessment of a hoard of later medieval gold rings and silver coins found near the River Thames, *Antiquaries Journal* 96, 117–42.

Standley, E. R. 2018. Coneys, coneygarths and cunnies: The rabbit and great households, *c*. 1080–1600, 372–92 in Woolgar (ed.).

Statham, M. 1998. The medieval town of Bury St Edmunds, 98–110 in Gransden (ed.).

Steane, J. 1993. *The Archaeology of the Medieval English Monarchy* (London: B. T. Batsford).

Steane, J. 2001. *The Archaeology of Power* (Stroud: Tempus).

Steedman, K., Dyson, T., and Schofield, J. 1992. *Aspects of Saxo-Norman London: III. The Bridgehead and Billingsgate to 1200*, London and Middlesex Archaeological Society Special Paper 14 (London: L. A. M. A. S.).

Stenning, D. F. 2003. Small aisled halls in Essex, *Vernacular Architecture* 34, 1–19.

Stevens, L. 1982. Some windmill sites in Friston and Eastbourne, Sussex, *Sussex Archaeological Collections* 120, 93–138.

Stevens, M. F. 2016. London creditors and the fifteenth-century depression, *Economic History Review* 69iv, 1083–107.

Stewart, I. 1988. Note on the *tabula* set, 31–6 in Darvill.

Stewart, I. and Watkins, M. J. 1984. An eleventh-century bone *tabula* set from Gloucester, *Medieval Archaeology* 28, 185–90.

Stirland, A. 2009. *Criminals and Paupers: The Graveyard of St Mary Fyebriggate* in combusto, *Norwich*, East Anglian Archaeology 129 (Gressenhall: Norfolk Museums and Archaeology Service).

Stocker, D. 1991. *St Mary's Guildhall, Lincoln*, Archaeology of Lincoln 17/1 (London: Council for British Archaeology).

Stocker, D. 2005. The quest for one's own front door: Housing the vicars choral at the English cathedrals, *Vernacular Architecture* 36, 15–31.

Stocker, D. 2013. Aristocrats, burghers and their markets: Patterns in the foundation of Lincoln's early churches, 119–43 in Hadley and ten Harkel (eds).

Stocker, D. 2018. Stranger on the shore: Gainsborough Old Hall: Yorkist 'merchant clique' in Lancastrian Lincolnshire?, 56–74 in Woolgar (ed.).

Stocker, D. and Vince, A. G. 1997. The early Norman castle at Lincoln and a re-evaluation of the original west tower of Lincoln Cathedral, *Medieval Archaeology* 41, 223–33.

Stone, D. 2005. *Decision-Making in Medieval Agriculture* (Oxford: Oxford University Press).

Stone, D. 2014. The impact of drought in early fourteenth-century England, *Economic History Review* 67ii, 435–62.

Stone, R. and Appleton-Fox, N. 1996, *A View from Hereford's Past: A Report on the Archaeological Investigations in Hereford Cathedral Close in 1993* (Woonton Ameley: Logaston Press).

Stoodley, N. 1999. *The Spindle and the Spear: A Critical Enquiry into the Construction and Meaning of Gender in the Early Anglo-Saxon Burial Rite*, British Archaeological Reports British Series 288 (Oxford: B. A. R.).

Stoodley, N. 2000. From the cradle to the grave: Age organization and the anglo-saxon burial rite, *World Archaeology* 31i, 456–72.

Stopford, J. (ed.) 1999. *Pilgrimage Explored* (York: York University).

Stoyle, M. 2014. *Water in the City: The Aqueduct and Underground Passages of Exeter* (Exeter: Exeter University Press).

Stratford, J. 2013. *Richard II and the English Royal Treasure* (Woodbridge: Boydell Press).

Sturdy, D. and Munby, J. 1985. Early domestic sites in Oxford: Excavations in Cornmarket and Queen Street, *Oxoniensia* 50, 47–94.

Suggett, R. 2013. Peasant houses and identity in medieval Wales, *Vernacular Architecture* 44, 6–18.

Summerson, H., Trueman, N., and Harrison, S. 1998. *Brougham Castle, Cumbria*, Cumberland and Westmorland Antiquarian and Archaeological Society Research Series (Carlisle: C. W. A. A. S.).

Swabey, ff. 1999. *Medieval Gentlewoman: Life in a Widow's Household in the Later Middle Ages* (Stroud: Sutton Publishing).

Swallow, R. 2014. Gateways to power: The castles of Ranulf III of Chester and Llywelyn the Great of Gwynedd, *Archaeological Journal* 171, 289–311.

Swallow, R. 2016. Cheshire Castles of the Irish Sea cultural zone, *Archaeological Journal* 173, 288–341.

Swanson, H. 1988. The illusion of economic structure: Craft guilds in late medieval English towns, *Past and Present* 121, 29–48.

Swanson, H. 1989. *Medieval Artisans* (Oxford: Blackwell).

Swanson, R. N. 1999. *The Twelfth-Century Renaissance* (Manchester: Manchester University Press).

Swanton, M. trans. and ed. 1996. *The Anglo-Saxon Chronicles* (London: J. M. Dent).

Sweetinburh, S. 2015. A tale of two mazers: Negotiating donor recipient relationships at Kentish medieval hospitals, *Archaeologia Cantiana* 136, 117–38.

Swift, E. 2000. *Regionality in Dress Accessories in the Late Roman West* (Montagnac: éditions monique mergoil).

Swift, E. 2019. Re-evaluating the quoit-brooch style: Economic and cultural transformations in the fifth century A.D., *Medieval Archaeology* 63i, 1–55.

Sykes, N. J. 2004. The dynamics of status symbols: Wildfowl exploitation in England, A.D. 410–1550, *Archaeological Journal* 161, 82–105.

Sykes, N. J. 2006. From *cu* and *sceap* to *beffe* and *motton*: The management, distribution, and consumption of cattle and sheep in medieval England, 56–71 in Woolgar *et al.* (eds).

Sykes, N. J. 2007. *The Norman Conquest: A Zooarchaeological Perspective*, British Archaeological Reports International Series 1656 (Oxford: B. A. R.).

Tatton-Brown, T. 1989. Church building on Romney Marsh in the later Middle Ages, *Archaeologia Cantiana* 107, 253–65.

Tatton-Brown, T. and Crook, J. 2002. *The English Cathedral* (London: New Holland).

Taylor, C. 1983. *Village and Farmstead: A History of Rural Settlement in England* (London: George Philip).

Taylor, C. 2010. 'A place there is where liquid honey drops like dew': The landscape of Little Downham, Cambridgeshire, in the twelfth century, *Landscape History* 31, 5–24.

Taylor, H. M. 1971. Repton reconsidered, 35–89 in Clemoes and Hughes (eds).

Taylor, H. M. and Taylor, J. 1965. *Anglo-Saxon Architecture* (Cambridge: Cambridge University Press).

Teague, S. and Brown, R. 2020. Anglo-saxon to post-medieval occupation at the Provost's Garden, the Queen's College, 139–200 in Dodd *et al.* (eds).

Teague, S., Biddulph, E., and Champness, C. 2020. Anglo-saxon to post-medieval occupation and evidence for the medieval Jewry at Nos 114–119 St Aldate's and Nos 4–5 Queen Street, 73–126 in Dodd *et al.* (eds).

Tebbutt, C. F. 1982. A middle Saxon iron-smelting site at Millbrook, Ashdown Forest, Sussex, *Sussex Archaeological Collections* 120, 20–35.

Tedeschi, C. 2001. Some observations on the palaeography of early christian inscriptions in Britain, 16–25 in Higgitt *et al.* (eds).

Telfer, A. 2010. New evidence for the transition from the late Roman to the Saxon period at St Martins-in-the-Fields, London, 49–58 in Henig and Ramsay (eds).

Tester, A., Anderson, S., and Carr, R. D. 2014. *Staunch Meadow, Brandon, Suffolk: A High-Status Middle Saxon Settlement on the Fen Edge*, East Anglian Archaeology 151 (Bury St Edmunds: Suffolk County Council Archaeological Service).

Thaudet, O. and Webley, R. 2019. Interrogating the diffusion of metal artefacts: A case-study of a particular type of copper-alloy buckle, *Medieval Archaeology* 63ii, 375–402.

Thier, K. 2011. Steep vessel, high horn-ship: Water transport, 49–72 in Clegg Hyer and Owen-Crocker (eds).

Thomas, C. 1988. Tintagel Castle, *Antiquity* 62 no. 236, 421–34.

Thomas, G. 2010. *The Later Anglo-Saxon Settlement at Bishopstone: A Downland Manor in the Making*, Council for British Archaeology Research Report 163 (York: C. B. A.).

Thomas, G. 2013a. Life before the minster: The social dynamics of monastic foundation at anglo-saxon Lyminge, Kent, *Antiquaries Journal* 93, 109–45.

Thomas, G. 2013b. A casket fit for a West Saxon courtier? The Plumpton hoard and its place in the minor arts of late Saxon England, 425–58 in Reynolds and Webster (eds).

Thomas, G. 2017. From tribal centre to royal monastery: Anglo-saxon Lyminge explored through its archaeology, *Anglo-Saxon Studies in Archaeology and History* 20, 97–148.

Thomas, G. 2018. Mead-halls of the *Oiscingas*: A new Kentish perspective on the anglo-saxon great hall complex phenomenon, *Medieval Archaeology* 62ii, 262–303.

Thomas, G., McDonnell, G., Merkel, J., and Marshall, P. 2016. Technology, ritual and anglo-saxon agriculture: The biography of a plough coulter, *Antiquity* 90 no. 351, 742–58.

Thomas, R., Holmes, M., and Morris, J. 2013. 'So bigge as bigge may be': Tracking size and shape change in domestic livestock in London (A.D. 1220–1900), *Journal of Archaeological Science* 40, 3309–25.

Thompson, J. D. A. 1956. *Inventory of British Coin Hoards A.D. 600–1500*, Royal Numismatic Society Special Publications 1 (R. N. S.).

Thompson, M. W. 1998. *Medieval Bishops' Houses in England and Wales* (Aldershot: Ashgate).

Thompson, V. 2004. *Dying and Death in Later Anglo-Saxon England*, Anglo-Saxon Studies 4 (Woodbridge: Boydell Press).

Thorn, F. and Thorn, C. (ed.) 1982. *Domesday Book: Worcestershire* (Chichester: Phillimore).

Thornton, M. 2014. Feloniously slain, *Northamptonshire Past and Present* 67, 46–56.

Tipton, P. J. 2012. Surrey-Hampshire Border Ware production in Cove, Hampshire, *Post-Medieval Archaeology* 46ii, 341–6.

Townsend, E. 2003. Pilgrimage, 424–35 in Marks and Williamson (eds).

Treen, C. and Atkin, M. 2005. *Water Resources and Their Management*, Wharram: A Study of Settlement on the Yorkshire Wolds, 10, York University Archaeological Publications 12 (York: University of York).

Turner, H. L. 1971. *Town Defences in England and Wales* (London: John Baker).

Turner, J. 2020. Bamburgh's Bowl Hole burials, *Current Archaeology* 360, 28–34.

Turner, R. C. 2004. The great tower, Chepstow, Wales, *Antiquaries Journal* 84, 223–318.

Turner, S. (2006) *Making a Christian Landscape: The Countryside in Early Medieval Cornwall, Devon and Wessex* (Exeter: University of Exeter Press).

Tweddle, D. 1992. *The Anglian Helmet from Coppergate*, Archaeology of York 17/8 (York: Council for British Archaeology).

Tweddle, D. 1995. *Corpus of Anglo-Saxon Stone Sculpture Volume 4: South-East England* (Oxford: Oxford University Press).

Tweddle, D., Moulden, J., and Logan, E. 1999. *Anglian York: A Survey of the Evidence*, Archaeology of York 7/2 (York: Council for British Archaeology).

Tyers, I. and Hibberd, H. 1993. Tree-ring dates from Museum of London Archaeology Service, *Vernacular Architecture* 24, 50–4.

Tyers, I., Groves, C., Hillam, J., and Boswijk, G. 1997. Tree-ring dates from Sheffield University, *Vernacular Architecture* 28, 138–58.

Tyler, E. 1999. 'The eyes of the beholder were dazzled': Treasure and artifice in *Encomium Emmae Reginae*, *Early Medieval Europe* 8, 247–70.

Tyler, E. 2000. 'When wings incarnadine with gold are spread': The *Vita Aedwardi Regis* and the display of treasure at the court of Edward the Confessor, 83–107 in Tyler (ed.).

Tyler, E. (ed.) 2000. *Treasure in the Medieval West* (Woodbridge: York Medieval Press).

Tyrell, A. and Frazer, W. O. (eds) 2000. *Social Identity in Early Medieval England* (Leicester: Leicester University Press).

Tyson, R. 2000. *Medieval Glass Vessels Found in England* c. *A.D. 1200–1500*, Council for British Archaeology Research Report 121 (York: C. B. A.).

Ulmschneider, K. 2010. More markets, minsters, and metal-detected finds: Middle Saxon Hampshire a decade on, 87–98 in Henig and Ramsay (eds).

Underwood, R. 1999. *Anglo-Saxon Weapons and Warfare* (Stroud: Tempus).

Unger, R. W. 1980. *The Ship in the Medieval Economy, 600–1600* (Montreal: McGill-Queens Press).

Unger, R. W. 2004. *Beer in the Middle Ages and Renaissance* (Philadelphia: University of Pennsylvania Press).

Uzzell, H. 2012. Dyeing, 175–80 in Owen-Crocker *et al.* (eds).

Vince, A. G. 1985. The Saxon and medieval pottery of London: A review, *Medieval Archaeology* 29, 25–93.

Vince, A. G. 2003. Lincoln in the early medieval era, 141–56; The new town: Lincoln in the high medieval era, 159–25; Lincoln in the early modern era, 303–28 in Jones, Stocker, and Vince.

Vince, A. G. 2006. Coinage and urban development: Integrating the archaeological and numismatic history of Lincoln, 525–44 in Cook and Williams (eds).

Vince, A. G. and Jenner, A. 1991. The Saxon and early medieval pottery of London, 19–119 in Vince (ed.).

Vince, A. G. and Mould, Q. 2007. New thoughts on the chronology of Saddler Street, Durham: Pottery, leatherwork and some implications, *Archaeologia Aeliana* 36, 79–92.

Vince, A. G. (ed.) 1991. *Aspects of Saxo-Norman London: 2. Finds and Environmental Evidence*, London and Middlesex Archaeological Society Special Paper 12 (London: L. A. M. A. S.).

Vyner, B. (ed.) 1990. *Medieval Settlement in North-East England*, Archaeological and Antiquarian Society of Durham and Northumberland Report 2 (Newcastle: A. A. S. D. N.).

Vyner, B. (ed.) 1994. *Building on the Past: Papers Celebrating 150 Years of the Royal Archaeological Institute* (London: Royal Archaeological Institute).

Wade-Martins, P. 1980. *Excavations in North Elmham Park, 1967–72*, East Anglian Archaeology Report 9 (Gressenhall: Norfolk Archaeological Unit).

Wadge, R. 2008. Medieval arrowheads from Oxfordshire, *Oxoniensia* 73, 1–16.

Waldron, T. 2006. Nutrition and the skeleton, 254–66 in Woolgar *et al.* (eds).

Walker, D. 2006. A soldier's life? Multiple crania trauma from medieval London, *The Archaeologist* 59, 29.

Walker, K., Clough, S., and Clutterbuck, J. 2020. *A Medieval Punishment Cemetery at Weyhill Road, Andover, Hampshire*, Cotswold Archaeology Monograph 11 (Cirencester: Cotswold Archaeology).
Waller, P. (ed.) 2000. *The English Urban Landscape* (Oxford/New York: Oxford University Press).
Wallis, R. J. 2017. 'As the falcon her bells' at Sutton Hoo? Falconry in early anglo-saxon England, *Archaeological Journal* 174, 409–36.
Wallis, R. J. 2020. The 'north-west Essex anglo-saxon ring': Falconry and pagan-christian discursive space, *Cambridge Archaeological Journal* 30iii, 413–32.
Wallis, S. 2014. *The Oxford Henge and Late Saxon Massacre: With Excavations of Medieval and Post-Medieval Occupation at St John's College, Oxford*, Thames Valley Archaeological Services Monograph 17 (Reading: T. V. A. S.).
Walton, P. 1989. *Textiles, Cordage and Raw Fibre from 16–22 Coppergate*, Archaeology of York 17/5 (London: Council for British Archaeology).
Walton Rogers, P. 1997. *Textile Production at 16–22 Coppergate*, Archaeology of York 17/11 (York: Council for British Archaeology).
Walton Rogers, P. 2002. Textile production, 2732–45 in Ottaway and Rogers.
Walton Rogers, P. 2007. *Cloth and Clothing in Early Anglo-Saxon England, A.D. 450–700*, Council for British Archaeology Research Report 145 (York: Council for British Archaeology).
Wanostrocht, C. A. 1992. Discovery of a thirteenth-century hoard of silver coins in the chapel of St Bartholomew's Hospital, Sandwich, *Archaeologia Cantiana* 110, 153–9.
Ward, M. 2019. Hard questions about hard woods: The exclusions in the Old English '*Aecerbot*' charm, *Landscape History* 40, 3–14.
Ward-Perkins, B. 2005. *The Fall of Rome and the End of Civilization* (Oxford: Oxford University Press).
Watkins, D. R. 1994. *The Foundry: Excavations on Poole Waterfront 1986/7*, Dorset Natural History and Archaeological Society Monograph 14 (Dorchester: D. N. H. A. S.).
Watson, B. 2014. Hanging lamps, 78–93 in Cotton (ed.).
Watts, D. G. 1982. Peasant discontent on the manors of Titchfield Abbey, *Proceedings of the Hampshire Field Club and Archaeological Society* 39, 121–35.
Watts, L. and Leach, P. 1996. *Henley Wood, Temples and Cemetery: Excavations 1962–69 by the Late Ernest Greenfield and Others*, Council for British Archaeology Research Report 99 (York: C. B. A.).
Watts, M. 2017. Watermills and waterwheels, 167–86 in Clegg Hyer and Hooke (eds).
Webster, C. J. (ed.) 2008. *The Archaeology of South West England: South West Archaeological Research Framework, Resource Assessment and Research Agenda* (Taunton: Somerset County Council).
Webster, L. 2012. *Anglo-Saxon Art: A New History* (London: British Museum Press).
Webster, L. 2017. *Wundersmiþa geweorc*, a Mercian sword-pommel from Oxfordshire, 178–200 in Cambridge and Hawkes (eds).
Webster, L. and Backhouse, J. (eds) 1991. *The Making of England: Anglo-Saxon Art and Culture A. D. 600–900* (London: British Museum Press).
Weddell, P. 2000. Braunton Great Field, *Archaeological Journal* 157, 440–5.
Weetch, R. 2017. Tradition and innovation: Lead-alloy brooches and urban identities in the eleventh century, 263–82 in Hadley and Dyer (eds).
Weikert, K. 2018. Of pots and pins: The households of late anglo-saxon Faccombe Netherton, 57–70 in Jervis (ed.).

Welch, C. M. 1997. Glass-making in Wolseley, Staffordshire, *Post-Medieval Archaeology* 31, 1–60.

West, C. 2011. Urban populations and associations, 198–207 in Crick and Van Houts (eds).

West, S. 1985. *West Stow: The Anglo-Saxon Village*, East Anglian Archaeology Report 24 (Gressenhall: Norfolk Archaeological Unit).

Wheatley, A. 2004. *The Idea of the Castle in Medieval England* (Woodbridge/New York: York Medieval Press/ Boydell Press).

White, A. J. 1988. Medieval fisheries in the Witham and its tributaries, *Lincolnshire History and Archaeology* 19, 29–35.

White, P. and Cook, A. 2015. *Sherborne Old Castle, Dorset: Archaeological Investigations 1930–90* (London: Society of Antiquaries of London).

White, S., Manley, J., Jones, R., Orna-Ornstein, J., Johns, C., and Webster, L. 1999. A mid fifth-century hoard of Roman and pseudo-Roman material from Patching, West Sussex, *Britannia* 30, 301–5.

White, W. J. 1985. Changing burial practice in later medieval England, 370–9 in Petre (ed.).

White, W. J. 1988. *Skeletal Remains from the Cemetery of St Nicholas Shambles, City of London* (London: Museum of London/London and Middlesex Archaeological Society).

Wickham, C. 2005. *Framing the Early Middle Ages: Europe and the Mediterranean, 400–800* (Oxford: Oxford University Press).

Wild, B. L. 2010. A gift inventory from the reign of Henry III, *English Historical Review* 125 (515), 529–69.

Wilkinson, D. and McWhirr, A. 1998. *Cirencester Anglo-Saxon Church and Medieval Abbey*, Cirencester Excavations 4 (Cirencester: Cotswold Archaeological Trust).

Wilkinson, L. J. 2018. The great household in wartime: Eleanor de Montfort and her *familia*, 29–55 in Woolgar (ed.).

Williams, A. 2008. *The World before Domesday* (London: Continuum).

Williams, D. 1983. 16 Bell Street, Reigate, *Surrey Archaeological Collections* 74, 47–89.

Williams, D. 1997. *Late Saxon Stirrup-Mounts: A Classification and Catalogue*, Council for British Archaeology Research Report 111 (York: C. B. A.).

Williams, D. 2018. *Datasheet 50: Copper-Alloy Purse Components: A New Classification* (The Finds Research Group A.D. 700–1700).

Williams, D. F. and Vince, A. G. 1997. The characterization and interpretation of early to middle Saxon granitic tempered pottery in England, *Medieval Archaeology* 41, 214–20.

Williams, E. H. D., Penoyre, J., and Hale, B. C. H. 1987. The George Inn, Norton St Philip, Somerset, *Archaeological Journal* 144, 317–27.

Williams, G. 2013. The 'northern hoards' revisited: Hoards and silver economy in the northern Danelaw in the early tenth century, 459–86 in Reynolds and Webster (eds).

Williams, G. 2019. The gold coins, 146–51 in Blackmore *et al.*

Williams, G. (ed.) 2020. *A Riverine Site near York: A Possible Viking Camp*, British Museum Research Publications 224 (London: British Museum Press).

Williams, G. and Naylor, J. 2016. *King Alfred's Coins: The Watlington Viking Hoard* (Oxford: Ashmolean Museum).

Williams, H. 2003a. Material culture as memory: Combs and cremation in early medieval Britain, *Early Medieval Europe* 12ii, 89–128.

Williams, H. 2003b. Remembering and forgetting the medieval dead, 227–54 in Williams, H. (ed.).

Williams, H. (ed.) 2003. *Archaeologies of Remembrance: Death and Memory in Past Societies* (New York: Plenum).

Williams, J. H. 1979. *St Peter's Street, Northampton: Excavations 1973–1976*, Archaeological Monograph 2 (Northampton Development Corporation).
Williams, J. H., Shaw, M., and Denham, V. 1985. *Middle Saxon Palaces at Northampton*, Archaeological Monograph 4 (Northampton: Northampton Development Corporation).
Williamson, P. 2003. The parish church, 375–423 in Marks and Williamson (eds).
Williamson, T. 1988. Settlement chronology and regional landscapes: The evidence from the claylands of East Anglia, 153–75 in Hooke (ed.).
Williamson, T. 2010. 'At pleasure's lordly call': The archaeology of emparked settlements, 162–81 in Dyer and Jones (eds).
Williamson, T. 2013. *Environment, Society and Landscape in Early Medieval England: Time and Topography*, Anglo-Saxon Studies 19 (Woodbridge: Boydell Press).
Willmoth, F. and Oosthuizen, S. (eds) 2015. *The Ely Coucher Book, 1249–50: The Bishop of Ely's Manors in the Cambridgeshire Fenland* (Cambridge: Cambridgeshire Record Society).
Willmott, H. 2018. Cooking, dining, and drinking, 697–712 in Gerrard and Gutiérrez (eds).
Willmott, H. and Daubney, A. 2020. Of saints, sows or smiths? Copper-brazed handbells in early medieval England, *Archaeological Journal* 177i, 326–55.
Willmott, H. *et al*. 2020. A Black Death mass grave at Thornton Abbey: The discovery and examination of a fourteenth-century catastrophe, *Antiquity* 94 no. 373, 179–96.
Willmott, T. 2010. The late Roman frontier: A structural background, 10–16 in Collins and Allason-Jones (eds).
Willmott, T. 2017. The Anglian abbey of *Streonæshalch*-Whitby: New perspectives on topography and layout, *Anglo-Saxon Studies in Archaeology and History* 20, 81–94.
Wilson, C. 1997. Rulers, artificers and shoppers: Richard II's remodelling of Westminster Hall 1393–9, 33–59 in Gordon *et al*. (eds).
Wilson, C. 2003a. 'Excellent, new and uniforme': Perpendicular architecture *c*. 1400–1547, 98–119 in Marks and Williamson (eds).
Wilson, C. 2003b. Royal patronage of the visual arts, 142–69 in Marks and Williamson (eds).
Wilson, D. M. 1964. *Catalogue of Antiquities of the Later Saxon Period, 1: Anglo-Saxon Ornamental Metalwork 700–1100 in the British Museum* (London: Trustees of the British Museum).
Wilson, D. M. 1965. Some neglected late anglo-saxon swords, *Medieval Archaeology* 9, 32–54.
Wilson, P. R. *et al*. 1996. Early Anglian Catterick and *Catraeth*, *Medieval Archaeology* 40, 1–61.
Wood, D. (ed.) 2004. *Medieval Monetary Matters* (Oxford: Oxbow Books).
Woodburn, B. and Guy, N. 2006. Arundel Castle, *Castle Studies Group Bulletin* 19, 9–24.
Woodcock, A. 2005. *Liminal Images: Aspects of Medieval Architectural Sculpture in the South of England from the Eleventh to the Fifteenth Century*, British Archaeological Reports British Series 386 (Oxford: B. A. R.).
Woodfield, C. 2005. *The Church of Our Lady of Mount Carmel, Whitefriars, Coventry*, British Archaeological Reports British Series 389 (Oxford: B. A. R.).
Woodiwiss, S. (ed.) 1992. *Iron Age and Roman Salt Production and the Medieval Town of Droitwich*, Council for British Archaeology Research Report 81 (London: C. B. A.).
Woods, D. 2013. The *Agnus Dei* penny of King Aethelred II: A call to hope in the Lord (Isaiah XL)?, *Anglo-Saxon England* 42, 299–309.

Woods, D. 2016. Hammer and sword on the coinage of viking York *c.* 919–27, *Numismatic Chronicle* 176, 271–81.

Woodward, A. 1992. *Shrines and Sacrifice* (London: B. T. Batsford/English Heritage).

Woolgar, C. M. 1999. *The Great Household in Late Medieval England* (New Haven/London: Yale University Press).

Woolgar, C. M. 2006. *The Senses in Late Medieval England* (New Haven/London: Yale University Press).

Woolgar, C. M. 2016. *The Culture of Food in England 1200–1500* (New Haven/London: Yale University Press).

Woolgar, C. M. 2018. Heirlooms and the great household, 432–55 in Woolgar (ed.).

Woolgar, C. M., Serjeantson, D., and Waldron, T. 2006. Conclusion, 267–80 in Woolgar *et al.* (eds).

Woolgar, C. M. (ed.) 1993. *Household Accounts from Medieval England*, two parts, Records of Social and Economic History n.s. 18 (Oxford: Oxford University Press).

Woolgar, C. M. (ed.) 2018. *The Elite Household in England, 1100–1500*, Harlaxton Medieval Studies 28 (Donington: Shaun Tyas).

Woolgar, C. M., Serjeantson, D., and Waldron, T. (eds) 2006. *Food in Medieval England: Diet and Nutrition* (Oxford: Oxford University Press).

Woolhouse, T., Hinman, M., and Sudds, B. 2019. Recent discoveries at Ely Cathedral, Cambridgeshire: Aetheldreda's Gate, the church of Holy Cross and the possible boundary of the anglo-saxon monastery, *Archaeological Journal* 176, 159–95.

Wrathmell, S. 2012a. Dating the foundation of the medieval village, 203–8; Lords and manors from the twelfth to the fifteenth centuries, 222–39 in Wrathmell (ed.).

Wrathmell, S. 2012b. Northern England: Exploring the character of medieval rural settlement, 249–65 in Christie and Stamper (eds).

Wrathmell, S. (ed.) 2012. *A History of Wharram Percy and Its Neighbours*, Wharram: A Study of Settlement on the Yorkshire Wolds, 13, York University Archaeological Publications 15 (York: University of York).

Wright, D. W. 2015. *'Middle Saxon' Settlement and Society* (Oxford: Archaeopress).

Wright, D. W. 2019. Crafters of kingship: Smiths, elite power, and gender in early medieval Europe, *Medieval Archaeology* 63ii, 271–97.

Wright, J. and Gaunt, A. 2013–14. A palace for our kings: A decade of research into a royal residence in the heart of Sherwood Forest at Kings Clipstone, Nottinghamshire, *Castle Studies Group Journal* 27, 234–51.

Wright, S. M. 1982. Much Park Street, Coventry: The development of a medieval street: Excavations 1970–74, *Transactions of the Birmingham and Warwickshire Archaeological Society* 1982, 1–133.

Yeoman, P. 2018. An archaeology of pilgrimage, 641–57 in Gerrard and Gutiérrez (eds).

Yorke, B. 1990. *Kings and Kingdoms of Early Anglo-Saxon England* (London: Seaby).

Yorke, B. 2000. Political and ethnic identity: A case study of anglo-saxon practice, 69–89 in Frazer and Tyrrell (eds).

Yorke, B. 2017. Queen Balthild's 'monastic policy' and the origins of female religious houses in southern England, *Anglo-Saxon Studies in Archaeology and History* 20, 7–16.

Yorke, B. 2021. Hamwic and the origins of Wessex revisited, 29–40 in Richardson, A.[a] and Allen (eds).

Youngs, S. 1989. Fine metalwork to *c.* A.D. 650, 20–71 in Youngs (ed.).

Youngs, S. 1995. A penannular brooch from near Calne, Wiltshire, *Wiltshire Archaeological and Natural History Magazine* 88, 127–31.

Youngs, S. (ed.) 1989. *'The Work of Angels': Masterpieces of Celtic Metalwork, Sixth to Ninth Centuries A.D.* (London: British Museum Publications).

Zeigler, V. 2019. From *wic* to *burh*: A new approach to the question of the development of London, *Archaeological Journal* 176, 336–68.

Index

Note: Page numbers in *italics* indicate an illustration on the corresponding page.

Taylor & Francis Group
an **informa** business

Taylor & Francis eBooks

www.taylorfrancis.com

A single destination for eBooks from Taylor & Francis with increased functionality and an improved user experience to meet the needs of our customers.

90,000+ eBooks of award-winning academic content in Humanities, Social Science, Science, Technology, Engineering, and Medical written by a global network of editors and authors.

TAYLOR & FRANCIS EBOOKS OFFERS:

A streamlined experience for our library customers

A single point of discovery for all of our eBook content

Improved search and discovery of content at both book and chapter level

REQUEST A FREE TRIAL

support@taylorfrancis.com

Routledge
Taylor & Francis Group

CRC Press
Taylor & Francis Group